THE ROUTLEDGE COMPANION TO INNOVATION MANAGEMENT

Innovation contributes to corporate competitiveness, economic performance and environmental sustainability. In the Internet era, innovation intelligence is transferred across borders and languages at an unprecedented rate, yet the ability to benefit from it seems to become more divergent among different corporations and countries. How much an organization can benefit from innovation largely depends on how well innovation is managed in it. Thus, there is a discernible increase in interest in the study of innovation management. This handbook provides a comprehensive guide to this subject.

The handbook introduces the basic framework of innovation and innovation management. It also presents innovation management from the perspectives of strategy, organization and resource, as well as institution and culture. The book's comprehensive coverage on all areas of innovation management makes this a very useful reference for anyone interested in the subject.

Jin Chen is Professor at Tsinghua University, Beijing, China.

Alexander Brem is Professor at Friedrich-Alexander-Universität Erlangen-Nürnberg and University of Southern Denmark.

Eric Viardot is Director of the Global Innovation Management Centre and Permanent Professor of Strategy and Marketing at EADA Business School in Barcelona, Spain.

Poh Kam Wong is Professor in Entrepreneurship and Innovation strategy at the NUS Business School, National University of Singapore.

ROUTLEDGE COMPANIONS IN BUSINESS, MANAGEMENT AND ACCOUNTING

Routledge Companions in Business, Management and Accounting are prestige reference works providing an overview of a whole subject area or sub-discipline. These books survey the state of the discipline, including emerging and cutting-edge areas. Providing a comprehensive, up-to-date, definitive work of reference, Routledge Companions can be cited as an authoritative source on the subject.

A key aspect of these Routledge Companions is their international scope and relevance. Edited by an array of highly regarded scholars, these volumes also benefit from teams of contributors which reflect an international range of perspectives.

Individually, Routledge Companions in Business, Management and Accounting provide an impactful one-stop-shop resource for each theme covered. Collectively, they represent a comprehensive learning and research resource for researchers, postgraduate students and practitioners.

Published titles in this series include:

THE ROUTLEDGE COMPANION TO MANAGEMENT BUYOUTS
Edited by Mike Wright, Kevin Amess, Nick Bacon and Donald Siegel

THE ROUTLEDGE COMPANION TO CO-OPETITION STRATEGIES
Edited by Anne-Sophie Fernandez, Paul Chiambaretto, Frédéric Le Roy and Wojciech Czakon

THE ROUTLEDGE COMPANION TO REWARD MANAGEMENT
Edited by Stephen J. Perkins

THE ROUTLEDGE COMPANION TO ACCOUNTING IN CHINA
Edited by Haiyan Zhou

THE ROUTLEDGE COMPANION TO CRITICAL MARKETING
Edited by Mark Tadajewski, Matthew Higgins, Janice Denegri Knott and Rohit Varman

THE ROUTLEDGE COMPANION TO THE HISTORY OF RETAILING
Edited by Jon Stobart and Vicki Howard

THE ROUTLEDGE COMPANION TO INNOVATION MANAGEMENT
Edited by Jin Chen, Alexander Brem, Eric Viardot and Poh Kam Wong

For more information about this series, please visit: www.routledge.com/Routledge-Companions-in-Business-Management-and-Accounting/book-series/RCBMA

THE ROUTLEDGE COMPANION TO INNOVATION MANAGEMENT

Edited by Jin Chen, Alexander Brem, Eric Viardot and Poh Kam Wong

LONDON AND NEW YORK

First published 2019
by Routledge
2 Park Square, Milton Park, Abingdon, Oxon OX14 4RN

and by Routledge
52 Vanderbilt Avenue, New York, NY 10017

Routledge is an imprint of the Taylor & Francis Group, an informa business

© 2019 selection and editorial matter, Jin Chen, Alexander Brem, Eric Viardot and Poh Kam Wong; individual chapters, the contributors

The right of Jin Chen, Alexander Brem, Eric Viardot and Poh Kam Wong to be identified as the authors of the editorial material, and of the authors for their individual chapters, has been asserted in accordance with sections 77 and 78 of the Copyright, Designs and Patents Act 1988.

All rights reserved. No part of this book may be reprinted or reproduced or utilised in any form or by any electronic, mechanical, or other means, now known or hereafter invented, including photocopying and recording, or in any information storage or retrieval system, without permission in writing from the publishers.

Trademark notice: Product or corporate names may be trademarks or registered trademarks, and are used only for identification and explanation without intent to infringe.

British Library Cataloguing-in-Publication Data
A catalogue record for this book is available from the British Library

Library of Congress Cataloging-in-Publication Data
Names: Chen, Jin, editor. | Brem, Alexander, editor. | Viardot, Eric, editor.
Title: The Routledge companion to innovation management / edited by Jin Chen, Alexander Brem, Eric Viardot and Poh Kam Wong.
Description: New York : Routledge, 2019. | Series: Routledge companions in business, management and accounting | Includes bibliographical references and index.
Identifiers: LCCN 2018046350| ISBN 9781138244719 (hardback) | ISBN 9781315276670 (ebook)
Subjects: LCSH: Technological innovations—Management. | Organizational change.
Classification: LCC HD45 .R756 2019 | DDC 658.4/063—dc23
LC record available at https://lccn.loc.gov/2018046350

ISBN: 978-1-138-24471-9 (hbk)
ISBN: 978-1-315-27667-0 (ebk)

Typeset in Bembo
by Apex CoVantage, LLC

CONTENTS

List of figures viii
List of tables xi
List of contributors xiii

PART I
Introduction to innovation and innovation management 1

1 Innovation and innovation management 3
   Jin Chen, Eric Viardot and Alexander Brem

2 Deliberate and spontaneous: the impact of cognitive disinhibition on people management 17
   Franc Ponti

3 Connotation and types of innovation 26
   Jin Chen and Ximing Yin

4 The fundamentals of innovation management 55
   Petra A. Nylund

5 The systems approach to innovation management 73
   Magnus Karlsson and Mats Magnusson

6 Innovation and innovation management in an age of changes 91
   Jin Chen and Liang Mei

PART II
The strategic perspective of innovation — 105

7 Strategic management of innovation — 107
Emigdio Alfaro, Fei Yu, Naqeeb Ur Rehman, Eglantina Hysa and Patrice Kandolo Kabeya

8 The free innovation paradigm — 169
Eric von Hippel

9 Open innovation — 180
Yufen Chen and Wim Vanhaverbeke

10 Bringing open innovation into practice: methods and approaches — 204
Frank Piller, Sumit Mitra, and Susanna Ghosh Mitra

11 R&D strategies for disruptive innovation — 220
Chang-Chieh Hang and Yi Ruan

12 Smart prototyping — 237
Fei Yu and Bastian Enste

13 Frugal innovation: developing and managing innovations in resource-constrained settings — 269
Eugenia Rosca, Nivedita Agarwal, and Jakob Schlegel

14 Innovation in the digital age — 278
Michael Dowling, Elisabeth Noll, and Kristina Zisler

15 Perspectives on policies to promote convergence in innovation — 297
Kong-rae Lee

16 Responsible innovation: origin, attribution and theoretical framework — 307
Liang Mei and Jin Chen

17 Serendipity and innovation: beyond planning and experimental-driven exploration — 343
Martin Kamprath and Tassilo Henike

PART III
The organizational perspective of innovation — 361

18 Innovation management within the organisation — 363
Regina Lenart-Gansiniec

19	Interorganizational relations within innovation systems *Terje Grønning and Parisa Afshin*	377
20	The crucial human factor in innovation *Georges Haour*	393

PART IV
Institutions and norms for innovation management   **413**

21	Institutional design of innovation towards the 'active innovation paradigm' *Dirk Meissner*	415
22	Ethics in innovation management as meta-responsibility: the practice of responsible research and innovation in human brain simulation *Bernd Carsten Stahl, Jos Timmermans, Stephen Rainey and Mark Shaw*	435
23	Intellectual property and innovation management *Can Huang and Suli Zheng*	457

PART V
Methodologies for innovation management   **477**

24	Standards, models, and methodologies for innovation management *Emigdio Alfaro*	479
25	Technological innovation audit *Xuesong Geng*	516
26	Innovation management simulations using agent-based modelling *Petra Ahrweiler*	539
27	Technology innovation investment portfolio planning: a systems approach with application examples *Oliver Yu*	560

Index   *590*

FIGURES

1.1	Evolution of corporate management	7
1.2	Evolution of the corporate development model	9
1.3	Sketch map of the innovation funnel model (using new drug development as an example)	10
1.4	Holistic framework for corporation innovation management integration	11
3.1	Connotation meaning of innovation	28
3.2	Knowledge–capital interaction	33
3.3	What's critical to innovation success – linking strategy and creativity, R&D, production and marketing	33
3.4	Innovation matrix	37
3.5	Incremental innovation vs. radical innovation	44
3.6	Incremental innovation and radical innovation: technology trajectory	45
3.7	Continuous innovation and discontinuous innovation	48
3.8	Summary of innovation classifications	48
3.9	Theoretical framework of HI: an emerging innovation paradigm in open environments	52
4.1	Knowledge micro processes	57
5.1	Principled outline of an integrated framework for innovation management	84
6.1	'Internet+': connotation and action plan	95
6.2	Four-dimensional framework of responsible innovation	102
6.3	Research framework of responsible innovation	103
6.4	Theoretical framework of responsible innovation	103
7.1	"Big-I" innovation and "small-i" innovation	147
7.2	GEM conceptual model	149
8.1	The free innovation and the producer innovation paradigms	171
10.1	Open innovation as a process of search: two approaches	209
12.1	From left to right: Original design of the table; define constraint and apply generative design algorithm; generative design model	240
12.2	Prototyping for X structure and integration into the design process	242
12.3	Classification of prototyping activities	244
12.4	Two-group simple randomized experimental design (in diagram form)	245

12.5	Prototyping activity assessment form	247
12.6	Chosen experimental design	249
12.7	Extract of the pair plot of the collected data	254
12.8	Distribution plot of the data	254
12.9	Count plot of the given data	256
12.10	K-nearest neighbor classification	257
12.11	Artificial neural network	258
12.12	Process of importing and fitting the model and generating predictions	259
12.13	Visualization of the decision tree classifier	260
13.1	Frugal innovation – a simple definition	270
13.2	Overview of initiatives of frugal innovation – from survival entrepreneurs to MNC	271
14.1	The generic innovation process for digital innovation	291
15.1	Process of convergence between Technology A and Technology B	300
16.1	Interactive mechanism of institutional levels from the perspective of interactive framework theory	319
16.2	Assessment standards of innovative activities	320
16.3	Theoretical framework of responsible innovation	324
16.4	Responsible governance of nanotechnology product risk management based on generation	326
17.1	Typology of exploration	350
17.2	Locus of serendipity	354
20.1	Management development as an agent of change	397
20.2	Increasing complexity of managing the innovation process	403
20.3	Entrepreneurial development of the offering draws on sources of technology distributed inside and outside the firm	404
20.4	Firms engage with universities in many different ways	406
20.5	Steps in spinning off a technical start-up company	409
21.1	Key issues for determining the company's innovation management role	417
21.2	Company innovation management in the light of open innovation	419
21.3	Characteristics of an innovation management organization	422
21.4	Innovation process stages and organizational meaning	425
21.5	IM from a service to a driver role	426
22.1	Basic structure of responsibility	438
22.2	Responsibility structure including authority	438
22.3	Components and dimensions of responsibility	440
22.4	Graphical representation of the HBP ethics map	449
23.1	Number of IP-related articles published in selected journals	460
23.2	Number of citations to the IP-related articles in selected journals	460
23.3	Number of publications in selected journals	461
23.4	Number of citations to publications in selected journals	462
25.1	The chain model of technological innovation	519
25.2	The new product performance triangle	519
25.3	Technological innovation measurement indicator system in the Oslo Manual	520
25.4	The stage-based technological innovation process measurement framework	521
25.5	The TIA theoretical model	522
25.6	The effect of technical and market maturity on technology innovation	526
27.1	A systematic planning process	562

27.2	The traditional Maslowian hierarchical model of human needs	562
27.3	Broad categorization of human needs based on the new model	564
27.4	Details of human needs based on the new model	565
27.5	Extension of the new model to the needs of an organization	566
27.6	Extension of the new model to the needs of a society	567
27.7	Application of the new model to a small Asian country	567
27.8	Scenario analysis process	572
27.9	Example of external forces	573
27.10	Axes of uncertainty	575
27.11	Graphical representation of factors	578
27.12	STRATEGY MAP: illustrative example 1	579
27.13	STRATEGY MAP: illustrative example 2	579
27.14	STRATEGY MAP: illustrative example 3	580
27.15	STRATEGY MAP: illustrative example 1 for qualitative portfolio evaluation	580
27.16	STRATEGY MAP: illustrative example 2 for qualitative portfolio evaluation	581
27.17	STRATEGY MAP: combined importance vs. combined risk	582
27.18	Modern portfolio theory	583
27.19	Portfolio revised for government investment	584
27.20	Implementation policy implications: government policy opportunities	585
27.21	Policy levers: risk reductions for high-risk clusters	586
27.22	Policy levers: commercialization of medium-risk clusters	587
27.23	Policy levers: observing and assisting low-importance clusters	588

TABLES

1.1	Nine strategic areas in the Strategy for American Innovation	4
1.2	Twelve disruptive technologies	5
1.3	Significant technological innovations in history	8
1.4	The 50 most innovative companies for 2018	8
2.1	Deliberate style and spontaneous style	21
2.2	Four large zones	22
3.1	Technology leadership does not mean successful innovation	29
3.2	Technological innovation vs. similar concepts	32
3.3	CoPS examples	36
3.4	Service industry vs. manufacturing	39
3.5	Incremental innovation vs. radical innovation	46
3.6	Paradigm shift of innovation by country or region	49
4.1	Micro- and macro-level research on functional constructs	58
5.1	Overview of selected system-related frameworks for innovation management introduced between 1997 and 2018	83
5.2	Examples of system elements for each theme of the framework for innovation management	83
6.1	Comparison between industrial thinking and Internet thinking	92
6.2	Innovative application of Internet+ to traditional industries	96
6.3	Environmental and eco-innovation assessment dashboard	99
6.4	Responsible innovation policies and activities conducted by developed countries	100
6.5	Lines of questioning on responsible innovation	101
7.1	Studies related to the impact of leadership styles on innovation	114
7.2	Entrepreneurial behavior and attitudes in developing countries (figures are in percent) in 2007	151
7.3	Entrepreneurial behavior and attitudes in developed countries (figures are in percent) in 2007	152
8.1	The extent of consumer innovation in six countries	170
8.2	Sources of scientific equipment innovations by nature of improvements effected	176
10.1	Differentiation of open innovation methods	210
11.1	Postulation of the abstracted R&D strategies	222

Tables

11.2	Application frequency of the four R&D strategies	226
11.3	Summary of cases and strategies in India and China	233
12.1	Experiment participant data	249
12.2	Arithmetic mean and standard deviation of 17 observations after the experiment	251
12.3	Prototyping data correlation matrix	253
12.4	Performance of the four machine learning algorithms on the testing set	261
12.5	Made predictions using the K-nearest neighbors algorithm	262
16.1	Concept analysis of responsible innovation	311
16.2	Comparison and summary of attribution perspectives of responsible innovation	313
16.3	Reflection of construction elements of responsible innovation in levels of institutional situations	322
16.4	Description of China's science and technology policies based on the responsible innovation perspective	331
16.5	Comparison and summary of nanotechnology innovation and governance based on the responsible innovation perspective	333
17.1	Patterns of serendipitous discoveries	348
17.2	Comparison of exploration approaches	352
23.1	Source journals of IP and innovation studies	458
23.2	List of 48 most-cited articles between 2000 and March 2018	463
24.1	Identified problems associated with the lack of standards, models, and methodologies for managing organizational innovation	486
24.2	Identified standards for managing innovation	488
24.3	Identified models for innovation management	499
24.4	Identified methodologies for innovation management	505
25.1	Technological innovation process audit metrics	529
25.2	Overall technological innovation performances audit for an enterprise	533
25.3	Innovation process performance assessment indicators	533
25.4	Performance indicators measuring competitiveness	534
27.1	Summary of major forecasting techniques	570
27.2	Example of plausible extreme futures of an axis	575
27.3	Another example of plausible extreme futures of an axis	575
27.4	Candidate scenarios	576
27.5	Final scenarios	576
27.6	Example of factor measures	577

CONTRIBUTORS

Parisa Afshin is a Doctoral Fellow, Department of Education, University of Oslo.

Nivedita Agarwal is Assistant Professor at the Chair of Technology Management at the Friedrich-Alexander-Universität Erlangen-Nürnberg (FAU), Germany.

Petra Ahrweiler is Professor at Johannes Gutenberg University Mainz, Germany.

Emigdio Alfaro is Professor and Researcher of CENTRUM Católica Graduate Business School of Pontificia Universidad Católica del Perú, Lima, Peru.

Alexander Brem is Professor at Friedrich-Alexander-Universität Erlangen-Nürnberg at the University of Southern Denmark.

Jin Chen is Professor in School of Economics and Management at Tsinghua University, Beijing, China.

Yufen Chen is Professor at Zhejiang Gongshang University, China.

Michael Dowling is a Professor for Innovation and Technology Management in the Faculty of Business and Economics at the University of Regensburg, Germany.

Bastian Enste is an MSc student of Innovation and Business at Mads Clausen Institute, University of Southern Denmark.

Xuesong Geng is Professor in the Lee Kong Chian School of Business at Singapore Management University, Singapore.

Terje Grønning is Professor in Work Society and Learning, Department of Education, University of Oslo.

Contributors

Chang-Chieh Hang is Executive Director at the Institute for Engineering Leadership, and Professor at the Department of Industrial Systems Engineering & Management, National University of Singapore.

Georges Haour is Professor of Management at IMD, Switzerland, and advisor to numerous organizations.

Tassilo Henike is Teaching Assistant and PhD Candidate at the Chair for Innovation Management and Entrepreneurship, University of Potsdam, Germany.

Can Huang is Professor at the Institute for Intellectual Property Management, School of Management, Zhejiang University, Hangzhou, China.

Eglantina Hysa is Associate Professor of Head of the Department of Economics at Epoka University, Tirana, Albania.

Poh Kam Wong is Professor in Entrepreneurship and Innovation Strategy at the NUS Business School, National University of Singapore.

Martin Kamprath is Senior Program Manager of Transfer and Innovation at the Helmholtz Association of German Research Centres and Lecturer at the Chair for Innovation Management and Entrepreneurship, University of Potsdam, Germany.

Patrice Kandolo Kabeya is Lecturer in Economics, Department of Banking and Finance at Epoka University, Tirana, Albania.

Magnus Karlsson is Adjunct Professor in Innovation Management at KTH Royal Institute of Technology, Stockholm, Sweden, and formerly Director of Innovation Management at Group Function Strategy, Ericsson.

Kong-rae Lee is Professor at Daegu Gyeongbuk Institute of Science and Technology (DGIST).

Regina Lenart-Gansiniec is Assistant Professor at Jagiellonian University in Krakow, Institute of Public Affairs, Poland.

Mats Magnusson is Professor at KTH Royal Institute of Technology, Stockholm, Sweden, and Permanent Visiting Professor at LUISS School of Business and Management, Rome, Italy.

Liang Mei is Associate Research Fellow at the National School of Development, Peking University, Beijing, China.

Dirk Meissner is Professor at National Research University Higher School of Economics, Laboratory for Economics of Innovation, Moscow, Russia.

Sumit Mitra is Professor of Strategic Management at Indian Institute of Management Kozhikode, Kerala, India.

Contributors

Susanna Ghosh Mitra is an Independent Researcher in India. She received her PhD from the University of Manchester, UK.

Elisabeth Noll is a management consultant in the automotive industry in Germany.

Petra A. Nylund is a researcher at Friedrich-Alexander-Universität Erlangen-Nürnberg (FAU).

Frank Piller is Professor of Technology and Innovation Management, RWTH Aachen University, Germany.

Franc Ponti is Professor of Innovation at EADA Business School.

Stephen Rainey is Research Fellow in the Centre for Computing and Social Responsibility of De Montfort University, Leicester, UK.

Naqeeb Ur Rehman is Lecturer in Economics at Epoka University, Tirana, Albania.

Eugenia Rosca is Lecturer in Supply Chain Management in the Department of Management, School of Economics and Management, Tilburg University, the Netherlands.

Yi Ruan is Assistant Professor in the International Business Management Department at University of Nottingham Ningbo China.

Jakob Schlegel is a Masters Student at the School of Business and Economics, Friedrich-Alexander-Universität Erlangen-Nürnberg (FAU), Germany.

Mark Shaw is Senior Research Fellow at the Centre for Computing and Social Responsibility of De Montfort University, Leicester, UK.

Bernd Carsten Stahl is Professor of Critical Research in Technology and Director of the Centre for Computing and Social Responsibility of De Montfort University, Leicester, UK.

Jos Timmermans is Researcher in the Faculty of Technology, Policy and Management in Delft University of Technology.

Wim Vanhaverbeke is Professor of Innovation Management and Strategy at Hasselt University, Visiting Professor at ESADE Business School, and Visiting Professor at National University of Singapore.

Eric Viardot is Director of the Global Innovation Management Centre and Permanent Professor of Strategy and Marketing at EADA Business School in Barcelona, Spain.

Eric von Hippel is Chair Professor of Woodrow Wilson Center, Sloan School of Management, Massachusetts Institute of Technology.

Ximing Yin is a PhD candidate at the School of Economics and Management at Tsinghua University, Beijing, China.

Contributors

Fei Yu is Associate Professor in Prototyping at Mads Clausen Institute, University of Southern Denmark.

Fei Yu is Associate Researcher, Research Center for Technological Innovation, Tsinghua University, China.

Oliver Yu is President and CEO, The STARS Group; Chairman of the Board, Global Alliance of Innovators & Entrepreneurs; and Board Member, IEEE Technology & Engineering Management Society.

Suli Zheng is Professor of School of Economics and Management, China Jiliang University, Hangzhou, China.

Kristina Zisler is a management consultant in the financial services industry in Germany.

PART I

Introduction to innovation and innovation management

1
INNOVATION AND INNOVATION MANAGEMENT

Jin Chen, Eric Viardot and Alexander Brem

Value of innovation

Innovation and human development

The history of mankind is one of innovation, especially our great economic leaps over the past two centuries (Fu and Gong, 2011). The Renaissance in the 14th century shattered backward thoughts by introducing new thinking. The navigation rush in the 15th century expanded the bounds of human civilization. The scientific revolution, which began in the 16th century, laid the foundation for the technological revolution. The capital market, which was born in the beginning of the 17th century, made financial activities a widespread phenomenon in society. The Industrial Revolution, which began in the 18th century, gave a great impetus to economies around the world. Although current economic theories and other doctrines fail to explain all these phenomena perfectly, many scholars have identified a common factor – innovation – in the chain of historical events (Chen, 2017b).

Alec Foege, author of *The Tinkerers: The Amateurs, DIYers, and Inventors Who Make America Great*, referred to innovators – amateurs, DIYers and inventors who enjoyed fiddling with small devices and inventions – as "tinkerers" (meaning "工匠" when translated into Chinese), to whom he attributed the miracle of America: "American tinkerers are a group of independent people who make world-changing inventions and innovations with sheer willpower and tenacity". For example, Benjamin Franklin, Eli Whitney, Cyrus McCormick, Thomas Edison and the Wright brothers were outstanding innovators in human history. Such inventors come these days from emerging markets like India ("jugaad") and Brazil ("gambiarra") but also from China (Agarwal, Grottke, Mishra, and Brem, 2017; Wimschneider, Agarwal, and Brem, 2018).

There, a new round of technological and industrial revolutions is forthcoming as a radical change in the global industrial structure and competition pattern begins to arise (Chen, Zhao, and Wang, 2014). Disruptive innovations that may make a breakthrough in the future are of great importance to our "technology-economy-society" pattern (Christensen, Baumann, Ruggles, and Sadtler, 2006).

The National Economic Council and the Office of Science and Technology Policy issued the newest version of the Strategy for American Innovation at the end of October 2015, announcing the commitment to the development of nine strategic areas (as shown in Table 1.1).

Table 1.1 Nine strategic areas in the Strategy for American Innovation

S. No.	Area	Description
1	Advanced manufacturing	A National Network for Manufacturing Innovation will be launched to restore the nation's lead at the cutting edge of manufacturing innovation.
2	Precision medicine	Precision medicine will boost developments in genomics, large data sets and health information technology while protecting privacy. It gives clinicians tools to better understand the complex mechanisms underlying a patient's health, disease or condition and to better predict which treatments will be most effective.
3	Brain initiative	A deepened knowledge of how brains work, based on genetics, will help scientists and doctors diagnose and treat neurological disorders.
4	Advanced vehicles	Breakthrough developments in sensing, computing and data science will bring vehicle-to-vehicle communication and cutting-edge autonomous technology safety features into commercial deployment.
5	Smart cities	An emerging community of civic leaders, data scientists, technologists and companies are joining forces to build "smart cities".
6	Clean energy and energy-efficient technologies	The administration will continue to deploy and develop clean energy technologies, fund climate-change solutions and increase new energy production while improving America's energy security.
7	Educational technology	The president has proposed to give 99 percent of students access to high-speed broadband by 2018. And the 2016 budget includes $50 million for the creation of an Advanced Research Projects Agency for Education.
8	Space	America will make core investments in the development of commercial crew space transportation capability by 2017. America will also invest in research on the protection of astronauts from space radiation, on advanced propulsion systems and on technologies that allow humans to live in outer space.
9	New frontiers in computing	In July 2015, the president created the National Strategic Computing Initiative to spur the creation and deployment of computing technology at the leading edge, helping advance administration priorities for economic competitiveness, scientific discovery and national security.

In May 2013, McKinsey Global Institute released *Disruptive Technologies: Advances That Will Transform Life, Business and the Global Economy by 2025*,[1] a report that estimated the direct impact of these technologies on the global economy between $14 and $33 trillion. Table 1.2 provides the details on the major technologies and areas.

Innovation and national/regional competitiveness

Currently scientific progress and innovation play a decisive role in economic and social development in the world (Chen, Yin, and Mei, 2018). An entity, whether as big as a country or as small as an enterprise, will miss the opportunity of proactive future development if it fails to grab

Table 1.2 Twelve disruptive technologies

S. No.	Area	Description	Potential economic impact on the world by 2025
11	Mobile Internet	Smaller, viewable, wearable and more powerful mobile computing devices with more sensors benefit consumers with improved medical and educational services, and elevate employee productivity.	$373 mln–$10.8 tln
22	Automation of knowledge work	This automation technology applies primarily to ordinary business operation (e.g. marketing, customer service and administrative support), social services (e.g. education and medical care), technology industries (e.g. science, engineering and IT) and professional services (law and finance).	$523 mln–$6.7 tln, equivalent to 120 mln–140 mln full-time jobs
33	IoT (Internet of Things)	IoT has the biggest economic impact on medical care and manufacturing. It is also applied to smart grids, urban infrastructure, resource exploitation, agriculture and automobiles.	$273 mln–$6.2 tln
44	Cloud	Cloud technology means a simpler, faster, more powerful and more efficient digital world that creates great value for consumers as well as enterprises, which can manage information more efficiently and flexibly.	$173 mln–$6.2 tln
55	Advanced robotics	Advanced robotics covers primarily industrial robotics, surgical robotics, exoskeleton robotics, prosthetic robotics, service robotics and domestic robotics.	$173 mln–$4.5tln
66	Autonomous and near-autonomous vehicles	Safer, less congestion, more time savings, less fuel consumption and less emissions.	$23 mln–$1.9 tln; can save 30,000–150,000 lives
77	Next-generation genomics	Next-generation genomics quickens advances in biology and applies primarily to the diagnosis and treatment of diseases, agriculture and biofuel production.	$70 mln–$1.6 tln
88	Energy storage	The technology applies primarily to electrical/hybrid vehicles, distributed energy, utilities and energy storage.	$90 bln–$635 bln
99	3D printing	Major applications include consumers, direct product manufacturing, tool and die making and bioprinting of tissue and organs.	$230 bln–$550 bln
110	Advanced nanomaterials	Advanced nanomaterials have found extensive application in medical care, electronics, composite materials, solar cells, desalination and catalyzers, but the cost is higher. Nanomedical materials have very great potential to be used for targeted cancer therapy.	$150 bln–$500 bln
111	Advanced oil and gas exploration and recovery	Shale gas and light crude oil exploration and recovery, primarily in North America.	$95 bln–$460 bln
112	Renewable energy	By 2025 wind power and solar power may increase from 2% to 16% of global electricity generation.	$165 bln–$275 bln; equivalent to 1 bln to 1.2 bln less tons of carbon emissions

Source: Chunping (2016).

self-developed core technology or intellectual property (IP) assets instrumental in innovation activities. Economists have attributed the fast growth of the world economy following World War II to a push for technological innovation.

Innovation has been widely recognized as the main driver and first impetus for a sustainable regional or national economic growth, as well as global competency (Acs, Audretsch, Lehmann, and Licht, 2017; Brem and Viardot, 2017). Especially for those emerging economies, it's no longer a useful tool for them to depend on international trade or labor-intensive work such as manufacturing. The marginal benefit from labor investment is decreasing, while the returns of investment in new technology are increasing, which becomes a new driving force for the emerging economics to obtain a competitive advantage in the global market (Aguirre-Bastos and Weber, 2018). Both developed and developing countries are trying to build up their national innovation system in order to cultivate creative talents, high-tech based start-ups and new technology that could be translated into sustainable power for industrial upgrading and economic growth (Chen, 2017a). This is also the main reason why Asian countries such as South Korea, Japan, China and India continue to increase their domestic expenditure on research and development (R&D), sharing the largest proportion of the worldwide R&D expenditure, about 42.9 percent in 2017, according to the 2017 Annual Global R&D Funding Forecast.[2] For example, South Korea ranks number one in national innovation competitiveness among all the countries in 2018, according to the 2018 Bloomberg Innovation Index.[3] China moved up two spots to 19th, buoyed by its high proportion of new science and engineering graduates in the labor force and an increasing number of patents by innovators such as Huawei Technologies Co., and is the first-ever developing country who gets a position in the top 20 most innovative countries in history.

Innovation is a double-edged sword in terms of social impact (Martin, 2016). On the one hand, many innovative products make our life better. For example, the plane and the high-speed rail make travel faster, and Apple smart devices have changed our lifestyle fundamentally. A large number of new products and services are delivered to every corner of the world. An increasing share of the public can have access to more plentiful food, life necessities and better medical services.

But innovation means possible negative effects as well. For example, industrial technologies may cause pollution, agricultural and fishing technologies may aggravate ecological problems and medical technologies may involve drug-resistance problems and bioethical issues (like genetic engineering). However, technology is essentially a knowledge-based means of solving problems and achieving goals. Overall, innovation, if effectively managed, will minimize its negative effects to better serve mankind, in which case we call it an inclusive innovation or responsible innovation (George, McGahan, and Prabhu, 2012; Stilgoe, Owen, and Macnaghten, 2013; Timmermans, Yaghmaei, Stahl, and Brem, 2017).

Innovation and corporate competitiveness

Innovation creates inexhaustible energy for corporate existence and development

The global competition pattern is now reducing down to economic and technology competition, which is increasingly drawing momentum from technological innovation (Chen, Yin, and Zhao, 2019; Kumpe and Bolwijn, 1994). More and more firms have found high production efficiency, quality and even flexibility to be insufficient to maintain competitive advantages. Instead, innovation is increasingly creating an inexhaustible energy for corporate existence and development (see Figure 1.1).

Innovation and innovation management

Time	Market requirement	Corporate management focus	Firm type	Management feature
1960s–1970s	Price	Production efficiency (cost reduction)	Efficient firm	Fordism (standardization and mass production)
1980s	Price + quality	Efficiency + quality	Quality firm	Total quality management
1990s	Price + quality + product line	Efficiency + quality + flexibility	Flexible firm	Flexible manufacturing system; JIT (just in time)
Late 1990s–present	Price + quality + product line + uniqueness	Efficiency + quality + flexibility + innovativeness	Innovative firm	Total innovation management

Figure 1.1 Evolution of corporate management
Source: Kumpe and Bolwijn (1994).

Increasingly shorter technology life cycle

Whereas it took typically several decades to successfully commercialize a technological invention in the first half of the 20th century, the cycle shortened significantly beginning in the second half. The telephone took as long as 60 years to enter 50 percent of American homes in the first half of the 20th century, but the Internet took only 5 years to enter most American homes. Corroborating the increasingly fast cycle, Moore's law observes that the storage capacity per unit area of a chip doubles every 18 months and that the bandwidth of a backbone network doubles every 6 months (see Table 1.3).

The life cycle of software products, measured in terms of the duration from introduction to exit or replacement by other products, has dropped to 4 to 12 months. Similarly, the time is 12 to 24 months for hardware and consumer electronics products, and 18 to 36 months for white goods. The firm is therefore compelled to adopt an innovation strategy. Without fast innovation, a firm would end up losing market share as its products become out of date.[4]

Towards an innovative firm

The Boston Consulting Group (BCG) issued The 50 Most Innovative Companies in December 2018, ranking Apple on top for one more year and including three Chinese companies[5] (see Table 1.4).

The companies on the list were generally believed to have four elements essential to success: high speed of innovation, good and simple R&D procedure, employment of a technology platform and systematic development of neighboring markets.

If we look back on the rankings over the past decade, we would find that many regular winners are masters of innovation, the power that drives continually growing proceeds. These include Apple, Google, Microsoft, Samsung, Tesla, BMW, Amazon, IBM, Hewlett-Packard, SpaceX, General Electric, Cisco, Huawei, Alibaba and Tencent.

Table 1.3 Significant technological innovations in history

Technology or product	Year of invention	Year of innovation	Invention-innovation cycle (y)
Fluorescent lamp	1859	1938	79
Compass	1852	1908	56
Zipper	1891	1918	27
Television	1919	1941	22
Jet engine	1929	1943	14
Copy machine	1937	1950	13
Steam engine	1764	1775	11
Turbine engine	1934	1944	10
Radiogram	1889	1897	8
Triode	1907	1914	7
DDT	1939	1942	3
Freon	1930	1931	1

Source: Qingrui (2000)

Table 1.4 The 50 most innovative companies for 2018

1. Apple	18. General Electric	35. Adidas
2. Google	19. Orange	36. BMW
3. Microsoft	20. Marriott	37. Nissan
4. Amazon	21. Siemens	38. Pfizer
5. Samsung	22. Unilever	39. Time Warner
6. Tesla	23. BASF	40. Renault
7. Facebook	24. Expedia	41. 3M
8. IBM	25. Johnson & Johnson	42. SAP
9. Uber	26. JPMorgan Chase	43. DuPont
10. Alibaba	27. Bayer	44. InterContinental Hotels Group
11. Airbnb	28. Dow Chemical	45. Disney
12. SpaceX	29. AT&T	46. Huawei
13. Netflix	30. Allianz	47. Procter & Gamble
14. Tencent	31. Intel	48. Verizon
15. Hewlett-Packard	32. NTT Docomo	49. Philips
16. Cisco Systems	33. Daimler	50. Nestle
17. Toyota	34. AXA	

Source: Michael Ringel and Hadi Zablit. Published online at January 17, 2018. www.bcg.com/en-us/publications/2018/most-innovative-companies-2018-innovation.aspx

According to the analysis of American scholars Kumpe and Piet, the mainstream model of corporate development has evolved from the effective firm to the quality firm, and then to the flexible firm; now the flexible firm is on the road to becoming the innovative firm (Kumpe and Bolwijn, 1994) (as shown in Figure 1.2). It's worth noting that Chinese firms are typically 10 to 20 years behind the international firms with regard to a development model due to historical reasons and technological strength.

The facts have shown that beginning in the 1990s (especially the 21st century), the majority of the most successful firms made it through cost reduction combined with quality and flexibility improvement. However, increasing economic globalization and competition have driven some firms to look beyond the relentless pursuit of quality and flexibility. They put a premium

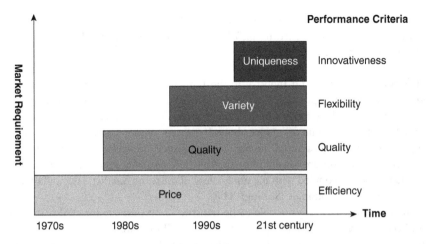

Figure 1.2 Evolution of the corporate development model
Source: Kumpe and Bolwijn (1994)

on innovation in order to compete with their rivals for market share as innovative organizations. Fast innovation has gradually emerged as a key weapon of market competitiveness as the one-time flexible firms find they are losing market share to more innovative firms. Of course, high efficiency, quality and flexibility remain the pillars of innovative firms.

Typically, an innovative firm makes a consistent effort to seek new breakthroughs in the area of its specialty to reduce cost, improve quality and flexibility and, finally, provide the market with products of outstanding price, quality and performance. The firm encourages an innovation culture and is equipped with an organizational structure and a stimulation mechanism conducive to effective communication and fast innovation (Greve, 2003).

The common belief of the innovative firms is that innovativeness has become the factor most critical to business success. An innovative organization is a learning organization as well. Innovation means not only the development of new products and technologies but also of new markets, of new material sources and of new uses for the same products (Schumpeter, 1934).

At present, most of the Chinese firms run in a model of efficiency and quality; a number of leading firms are characterized by flexibility; only a limited few of the leading firms have got on the road to innovativeness (Chen, Tong, and Ngai, 2007).

Overall, the innovative firm is a new type of firm as opposed to its counterparts focused on efficiency, quality and flexibility. Some prominent features of an innovative firm include the focus on such core values as innovativeness; the integration of global innovative resources (including the staff); a coordinated innovation model that covers tactics, strategy, culture, institutions, markets, organization and processes in a ubiquitous range; and self-developed IP assets and core technology needed to maintain a consistent competitive advantage.

The importance of innovation management

In *The Innovator's Solution* (Christensen and Raynor, 2013), Christensen writes:

> No matter how hard the gifted people are, many of the attempts to create new products have failed at last. 60% of the new products died before they are listed, and in the

rest 40% of products that can be seen in the market, 40% of them are unprofitable and withdrawn from the market. In all, 75% of the investment in product development ended in failure at last.

The Department of Trade and Industry in the United Kingdom once conducted a survey of 14,000 organizations that purchased computer software and found that 80 to 90 percent of projects did not achieve the expected performance goals, about 80 percent of projects exceed the scheduled development time or budget, about 40 percent of projects end in failure and only 10 to 20 percent of projects achieved the expected goal successfully. In the process of innovation, various unknown factors are usually unpredictable. The results of innovation investment efforts are generally random, coupled with the uncertainty of the future market – thus, all of these make innovation a very risky business (Stirling, 2008).

Many innovative ideas are not able to be translated into new products. Also, many projects cannot become technically feasible products. And even if they are technically feasible, they may not necessarily get market recognition. The success rate of innovation in some industries is very low. Taking new drug development as an example, commonly, only 1 of 3,000 initial innovative ideas is able to be commercially successful. And it often takes 12 years or even longer from the discovery to listing of the new drug and costs hundreds of millions of dollars. Therefore, the innovation process is often seen as a funnel, and there are many new ideas with potential for development at the beginning, but only a few successes can be achieved in the end (see example in Figure 1.3).

In order to achieve better market success for innovation, Brem and Viardot (2015) underline the importance of the downstream activities of the innovation process, namely marketing and commercialization; they suggest adopting innovation as a priority in the innovation strategy of firms and governments, as the European Union has done in its Horizon 2020 innovation plan (Salmelin, 2013). Similarly, the importance of the adoption of innovation by consumers has been acknowledged with the emergence of the conceptual model of Quadruple Helix Innovation, where citizens are adding a fourth element to the more traditional combination of partnership for innovation between the industry, the government and the universities (Carayannis and Campbell, 2009).

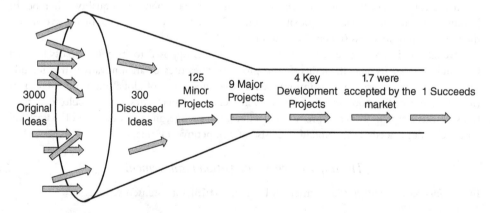

Figure 1.3 Sketch map of the innovation funnel model (using new drug development as an example)
Source: Jin (2002)

Innovation and innovation management

Innovation management: an integration framework

In order to complete the transformation of idea to market value, innovation management needs careful design in terms of strategy, organization, resource and culture (institution), which means the "creative destruction" based on deconstruction and the "organizational reconstruction and regularization" management activities based on construction are reasonably interacted to continuously promote the evolution of the company (Chen, Huang, and Xu, 2015). In general, innovation requires "horizontal-vertical theory", or in other words, a holistic innovation framework (Chen, Yin, and Mei, 2018). Horizontal management is the combination of vision and creativity, R&D, manufacturing and sales; vertical management requires the coordination of strategy, organization, resources and culture (institution) (see Figure 1.4).

Innovation strategy

Innovation requires the overall strategic guidance of the company. From the perspective of the logical structure and way of thinking of the discipline, innovation and strategy are almost the same. Or, at least, innovation should be taken into consideration when designing the corporate-level strategy. There is a strong correlation between the lack of indigenous innovation of Chinese companies and the weakness of their own strategic management capabilities, whereby indigenous innovation is a specific Chinese innovation term (Brem, 2009). Many companies only have profit and sales targets but no growth indicators based on indigenous intellectual property rights and technological innovation. Therefore, Chinese companies have always been unbalanced between their investment in growth (such as innovation) and their investment in shareholder or financial returns. There is no such strategic arrangement. A company that is eager to innovate must go beyond its traditional development model and realize the transformation from a business model based on introduction and simple manufacturing to the business model that integrates external emerging, breakthrough science technology and commercial resources to

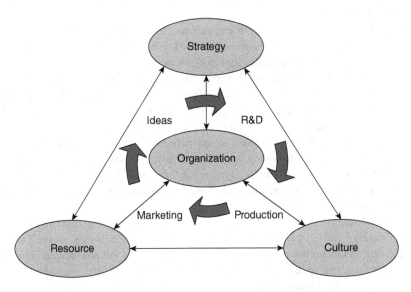

Figure 1.4 Holistic framework for corporation innovation management integration
Source: Chen (2002)

create higher value-added, more environmentally friendly products or services. In other words, companies that integrate innovation strategy, culture, resources and traditional strategic tools could achieve superior economic rents than the ones who don't (Chen, Huang, and Xu, 2015).

3M, the model of world-class innovation, has been strategically demanding that new products and services developed during the year should contribute 10 percent of the sales revenue for the next year, which makes 3M develop 1,500 new products each year. Some leading Chinese companies, such as China International Marine Containers (Group) Co., Ltd., have been transforming from the early stage of simply copying foreign samples to the development of high-quality products and strive to master the core patents, formulating or participating in the formulation of international standards for containers more actively, reflecting some Chinese enterprises' new understanding and actions in terms of innovation competition. Therefore, strengthening strategic management capabilities, enhancing strategic innovation capabilities and strengthening the benign interaction between corporate strategy and technological innovation are important conditions for the implementation of indigenous innovation. Without strategic analysis of corporate strategy, product design and technology realization, it is nearly impossible for Chinese companies to achieve indigenous innovation in a real sense.

Innovative organization

In order to realize indigenous innovation, a company should focus on optimizing the frame of innovative organization. Traditional Chinese companies continue the bureaucratic and hierarchical organizational structure of industrial society, which makes the connection between R&D, production and marketing very unstable. Even the high-intensity R&D is not enough to break the barriers (Baldwin and von Hippel, 2011). Besides, since market demand and technology supply cannot be matched appropriately, technological achievements are difficult to translate into new products and productivity. A modern innovative company must reform its organizational structure fundamentally and rebuild a customer-oriented and process-oriented organizational form, so as to translate ideas into products that are manufacturable and commercially valuable more quickly and efficiently.

The Haier Group constantly adjusts its organizational structure and strives to achieve a harmonious unity of business stream, product stream and logistics. This customer-oriented adaptive structure matches business orders with employees' work tasks, and even goes one step further in terms of the organizational structure that is visible and nonexecutive, or what we call it "flat organization" (Kanter and Dai, 2018; Lewin, Välikangas, and Chen, 2017). These actions played an important role in starting innovation and realizing the final value or innovation. The BMW Group is meticulous about its coordination of innovations. Every time BMW starts to develop a new type of car, 200 to 300 project team members from the engineering, design, production, marketing, procurement, and financing departments of the BMW Group will gather in the research and innovation center and work together for three years. This kind of close relationship can promote face-to-face communication, thus avoiding contradictions between marketing and engineering departments later on.

Companies should continue to strengthen organizational transforming in terms of innovation and build a superior process platform in order to turn new ideas into new values. The organizational structure is further oriented toward customers, flattening and reducing the bureaucratic control of the organization and enhancing the service function of the organization – it is a good method for the promotion of indigenous innovation of Chinese companies (Baldwin and von Hippel, 2011). In order to achieve this type of organizational transformation, future corporate managers should be led by the chief operating officer, chief innovation officer and chief resource officer. The main responsibility of the chief executive officer is to exert the enthusiasm and creativity of these three managers. We believe that the value creation of a company will be completed by operations-related and innovation-related activities. Operations (which mainly includes current products, markets, manufacturing, logistics, etc.) are mainly responsible for the creation of corporate cash flow and profits, while innovation (with an emphasis on strategy, technology, future R&D and market development) focuses on gaining potential and more options for future sustainable development. In order to achieve the value creation, a company must build or acquire powerful resources and capabilities and conduct management and service work appropriately. What's more, the chief innovation officer needs to integrate the capabilities of marketing expert, technical expert, strategist and industrialist.

Innovation of resources

Resource refers to the core assets for a company to obtain a competitive advantage (Barney, 2001), while at the same time, innovation is a creative recombination of resources (Schumpeter, 1934). The resources include a series of tangible and intangible ones, such as information, capital, talent, brand and intellectual property (Barney, 2001). Realizing indigenous innovation of a company requires it to continuously enrich and expand its innovation resources, especially information and knowledge sources. In order to speed up this process, a company needs to fully mobilize the enthusiasm of employees to participate in innovation and gradually realize the full participation of the company's indigenous innovation (Xu et al., 2007). The Baosteel Group Corporation' requires four annual rationalization suggestions from each person, and more people are engaged in competitive information development every year, which is a valuable attempt among domestic companies in this regard. Toyota has become the most innovative company in the world, with 35 suggestions per person every year and a total of 2,000,000 suggestions, which helps Toyota generate continuous creative and valuable ideas that could be commercialized into profitable products.

The market research ability of Chinese companies is still weak. Regarding the condition that market demand is increasingly segmented, relying solely on operator intuition is not enough. Most Chinese companies still don't know how to apply the scenario analysis method yet. Technology foresight, competitive intelligence tools that should be used for the analysis of strategy and market or overall information and intelligence resources of enterprises are still scarce. Compared to all computer publications ordered by IBM and the knowledge library of Huawei, most of the files and information bases of Chinese companies still need to be improved.

In the open innovation era, companies cannot just rely on internal limited resources to achieve innovation (Chesbrough, Vanhaverbeke, and West, 2006). The ability of acquiring external knowledge becomes more and more important. Interactive learning is an important condition for acquiring external resources to create innovation (Berchicci, 2013). Therefore, learning and R&D will become two important aspects of innovation. At the same time, users, especially the leading users who are directly involved in innovation, will accelerate the process of innovation and increase the success rate (Foxall and Johnston, 1987; Brem, Bilgram, and Gutstein, 2018). We believe that user-based democratized innovation will have a great influence on China's innovation practice. Similarly, suppliers are also major innovators. For companies with strong capital capability, they can help small, technologically advanced companies develop innovative projects via seed funding and venture capital. In this way, big companies could obtain technological capabilities through the successful R&D of small companies, who are suppliers for them. In order to avoid duplication of R&D or to offset for deficiencies in the company's technology, companies can also acquire advanced technologies and key technologies efficiently and economically through the purchase of external technologies or technology mergers to accelerate technological innovation.

In short, the process of diversification and integration of corporate innovation resources should also be part of the process of establishing a corporation innovation network. Innovation resources and innovation networks complement each other and jointly promote corporation innovation, in which efficient flow and recombination of resources through internal and external networks could accelerate the innovation and commercialization process.

Innovation culture

An innovation culture plays an important role in the effective development of technological innovation (Kratzer, Meissner, and Roud, 2017). Compared with information, capital and organizational structure, innovation culture is called the other side of technological innovation. The reason why the innovation of Haier succeeded is because it effectively integrates Confucian culture (a suitable hierarchy), American entrepreneurial spirit, Japanese team culture and German quality culture. Emphasis on innovation culture can have a greater significance. Zhang Ruimin defined himself as a chief cultural officer, which gave him a higher vision than the general CEO. Therefore, he further promoted Haier's innovation via pushing and building a culture that attracts full participation and encourages both exploitation and exploration.

Values, institutional systems, behavioral norms and physical carriers are the four aspects of innovation culture and must be highly emphasized by the top management team. Values are the basic characteristics of culture, and contemporary culture innovation should take entrepreneurship as the core and pursue a culture of advancement, development, change and excellence. Innovation culture determines the value orientation of technological innovation. The scale, level, focus and method of technological innovation are often determined by its value orientation. Sony Corporation has always taken "technical leading" as the fundamental orientation of its innovation culture, and its technological innovation is very active. 3M takes "proportion of new products/new business income to sales revenue" as the main goal of business operations, which made it one of the most successful innovation companies in the world.

In order to run the innovation culture, it must be based on a certain system. The communication system of technology and market and the management system of technical human resources are two systems related to technological innovation. The human resource (HR) systems in Chinese companies need revising. The HR system that truly suits innovation is flexible, whereas the hierarchical solidification makes people unwilling to change themselves. At Microsoft, employees are divided into 15 levels that vary from year to year, and salaries are set according to grade. Innovative companies often implement multihierarchy career systems, such as the 15 levels of Microsoft and the 27 levels of Haier.

A behavioral norm is the basic characteristic and specific appearance of culture (Greve, 2003). The innovation culture manifests itself in behavioral norms for entrepreneurs and corporate employees, and the key is to embrace innovation, understand innovation, participate in innovation, value innovation, tolerate failure and have respect for employees' backgrounds (nationality, regions, family, etc.).

The physical carrier is an objective symbol of innovation culture and has obvious guidance and demonstration effects. For example, many innovative companies strongly encourage the establishment of individualized offices, setting up clear signs for the most creative employees and constructing exhibition venues for innovative products for companies. These venues should be displayed to people inside and outside the company to establish the employees' sense of honor in the innovative products.

The best embodiment of a flexible culture of innovation is 3M, while the best embodiment of innovation and cultural discipline is some of China's outstanding companies. Companies such as Huawei and Haier have strict disciplines and even some militarized management styles. Disciplinary culture ensures that all kinds of resources are unimpeded and decisions are implemented.

In general, the culture of innovation should be a unique dualistic culture. On the basis of maintaining unity and coordination, appropriately increasing the connotation of individuality and tolerance for failure is the cultural foundation for companies to achieve indigenous innovation.

Notes

1 See also: www.mckinsey.com/business-functions/digital-mckinsey/our-insights/disruptive-technologies
2 See also: https://learn.rdmag.com/20180112_gff_2018_rd_lp
3 See also: www.bloomberg.com/news/articles/2018-01-22/south-korea-tops-global-innovation-ranking-again-as-u-s-falls
4 Schilling, Melissa A., *Strategic Management of Technological Innovation*. Translated by Xie Wei and Wang Yi. Tsinghua University Press, 2005.
5 See also: www.bcg.com/en-us/publications/2018/most-innovative-companies-2018-innovation.aspx

References

Acs, Z. J., Audretsch, D. B., Lehmann, E. E. and Licht, G. (2017). National systems of innovation. *The Journal of Technology Transfer*, 42(5), 997–1008. https://doi.org/10.1007/s10961-016-9481-8.

Agarwal, N., Grottke, M., Mishra, S. and Brem, A. (2017). A systematic literature review of constraint-based innovations: state of the art and future perspectives. *IEEE Transactions on Engineering Management*, 64(1), 3–15.

Aguirre-Bastos, C. and Weber, M. K. (2018). Foresight for shaping national innovation systems in developing economies. *Technological Forecasting and Social Change*, 128, 186–196. https://doi.org/10.1016/j.techfore.2017.11.025.

Baldwin, C. and von Hippel, E. (2011). Modeling a paradigm shift: from producer innovation to user and open collaborative innovation. *Organization Science*, 22(6), 1399–1417. https://doi.org/10.1287/orsc.1100.0618.

Barney, J. B. (2001). Resource-based theories of competitive advantage: a ten-year retrospective on the resource-based view. *Journal of Management*, 27(6), 643–650. https://doi.org/10.1016/S0149-2063(01)00115-5.

Berchicci, L. (2013). Towards an open R&D system: internal R&D investment, external knowledge acquisition and innovative performance. *Research Policy*, 42(1), 117–127. https://doi.org/10.1016/j.respol.2012.04.017.

Brem, A. (2009). The term innovation and its front end – is there a specific asian view? In *The China information technology handbook*. Boston, MA: Springer, pp. 1–12.

Brem, A., Bilgram, V. and Gutstein, A. (2018). Involving lead users in innovation: a structured summary of research on the lead user method. *International Journal of Innovation and Technology Management*, 15, 3, Article Nr. 1850022.

Brem, A. and Viardot, E. (2015). *Adoption of innovation. Balancing internal and external stakeholders interest for the management of innovation*. Springer-Verlag.

Brem, A. and Viardot, E. (2017). *Revolution in innovation management: internationalization and business models with A. Brem*. Palgrave Macmillan.

Carayannis, E. G. and Campbell, D. F. J. (2009). Mode 3 and 'Quadruple Helix': toward a 21st century fractal innovation ecosystem. *International Journal of Technology Management*, 46(3), 201–234.

Chen, J. (2017a). *Theory of firm innovation system* (1st ed.). Science Publisher.

Chen, J. (2017b). Towards new and multiple perspectives on innovation. *International Journal of Innovation Studies*, 1(1), 1. https://doi.org/10.3724/SP.J.1440.101001.

Chen, J., Huang, S. and Xu, Q. (2015). Firm innovation systems: perspectives of researches on state-owned key enterprises. *Frontiers of Engineering Management*, 2(1), 64. https://doi.org/10.15302/J-FEM-2015017.

Chen, J., Tong, L. and Ngai, E. W. T. (2007). Inter organizational knowledge management in complex products and systems: challenges and an exploratory framework. *Journal of Technology Management in China*, 2(2), 134–144. https://doi.org/10.1108/17468770710756077.

Chen, J., Yin, X. and Mei, L. (2018). Holistic innovation: an emerging innovation paradigm. *International Journal of Innovation Studies*, 2(1), 1–13. https://doi.org/10.1016/j.ijis.2018.02.001.

Chen, J., Yin, X. and Zhao, C. (2019). Firm technological innovation system: perspectives of enhancing corporate indigenous innovation capability. In *The Routledge companion to innovation management* (1st ed., in press). Routledge Companions.

Chen, J., Zhao, X. and Wang, Y. (2014). A new measurement of intellectual capital and its impact on innovation performance in an open innovation paradigm. *International Journal of Technology Management*, 67(1), 1–25. https://doi.org/10.1504/IJTM.2015.065885.

Chesbrough, H., Vanhaverbeke, W. and West, J. (2006). *Open innovation: researching a new paradigm*. Oxford: Oxford University Press. https://books.google.com/books?hl=en&lr=&id=lgZAyauTEKUC&oi=fnd&pg=PT2&dq=open+innovation&ots=7r7KKVNykp&sig=f1aWJZMJjbnkkql-1IKWovzNv1M.

Christensen, C. M., Baumann, H., Ruggles, R. and Sadtler, T. M. (2006, December 1). Disruptive innovation for social change. March 9, 2018 https://hbr.org/2006/12/disruptive-innovation-for-social-change.

Christensen, C. M. and Raynor, M. E. (2013). *The innovator's solution: creating and sustaining successful growth* (1 ed.). Harvard Business Review Press.

Chunping, L. (2016) "National Academy of Innovation Strategy", *Innovation Research Report* (Issue 11, 2016)

Foxall, G. and Johnston, B. (1987). Strategies of user-initiated product innovation. *Technovation*, 6(2), 77–102.

Fu, X. and Gong, Y. (2011). Indigenous and foreign innovation efforts and drivers of technological upgrading: evidence from China. *World Development*, 39(7), 1213–1225. https://doi.org/10.1016/j.worlddev.2010.05.010.

George, G., McGahan, A. M. and Prabhu, J. (2012). Innovation for inclusive growth: towards a theoretical framework and a research agenda. *Journal of Management Studies*, 49(4), 661–683. https://doi.org/10.1111/j.1467-6486.2012.01048.x.

Greve, H. R. (2003). *Organizational learning from performance feedback: a behavioral perspective on innovation and change*. Cambridge; New York: Cambridge University Press.

Kanter, R. M. and Dai, N. H. (2018). Haier: incubating entrepreneurs in a Chinese giant. www.hbs.edu/faculty/Pages/item.aspx?num=54098.

Kratzer, J., Meissner, D. and Roud, V. (2017). Open innovation and company culture: internal openness makes the difference. *Technological Forecasting and Social Change*, 119, 128–138. https://doi.org/10.1016/j.techfore.2017.03.022.

Kumpe, T. and Bolwijn, P. T. (1994). Toward the innovative firm – challenge for R&D management. *Research-Technology Management*, 37(1), 38–44. https://doi.org/10.1080/08956308.1994.11670953.

Lewin, A. Y., Välikangas, L. and Chen, J. (2017). Enabling open innovation: lessons from Haier. *International Journal of Innovation Studies*, 1(1), 5–19. https://doi.org/10.3724/SP.J.1440.101002.

Martin, B. R. (2016). Twenty challenges for innovation studies. *Science and Public Policy*, 43(3), 432–450. https://doi.org/10.1093/scipol/scv077.

Salmelin, B. (2013). Innovation in Horizon 2020 – reflections from open innovation 2.0 paradigm. *Open Innovation 2.0 Conference*, Brussels, November 28, 2013. September 17, 2014. www.euris-programme.eu/.

Schumpeter, J. A. (1934). *Theory of economic development* (New ed.). New Brunswick, NJ: Routledge.

Stilgoe, J., Owen, R. and Macnaghten, P. (2013). Developing a framework for responsible innovation. *Research Policy*, 42(9), 1568–1580. https://doi.org/10.1016/j.respol.2013.05.008.

Stirling, A. (2008). Science, precaution, and the politics of technological risk. *Annals of the New York Academy of Sciences*, 1128(1), 95–110. https://doi.org/10.1196/annals.1399.011.

Timmermans, J., Yaghmaei, E., Stahl, B. C. and Brem, A. (2017). Research and innovation processes revisited – networked responsibility in industry. *Sustainability Accounting, Management and Policy Journal*, 8(3), 307–334.

Wimschneider, C., Agarwal, N. and Brem, A. (2018). Gambiarra – the Brazilian Jugaad innovation? An empirical examination of the antecedents of constraint-based innovations in two cultures, IEEE TEMS-ISIE (International Symposium on Innovation and Entrepreneurship), Beijing.

Xu, Q., Chen, J., Xie, Z., Liu, J., Zheng, G. and Wang, Y. (2007). Total innovation management: a novel paradigm of innovation management in the 21st century. *The Journal of Technology Transfer*, 32(1–2), 9–25. https://doi.org/10.1007/s10961-006-9007-x.

2

DELIBERATE AND SPONTANEOUS

The impact of cognitive disinhibition on people management

Franc Ponti

The human brain is a gray mass full of folds, and it weighs approximately 1,300 grams. All brains are equal in appearance, or almost. In actual fact, the brain of each person is extraordinarily different from the rest. Our connectome (map of neural connections) differs from that of all other people in many ways. In it are deposited our experiences, our particular vision of the world, our knowledge and many more elements. We are the carriers of a brain of which there are no replicas (for the time being).

Every brain houses around 90 billion neurons. Although this figure may vary depending on the source, this is obviously an astronomical amount. If we consider the potential number of connections that can be established among all these neurons, then the figure is mind boggling: between 100 and 500 trillion synapses.

These figures are impressive because, as in the case of the immensity of the universe, they are beyond our routine intuitive comprehension. Modern neuroscience is constantly surprising us with new data on the subject: it seems that neurons are not only found in the brain but that the brain prolongs itself in remote places in our body such as the heart and the stomach. In fact, both these organs help us to perceive reality in a specific way. We often feel emotion with our heart (love, hope, joy) and we experience sensations with our stomach (satiety, security, fear). Some scientists have even gone so far as to affirm that in certain cases the orders that the neurons from these two organs send to the brain may be stronger than those being sent in the opposite direction.

To start with, the brain is a conservative organ. Its main functions are to control, both internally (the body's homeostasis in all the senses) and externally (detecting dangers and sending out alarm signals). Hence, if we suddenly bump into an infuriated wild boar in an isolated spot in the woods, this triggers a series of mechanisms, which are regulated by brain functions (especially the emotional brain) that in turn articulate protection and defense mechanisms: adrenaline secretions, a change in blood flow, a faster pulse, etc. However, our brain is able to adapt with more or less effort to any new task we propose: learning a language, studying a subject or quitting something (smoking, for example). This is made possible thanks to what is known as neuroplasticity, in other words, the brain's capacity to regenerate itself and form new neural connections, which subsequently incorporate and fix new learnings and experiences.

Its degree of plasticity will depend in any event on how trained the brain is to register changes and proceed to process and integrate them. In this respect, young brains start off with a certain advantage: we all know from experience that it is better to learn a language at the age of seven than at the age of seventy. Having said this, a trained brain of an elderly person can still learn, change and constantly adapt itself.

From the standpoint of creativity, the brain also acts as a sound box of each person's immediate environment. Leaving genetics aside, the creative brain continues to build itself throughout a person's lifetime, but the experiences during the first fifteen or twenty years of one's life are certainly very important. Lives that are led under controlled parameters and excessive security tend not to be as creative as others. By contrast, life trajectories rooted in exploration and play tend to express greater creativity.

It is said that the creator of the video game *Super Mario Bros.*, Shigeru Miyamoto, spent his childhood playing with sticks and strings near the riverside in Kyoto, Japan. He used to make dolls and puppets and performed shows for his friends. One day he discovered a cave and began spending hours and hours in the dark, letting his imagination run wild. The childhood accounts of many highly creative individuals underline the fundamental importance of play and of transgressing the limits of normality in forging an innovative trajectory. These words uttered by George Bernard Shaw are very much to the point here: "We do not cease to play because we become adults; we become adults when we stop playing".[1]

A large number of people, for different reasons, do not manage to exploit their creative potential to the full. Either out of personal choice or due to factors related to their environment, these people are being towed along, simply letting things happen to them throughout the course of their lives. They are always expecting things to happen and often opt out when it comes to their creative capacities, passing on the challenge to other people. Others, on the other hand, act as leaders of their own creativity, challenging conventions, breaking barriers, overcoming their fears and generating an extraordinary attitude of vital creativity. These are people who build their own lives.

Why are there so many differences between people with regard to creativity? Why are some people very creative, whereas others aren't or don't show it? Does this depend solely on genetic factors? Does it have to do with a person's learnings, experiences and attitude towards life? Most probably it's a bit of everything. However, the great majority of experts in creativity attach relatively little importance to genetics while emphasizing the relevance of environmental factors. At the end of the road (or at the beginning, as one prefers), creativity is something that we build, design, live and dream.

Generally speaking, which factors determine personal creativity?

- Enjoying a childhood (at home or at school) full of opportunities to explore, dare, cross limits and discover things through constant play and experimentation. The findings of some studies confirm that children with a rigid learning environment (with too many restrictions on how to do things) end up losing their curiosity and the excitement of coming up with answers on their own.
- Living in an environment that facilitates and fosters creativity, be it at school, in the workplace or any other social circumstances. Unfortunately, this very familiar sentence is still echoed throughout many organizations: "You are not being paid to be creative but to do your job properly". At the other end of the scale, cutting-edge organizations do away with rigid hierarchies, create collaboration and experimentation spaces and succeed in promoting creative trust among their members.

- Enjoying "T"-shaped learning, whereby the top part of the letter consists of various types of knowledge (music, history, comics, gardening, etc.) and the vertical part corresponds to intensive specialization (in industrial engineering, for example). The combination of directions in knowledge (horizontal-vertical) means that people combine their specialization with transversality. New combinations and different perspectives spring up as a result, and these constitute the basic elements for creative action.
- Having great passion, accompanied by curiosity, for either one particular field or various fields. People who tend to flow, as Csikszentmihalyi[2] has very aptly defined it, are usually much more creative than people who do things simply because they have to do them. An individual who has mastered a particular talent (dance, for example), who incorporates elements of creativity in their activity and who happens to be in the right place at the right time to fulfill their dream, has all the chances of situating themselves in their "element" or "creativity zone" (a term coined by Ken Robinson).[3]
- In addition to this, there may be some genetic factors that highlight our creative potential. The real query in this respect is whether this simply has to do with genetic "determinants" or a combination of these and environmental factors.

Obviously this is not an exhaustive list. Creativity is so slippery, elusive and complex that it would be pretentious to draw up a totally comprehensive list of factors that promote it. Having said this, we have most probably mentioned some of the most significant ones. In this chapter we are going to look into one of the most important concepts for being creative, what is known as cognitive disinhibition (CD), and we will also present the results of a recent study on this subject,

What is cognitive disinhibition?

We can define CD as the brain's incapacity to filter irrelevant information for a specific practice or for survival.[4] Expressed in other words, our brain tends to select information that is relevant or useful for a given daily task: grooming, going down a staircase or thinking creatively. If, for example, we intend to come up with ideas on how to improve a ballpoint pen, our brain automatically filters everything that is irrelevant to this specific task while we come up with improvement ideas for the ballpoint pen, for example, a giraffe, our grandmother's face or baked onions.

Experts in creativity point out – and there is quite a lot of consensus on this – that there are two clearly differentiated pathways towards creative thinking: the deliberate pathway and the spontaneous pathway.[5] Deliberate thinkers are sequential, logical and structured. They focus their attention on the object or process that needs to be improved and exercise conscious creative control over it. Observation using neuroimaging shows that the active brain areas during a deliberate episode are the left prefrontal cortex and certain areas of the left parietal and temporal cortexes (the executive control network). In contrast, spontaneous thinkers find it difficult to focus their attention on the selected object or process, and their minds tend to wander and mix different pieces of information. Ideas do not occur directly or consciously but pop up suddenly and unexpectedly. The brain areas activated in the case of spontaneous thinkers are the alternative brain areas: interhemispheric associative thinking zones, the limbic system, etc. (the default network).

CD takes place much more frequently in spontaneous thinkers than in deliberate thinkers. The default network, the alternative brain system to that of the executive control network, far from filtering irrelevant information, allows concepts coming from the brain's implicit (unconscious) structures to combine in unusual ways and enable more imaginative and transgressive solutions.

There is sufficient scientific evidence confirming that the majority of highly creative individuals activate their spontaneous networks more often, although they are also able to engage in both types of thinking simultaneously, which allows them to fantasize and play around with concepts and, at the same time, to evaluate information critically and come up with solutions adapted to the real world.

Having said this, in order to construct a creative or innovation team, it is important to have a combination of people of both styles, as long as they share a common denominator: the ability to listen, respect and integrate ideas. The deliberate–spontaneous conflict can prove to be very productive if it is managed in an appropriate fashion: building on the other person's ideas through dialogue and collaboration. The efficacy of creative disciplines such as design thinking, one of most successful innovation methodologies around today, is grounded on combining deliberate phases (empathy towards users, defining the user's point of view) with spontaneous phases (coming up with new concepts and prototyping). It is therefore important for a design thinking team to incorporate profiles that are as diverse as possible (spontaneous, deliberate, visual, emotional, cognitive, etc.), always on the condition that its members overcome the limitations of their egos and embrace the cooperative dimension and a collective win-win mind-set.

In addition to the two general styles we have discussed, some authors state that creativity can be expressed through seven different and complementary brainsets: connecting (establishing remote associations between ideas), reasoning (using memory and logic to argue), visualizing (perceiving reality in a visual and metaphoric way), absorbing (leaving the mind in a state of repose), transforming (creating through negative emotional states), evaluating (judging ideas critically and taking decisions) and flowing (a state of motivation that leads to alterations with the passing of time and provides a sensation of union with the creative activity). Highly creative individuals would be able to switch in and out of a greater number of brainsets than less creative people, who would be settled in a more reduced comfort zone.

Evidently, both the general creative style and the previously mentioned brainsets can be developed in each individual. Generally speaking, creative genius would obtain the greatest possible number of creative registers; in other words, it would be able to achieve the largest number of combinations and maximum intensity by spanning across all the generated creativity options.

Due to the brain's neuroplasticity, understood as the brain's capacity to create new connections arising from different vital experiences and learnings, we can develop both the general creative style (deliberate or spontaneous) and the different brainsets. Table 2.1 outlines different practices, habits or exercises that can help anyone work on their failings or consolidate their strengths. In this respect, this constitutes a real "personal creative development plan", which would enable the person to evolve creatively in the desired direction (see Table 2.1):

Associated concepts

It is worthwhile going over a series of concepts that are very closely related to CD: divergent thinking, meditation, mindfulness and psychopathology.

With regard to divergent thinking, which consists of coming up with several ideas or solutions to open-ended problems (alternative uses for a plastic cup, for example), it seems logical that CD tends to favor the quantity of ideas that are generated and at the same time allows these ideas to be more original. In fact, if CD enables more heterogeneous interaction between the elements of information which are able to cross the brain filters, it seems evident that the degree of originality of the ideas will be greater. A plastic cup, for example, could easily be converted

Table 2.1 Deliberate style and spontaneous style

Deliberate style	Spontaneous style
– Putting forward hypotheses, rejecting them or validating them – Learning to solve closed problems (with a single solution) – Learning to work using a project methodology (project management) – Practicing meditation techniques (mindfulness) based on concentrating on a stimulus – Familiarizing oneself with idea selection and evaluation techniques (PMI, etc.) – Familiarizing oneself with structured creativity techniques (SCAMPER, Idea Box, etc.) – Practicing systematic trial and error – Learning how to order an activity using task lists (checklist) – Controlling body movements (yoga, Pilates) – Analyzing information, big data, etc.	– Solving open-ended problems (many solutions) – Thinking and decision making based on intuition – Default mode network, meditation (imaginative) – Seeking and immersing oneself in moments that foster creative insight (walks, outdoor activities, etc.) – Practicing intuitive techniques (Ideart, color bath, etc.) – Coming up with hypotheses (what-if questions) – Generating ideas without conscious control (mind wandering) – Creative inspiration based on emotions – Creative visualization – Altered states of awareness – Developing sensibility (outer and inner) – Promoting daydreaming

into a flashing light on a police patrol car. This aspect becomes especially relevant during brainstorming processes in teams. Many individuals often feel awkward in such situations because their brain tends to function in "problem solving" mode (convergence) and not by seeking out different approaches in order to achieve flow, variety and flexibility of ideas (divergence). Recent studies on brain connectivity have found that divergent thinking and originality are common among more creative individuals, whereas the connections of less creative people take place between the brain zones associated with memory and thinking about the past (lived experiences)[6]

Furthermore, according to certain studies, practicing meditation or mindfulness on a regular basis has a positive impact on CD.[7] In fact, when one is able to attain states of mental calm or "absorption" with relative ease, this means that less information is filtered and consequently one can achieve a greater amount of unexpected combinations, which in turn facilitates creative originality. In this respect, as some experts point out,[8] meditation, the main objective of which is to focus attention on a particular stimulus (breathing, sound, etc.), would create new connections in the executive control network akin to those of deliberate thinkers, whereas imaginative meditation (fostering modifications of the initial stimulus, for example, the flight of a butterfly) would have beneficial effects on the default network, typical of spontaneous thinkers, thus facilitating the development of radical imagination. Practicing both types of meditation regularly would therefore be extraordinarily beneficial from the point of view of creativity, in that it would consolidate the interrelations between the two big brain networks linked to creativity.

Finally, some researchers have found sufficient scientific evidence that establishes a link between CD and a tendency towards eccentricity or, taken to its extreme, towards psychopathology (schizophrenia, bipolar disorders and neuroses).[9] When filtering irrelevant information becomes too difficult, this may lead to mental confusion and a tendency to construct alternative realities, especially if the individual is not equipped with protective factors such as a high

Table 2.2 Four large zones

High GI and low CD Associated with individuals with management and decision-making capacity but who have difficulties when it comes to accessing advanced creative states.	**High GI and high CD** The high creativity zone, given that it combines high doses of CD with the protection factors (GI, memory, mental flexibility). Most highly creative people fall into this zone.
Low GI and low CD This corresponds to barely creative individuals who tend towards routine. Their intellectual performance is clearly below average.	**Low GI and high CD** Individuals with high CD but without protection factors. A tendency towards delirium and disordered schizoid thinking.

intellectual coefficient or mental flexibility. We can take the two key concepts (cognitive disinhibition and general intelligence) to draw up an explanatory table that features four large zones (see Table 2.2).

The research study findings

A research study that was carried out recently set out to find out whether the results of a CD test correlate with another test of creative flow. The working hypothesis was that a relationship exists between the two variables.

After preparing the tests (Shelley Carson's Creative Mindsets Questionnaire for evaluating CD and Robert McKim's Creative Flow Test to evaluate general creativity), they were handed out to 237 people who at the time of completing the questionnaires were taking a business education program in the EADA Business School in Barcelona. The sample was made up of adults with management responsibilities in companies from different sectors. All of them took part voluntarily.

The tests were handed out during the sessions that the author of this study had with the participants on different courses and programs at the center of education. It is worth mentioning here that the participants were allowed to ask questions during the process, which tends to improve the reliability and the consistency of the results.

The findings proved that the individuals who obtained high scores on Shelley Carson's Creative Mindsets Questionnaire, which assesses CD, also obtained high scores on Robert McKim's Creative Flow Test. More specifically, a significant correlation was found of 0.043 (chi-square), which proved that the two variables under study were not independent of each other, confirming the alternative hypothesis (that the two variables are related). Therefore, the differences observed in the distribution of the groups cannot be regarded as random. Consequently, the study's main hypothesis was confirmed.

The most important conclusions that can be drawn from the study, as well as from other research studies with similar findings, are:

- Spontaneous creativity in any context is as valid for solving complex problems or coming up with ideas as deliberate creativity. Undoubtedly, by combining the two we can achieve greater creative capacity at all levels. The research points out that people with higher levels of CD tend to obtain higher creativity scores when given a standard creativity test. What's more, in real situations where the need arises to come up with ideas for solving problems or giving birth to new concepts, these people may be more efficacious.

- In the corporate environment we need to learn how to manage and recognize the value of the sources of spontaneous creativity (intuition, meditation, playing, etc.) in the same way as we have valued the sources of deliberate creativity up to now (reasoning, logic, planning, etc.). These should not be two closed off and barely interrelated realities. Deliberate individuals should open themselves up to the spontaneous dimension of their being and vice versa. Creative complementariness needs to be regarded as a powerful tool for personal and consequently for professional growth.
- The study opens up the door to new considerations concerning aspects related to people management inside organizations, which we will review in detail further on.

Some of the drawbacks of the study have to do with the lack of existing tests for measuring or estimating the CD levels of the examined individuals. Furthermore, in order to obtain even more significant results, we need to enlarge the study sample, stratify it and even carry out studies by different age groups and in different cultural contexts.

The implications for people management

CD has relevant implications for improving people management and administration. To this end, we need to reflect upon the need to set up mechanisms inside the company that allow both pathways towards creativity, the deliberate and the spontaneous (as well as the different brainsets), to be expressed under equal conditions:

- The total or partial doing away with "hard" organizational structures, such as organizational charts or hierarchies, in order to progressively promote the expression of different creative sensibilities. A spontaneous individual, for example, needs fewer rigid plannings, deadlines, formal meetings, etc., so as to be able to give free rein to his or her creativity. By progressing towards a greater balance between control and an attitude of open listening, we can foster a better understanding between deliberate and spontaneous people. Cutting-edge company management models such as the one put forward by Frederic Laloux share three key common features: In the first place these companies have a clear "organisational purpose", a kind of "soul" which gives meaning to their existence and especially gives meaning to the work of their members. Patagonia, a US firm dedicated to manufacturing and commercializing mountaineering gear, has a healthy obsession with producing long-lasting, environmentally friendly products, which can be regarded as a highly inspiring ongoing purpose. Second, state-of-the-art companies allow their members to be themselves, entirely stripped of masks and hypocritical behaviors. The purpose here is to replace behaviors of submission to power with others based on genuine relationships among peers. Whole Foods supermarkets, recently acquired by Amazon, is a good example of an integral company. Finally (what is perhaps its distinctive feature), the model put forward by Laloux calls for the total or partial doing away of hierarchies and their corresponding organizational charts. In order to counter the logical fear that such a measure would lead to chaos or a permanent incapacity to take decisions, Laloux is in favor of holocratic structures based on self-managed teams. The case of the nonprofit Dutch organization, Buurtzorg, is very representative in this respect. Buurtzorg is made up of over 200 self-organized teams of nurses who provide home nursing services. Each team makes its own decisions, and Buurtzorg only has a small coordination and support structure. Instead of working driven by cost and efficiency criteria, Buurtzorg provides a service focused on optimizing quality care for customers: their maxim is "sit down and have a cup of tea with each patient and listen to their problems with understanding". Subsequently, the leadership in such organizations is substantially altered. Far from pointing the way or giving orders, the leaders, along with their people, "feel and respond" to changes.

- Changes to training plans in order to introduce spontaneous skills to compensate the excess of deliberate skills: meditation, self-awareness, sensorial awareness, lateral thinking, etc. In short, the long-term trend should be towards a greater balance between the two modalities. A holistic training plan should therefore combine knowledge, tools and skills related to the deliberate stream with competencies and the acquisition of sensibilities of a more spontaneous nature. Taking the Google company as an example, it should be every company's responsibility to set up an optional training system that, in addition to the skills and knowledge required to fulfill each employee's functions, will be in charge of organizing seminars, workshops and personal growth forums to offer integral training for each person and provide them with a holistic vision of their work, interests and life objectives. We are not dealing here with a traditional training plan (where company employees may even be obliged to participate in an activity). Instead, each person should be able to draw up their own personal growth plan adapted to their specific goals. The company therefore wouldn't be in charge of preparing a more or less standardized training proposal, which its employees would have to adapt to, but rather things would be the other way round: employees' requests would gradually configure a heterodox, dynamic and flexible training space.
- Introducing work spaces and methodologies that facilitate more interaction between the two creative modes: from experimentation areas or creativity laboratories right up to a comprehensive remodeling of the company's office spaces so as to foster interpersonal relationships and interdisciplinary cooperation while removing what are often very important status symbols. These spaces would fulfill a double purpose: On the one hand, they can provide the organization's employees with a space to work on innovation projects and where they can disconnect from their daily tasks. They would also be curiosity and experimentation areas for testing out extreme ideas, prototyping solutions to problems, etc. With regard to the work methodologies, companies should promote those that facilitate greater interaction between deliberate and spontaneous thinkers – for example, design thinking, which, as we have already seen, combines analytical and disruptive competencies.[10] In the coming years setting up such spaces (both physical and virtual) will make the difference between more traditional and more advanced companies.

Notes

1 Phrase attributed to George Bernard Shaw. Its origins are not clear.
2 See the book "Flow: the psychology of happiness", by Mihaly Csikszentmihalyi (2002). Rider.
3 See "The element: how finding your passion changes everything", by Ken Robinson (2009). Penguin Books.
4 See "Your creative brain", by Shelley Carson (2013). Harvard Health Publications.
5 See "How creativity happens in the brain" by Arne Dietrich (2015). Palgrave Macmillan.
6 See the article "Robust prediction of individual creative ability from brain functional connectivity" by Roger E. Beaty, Yoed N. Kenett, Alexander P. Christensen, Monica D. Rosenberg, Mathias Benedek, Qunlin Chen, Andreas Fink, Jiang Qiu, Thomas R. Kwapil, Michael J. Kane, and Paul J. Silvia. PNAS January 16, 2018; published ahead of print January 16, 2018.
7 See "Mindfulness: a practical guide to finding peace in a frantic world", by M. Williams and D. Penman (2011). Piatkus.

8 See "Wired to create", by SB Kaufman (2015), especially the chapter on meditation and its effects on creativity. Vermilion.
9 See "Creativity and mental illness", compiled by J. Kaufman (2014). Cambridge University Press.
10 See "Reinventing organizations" by Frederic Laloux (2014), an excellent practical treatise on how to gradually leave aside what until very recently were considered immovable truths of management. Published by Nelson Parker.

3
CONNOTATION AND TYPES OF INNOVATION

Jin Chen and Ximing Yin

Basic definition and nature of innovation

Innovation has been widely regarded as the central process driving economic growth and the sustainable competitive advantages of both companies and nations, as well as global sustainable growth, while the key precondition to conducting innovation management effectively is to have a big picture and deep insight of the concept: the nature of innovation (Schumpeter, 1934). This chapter will introduce the connotation and types of innovation, as well as the latest trend and emerging paradigm of innovation (Chen, Yin, and Mei, 2018; Martin, 2016).

Basic definition of innovation

Innovation is a very ancient English word which stemmed from the Latin word "innovare", meaning renewal, making of new stuff or change.

Joseph Schumpeter, a professor from Harvard University and an Austrian American, was the first scientist to introduce the innovation theory (Fagerberg, 2003). In the German edition of *The Theory of Economic Development*, published in 1912, he systematically defined the word "innovation" as the introduction of an unprecedented "new combination of production factors" into the production system. Innovation is made in order to obtain potential profit (Chen, 2017).

In putting forward the innovation theory, Schumpeter was motivated primarily to provide an all-new interpretation of the internal mechanism of economic growth and economic cycles. Based on the internal mechanism of innovation, he explained why a capitalist economy assumed a "boom-recession-depression-recovery" cycle, adding that innovation at different levels contributed to three economic cycles of varying lengths (Schumpeter, 1934).

Schumpeter summarized the following five forms of innovation:

- Introducing new products or improving product quality;
- Adopting new production methods and processes;
- Developing new markets;
- Exploiting new sources of supply of new material or partly finished products;
- Implementing new organizational forms.

However, his original thoughts on innovation were difficult for most people and mainstream economists to accept for a very long time, until the 1950s, when science and technology began to play an increasingly independent and outstanding role, drawing a lot of attention to innovation theory research. From the 1980s onwards, researchers went deeper into and applied theories of technological innovation to many realistic phenomena in economic development. The significant place and systematic theory of innovation gradually began to be established.

Initially, innovation was used primarily to define technological innovation, namely, the creation and introduction of new technology into a product, process or business system. The invention of an all-new product or process is an important technological improvement on the existing ones, or the launch of a new product into the market (product innovation), or the application of a new production process (process innovation).

The Organisation for Economic Co-operation and Development (OECD) issued the first edition of the *Oslo Manual: Proposed Guidelines for Collecting and Interpreting Technological Innovation Data* in 1992, updated in 1997 and 2005, in which it broadly defines technological innovation as: "An innovation is the implementation of a new or significantly improved product (good or service), or process, a new marketing method, or a new organizational method in business practices, workplace organization or external relations" (OECD/Eurostat, 2005, p. 46). The narrower definition of innovation could be "the implementation of one or more types of innovations, for instance, product and process innovations". An innovation is deemed to have been realized if a product was launched into the market or a process was applied to production. Therefore, innovation spans a range of activities, whether scientific, technological, organizational, financial or commercial.

In addition, the scholars defined innovation differently:

- American scholar Mansfield held that an invention could be termed a technological innovation the first time it was applied (Mansfield, 1968).
- British technology policy expert Prof. Christophe Freeman regarded innovation as the many steps (e.g. technology, design, manufacturing, finance, management and marketing) that took place the first time a new product or process was initiated (Freeman, 1987).
- American scholar Chesbrough defined innovation as the creation and commercialization of an invention (Chesbrough, 2003).
- American scholar Drucker considered innovation a special tool an entrepreneur applies in order to turn changes into different business and service opportunities. Innovation can be a discipline, an academic field or a practice (Drucker, 2009).
- The China's Central Committee and State Council defined technological innovation more systematically in *The Resolution on the Further Development of Technological Innovation, High Technology and Industrialization*,[1] issued in 1999:
    - Technological innovation is the application of innovative knowledge, new technologies and processes by an enterprise. It also encompasses the adoption of new production methods and management models to improve product quality, develop new products, provide new services, occupy new market share and realize market value.

In this book, the author defines innovation as an entire procedure encompassing the genesis, design, R&D, trial production, production and commercialization of new thoughts and ideas. It symbolizes the ability to transform foresight, knowledge and enterprise into wealth, especially the ability to combine technical knowledge efficiently with commercial knowledge to derive value. In a broader sense, all the undertakings aimed at creating new economic or social value can be termed innovation.

At the outset of an innovation initiative, problem orientation and strategic foresight are equally important to clarifying the strategic direction. One should apply a holistic thinking mind-set to manage the tension and paradox between short-term problem-driven and long-term future-prospect thinking processes. While innovation is under way, it is very necessary to keep in close touch with the team members and stakeholders (e.g. the user, joint venture, university and investor). When it comes to state of mind, freewill, great courage to take a risk and a positive attitude to setbacks are requisites. When it comes to performance, a lot of attention should be paid to the contribution of innovation to social development and environmental protection, as well as to the materialization of commercial value. See Figure 3.1.

Innovation does not necessarily involve technological changes

Innovation does not necessarily have a technological or physical nature. It may be an invisible asset or approach (Rogers, 2010). It's not technology, but the online business model of Google, Amazon and Alibaba that contributes most to the prevalent success of the World Wide Web. Since China marketized the electrical power industry with a competitive feed-in tariff mechanism, the policy has led to a prolonged wave of corporate innovation in strategy, organizational structure, management and operation. It's very clear that innovation is a prevalent trend in many forms and fields. Compared with technological innovation, institutional innovation is more important, although more difficult to achieve. One example is Shenzhen, a fast-growing city, which rose over two decades ago in economic reform and derives its success from the establishment of the Shenzhen economic and technological development zone (ETDZ) in the 1980s. According to the report released by the World Economic Forum in 2018, Shenzhen ranks number one among emerging cities with its global networks of innovation. Shenzhen has built on its reputation for hardware manufacturing to develop its own internationally

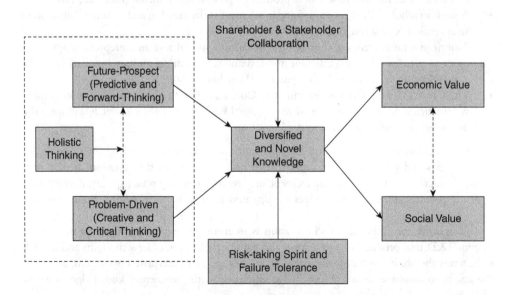

Figure 3.1 Connotation meaning of innovation

competitive innovation ecosystem. Internet giant Tencent is based in the city, as are the global hardware firms of Huawei and ZTE. As a result, the city sees the third-highest number of patent applications of any city in the world. As China's capabilities grow, Shenzhen is likely to be at the center of this.[2]

Technology leadership does not equal successful innovation

Technology leadership does not necessarily mean successful innovation. See Table 3.1.

These technology leaders failed in their products and programs primarily because of poor coordination of nontechnological factors with technological factors, marketing and manufacturing capacity. Take Wanyan, for example, the company that unveiled the world's first VCD in 1994. However, it dropped behind in the ensuing campaigns on market expansion, marketing and manufacturing capacity and ended up falling out in a VCD war. On the contrary, Intel and Haier succeeded in transforming technological advantages into market advantages through effective coordination of technological and nontechnological factors.

Success factors in innovation

Over the past decades, scholars have summarized some important success factors for innovation, including:

- **Integration of departmental responsibilities**: The various departments converge functionally in an effective manner so that all the departments are involved as an integrated body in the innovation program from the outset to make highly manufacturable designs.
- **Strong market orientation:** Potential users are allowed to participate or get involved in as many R&D programs as possible to play a pioneering role.
- **Good external communication**: The innovator keeps in effective touch with external scientific and technological sources and remains receptive to new thoughts from without.
- **Ingenious plans and more program control procedures:** Resources are deployed so as to select new program procedures. Program assessments are made in order to manage and control programs effectively.
- **Key persons:** Such persons include influential program advocates and technological gate keepers. There must be energetic managers. Talented managers and researchers must be retained.

Table 3.1 Technology leadership does not mean successful innovation

	Leader	*Follower*
Winner	Pilkington (float glass process)	Mitsubishi (VHS video recorder)
	Intel (CPU)	IBM (PC)
	Founder (laser typesetting)	Lenovo (PC)
	Haier (water heater safety device)	Eastcom (cellphone)
Loser	EMI (scanner)	Nokia (smart phone)
	Xerox (PC, mouse, etc.)	Letv (Internet + TV)
	Wanyan (VCD)	GREE (mobile phone)
	XH Electronics (color TV)	Baidu (take-out platform)
	Motorola (iridium)	Solyndra (solar power)

Apart from these, certain strategic factors are also a precondition to successful innovation:

- The senior management team gives a pledge of commitment to support an innovation program.
- A long-term corporate strategy must be positioned to play a key role.
- For significant projects, long-term resource planning must not be based solely on a short-term payback period but on future market penetration and growth.
- The firm must be flexible and responsive to changes. There must be a sensible internal innovation mechanism.
- The senior management is risk tolerant.
- There must be an innovation-receptive corporate culture fit for innovator development.
- The entrepreneurial, institutional and financial environment must be supportive. Effective external incentives are important as well.
- There must be close ties between R&D and other corporate divisions, as well as a sensible R&D structure.

Innovation and relevant concepts

Innovation and creation

Putting it simply, innovation is the proposal and commercialization of a creative idea. There will be no innovation without creative ideas. Creativity differs from innovation, in that the former involves only putting forward creative ideas, while the latter materializes and commercializes the ideas.

Innovation and invention

Innovation and invention often interweave with each other, so many confound them. But the two concepts are fundamentally distinct. Some innovations include no invention at all. A certain innovation that concerns an invention may encompass more than the latter. A measure of invention is the number of patents, or the wave of cheers from secluded laboratories. Innovation, however, means the translation of an invention into application; as Einstein cautioned his assistants: "We must achieve concrete results. We're not those German professors wasting their life on bee hairs".

Schumpeter, who first differentiated invention from innovation, held that one of an entrepreneur's responsibilities is to introduce new inventions into the production system and that innovation is the first-time commercialization of an invention (Fagerberg, 2003; Schumpeter, 1934).

It's natural that a time lag exists between the invention of a technology and its commercialization as an innovation. By and large, a period of technology diffusion or adjustment typically comes before an innovation produces a remarkable economic impact (Andergassen, Nardini, and Ricottilli, 2017). For example, the fax machine took 145 years to really commercialize.

The chance that an invention successfully turns into a commercial innovation is small. In the United States, a meager average of 12 to 20 percent of all R&D projects stand a chance of turning out successful commercial goods or processes.

Innovation and entrepreneurship

The concept of entrepreneur was first put forth in the 1730s by French economist Richard Cantillon, who believed that an entrepreneur worked to improve the efficiency of economic resources. Entrepreneurship is a set of special skills of a spiritual and technical nature. In other words, entrepreneurship is used to describe the versatile talent an entrepreneur exhibits in the creation, management and operation of an enterprise (Drucker, 2009). It is an invisible, singularly critical production factor, and innovation lies at its core. Besides, entrepreneurship normally encompasses such traits as risk taking, courage to explore, learning ability, persistence, devotion, cooperation and integrity.

Innovation and R&D

Since Thomas Edison made innovative invention a branch of science in the 19th century, R&D has served as an important measure of the innovation capability of a country or enterprise (Belderbos, Carree, and Lokshin, 2004).

There are many definitions of the word. The OECD defines R&D as systemic creative work aimed at enriching the knowledge repository regarding humans, culture and society, as well as the utilization of such knowledge for new inventions and applications.

The OECD classifies R&D activities into three types: basic research, applied research and experimental development. Basic research refers to experiments or theoretical research, which, based on phenomena and facts, aims primarily to acquire new knowledge and has no concrete application purposes. Basic research is conducted to generate new knowledge and discover truths and has no directionality. Although much of the basic research in the United States is funded by the federal government, a large number of top-of-the-line firms are also very successful in this area. Take Johnson & Johnson, for instance. The conglomerate spent $US10.554 billion on R&D in 2017, taking about 12.7 percent of its total revenue. At the same time, Merck, an emerging leader of innovative medicines, vaccines and animal health products, spent $US7.5 billion on R&D in 2017, taking about 17.2 percent of its total revenue.[3] Researchers have reached one consensus: basic R&D on the existing platform of technological knowledge is the one way potential invention opportunities can be quickly discovered and utilized. The viewpoint hypothesizes that technology drives innovation.

Applied research refers to investigation on raw data and deals primarily with the acquisition of new knowledge on a specific applied or pragmatic field. The objective of applied research is clearly defined, and the resulting inventions, if any, may be commercialized, since it is oriented to solving practical problems a firm faces. Applied research proponents don't think basic research is necessary because they have a sufficiently large stock of knowledge for their businesses.

Experimental development refers to systematic trials that convert knowledge derived from scientific research and experience on new material/product/equipment manufacturing to the development of new processes, products, systems and services, or to the improvement of existing processes, products and services.

R&D starts from creative ideas, extending all the way through research, development and success of trial production. The center of R&D lies in process and output.

An increasing number of companies are paying more attention to R&D capabilities. Major corporations across the world run their own research bodies, like IBM, Microsoft, Siemens, Huawei and Haier. A firm may encounter huge problems buying advanced technology from the market, especially in an era full of cutthroat competition when the owners of cutting-edge technology will not choose to part easily with the huge profits before strong competitors appear. Even if traditional technology can be bought, it is usually expensive. With the development of technology and the escalation of market competition, firms will need more advanced technology, which requires much more expenditure. Furthermore, some technologies may not be applicable upon introduction. They have to be assimilated and adapted to the production and management system of the firm before achieving business profit.

Overall, technological knowledge constitutes an integral part of a company's core capabilities. A company cannot maintain long-lasting competitive advantages unless it carries out R&D activities to accumulate unique technological knowledge (and especially its own R&D talent resources) in order to avoid being emulated by competitors.

Table 3.2 outlines the difference between technological innovation and some similar concepts.

Nature of innovation

Innovation spans the whole process from basic research through to applied research, with a "Death Valley" in between. To be effective, an innovation should have some kind of a bridge to connect basic research to applied research, or else ultimate commercialization efforts will end up in failure and the innovation will not realize its value. Therefore, how to establish ties between basic research and commercial applied research is very critical to innovation.

Innovation can also be depicted in terms of the knowledge–capital interaction process. As an essential part of innovation, research relies on capital input to deliver knowledge output, which lays the foundation for innovation. Innovation as a new capital eventually contributes to a greater capital spillover. See Figure 3.2.

Table 3.2 Technological innovation vs. similar concepts

Concept	Simple definition	Distinction from technological innovation
Invention	Propound a new concept, thought or doctrine for the first time.	No mass production and commercialization.
Basic research	Explore the world and technological advances. No specific commercial goals.	No intensive trial production, mass production and commercialization.
Applied research	Systematic creation activities aimed at acquiring more technical knowledge by working towards specific goals.	Inadequate links with the production and market sectors.
Experimental development	Employ the knowledge derived from basic/applied research to develop new materials, products and equipment.	No consideration for commercialization.
Technology introduction	Introduce new equipment and talent to improve production capacity and marketability.	No guarantee for market entry.
Technological renewal	Involve primarily systematic or partial renewal of production equipment.	Can improve production capacity, but commercialization possibility remains unknown.
Technological revolution	Strictly speaking, technological revolution encompasses the whole span from invention, to innovation, to diffusion.	Takes a longer time than innovation. An economic concept. Less operable in reality.
Technological progress	The process wherein innovations mass and consolidate over years.	Post-innovation summation of innovation history.

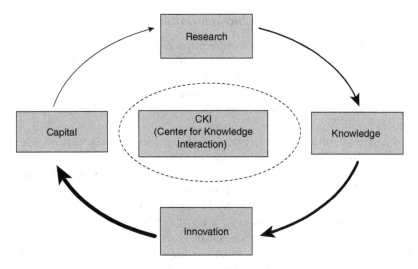

Figure 3.2 Knowledge–capital interaction

Source: Adapted from the web content of the Technical University of Munich, www.tum.de/

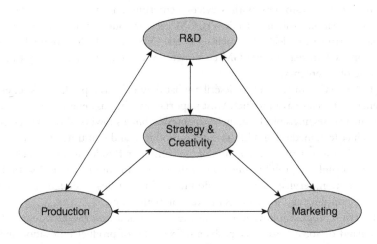

Figure 3.3 What's critical to innovation success – linking strategy and creativity, R&D, production and marketing

From the perspective of organizational management, innovation pays attention to the effective coordination of strategy and creativity, R&D, production and marketing. Typically, effective synergism and coordination among the four divisions are very important to a firm and require great emphasis. Generally speaking, the vast majority of the innovation failures are not attributed to technological factors, but to defective strategy, market survey, sales management and organizational management. See Figure 3.3.

Basic types of innovation

Innovation can be classified in different terms. In terms of content it can be classified into product innovation, process innovation, service innovation and business model innovation.

Product innovation

A product in the traditional sense is any tangible physical good or raw material, ranging extensively from everyday products (e.g. toothpaste) to industrial goods (e.g. steel pipes) (Gao et al., 2017). At the early stage of the product lifecycle, there is no prevalent design in the market and products are subject to major changes. Therefore, a firm must constantly improve on an innovation to meet customer demand, expand the customer base and build up greater market advantages.

There is a recent trend among service companies (e.g. insurers, financial firms, telecommunications carriers and other professional service firms) to promote their services as "products". One case in point is the successful launch of Alipay, an online financing product, by Ant Financial Company in 2004, which is trying to bring inclusive financial services to the world. As described by Fortune's Annual Change the World List 2017, Ant Financial's Ant Forest app has encouraged 450 million users in China to do just that in fulfillment of parent Alibaba Group's pledge to use financial technology to tackle climate change. Users earn points toward planting virtual trees by adopting earth-friendly habits. The company plants a real tree for every 17.9 kg of carbon saved: over 8 million were planted in 2017. And the engagement keeps customers loyal to Ant's widely used payment app.[4]

In order to break the traditional bounds of industry, a growing number of producers are beginning to provide customers with services centering on their products. For example, automakers offer roadside assistance to drivers. GM sells cars, but customers buy service as well, which is sold as part of the deal. One such service is OnStar, a vehicle-mounted GPS satellite communications system that enables GM customers to locate themselves at any time and call for help in case of emergency.

Although the service firms tend to describe what they offer as a product, it's different from what we generally perceive as a product. Most importantly, whereas generic products are visible, service is, in many cases, invisible. Insurance is intangible, but a snowboard is physical and visible. A service product (e.g. medical and health care) is produced and consumed simultaneously, and its delivery requires very active participation of the consumer. Besides, it is extremely difficult, if not virtually impossible, to prohibit imitation by the establishment of a patent law. In the model of product innovation, service takes the predominant form of tie-ins designed to increase the value-added of a product and improve its market competitiveness.

In simple terms, product innovation means the release of a new product designed to meet customer demand or solve customers' problems. Examples of product innovation include the Apple iPhone, Haier's environmentally friendly twin tub washing machine (no need for washing powder) and the Huawei Mate 8 fingerprint recognition smart phone. Product innovation can be subdivided into component innovation, architectural innovation and complex products and systems (CoPS) innovation (Chen, Tong, and Ngai, 2007; Hobday, 2000).

Component innovation

The vast majority of products and processes are hierarchically nested systems; that is to say, the product or process as an entity is a system made up of components, each of which is in turn made up of a lower hierarchy of components until the hierarchical structure ends at an indivisible level. One example is the bike, which is a system comprising the frame, wheels, tires, seat, brake discs and other components. Each of these components is an independent system. For example, the seat can be considered a system comprising the metal and plastic frame, stuffing and nylon cover.

Innovation may lead to changes to an individual component, or the entire structure where a component works, or both. If an innovation leads to changes to one or more components without severely compromising the entire system structure, it's termed a component innovation. One case in point is an innovative bike seat that introduces gel stuffing as an enhanced dampening material while involving no further structural change to the bike.

Architectural innovation

In contrast to component innovation, architectural innovation drives changes to the entire system structure or to the action mechanism governing two or more components (Wilden, Devinney, and Dowling, 2016). While a stringent architectural innovation may change how the components interact as a system, no substantial change occurs to the components themselves. Moreover, most architectural innovations not only change the interaction but also change the components themselves, leading to a fundamental system change. Architectural innovation may have a far-reaching complex impact on the market competitors and technology users. One example is the transition from a functional cellphone to a smart cellphone. This architectural innovation requires not just applicable changes to many components but also changes to how the cellphone is operated.

Whereas a single-component innovation requires a firm to master the expertise about the component, initiating or introducing an architectural innovation requires the mastery of how to assemble and integrate the components structurally into the system. The firm must learn about the features of the various components, how they work together and how some system feature changes trigger substantial system changes or structural feature changes to individual components.

CoPS innovation

The CoPS evolved from the LTS (Large Technical System), a concept which originated from the US military's technology development system. The CoPS remained a relatively new concept even to Western countries until the late 1990s when clearer definitions were suggested (Hobday, 2000). A CoPS refers to a huge product, system or piece of infrastructure that involves enormous R&D spending and high technology and is job-produced or custom-made in small batches (Chen, Tong, and Ngai, 2007; Hobday, 2000). The concept encompasses large telecommunications systems, mainframe computers, aeronautical and space systems, smart buildings, power grid control systems, large vessels, high-speed trains, semiconductor production lines, information systems and other systems inseparable from modern industrial uses (see Table 3.3). In spite of its small production, the CoPS industry accounts for a significant share of gross domestic product (GDP) and played a very critical role in the modern economy due to the bulky size and high unit cost of the products.

In an investigation into diverse product data in the UK, Miller and Hobday, researchers in the Science Policy Research Unit (SPRU) of the University of Sussex, found CoPSs to have contributed to at least 11 percent of GDP, creating at least 1.4 million to 4.3 million jobs. Their further research pointed out that the role of the CoPS industry was not to be overlooked in maintaining the UK's leadership in the world economy. As a very sophisticated system consisting of numerous subsystems and components, a CoPS, if successfully developed, can give an impetus to the other industries and common mass production industries. For example, it drives the development and application of more advanced mass production lines.

Table 3.3 CoPS examples

Aircraft flight control system	Aircraft engine	Runway
Airport	Navigation system	Large ship (vessel)
Baggage handling system for airports	Bank transaction processing system	Observatory
Business information network	Large chemical plant	Mainframe computer
Power grid control system	Big bridge	SPC exchange
Flight simulator	Ship dock	Space station
High-speed train	Flexible manufacturing system	Synchrotron
Smart building	Helicopter	Telecommunications transaction processing systems
Semiconductor workshop	Fighter jet	Water filtration system
Microchip workshop	Guidance system	Water supply system
Nuclear power plant	Nuclear fusion reactor	Wastewater treatment plant
Offshore drilling platform	Port cargo handling system	Microwave tower
Passenger aircraft	Semiconductor lithography system	

Source: Authors' design, based on Hobday (1998)

In terms of technology diffusion (Andergassen, Nardini, and Ricottilli, 2017), a CoPS involves a wide variety of high technologies that directly cause its embedded technology modules to be applied in other fields. This technology diffusion is faster than normal product innovation, thus bringing about technological updates to the whole industry and improving the competitive power of a country.

Process innovation

Process innovation is a new mode of producing or delivering a new product or service, for example, innovation in production processes, technological roadmaps or production equipment (Pilav-Velić) and Marjanovic, 2016).

For a manufacturer, process innovation includes the adoption of new processes, techniques, manufacturing methods and technologies to achieve advantages in cost, quality, lead time, development cycle and delivery speed, or to improve the custom-making capacity of products and services. In the case of washing machine manufacturing, a process innovation may take the form of the adoption of a new sheet material or the replacement of a traditional machine tool with a computerized numerical control (CNC) machine tool, which contributes to 50 percent cost reduction or threefold productivity or more.

The purpose of product innovation is to optimize product design and performance singularity, whereas the purpose of process innovation is to improve product quality, reduce production cost, maximize productivity, minimize energy consumption and upgrade the working environment.

Process innovation delivers multiple benefits (e.g. larger margin, less cost, higher productivity and higher employee satisfaction), makes value delivery more stable and reliable and benefits the customer as well. Process innovation is unique in that it's normally invisible to the customer; in other words, it occurs at the backstage of the firm. Only when a mishap of the corporate internal procedure causes a failed delivery of products or services will the customer take notice of the problematic procedure.

Product innovation and process innovation usually alternate. On the one hand, a new process makes the production of new products possible. For example, when a new metallurgical process makes bike chain production possible, the development of shaft-driven bikes with a gear train becomes possible in due course. On the other hand, a state-of-the-art workstation helps a firm realize computer-aided manufacturing (CAM), which is a boost to speed and efficiency. In addition, a product innovation developed by a firm may be a process innovation for another. For example, when an innovative CNC lathe developed by a manufacturer is used by a firm for machining, it is considered a process innovation for the latter since it improves speed, quality and efficiency.

A service firm employs process innovation to improve frontstage service and launch novel services or new "products" visible to the customer. In 1986, FedEx released a unique parcel tracking system to the market. What the customer saw was only a small barcode reader the operator used for parcel scanning, while the rest of the sophisticated system was invisible to the customer, who knew only the real-time state of the parcel on its way. The value-added service helped FedEx secure temporary advantages over its competitors.

Innovation matrix

Based on the basic types and characteristics of innovation, we can infer the category under which the innovation of an organization or firm falls. The categorization matrix pertinent to innovation management optimization is suggested as follows (see Figure 3.4).

Service innovation

One hallmark of modern economy is a fast-growing service sector which gains in increasing significance in the national economy. Lying at the core of the world economy, the service sector is the driving force behind economic globalization. A growing number of firms in the service

	Technological Innovation		Non-Technological Innovation	
	Product Innovation	Process Innovation	Service Innovation	Business Model Innovation
Radical Innovation				
Significant Innovation				
Incremental Innovation				

(Level of Innovation / Nature of Innovation)

Figure 3.4 Innovation matrix

sector are making service innovations to render high-quality services and products, cut costs and develop new service philosophies.

Service innovation is a dynamic process a firm takes to implement purposeful, organized changes to a service system with the aim of improving service quality, creating new market value and introducing changes to service factors. While the service innovation theory evolved from the technological innovation theory and the two are inseparably correlated, service innovation distinguishes itself from the latter (especially innovation in manufacturing technology) by its unique innovation strategy.

Basic characteristics of service innovation

Intangibility

In the first place, in contrast to a tangible consumer product or industrial product, service and its components are in many cases intangible, incorporeal and invisible to the naked eye. This hallmark makes service not easy to evaluate or validate.

In the second place, customer services are sold as a tie-in bundled with many consumer and industrial products. For the customer, the service or utility attached to these vehicles matters much more. From this standpoint, intangibility is not unique to service.

Inseparability

The production and consumption of a service are not to be clearly differentiated. They take place at the same time. In other words, the customer consumes a service at the moment he or she receives it from the service firm. There is no chronological order as to the production and consumption of a service. This characteristic indicates that the customer cannot eventually enjoy the service unless he or she participates in the production of the service. The characteristic makes the service industry more discrete, localized and distinct from manufacturing.

Heterogeneity

Heterogeneity means persistent incoherence in terms of service composition and quality that is hard to generalize. Because the service industry is centered around humans, the individuality of humans makes it very hard to adopt a uniform service quality standard. For one thing, the quality of a service provided by the same service provider may vary from time to time due to individual factors (e.g. state of mind); for another, the factors (e.g. knowledgeability, interest and hobby) of the customer, who participates directly in the production and consumption of the service, may have a direct impact on service quality and effect. Heterogeneity may cause the customer to confuse the image of the firm with its service.

Perishability

Perishability requires a service firm to address how to address understock problems and the resulting undersupply problems, develop a distribution strategy, select distributors and distribution channels, design production processes and address passive service demand in a flexible and effective manner.

Absence of ownership

The absence of ownership means that in the production and consumption of a service, the ownership transfer that concerns no physical stuff. Since the service is intangible and perishable, it disappears upon the completion of the deal and the consumer has not physically owned it. The ownership of the service is not readily transferable.

The differences between service and manufacturing are presented in Table 3.4.

The success of the service industry is built on innovation and skilled management, which play an ongoing role in enhancing service quality and productivity. A firm gets the upper hand in competition through innovation activities that add to product value.

In the United States and European developed countries, the service sector takes the lead in economy, contributing to 60 to 80 percent of the GDP. Therefore, service innovation is no less important than technological innovation for manufacturing. Of course, a service innovation may be of a technological nature, but in most cases it is social or nontechnological. It is not to be understood in the narrow sense as a "supplement" to technological innovation.

- Service innovation is more incremental than radical. Service innovation is in more cases incremental because it normally involves very tiny process changes and almost no breakthrough innovation. Service innovation is introduced to curtail cost, enhance product differentiation, improve the flexibility of reaction to customer questions, develop new markets and maximize customer loyalty.
- In the service sector product innovation and process innovation are usually integrated. Service innovation may take the form of the launch of a new service product, the production or delivery of a new service or the generalization of a new technology. The service is

Table 3.4 Service industry vs. manufacturing

Manufacturing	Service
A product is tangible	A service is intangible
Ownership transfer takes place when the deal is made	The ownership of a service is normally not transferred
A product is verifiable	A service is not easily verifiable
A product can be traded for many times	The trading of a service is unrepeatable
Both the buyer and seller can store a product	A service cannot be stored
A product is produced before consumption	A service is normally produced and consumed at the same time
A product is produced, sold and consumed separately	A service is produced, sold and consumed at the same time
A product is transportable	A service is not transportable
The supplier sells a product, while the customer generally does not participate in production	The customer participates in the delivery of a service
A product may become an indirect link between the producer and the user	A service is often a direct link between the provider and the user
The core value is produced in a factory	The core value is produced when the buyer communicates with the seller

nonstorable, so it cannot be entirely dissociated from the product, and innovation in the service product is indissociable from innovation in the service process. That explains why the service innovation often comes with the changes to many factors, like the service production process and the service product.
- Service innovation is customer-oriented. While it's based primarily on customer demand, service innovation may also originate in the evolution of corporate philosophy. The less standardized the service, the higher the customization requirements and the more important the customer's decision in service innovation.
- Service innovation may form new knowledge or information. For example, the service staff, when delivering services, devise new methods or build up new knowledge and information. As the gathering of and investigation on scientific knowledge is not necessary, service innovation requires a relatively short time.
- Innovation teams are usually more flexible. By and large, no or very few service firms have R&D units. Their innovation team, responsible for conception and blueprints, is normally an improvised project team of employees temporarily drafted from the various departments. Once the innovation plan has come into operation or been harmonized with the routine business procedure, the team dissolves.

Servitization of manufacturing

Service innovation is not unique to the service industry. Servitization has become a predominant trend across the global manufacturing sector since the 1980s, a phenomenon proven by a growing share contributed by sheer manufacturing to the value-added of industrial goods and a shrinking share by service (e.g. R&D, industrial design, logistics, marketing, brand management, intellectual property management and product maintenance). Take the automotive industry, for instance. The return on investment (ROI) stands at only 3 to 5 percent for manufacturing, while the figure stands at up to 7 to 15 percent for vehicle service. Excellent manufacturers are turning from production-centered to service-centered.

Servitization of manufacturing is a business model wherein the manufacturer reorients the core of its value chain from manufacturing to service. The service industry contributes to about 70 percent of the GDP of developed countries, with producer services accounting for about 60 percent. However, in China, producer services are still a backward industry, accounting for an insignificant share of the economy. Still, the emphasis on producer services has emerged as the consensus across the society at large.

Producer services include primarily R&D, design, third-party logistics, lease financing, IT service, energy conservation and environmental service, testing and certification, e-commerce, consulting, service outsourcing, after-sales service, HR service and brand building.

GE is the largest manufacturer of electrical equipment and electronics in the world. It is not only a producer of consumer and industrial electrical equipment but also a giant military contractor of space exploration and aeronautical instruments, jet navigation systems, multiwarhead ballistic missile systems, radars and spaceflight systems. However, it reaps the majority of its revenue from various services, which accounted for 59.1 percent of its total revenue in 2006 alone. The present-day GE is a conglomerate branching extensively into commercial finance, consumer finance, medical care, industry, infrastructure and NBA Universal.

Classification of service innovation

There are five types of service innovation.

Service product innovation

Service product innovation refers to innovation in the content or product of a service. This type of innovation is centered around product design and production capacity. Examples include People's Uber launched by Uber China and MI Roam launched by MI.

Service process innovation

Service process innovation refers to innovation in the production and delivery process of a service product. It is subdivided into production process innovation, or backstage innovation, and delivery process innovation, or frontstage innovation. Sometimes it is very difficult to discriminate between service process innovation and service product innovation. Where the supplier (firm) and the customer liaise very closely, the customer will participate in the rendering of the service, a situation that requires both sides to contribute to providing the product. In this case, the product is virtually indistinguishable from the process. For such firms, it's very difficult to distinguish product innovation from process innovation.

Service management innovation

Service management innovation refers to innovation models of service organization or management. A service firm adopting total quality management (TQM) practices well deserves the title of a service management innovator. One example is Hai Di Lao, a hot pot brand renowned for ingenious staff management.

Service technology innovation

Service technology innovation refers to innovation in service-supporting technologies, such as Alipay Facial Scan, Huawei Mate 8 fingerprint recognition and the online seat reservation service of movie theaters.

Service model innovation

Service model innovation refers to innovation in the model of the services provided by a service firm. One example is the O2O home wash service introduced by traditional car detailing stores.

Business model innovation

Peter Drucker, a master of management, once said: "The current competition among companies is not the competition between products but the competition between business models". Business model innovation refers to challenges in the ways to create value for customers that are common in the industry today. It strives to meet the changing needs of customers, provide more value for customers, open up new markets for enterprises and attract new customers. A simple example is that compared with traditional bookstores, Amazon and Dangdang.com are business model innovations.

There are many definitions of the business model, but the management academic community primarily accepts the "clarification of business model" published in 2005: the definition in the article "The origin, current status, and future" is as follows:

> [T]he business model is a conceptual tool that contains a series of elements and their relationships that shed light on the business logic of a particular entity. It describes

the value companies can provide to their customers, as well as the company's internal structure, partner networks, and relationship capital to achieve (create, market, and deliver) this value and generate sustainable, profitable revenue.

(Osterwalder, Pigneur, and Clark, 2010)

This defines the characteristics of the business model. The business model shows the relationships and elements that a company depends on to create and sell value. It can be subdivided into nine areas:

- Value proposition. The value that the company can provide to consumers through its products and services. The value proposition confirms the practical significance of the company to consumers.
- Target customer segments. The company's targeted consumer groups. These groups have certain commonalities that allow companies to create value (for these commonalities). The process of defining consumer groups is also referred to as market segmentation.
- Distribution channels. Various ways companies use to reach consumers. Here is how the company develops its market. It involves the company's marketing and distribution strategy.
- Customer relationships. The links established between the company and its consumer groups. What we call customer relationship management is related to this.
- Value configurations. The configuration of resources and activities.
- Core capabilities. The ability and qualifications companies need to implement their business model.
- Partner network. A network of partnerships between the company and other companies to effectively provide value and realize its commercialization. This also describes the company's business alliances.
- Cost structure. The currency description of the tools and methods used.
- Revenue streams. The company creates wealth through a variety of revenue flows.

We can use these nine factors to measure whether a business model is qualified and take further action to improve the business model.

Every innovation of the business model can bring the company a competitive advantage for a certain period. But over time, companies must continually rethink their commercial designs.

Levels of innovation

Since Schumpeter put forward the innovation theory, scholars worldwide have been attaching extensive importance to research on content-centered innovation (e.g. product and process innovation). In order to carry out in-depth research and increase the pertinence of innovation policy, scholars classify innovation based on different standards and dimensions.

Classification by the level of innovation

Scholars divide innovation levels into incremental innovation and breakthrough innovation (or radical innovation) (Prahalad, 2012; Ritala and Hurmelinna-Laukkanen, 2013; Van Lancker, Mondelaers, Wauters, and Van Huylenbroeck, 2016).

Incremental innovation

Incremental innovation refers to minor improvements and updates on a product or process along the initial technology trajectory. The general opinion is that incremental innovation can maximize the potential of an existing technology while adding to the advantages (especially organizational capabilities) of the existing mature firm. Incremental innovation has a lesser requirement on the size and technological capability of a company.

Research on the rocket engine, computer and synthetic fiber suggests that incremental innovation has a remarkable impact on product cost, reliability and other performance parameters. Despite the fact that single innovations mean only very small changes, the cumulative effect normally surpasses that of the initial innovation. That is the trend typical of the price cuts and reliability improvements of the early Ford Model T, which plummeted from $1,200 to $290 during 1908–1926 amid remarkable rises in labor productivity and capital productivity. Ford's successful cost reduction resulted from numerous improvements of processes (e.g. welding, casting, assembly and material substitution). One more feat of the Model T is the better performance and reliability attributed to improved product design, which made the car more captivating.

Although incremental innovation typically has insignificant effects on the firm's profitability, it works to improve customer satisfaction, add to product or service utility and generate a positive impact. Similarly, incremental innovation lends itself to improving productivity and cutting costs.

From the theoretical perspective, incremental innovation does not seem to have applied new scientific knowledge on a significant scale, but over time it will build up a tremendous cumulative economic effect. Many companies and their managers prefer the cumulative model to the radical model when it comes to innovation, considering that the latter may imperil the company and land it in dire straits.

Nevertheless, a lot of empirical researches have shown that incremental innovation maintains the competitive advantage of a firm's products only for the time being. When a rival rises with a disruptive innovation, an established large corporation will likely lose ground and market leadership. The invention of the transistor almost crushed all the vacuum tube manufacturers who had been working devotedly on incremental innovation. Another example is Japan's quartz clock technology, which dealt a lethal blow to the Swiss horological industry. Ironically, the quartz clock had its origin in Switzerland, and excellent Swiss scientists and horologists had been refining their incremental innovations time and again for higher performance. These lessons prove that while incremental innovation helps a company maintain a temporary advantage, it may be easily beaten by radical innovation.

Incremental service innovations include simplified hotel check-in and check-out procedures, refit of a bank hall, installation of conspicuous signs in a rest home to aid elderly people with poor eyesight and USB charging ports fitted on aircraft seats by international airlines.

Constant innovation is very essential to the success of firms committed to developing new products and markets. Their awareness of the essentiality of each increment of progress to an innovation as a whole explains why incremental innovation well deserves its endorsement as an indispensable and valuable tool. However, there is one limitation to sole attention to incremental innovation. The firm may be impeded from making further progress in products, services or market.

Radical/breakthrough innovation

Radical or breakthrough innovation is a type of innovation that leads to an enormous progress in the primary performance indicators of a product, a decisive impact on market rules, competition environment and industry structure, or even a thorough reshuffle of the industry pattern.

As they typically involve all-new concepts, significant technological breakthroughs, foremost scientists or engineers and great spending, radical innovations may take eight to ten years or longer to materialize. A radical innovation usually comes with a series of product, process and business organizational innovations, or even revolutions in industry structure. It's very hard to define the expression in terms of revenue increases since that depends on the size and spending of a firm. As such, a radical innovation could be understood only as a so-called "breakthrough". Any attempt at a definition, if applicable, could only be based on the term itself. If a process improvement reduces cost or increases production significantly, it can also be termed a breakthrough. See Figure 3.5.

Sometimes a radical invention also secures a radical innovation for an enterprise. Radical innovation is a great stride forward by humans. While it may not secure first-comer advantage for a firm, in many cases it gives birth to an all-new industry. The automobile, electricity, penicillin and the Internet are all radical inventions and discoveries.

All the successful technological firms need continuous or incremental innovation to fulfill the varying demands of existing customers and therefore realize continuous business growth. However, incremental innovation needs to be complemented periodically by discontinuous innovation, including radical innovation, one of the major types of discontinuous innovation. To qualify as a "breakthrough", an innovation must have the potential of achieving at least one of the three following goals:

- Brand-new set of performance features;
- At least five-fold improvement or more on the existing performance indicators; or
- Cost reduction by a large margin (>30%).

Long-established multinational corporations, like IBM, GE, Motorola, HP, Siemens, Philips, 3M, GM and DuPont, regularly interrupt incremental innovations in a process with radical innovations.

Nevertheless, failures predominate over successes when it comes to attempts on significant radical innovation. Although many small startup firms (especially Silicon Valley firms) seem to

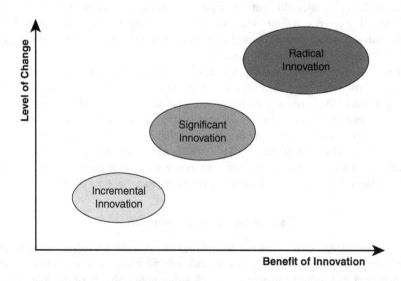

Figure 3.5 Incremental innovation vs. radical innovation

have experimented with and commercialized radical innovation, most fail in the end. According to recent research, only a small portion of the venture capital (VC)–funded innovations in the United States belong to the first type (true breakthrough) and the second type (fundamental technological improvement), because VC funds have a short lifecycle (normally eight years) and do not opt for long-term, high-risk investments despite the high potential for profitability.

Obviously, radical innovation, which involves a lot of time, investment and concern from top management, is a very thorny undertaking even in the United States, Europe, Japan and other developed countries. That explains why it is very important for developing countries to grasp the essence of breakthroughs and implement innovation methods from an open-minded perspective. Disruptive innovation, another model of discontinuous innovation put forward by Harvard professor Clayton M. Christensen, might be a more sensible, realistic practice to introduce and popularize for developing countries.

The main distinction between radical innovation and incremental innovation can be understood from the perspective of the technology trajectory. As shown in Figure 3.6, when Technology I enters the incremental innovation stage, a new idea (Technology II) different from Technology I is introduced and attempts on a radical innovation must be made, even though the initial outcome may be less satisfactory than the preceding product. An example is the earliest train, which did not run as fast as a horse-drawn carriage. However, after more stable principal technical performance parameters were achieved through significant innovation, there was a period when technology and product performance experienced a sharp increase until the principal technical performance parameters stabilized, which we may call the radical innovation

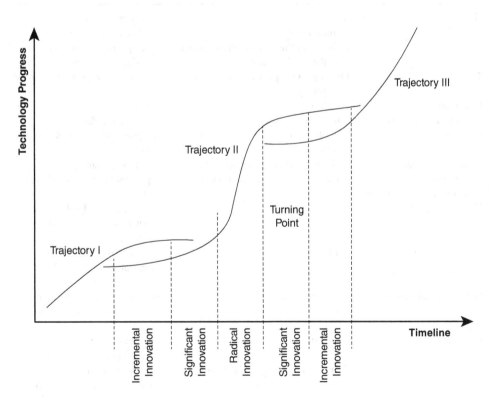

Figure 3.6 Incremental innovation and radical innovation: technology trajectory

source: Authors' design, based on Christensen (1997).

stage. During the radical innovation stage, Technology II experienced a turning point where the marginal increase rate of performance decreases but the overall performance still increases. Then the firm entered another significant innovation period, which we can call the radical-incremental innovation transition stage. Finally, the firm entered a stage of incremental innovation until a new technological trajectory appeared (Technology III). When the product of Technology III overtook that of Technology II, the incremental innovation ended in decline. If a firm does experiment with incremental innovation (Technology II) and radical innovation (Technology III) at the same time, the chance is greater that it can maintain a consistent competitive advantage. If a firm has a leading advantage in Technology II but gives no consideration to Technology III, it has to face the challenge from a latecomer, which may result in the reshuffle of the market in the middle of the trajectory of Technology III.

Radical innovation is significantly different from incremental innovation with regard to goals, organizational structure, processes and uncertainties (see Table 3.5). Further statistical research has proven the two differ also in target firms. In more cases, radical innovation takes place in small and medium enterprises(SMEs) while large firms prefer incremental innovation. Academic research based on a technology history perspective has also found out that large mature companies frequently lose to smaller ones due to radical innovation. This is due

Table 3.5 Incremental innovation vs. radical innovation

Difference	Incremental innovation	Radical innovation
Goal	Maintain and consolidate the existing market position	Change the rule of game and realize transcendence
Focus	Improve on the cost and performance of the original product	Development of a new industry, product or process
Technology	Develop and exploit the existing technology	Research and exploration of new technology
Uncertainty	Low level	High level
Technology trajectory	Linear and continuous	Divergent and discontinuous
Business plan	The plan is made immediately the innovation begins	The plan evolves as exploratory learning occurs
Generation of new thoughts and opportunity recognition	New thoughts are generated at the end of the previous innovation	New thoughts are generated spontaneously in the lifecycle
Main participant	Cross-functional teams (CFT)	Versatile, knowledgeable individuals and informal networks
Procedure	Formal phase model	Informal flexible model at the early phase and formal model at the late phase
Organizational structure	CFTs inside the business unity	From thinker to incubator and then to target-driven project team
Resources and capability	Standard resource allocation	Acquisition of resources and capability in a creative way
Operator involvement	Formal involvement from the very beginning	From informal involvement at the early phase to formal involvement at the late phase

Source: Authors' design, based on Leifer (2000)

primarily to the fact that the institutions – rules of business conduct, corporate culture, incentive mechanism, operational strategy and organizational capability – were based on the preceding generation's technology trajectory and were suited to the incremental innovation processes at the later part of the preceding generation's technology. Therefore, the successful experience, core capability and competitive advantage work to impede a new round of competition (Christensen, 1997).

Richard Leifer and his fellow researchers investigated the inherent laws of radical innovation from the lifecycle perspective, discovering some generic characteristics that distinguished radical innovation from incremental innovation(Leifer et al., 2000):

- Radical innovation often takes a long time (10 years or longer).
- Radical innovation is highly uncertain and unpredictable.
- Radical innovation is sporadic. Stops and starts alternate. So do discontinuation and recommencement.
- Radical innovation assumes a nonlinear trend. It involves the recurrence of some activities and feedback as a response to discontinuation, as well as the constant employment of all the crucial radical innovation management capabilities.
- Radical innovation is random. There is not a fixed team of main participants, and the focus of research varies. Radical innovation is susceptible to external environmental changes.
- Radical innovation is background-dependent. Many factors, for example, history, experience, corporate culture, individuality and informal relations, interrelate and produce various positive or negative effects.

Classification by continuity and the target market

Continuous innovation

For a particular firm, if an innovation based on one technology trajectory and knowledge bank involves the constant improvement of existing products and launch of new products, it is termed a continuous innovation or sustaining innovation (Corso and Pellegrini, 2007). One example is Haier's Prodigy washing machine. Now in its 18th generation, Prodigy has undergone years of technological upgrades, incorporating many outstanding features (e.g. summer-adapted barrel volume, sterilization, no use for detergent and better performance). See Figure 3.7.

Discontinuous innovation

Also termed intermittent innovation, discontinuous innovation encompasses innovation models that diverge from the initially continuous technology trajectory, such as radical innovation and disruptive innovation (Lynn, Morone, and Paulson, 1996). A disruptive innovation targets new market segments, assumes a new technology trajectory and is founded on a new knowledge base. One example is the UTStarcom Personal Handy Phone, a mobile version of a fixed-line phone, which came as a disruptive innovation compared with the original fixed-line technology trajectory.

Figure 3.8 summarizes the types of innovation based on this analysis and tries to classify innovation in three dimensions (i.e. content, level and market positioning). By using content as a dimension, innovation can be classified into product innovation, process innovation, service innovation and business model innovation. By using level of innovation as a dimension, innovation can be classified into incremental innovation and radical innovation, based on the degree of improvement. By using market positioning as another dimension, innovation can be classified

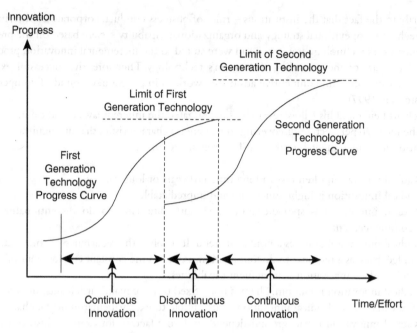

Figure 3.7 Continuous innovation and discontinuous innovation

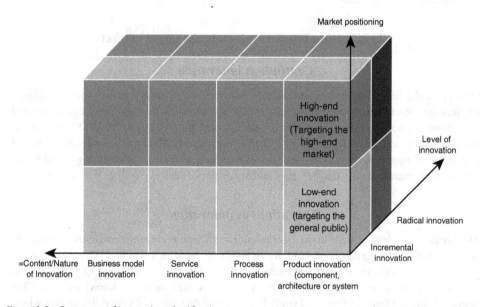

Figure 3.8 Summary of innovation classifications

into high-end innovation, which targets the high-end market, and low-end innovation, which targets the general public.

A firm may have a bias for a particular content, level and market positioning of innovation at a particular growth stage. Traditional manufacturing more often than not pays more regard to product innovation and process innovation and tries to reduce risks by incremental improvements.

In addition, it is oriented to the general public in the low-end market in an effort to achieve economies of scale. Apple and other high-tech giants, intent on business model innovation, prefer a development strategy that combines incremental innovation with radical innovation in different product families while targeting such high-end markets as smart phones and tablets to achieve high innovation efficacy. A firm needs to balance among content, level of innovation and market positioning resource and select an appropriate path for sustained competitive advantage.

Holistic innovation

Innovation paradigm shift

With the recent advancement of the global and regional economies have come environmental problems, climate change and poverty that leave a big challenge for science, technology and innovation (Hekkert et al., 2007). Though researchers in the field of innovation made many advances (Martin, 2016), issues such as the Sustainable Development Goals (SDGs) induced more reflection on the paradigm of innovation and development. The traditional paradigms of innovation typically introduced by Western scholars are rooted in the Industrial Revolution and information technology. These traditional paradigms focus mostly on science, technology and the economy, and have limited responses to the process of global economic and institutional change. The recent paradigm of technological innovation shifted towards a broader dialogue between scientific research, technological innovation and social development (Stilgoe, Owen, and Macnaghten, 2013). Additionally, beyond achieving scientific and technological progress and economic growth, the goals aim for ethical and social fulfillment (Pandza and Ellwood, 2013), therefore achieving a sustainable transformation.

Thomas Kuhn's (1970) book, *The Structure of Scientific Revolutions*, brought about a paradigm shift in how philosophers thought about science. Drawing from Kuhn's classical perspective of a paradigm shift, we can observe paradigm shifts related to innovation by country or region (see Table 3.6).

Table 3.6 Paradigm shift of innovation by country or region

Country/region	Main innovation paradigm	Scholars
North America	User innovation	von Hippel (1986)
	Disruptive innovation	Christensen (1997)
	Open innovation	Chesbrough (2003)
Europe	Design-driven innovation	Verganti (2009)
	Social innovation	Nicholls and Murdock (2012)
	Common innovation	Swann (2014)
	Responsible innovation	Owen, Behun, Manning, and Reid (2012)
		Stilgoe, Owen, and Macnaghten (2013)
Asia	Lean production	Womack, Jones, and Roos (1990)
	Knowledge-creating company	Nonak and Takeuchi (1995)
	Jugaad innovation	Radjou, Prabhu, and Ahuja (2012)
	Imitation	Linsu Kim (2000)
	Convergence innovation	Kong-rae Lee (2015)
	Indigenous innovation	Jin Chen (1994)
	Total innovation	Qingrui Xu (2007)
	Secondary innovation	Xiaobo Wu (2009)
	Embracing innovation	Richard Li-Hua (2014)

The deficiencies of existing innovation paradigms

Reviewing the evolution of the innovation paradigms, we can divide the existing innovation paradigms into three main categories. The first is based on partial elements such as user innovation (von Hippel, 1986) and disruptive innovation (Christensen, 1997) proposed by American scholars, design-driven innovation (Verganti, 2009) and public innovation (Swann, 2014) advanced by European scholars, knowledge innovation proposed by Japanese scholars (Nonaka and Takeuchi, 1995), imitation-based innovation introduced by Korean scholars (Kim and Nelson, 2000) and secondary innovation introduced by Wu Xiaobo (Wu, Ma, Shi, and Rong, 2009). The second category includes paradigms focusing on the horizontal interaction and integration of factors such as knowledge, resources and so on. This category, such as open innovation by American scholars (Chesbrough, 2003) and total innovation by Chinese scholars (Xu et al., 2007), as well as convergence innovation by Korean scholars (Lee, 2015), does not consider vertical integration and may therefore risk being too open and lacking a core competence. The third category includes responsible innovation and public innovation by European scholars (Nicholls and Murdock, 2012; Owens, Behun, Manning, and Reid, 2012; Stilgoe, Owen, and Macnaghten, 2013) and Jugaad innovation by Indian scholars (Radjou, Prabhu, and Ahuja, 2012), embracing innovation by Chinese scholars (Li-Hua, 2014) and focusing merely on the conceptual, cultural or societal aspect of innovation, thus ignoring the importance of technological factors.

Existing innovation paradigms focus on understanding the innovation process from the perspectives of specific innovation behaviors, methods or aspects of innovation, but they cannot escape the atomistic innovative thinking mind-set. Reviewing the road to innovation of world-class enterprises, new products, new elements, new methods, new processes and even new ways of organizing do not depend on individual improvements or enhancements, nor are they spontaneous – rather, they result from organized innovation (Currall, Frauenheim, Perry, and Hunter, 2014). These three types of traditional innovation paradigms ignore the leading and essential role of strategic design and strategic implementation in promoting the implementation of ideas, obtaining innovation and transforming innovative values. Gary Hamel, the guru of modern management, introduced an innovative four-level model in his book, *Big Future of Management* (Hamel, 2008), including technological innovation, operational innovation, strategic and business model innovation and management innovations, which call for more emphasis on strategic design for innovation in terms of important leadership and driving value. Phillip also points out that holistic thinking is very important to leverage correctly both sides of the brain for knowledge workers from a consulting perspective (Andrews and Wall, 2017), which predicts the importance of strategic integration for enterprises. In addition, these three traditional innovation paradigms lack the long-standing global view of Eastern philosophy (Chinese traditional culture, Buddhist wisdom, etc.), such as overall thinking, unity of opposites, organic integration and dynamic development. They fail to embody the dynamic integration of yin-yang evolution, the harmony between man and nature advocated by Taoism, the "middle course (Zhong Dao)" philosophy advocated by Confucianism, the concept of "harmonious but different (He Er Bu Tong)" and the overall strategic concept introduced by the ancient Chinese book *Art of War* (Tzu, 2005).

Holistic innovation: new innovation paradigm based on Eastern wisdom

In light of the deficiency of existing innovation paradigms in the Chinese context, drawing from the advantages of Eastern philosophy and traditional Chinese culture, Chen, Yin, and Mei

(2018) proposed a new paradigm of innovation, holistic innovation (HI), which is total and collaborative innovation driven by a strategic vision in an era of strategic innovation, which aims for a sustainable and competitive advantage. An innovative management paradigm based on HI is called holistic innovation management (HIM).

The four core elements of HI are strategic, total, open and collaborative; that is, total innovation, open innovation and collaborative innovation driven by the strategic vision. The four elements are interrelated and indispensable pillars within the helix of holistic innovation.

Framework of holistic innovation

In the innovation-driven era, HI is a new paradigm rooted in overall management change. It is a trinity based on the integration of the natural sciences and social sciences under the guidance of Eastern and Western philosophies. The helix concept of HI embodies a global outlook, an overall outlook and a peaceful outlook, which is in line with the common core values across Eastern and Western philosophies. It is conducive to achieving an organic co-evolution among engineering, technology, science and humanities, arts and markets in a cross-cultural competitive environment. Additionally, HI goes beyond the traditional boundaries of organizations, pushing companies to interact with the external partners, including the demand side, the supply side and even the domestic and foreign policy side and other relevant subjects and interests. By doing this, companies can build a vertical and horizontal innovation ecosystem. This system aims to exploit and create market opportunities and technology potential in a dynamic collaborative model to enhance product and technology novelty through cross-border innovation and competition and cooperation. Finally, HI could contribute to the goal of "Innovation for Peace" (Miklian and Hoelscher, 2018), an innovation to achieve global sustainable development and fulfill the value of humanity (Pandza and Ellwood, 2013) (see Figure 3.9).

Companies should think big, aim high and try to lead their own internal evolution in their ecosystems through forward-looking strategic design. Moreover, companies should also act boldly in their strategic implementation. Through horizontal resource integration, longitudinal vertical integration of capabilities and relying on collaborative innovation thinking, companies can achieve overall technology integration and product innovation and a competition-cooperation win-win situation (Ming-Jer Chen, 2014).

At the regional and national level, governments should realize that in the strategic fields of major scientific and technological innovation such as aerospace systems, high-speed railway technology, quantum communication, artificial intelligence and the Industrial Internet, they need more than simple technological innovation, they also need a long-term development strategy that is embedded with innovation strategy for the nation. Only through such a holistic thinking process can we achieve the organic integration of science and technology strategy, education strategy, industrial strategy, financial strategy and talent and diplomatic strategy. At the same time, a strategic vision can drive the horizontal integration and vertical promotion of all elements to provide an inexhaustible source of power to build the most innovative nation in the world. This will serve as a powerful engine for a global campaign of anti-poverty and peace. Finally, it will make a significant leading contribution to global sustainable development (Miklian and Hoelscher, 2018).

The holistic innovation theory calls for more attention from academics and public policy areas. Because holistic innovation provides enterprises with a systematic and holistic view of combining strategic management, organizational design, cultural construction and industrial trends, it can help realize the divergent thinking of engineering and social sciences in the natural sciences. It will help enterprises seize the "window of opportunity" during the process of

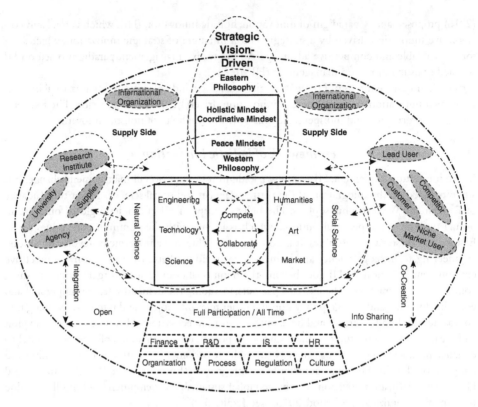

Figure 3.9 Theoretical framework of HI: an emerging innovation paradigm in open environments
Source: Chen, Yin, and Mei (2018)

industrial transformation and technological innovation. It is a new paradigm for enterprises to reshape their sustainable innovation capability and core competence. It is worthwhile for enterprise managers to engage in practical exploration and for scholars to follow up. As for the policy aspect, holistic innovation theory provides an innovative policy design perspective based on global and integrated views. Innovation policy should not be limited to science and technology. Science and technology, education, economy, culture, people's livelihood and ecology should be combined to create a synergy to promote total and collaborative innovation driven by strategic design. Only in this way can China realize the national, industrial and enterprise innovation strategies. We can then systematically upgrade the national and regional innovation system and technology transfer system to provide the nation with assistance in major technological fields and strategic industries, and empower enterprises in emerging markets to win the advantages of global innovation and leadership.

Notes

1 See also: http://cpc.people.com.cn/GB/64184/64186/66689/4494528.html
2 See also: www.weforum.org/agenda/2018/01/worlds-most-innovative-cities-jll/
3 For more details, please see the European Innovation Scoreboard 2017.
4 See also: http://fortune.com/change-the-world/alipayant-financial/

References

Andergassen, R., Nardini, F. and Ricottilli, M. (2017). Innovation diffusion, general purpose technologies and economic growth. *Structural Change and Economic Dynamics*, 40, 72–80. https://doi.org/10.1016/j.strueco.2016.12.003.

Andrews, P. and Wall, K. J. (2017). *Holistic innovation: the new driver for excellent enterprises*. CreateSpace Independent Publishing Platform.

Belderbos, R., Carree, M. and Lokshin, B. (2004). Cooperative R&D and firm performance. *Research Policy*, 33(10), 1477–1492. https://doi.org/10.1016/j.respol.2004.07.003.

Chen, J. (1994). From technology importing to indigenous innovation learning model. *Science Research Management*, 15(2), 32–34+31.

Chen, J. (2017). Towards new and multiple perspectives on innovation. *International Journal of Innovation Studies*, 1(1), 1. https://doi.org/10.3724/SP.J.1440.101001.

Chen, J., Tong, L. and Ngai, E. W. T. (2007). Inter organizational knowledge management in complex products and systems: challenges and an exploratory framework. *Journal of Technology Management in China*, 2(2), 134–144. https://doi.org/10.1108/17468770710756077.

Chen, J., Yin, X. and Mei, L. (2018). Holistic innovation: an emerging innovation paradigm. *International Journal of Innovation Studies*, 2(1), 1–13. https://doi.org/10.1016/j.ijis.2018.02.001.

Chesbrough, H. W. (2003). The era of open innovation. *MIT Sloan Management Review*, 44(3), 35–41.

Christensen, C. M. (1997). *The innovator's dilemma: when new technologies cause great firms to fail*. Harvard Business School Press.

Corso, M. and Pellegrini, L. (2007). Continuous and discontinuous innovation: overcoming the innovator dilemma. *Creativity and Innovation Management*, 16(4), 333–347. https://doi.org/10.1111/j.1467-8691.2007.00459.x.

Currall, S. C., Frauenheim, E., Perry, S. J. and Hunter, E. M. (2014). *Organized innovation: a blueprint for renewing America's prosperity*. Oxford: Oxford University Press.

Drucker, P. F. (2009). *Innovation and entrepreneurship* (Reprint ed.). HarperCollins e-books.

Fagerberg, J. (2003). Schumpeter and the revival of evolutionary economics: an appraisal of the literature. *Journal of Evolutionary Economics*, 13(2), 125–159. https://doi.org/10.1007/s00191-003-0144-1.

Freeman, C. (1987). *Technology, policy, and economic performance: lessons from Japan*. Pinter Publishers.

Gao, Y., Shu, C., Jiang, X., Gao, S. and Page, A. L. (2017). Managerial ties and product innovation: the moderating roles of macro- and micro-institutional environments. *Long Range Planning*, 50(2), 168–183. https://doi.org/10.1016/j.lrp.2016.11.005.

Hamel, G. (2008). The future of management. *Human Resource Management International Digest*, 16(6). https://doi.org/10.1108/hrmid.2008.04416fae.001.

Hekkert, M. P., Suurs, R. A. A., Negro, S. O., Kuhlmann, S. and Smits, R. E. H. M. (2007). Functions of innovation systems: a new approach for analysing technological change. *Technological Forecasting and Social Change*, 74(4), 413–432. https://doi.org/10.1016/j.techfore.2006.03.002.

Hobday, M. (1998). Product complexity innovation and industrial organization. *Research Policy*, 26(6), 689–710.

Hobday, M. (2000). The project-based organisation: an ideal form for managing complex products and systems? *Research Policy*, 29(7–8), 871–893. https://doi.org/10.1016/S0048-7333(00)00110-4.

Kim, L. and Nelson, R. R. (2000). *Technology, learning, and innovation: experiences of newly industrializing economies*. Cambridge: Cambridge University Press.

Kuhn, T. S. (1970). *The structure of scientific revolutions* (2nd ed.). Chicago: University of Chicago Press.

Lee, K. (2015). Toward a new paradigm of technological innovation: convergence innovation. *Asian Journal of Technology Innovation*, 23(sup1), 1–8. https://doi.org/10.1080/19761597.2015.1019226.

Leifer, R., McDermott, C. M., O'Connor, G. C., Peters, L. S., Rice, M. P. and Veryzer, R. W., Jr. (2000). *Radical innovation: how mature companies can outsmart upstarts*. Harvard Business Press.

Li-Hua, R. (2014). Embracing contradiction. In *Competitiveness of Chinese firms*. London: Palgrave Macmillan, pp. 87–104. https://doi.org/10.1057/9781137309303_5.

Lynn, G. S., Morone, J. G. and Paulson, A. S. (1996). Marketing and discontinuous innovation: the probe and learn process. *California Management Review*, 38(3), 8–37. https://doi.org/10.2307/41165841.

Mansfield, E. (1968). *Industrial research and technological innovation: an econometric analysis*. W.W. Norton.

Martin, B. R. (2016). Twenty challenges for innovation studies. *Science and Public Policy*, 43(3), 432–450. https://doi.org/10.1093/scipol/scv077.

Miklian, J. and Hoelscher, K. (2018). A new research approach for peace innovation. *Innovation and Development*, 8(2), 189–207. https://doi.org/10.1080/2157930X.2017.1349580.

Ming-Jer, C. (2014). Becoming ambicultural: a personal quest, and aspiration for organizations. *Academy of Management Review*, 39(2), 119–137. https://doi.org/10.5465/amr.2013.0493.

Nicholls, A. and Murdock, A. (2012). The nature of social innovation. In Nicholls, A. and Murdock, A. (Eds.), *Social innovation: blurring boundaries to reconfigure markets*. London: Palgrave Macmillan, pp. 1–30. https://doi.org/10.1057/9780230367098_1.

Nonaka, I. and Takeuchi, H. (1995). *The knowledge-creating company: how Japanese companies create the dynamics of innovation*. Oxford: Oxford University Press.

OECD/Eurostat (2005). *Oslo manual: guidelines for collecting and interpreting innovation data*, 3rd edition, The Measurement of Scientific and Technological Activities, OECD Publishing, Paris. https://doi.org/10.1787/9789264013100-en

Osterwalder, A., Pigneur, Y. and Clark, T. (2010). *Business model generation: a handbook for visionaries, game changers, and challengers*. Hoboken, NJ: John Wiley & Sons Ltd.

Owens, E. W., Behun, R. J., Manning, J. C. and Reid, R. C. (2012). The impact of internet pornography on adolescents: a review of the research. *Sexual Addiction & Compulsivity*, 19(1–2), 99–122. https://doi.org/10.1080/10720162.2012.660431.

Pandza, K. and Ellwood, P. (2013). Strategic and ethical foundations for responsible innovation. *Research Policy*, 42(5), 1112–1125. https://doi.org/10.1016/j.respol.2013.02.007.

Pilav-Velić, A. and Marjanovic, O. (2016). Integrating open innovation and business process innovation: insights from a large-scale study on a transition economy. *Information and Management*, 53(3), 398–408. https://doi.org/10.1016/j.im.2015.12.004.

Prahalad, C. K. (2012). Bottom of the pyramid as a source of breakthrough innovations. *Journal of Product Innovation Management*, 29(1), 6–12. https://doi.org/10.1111/j.1540-5885.2011.00874.x.

Radjou, N., Prabhu, J. and Ahuja, S. (2012). *Jugaad innovation: think frugal, be flexible, generate breakthrough growth*. John Wiley & Sons Ltd.

Ritala, P. and Hurmelinna-Laukkanen, P. (2013). Incremental and radical innovation in coopetition-the role of absorptive capacity and appropriability: incremental and radical innovation in coopetition. *Journal of Product Innovation Management*, 30(1), 154–169. https://doi.org/10.1111/j.1540-5885.2012.00956.x.

Rogers, E. M. (2010). *Diffusion of innovations* (4th ed.). Simon and Schuster.

Schumpeter, J. A. (1934). *The theory of economic development: an inquiry into profits, capital, credit, interest, and the business cycle*. Transaction Publishers.

Stilgoe, J., Owen, R. and Macnaghten, P. (2013). Developing a framework for responsible innovation. *Research Policy*, 42(9), 1568–1580. https://doi.org/10.1016/j.respol.2013.05.008.

Swann, G. M. P. (2014). *Common innovation: how we create the wealth of nations*. Cheltenham: Edward Elgar Publishing.

Tzu, S. (2005). *The art of war: complete texts and commentaries*. Shambhala Publications.

Van Lancker, J., Mondelaers, K., Wauters, E. and Van Huylenbroeck, G. (2016). The organizational innovation system: a systemic framework for radical innovation at the organizational level. *Technovation*, 52–53, 40–50. https://doi.org/10.1016/j.technovation.2015.11.008.

Verganti, R. (2009). *Design-driven innovation: changing the rules of competition by radically innovating what things mean*. Harvard Business Press.

von Hippel, E. (1986). Lead users: a source of novel product concepts. *Management Science*, 32(7), 791–805. https://doi.org/10.1287/mnsc.32.7.791.

Wilden, R., Devinney, T. M. and Dowling, G. R. (2016). The architecture of dynamic capability research identifying the building blocks of a configurational approach. *The Academy of Management Annals*, 10(1), 997–1076. https://doi.org/10.1080/19416520.2016.1161966.

Womack, J. P., Daniel T. J. and Daniel R. (1990). *The machine that hanged the world: the story of lean production*. New York: Harper Collins.

Wu, X., Ma, R., Shi, Y. and Rong, K. (2009). Secondary innovation: the path of catch-up with 'Made in China'. *China Economic Journal*, 2(1), 93–104. https://doi.org/10.1080/17538960902860147.

Xu, Q., Chen, J., Xie, Z., Liu, J., Zheng, G. and Wang, Y. (2007). Total innovation management: a novel paradigm of innovation management in the 21st century. *The Journal of Technology Transfer*, 32(1–2), 9–25. https://doi.org/10.1007/s10961-006-9007-x.

4
THE FUNDAMENTALS OF INNOVATION MANAGEMENT

Petra A. Nylund

This chapter presents the building blocks of innovation management from a micro to macro level, explaining how innovation management has grown through incorporating a wide set of theoretical frameworks. Our voyage through the fundamentals of innovation management begins with the individual-level micro foundations; passes through firm-level knowledge and learning processes; and ends with systems of innovation on a national, regional, technological, and sectoral scale. We discuss how innovation management has used these building blocks and identify ideas that could be better implemented in innovation research and practice, such as the cyclic nature of the innovation process and the reuse of knowledge and innovation on all levels. We conclude by considering these issues in the recent studies of innovation ecosystems.

The micro foundations of innovation management

Innovation is usually treated on the organizational level and is only exceptionally considered on the level of the individual (Crossan and Apaydin, 2010). Underlying constructs (i.e. knowledge) are seen as transferred between firms (Kogut and Zander, 1993), and capabilities are based on organizational rather than individual skills, resources, and competences (Teece and Pisano, 1998). However, organization-level innovation ultimately depends on how individuals create, transfer, conserve, and use knowledge (Simon, 1991). Accounting for the relevant micro mechanisms would enable us to better define and understand collective-level constructs (Foss, 2006; Peteraf, Pitelis, and Zollo, 2008). Through explicitly linking the individual and collective levels, we can apply learnings from psychology and other disciplines to the salient questions regarding innovation (Crossan and Apaydin, 2010). Focusing on the micro foundations of the firm, however, is more than simply importing individual-level psychological theories and using them at the organizational level (Felin and Foss, 2005). When investigating the micro-level foundations of innovation, it is important to focus on how individual-level constructs affect firm behavior.

Knowledge is a necessary ingredient in the innovation process (Quintane, Casselman, Reiche, and Nylund, 2011). It can be seen as residing within the organization (March, 1991) and may be stored in the organization, for example, in its routines (Nelson and Winter, 1982), but the communication, coordination, and combination of knowledge are carried out by individuals (Grant, 1996). Therefore, understanding how individuals process knowledge is central to advancing our understanding of innovation. On the micro level, knowledge processes take place within the individual. We will identify the micro-level knowledge processes of motivation, attention, cognition, memory, creativity, and articulation. Innovation depends on how individuals create knowledge and on how this individual knowledge is integrated into firm-level innovation processes. Individual-level micro foundations of innovation form a circular feedback loop with six underlying processes:

- Motivation: Individual innovation processes are induced by motivation, which is often intrinsically generated by the joy of innovating, but is also influenced by the normative pressures and extrinsic compensation offered by the firm.
- Attention: Out of all the ideas generated by individuals and groups, some are selected for further attention and become a focus of time and resources.
- Cognition: Individuals structure knowledge in order to process and understand it, converting it to innovation input.
- Memory: Here we explain the processes for storing knowledge on the individual level in preparation for innovation.
- Creativity: Individuals need to convert the stored knowledge into new ideas to foment innovation.
- Articulation: For an idea to travel from the individual level and become a firm-level innovation, it needs to be articulated and understood by others so that their feedback can generate new motivation and new individual-level innovation processes.

We review literature on the constituting micro processes of firm-level innovation and conduct a composition analysis comparing the definition of each construct at the individual and organizational level. We then study the cross-level effects of the individual-level constructs in the composition model on firm-level knowledge processes. To conclude this section, we identify the contributions of this chapter, as well as directions for future research and practice.

Knowledge micro processes and their role in firm-level innovation

Individual knowledge micro processes form the foundation of an individual's engagement in a firm's knowledge processes. Attention is the linchpin between motive and emotion, on the one hand, and cognition, on the other (Simon, 1994). The organizational knowledge processes may have different ends such as building dynamic capabilities or transferring knowledge. However, the underlying micro processes of organizational knowledge processes are similar. The knowledge-related micro processes are distinguished in neuroscience. Knowledge is represented in neural networks (Hayek, 1952; Edelman and Mountcastle, 1978). These networks consist of neurons (brain cells) connected by synapses (Hebb, 1949). The form and meaning of knowledge are conveyed through neural signaling, neural adaptation, and neural growth (Feldman, 2006). The neural networks are thus created and reconfigured in a continuous dynamic process (Fuster, 2006). This process can be divided into six steps (Figure 4.1).

For an innovation process to begin, motivation is needed. The motivational significance of a neural network is conveyed by a region of the brain called the amygdala. Motivation directs attention so that some knowledge is selected for processing in favor of other knowledge. The motivational signals will cause some of the existing neural networks to provide inputs with active neurons to synaptically latch on to. The activation of neural networks corresponds to attention. The focused attention enables a cognitive process, wherein the new stimulus becomes part of the neural network. Cognition thus takes place as a synapse that is formed to link the new neuron with the network. The neural networks persist in time and constitute the memory

Fundamentals of innovation management

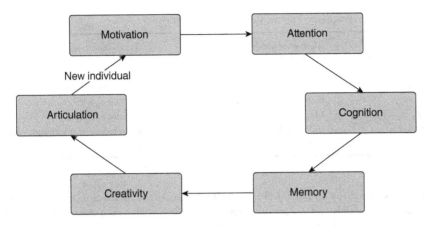

Figure 4.1 Knowledge micro processes

of the individual. The knowledge in the memory may then be used creatively. Creativity involves the restructuring of established memory networks. The knowledge is then articulated in order to be processed by additional individuals. Articulation of knowledge requires a connection with the neural networks for language and speech. When the processed knowledge is transferred, it can become an input in the knowledge process of another individual.

In the following, we will describe each micro process. First, we review the research about each construct on both micro and macro levels. From a multilevel perspective, the organization is understood as a nested arrangement of organizational entities. Individuals are located in groups, which in turn are located in subunits, organizations, and interorganizational networks (Hitt, Beamish, Jackson, and Mathieu, 2007). The locus of knowledge in this nested arrangement is crucial for how firms create value (Felin and Hesterley, 2007). We use psychological constructs that have been employed to explain both the behavior of individuals and that of organizations. The meaning attributed to these constructs is often quite different at the organizational level compared to the original psychological conception. In Rousseau's (1985) typology of multilevel models, composition models describe variables at multiple levels of analysis that are functionally similar. We identify the principal differences between the research at the micro and macro levels. These differences are summarized in Table 4.1.

Second, we describe the role of each micro construct in the knowledge processes of a firm. This analysis situates the micro processes within the higher-level processes of the organization. Cross-level models specify the effects that phenomena at one level have on those of another level (Klein and Kozlowski, 2000; Rousseau, 1985). These models usually describe the effects of the organization on the individual, but can likewise study the reverse effects (Behling, 1978; Hitt, Beamish, Jackson, and Mathieu, 2007).

Motivation and knowledge

Individual actions, including knowledge processes, are induced by some form of motivation. Motivation is the influence of needs and desires on the intensity and direction of behavior (Slavin, 2005). It can be either extrinsic or intrinsic. Extrinsic motivation is driven by factors external to the activity such as monetary rewards. Intrinsic motivation, on the other hand, is aroused by factors inherent in the activity and result in spontaneous, expressive, and often

Table 4.1 Micro- and macro-level research on functional constructs

Function	Micro-level research	Macro-level research
Motivation	Psychological needs	Motivating
Attention	Selecting information	Directing attention
Cognition	Knowledge structure	Knowledge structure
Memory	Memory retrieval	Memory storage
Creativity	Individual characteristics	Generation of novel and useful ideas
Articulation	Combination of sounds	Interactive definition of concepts

pleasurable behavior (Deci, 1975; Kehr, 2004). Individual-level motivation research focuses on the psychological needs and desires underlying motivation such as self-determination, competence, and interpersonal relatedness (Deci and Ryan, 1985).

On the organizational level, extant research examines how firms can fulfill needs and desires and thus generate motivation. This research looks at motivators such as job enrichment (Hackman and Oldham, 1976) or incentive schemes (Baker, Jensen, and Murphy, 1988). Organizational motivation is thus conceptualized as the action or process of motivating, whereas individual motivation focuses on the characteristics of the psychological needs.

Motivation has an initiating role in organizational knowledge processes. Organizational knowledge transfer, knowledge creation, and the generation of knowledge networks all need to be initiated by motivation. For knowledge transfer to occur, both the source and the recipient of knowledge must be motivated, intrinsically or extrinsically, to collaborate and to exert the effort required for knowledge transfer (Szulanski, 2000). Other knowledge processes also require effort from the individual who needs to be motivated. Intrinsic motivation for knowledge processes can stem from the knowledge or from the act of processing it. Knowledge creation has been found to be largely intrinsically motivated (Mudambi, Mudambi, and Navarra, 2007; Teigland and Wasko, 2009). Moreover, the generation of knowledge networks depends on the accessibility and valuation of knowledge, both of which are related to motivation (Borgatti and Cross, 2003; Nebus, 2006). Knowledge will be accessible only if the knowledge transferring parties are motivated, whereas the valuation of knowledge can be seen as the sum of the motivation to either transfer or protect it. The motivators to transfer knowledge through strong and weak ties could be very different. Strong ties presuppose frequent and prolonged interaction, which could yield intrinsic motivation. Weak ties, on the other hand, provide less motivation through interaction and should therefore be extrinsically motivated by the purpose they serve (Granovetter, 1973). However, when firms move towards alliances and resource interdependence, the existence of even very strong ties could be based on extrinsic motivation.

For knowledge to benefit the organization, individuals must also be motivated to use this knowledge within the organization instead of outside it. Individual intellectual capital can be acquired when individuals enter the firm, or it can be built over time through formation and experience. Individuals must thus be motivated to join and remain within the firm, as well as to continue acquiring knowledge once in the firm. The intellectual capital of an organization further depends upon individuals being motivated to convert individual social capital into the social capital of the organization (Reiche, Harzing, and Kraimer, 2009). Dynamic capabilities likewise require the willingness of individuals to build and sustain configurations of skills, resources, and competences. Skills and competences ultimately reside within the individual. This means that although capabilities cannot be appropriated by another firm, they are nevertheless volatile and subject to the employees remaining within the organization. The common use of large firm empirical samples represents employee turnover as a minor issue, but in smaller firms a breakout or renunciation of one or a few employees may deteriorate organizational capabilities significantly (Dess and Shaw, 2001).

The scarce literature available on motivational micro foundations of the firm confers the existence of the firm to the access to intrinsic motivational factors unavailable to the market (Osterloh and Frey, 2000). Firms can use both normative intrinsic motivation based on values and norms and hedonic intrinsic motivation, which comes from the enjoyment of carrying out the task at hand (Lindenberg, 2001). Relations and norms are mechanisms more readily available to the firm than to the market (Fauchart and von Hippel, 2008). Kogut and Zander (1996) perceive the firm as a social community specializing in knowledge transfer by providing a normative territory to which members identify and project their longing to belong.

Attention and knowledge

Attention is a crucial step in individual knowledge processes. Individual attention means that some information is selected for processing at the expense of less-than-optimal processing of other information (Cowan et al., 2005). Attention enables the individual to shut out distractions and effectively carry out the desired action (James, 1890). Attention is necessary since the human mind can only process a limited amount of information (Simon, 1947, 1991). The individual thus has to select certain items in favor of others. Needs, desires, and preferences determine which items receive attention and which items are ignored.

An organization needs to focus attention of the participating individuals on the needs of the organization, which may be contrary to the needs of the individuals. Attention at the organizational level is thus not only about selecting the information to attend to but also about directing the attention of employees. The organization directs attention, which in turn stimulates action (Simon, 1947). The firm focuses attention on the more important knowledge. Attention is then situated in the procedural and communication channels of the organization and is distributed by the rules, resources, players, and social positions of the organization (Ocasio, 1997). Jacobides (2007) refines the role of the firm as that of structuring attention through the organizational structure. The structure, locus, and focalization of attention are all elements at the organizational level. However, only an individual can ultimately pay attention. To understand what is required to focus attention, we must understand attention itself as a lower-level phenomenon.

The role of attention in organizational knowledge processes is to select certain knowledge. Selecting inadequate input for a knowledge process necessarily leads to suboptimal output. Erroneously processing irrelevant information instead of important items will waste scarce resources. Not only may the resources for knowledge processes be put to inefficient use but as a result of misdirected attention, resources may be spent on useless or damaging actions. When omitted information is crucial to the understanding of an issue, processed knowledge may be flawed. If this defective knowledge is acted upon, undesired results are probable. We know little about how to direct attention so that it benefits competitiveness.

Cognition and knowledge

Individual knowledge processes necessarily include a cognitive step. Cognition is the ingestion of information for subsequent processing. Individual-level cognitive processes have been thoroughly researched by management scholars basing their work on that of psychologists. Much of the cognition literature is centered on how individuals structure knowledge in order to understand it (Neisser, 1976; Walsh, 1995). Knowledge is understood by the individual through interpretative processes such as noticing, bracketing, and labeling (Weick, 1979). Meaning is conferred to information by ascribing labels to it (Dutton and Jackson, 1987; Taylor and Fiske, 1978). The mental template that individuals impose on knowledge to give it form and meaning is called a knowledge structure (Walsh, 1995).

Organizational cognition is often modeled through aggregating the cognitive processes of the individuals within the organization. Cognitive maps are representations of individual-level knowledge structures that are simply applied to a collective level through aggregating the individual-level constructs (Schneider and Angelmar, 1993). However, the average of individual cognitive maps (Bougon, Weick, and Binkhorst, 1977; Walsh, Henderson, and Deighton, 1988) is not necessarily representative of an organizational map. Organizations have a history, environment, and internal social relationships which may not directly affect individual maps, but could affect how individual maps are related and put together at the organizational level. The interaction of individuals can yield cognitive processes far beyond the sum of individual processes (Weick, 1979; Weick, Sutcliffe, and Obstfeld, 2005). In the case of cognition, the micro- and macro-level constructs are perhaps excessively aligned to the extent of an anthropomorphic fallacy (i.e. treatment of the organization as a human being).

The role of cognition is to prepare for organizational knowledge processes through ingesting and categorizing knowledge. The understanding of information thus does not only depend on the information itself but also on the knowledge structures of the individual and the organization. Different cognitive processes will result in different knowledge which will prompt different actions. When knowledge structures are aligned with the objective of the knowledge process, cognition enables subsequent processes. Knowledge will then be understood in a way that prepares it for future knowledge creation, transfer, capability building, etc. Knowledge may be structured, for example, according to whether it concerns a threat or an opportunity (Dutton and Jackson, 1987), or according to probable future use.

Cognitive errors, and consequent erroneous knowledge processes, occur when knowledge is wrongly categorized. For example, individuals' cognitive representation of the organization influences which capabilities an organization will build (Adner and Helfat, 2003; Gavetti, 2005; Helfat and Peteraf, 2003). Even when individuals are motivated to act in accordance with the interest of the organization, misconceptions of what those interests are may hinder capability building. Also, the different cognitive structures of the individuals in the organization may give rise to conflict or miscommunication, which hinders the adaptation of capabilities to a dynamic environment. Cognitive difficulties can also impede knowledge transfer since they hamper reception of knowledge. Cognitive barriers can result from knowledge being tacit, that is, not codified (Polanyi, 1966), concealed, complex, or system embedded (Winter, 1987), or from knowledge lacking an apprehensible underlying structure (Boisot and Child, 1999).

Memory and knowledge

Memory is the micro process that makes knowledge last over time. The act of remembering includes the perception, storage, and retrieval of past events. Research on individual and organizational memory has shown that they share the function of recollecting past events and situations but differ in the manner in which this function is carried out (Morgeson and Hofmann, 1999).

Individual memory research centers on the psychological processes of retrieval (Craik, 1979; Lockhart, 2001), whereas perception is covered by the cognition literature. Retrieval is an evolving process where events are affected by context and culture in reconstructing a memory (Bartlett, 1932).

Research on organizational memory is focused on the storage of knowledge more than on the retrieval. Organizational memory can be seen as located in procedures (March and Simon, 1958); in structural artifacts (Starbuck and Hedberg, 1977); or within the individuals, culture, transformations, structures, ecology, and archives of the organization (Walsh and Ungson, 1991). The variation in storage bins for organizational memory could explain why storage is a more frequent object for study at the macro level, while retrieval dominates micro-level research. Understanding knowledge retrieval at the organizational level would, however, aid the study of how existing knowledge is recombined in organizations (Nonaka, 1994; Kogut and Zander, 1996).

Memory has an essential role in accumulating knowledge within organizations. This role is evident in the literature on, for example, the generation of organizations' intellectual capital, the transfer of knowledge, and the evolution of knowledge networks. To generate intellectual capital, knowledge must be remembered by employees. Social capital is stored in the relationships maintained by the employees of the organization. It can encompass external relationships, including those with customers (Bontis, 1996), but also the internal relationships between employees (Leana and Van Buren, 1999; Nahapiet and Ghoshal, 1998). An organization's intellectual capital is stored in the systems and processes of the organization. Since it is largely impersonal, it is less prone to deterioration through the moves of individuals than individual intellectual capital. The generation of organizational intellectual capital requires individual memory to be converted into organizational memory. Individual knowledge can be converted into institutionalized processes, and interpersonal relationships can become organizational social capital (Reiche, Harzing, and Kraimer, 2009).

Knowledge transfer involves conveying knowledge from the memory of one unit to another. According to Argote and Ingram (2000), knowledge is stored in reservoirs consisting of individuals, tools, and tasks. Knowledge can be transferred by moving reservoirs or by modifying their content. Individuals can thus act as knowledge reservoirs, which makes the function of individual memory vital to knowledge transfer. Moving individuals is a powerful mechanism for knowledge transfer since individuals are able to adapt the knowledge to its new context. Brown and Duguid's (1991, 2001) conception of firms as communities-of-practice emphasizes that knowledge travels easily between individuals of the same trade, while it is difficult to transfer across practice groups even within one firm. The difference in the ease of knowledge transfer could be explained by the shared memories within communities of practice.

Memory is also an important foundation to the study of knowledge networks. Social network theory builds on the notion of ties that last over time in spite of changes in the environment (Granovetter, 1973). This would require networks to have memory in addition to that of individuals or organizations. Memory should affect how networks adapt knowledge transfer to the loss or addition of a node. Particularly in the case of the loss of central nodes, the constitution of the network memory may affect whether the network survives or not.

Creativity and knowledge

Retrieved knowledge must undergo a creative process if knowledge processes are to yield a result different from the original input. Individual creativity has been examined by psychology researchers with a focus on the characteristics of creative individuals (Barron, 1955; MacKinnon, 1965).

At the organizational level, creativity is usually defined as the production of novel and useful ideas (Oldham and Cummings, 1996; Scott and Bruce, 1994; Stein, 1974; Woodman, Sawyer, and Griffin, 1993). This collective creativity is based on individual creativity (Amabile, 1988) but also on other individual-level constructs such as motivation and cognition (George, 2007). Instead of centering on the outcome when defining creativity, some authors focus on the creative process. Creativity is then defined as the engagement of an individual in a creative act (Ford, 1996; Drazin, Glynn, and Kazanjian, 1999; Torrance, 1988). Collective-level creativity is then a process that maps who engages in creative acts and when they engage. Individual-level creativity as a process rather than an outcome should be useful not merely to explain collective-level creativity, but may also provide a micro foundation for knowledge transfer and learning.

Creativity performs a crucial role in knowledge creation. It is essential for current knowledge to be converted to new knowledge (Nonaka, 1994). For knowledge to benefit the organization, it must be adapted to the task and situation, which also requires creativity. The understanding of why certain individuals are more creative than others helps firms put together creative teams. Furthermore, comprehension of the circumstances that bring out the creativity in any individual enables firms to leverage their intellectual capital.

Articulation and knowledge

At the individual level, articulation is the intelligent combination of sounds for the purpose of speech (Whitney, 1881). Levelt (1995) further defines the construct as the process of forming words from intentions or thoughts. The articulation of knowledge implies combining words into concepts. The individual process is contained within the human mind.

At the organizational level, articulation develops when organizational members engage in dialogical exchanges (Tsoukas, 2009). Articulation is hence the interactive and collaborative process of defining shared concepts. Concepts are formed and understood when individuals exchange opinions and challenge preconceptions (Argyris and Schön, 1978). In an organization, power struggles may distort the process of articulation (March, 1962; Eisenhardt and Zbaracki, 1992). Organizational articulation is a complicated process that is quite understudied (Zollo and Winter, 2002; Nonaka, 1994).

The role of articulation in organizational knowledge processes is to externalize knowledge and facilitate collaboration (Nonaka, 1994). Knowledge processes can take place without articulation, as is the case in the transfer of tacit knowledge through joint work and other social processes (Nonaka, 1994). When the organization acts as a knowledge protector, articulation becomes an obstacle rather than an enabler. Articulated, explicit knowledge is easy to transfer and difficult to protect (Liebeskind, 1996; Winter, 1987). However, many knowledge processes require knowledge to be articulated at some point. For example, articulation is central to the conversion of individual intellectual capital into organizational intellectual capital. The strategy process literature implicitly elaborates on the processes of organizational articulation. Strategy can be deliberately formulated or emerge unintentionally (Mintzberg and Waters, 1985; Mintzberg, Ahlstrand, and Lampel, 1998).

The impact of individual-level foundations on firm-level innovation management

This section contributes to our understanding of the micro-foundational constructs of innovation management. It highlights the similarities and differences between salient constructs at each level, and thus enables us to better take advantage of both individual- and organization-level research on these constructs. Often, the research at different levels is complementary, and a unified approach enables us to benefit from synergy effects and extend the reasoning to firm- and system-level innovation. Motivation, for example, is crucial for the initiation of all knowledge processes. Therefore, research on motivation at different levels in the organization will benefit innovation studies.

Further, we model the sequence of micro processes that form the individual innovation process. Thus, we investigate the relations between the micro constructs. By linking the neural level to first the individual and then the organizational level, we show how neural processes affect firm-level innovation processes.

The individual-level foundations are shared by other knowledge-based macro processes such as knowledge acquisition (Huber, 1991), knowledge creation (McFadyen and Cannella, 2004; Nonaka, 1994), generation of knowledge networks (Borgatti and Cross, 2003; Granovetter, 1973; Nebus, 2006), organizational learning (Argyris and Schön, 1978; Crossan, Lane, and White, 1999; Hilgard and Bower, 1966; Zollo and Winter, 2002), creation of intellectual capital (Bontis, 1996; Nahapiet and Ghoshal, 1998), and building of dynamic capabilities (Eisenhardt and Martin, 2000; Kogut and Zander, 1992; Teece, 1982, 1986; Teece and Pisano, 1998). Common micro foundations thus offer ground for cross-fertilization between research streams and for a more integrated approach to innovation. For example, efforts regarding the cognitive foundations of capabilities (Adner and Helfat, 2003; Helfat and Peteraf, 2003; Gavetti, 2005) could be used in innovation research.

In practice, an understanding of how individual-level processes affect firm behavior enables managers to influence individuals to act in accordance with firm needs. Managers can work to align the motivation of employees with that of the firm. Moreover, they can consciously direct attention, clarify and coordinate knowledge structures, facilitate the storage and retrieval of knowledge in the organizational memory, encourage creativity, and enable interactive articulation. Finally, by understanding how individuals process knowledge, managers can determine which innovation processes to carry out within the firm and which processes to outsource, thereby increasing the competitiveness of the firm.

Knowledge, learning, and innovation management

Innovation management is to some extent an application of the more basic research on knowledge and learning. In this section, we review literature on knowledge and learning in organizations to discover what innovation management has learned and what it still needs to learn from these foundations. Whereas the knowledge-based processes in general, and organizational learning in particular, are perceived as circular feedback loops, innovation management still has a lot to learn about circularity and reuse of innovation and knowledge.

The knowledge-based view

The knowledge-based view rests on the assumption that firm resources are the main sources leading to competitive advantage (Barney, 1991; Collis and Montgomery, 1995, 1998; Prahalad and Hamel, 1990; Rumelt, 1984; Teece, 1984; Wernerfelt, 1984). Knowledge is proposed as the core resource for obtaining competitive advantage (Conner and Prahalad, 1996; Grant, 1996; Kogut and Zander, 1992). However, the knowledge-based view has expanded beyond viewing knowledge as a mere, but important, asset. Thus, it also goes beyond viewing the transfer of knowledge as a transaction of assets in which the firm can minimize transaction costs (Coase, 1937; Williamson, 1975).

Whereas information is a flow of messages or meanings that might add to, restructure, or change knowledge (Machlup, 1983), knowledge is created and organized by the very flow of information, anchored in the commitment and beliefs of its holder (Nonaka, 1994). Examples of knowledge are facts, opinions, ideas, theories, principles, models, experiences, values, contextual information, expert insight, and intuition (Mitri, 2003). Knowledge is the skilled process of leveraging resources (Penrose, 1959), and thus the component that enables the firm to organize resources to create competitive advantage (Conner and Prahalad, 1996; Grant, 1996; Nonaka and Takeuchi, 1995).

The antecedents of knowledge creation depend on a number of factors, such as which form of knowledge is created (Teece, 1977), by whom (Dahlin, Weingart, and Hinds, 2005), for what purpose (Siggelkow and Levinthal, 2003), and in what context (Håkanson, 2010). Understanding the communication, coordination, and combination of knowledge as the core of the firm has enabled us to explain many aspects of the existence, structure, and strategy of organizations (Arrow, 1974; Conner and Prahalad, 1996; Kogut and Zander, 1996).

One of the fundamental concepts of knowledge creation is the epistemic distinction between explicit and tacit knowledge (Polanyi, 1966). The firm can be perceived as a unique configuration of explicit and tacit knowledge (Spencer, 2008). Explicit knowledge is codified and can be communicated using formal language, whereas tacit knowledge is personal and related to action and emotion. Tacit knowledge is not articulated and is difficult to transmit (Winter, 1987).

In Nonaka's SECI model for knowledge conversion (1994), tacit knowledge is renewed through *socialization*, while previous explicit knowledge is *combined* into new explicit knowledge. New knowledge is also created through *externalization* of tacit knowledge to explicit, and through *internalization* of explicit knowledge to *tacit*.

In the socialization mode, several individuals work together over time. Knowledge is created in relationships where these individuals are confronted with the different work methods of others and when the individuals adapt to each other (Oluikpe, 2015). Combining explicit knowledge into new concepts is faster and requires fewer resources. The combination of explicit knowledge requires that knowledge has previously been externalized, that is, articulated from tacit knowledge to explicit knowledge present in plans, drawings, etc. Tacit knowledge is often difficult to articulate since it is based on action and emotion. Externalization can thus also be a time-consuming and costly process (Cowan, David, and Foray, 2000). Furthermore, explicit knowledge is difficult to protect precisely because it is so easy to transfer (Winter, 1987).

Individual knowledge can be created in any of the four modes, but organizational knowledge creation requires the dynamic interaction between the modes in a continual cycle. Nonaka (1994) sees this cycle as an upward spiral starting from knowledge at the individual level and progressing to organizational or interorganizational knowledge.

Organizational learning

Whereas the knowledge-based view primarily sees knowledge as an asset that yields competitive advantage, organization-learning literature focuses on how this asset affects organizational behavior (Levitt and March, 1988). Organizational learning can be defined as the origination or change of an activity as a reaction to an encountered situation (Hilgard and Bower, 1966). It is thus organizational change resulting from experience (Argote and Miron-Spektor, 2011). Organizational learning occurs when learning leads to a modification not only of actions but also of the organization structure, including norms, policies, and objectives (Argyris and Schön, 1978). It thus involves changing the knowledge of the organization (Fiol and Lyles, 1985).

Similar to other knowledge-based processes, organizational learning is described as a cycle wherein the organizational context triggers experience, which yields knowledge that in turn affects the context (Argote and Miron-Spektor, 2011). The articulation of knowledge enables the organization to use and share it, which is what finally triggers change in both the actions and structure of the firm (Zollo and Winter, 2002). The individual-level learning must thus be followed by an organization-level institutionalization of the new knowledge (Crossan, Lane, and White, 1999).

Implications for innovation management

The circular thinking that characterizes the knowledge and learning literature has not yet been fully embraced by the innovation literature. Already in the early works of Schumpeter (1934), innovation was seen as a cycle or a circular flow, with the firm adapting to external changes through innovation, thus gaining a competitive edge which would gradually wear off, requiring further innovation (Hagedoorn, 1996). The cyclic ideas of the knowledge-based view and organizational learning are included in innovation management insofar that firms innovate based on experience with previous, similar innovations (Lee, Rho, Kim, and Jun, 2007). However, whereas the knowledge-based view treats storage and recombination of knowledge extensively, and the organizational learning literature studies knowledge repositories and reuse of knowledge, the understanding of knowledge reuse for the purpose of innovation is still in its infancy.

One reason for the relative absence of a broader conceptualization of knowledge reuse in the innovation management literature may be the more applied character of innovation compared to its theoretical knowledge-based and organizational-learning underpinnings. Although knowledge reuse seems appropriate for many firms, these mechanisms are scarcely used in reality. Novelty-seeking behavior should be especially prominent in individuals seeking to innovate, as their quest is to come up with new solutions (Schweizer, 2006), and therefore they may be biased towards using new knowledge, rather than retrieving existing solutions and applying them new problems. For radical innovation, resorting to knowledge reuse requires first exhausting other possible solutions (Majchrzak, Cooper, and Neece, 2004). The adoption of cyclic ideas from knowledge and learning literature in the practice of innovation is thus hindered by the novelty seeking of innovators. Capabilities and routines for knowledge reuse may be needed to overcome this bias, for example, capturing knowledge generated in innovation projects through postmortems, after-action reviews, and lesson-learned books. Companies today cannot afford to reinvent the wheel over and over. Instead, they may want to institutionalize knowledge reuse.

Innovation management and innovation systems

The work on innovation systems is very much concerned with how firms learn from each other and how different components contribute to advancing the competitiveness of the system as a whole. The recent conceptualization of the innovation ecosystem allows us to better understand the key concepts of knowledge storage and reuse on the system level.

Systems of learning and innovation

The study of systems of innovation conceptualizes interactive learning processes at the core of innovation processes (Edquist, 1997). The system is thus composed of components that learn from each other. The interconnection of individuals and organizations today requires firms to consider external knowledge for innovation (Castells, 2000). The use of external knowledge improves innovative performance (Ahuja, 2000; Laursen and Salter, 2006), and open innovation processes that cross firm boundaries is an increasingly vibrant topic (Chesbrough, 2003; Bogers et al., 2017). More than ever, a systemic view of learning and innovation is necessary.

This requires an understanding of how people learn and interact in innovation systems with different cultures. We also need to learn more about the different roles assumed by firms in innovation systems, such as lead innovators who introduce radically new technology or technology modifiers who are more focused on incremental innovation (Arundel, Lorenz, Lundvall, and Valeyre, 2007). With a system view, we can begin to understand how innovation emerges in the interaction of firms with different drivers, focus, and roles. Knowledge today is too vast for one firm, let alone one individual, to grasp all that is necessary for innovation. Firms thus do not need to interact only in order to access knowledge, but to use this knowledge and turn it into innovation. Customers, suppliers, universities, competitors, etc., all contribute pieces to the complex innovation puzzle. Today firms are particularly keen on learning from users and innovate to improve the user experience (Von Hippel, 1986; Gambardella, Raasch, and von Hippel, 2016).

The scope of innovation management systems

Scholars began studying systems of innovation at a national level (Freeman, 1995; Lundvall, 1992; Nelson and Rosenberg, 1993). The definition of national innovation systems rests on the activities and interactions of the participating institutions and organizations within a country (Freeman, 1987). An emphasis is placed on how institutions and infrastructure can aid innovation processes. Others find the nations to be a too wide and complex unit of analysis and prefer to discuss the mechanisms of regional innovation systems (Cooke, Uranga, and Etxebarria, 1997). With increasing internationalization, levels above the national have also become of interest (e.g. continental innovation systems) (Freeman, 2002). Innovation systems have also been studied in the context of a specific technology or sector (Carlsson, 1995). In sectoral systems, the components share the same knowledge base, technologies, inputs, and demand (Malerba, 2002). Limiting the study of innovations to specific sectors thus enables a deeper study of the systemic knowledge processes that precede innovation. Recently, authors have contended that a combined focus on technology and geographical space is necessary to capture the nature of innovation processes (Binz, Truffer, and Coenen, 2014).

Innovation ecosystems

Technical change can be studied as an evolutionary process, where solutions are superior to those previously available, but not necessarily optimal, so that there remains a gap for further development (Nelson and Winter, 1977). Growth of an ecosystem requires increased diversity of the components (Saviotti, 1988), but also a selection of dominant designs that provide common ground for new innovations (Abernathy and Utterback, 1978).

Innovation ecosystems are loose networks of organizations and individuals that interact and coevolve to create and capture value from innovation (Moore, 1993; Iansiti and Levien, 2004; Adner and Kapoor, 2010). In addition to characteristics of innovation systems in general, innovation ecosystems require a focal firm or platform (Autio and Thomas, 2014). Platforms are products, services, or technologies upon which firms can develop complementary innovations (e.g. specific products, related services, or component technologies) (Gawer and Cusumano, 2002, 2014). Platforms can be purposively constructed as a basis for the innovation of others, for example, in the case of programming languages such as SQL or Java which serve as a tool for innovation for anyone dominating that language. Platforms can also emerge over time, when a dominant design is established. A dominant design is a product that synthesizes earlier innovations and forms a standard (Abernathy and Utterback, 1978). It stops parallel innovation projects for similar products and enables the industry to move forward with complementary innovations or by focusing efforts on different, unsolved challenges.

The antecedents of the crucial role of ecosystem platforms are an area that scholars are just beginning to delve into. We argue that it is the platform's ability to encapsulate prior knowledge and enable others to build on that knowledge that foments ecosystem growth. Organizational learning causes knowledge to become embedded in the organization's context and thus changes that context (Argote and Miron-Spektor, 2011). Similarly, knowledge of the members in an innovation ecosystem should become embedded in the ecosystem, spurring innovation and growth. Specifically, platforms can act as a knowledge artifact, which allows firms to use knowledge without previously understanding or processing it (Starbuck and Hedberg, 1977). Because companies do not have to comprehend the details of the basis for their innovation, they can focus on new ways to create and capture value in innovative business models.

Platform innovations become catalytic to market growth in that they enable firms with few resources to overcome barriers to market entry (Christensen, 2006). The explosion of the app ecosystem has been enabled not only by operating system platforms such as iOS and Android but also by the corresponding commercialization platforms App Store and Google Play. Apple, Google, Airbnb, Uber, and Lyft are but a few examples of companies that assume keystone roles in innovation ecosystems and thus assume a responsibility for creating the conditions for sustainable business opportunities for other companies and entrepreneurs.

In conclusion, this chapter attempts to understand the gap in innovation management research and practice regarding the reuse of knowledge and innovation. We conceptualize innovation ecosystem platforms as enablers of innovation that reuse knowledge without prior processing of this knowledge by the innovator. Innovation ecosystems can therefore overcome the novelty bias that hinders circular knowledge and learning processes within innovation.

References

Abernathy, W. J. and Utterback, J. M. (1978). Patterns of industrial innovation. *Technology Review*, 80(7), 40–47.

Adner, R. and Helfat, C. E. (2003). Corporate effects and dynamic managerial capabilities. *Strategic Management Journal*, 24, 1011–1025.

Adner, R. and Kapoor, R. (2010). Value creation in innovation ecosystems: how the structure of technological interdependence affects firm performance in new technology generations. *Strategic Management Journal*, 31(3), 306–333.

Ahuja, G. (2000). Collaboration networks, structural holes, and innovation: a longitudinal study. *Administrative Science Quarterly*, 45, 425–455.

Amabile, T. M. (1988). A model of creativity and innovation in organizations. In Staw, B. M. and Cummings, L. L. (Eds.), *Research in organizational behavior*, 10, 123–167. Greenwich, CT: JAI Press.

Argote, L. and Ingram, P. (2000). Knowledge transfer: a basis for competitive advantage in firms. *Organizational Behavior and Human Decision Processes*, 82, 150–169.

Argote, L. and Miron-Spektor, E. (2011). Organizational learning: from experience to knowledge. *Organization Science*, 22(5), 1123–1137.

Argyris, C. and Schön, D. (1978). *Organizational learning: a theory of action perspective*. Reading, MA: Addison Wesley.

Arrow, K. J. (1974). *The limits of organization*. New York: Norton.

Arundel, A., Lorenz, E., Lundvall, B-Å. and Valeyre, A. (2007). How Europe's economies learn: a comparison of work organization and innovation mode for the EU-15. *Industrial and Corporate Change*, 16(6), 1175–1210.

Autio, E. and Thomas, L. (2014). *Innovation ecosystems: the Oxford handbook of innovation management*. Oxford University Press, pp. 204–288.

Baker, G., Jensen, M. and Murphy, K. (1988). Compensation and incentives: practice versus theory. *Journal of Finance*, 43, 593–616.

Barney, J. (1991). Firm resources and sustained competitive advantage. *Journal of Management*, 17, 99–120.
Barron, F. (1955). The disposition toward originality. *The Journal of Abnormal and Social Psychology*, 51(3), 478.
Bartlett, F. C. (1932). *Remembering*. Cambridge, MA: Cambridge University Press.
Behling, O. (1978). Some problems in the philosophy of science in organizations. *Academy of Management Review*, 3, 193–201.
Binz, C., Truffer, B. and Coenen, L. (2014). Why space matters in technological innovation systems – mapping global knowledge dynamics of membrane bioreactor technology. *Research Policy*, 43(1), 138–155.
Bogers, M., Zobel, A. K., Afuah, A., Almirall, E., Brunswicker, S., Dahlander, L., Frederiksen, L., Gawer, A., Gruber, M., Haefliger, S., Hagedoorn, J., Hilgers, D., Laursen, K., Magnusson, M. G. Majchrak, A., McCarthy, I. P., Moeslein, K. M., Nambisan, S., Piller, F. T., Radziwon, A., Rossi-Lamastra, C., Sims, J. and Ter Wal, A. L. T. (2017). The open innovation research landscape: established perspectives and emerging themes across different levels of analysis. *Industry and Innovation*, 24(1), 8–40.
Boisot, M. and Child, J. (1999). Organizations as adaptive systems in complex environments: the case of China. *Organization Science*, 10, 237–252.
Bontis, N. (1996). Intellectual capital: an exploratory study that develops measures and models. *Management Decision*, 36(2), 63–76.
Borgatti, S. P. and Cross, R. (2003). A relational view of information seeing and learning in social networks. *Management Science*, 49, 432–445.
Bougon, M., Weick, K. E. and Binkhorst, D. (1977). Cognition in organizations: analysis of the Utrecht Jazz Orchestra. *Administrative Science Quarterly*, 22, 606–631.
Brown, J. S. and Duguid, P. (1991). Organizational learning and communities-of-practice: toward a unified view of working learning and innovation. *Organization Science*, 2, 40–57.
Brown, J. S. and Duguid, P. (2001). Knowledge and organization: a social-practice perspective. *Organization Science*, 12(2), 198–213.
Carlsson, B. (Ed.) (1995). *Technological systems and economic performance: the case of factory automation*. Dordrecht: Kluwer.
Castells, M. (2000). *The rise of the network society* (2nd ed.). Oxford and Malden, MA: Blackwell Publishers.
Chesbrough, H. W. (2003). *Open innovation: the new imperative for creating and profiting from technology*. Cambridge, MA: Harvard Business School Publishing.
Christensen, C. M., Baumann, H., Ruggles, R. and Sadtler, T. M. (2006). Disruptive innovation for social change. *Harvard Business Review*, 84(12), 94.
Coase, R. H. (1937). The nature of the firm. *Economica*, 4, 386–405.
Collis, D. J. and Montgomery, C. A. (1995). Competing on resources: strategy in the 1990's. *Harvard Business Review*, 73(4), 118–130.
Collis, D. J. and Montgomery, C. A. (1998). Creating corporate advantage. *Harvard Business Review*, 76(3), 70–83.
Conner, K. and Prahalad, C. K. (1996). A resource based theory of the firm: knowledge versus opportunism. *Organization Science*, 7, 477–501.
Cooke, P., Uranga, M. G. and Etxebarria, G. (1997). Regional innovation systems: institutional and organisational dimensions. *Research Policy*, 26(4–5), 475–491.
Cowan, N., Elliot, E. M., Saults, J. S., Morey, C. C., Mattox, S., Hismjatullina, A. and Conway, A. R. A. (2005). On the capacity of attention: its estimation and its role in working memory and cognitive aptitudes. *Cognitive Psychology*, 51, 42–100.
Cowan, R., David, P. A. and Foray, D. (2000). The explicit economics of knowledge codification and tacitness. *Industrial and Corporate Change*, 9(2), 211–253.
Craik, F. I. M. (1979). Human memory. In Rosenzweig, M. R. and Porter, L. M. (Eds.), *Annual Review of Psychology*, 30, 63–102. Palo Alto, CA: Annual Reviews.
Crossan, M. M. and Apaydin, M. (2010). A multi-dimensional framework of organizational innovation: a systematic review of the literature. *Journal of Management Studies*, 47(6), 1154–1191.
Crossan, M. M., Lane, H. W. and White, R. E. (1999). An organizational learning framework: from intuition to institution. *Academy of Management Review*, 24, 522–537.
Dahlin, K. B., Weingart, L. R. and Hinds, P. J. (2005). Team diversity and information use. *Academy of Management Journal*, 48, 1107–1123.
Deci, E. L. (1975). *Intrinsic motivation*. New York: Plenum Press.
Deci, E. L. and Ryan, R. M. (1985). *Intrinsic motivation and self-determination in human behavior*. New York: Plenum Press.

Dess, G. G. and Shaw, J. D. (2001). Voluntary turnover, social capital, and organizational performance. *Academy of Management Review*, 26, 446–456.
Drazin, R., Glynn, M. A. and Kazanjian, R. K. (1999). Multilevel theorizing about creativity in organizations: a sensemaking perspective. *Academy of Management Review*, 24, 286–307.
Dutton, J. E. and Jackson, S. E. (1987). Categorizing strategic issues: links to organizational action. *Academy of Management Review*, 12, 76–90.
Edelman, G. M. and Mountcastle, V. B. (1978). *The mindful brain*. New York: Plenum Press.
Edquist, C. (1997). *Systems of innovation: technologies, institutions, and organizations*. Psychology Press.
Eisenhardt, K. M. and Martin, J. A. (2000). Dynamic capabilities: what are they? *Strategic Management Journal*, 21, 1105–1121.
Eisenhardt, K. M. and Zbaracki, M. J. (1992). Strategic decision making. *Strategic Management Journal*, 13, 17–37.
Fauchart, E. and von Hippel, E. (2008). Norms-based intellectual property systems: the case of French chefs. *Organization Science*, 19, 187–201.
Feldman, J. A. (2006). *From molecule to metaphor: a neural theory of language*. Cambridge, MA, and London: MIT Press.
Felin, T. and Foss, N. J. (2005). Strategic organization: a field in search of micro-foundations. *Strategic Organization*, 3, 441–455.
Felin, T. and Hesterley, W. S. (2007). The knowledge-based view, nested heterogeneity, and new value creation: philosophical considerations on the locus of knowledge. *Academy of Management Review*, 32, 195–218.
Fiol, C. M. and Lyles, M. A. (1985). Organizational learning. *Academy of Management Review*, 10(4), 803–813.
Ford, C. M. (1996). A theory of individual creativity in multiple social domains. *Academy of Management Review*, 21, 1112–1134.
Foss, N. J. (2006). Knowledge and organization in the theory of the multinational corporation: some foundational issues. *Journal of Management and Governance*, 10, 3–20.
Freeman, C. (1987). *Technology policy and economic performance: lessons from Japan*. London: Pinter.
Freeman, C. (1995). The national system of innovation: in historical perspective. *Cambridge Journal of Economics*, 19(1), 5–24.
Freeman, C. (2002). Continental, national and sub-national innovation systems – complementarity and economic growth. *Research Policy*, 31(2), 191–211.
Fuster, J. M. (2006). The cognit: a network model of cortical representation. *International Journal of Psychophysiology*, 60, 125–132.
Gambardella, A., Raasch, C. and von Hippel, E. (2016). The user innovation paradigm: impacts on markets and welfare. *Management Science* 63(5), 1450–1468.
Gavetti, G. (2005). Cognition and hierarchy: rethinking the microfoundations of capabilities' development. *Organization Science*, 16, 599–617.
Gawer, A. and Cusumano, M. A. (2002). *Platform leadership: how Intel, Microsoft, and Cisco drive industry innovation*. Boston, MA: Harvard Business School Press.
Gawer, A. and Cusumano, M. A. (2014). Industry platforms and ecosystem innovation. *Journal of Product Innovation Management*, 31(3): 417–433.
George, J. M. (2007). 9 Creativity in organizations. *The Academy of Management Annals*, 1, 439–477.
Granovetter, M. (1973). The strength of weak ties. *American Journal of Sociology*, 78, 1360–1380.
Grant, R. M. (1996). Toward a knowledge-based theory of the firm. *Strategic Management Journal*, 17, 109–122.
Hackman, J. R. and Oldham, G. R. (1976). Motivation through the design of work. *Organizational Behavior and Human Performance*, 16, 250–279.
Hagedoorn, J. (1996). Innovation and entrepreneurship: Schumpeter revisited. *Industrial and Corporate Change*, 5(3), 883–896.
Håkanson, L. (2010). The firm as an epistemic community: the knowledge-based view revisited. *Industrial and Corporate Change*, 19(6), 1801–1828.
Hayek, F. A. (1952). *The sensory order*. Chicago: University of Chicago Press.
Hebb, D. O. (1949). *The organization of behavior*. New York: John Wiley and Sons.
Helfat, C. E. and Peteraf, M. A. (2003). The dynamic resource-based view: capability lifecycles. *Strategic Management Journal*, 24, 997–1010.
Hilgard, E. R. and Bower, G. H. (1966). *Theories of learning*. New York: Meredith.

Hitt, M. A., Beamish, P. W., Jackson, S. E. and Mathieu, J. E. (2007). Building theoretical and empirical bridges across levels: multilevel research in management. *Academy of Management Journal*, 50, 1385–1399.

Huber, G. P. (1991). Organizational learning: the contributing processes and the literatures. *Organization Science*, 2(1), 88–115.

Jacobides, M. G. (2007). The inherent limits of organizational structure and the unfulfilled role of hierarchy: lessons from a near-war. *Organization Science*, 18, 455–477.

Iansiti, M. and Levien, R. (2004). Strategy as ecology. *Harvard Business Review*, 82(3), 68–81.

James, W. (1890). The principles of psychology, I. http://psychclassics.yorku.ca. 11/17/08.

Kehr, H. M. (2004). Integrating implicit motives, explicit motives and perceived abilities: the compensatory model of work motivation and volition. *Academy of Management Review*, 29, 479–499.

Klein, K. J. and Kozlowski, S. W. J. (2000). From micro to meso: critical steps in conceptualizing and conducting multilevel research. *Organizational Research Methods*, 3, 211–236.

Kogut, B. and Zander, U. (1992). Knowledge of the firm, combinative capabilities, and the replication of technology. *Organization Science*, 3, 383–397.

Kogut, B. and Zander, U. (1993). Knowledge of the firm and the evolutionary theory of the multinational corporation. *Journal of International Business Studies*, 24, 625–645.

Kogut, B. and Zander, U. (1996). What firms do? coordination, identity, and learning. *Organization Science*, 7, 502–518.

Laursen, K. and Salter, A. J. (2006). Open for innovation: the role of openness in explaining innovation performance among UK manufacturing firms. *Strategic Management Journal*, 27, 131–150.

Leana, C. R. and Van Buren, H. J. III. (1999). Organizational social capital and employment practices. *Academy of Management Review*, 24, 538–555.

Lee, K., Rho, S., Kim, S. and Jun, G. J. (2007). Creativity-innovation cycle for organisational exploration and exploitation: lessons from Neowiz-a Korean internet company. *Long Range Planning*, 40(4), 505–523.

Levelt, W. J. M. (1995). *Speaking. From intention to articulation*. Cambridge, MA: MIT Press.

Levitt, B. and March, J. G. (1988). Organizational learning. *Annual Review of Sociology*, 14, 319–340.

Liebeskind, J. P. (1996). Knowledge, strategy, and the theory of the firm. *Strategic Management Journal*, 17, 93–107.

Lindenberg, S. (2001). Intrinsic motivation in a new light. *Kyklos*, 54, 317–342.

Lockhart, R. S. (2001). Commentary: levels of processing and memory theory. In Craik, F. I. M., Naveh-Benjamin, M., Moscovitch, M. and Roediger, H. L. (Eds.), *Perspectives on human memory and cognitive aging: essays in honour of Fergus Craik*. New York: Psychology Press, pp. 99–104.

Lundvall, B.-Å. (Ed.). (1992). *National systems of innovation: towards a theory of innovation and interactive learning*. London: Pinter.

Machlup, F. (1983). Semantic quirks in studies of information. In Machlup, F. and Mansfield, U. (Eds.), *The study of information*. New York: John Wiley & Sons Ltd.

MacKinnon, D. W. (1965). Personality and the realization of creative potential. *American Psychologist*, 20, 622–629.

Majchrzak, A., Cooper, L. P. and Neece, O. E. (2004). Knowledge reuse for innovation. *Management Science*, 50(2), 174–188.

Malerba, F. (2002). Sectoral systems of innovation and production. *Research Policy*, 31(2), 247–264.

March, J. G. (1962). The business firm as a political coalition. *The Journal of Politics*, 24, 662–678.

March, J. G. (1991). Exploration and exploitation in organizational learning. *Organization Science*, 2, 71–87.

March, J. G. and Simon, H. A. (1958). *Organizations*. New York: John Wiley & Sons Ltd.

McFadyen, M. A. and Cannella, A. A. (2004). Social capital and knowledge creation: diminishing returns of the number and strength of exchange relationships. *Academy of Management Journal*, 47(5), 735–746.

Mintzberg, H., Ahlstrand, B. and Lampel, J. (1998). *Strategy safari: a guided tour through the wilds of strategic management*. Hertfordshire: Prentice Hall.

Mintzberg, H. and Waters, J. (1985). Of strategies, deliberate and emergent. *Strategic Management Journal*, 6, 257–272.

Mitri, M. (2003). A knowledge management framework for curriculum assessment. *Journal of Computer Information Systems*, 43(4), 15–24.

Moore, J. F. (1993). Predators and prey: a new ecology of competition. *Harvard Business Review*, 71(3), 75–86.

Morgeson, F. P. and Hofmann, D. A. (1999). The structure and function of collective constructs: implications for multilevel research and theory development. *Academy of Management Review*, 24, 249–265.

Mudambi, R., Mudambi, S. and Navarra, P. (2007). Global innovation in MNCs: the effects of subsidiary self-determination and teamwork. *Product Innovation Management*, 24, 442–455.

Nahapiet, J. and Ghoshal, S. (1998). Social capital, intellectual capital, and the organizational advantage. *Academy of Management Review*, 23, 242–266.

Nebus, J. (2006). Building collegial information networks: a theory of advice network generation. *Academy of Management Review*, 31, 615–637.

Neisser, U. (1976). *Cognition and reality: principles and implications of cognitive psychology*. San Francisco, CA: Freeman.

Nelson, R. R. and Rosenberg, N. (1993). Technical innovation and national systems. In Nelson, R. R. (Ed.), *National innovation systems – a comparative analysis*. Oxford: Oxford University Press.

Nelson, R. R. and Winter, S. (1977). In search of a useful theory of innovation. *Research Policy*, 6 (I), 36–76.

Nelson, R. R. and Winter, S. G. (1982). *An evolutionary theory of economic change*. Cambridge, MA: Harvard University Press.

Nonaka, I. (1994). A dynamic theory of organizational knowledge creation. *Organization Science*, 5, 14–37.

Nonaka, I. and Takeuchi, H. (1995). *The knowledge creating company*. New York: Oxford University Press.

Ocasio, W. (1997). Towards an attention-based view of the firm. *Strategic Management Journal*, 18, 187–206.

Oldham, G. R. and Cummings, A. (1996). Employee creativity: personal and contextual factors at work. *Academy of Management Journal*, 39, 607–634.

Oluikpe, P. I. (2015). Knowledge creation and utilization in project teams. *Journal of Knowledge Management*, 19(2), 351–371.

Osterloh, M. and Frey, B. S. (2000). Motivation, knowledge transfer, and organizational forms. *Organization Science*, 11, 538–550.

Penrose, E. T. (1959). *The theory of the growth of the firm*. New York: John Wiley & Sons Ltd.

Peteraf, M., Pitelis, C. N. and Zollo, M. (2008). On 'the metamorphosis of (the theory of) the firm': an introduction. *Organization Studies*, 29, 1109–1115.

Polanyi, M. (1966). *The tacit dimension*. New York: Anchor Day.

Prahalad, C. K. and Hamel, G. (1990). The core competence of the corporation. *Harvard Business Review*, 68(3), 79–91.

Quintane, E., Casselman, M. R., Reiche, S. B. and Nylund, P. A. (2011). Innovation as a knowledge-based outcome. *Journal of Knowledge Management*, 15(6), 928–947.

Reiche, B. S., Harzing, A-W. and Kraimer, M. L. (2009). The role of international assignees' social capital in creating inter-unit intellectual capital: a cross-level model. *Journal of International Business Studies*, 40, 509–526.

Rousseau, D. M. (1985). Issues of level in organizational research: multi-level and cross-level perspectives. In Cummings, L. L. and Staw, B. M. (Eds.), *Research in organizational behavior*, 7, 1–37. Greenwich, CT: JAI Press.

Rumelt, R. P. (1984). Towards a strategic theory of the firm. In Lamb, R. B. (Ed.), *Competitive strategic management*. Englewood Cliffs, NJ: Prentice-Hall.

Saviotti, P. P. (1988). Information, entropy and variety in technoeconomic development. *Research Policy*, 17(2), 89–103.

Schneider, S. C. and Angelmar, R. (1993). Cognition in organizational analysis: who's minding the store? *Organization Studies*, 14, 347–374.

Schumpeter, J. A. (1934). *The theory of economic development: an inquiry into profits, capital, credit, interest, and the business cycle*. Cambridge, MA: Harvard University Press.

Schweizer, T. S. (2006). The psychology of novelty seeking, creativity and innovation: neurocognitive aspects within a work-psychological perspective. *Creativity and Innovation Management*, 15(2), 164–172.

Scott, S. G. and Bruce, R. A. (1994). Determinants of innovative behaviour: a path model of individual innovation in the workplace. *Academy of Management Journal*, 37, 580–607.

Siggelkow, N. and Levinthal, D. A. (2003). Temporarily divide to conquer: centralized, decentralized, and reintegrated organizational approaches to exploration and adaptation. *Organization Science*, 14(6), 650–669.

Simon, H. A. (1947). *Administrative behavior*. New York: Palgrave Macmillan.

Simon, H. A. (1991). Bounded rationality and organizational learning. *Organization Science*, 2, 125–134.

Simon, H. A. (1994). The bottleneck of attention: connecting thought with motivation. In Spaulding, W. D. (Ed.), *Integrative views of motivation, cognition and emotion*. Lincoln, NE: University of Nebraska Press, pp. 1–22.

Slavin, R. E. (2005). *Educational psychology: theory and practice*. Boston, MA: Allyn and Bacon.

Spencer, J. W. (2008). The impact of multinational enterprise strategy on indigenous enterprises: horizontal spillovers and crowding out in developing countries. *Academy of Management Review*, 33(2), 341–361.

Starbuck, W. and Hedberg, B. (1977). Saving an organization from a stagnating environment. In Thorelli, H. (Ed.), *Strategy + structure = performance*. Bloomington: Indiana University Press, pp. 249–258.
Stein, M. I. (1974). *Stimulating creativity*, 1. New York: Academic Press.
Szulanski, G. (2000). The process of knowledge transfer: a diachronic analysis of stickiness. *Organizational Behavior and Human Decision Processes*, 82(1), 9–27.
Taylor, S. E. and Fiske, S. T. (1978). Salience, attention and attribution: top of the head phenomena. In Berkowitz, L. (Ed.), *Advances in Experimental Social Psychology*, 1, 249–288. New York: Academic Press.
Teece, D. J. (1977). Technology transfer by multinational corporations: the resource cost of transferring technological know-how. *Economic Journal*, 87, 242–261.
Teece, D. J. (1982). Towards an economic theory of the multiproduct firm. *Journal of Economic Behavior and Organization*, 3, 39–63.
Teece, D. J. (1984). Economic analysis and strategic management. *California Management Review*, 26(3), 87–110.
Teece, D. J. (1986). Transactions cost economics and the multinational enterprise. *Journal of Economic Behavior and Organization*, 7, 21–45.
Teece, D. J. and Pisano, G. (1998). The dynamic capabilities of firms: an introduction. In Dosi, G., Teece, D. J. and Chytry, J. (Eds.), *Technology, organization and competitiveness: perspectives on industrial and corporate change*. Oxford: Oxford University Press, pp. 193–212.
Teigland, R. and Wasko, M. (2009). Knowledge transfer in MNCs: examining how intrinsic motivations and knowledge sourcing impact individual centrality and performance. *Journal of International Management*, 15, 15–31.
Torrance, E. P. (1988). The nature of creativity as manifest in its testing. In Sternberg, R. J. (Ed.), *The nature of creativity: contemporary psychological reviews*. Cambridge: Cambridge University Press, pp. 43–75.
Tsoukas, H. (2009). A dialogical approach to the creation of new knowledge in organizations. *Organization Science*, 20(6), 941–957.
Von Hippel, E. (1986). Lead users: a source of novel product concepts. *Management Science*, 32(7), 791–805.
Walsh, J. P. (1995). Managerial and organizational cognition: notes from a trip down memory lane. *Organization Science*, 6, 280–321.
Walsh, J. P., Henderson, C. M. and Deighton, J. A. (1988). Negotiated belief structures and decision performance: an empirical investigation. *Organizational Behavior and Human Decision Processes*, 42, 194–216.
Walsh, J. P. and Ungson, G. R. (1991). Organizational memory. *Academy of Management Review*, 16, 57–91.
Weick, K. E. (1979). *The social psychology of organizing*. Reading, MA: Addison-Wesley.
Weick, K. E., Sutcliffe, K. M. and Obstfeld, D. (2005). Organizing and the process of sensemaking. *Organization Science*, 16, 409–421.
Wernerfelt, B. (1984). A resource-based view of the firm. *Strategic Management Journal*, 5, 171–180.
Whitney, W. D. (1881). What is articulation? *The American Journal of Philology*, 2(7), 345–350.
Williamson, O. (1975). *Markets and hierarchies: analysis and anti-trust implications*. New York: Free Press.
Winter, S. G. (1987). Knowledge and competence as strategic assets. In Teece, D. J. (Ed.), *The competitive challenge: strategies for industrial innovation and renewal*. Cambridge, MA: Ballinger.
Woodman, R. W., Sawyer, J. E. and Griffin, R. W. (1993). Toward a theory of organizational creativity. *Academy of Management Review*, 18, 293–321.
Zollo, M. and Winter, S. G. (2002). Deliberate learning and the evolution of dynamic capabilities. *Organization Science*, 13, 339–351.

5
THE SYSTEMS APPROACH TO INNOVATION MANAGEMENT

Magnus Karlsson and Mats Magnusson

Introduction

The environment in which a company or organization operates today can be characterized by accelerating change, the globalization of markets, the emergence of new technologies and competitors, new regulatory requirements and ever more demanding users and citizens. In this environment, the ability to innovate becomes a key success factor for most organizations. They seek to continuously create and realize value by introducing new or changed products, services, processes, models, methods, etc.

The reasons for an organization to innovate are many and can include to increase revenues, growth and profitability, reduce costs and waste, increase the satisfaction of users, customers and citizens, motivate employees and attract partners, collaborators and funding, and so on. Engaging in innovation activities is thus a way for an organization to be future focused and effectively deliver on its overall objectives to secure prosperity and longer-term relevance and survival.

The ability to innovate and to make it a core organizational capability is increasingly becoming the most important differentiator and dominant success factor of organizations. Failing to capture new opportunities and to respond to innovation challenges may consequently lead to stagnation, irrelevance and ultimately to the demise of the organization.

Why a systems approach?

In their efforts to address opportunities and challenges, companies and organizations have been using many different innovation approaches. These include brainstorming sessions, idea management platforms, hackathons, design thinking labs, start-up accelerators and corporate venture funds, to name a few. Very often these efforts have not led to the desired innovation performance and they are therefore discontinued or they simply fade away. Some of the reasons for these efforts not living up to expectations can be the lack of necessary resources and competences, not setting a clear direction to guide creativity, failure in providing the required organizational structures, missing appropriate measurements, insufficient senior management commitment or the lack of providing appropriate end-to-end processes or ways of working for the innovation initiatives to succeed.

Organizations are generally underestimating what it takes to make their innovation efforts successful, especially when they are seeking more radical, disruptive or transformative innovations. Innovation attempts tend to be fragmented, ad hoc and episodic. There is thus a need to find approaches that are more holistic, systematic and sustainable over time, and that changes the focus from singular events and projects to building longer-term innovation capabilities.

This chapter is addressing these issues by taking a systems approach to innovation management. Such an approach recognizes that the different activities and the support necessary for an organization to innovate are interrelated and interacting and can be managed more effectively as a system. This holistic view recognizes the systemic nature of innovation capabilities of an organization. The focus is on both removing barriers and putting enablers in place.

A systems approach can, for example, better guide the organization to assess and evaluate the innovation performance of the system and make adjustments with a focus on the most critical innovation capability gaps.

In this chapter, an exposition of systems-focused innovation management research and an overview of selected system-related innovation management frameworks from the literature provide the basis for a principled outline of an integrated framework for innovation management.

Exposition of systems-focused innovation management research

The field of organization studies and management has been enriched by systems theory for more than half a century. A key insight in this literature is that organizations can be seen as systems consisting of interrelated and interacting elements, where changes to one element of the system influence the whole. Hence, decisions need to be made based on holistic considerations, even if a complete understanding of systems is often beyond the bounded rationality of individuals (Simon, 1947). As Scott (1981) points out, the notion of systems used in organization studies has shifted over time, from a view of organizations as rational or natural systems, to the view of organizations as open systems that is commonly found today. A seminal work in this field is the one by Katz and Kahn (1966). Their contribution highlighted the view of organizations as open systems, having the capability to reduce entropy by exchanging energy with their environment. According to this perspective, organizations interact with their environment and need to continuously adapt to its changes.

Given the importance for organizations to respond to changes to their environment, the capacity to identify such changes and act upon them through learning and adaptation stand out as particularly important. This also underlines the importance of innovating in terms of changes to existing systems and their related behaviors. Some of the key concepts in systems theory can be used to explain the role innovation activities play in organizations, as well as some of their boundary conditions. In a stable environment, one of the important functions of an organization is homeostasis – constantly bringing the system back to its desired state. However, in order for an organization to survive in a nonstable environment, it must continuously adapt to changes in the environment. In order to do so in a sustained manner, an organization must have sufficient requisite variety (Ashby, 1956), implying that it must have a higher capacity to change and adapt than its surrounding environment. However, adaptation and change are dependent on energy, which must consequently be provided by productive behavior. Thus, we can regard an organization as a system handling certain productive functions, and innovation efforts modify these functions in order to fit the organization to its external environment. This is at the core of Burns and Stalker's (1961) seminal work "Management of Innovation", in which they point out the different needs for innovating in environments with different dynamics and corresponding suitable ways of organizing. In a stable environment, the main focus of an organization is to perform defined tasks in an efficient manner, implying a mechanistic organizational structure. In a changing environment, on the contrary, the main focus of an organization has to be to adapt its tasks and output to match its changing environment, requiring an organic organizational structure (Burns and Stalker, 1961).

Towards more adaptive and networked systems

In order to match a changing environment, organizations need to continuously adapt their goals and hold control mechanisms that render such actions possible. This view is clearly reflected in the concept of homeorhesis proposed by Burgelman (1983). Burgelman regards organizations as continuously evolving systems, driven by both so-called induced strategic behavior (top-down) and autonomous strategic behavior (emergent changes driven bottom-up, often by innovation activities). This theory highlights the importance of emergent strategy (Mintzberg, Ahlstrand, and Lampel, 1998) in order to allow for sufficient adaptability under conditions where it is difficult to foresee developments and trends.

The difficulties in anticipating future development in the environment imply that innovation efforts do not only aim at adapting to change but that they can also change the environment indirectly through the organization. This also suggests that traditional strategic management frameworks have a somewhat limited usefulness for innovation purposes (see e.g. Brown and Eisenhardt, 1998) and that companies and organizations either need to include innovation activities as an explicit part of their strategies or complement them with an explicit innovation strategy.

Brown and Eisenhardt (1998) argue that dominant strategic management theories such as the positioning school (Porter, 1980) and the resource-based view (Wernerfelt, 1984; Barney, 1991; Grant, 1991) are both overly static. The focus in the positioning school is put on external factors and then, in particular, on analyzing competitive forces in order to identify positions where market imperfections can be used to make above-normal rents. Given the implicit focus on monopoly rents, relatively little attention is paid to innovation activities, apart from highlighting the need to make a choice between innovation followership and innovation leadership, respectively. Compared to the positioning school, the resource-based view (RBV) has a much closer relationship to both innovation and systems theory. Here, the view of rents is a Ricardian one, basically stressing that organizations have idiosyncratic resources and capabilities, and as a consequence, different performances. Apart from the key role played by resources and capabilities, other systemic characteristics such as values and systems are also addressed. An even stronger connection to the earlier mentioned works on organizations as systems is found in the work by Amit and Schoemaker (1993), who point out the necessity to combine a strictly internal focus on resources with the key industry factors represented in Porter's (1980) five forces framework. The matching of strategic assets and key environmental factors directly reflects the basic ideas about the necessity of fit between a system and its external environment.

As mentioned earlier, a clear shortcoming of both the positioning school and RBV is their limited attention to dynamics and change. Brown and Eisenhardt (1998) underline these frameworks' tendency towards statical optimization and argue for a new approach to strategic management with an emphasis on continuous reinvention and change. This focus on innovation activities and change is also found in the dynamic capabilities framework, which has sprung out of the RBV. The earliest works in this stream of literature introduced the notions of position, process and path to explain the dynamic capabilities that over time alter an organization's base of resources and capabilities (Teece, Pisano, and Shuen, 1997). Further development by Teece (2007) has combined traditional strategic management thinking with components from entrepreneurship theory, bringing in the importance of identifying and seizing opportunities as a fundamental part of a more emergent and innovation-oriented strategy. This view echoes the need for a more dynamic approach to strategic management. This is also reflected in works addressing innovation strategy and its relationship to business and corporate strategy. In particular, we here observe the notions of "competing for the future" (Hamel and Prahalad, 1994) and "discovery-driven planning" by McGrath (2010), where innovation efforts are seen as explicit parts of strategy.

Another observation is the need to address capabilities in a systemic manner, given that these tend to be constituted by bundles of resources, which are distributed throughout the organization and include substantial mutual interdependencies (Thompson, 1967). This implicitly calls for improved integration mechanisms (Lawrence and Lorsch, 1967; Bhidé, 2000) in order to purposefully bring together the increasingly heterogeneous resources of a larger system.

Altogether, we see that the systems perspective has a long tradition in organization studies, among other things highlighting systemic properties needed to cope with continuous change, adaptation and renewal. Also in strategic management theory it is possible to identify a stream of contributions emphasizing both the systemic nature of capabilities and the requirements in terms of dynamics. A notable limitation to the mentioned theoretical aspects is the clear focus on single organizations as the unit of analysis. Works with a somewhat more open view on development in the fields of organization and management emphasize the boundary-spanning nature of business and other value-realizing activities, explicitly focusing on systems larger than the single organization and the capabilities related to a networked way of working (see e.g. Lorenzoni and Lipparini, 1999). An innovation-related area of investigation addressing these questions is, without a doubt, open innovation (Bogers et al., 2017), which basically argues for a change of the systems boundaries considered by management with respect to innovations. By extending the innovation management focus to include suppliers, customers, users and collaborators, new opportunities can be identified, but at the cost of increased complexity. An even more explicit tendency to extend systems boundaries we see is the present interest in so-called innovation ecosystems (Adner and Kapoor, 2010). Although the "eco-" part of this concept may indeed be questioned, given fundamental differences between the biological world and the business world (Oh, Phillips, Park, and Lee, 2016), the explicit focus on systems can lead to new innovation insights.

The need to address interdependencies between internal resources and activities is frequently highlighted in existing literature on organizing and organizational learning. This is seen both in Senge's (1990) explicitly systemic view of organizational learning and in Nonaka's (1994) theory of organizational knowledge creation. The latter explicitly underscores the importance of typical systems theory constructs such as redundancy and requisite variety and how these factors influence innovation efforts. In the broad field of R&D management the literature on multi-project management (Cusumano and Nobeoka, 1998) and portfolio management (Nagji and Tuff, 2012) also reflects a systems perspective by widening the management focus from single-innovation projects to portfolios comprising sets of such projects and initiatives. An extension of this view has resulted in a focus on technology and other types of platforms, which today constitute a key factor in many industries and sectors.

Structure, strategy and process perspectives

As can be seen from the exposition of theory earlier, the use of a systems perspective in different streams of management research and thinking is not new but has been explicitly addressed and used in both strategic management, organization theory and design, as well as in project management, quality management, knowledge management and organizational learning, for example. Innovation management theory and practice can benefit greatly from building on this established wealth of knowledge. As stated already in the 1980s by Peter Drucker, we can conclude that innovating is a systemic practice (Drucker, 1985) and will thus benefit from insights from systems theory and thinking. Some authors (see e.g. Janszen, 2000) even go so far as to suggest that organizational innovation should be viewed as a complex self-adapting system. Many managerial systems are exhibiting systemic characteristics in terms of them being uncertain, interactive, nonlinear and distributed. This implies that they require real-time and dynamic coordination and integration of strategy, structure, process, culture and people (van de Ven, Polley, Garud, and Venkataraman, 1999). We will here summarize some of the main implications for innovation management from extant systems-focused theory in the broader management field. These insights are presented in relation to structure, strategy and processes, respectively.

Structure

In terms of structure, we need to consider both organizational structures and product structures, as well as their interrelationships. As pointed out by Henderson and Clark (1990), product architectures and organizational structures come to reflect each other, and this has implications for the innovations that organizations tend to generate. As a consequence, there is a need to actively design organizations so that they become more permeable for innovations, that is, by setting up ambidextrous structures (Tushman and O'Reilly, 1996). Important here is to enable not only the differentiation aspect of such solutions but also to manage the required integration through the use of suitable integration mechanisms. At the core of this issue we find the combination of exploitation of an organization's assets and the exploration of new knowledge and opportunities (March, 1991). At a certain point in time, revenues result from the match an organization makes between its existing strategic assets and the specific characteristics of its external environment (Amit and Schoemaker, 1993). However, this operative system needs to be continuously renewed in order to continuously have a good fit with a changing environment. Dynamic capabilities are used to revitalize this base of strategic assets, thus acting as a type of meta-capabilities, which are applied to existing operations and capabilities and thus indirectly contribute to short-term exploitation.

Another important implication from extant theory is the need to manage the overall portfolio of innovation projects and initiatives in a holistic and systemic way. The exact organizational design that should be used for this purpose needs to be based on an evaluation of available synergies between projects and the conflicting need for product and service integrity (Clark and Fujimoto, 1990). A frequently used approach to reconcile these different objectives is the use of product platforms or modularization. Depending on the specific needs, the use of one of these approaches, or their combination, may be appropriate (Magnusson and Pasche, 2014).

Recently, the organizing of innovation efforts has been subject to substantial changes, as increased connectivity and new business models create a tendency towards more open and collaborative ways of innovating. This has given rise to the notion of innovation ecosystems (Adner and Kapoor, 2010), which arguably in many cases is a more relevant unit of analysis than the single organization in order to understand how innovations are achieved. In this setting, the establishing of a fruitful technology platform (Cusumano and Gawer, 2002) often plays a fundamental role in achieving competitiveness through network externalities (see e.g. Schilling, 2010) and resulting complementarities.

Strategy

Although there are numerous writings underlining the spontaneous and emergent nature of innovating, we would first of all like to challenge the reliance on such an ad-hoc approach. Even if a hands-off approach may historically have worked in a few companies and organizations, the changed situation in most workplaces makes this approach questionable today, as there is less time available to spend on innovation activities outside defined job roles and a more pronounced need for collaboration with others due to increased openness and multitechnology products, services and processes. Rather than leaving innovation success to chance, it is necessary to address innovation efforts in strategic terms, making innovation objectives explicit and shared and including mechanisms that can direct creativity to valuable areas and capture relevant bottom-up initiatives.

The field of strategic management has undergone a radical transformation in the last few decades. The strong focus on industries and competition seen in the positioning school (Porter, 1980) has gradually been complemented with a focus on distinctive (or core) capabilities (Barney, 1991; Grant, 1991; Prahalad and Hamel, 1990), leading to the need for combined and more systemic approaches, in line with the suggestions by Amit and Schoemaker (1993). As pointed out in the discussion on dynamic capabilities theory, managers "integrate, build and reconfigure internal and external competencies to address rapidly changing environments" (Teece, Pisano, and Shuen, 1997) to build sustainable or temporary competitive advantages. Following this view, innovation management can be viewed as a form of organizational capability, and as highlighted by Lawson and Samson (2001), organizations should thus focus on building innovation capabilities.

Another important development is the increased emphasis on dynamics (Brown and Eisenhardt, 1998; Teece, Pisano, and Shuen, 1997; Teece, 2007), leading to a closer and more bidirectional relationship between strategy and innovation activities. Consequently, there is a need to establish closer links between strategic management and innovation efforts, either in terms of innovation components in the strategies of the companies or organizations, or in terms of explicit innovation strategies.

Process

Innovation management has drawn upon process models and standards from adjacent management fields, such as product development management and quality management.

The development of an innovation always comprises a certain level of uncertainty, and this implies that there is a need for processes and ways of working that enable fast experimentation and adaptation. This does not exclude that planning is useful, but simply that a complete reliance on plans may lead organizations to miss out on innovations. Moreover, it is important to stay open to emergent insights, ideas and initiatives and align them with strategies as a complement to what is part of the induced strategy. This shift from planning to increased experimentation is clearly reflected in the change of dominant process models used in innovation and product development management. The well-established stage-gate model of Cooper (1990) has thus been complemented by other, more iterative and flexible approaches, such as agile development models, and lately also the use of so-called devops. Among these adaptive models for performing innovation activities we also note design thinking and lean startup. The process of design thinking usually involves the following steps: empathize, define, ideate, prototype and test. Unlike the stage-gate system that moves from idea to launch, design thinking starts by discovering customer needs (see e.g. Geissdoerfer, Bocken, and Hultink, 2016; Luebkeman and Brown, 2015). The lean startup (Erickson, 2015; Hart, 2012; Ries, 2011) approach to innovation management is another methodology that is gaining ground, especially in software-intensive industries. The lean startup methodology has emerged from the concepts of lean manufacturing and product development (Liker, 2004), agile software development (Cohen, Lindvall, and Costa, 2003) and customer development (Blank, 2013). The lean startup methodology uses a build–measure–learn process and in that way also has some similarities with design thinking. Apart from proposing a more iterative and agile way of controlling innovation activities than traditional development models, the mentioned approaches also share a clear focus on user and customer value and the need for experimentation to find this value. Hence, we can observe a shift from more resource-driven and push-oriented innovation models to more demand-driven and pull-based ones. These characteristics are also shared by lean approaches to product development and innovation activities (see e.g. Reinertsen, 1999), in which the cost of delays and the consequent need for innovation flow are underlined.

Summarizing the broad systems-based management literature with a high relevance for innovation management, we can conclude that there is a clear need for a systemic and systematic approach to guide innovation activities. Although we find numerous useful components in the extant management theory, we need to turn to more applied works in order to develop an applicable framework that can be fruitfully used in practice.

Selected frameworks from the literature

Around the 2000s, research shifted from a focus on individual processes, activities and elements to the integration of these elements into a system and the interactive relationships between them. As the scope of innovation management expanded to include multiple types of innovations, involving more and more stakeholders and drawing on a broader range of organizational capabilities, an integrative and systemic approach was required to ensure both the effectiveness and efficiency of innovation efforts of a company or organization.

The following is an overview of selected frameworks with a systems approach to innovation management. The overview does not have the ambition to be complete but to illustrate the diversity of frameworks that have been proposed during the last 20 years. The purpose is to extract common themes as an input to the framework outlined in the next section. The frameworks that have been surveyed have been developed in three main contexts: (1) academic works based on previous research or empirical studies, (2) national and international standardization activities based on the evolution of management systems and (3) practical experience and good practices from consultants and industrial research reports.

Academic works

In the context of academic works, the first edition of the popular textbook *Managing Innovation* (Tidd, Bessant, and Pavitt, 1997) provides a good starting point. The authors emphasize the inherently interdisciplinary and multifunctional nature of the management of innovation and propose a coherent framework based on the systematic analysis of the latest management research at the time. In short, Tidd et al. identified four generic phases of the innovation process: (1) scanning of the environment (internal and external), (2) deciding (on the basis of a strategic view) what signals to respond to, (3) obtaining the resources to enable the response and (4) implementing projects to respond effectively. To complete the framework, four clusters of behaviors or routines were suggested to support the process model: (5) taking a strategic approach to innovation efforts, (6) effective implementation mechanisms and structures, (7) supporting organizational context and (8) effective external linkages (Tidd, Bessant, and Pavitt, 1997).

The original framework has evolved but essentially stayed the same in subsequent editions (Tidd and Bessant, 2013), and similar frameworks have been put forward by, for example von Stamm (2003) and Goffin and Mitchell (2005).

The innovation management system proposed by Tuominen, Piippo, Ichimura, and Matsumoto (1999) had some similar elements but put a greater emphasis on customer needs and requirements and how technological opportunities can be matched to meet those needs. The system was influenced by the "fusion model" based on the works of Knut Holt (Holt, Geschka, and Peterlongo, 1984) and described in, for example, Muramatsu, Ichimura, and Ishii (1990).

A comprehensive research program with a focus on breakthrough innovation in established companies was conducted at the Rensselaer Polytechnic Institute. Approximately 30 large companies were studied during a 10-year period starting in 1995. The proposed management system for breakthrough innovation was made up of three distinct elements or sets of activities: (1) discovery with focus on conceptualization, (2) incubation with focus on experimentation and finally (3) acceleration with focus on commercialization. Each element has interfaces with one another and to the rest of the organization, and these relationships need to be managed by an overall orchestrating function. In a matrix-like structure, each element has its own expression of the innovation management system in terms of (a) structure and location, (b) mandate, (c) leadership and governance, (d) roles and responsibilities, (e) processes and (f) metrics (O'Connor, Leifer, Paulson, and Peters, 2008). The framework has been further elaborated based on additional research during the last 10 years (O'Connor, Corbett, and Peters, 2018).

The framework developed by the Center for Innovation Management Studies (CIMS) at North Carolina State University has a similar matrix-like structure but takes a broader scope and includes innovation management not only at the organizational level but also at the industry and macro-environment level. A comprehensive meta-analysis of innovation management research revealed key dimensions and competencies that successful innovating companies possess. The five elements or dimensions were strategy, organization and culture, processes, techniques and tools, and metrics. For each level and dimension, five management competencies were identified, forming a three-dimensional model: the management of ideas, markets, portfolios, platforms and projects (Mugge and Markham, 2013).

Another three-dimensional approach was developed by scholars at the Institute of Management Science & Strategy of Zhejiang University. The total innovation management (TIM) framework was introduced in 2002 and was inspired by the resource-based view of organizations, complexity theory, and the works of Shapiro (2001), Bean and Radford (2001) and Tucker (2002), among others. The first dimension of the framework outlines different types of innovations as sources for competitive advantage: (1) technology innovation is the foundation, supplemented with (2) marketing, (3) organizational and (4) institutional innovation, and all are supported by the elements of (5) strategy and (6) culture. The second dimension emphasized the broad involvement of all (7) people in innovation activities in the organization. The final dimension extends the framework in time and space, indicating that innovation activities are actually executed all the time and everywhere (Xu, Yu, Zheng, and Zhou, 2002; Xu, Chen et al., 2007). The framework has been applied in several empirical studies of companies in China (Chen, Jin, He, and Yao, 2006; Xu, Zhu, Zheng, and Wang, 2007), the United States (Menke, Xu, and Gu, 2007) and Japan (Mao and Wang, 2012).

The TIM framework has been further extended by Chen, Yin, and Mei (2018) to include a strategic vision with a focus on purpose and meaningfulness, forming a holistic innovation system.

National and international standardization

The concept of management systems emerged in the context of standardization during the 1980s. The International Organization for Standardization (ISO) published the first version of the ISO 9000 series of standards in 1989, based on the philosophy of quality management developed since the 1950s. Quality management systems introduced the process-based view of the organization and the plan–do–check–act cycle for continuously improving the system, see ISO 9001 (ISO, 2015).

In parallel, the British Standards Institute (BSI) published the first standard for design management in 1989 that was developed into a series of design management system standards in the following years. BS 7000–1:2008 Part 1: Guide to managing innovation was published in 1999 (BSI, 2008). The standards were developed based on the concept of total design, a structured process for product design and development introduced by Stuart Pugh in the 1980s (Hollins, 2000).

Standardization activities in the area of innovation management started in the late 1990s. Requirements of a research and development and innovation (R&D&I) management system were developed by the Spanish Association for Standardisation and Certification (AENOR). The first management system standard, UNE 166002, was published in 2002 for a trial period, followed by the definitive requirement standard in 2006 (Mir and Casadesús, 2011; AENOR, 2006).

The standard included a development of the original innovation model of Kline (1985), had linkages to the British standard on managing innovation (BSI, 2008) and was designed by analogy with the international quality management system standard (ISO 9001). The Spanish standard was adopted and modified by several countries, including Portugal, Mexico and Brazil (Mir and Casadesus, 2011; Caetano, 2017). Several studies of Spanish companies have been made looking at the impact of the standard, for example, Mir, Casadesús, and Petnji (2016); Yepes, Pellicer, Alarcon, and Correa (2016); and Garechana, Río-Belver, Bildosola, and Salvador (2017).

In 2007, initiatives were taken by the European Committee for Standardization (CEN), which resulted in the creation of a technical committee on innovation management in 2008, led by AENOR. The committee published a technical specification: Innovation Management – Part 1: Innovation Management System, in 2013, CEN/TS 16555–1:2013 (CEN, 2013; Caetano, 2017).

The ISO set up a committee (ISO/TC 279) for innovation management in 2013, led by the French secretariat of AFNOR (the French Association for Standardization). Like the approach taken at the European level, the aim was to develop guidance standards that provided recommendations rather than requirements. The first international management system standards for innovation management will be published in 2019.

Rebelo, Santos, and Silva (2015) discuss the possibilities for organizations to establish an integrated management system (IMS), incorporating different individual management system standards (MSS), including an innovation management system.

Consultants and industrial research reports

Another context for the development of the systems approach to innovation management is constituted by the consultants and industrial research reports, which are mainly based on practical experience and good practices.

Based on the practices of the consulting company Strategos and the thinking of Gary Hamel, Skarzynski and Gibson (2008) outlined a systems approach to innovation management in their book *Innovation to the Core*. Four main groups of elements are suggested: (1) leadership and organization, (2) processes and tools, (3) people and skills and (4) cultures and values.

The Boston Consulting Group suggested a similar approach, focusing on innovation strategy, research and product development processes and a comprehensive set of organizational enablers (Taylor and Wagner, 2014). Other examples are software companies Microsoft and SAP, which have published their versions of frameworks (Microsoft, 2013; Cigaina, 2013).

A comprehensive effort to develop an innovation management standard was undertaken by the Total Innovation Management (TIM) Foundation (different from the TIM framework discussed earlier and independent of the work by ISO). The set of documents was described as an advisory standard with a maturity model and a management system approach and was published through the Product Development and Management Association (PDMA) in 2013 (PDMA and TIM, 2013).

Badrinas and Vila (2015) used the PDMA and TIM framework, with adaptations based on Vila and Munoz-Najar (2002), in an empirical study of six successful European companies. Seven "steps" were identified, together forming an integrated innovation management system: (1) management commitment, (2) stakeholders' influence, (3) statements: mission, vision and values, (4) strategy and objectives, (5) management review and communications, (6) people and competences, and (7) front-end innovation drive.

A system-related framework was developed in 2013 by the Japan Innovation Network (JIN) following a research committee report by the Ministry of Economy, Trade and Industry (METI) in Japan. The Innovation Compass framework was launched in 2014 and was based on a "two-layered management" model – the systematic approach to managing creativity and productivity in parallel in an organization. In the framework, three process elements: (1) idea generation, (2) business model building and (3) commercialization, are implemented through (4) training programs, (5) acceleration programs and (6) networks. The system is governed by top management through (7) a vision, goals and performance indicators, and implemented using (8) a supporting mechanism, including e.g. knowledge management (Nishiguchi and Konno, 2018).

As a final example, in the context of the European Foundation for Quality Management (EFQM), an innovation capability assessment framework was developed. The framework included several elements discussed earlier but put a specific focus on data analytics and management style (Hakes, 2014).

Common themes

As seen from the earlier discussion, a number of system-related frameworks for innovation management have been proposed in the literature during the last 20 years. See Table 5.1 for an overview of the 19 selected frameworks that have been discussed in this chapter.

A review of the frameworks reveals a number of common elements that should be considered by a company or organization for successfully achieving innovation. These elements can be categorized into eight themes: context, direction, leadership, culture, processes, structures, support and resources, and evaluation. Table 5.2 provides examples of elements for each theme based on the literature review.

Principled outline of an integrated framework for innovation management

It is beyond the scope of this chapter to make a comprehensive synthesis of the reviewed literature and propose a definitive framework for innovation management. As seen from the review, the system-related frameworks are evolving as more and more knowledge from research and practice become available. The scope and purpose of such frameworks are also changing over

Table 5.1 Overview of selected system-related frameworks for innovation management introduced between 1997 and 2018

Framework	References
Innovation Management Process Model	Tidd, Bessant, and Pavitt (1997)
Product Innovation Management System	Tuominen, Piippo, Ichimura, and Matsumoto (1999)
Requirements of an R&D&I Management System, UNE 166002:2002/6	AENOR (2006), first published 2002
Total Innovation Management	Xu, Yu, Zheng, and Zhou (2002); Xu, Chen et al. (2007)
Bettina von Stamm (BvS) Innovation Framework	von Stamm (2003)
Innovation Pentathlon Framework	Goffin and Mitchell (2005)
Management System for Breakthrough Innovation	O'Connor, Leifer, Paulson, and Peters (2008)
Innovation to the Core	Skarzynski and Gibson (2008)
Innovation Management System, CEN/TS 16555–1:2013	CEN (2013)
Innovation Management Standard	PDMA and TIM (2013)
Microsoft's Innovation Management Framework	Microsoft (2013)
Innovation Management Framework, by SAP	Cigaina (2013)
Innovation Management Framework, by the Center for Innovation Management Studies (CIMS)	Mugge and Markham (2013)
Innovation as a System, by Boston Consulting Group	Taylor and Wagner (2014)
Innovation Compass, by Japan Innovation Network (JIN)	Nishiguchi and Konno (2018)
Innovation Capability Assessment Framework (EFQM)	Hakes (2014)
Integrated Innovation Management System	Badrinas and Vila (2015)
Holistic Innovation	Chen, Yin, and Mei (2018)
Innovation Management System	O'Connor, Corbett, and Peters (2018)

Table 5.2 Examples of system elements for each theme of the framework for innovation management

Theme	Examples of elements
Context	Scanning of the external and internal environment. Identification of trends, opportunities and challenges, technologies, user and customer needs and requirements, and stakeholders.
Direction	Vision and direction, managerial goals, objectives and strategies. Strategic and tactical planning.
Leadership	Commitment, mandate, engagement, future focus and communication. Incentives, leadership styles and values.
Culture	Work environment, social context, values and organizational culture supporting innovation activities.
Processes	Innovation processes, including insights from the context, idea generation, prioritization and selection, validation, experimentation and prototyping, business modelling, incubation, commercialization and implementation. Innovation projects, initiatives and portfolios.
Structures	Organizational setup, governance, roles and responsibilities. Internal and external linkages, networks and collaboration (customers, partners, suppliers, etc.).
Support and resources	Funding, people and time. Tools and methods, competences and skills. Intellectual property management and data analytics.
Evaluation	Innovation metrics, indicators, monitoring, assessment, evaluation, management review, feedback. Improvement of the system.

time. However, a few key observations that are relevant for future research and practice can be made. These observations taken together can be summarized by a principled outline of an integrated framework for innovation management (see Figure 5.1).

The purpose of such a framework is to ensure the sustained buildup of renewal capabilities and continuous creation and realization of value for the organization and its stakeholders. It is argued that the proposed outline is fulfilling the general criteria of a well-functioning system: (1) comprehensiveness: all the necessary elements are included to achieve the purpose of the system, (2) coherence: all the elements are contributing to the same purpose, and (3) consistency: elements are aligned and are not conflicting.

Management systems of the organization

For the purpose of this summary, innovation management is considered at the level of the organization, based on the notion that the organization can control its own destiny (i.e. can be managed as an autonomous entity). The systems approach can be applied to any organization, public or private, of any size and in any sector. It can be used also for a set of organizations if they can be managed as one entity to a certain degree.

Based on the discussion earlier, two management systems of the organization are considered: the system for managing operations and the system for managing innovations (see for example March, 1991; Tushman and O'Reilly, 1996; Martinich, 2004; Nishiguchi and Konno, 2018). The systems are interrelated and interacting and can be implemented in one integrated or two separated hierarchies. They represent two modes of operation that require different adaptations and approaches to the themes: context, direction, leadership, culture, processes, structures, support and resources, and evaluation.

The system for managing operations is operating under conditions of relative certainty and decision-making can generally be based on knowledge and facts. The system is primarily

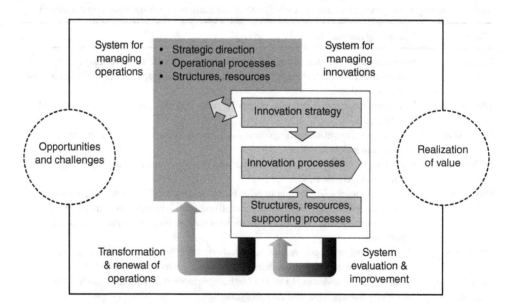

Figure 5.1 Principled outline of an integrated framework for innovation management

designed to support existing offerings, processes and value realization models for existing markets, customers and users.

The system for managing innovations is operating under conditions of higher uncertainty, and decision-making must therefore to a large degree be based on assumptions. Uncertainties can relate to any dimension of the innovation or the innovation process, for example, strategic fit, feasibility to realize, cost and resources, value for the user, etc. The system is primarily designed to introduce new offerings, processes and value realization models, targeting existing as well as new markets, customers and users.

Elements of the system for managing innovations

Both management systems are dependent on effective and timely scanning and identification of opportunities and challenges of the *context*. The scanning, scanning can, for example, reveal new technologies, new user patterns and needs, as well as new customers, partners, competitors and other stakeholders. The context can also include issues internal to the organization related to assets, competences and other capabilities.

The *direction* for innovation activities, based on an understanding of the context, can be defined in terms of innovation objectives and one or more innovation strategies. An innovation strategy is typically designed both to contribute to and to challenge and extend beyond the overall strategic direction of the organization. The strategy can help to allocate resources and to ensure that innovation opportunities can move between the two management systems, depending on where they can be most effectively addressed.

Leadership commitment at different levels of the organization plays an important role in executing the strategy by inspiring and engaging people, promoting internal and external collaboration, balancing incentives and recognition for exploration and exploitation, communicating and creating awareness and fostering a *culture* supporting innovation activities, including risk taking and learning from failures.

Innovation *processes* are designed to achieve innovations according to the innovation strategy. Innovation initiatives in the form of projects, programs, etc., are implemented through these processes and may constitute one or more innovation portfolios. A set of generic innovation processes can be identified: (1) seek insightful knowledge to identify opportunities, (2) generate concepts and solutions based on these insights, (3) validate the concepts using experimentation and prototyping for example, (4) develop concepts into mature solutions and (5) deploy solutions to realize value. Deployment also includes capturing feedback from the diffusion of the innovations as well as lessons learned to improve the management systems.

The mentioned processes can be viewed as learning processes, designed to manage uncertainty by systematically converting assumptions into knowledge. They can be configured in different sequences, be executed iteratively, be implemented both internally and externally to the organization and be a combination of processes related to the system for managing operations and to the system for managing innovations.

Organizational *structures* are supporting and contributing to the innovation processes. Separated structures can be considered when the organization is aiming for innovations that are disruptive with respect to, or may be competing with, existing offerings, or when support and resources need to be protected from the influence of existing operations of the organization. Structures can involve external stakeholders, as in the case of collaborative, open or ecosystem innovation.

Resources that are necessary for facilitating the innovation processes can include people, time, funding, knowledge and infrastructures. Examples of other relevant *support* are tools and methods, competence development, knowledge management, strategic intelligence, portfolio management and intellectual property management.

Performance evaluation and feedback processes

A set of indicators can be established at different levels and for different parts of the systems for *evaluating* the overall performance of the organization. The evaluation can be related to the innovation performance of the organization, that is, the measurable results of innovation activities, or the innovation capabilities of the organization, that is, its ability to perform innovation activities in relation to its purpose and objectives.

Two feedback processes are important to consider within and between the two management systems of the organization. The system for managing innovations is evaluated and improved related to all its elements (i.e. context, direction, leadership, culture, processes, structures, support and resources, and evaluation). This feedback process is designed to continuously improve the system both in terms of efficiency and effectiveness.

The second feedback process captures learnings from the system for managing innovations and provides input to the renewal and transformation of the system for managing operations. In this way, the two systems are continuously evolving while adapting to changes external and internal to the organization (see Figure 5.1).

Implications and conclusions

Implications for future research

This chapter provides a broad exposition of systems-oriented management works, with the aim of deriving implications for management theory and practice through the principled outline of an integrated framework for innovation management. Given the abundance of systems-based management theories, it is not possible to perform a truly comprehensive review in a short chapter like this, but the selected literature should merely be seen as a way of deriving important characteristics that an integrated innovation management framework needs to include. Hence, rather than calling for more research scrutinizing the comprehensiveness of the literature exposition, we see it as more important to study and evaluate what results can be gained by organizations adopting more systemic and systematic approaches to innovation management. Important aspects include the influence such approaches may have on the type of innovation that are generated and how they affect innovation efficiency and effectiveness. There are, of course, also potential downsides with systemic and systematic approaches to innovation management, as these may hamper innovation activities if they are not questioned and improved.

Implications for practice

The systems approach to innovation management provides companies and organizations with a guiding framework that can serve as a checklist of what elements should be considered to improve innovation performance and capabilities. It can help organizations move beyond simplistic and episodic efforts and adopt a more systemic, systematic and sustainable approach. A systems approach can also form the basis for innovation management assessments, management reviews and maturity models to assist organizations in identifying critical issues and developing action plans.

With the emerging system frameworks at the European and international level, common and more credible reference frameworks are established. They can be used for independent audits of an organization, benchmarking and comparisons between organizations, as well as for providing innovation management support and consulting services.

Commonly shared system frameworks and a common language for innovation management can help facilitate awareness and drive the adoption and integration of innovation activities in all management practices of any organization.

References

Adner, R. and Kapoor, R. (2010). Value creation in innovation ecosystems: how the structure of technological interdependence affects firm performance in new technology generations. *Strategic Management Journal*, 31(3), 306–333.
AENOR (2006). R&D&i management: R&D&i management system requirements. *Spanish Standard UNE 166002*, AENOR (Spanish version).
Amit, R. and Schoemaker, P. J. (1993). Strategic assets and organizational rent. *Strategic Management Journal*, 14, 33–46.
Ashby, W. R. (1956). *An introduction to cybernetics*. London: Champan & Hall.
Badrinas, J. and Vilà, J. (2015). An innovation management system to create growth in mature industrial technology firms. *International Journal of Innovation Science*, 7(4), 263–279.
Barney, J. B. (1991). Firm resources and sustained competitive advantage. *Journal of Management*, 17, 99–120.
Bean, R. and Radford, R. W. (2001). *The business of innovation: managing the corporate imagination for maximum results*. New York: AMACOM.
Bhidé, A. (2000). *The origin and evolution of new businesses*. New York: Oxford University Press.
Blank, S. (2013). Why the lean start-up changes everything. *Harvard Business Review*, 91(5), 63–72.
Bogers, M., Zobel, A-K., Afuah, A., Almirall, E. Brunswicker, S., Dahlander, L., Frederiksen, L., Gawer, A., Gruber, M., Haefliger, S., Hagedoorn, J., Hilgers, D., Laursen, K., Magnusson, M., and Majchrzak, A., McCarthy, I. P., Moeslein, K. M. and Nambisan, S., Piller, F. T., Radziwon, A., Rossi Lamastra, C., Sims, J. and Ter Wal, A. L. J. (2017). The open innovation research landscape: established perspectives and emerging themes across different levels of analysis, *Industry and Innovation*, 24(1), 8–40.
Brown, S. L. and Eisenhardt, K. M. (1998). *Competing on the edge: strategy as structured chaos*. Boston, MA: Harvard Business School Press.
BSI (2008). Design management systems – part 1: guide to managing innovation. British Standard BS 7000–1:2008, BSI.
Burgelman, R. A. (1983). Corporate entrepreneurship and strategic management: insights from a process study. *Management Science*, 29(12), 1349–1364.
Burns, T. and Stalker, G. M. (1961). *Management of innovation*. London: Tavistock Publications.
Caetano, I. (2017). Standardization and innovation management. *Journal of Innovation Management*, 5(2), 8–14.
CEN (2013). Innovation management – part 1: innovation management system. CEN/TS 16555–1.
Chen, J., Jin, X., He, Y.-B. and Yao, W. (2006). TIM based indigenous innovation: experiences from Haier Group. *2006 IEEE International Conference on Management of Innovation and Technology*, 207–210, June 21–23, Singapore.
Chen, J., Yin, X. and Mei, L. (2018). Holistic innovation: an emerging innovation paradigm. *International Journal of Innovation Studies*, 2(1), March, 1–13.
Cigaina, M. (2013). *Innovation management framework: enabling and fostering innovation in your company*. Epistemy Press.
Clark, K. B. and Fujimoto, T. (1990). The power of product integrity. *Harvard Business Review*, 68(6), 107–118.
Cohen, D., Lindvall, M. and Costa, P. (2003). *A state of the art report: agile software development, data and analysis center for software 775 Daedalian Dr. Rome*. New York 13441–4909.
Cooper, R. G. (1990). Stage-gate systems: a new tool for managing new products. *Business Horizons*, 33(3), May–June, 44–54.
Cusumano, M. and Nobeoka, K. (1998). *Thinking beyond lean: how multi-project management is transforming Toyota and other companies*. New York: The Free Press.

Cusumano, M. A. and Gawer, A. (2002). The elements of platform leadership. *MIT Sloan Management Review*, 51–58.

Drucker, P. F. (1985). *Innovation and entrepreneurship: practices and principles.* New York: Harper & Row.

Erickson, L. B. (2015). The innovator's method: bringing the lean startup into your organization. *Research-Technology Management*, 58(1), January–February.

Garechana, G., Río-Belver, R., Bildosola, I. and Salvador, M. R. (2017). Effects of innovation management system standardization on firms: evidence from text mining annual reports. *Scientometrics*, 111, 1987–1999.

Geissdoerfer, M., Bocken, N. M. P. and Hultink, E. J. (2016). Design thinking to enhance the sustainable business modelling process – a workshop based on a value mapping process. *Journal of Cleaner Production*, 135, 1218–1232.

Goffin, K. and Mitchell, R. (2005). *Innovation management: strategy and implementation using the pentathlon framework* (1st ed.). London: Palgrave Macmillan.

Grant, R. M. (1991). A resource based theory of competitive advantage: implications for strategy formulation. *California Management Review*, 33, 114–135.

Hakes, C. (2014). *Innovation reboot: how to build, manage and assess innovation capability in organisations and teams.* Somersham: Leadership Agenda Limited, The Innovation Reboot Project.

Hamel, G. and Prahalad, C. K. (1994). *Competing for the future.* Boston, MA: Harvard Business School Press.

Hart, M. (2012). The lean startup: how today's entrepreneurs use continuous innovation to create radically successful businesses. *Journal of Product Innovation Management*, 29(3), 506–510.

Henderson, R. M. and Clark, K. B. (1990). Architectural innovation: the reconfiguration of existing product technologies and the failure of established firms. *Administrative Science Quarterly*, 35, 9–30.

Hollins, B. (2000). The development of a British standard for innovation management. *The Design Journal*, 3(2), 27–35.

Holt, K., Geschka, H. and Peterlongo, G. (1984). *Need assessment: a key to user-oriented product innovation.* New York: John Wiley & Sons Ltd.

ISO (2015). Quality management systems – requirements. International Standard, ISO 9001:2015.

Janszen, F. (2000). *The age of innovation.* London: Prentice Hall.

Katz, D. and Kahn, R. L. (1966). *The social psychology of organizations.* New York: John Wiley & Sons Ltd.

Kline, S. J. (1985). Innovation is not a linear process. *Research Management*, 28(4), 36–45.

Lawrence, P. R. and Lorsch, J. W. (1967). *Organization and environment: managing differentiation and integration*, Division of Research, Graduate School of Business Administration. Boston, MA: Harvard University Press.

Lawson, B. and Samson, D. (2001). Developing innovation capability in organisations: a dynamic capabilities approach. *International Journal of Innovation Management*, 5, 377–400.

Liker, J. K. (2004). *The Toyota way: fourteen management secrets from the world's greatest manufacturer.* New York: McGraw-Hill.

Lorenzoni, G. and Lipparini, A. (1999). The leveraging of interfirm relationships as a distinctive organizational capability: a longitudinal study. *Strategic Management Journal*, 20(4), 317–338.

Luebkeman, C. and Brown, T. (2015). Design is our answer an interview with leading design thinker Tim Brown. *Architectural Design*, 85, 34–39.

Magnusson, M. and Pasche, M. (2014). A contingency-based approach to the use of product modules and platforms. *Journal of Product Innovation Management*, 31(3), 434–450.

Mao, W. and Wang, P. (2012). Innovation management in Japanese Electronics Companies: a perspective of Total Innovation Management (TIM). *Proceedings of the 2012 IEEE ISMOT*, 518–521, November 8–9, Hangzhou, Zheijiang, China.

March, J. G. (1991). Exploration and exploitation in organizational learning. *Organization Science*, 2(1), February.

Martinich, L. (2004). An innovation framework: the foundation for two complementary approaches to innovation management. *IEEE/UT Engineering Management Conference*, August 12–13, Austin, TX.

McGrath, R. G. (2010). Business models: a discovery driven approach. *Long Range Planning*, 43, 247–261.

Menke, M., Xu, Q. and Gu, L. (2007). An analysis of the universality, flexibility, and agility of total innovation management: a case study of Hewlett – Packard. *Journal of Technology Transfer*, 32, 49–62.

Microsoft. (2013). Best practices for innovation: Microsoft's innovation management framework, Microsoft, June 2013.

Mintzberg, H., Ahlstrand, B. and Lampel, J. (1998). *Strategy safari: a guided tour through the wilds of strategic management.* New York: The Free Press.

Mir, M. and Casadesús, M. (2011). Standardised innovation management systems: a case study of the Spanish Standard UNE 166002:2006. *Revista Innovar Journal*, 21(40), 171–187.

Mir, M., Casadesús, M. and Petnji, L. H. (2016). The impact of standardized innovation management systems on innovation capability and business performance: an empirical study. *Journal of Engineering Technology Management*, 41, 26–44.

Mugge, P. and Markham, S. K. (2013). An innovation management framework: a model for managers who want to grow their businesses. In Kahn, Kenneth B. (Ed.), *The PDMA handbook of new product development*. New York: John Wiley & Sons Ltd.

Muramatsu, R., Ichimura, T. and Ishii, K. (1990). An analysis of needs assessment and information behavior in product development based on the fusion model. *Technovation*, 10(5), 305–317.

Nagji, B. and Tuff, G. (2012). Managing your innovation portfolio. *Harvard Business Review*, 90(5), 66–74.

Nishiguchi, H. and Konno, N. (2018). *Double-decker innovation management*. Tokyo: Nikkei Newspaper Publisher.

Nonaka, I. (1994). A dynamic theory of organizational knowledge creation. *Organization Science*, 5(1), 14–37.

O'Connor, G., Leifer, R., Paulson, A. and Peters, L. (2008). *Grabbing lightning: building a capability for breakthrough innovation*. San Francisco, CA: Jossey-Bass.

O'Connor, G. C., Corbett, A. C. and Peters, L. S. (2018). *Beyond the champion: institutionalizing innovation through people*. Stanford: Stanford University Press.

Oh, D. S., Phillips, F., Park, S. and Lee, E. (2016). Innovation ecosystems: a critical examination. *Technovation*, 54, 1–6.

PDMA & TIM (2013). Innovation Management Standard, TIM-PD-001-STD, Product Development and Management Association (PDMA), Total Innovation Management (TIM) Foundation.

Porter, M. E. (1980). *Competitive strategy: techniques for analyzing industries and competitors*. New York: Free Press.

Prahalad, C. K. and Hamel, G. (1990). The core competence of the corporation. *Harvard Business Review*, May–June, 79–91.

Rebelo, M. F., Santos, G. and Silva, R. (2015). Integration of standardized management systems: a dilemma? *Systems*, 3, 45–59.

Reinertsen, D. G. (1999). Taking the fuzziness out of the fuzzy front end. *Research Technology Management*, November–December, 25–31.

Ries, E. (2011). *The lean startup: how today's entrepreneurs use continuous innovation to create radically successful businesses*. New York: Crown Business.

Schilling, M. A. (2010). *Strategic management of technological innovation* (4th ed., international version). New York: McGraw-Hill.

Scott, W. R. (1981). *Organizations: rational, natural and open systems*. Englewood Cliffs, NJ: Prentice-Hall.

Senge, P. M. (1990). *The fifth discipline. The art and practice of the learning organization*. London: Random House.

Shapiro, S. M. (2001). *24/7 Innovation: a blueprint for surviving and thriving in an age of change*. New York: McGraw Hill.

Simon, H. A. (1947). *Administrative behavior* (1st ed.). New York: Free Press,.

Skarzynski, P. and Gibson, R. (2008). *Innovation to the core: a blueprint for transforming the way your company innovates*. Boston, MA: Harvard Business School Press.

Taylor, A. and Wagner, K. (2014). Rethinking your innovation system. *Boston Consulting Group*, October.

Teece, D. J. (2007). Explicating dynamic capabilities: the nature and microfoundations of (sustainable) enterprise performance. *Strategic Management Journal*, 28(13), 1319–1350.

Teece, D. J., Pisano, G. and Shuen, A. (1997). Dynamic capabilities and strategic management. *Strategic Management Journal*, 18, 509–533.

Thompson, J. D. (1967). *Organizations in action*. New York: McGraw Hill.

Tidd, J. and Bessant, J. (2013). *Managing innovation: integrating technological, market and organizational change* (5th ed.). New York: John Wiley & Sons Ltd.

Tidd, J., Bessant, J. and Pavitt, K. (1997). *Managing innovation: integrating technological, market and organizational change* (1st ed.). New York: John Wiley & Sons Ltd.

Tucker, R. B. (2002). *Driving growth through innovation: how leading firms are transforming their futures*. San Francisco: Berrett-Koehler Publishers Inc.

Tuominen, M., Piippo, P., Ichimura, T. and Matsumoto, Y. (1999). An analysis of innovation management systems' characteristics. *International Journal of Production Economics*, 60–61, 135–143.

Tushman, M. L. and O'Reilly, C. A. (1996). Ambidextrous organizations: managing evolutionary and revolutionary change. *California Management Review*, 38(4), 8–30.

van de Ven, A. H., Polley, D. E., Garud, R. and Venkataraman, S. (1999/2008). *The innovation journey*. New York, NY: Oxford Univ. Press.

Vilà, J. and Muñoz-Nájar, J. A. (2002). The innovation system: organizational and managerial competencies to innovate. *IESE Alumni Magazine*, March.

von Stamm, B. (2003). *The innovation wave: meeting the corporate challenge*. New York: John Wiley & Sons Ltd.

Wernerfelt, B. (1984). A resource-based view of the firm. *Strategic Management Journal*, 5, 171–180.

Xu, Q., Chen, J., Xie, Z., Liu, J., Zheng, G. and Wang, Y. (2007). Total innovation management: a novel paradigm of innovation management in the 21st century. *Journal of Technology Transfer*, 32, 9–25.

Xu, Q., Yu, Z., Zheng, G. and Zhou, Z. (2002). *Towards capability-based Total Innovation Management (Tim): the emerging new trend of innovation management – a case study of Haier Group*. ISMOT & ICMIT'02, Hangzhou, Zhejiang, China: Zhejiang University Press.

Xu, Q., Zhu, L., Zheng, G. and Wang, F. (2007). Haier's Tao of innovation: a case study of the emerging total innovation management model. *Journal of Technology Transfer*, 32, 27–47.

Yepes, V., Pellicer, E., Alarcon, L. F. and Correa, C. L. (2016). Creative innovation in Spanish construction firms. *Journal of Professional Issues in Engineering Education and Practice*, 142, 1.

6
INNOVATION AND INNOVATION MANAGEMENT IN AN AGE OF CHANGES

Jin Chen and Liang Mei

Innovation and innovation management in the 'Internet+' Age

In 2012, Alibaba Chairman Ma Yun and Wanda Chairman Wang Jianlin entered into a ¥100M VAM (Valuation Adjustment Mechanism) agreement to challenge the possibility of e-commerce grabbing a 50+ percent share of the Chinese retail market by 2020. In the following year, Gree Chairman Miss Dong Mingzhu entered into a ¥1B VAM agreement with MI Chairperson Lei Jun on Gree's traditional marketing model and MI's e-marketing model. Symbolizing the clash between the new and old thoughts of economic and industrial transformation, the two events provide an insight into how to innovate in corporate technology, markets, organizational management and business models in the Internet revolution. How to initiate new innovation and innovation management in an Internet era is emerging as the leading edge of research and practice.

Internet thinking

Innovation and innovation management in the 'Internet+' age focused primarily on a revolution in the business thinking model and resulted in Internet thinking, one that reviews the market, the user, the product, the corporate value chain and the entire business ecosystem with the continuation of technological developments, including mobile Internet, big data and cloud computing.

Embedded in the chain that links up products, production, service, marketing, strategy and business model design, Internet thinking represents the paradigm shift from linear thinking, oriented to traditional industries, to circular thinking, oriented to the Internet. Table 6.1 compares the two thinking models.

Considering the shift in business logic from linear industrial thinking to circular Internet thinking, Internet thinking is further dissected.

User-first

At the core of Internet thinking is the user, who plays an ongoing critical role in business operations and the value chain. To orient the products, services and business models of a firm to the user means to put the firm in the user's place in addressing such problems as product innovation,

Table 6.1 Comparison between industrial thinking and Internet thinking

	Industrial thinking	Internet thinking
Mind-set	Linear thinking	Circular thinking
Characterization	Forward, irreversible, one-step	Cyclical, evolutionary
Risk characteristics	Massive, less change resistant	Staged, controllable
Visualization	Wool is shorn from sheep	Wool is shorn from pigs
Marketing model	Massive investment in advertising	Word-of-mouth marketing, social media marketing
Innovation model	Closed innovation	Open innovation
Innovator	R&D staff	User participation
Financial philosophy	Make profit from products	Products can be free

Source: Sun and Gang (2015)

pricing and brand promotion. Upmarket demand is developed, users are led to 'vote by foot' and competitive advantages are secured through organizational innovation. For example, the 'user cult' philosophy of Qihoo 360 placed user experience as the cardinal principle of product and service innovation. The development of free PC and cellphone antivirus and security packages assured Internet users of network security and emotional security to the greatest extent. That's why Qihoo 360 succeeded in its business model in a highly competitive market.

Big data

The Internet as a tool enables a firm to accumulate countless market users as well as mass data on suppliers, partners and competitors that transfers into core corporate assets and sources for competitive advantages. When applied to the whole value chain of the corporate business model, big data analysis and mining contribute to matching supply precisely with demand, to locating markets and consumer preferences precisely to formulate systemic market strategy, to classifying cooperators' information and allocating knowledge resources effectively and to optimizing logistics information and improving cost and operational advantages. Ultimately, big data infusion into the value chain creates competitive advantages for a firm.

Interdisciplinarity

Interdisciplinarity drives a firm to go beyond or restructure the bounds of the original business model with the assistance of Internet technologies and platforms. The increase to the business value of its products and services earns paybacks and competitive advantages. For example, Tencent and Alibaba use the Internet and the e-commerce platform to link WeChat and Alipay online payment tools with our everyday life. DiDi and KuaiDi are also popular apps that have won a wider user base and many more stickier customers. Interdisciplinarity based on Internet technology has therefore been realized.

Simplicity

Simplicity stresses minimalism in R&D, product design, production and service to maximize user experience to the greatest extent. The technological complexity of Internet technology is prevented from compromising user experience and satisfaction

Extremity

Ongoing investment of financial capital in the Internet age gave rise to fierce competition among firms. Focusing on developing customer demand deeply, and providing best experience by products and services for customers, so as to achieve customer stickiness.

Iteration

Thanks to Internet technology, innovation in products and services further improves information asymmetry and innovation efficiency for a firm while in the course of research, development and innovation. At the same time, intense competition and ongoing development of the user market further drive the demand for new, diverse individualized products and services. Under these circumstances, firms should not get into a rut, but rather pay attention to an iteration procedure as a means of evolving from old products and services to new ones. Fast iteration enables user demand to be met continually and dynamically.

Platform

The 'platform awareness', oriented to the organizational strategy, business model and organizational form, emphasizes a self-contained business ecosystem built on the Internet. It's an interactive platform involving competition and collaboration with the stakeholders in the business ecosystem in order to get an advantage. One example is Taobao, an online e-commerce platform that charges fees from countless small- and medium-sized enterprises (SMEs), startups and mini-shopkeepers. Taobao is renowned for its good service, network security, rules and a culture promoting both competition and collaboration. This e-commerce platform grabs the advantage due to the prosperity of SMEs in the business ecosystem as a whole.

Socialization

What the Internet emphasizes as interconnection among people is a web-like relationship in nature. Information communication, relationship introduction and word of mouth are similar in that they depend on interconnection. Interconnection is responsible for the externality of the Internet; that is to say, every new customer will create positive value to the whole Internet, resulting in a spillover effect at the society level. Firms should take notice of the spillover effect and use the Internet as an effectual socialization tool to introduce innovative models, such as crowd sourcing and crowd funding.

Network traffic

Network traffic concerns primarily service operations, such as specific marketing and service models. A firm should pay close attention to network traffic because it means financial returns and is key to the success of a business model. Take Qihoo 360, for example. At first its free antivirus engine drew objections from investors and competitors. However, the free service enabled Qihoo 360 to accumulate a very large clientele and create a brand effect founded on a sense of identity. The company went on to pursue such core service modules as a search engine, earning handsome returns in the form of network traffic.

'Internet+'

To put it simply, 'Internet+' means the "Internet plus traditional industries". But it's not simply the addition but also the employment of IT and the Internet platform to apply the Internet to the traditional industries to create new development opportunities. Internet+ is characteristic of a new form of society where the role of the Internet in social resource optimization and integration is maximized since Internet innovations are introduced into the society, economy, etc. Internet+ enhances the innovativeness and productivity of a society to form a new economic model built on the Internet as a medium and infrastructure.

Prime Minister Li Keqiang stated with clarity in a 2015 government report that "the 'Internet+' Action Plan is intended to apply mobile web, cloud computing, big data and IoT (Internet of Things) to modern manufacturing, to accelerate the development of e-commerce, the industrial Internet and Internet finance, and to guide Internet companies in expanding into the international market".[1] Figure 6.1 analyzes Internet+ from three perspectives: connotation, philosophy and action plan.

National strategy drives industry, society, transport, finance, government, education, medical care and agriculture to press ahead with innovations in technological, service and business models in an Internet context. The Internet platform is joined by IT with the various traditional industries to create many new business models in both traditional and new areas. Table 6.2 lists some typical cases of innovative application of 'Internet+' to traditional areas.

Green innovation management

Beyond the innovation models driven by conventional technological feasibility and economic benefit, the environmental impact of innovation is beginning to gain attention as an important powerhouse for sustainable social development. New innovation paradigms, such as eco-innovation and environmental innovation, are proliferating in recent years.

With the rising negative externalities of innovative and economic activities, the world is paying more and more attention to environmental and ecological issues and their challenges. Take China, for example. Over the past three decades, rapid economic reforms have caused and aggravated such social problems as environmental pollution and economic inequality. The move of national innovation and institutional transformation faces the dual objective of economic growth and environmental conservation. Beginning from the end of the 1980s, the policy of environmental conservation and sustainable development underwent five changes (Zhang and Wen, 2008):

- From environmental conservation as a fundamental policy to sustainable development as a national strategy;
- From pollution control to ecological protection;
- From end-of-pipe treatment to control at the source;
- From waste discharge points to regional environmental restoration;
- From regulatory measures to economic and legal steps.

Connotation of environmental and eco-innovation

This part deals with the significant environmental impact of four innovation concepts and their management models from a social perspective. These core concepts include sustainable innovation, ecological innovation (or eco-innovation), environmental innovation and green innovation.

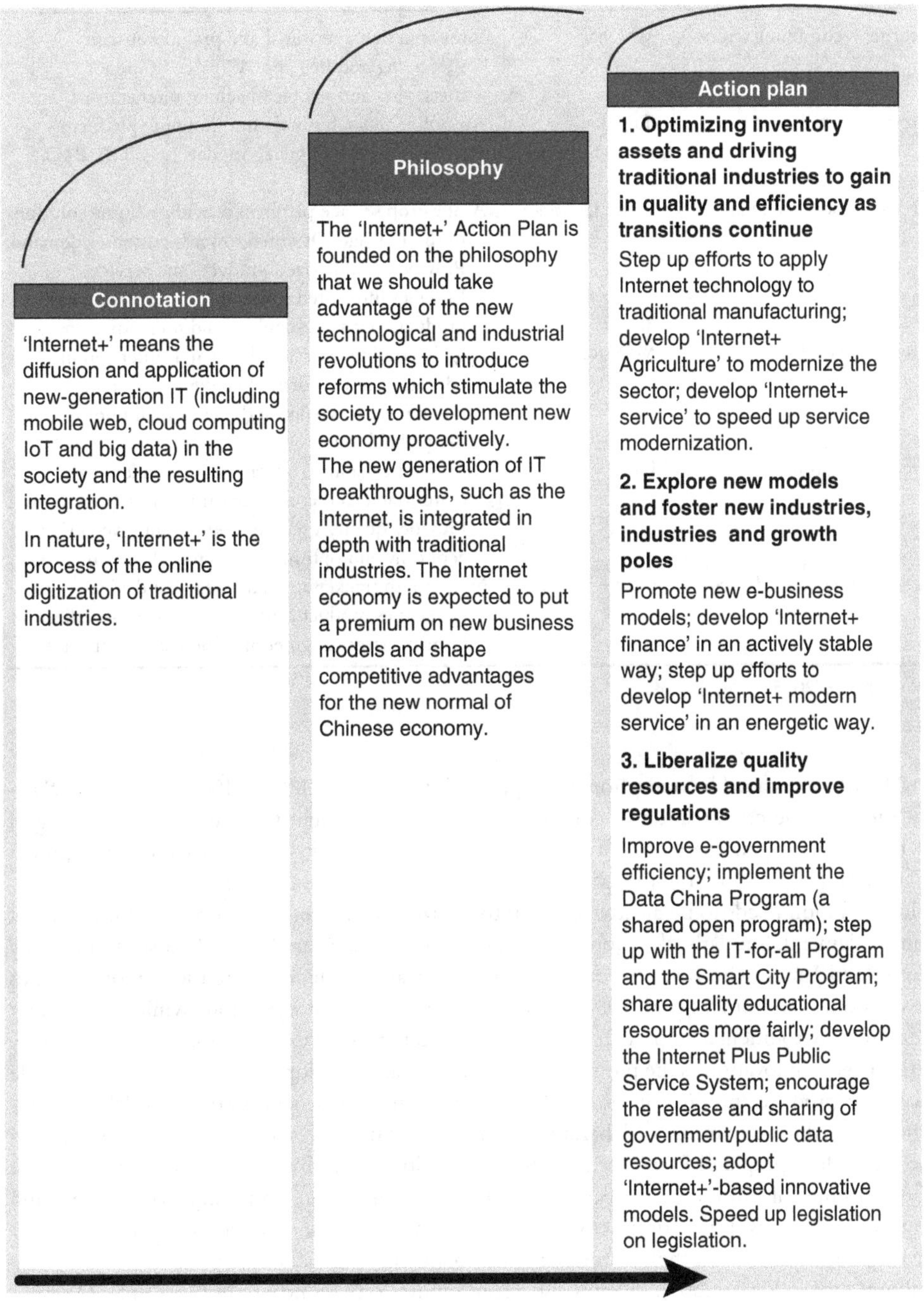

Connotation

'Internet+' means the diffusion and application of new-generation IT (including mobile web, cloud computing IoT and big data) in the society and the resulting integration.

In nature, 'Internet+' is the process of the online digitization of traditional industries.

Philosophy

The 'Internet+' Action Plan is founded on the philosophy that we should take advantage of the new technological and industrial revolutions to introduce reforms which stimulate the society to development new economy proactively.
The new generation of IT breakthroughs, such as the Internet, is integrated in depth with traditional industries. The Internet economy is expected to put a premium on new business models and shape competitive advantages for the new normal of Chinese economy.

Action plan

1. Optimizing inventory assets and driving traditional industries to gain in quality and efficiency as transitions continue

Step up efforts to apply Internet technology to traditional manufacturing; develop 'Internet+ Agriculture' to modernize the sector; develop 'Internet+ service' to speed up service modernization.

2. Explore new models and foster new industries, industries and growth poles

Promote new e-business models; develop 'Internet+ finance' in an actively stable way; step up efforts to develop 'Internet+ modern service' in an energetic way.

3. Liberalize quality resources and improve regulations

Improve e-government efficiency; implement the Data China Program (a shared open program); step up with the IT-for-all Program and the Smart City Program; share quality educational resources more fairly; develop the Internet Plus Public Service System; encourage the release and sharing of government/public data resources; adopt 'Internet+'-based innovative models. Speed up legislation on legislation.

Figure 6.1 'Internet+': connotation and action plan

Table 6.2 Innovative application of Internet+ to traditional industries

Internet+ (traditional industry)	Typical case	Description
Internet+ communications	WeChat	Run on a smart terminal and provides instant messaging and free apps. Capable of instant messaging and people–machine interaction.
Internet+ retail	Taobao	An online retail, business and shopping platform supporting e-commerce models (e.g. B2B, B2C, C2C and O2O).
Internet+ home appliance	Haier U-home	A one-stop service platform providing home solutions in the IoT age. Oriented towards customer demand. Provides modularized products and services. Provides integrated solutions on the platform of products, services, suppliers and user experience.
Internet+ education	MOOC	A global online learning platform. It offers online education in the form of credit courses and integrates knowledge and educational resources at the global level.
Internet+ transport	Uber	An instant e-hailing software that provides a safe, comfortable and convenient urban transport service. Provides quality user experience, improves a sharing economy and optimizes resource allocation.
Internet+ personal devices	Nike+	Nike health tracker apps and wearable devices. Diversifies product functions. Improves socialization, human-factors engineering and user experience.

Source: Ning (2015)

The term 'sustainable innovation' first appeared in the 1980 IUCN *World Conservation Strategy*, meaning the combination of conservation with development to ensure the well-being of all human beings on the globe. At the same time, sustainability stresses that the development of modern people should not be at the expense of the interests of posterity. Therefore, sustainable innovation needs to be creative enough to realize sustainable social development and meet human demand. Similarly, the word 'eco-innovation' first appeared in a 1996 study made by Fussler and James, who held that research and practical experience should lean more towards new products and processes that create value for customers and operations while significantly reducing environmental impact. Famous scholars Kemp and Pearson took a further step by defining eco-innovation as the production, assimilation and development of activities that, while related to products, production processes, services, management and business models, can significantly reduce environmental hazards and negative pollution and resource externalities in the life cycle (Kemp and Pearson, 2007). Similarly, Oltra and Jean first put forward the concept of environmental innovation, a near-synonym of eco-innovation, proposing that the new and improved processes, innovation activities, innovation systems and products would ultimately have a positive impact on the environment and create ongoing value for environmental sustainability (Oltra and Jean, 2009). There is also green innovation, a concept put forward by Driessen and Hillebrand. In essence, green innovation does not imply that innovation activities oriented to sustainable development are meant to reduce environmental pressure, but that innovation activities in themselves create positive significance and value to the environment (Driessen and Hillebrand, 2002). Green innovation includes, for example, energy conservation, pollution protection, waste recycling, green product design and environmental management improvements (Chen, Lai, and Wen, 2006).

Process management for environmental/eco-innovation

While implementing product and process innovation for greater competitive advantages, environmentally and ecologically innovative firms pay a great deal of attention to the environmental impact of innovation activities. From the perspective of innovation, environmental and eco-innovation mark a major change in the corporate innovation concept.

Take the automotive value chain, for example. From a traditional closed perspective, the value chain is a fixed one, beginning from the auto parts maker and the automaker to the dealer and the user. The concerns of a traditional automotive business include toxic substances, atmospheric pollution and environmental law compliance in the course of manufacturing. However, from the standpoint of environmental and eco-innovation, an innovative value chain integrating environmental innovation requires all the participants to be environmentally responsible. Auto parts/material suppliers, automakers, dealers, users and life terminals are put wholly under environmental monitoring and management.

Core dimensions of environmental and eco-innovation

Economists and management experts underline the complexity and multidimensionality of innovation. Environmental innovation extends the dimensionality of innovative activities and behavior beyond such traditional dimensions as product and process.

Design dimension

The design dimension of environmental and eco-innovation determines the impact of innovation activities on the environment throughout the life cycle. Design comprises three ingredients: component addition, subsystem change and system change.

Component addition means the development of additional functions or components in the course of developing an innovative product in order to enhance its environmental performance and minimize the negative environmental impacts from product, process and system innovations. For example, the catalytic converter was developed and embedded in the vehicle exhaust purifier to control NOx/CO/hydrocarbon emissions. Subsystem change also improves the design to weaken environmental impacts while enhancing eco-efficiency and energy efficiency. System change involves a redesign of innovative products and processes so that they meet the requirements for eco-friendly development. Examples include waste reuse and recycling, dissemination of new-energy vehicle breakthrough innovations (e.g. new-energy vehicles) and innovations in and dissemination of solar products. All the steps are focused on the design concepts of environmental and eco-innovation when it comes to such system changes as energy use, energy conservation and emissions reductions, environmental friendliness and sustainable development.

User dimension

The user dimension covers two ingredients, namely, user development and user acceptance. User development highlights the important role of users in product definition, design improvement and R&D. The firm should attach great importance to the role of the users (especially lead users) in the entire stage from creative idea generation to product commercialization. The firm should collaborate effectively with the users throughout the entire product development stage, since they concern both the development and use of the products. However, although user participation improves product efficacy, it may fail to adequately meet the firm's need for breakthrough innovations, for the user may reject such innovations because of the limits of thinking on current products and a deficiency of knowledge about complicated products and processes. Therefore, it is necessary to balance exploration and utility when the firm relies on the user to convert innovative ideas into commercial products. In this manner, the user is effectively stimulated as a source of innovativeness to create significant value, and user feedback on environmental and ecological issues is used in the interests of innovation management in an environmental context. User acceptance of the application of innovation has a revolutionary impact on user behavior and user practice. Usually, fast and mass user application features successive innovation, and user acceptance of an innovation depends greatly on the influence of social values and norms. One example is the society-wide pursuit of health trends (e.g. eating more vegetables), which contributed to successful innovation in niche markets.

Product-service dimension

The product-service dimension covers the change in the product-service deliverable and the change in the value chain process and relations. The change in the product-service deliverable stresses the interaction between the products/services and the user, as well as the changes in the perception of customer relations. Environmentalism incorporated as a philosophy and mode of life into the user's cognitive and consuming habits lends itself to market feedback on the firm's environmental innovation behavior while dynamically and strategically promoting ongoing environmental innovation. For example, a firm may turn from selling products to selling service packs, leasing products, maintaining a product operating environment and recycling waste. Users are therefore influenced by a sense of environmental protection and maintain a prolonged interaction with the firm.

The change in the value chain process and relations stresses primarily whether the value networks and processes of the products and services can create a green, positive and environmental resource cycle. In the context of environmental protection, innovative management is centered on the sustainable development of firms and stakeholders. For example, competent environmental companies may monopolize the niche market by publicizing the value of green products and services. In doing so, the companies switch from environmental and eco-innovation to ongoing competitive advantages.

Governance dimension

The governance dimension of environmental and eco-innovation involves all innovative environmental solutions at the institutional and organizational levels aimed at achieving the dual objective – competitive advantage improvement at the firm level and positive environmental benefit at the social level. Governance interventions (e.g. environmental law, environmental codes and environmental assessment standards), as well as incentives (e.g. environmental subsidies and environmental innovation-related preferences), are adopted to encourage the firm and the society to review and strategically emphasize green and environmental innovation activities.

Based on the core dimension of environmental and eco-innovation, Javier Carrillo-Hermosilla created an assessment system for the environmental and eco-attributes of innovation activities. See Table 6.3.

Table 6.3 Environmental and eco-innovation assessment dashboard

Main dimension	Ranking				
	1	2	3	4	5
Component condition					
Subsystem change					
System change					
User development					
User acceptance					
Product-service deliverable					
Value chain change					
Governance					

Responsible innovation

In the course of human evolution and social development, innovation has served a sustained role in driving economic growth, facilitating sustainable social development and improving the life and well-being of the populace (Owen, Baxter, Maynard, and Depledge, 2009). Take the technological and industrial innovations in the 20th century, for example. Atomic energy, the internal combustion engine, molecular biology, nanoscience and the information revolution have done their significant share of work to boost sustained social progress and revolution.

On the other hand, despite the accompanying social progress, technological innovation is giving rise to increasingly hazardous social paradoxes, such as atomic energy development vs. nuclear security, genetic modification vs. bioethics and biosecurity regarding humans and other living beings, industrial innovation vs. environmental hazards, financial innovation vs. financial crisis, and IT vs. information security and privacy protection. These dual-nature challenges concern both social progress and social hazards and divert the attention of researchers and doers to 'responsible innovation'.

Under the Smart Growth strategy where knowledge and innovation drive economic growth, the Horizon 2020 Framework Program introduced the concept of 'responsible innovation', highlighting its global strategic importance. From the perspective of responsible innovation, research and innovation should be effective in reflecting social demand, social willingness, social values and social responsibilities. Policy makers are obligated to erect a governance framework on which to encourage responsible research and innovation activities (Mei, Chen, and Sheng, 2014).

To achieve this goal, innovation is supposed to be morally acceptable and socially intended, safe and sustainable (Von Schomberg, 2013). Based on the fundamental vision of the 2020 Smart Growth Strategy, responsible innovation requires research and innovation activities to review two basic questions: Are humans able to delineate the social impact and results on innovative activities? Will the support for an innovation cause it to evolve in a direction that is satisfactory to society?

In this case, the developed countries have tried out many responsible innovation programs at the national and regional levels. See Table 6.4.

Basic connotation of responsible innovation

Responsible innovation revisits the positive process of the traditional innovation paradigm from the viewpoint of idea creation and commercialization. By predicting the potentially negative

Table 6.4 Responsible innovation policies and activities conducted by developed countries

Policy and activity	Key goal and content description
The Netherlands Responsible Innovation Program	• Focusing on the design of innovation processes and integrating innovation research with social analysis and ethics study in order to ensure the coordinated development of science and technology
The Germany Action Plan Nanotechnology 2020	• Reducing the negative impact on the environment and health, exploring the potential value of nanotechnologies on sustainable development and improving the supportive public policies on the development of nanotechnologies. • Analyzing the potential risks for nanomaterial on the environment and human beings • Developing the approaches and proposals for responsible innovation of nanomaterial
The UK EPSRC Nanomedicine Public Dialogue	• Defining the focus and priority of nanotechnology on medical research • Describing the direction and decisions of nanomedicine research • Listening to public feedback on the research
Research on European Nano-Science and Technology Regulation	• Formulating European nanoscience and technology regulations and values • Discussing the ethical norms, research activities, stakeholders and governance mechanisms of the development of European nanoscience and technology and achieving the responsible innovation of nanoscience and technology • Exploring nanoscience and technology governance regulations and the responsible innovation on emerging technologies
Responsible Innovation Framework at the UK's Engineering and Physical Sciences Research Council (EPSRC)	• Combining the purpose, vision, impact, motivation and open dialogue of responsible innovation and achieving ethics, reflexivity and responsiveness of innovation governance
The U.S. Social-Technology Integration Research Program	• Integrating the technological research in labs with societal expectations and needs • Comparing and evaluating innovation activities in labs with public opinions • Conducting interdiscipline collaborative research on responsible innovation and relevant responsiveness mechanisms
The Hippocratic Oath for Scientists	• Scientists' responsibility in terms of both science and technology and other humanistic aspects involving care, respect, legitimacy, justice, love and avoiding harm
BASF Dialogforum Nano	• Formulating seven criteria of responsible innovation in nanotechnology
European Commission ETICA Project	• Discussions on ethical issues of emerging information and communication technology (ICT) involving technology classification, ethical observation, evaluation and practices of ICT • Introducing a multistakeholder reflexivity approach and promoting ethical discussions by multistakeholders

Source: Liang, Jin, and Weizhong (2014)

impacts of innovation activities, more heterogeneous stakeholders should be included and more responsive institutions should be constructed so as to lead innovation processes in directions that are satisfying socially and ethically acceptable, achieving the maximum public values (Mei and Chen, 2015).

As an emerging research and practice innovation paradigm, the questions of responsible innovation mainly focus on aspects involving product, process and purpose (see Table 6.5).

The relevant concepts of responsible innovation include responsible research and innovation (RRI) and responsible development (RD), which originates from contexts in the EU and the United States. As an emerging paradigm, the main characteristics of responsible innovation include:

- Focusing on the needs and challenges of a societal ecosystem and ethics;
- Making inclusiveness and multistakeholder participation a promise and promoting mutual learning and decision-making mechanisms;
- Focusing on the prediction of potential problems of innovation, evaluating value appropriation and revisiting potential value, propositions, beliefs and norms of innovations;
- Proposing and constructing mutual participation and adaptive mechanisms of responsible innovation (Wickson and Carew, 2014).

Frameworks of responsible innovation

Stahl (2013) proposed a three-dimensional framework of responsible innovation, including the actor of innovation, the activity of innovation and the norm of innovation, and argued that responsible innovation was a meta-responsibility.

Stilgoe, Owen, and Macnaghten (2013) constructed four dimensions of responsible innovation, involving anticipation, reflexivity, inclusion and responsiveness (see Figure 6.2).

However, the previous discussions on responsible innovation were mainly from geographical contexts like the EU and the United States. Embedded in such developed countries' contexts, the relevant institutions advocate potential priorities of specific technological and societal issues, implying an inclusive, democratic and just relationship between science and

Table 6.5 Lines of questioning on responsible innovation

Product questions	Process questions	Purpose questions
How will the risks and benefits be distributed?	How should standards be drawn up and applied?	Why are researchers doing it?
What other impacts can we anticipate?	How should risks and benefits be defined and measured?	Are these motivations transparent and in the public interest?
How might these change in the future?	Who is in control?	Who will benefit?
What do we know about?	Who is taking part?	What are they going to gain?
What might we never know about?	Who will take responsibility if things go wrong?	What are the alternatives?
	How do we know we are right?	

Source: Macnaghten and Chilvers (2013)

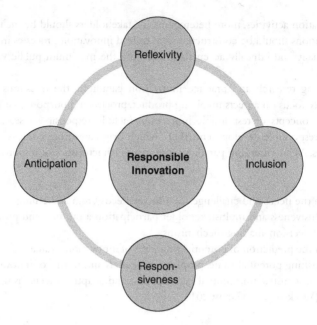

Figure 6.2 Four-dimensional framework of responsible innovation

society (Van Oudheusden, 2014). In contrast, responsible innovation in the developing countries' contexts is different. The relevant researches and practices require considerations of the heterogeneity of national, regional and organizational factors, as well as the relationship between science and technology, science and society and the influence of responsible innovation on poor regions in the context of constructing a framework of responsible innovation (Mei and Chen, 2014).

Thus, Liang Mei and Jin Chen (2014) integrated the three-dimensional and four-dimensional frameworks of responsible innovation and further complemented the contextual factor in a new theoretical framework of responsible innovation (see Figure 6.3).

The evaluation of responsible innovation

The lives of human beings and the development of society rely more and more on technological innovation. Responsible innovation triggers a consideration of the negative impacts and ethical concerns of innovation activities. Traditional innovation paradigms mainly focus on the two-dimensional evaluative criteria of innovation, involving the advance and feasibility of science and technology, and the economic efficiency and growth. With the evolution of responsible innovation, the criteria of innovation evaluation are extended. Previous responsible innovation literature argues that the research and innovation activities must meet two more basic criteria, namely ethical acceptance and social satisfaction. Based on the relevant academic discussions, the Chinese scholars Liang Mei and Jin Chen (2015) established the evaluative criteria of responsible innovation (see Figure 6.4).

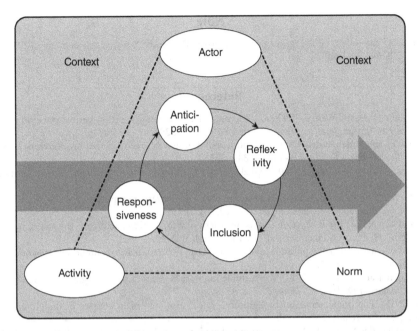

Figure 6.3 Research framework of responsible innovation
Source: Liang and Jin (2014)

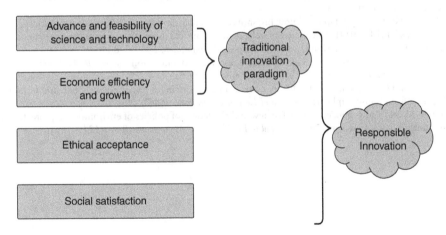

Figure 6.4 Theoretical framework of responsible innovation
Source: Liang and Chen Jin (2015)

Note

1 Report on the work of the government in 2015, People.cn: www.people.com.cn/n/2015/0305/c347407-26643598.html

References

Chen, Y.-S., Lai, S-B. and Wen, C-T. (2006). The influence of green innovation performance on corporate advantage in Taiwan. *Journal of Business Ethics*, 67(4), 331–339.

Driessen, P. H. and Hillebrand, B. (2002). Adoption and diffusion of green innovations. *Marketing for Sustainability: Towards Transactional Policy-Making*, 343–355.

Kemp, René and Pearson, Peter (2007). Final report MEI project about measuring eco-innovation. *UM Merit, Maastricht*, 10.

Macnaghten, P., and Chilvers, J. (2013). The future of science governance: publics, policies, practices. *Environment and Planning C: Government and Policy*, 32(3), 530–548.

Mei, L. and Chen, J. (2014). Reflection and reconstruction of innovation paradigm – the emerging research on responsible innovation. *Science and Management*, 34(3), 3–11.

Mei, L. and Chen, J. (2015). Responsible innovation: origin, attribution and theoretical framework. *Management World*, 263(8), 39–57.

Mei, L., Chen, J. and Sheng, W. (2014). Responsible innovation – emerging paradigm of research and innovation. *Studies in Dialectics of Nature*, 30(10), 83–89.

Ning, J. (2015). The implementation background, connotation and main content of the "Internet Plus" action plan. *E-government*, 6, 32–38.

Oltra, V. and Maïder, S. J. (2009). Sectoral systems of environmental innovation: an application to the french automotive industry. *Technological Forecasting and Social Change*, 76(4), 567–583.

Owen, R., Baxter, D., Maynard, T. and Depledge, M. (2009). Beyond regulation: risk pricing and responsible innovation, *Environmental Science & Technology*, 18(43), 6902–6906.

Stahl, B. C. (2013). Responsible research and innovation: the role of privacy in an emerging framework. *Science and Public Policy*, 40(6), 708–716.

Stilgoe, J., Owen, R. and Macnaghten, P. (2013). Developing a framework for responsible innovation. *Research Policy*, 42(9), 1568–1580.

Sun, L., and Wei, G. (2015). Do you know big shots are circular thinkers? *CEIBS Business Review*, 1, 29–33.

Van Oudheusden, M. (2014). Where are the politics in responsible innovation? European governance, technology assessments, and beyond. *Journal of Responsible Innovation*, 1(1), 67–86.

Von Schomberg, R. (2013). A vision of responsible research and innovation. *Responsible Innovation: Managing the Responsible Emergence of Science and Innovation in Society*, 51–74.

Wickson, F. and Carew, A. L. (2014). Quality criteria and indicators for responsible research and innovation: learning from transdisciplinarity. *Journal of Responsible Innovation*, 1(3), 254–273.

Zhang, K-M. and Zong-guo, W. (2008). Review and challenges of policies of environmental protection and sustainable development in China. *Journal of Environmental Management*, 88(4), 1249–1261.

PART II

The strategic perspective of innovation

7
STRATEGIC MANAGEMENT OF INNOVATION

Emigdio Alfaro, Fei Yu, Naqeeb Ur Rehman, Eglantina Hysa and Patrice Kandolo Kabeya

In this chapter, the importance and the components of the strategic management of innovation are detailed through the following sections: (a) corporate strategy and innovation; (b) leadership and innovation; (c) core competences and innovation; (d) patents, standards and innovation; (e) marketing strategy of innovation; and (f) entrepreneurship and innovation. Doğan (2017) indicated that "[t]he strategic management of innovation indicates an important component of the corporate strategy and an important factor that has a significant contribution to a company's competitive advantage" (p. 294) and that "[f]or this reason, the strategic management of innovation has become a fundamental issue in the field of strategic management" (p. 294). Today's organizations must include innovation management as an indispensable part of their strategic management and must be focused on the competitive advantages, which will contribute to their value generation. In this respect, Keupp, Palmié, and Gassmann, 2012 suggested that "strategic management of innovation is concerned with the use of appropriate strategic management techniques in order to increase the effect of [a] firm's innovation activities on [the] firm's growth and performance" (p. 368).

To better comprehend the strategic management of innovation, it is necessary to better comprehend both related concepts: the strategic management and the innovation. With regard to strategic management, Kohl, Orth, Riebartsch, and Hecklau, 2016 indicated that "strategic management systems have a remarkable impact on decision making processes, but lack in many cases of a long-term perspective, stakeholder-orientation and barely provide holistic solutions facilitating the establishment of innovations in a company" (p. 335). In addition, Grant (2010) explained that "[i]f strategic management is all about managing to achieve outstanding success then the essential tasks of strategy are to identify the sources of superior business performance and to formulate and implement a strategy that exploits these sources of superior performance" (p. xii). Additionally, Johnson, Scholes, and Whittington (2008) indicated that "strategic management is concerned with complexity arising out of ambiguous and non-routine situations with organisation-wide rather than operation-specific implications" (p. 11) and that "this is a major challenge for managers who are used to managing on a day-to-day basis the resources they control" (p. 11). Johnson, Scholes, and Whittington (2008) also indicated that "strategic management includes understanding the strategic position of an organisation, making strategic choices for the future and managing strategy in action" (p. 12).

Diverse authors explained the different focus of innovation as follows: (a) new or significantly improved products (Doğan, 2017; Grant, 2010; OECD and European Commission, 2005); (b) new or significantly improved processes (Doğan, 2017; OECD and European Commission, 2005); (c) distribution (Doğan, 2017); (d) learning perspective (Grant, 2010); (e) knowledge (Johnson, Scholes, and Whittington, 2008); (f) a new marketing method or a new organizational method in business practices, the workplace or external relations (OECD and European Commission, 2005); (g) outcomes, value creation and profitability (Grant, 2010; OECD and European Commission, 2005); and (h) strategic challenge (Ferrary, 2008). Doğan (2017) explained that "[i]nnovation has traditionally focused on products and processes, and then it has attracted attention as an area that will provide significant gains regarding innovation" (p. 294) and that "however, the combination of product, process and distribution hasn't reflected the sufficient potential for organizational innovation" (p. 294).

Grant (2010) emphasized that "[t]he innovation and learning perspective includes measures related to new product development cycle times, technological leadership and rates of improvement" (p. 51). Johnson, Scholes, and Whittington (2008) also pointed out that "[i]nnovation involves the conversion of new knowledge into a new product, process or service and the putting of this new product, process or service into use, either via the marketplace or by other processes of delivery" (p. 325).

The specialists of the Organisation for Economic Co-operation and Development (OECD) and the European Commission 2005 defined innovation as follows: "An innovation is the implementation of a new or significantly improved product (good or service), or process, a new marketing method, or a new organizational method in business practices, workplace organisation or external relations" (p. 46) and indicated that "[t]he minimum requirement for an innovation is that the product, process, marketing method or organisational method must be new (or significantly improved) to the firm" (p. 46). The specialists of the OECD and European Commission, 2005 also explained that "[a] common feature of an innovation is that it must have been implemented. A new or improved product is implemented when it is introduced on the market" and that "[n]ew processes, marketing methods or organisational methods are implemented when they are brought into actual use in the firm's operations" (p. 47). Additionally, the specialists of the OECD and European Commission, 2005 classified the types of innovation as follows: "Four types of innovations are distinguished: product innovations, process innovations, marketing innovations and organisational innovations" (p. 47).

Grant (2010) explained that "[t]he profitability of an innovation to the innovator depends on the value created by the innovation and the share of that value that the innovator is able to appropriate" (p. 299) and indicated that the created value by an innovation is distributed among (a) customers, (b) suppliers, (c) innovators and (d) imitators and other 'followers' (p. 299). Additionally, Grant (2010) commented that "[t]he extent to which a firm can establish clear property rights in an innovation critically determines the choice of strategy options" (p. 305). Regarding the features of innovation, OECD and European Commission, 2005 indicated the following: (a) "Innovation is associated with uncertainty over the outcome of innovation activities" (p. 34), (b) "Innovation involves investment" (p. 35), (c) "Innovation is subject to spillovers" (p. 35), (d) "Innovation involves the utilisation of new knowledge or a new use or combination of existing knowledge" (p. 35) and (e) "Innovation aims at improving a firm's performance by gaining a competitive advantage" (p. 35). Additionally, Ferrary (2008) explained that "[i]nnovation is a strategic challenge for high-tech companies and as such, justifies large investments in R&D" (p. 600).

Corporate strategy and innovation

In this section, the concept of the corporate strategy and the impact of corporate strategies on innovation are presented. The impact of some corporate strategies (the mergers and acquisitions and the spin-offs) on the innovation were found in a literature review with diverse results.

Corporate strategy

Regarding the term 'corporate strategy', Johnson, Scholes, and Whittington (2008) indicated that it "denotes the most general level of strategy in an organisation and in this sense embraces other levels of strategy" (p. 2). In this respect, Spear and Roper (2016) indicated that "[c]ommunicating corporate strategy to employees is critical, in order to guide their behaviour and drive organisational performance" (p. 518). For a better understanding of the concept of corporate strategy, it is necessary to understand first the concept of strategy in general.

Grant (2010) explained that "[i]n its broadest sense, strategy is the means by which individuals or organizations achieve their objectives" (p. 16). Grant (2010) also pointed out the following: (a) "Common to definitions of business strategy is the notion that strategy is focused on achieving certain goals" (p. 16); (b) "the critical actions that make up a strategy involve allocation of resources" (p. 16); and (c) "strategy implies some consistency, integration, or cohesiveness of decisions and actions" (p. 16). Along these same lines, Johnson, Scholes, and Whittington (2008)indicated that strategy is "the direction and scope of an organisation over the long term, which achieves [an] advantage in a changing environment through its configuration of resources and competences with the aim of fulfilling stakeholder expectations" (p. 3).

Johnson, Scholes, and Whittington (2008) explained that the levels of strategy in an organization are the following: (a) corporate-level strategy, (b) business-level strategy and (c) operational strategies (p. 7). Johnson, Scholes, and Whittington (2008)also emphasized that the corporate-level strategy is "concerned with the overall scope of an organisation and how value will be added to the different parts (business units) of the organization" (p. 7) and that "[t]his could include issues of geographical coverage, diversity of products/services or business units, and how resources are to be allocated between the different parts of the organisation" (p. 7). Finally, Johnson, Scholes, and Whittington (2008) pointed out: "Being clear about corporate-level strategy is important: determining the range of business to include is the basis of other strategic decisions" (p. 7). Then the corporate strategy could be defined as the strategy of the organization at the top level, which includes the allocation of resources, the processes and the products of the business units and the relationships with the organizations in its environment for obtaining or for improving the expected results.

The impact of corporate strategies on innovation

Various studies about the impact of mergers, acquisitions and spin-offs in different countries were found in the literature review. Those studies are detailed in the following paragraphs.

The impact of mergers and acquisitions on innovation

Some studies about the impact of mergers and acquisitions on innovation were found in the literature review with samples from such diverse sources as Securities Data Corporation Platinum, Center for Research in Security Prices and Compustat (Saboo, Sharma, Chakravarty, and

Kumar, 2017) and such diverse countries as Spain (Cefis and Triguero, 2016), the United States (Kern, Dewenter, and Kerber, 2016; Park and Sonenshine, 2012) and Taiwan (Lin, 2014, 2015). In this respect, Lin (2015) stated that "[o]ne of the innovation sources for firms is to acquire other technological firms" (p. 29).

Saboo, Sharma, Chakravarty and Kumar (2017) studied the effects of the degrees of overlap between the acquiring and target firms in terms of innovation and relational resources on acquisition outcomes using a sample of 129 unique acquirers and 319 targets of biopharmaceutical acquisitions; data were collected from multiple sources such as the Securities Data Corporation (SDC) Platinum, the Center for Research in Security Prices (CRSP) and Compustat (p. 220). The results of the study of Saboo, Sharma, Chakravarty and Kumar (2017, p. 219) revealed that (a) innovation overlap has a positive effect on acquisition outcomes, (b) relational overlap has a negative effect on acquisition outcomes, (c) the acquirer CEO's throughput background and acquisition experience negatively moderate the influence of innovation overlap, (d) the target's innovation resource quality and the acquirer's marketing intensity positively moderate the influence of innovation overlap and (e) "[t]he target's relational resource quality and the acquirer CEO's throughput background positively moderate the influence of relational overlap". Finally, Saboo, Sharma, Chakravarty, and Kumar (2017)stated "[W]e highlight the contingent roles of innovation and relational overlap in influencing acquisition performance and propose that managers should account for such constructs to assess possible means of achieving acquirer–target synergy" (p. 236).

Cefis and Triguero (2016) studied the impacts of mergers and acquisitions (M&A) on corporate R&D strategies with a sample of 4,629 Spanish manufacturing firms in every manufacturing sector since 1990 until 2008 (p. 176), considering the increase or the decrease of innovation input such as in-house R&D, external R&D or both (p. 175). The results of the study showed (a) "M&A has a negative and significant impact on R&D intensity, decreasing in-house R&D and external technological sourcing" (p. 175); (b) "M&A enables the rationalization of R&D capacity, implying a decrease in R&D efforts" (p. 175); and (c) "M&A negatively affects both types of R&D, but, on average, the effect is more negative on external R&D" (p. 175). Lastly, Cefis and Triguero (2016) commented that "M&A neither contributes to making or buying more R&D from third companies" (p. 194) and that "M&A is used to improve the use of existing assets to achieve lower costs and more efficiency derived from adjusting excess or duplicated resources after the acquisition, decreasing the R&D per employee" (p. 194).

Kern, Dewenter, and Kerber (2016) studied the effects of M&A on innovation with a sample of 135 M&A (including 341 different markets), which were listed in the U.S. antitrust agencies the Federal Trade Commission (FTC) and Department of Justice (DOJ) from1995 to2008, and in which the agencies mentioned innovation aspects in the market definition and/or anticompetitive effects. The results of the study of revealed (a) "in one third of all challenged mergers also innovation concerns have been raised (with no significant differences between the agencies)" (p. 373), (b) "[d]espite the wide-spread rejection of the 'innovation market approach' in the antitrust debate the agencies used more often an innovation-specific assessment approach that includes also innovation in the market definition than the traditional product market concept" (p. 373); and (c) "[o]verall, we found both significant similarities and differences as well as some convergence over time in regard to the specifics of the assessment of innovation effects of mergers between both agencies" (p. 373). Finally, Kern, Dewenter, and Kerber (2016) commented that "it is surprising how clearly the new U.S. Horizontal Merger Guidelines still stick to the old product market approach, with the consideration of innovation only in the competitive assessment part, because this contradicts to a large extent the practice of the agencies during our investigation period" (p. 397).

Lin (2015) studied the impact of acquisition on organizational learning with a sample of 224 information firms in Taiwan from the following sectors: computer and associated equipment manufacturing, integrated circuits, opto-electronics and telecommunication, and electronic components. The results of the study of demonstrated that "in the period of incremental change, firms usually adopt related acquisitions and enhance their innovation through exploitation" (p. 29) and that "[c]onversely, in the period of technological ferment, firms usually adopt unrelated acquisitions and enhance their innovation through exploration" (p. 29). Lastly, Lin (2015) commented:

> Longitudinal studies are important because every single acquisition by a large firm is merely a small part of a longitudinal sequence of acquisitions. Consequently, at least in the short term, integration mechanisms are unavoidably imperfect, which results in the decrease of short-term acquisition performance. Understanding acquisitions may hence warrant further investigations of intertemporal changes in strategy, structure, and culture.
>
> *(p. 42)*

Lin (2014) explained that "[c]oncurrent with increased acquisitions, technological development and organizational innovation has gained importance in recent decades" (p. 31) and that "[g]lobal technological change and keen competition have increased the value of technological innovation because it can help firms gain and maintain competitive advantages" (p. 31). Lin (2014) examined "how different M&A strategies affect exploration and exploitation of the combined firm, how post-acquisition integration affects exploration and exploitation of the combined firm, and how organizational ambidexterity affects post-acquisition performance" (p. 30) with a sample of the top 1,000 Taiwanese electronic and computer firms reported by China Credit Information Service in 2009. The results of the study revealed (a) "related acquisitions with high degrees of acquisition integration positively affect the combined firm's exploitation" (p. 30), (b) "unrelated acquisitions with high degrees of R&D expenditure and acquisition experience positively affect the combined firm's exploration" (p. 30) and (c) "[t]he firm's ability of simultaneously pursuing exploitation and exploration positively affects its post-acquisition performance" (p. 30). Finally, Lin (2014) indicated that "[p]erhaps a vertical/related/unrelated acquisition classification may provide better understandings for relationships among acquisition, exploration/exploitation, and performance" (p. 43).

Park and Sonenshine (2012) studied the effects of M&A on innovation activities (considering the R&D, patent grants and citation-weighted patent grants before and after the M&A) with a sample of 78 firms from the United States that were joined from 1989 to 2008 and included four groups: "the full sample of firms, non-merged firms, merged firms that were challenged by the authorities, and those merged firms that were not challenged" (p. 152). The results of the study revealed that "the post-merger innovation outcomes of firms whose mergers were challenged are lower than they would have been had the firms not merged" (p. 143) and (b) "for non-challenged mergers, or mergers that do not raise concerns about market concentration, post-merger innovation outcomes are not significantly different from what they would have been without a merger" (p. 143). Finally, for future researches, Park and Sonenshine (2012) recommended:

> First, our empirical analysis has some implications for theoretical research. Models studying the impact of market concentration on innovation should be conditioned on whether excessive market power results, perhaps due to the combination of mergers

and barriers to entry. Models should also study the effects of mergers beyond product markets and analyze the resulting concentration in innovation markets. The ultimate impact on innovation may reside in what transpires in the innovation market. Second, the empirical work could be extended to study the total factor productivity of challenged mergers versus non-challenged mergers (using the approach in Bertrand and Zitouna 2008) or to apply the innovation market analysis to cross border mergers and acquisitions.

(p. 164)

The impact of spin-offs on innovation

Some studies about the impact of spin-offs on innovation were found in the literature review with samples from such diverse countries as Germany (Abou, 2017), the United States (Woolley, 2017), Ireland (Curran, Van Egeraat, and O'Gorman, 2016) and Israel (Frenkel, Israel, and Maital, 2015). About the sources of spin-offs, Woolley, 2017 indicated that "[s]pin-off firms originate from several sources including universities, existing firms, and government research centers" (p. 64).

Abou (2017) explained that "[s]pinoffs represent an important means to introduce new technologies, products and services to the market that would otherwise be left unexploited" (p. 203) and that "[a]bundant opportunities within corporations as well as entrepreneurial-driven employees form the blend for spinoff foundations" (p. 203). Abou (2017)also explained that "[s]ince not every opportunity can be seized, thoroughly evaluated and realized within corporations, spinoffs are an alternative route for these opportunities to be exploited" (p. 203) and that "[s]pinoff founders thereby use the knowledge and experience gained during their previous employment" (p. 203). Abou (2017) studied innovation performance considering the product innovation and the corporate parent support with a sample of 1,325 spin-off observations of German startups in the year 2009 (p. 211). The results of the study revealed that "obstructive interference by a corporate parent is positively associated with innovation performance of a spinoff – especially compared to spinoffs that receive parent support" (p. 203) and that "results are mainly driven by high-tech industry branches" (p. 203).

Woolley (2017) studied "academic, corporate, and government spinoffs as well as other start-ups across five outcomes including firm cessation, acquisition, liquidation, bankruptcy, venture capital, and government small business innovation funding" (p. 64) with a sample of 226 US nanotechnology firms founded between 1981 and 2002. About the sample, Woolley (2017) indicated that "[t]he sample of firms here represents what are considered the 'hard sciences' such as engineering, physics, chemistry, and biology" (p. 85). The results of the study demonstrated that "lineage, both in terms of intellectual property and founder background, does influence outcomes; however, each type of firm origin has provocative distinctions" (p. 64). Lastly, Woolley (2017) stated "[t]hese findings unpack the categorization of spin-off firms to clarify the role of early knowledge transfer mechanisms and initial resource portfolios" (p. 64).

Curran, Van Egeraat and O'Gorman (2016) studied the spin-offs (university and private sector spin-offs) and the inherited competence (R&D competence and innovation competence) of the Irish biotech industry. About the data collection, Curran, Van Egeraat, and O'Gorman (2016) explained that "[q]ualitative data on the different types of knowledge and competence possessed by spin-off firms within the Irish biotech industry was collected via semi-structured interviews" (p. 448) and that "[i]nterviews were conducted with actors in 10 biotech spin-off firms, 2 venture capital firms, industrial development agencies and with other industry experts" (p. 448). The results of the study showed (a) "differences in pre-entry experience manifest themselves most markedly in terms of the firm's capacity to attract venture capital, with private sector spin-offs considerably outperforming university spin-offs" (p. 443) and (b) "the superior performance of the private sector spin-offs is explained by the nature of their inherited competence in that they are characterized by higher levels of innovation competence" (p. 443). Finally, Curran, Van Egeraat, and O'Gorman (2016) suggested the following:

> These findings have a number of implications for industrial policy in the context of the science-based industry. Recent policy in Ireland and elsewhere has been characterized by a strong focus on stimulating university spin-offs. The formative role of private sector spinoffs in industry evolution suggests that policymakers should at least pay as much attention to stimulating private sector spin-offs as to university spin-offs, and should be mindful of the proportion of industrial promotion agencies' resources that are directed to each of these cohorts. Government agencies should leverage the role of private sector spin-off processes and specifically, within that, the role of high competence parents such as Elan.
>
> *(p. 458)*

Frenkel, Israel, and Maital (2015) realized an in-depth analysis of RAD Bynet, an Israeli startup that was founded in 1981 and gave rise to 129 other startups employing 15,000 workers, according to the vision of its founder (p. 1646), with a sample of 57 firms in RAD's ecosystem. The results of the study of Frenkel, Israel, and Maital (2015) revealed (a) "social and technological proximity encourages the tendency of the companies to maintain business relationships that probably contribute to knowledge exchange, while technological diversity drives innovation and startup formation" (p. 1646) and (b) "firms will choose to cooperate on the basis of a shared past and personal proximity relations, as well as technological proximity at a certain level" (p. 1646). Lastly, Frenkel, Israel, and Maital (2015) commented that "'viral clouds' of startups like the one we studied can thus intentionally be designed and developed" (p. 1646).

Leadership and innovation

Eisele (2017) explained that "[a]lthough many factors besides leadership have been found to affect organizational innovation, leadership style has been identified as being one of the most important factor" (p. 478). For a better understanding of the impact of the leadership on innovation, first it is necessary to understand the concept of leadership and the diverse leadership styles. In this regard, Rajeh, Fais, Ali, and Abdullahi (2017) stated that "[l]eadership effectiveness is a complex concept that is very challenging to describe as it encapsulates varying components including several organizational contingencies interspersed with personal and interpersonal behaviors" (p. 392). Rajeh, Fais, Ali, and Abdullahi (2017) also indicated that an inclusive notable leadership effectiveness definition refers to "the successful exercise of personal influence by an individual or more that leads to the achievement of shared objectives in such a way that satisfies all the involved individuals" (p. 392). Additionally, Johnson, Scholes, and Whittington (2008) pointed out that "[l]eadership is the process of influencing an organisation (or group within an organization) in its efforts towards achieving an aim or goal" (p. 598). In this section, the details of the impacts of the leadership styles on innovation are presented. A list of the studies related to the impact of the leadership styles on innovation appears in Table 7.1.

Table 7.1 Studies related to the impact of leadership styles on innovation

Type of leadership	Related study
Directive	(Howaldt, Oeij, Dhondt, and Fruytier, 2016; Breevaart, Bakker, Demerouti, and Derks, 2016; Kesting, Ulhøi, Song, and Niu, 2015; Bell, Chan, and Nel, 2014; Somech, 2005, 2006)
Participative	(Lumbasi, K'Aol, and Ouma, 2016; Kesting, Ulhøi, Song, and Niu, 2015; Sagnak, 2016; Malik, 2013; Hoch, 2013; Somech, 2005, 2006)
Interactive	(Meier, Sachs, Stutz, and McSorley, 2017; Kesting, Ulhøi, Song, and Niu, 2015; Hussain, Ali, and Arshad, 2014)
Charismatic	(Lee, Chen, and Lee, 2015; Kesting, Ulhøi, Song, and Niu, 2015)
Transformational	(Kesting, Ulhøi, Song, and Niu, 2015; Oladimeji and Ndubuisi, 2017; Ullah, Ab Hamid, and Shahzad, 2016; Chen, Zheng, Yang, and Bai, 2016; Prasad and Junni, 2016; Khalili, 2016; Slåtten and Mehmetoglu, 2015; Kao, Pai, Lin, and Zhong, 2015; Sagnak, Kuruoz, Polat, and Soylu, 2015; Chang, 2014)
Transactional/Instrumental	(Sethibe and Steyn, 2015; Kesting, Ulhøi, Song, and Niu, 2015)
Strategic/CEO	(Kesting, Ulhøi, Song, and Niu, 2015)
Shared	(Kesting, Ulhøi, Song, and Niu, 2015)
Distributed	(Kesting, Ulhøi, Song, and Niu, 2015)
Family	(Nieto, Santamaria, and Fernandez, 2015; Lodh, Nandy, and Chen, 2014)
Paternalistic	(Fu, Li, and Si, 2013)
Ambidextrous	(Ahlers and Wilms, 2017; Zacher and Rosing, 2015)
Humorous	(Pundt, 2015; Ho, Wang, Huang, and Chen, 2011)
Authentic	(Zhou, Ma, Cheng, and Xia, 2014; Avolio et al., 2004)
Structuring	(Pei, 2017)
Entrepreneurial	(Bagheri and Akbari, 2018; Lope, Asimiran, and Bagheri, 2014)
Developmental	(Kwon and Cho, 2016; Keller, Fehér, Vidra, and Virág, 2015)
Female	(Flabbi, Piras, and Abrahams, 2016; Xie and Pang, 2018; Chao and Tian, 2011; Dezsö and Ross, 2012)

The impact of directive leadership on innovation

Howaldt, Oeij, Dhondt, and Fruytier (2016) stated that "hierarchical organisational structures may lead to more directive leadership styles and human resource management (HRM) practices that focus on a clear division of labour and control, whereas less hierarchical structures may lead to leadership styles" (p. 3). In this respect, Breevaart, Bakker, Demerouti, and Derks (2016) explained that "directive leadership had a stronger negative effect, when employees were high on the need for autonomy" (p. 312).

Kesting, Ulhøi, Song, and Niu (2015) stated that "[a]ccording to Lornikova et al. (2013, p. 573), directive leadership 'is associated with a leader's positional power and is characterized by behaviors aimed at actively structuring subordinates' work by providing clear directions and expectations regarding compliance with instructions'" (p. 26) and that in the directive leadership, "the final decision-making power rests with the leader" (p. 26). Bell, Chan, and Nel (2014) explained that "[d]irective leadership is defined as the process of providing the subordinates with a guideline for decision making and action that is in favour with a leader's perspective (Fiedler, 1995; Sagie, 1997)" (p. 1973). Bell, Chan, and Nel (2014) also explained that "directive leadership has a positive and significant impact on most of the facets of organisational culture with the exception of adaptability" (p. 1981). Additionally, the results of the study of Somech (2006) about the relationships of the participative and the directive leadership with the functionality of a heterogeneous team's process and outcomes (with a sample of 136 primary care teams of the largest health maintenance organization in Israel) showed that "[t]he impact of directive leadership was in promoting team reflection under the condition of low functional heterogeneity, whereas no such impact was found under the condition of high functional heterogeneity" (p. 132).

After a literature review, Somech (2005) commented that "[o]verall, the results indicated that a more participative style produced more creative and more worthwhile projects than a directive style" (p. 781). However, Somech (2005) studied the impact of the directive versus participative leadership on the effectiveness (team in-role performance and team innovation) with a sample of 140 teams of 140 different elementary schools in northern Israel. The results of the study revealed "a positive relation between directive leadership and organizational commitment, as well as a positive relation between directive leadership and school-staff team in-role performance" (p. 777) and that "[i]n addition, organizational commitment served as a mediator in the directive leadership–performance relationship" (p. 777).

The impact of participative leadership on innovation

Lumbasi, K'Aol, and Ouma (2016) explained that according to Malik (2013), participative leader behavior "is effective for attaining high employee performance because the leader consults with subordinates in setting, clarifying and achieving goals and also indicated that there is significant correlation between all the four path-goal leadership styles and employee performance" (p. 2348). Kesting, Ulhøi, Song, and Niu (2015) explained that "Somech (2006, p. 135) defines participative leadership as 'shared influence in decision making'" (p. 26) and that in participative leadership, "the final decision-making power rests with the leader" (p. 26).

Sagnak (2016) studied "the mediating role of intrinsic motivation on the relationship between participative leadership and change-oriented organizational behavior" (p. 200) with a sample of 850 teachers randomly selected from 68 elementary schools in Nigde, Turkey. The results of the study were as follows: (a) participative leadership was a significant predictor of change-oriented organizational citizenship behavior and intrinsic motivation (p. 200), (b) a significant relationship between change-oriented organizational citizenship behavior and intrinsic motivation was present (p. 200) and (c) intrinsic motivation fully mediated the relationship between participative leadership and change-oriented organizational behavior (p. 200).

> Hoch (2013) investigated the relationship between shared leadership and innovative behavior with a sample of 43 work teams (184 team members and their team leaders from two firms) with self-evaluations of team leaders and evaluations of the team members of the personality and shared leadership of the team leaders. The results of the study demonstrated (a) "[s]hared and vertical leadership, but not team composition, was positively associated with the teams' level of innovative behavior" (p. 159) and (b) "[v]ertical transformational and empowering leadership and team composition in terms of integrity were positively related to shared leadership" (p. 159). Finally, Hoch (2013) indicated the implications of the results of the study as follows:
>
>> Understanding how organizations can enhance their own innovation is crucial for the organizations' competitiveness and survival. Furthermore, the increasing prevalence of teams, as work arrangements in organizations, raises the question of how to successfully manage teams. This study suggests that organizations should facilitate shared leadership which has a positive association with innovation.
>>
>> *(p. 159)*

Somech (2006) studied the relationships of participative and directive leadership with the functionality of a heterogeneous team's process and outcomes, with a sample of 136 primary care teams of the largest health maintenance organization in Israel. The results of the study showed that "in high functionally heterogeneous teams, participative leadership style was positively associated with team reflection, which in turn fostered team innovation; however, this leadership style decreased team in-role performance" (p. 132). Additionally, the results of the study about the impact of the directive versus participative leadership on the effectiveness of team in-role performance and team innovation (with a sample of 140 teams of 140 different elementary schools in northern Israel) revealed "a positive relation between participative leadership and teachers' empowerment, and a positive relation between participative leadership and school-staff team innovation, and empowerment served as a mediator in the participative leadership–innovation relationship" (p. 777).

The impact of interactive leadership on innovation

Meier, Sachs, Stutz, and McSorley (2017) explained that "[t]he interactive leadership understanding allows the integration of such essential characteristics and effects of digitalization as network orientation, innovation capabilities or enhanced team cooperation" (p. 104). Meier, Sachs, Stutz, and McSorley (2017) also explained that

> In the more interactive understanding of leadership on which this project is based, a collective that shares work produces together in ongoing interactions three outcomes based on collective beliefs and practices: *Direction*, which means widespread agreement on goals, aims and the mission within the collective; *alignment*, which means the organization and coordination of knowledge and work; and *commitment*, which includes the willingness of collective-members to subsume their own interests.
>
> *(p. 104)*

Kesting, Ulhøi, Song, and Niu (2015) explained that in the study of Rosener (1990) four core characteristics of interactive leadership were found: "encouragement for participation, widespread sharing of information and power, efforts to enhance self-worth of employees, and energizing employees for different work tasks" (p. 27). Kesting, Ulhøi, Song, and Niu (2015) also explained that interactive leadership has an "unspecified positive effect on innovativeness and innovation success" (p. 28). Hussain, Ali, and Arshad (2014) indicated that "interactive leadership has its roots in participative management approaches, in transformational leadership theories, and in situation – contingent models of leadership" (p. 59).

The impact of charismatic leadership on innovation

Under the framework of internal marketing, the results of the study of Lee, Chen, and Lee (2015) revealed (a) "[i]nternal marketing will positively affect the organizational commitment" (p. 68), (b) "[o]rganizational commitment will positively affect performance" (p. 68) and (c) "[c]harismatic leadership will enhance the effect of organizational commitment and performance" (p. 68). Finally, Lee, Chen, and Lee (2015) concluded:

> This study finds out that when the organization provides education and training, reward system and good communication channels, employees can effectively improve organizational commitment, dedication to the organization over the long term and

are willing to stay; further increase their skills and knowledge of company, to bring better performance. In addition, managers can enhance the effect of organizational commitment to performance. In other words, charismatic leader can lead and influence employees, is the cornerstone of a successful business. Finally, the expected results of this study can provide a reference of charismatic leadership to academic, and also help companies improve their performance and to maintain the competitive advantage with the right thinking.

(p. 68)

Kesting, Ulhøi, Song, and Niu (2015)stated that "[a]ccording to Weber, charismatic leadership is 'resting on devotion to the exceptional sanctity, heroism or exemplary character of an individual person' (1921/78, p. 215)" (p. 28) and that "[i]n the same vein, Shamir et al., 1993 argue that creating a sense of collective identity is essential to being a charismatic leader" (p. 28). Kesting, Ulhøi, Song, and Niu (2015) also explained that "[t]here is ample evidence that charismatic leadership can increase commitment, generate energy, and direct individuals towards new objectives, values or aspirations (Nadler and Tushman, 1990; James and Lahti, 2011)" (p. 28). Additionally, Kesting, Ulhøi, Song, and Niu (2015) pointed out that "Avolio et al., 1991 have noted that charismatic leaders create admiration, respect, loyalty, and a collective sense of mission" (p. 28) and that "[i]n accordance with that, other studies have established a positive link between charismatic leadership and perceived team innovativeness (Eisenbach et al., 1999; Paulsen et al., 2009)" (p. 28). Finally, Kesting, Ulhoi, Song, and Niu (2015) commented:

However, there are strong indications that charisma alone is not sufficient to make innovations a commercial success (Nadler and Tushman, 1990). In a study by Bossink, 2004, the failure of an innovation project was found to be related to the inability of a charismatic leader to participate in a knowledge network and collect professional information. Bossink further supports this finding in a follow-up study (2007, p. 140), finding that a charismatic leader was not able to "absorb useful information and knowledge during the project".

(p. 28)

Impact of transformational leadership on innovation

Various authors have explained the relationships between transformational leadership and innovation (Kesting, Ulhøi, Song, and Niu, 2015; Oladimeji and Ndubuisi, 2017; Ullah, Ab Hamid, and Shahzad, 2016; Chen, Zheng, Yang, and Bai, 2016; Prasad and Junni, 2016; Khalili, 2016; Slåtten and Mehmetoglu, 2015; Kao, Pai, Lin, and Zhong, 2015; Sagnak, Kuruoz, Polat, and Soylu, 2015; Chang, 2014). In this regard, Kesting, Ulhøi, Song, and Niu (2015) explained: "Yukl 1989 sees the main motivation of transformational leadership research in the conceptualization of an appropriate style to transform organizations" (p. 29) and stated that "transformational leadership is also the most actively researched leadership style with regard to innovations and change" (p. 29).

Oladimeji and Ndubuisi (2017)evaluated the factors which determine employees' creative and innovative undertakings in the oil and gas industry in Nigeria with a sample of 414 randomly selected employees of four oil and gas service firms in Lagos between 19 and 61 years old with validated scales of employee creativity and innovation, transformational leadership and organizational culture. The results of the study of revealed (a) transformational leadership has a significant impact on employee creativity, (b) transformational leadership has a significant impact on employee innovation, (c) organizational culture has a significant impact on employee creativity, (d) organizational culture has a significant impact on employee innovation and (e) transformational leadership and organizational culture significantly interacted to affect employee creativity and employee innovation (p. 325). Finally, Oladimeji and Ndubuisi (2017) recommended that "oil and gas service companies can facilitate employee creativity and innovation by promoting and investing in transformational leadership training of their managerial staff as well as instituting [and] enabling an innovative organisational culture" (p. 325).

Ullah, Ab Hamid, and Shahzad (2016) studied the relationships between transformational leadership and knowledge sharing and innovative capability with a sample of 254 randomly selected managers and owners working in the dairy sector of Pakistan. The results of the study were as follows: (a) "leaders play [a] key role in the process of knowledge management, particularly in the knowledge sharing" (p. 94); (b) "[t]ransformational leadership encourages the employees to share their knowledge, skills and experiences with the other employees of the organization" (p. 94); (c) "knowledge sharing upturns the innovation capabilities of the organizations" (p. 95); and (d) "[t]he findings proved the mediation of knowledge sharing in the relationship between transformational leadership and organizational innovation capability" (p. 95). Lastly, Ullah, Ab Hamid, and Shahzad (2016) concluded that "[t]ransformational leaders enhance the knowledge sharing by motivating the followers to share knowledge. And, in turn, knowledge sharing upturns the innovation capabilities of the organization" (p. 95).

Chen, Zheng, Yang, and Bai (2016) investigated the forces driving organizational innovation (particularly CEO transformational leadership) and its effects on external and internal social capital in top management teams with questionnaires sent to 90 Chinese top management teams (p. 843). Chen, Zheng, Yang, and Bai (2016) concluded that "both internal and external social capital mediated the relationship between transformational leadership and organizational innovation" (p. 843). Chen, Zheng, Yang, and Bai (2016) also pointed out that "a social capital focus challenges the tacit assumption that transformational leadership has only internal influences by showing that it potentially spills over to the external domain" (p. 843).

Prasad and Junni (2016) studied the relationships of CEO transformational and transactional leadership with the organizational innovation with a sample of 163 firms in services, manufacturing, construction and other industries in the United States, and their results indicated that both leadership styles influence organizational innovation positively; however, "organizations benefit more from transformational leadership in dynamic environments" (p. 1542). Prasad and Junni (2016) also stated:

> Transformational leaders put in effort to communicate an inspiring shared vision and common goals concerning the firm's future. By communicating about the longer term firm strategy and goals, CEOs can inspire organizational members to think about how the organization could be renewed in order to meet future goals. CEOs that exhibit transformational leadership behaviors are also likely to promote risk-taking and experimentation relating to new activities, processes and tasks (Dess and Picken, 2000), which can promote organizational innovation.
>
> *(p. 1559)*

Khalili (2016) investigated "the association between transformational leadership and employees' creativity and innovation. Additionally, this study explored the moderating role of employees' perceptions of a supportive climate for innovation" (p. 2277) with a sample of 1,172 employees of various types of industries in Iran. Khalili (2016) also explained: "that the findings indicated a supportive climate for innovation moderated the transformational leadership-employees' creativity and transformational leadership-employees' innovation relationships" (p. 2277). Finally, Khalili (2016) pointed out: "Organisations should invest in transformational leadership training and in the selection of leaders with this leadership style if their aim is to foster and enhance employees' creativity and innovation" (p. 2277) and that "[t]hey also should invest in organisational climate improvement in order to provide a dynamic platform for being creative and innovative in the workplace" (p. 2277).

Slátten and Mehmetoglu (2015) studied the effects of transformational leadership and perceived creativity on innovation behavior in the hospitality industry with a sample of 345 hospitality frontline employees. The results of the study demonstrated that "both transformational leadership and employee service creativity influence innovative behavior significantly" (p. 195) and "these effects are indeed moderated by time in that despite initially different magnitudes, they approach each other over time" (p. 195). Finally, Slátten and Mehmetoglu (2015) indicated:

> One practical implication for hospitality managers is the importance of cultivating frontline employees' creativity. However, it is important to note that managers must consider the desire and need for creativity in relation to the type of job and specific work tasks. Clearly, for some types of jobs or work tasks, managers may not want their employees to do anything other than follow the policy manual. On the other hand, there could be types of jobs and work tasks where managers provide the opportunity for their employees to be creative and innovative in their behavior (e.g. when turning a dissatisfied customer into a satisfied customer and doing what is necessary to keep the customer loyal to the company). Consequently, managers must decide on the basis of the specific type of job, work task or company policy in general, whether their employees should either strictly follow the policy manual or be given (some degree of) freedom to be creative and innovative in performing their job or work task.
>
> (p. 212)

Kao, Pai, Lin, and Zhong (2015) studied the relationship between transformational leadership (TFL) and service innovation behavior with a dual-perspective approach that includes motivational and sociopolitical perspectives with a sample of 269 employees and 1,396 customers of hair salons in Taiwan. The results of the study showed (a) "the perceived organizational climate for innovation, creative self-efficacy, and expected image gains fully mediate the relationship between TFL and employees' service innovation behavior" (p. 448); (b) "TFL positively influences employees' perceived organizational climate for innovation, which in turn enhances the service innovation behavior of employees through both motivational (i.e. creative self-efficacy) and social political (i.e. expected image gains) mediating mechanisms" (p. 448); and (c) "image risks are found to have a non-significant relationship with service innovation behavior" (p. 448).

Sagnak, Kuruoz, Polat, and Soylu (2015) investigated "the mediating effect of psychological empowerment on the relationship between transformational leadership and innovative climate" (p. 150) with a sample of 301 teachers of Eskisehir Central Secondary School. The results of the study revealed (a) "there was a significant positive relationship between transformational leadership and psychological empowerment" (p. 150); (b) "[a] significant positive relationship was found between psychological empowerment and innovative climate" (p. 150); (c) "[t]he stepwise regression analysis showed a significant relationship between transformational leadership and innovative climate" (p. 150); (d) "[a]ccording to the Sobel test results, the relationship between transformational leadership and innovative climate was decreasing but significant" (p. 150); and (e) "[t]herefore, it has been determined that psychological empowerment partially mediated the relationship between transformational leadership and innovative climate" (p. 150). Finally, Sagnak, Kuruoz, Polat, and Soylu (2015) concluded and recommended:

> Transformational leadership affects [an] innovative climate both directly and indirectly through psychological empowerment. However, research about psychological empowerment in educational organizations and innovation and creativity at schools is very limited. In relation to this study, the effect of the leadership roles of principals, on the level of the psychological empowerment of teachers on their innovative and creative behaviors, can be examined.
>
> (p. 150)

Chang (2014) proposed a multilevel framework for studying the effects of multilevel TFL in management innovation and innovation in general, with a sample composed of 169 managers and 423 employees of 141 units from 21 banking service firms in an emerging economy and the application of the hierarchical linear modeling analysis (p. 265). The results of the study demonstrated (a) "unit-level TFL was positively related to unit-level management innovation" (p. 265); (b) "firm-level TFL was positively associated with [a] firm-level empowerment climate, which in turn enhanced unit-level management innovation" (p. 265); (c) "[a] firm-level empowerment climate strengthened the relationship between unit-level TFL and unit-level management innovation" (p. 265); and (d) "the unit-level trust mediates the relationship between [the] firm-level empowerment climate and unit-level management innovation" (p. 265). Lastly, Chang (2014) explained the practical implications of the results:

> Firms operate more effectively when they generate management innovation. To help ensure the effectiveness of management innovation, it is essential that firms, especially those from the banking sector, encourage their managers to engage in TFL behaviors. The managers must consider how to utilize their TFL behaviors to create trusting relationships in order to achieve the organizational goals. Firms can also take steps to develop a supportive climate of higher levels of autonomy, delegation, freedom and task accountability, in order to promote higher levels of trust at the lower levels of the organizational hierarchy.
>
> (p. 265)

The impact of transactional leadership on innovation

Sethibe and Steyn (2015) explained that "[t]ransactional leaders focus on individuals' self-interest" (p. 333). Sethibe and Steyn (2015) also explained that according to Howell and Avolio (1993), "transactional leadership as a leadership style in which a leader-follower relationship is based on a series of exchanges or bargains between leaders and followers" (p. 330) and that transactional leadership, according to Golla and Johnson (2013) is: "a style of leadership that focuses on individual self-interest and motivates individuals though rewards" (p. 330). After their systematic review, Sethibe and Steyn (2015) concluded that "innovation is significantly and positively related to superior organisational performance, and that, although [a] transformational leadership style is significantly and positively related to innovation, [a] transactional leadership style is more appropriate when the aim is to instil a culture of innovation" (p. 325).

Kesting, Ulhøi, Song, and Niu (2015) explained that "researchers agree that, unlike transformational leadership, transactional leadership is not focused on change" (p. 30) and indicated that "[i]ts basic approach is to lead by clear definition and communication of work tasks (Avolio et al., 1991) and rewards and punishments (Bass, 1990a; Eisenbach et al., 1999), focusing on the basic needs of the followers (Daft, 2001)" (p. 30). Kesting, Ulhøi, Song, and Niu (2015) also commented that "[t]he concept of instrumental leadership is less widespread in research. Like transactional leaders, instrumental leaders also employ rewards and punishments, but focus more on goal-setting and control (Nadler and Tushman, 1990)" (p. 30). Additionally, Kesting, Ulhøi, Song, and Niu (2015) pointed out that regarding the effects of transactional/instrumental leadership, the studies showed that "followers indeed develop expectations about rewards that they receive in exchange for meeting a transactional/instrumental leader's expectations (Tracey and Hinkin, 1998), and that they act rather rationally in accordance with this (Deluga, 1990)" (p. 30). Finally, Kesting, Ulhøi, Song, and Niu (2015) indicated:

> In general, transactional leadership is mostly seen as a means to keep things on track during the implementation phase (Howell and Avolio, 1993), and [is] less suitable for the stimulation of new ideas (Pieterse et al., 2010). Thus, Keller, 1992 stated that incremental innovations might be better led by transactional leaders, while radical innovations might be better led by transformational leaders. Sillince, 1994 suggests that transactional leadership might be particularly suited to product innovations and R&D teams, since it helps achieve straightforward goals. However, Bossink, 2004 presents a case where transactional leadership has worked during all the stages.
>
> (p. 31)

The impact of strategic or CEO leadership on innovation

Kesting, Ulhøi, Song, and Niu (2015) stated that "[t]he study of strategic leadership focuses on executives who have overall responsibility for an organization (Finkelstein and Hambrick, 1996, p. 2)" (p. 31) and explained that "[s]everal researchers have pointed to the particular importance of strategic decision-makers (and their hierarchical power) in advancing organizational innovation (Bossink, 2004; Michaelis et al., 2009; Makri and Scandura, 2010)" (p. 31). Kesting, Ulhøi, Song, and Niu (2015) also pointed out: "The basic idea here is that CEOs and other upper-echelon decision-makers can use their institutional power 'to initiate changes that will create a viable future for the organization' (Ireland and Hitt, 2005, p. 45)" (p. 31).

Kesting, Ulhøi, Song, and Niu (2015) explained that "strategic leaders shape the organizational environment by creating organizational structures, processes, and a culture that support innovation (Michaelis et al., 2009; Sternberg et al., 2004)" (p. 31). Kesting, Ulhøi, Song, and Niu (2015) also stated that "strategic leaders serve important innovation roles in that they advance new ideas from the conceptualization phase to the development and commercialization phase (Sternberg et al., 2004; Wong, 2013)" (p. 31) and that they "devote substantial time to discussing technical matters and detailed designs (Nam and Tatum, 1989)" (p. 31). Additionally, Kesting, Ulhøi, Song, and Niu (2015) pointed out: "Research has also shed light on the importance of personal traits that strategic decision-makers need to become successful strategic/CEO leaders" (p. 31). Finally, Kesting, Ulhøi, Song, and Niu (2015) explained that "[a]s regards the effects, Norrgren et al., 1999 found that strategic/CEO leadership generally facilitates employees' innovative capabilities" (p. 31) and that "[c]oncerning the goals, Elenkov et al., 2005 provide some indications that strategic/CEO leadership is suited to supporting both product and organizational innovations" (p. 31).

The impact of shared and distributed leadership on innovation

Kesting, Ulhøi, Song, and Niu (2015) indicated that "[b]oth shared and distributed leadership challenge the (often implicit) assumption of previous leadership styles, that there is only 'one person in charge and the others follow' (Pearce et al., 2009, p. 234)" (p. 32), because there are multiple leaders within a group, and explained that "[a]ccording to Pearce et al. (ibid.), 'Shared leadership can be understood as a dynamic, unfolding, interactive influence process among individuals, where the objective is to lead one another toward the achievement of collective goals'" (p. 32). Kesting, Ulhøi, Song, and Niu (2015) also explained that "[a]ccording to Harris, 2007, the main difference between the two styles is that distributed leadership focuses on the allocation of power and management skills, while shared leadership focuses on the mutual influences among team members or team leaders" (p. 32).

With respect to innovation, Kesting, Ulhøi, Song, and Niu (2015)stated that "research particularly emphasizes the importance of coaching and guidance in making sure that teams are on the right track (Muethel and Hoegl, 2010)" (p. 32) and explained that " Friedrich et al., 2010 point to the importance of rewards in motivating distributed leaders, thereby establishing a link between distributed and transactional/instrumental leadership" (p. 32). Finally, Kesting, Ulhøi, Song, and Niu (2015) pointed out:"Pearce and Manz, 2005 argue that shared leadership appears to be especially important for continuous innovation; but there is no further specification of innovation stages or types" (p. 32).

The impact of family leadership on innovation

Nieto, Santamaria, and Fernandez (2015) investigated innovation behavior in family firms with a sample of 15,173 Spanish manufacturing firms for the period from1998 to2007. The results of the study revealed:

- Regarding innovation effort in family firms:"The negative and significant impact of family firms on R&D intensity squares with the theoretical expectation, thus indicating that family firms undertake fewer innovation efforts than nonfamily firms" (p. 391), which implies that (a) "Regarding firm specificities, the effect of size is positive and highly significant, as would be expected" (p. 391); (b) "Other firm characteristics, such as age and export intensity, also have a positive and significant effect on the decision to perform innovation efforts" (p. 391); (c) "Concerning market characteristics, pressure from main suppliers is negatively related to innovation effort. As expected, higher demand (Expansion) exerts a positive and significant effect on innovation effort" (p. 391); and (d) "our measure of appropriability is negatively and significantly related to innovation effort" (p. 392).
- Regarding innovation sourcing in family firms:"the propensity of family firms to turn to external sources is significantly lower" (p. 392), which implies that (a) "family firms are significantly less prone to collaborate technologically than are nonfamily firms" (p. 392); (b) "the impact of size is positive and highly significant for selecting among the different sources of innovation" (p. 392); (c) "[t]he impact of age, export intensity, foreign capital, and market share are also positive and significant [in terms of]the likelihood of turning to any source of innovation" (p. 392); (d) "[f]inancial constraints have a negative and significant impact on the choice of different sources of innovation" (p. 393); (e) "[h]igher demand has a significant and positive effect on the likelihood of turning to any source of innovation" (p. 393); and (f) "our measure of appropriability is negatively and significantly related to innovation sourcing" (p. 393).

- Regarding innovation results in family firms: "family firms differ significantly from other firms in their innovation results" (p. 393), which implies that (a) "[t]he positive and significant effect of our key variable (Family) on incremental innovations shows that family firms are more likely to achieve incremental innovations than nonfamily firms" (p. 393); (b) "the negative and significant impact of Family on radical innovations shows that family firms are less likely to achieve radical innovations than nonfamily firms" (p. 393); and (c) "[i]nternal activities, contracted sources, and collaboration agreements clearly stand out as critical factors in the generation of product innovations with different degrees of novelty" (p. 394). Finally, Nieto, Santamaria, and Fernandez (2015) explained:

  - Of the controls for firm characteristics, whereas market power (Market share) exerts a positive and significant impact on both measures of product innovation, firm size (Size) only exerts a slightly positive impact on incremental product innovation. Age (Age) has a negative and significant impact on the achievement of incremental innovation. Although export intensity (Export) does not exercise any significant impact on the probability of achieving any type of innovation, the presence of foreign capital (Foreign) has a negative and significant impact on the probability of radical innovations. Regarding market characteristics, pressure from main clients (Client concentration) and suppliers (Supplier concentration) clearly hinders the generation of product innovations (for both degrees of novelty). Growth of demand (Expansion) has a positive and significant effect on the achievement of both types of product innovation. Lastly, appropriability conditions (Appropriability) exert a negative and significant impact on more radical innovations. (p. 394)

Lodh, Nandy, and Chen (2014)studied the direct effect of family ownership on innovation in emerging markets with a sample of a panel of 395 Indian family-controlled publicly listed firms of the Bombay Stock Exchange (BSE) from2001 to2008.The results of the study indicated that (a) "after controlling for possible endogeneity, the impact of family ownership on innovation productivity is positive" (p. 19); (b) "family CEOs reduce innovation activities in India and thus [provide]evidence against CEO duality from an emerging market perspective" (p. 19); and (c) "innovation is impacted by ownership structure and by the lack of supporting institutional frameworks in emerging markets with concentrated family ownership such as India" (p. 19). Finally, Lodh, Nandy, and Chen (2014) recommended that (a) "the Indian government should improve policies on information disclosure and establish more proper corporate governance mechanisms for family businesses" (p. 19); (b) "policymakers should consider improving the corporate governance code and further encourage family firms to have an independent and professional CEO" (p. 19); and (c) "policymakers must investigate the impact of institutional underdevelopment on innovation before reforming ownership structure" (p. 19).

The impact of paternalistic leadership on innovation

Fu, Li, and Si (2013)analyzed the impact of paternalistic leadership on innovation with a sample of 159 Chinese high-tech enterprises in a cross-sectional study. Fu, Li, and Si (2013) also indicated that paternalistic leadership is "the distinctive characteristics of leadership style of senior leaders of the Chinese enterprises" (p. 11) and that "[i]t refers to a similar patriarchal style and with a strong and clear authority, but also has the composition of care, understanding the subordinates, and moral leadership" (p. 11). Fu, Li, and Si (2013) also commented: "According to the magnitude of innovation and knowledge base, innovation can be divided into exploratory innovation and exploitative innovation (Benner and Tushman, 2003; Jansen et al., 2006)" (p. 11). Fu, Li, and Si (2013) further stated:

> The enterprise through exploratory innovation is to design new products, open up new market segments, develop new distribution channels, [and] provide services to new consumer groups. Exploratory innovation puts emphasis on accessing and creating new knowledge, and strives to out of and beyond the enterprise's existing knowledge base (Benner and Tushman, 2003; Jansen et al., 2006).
>
> (p. 11)

Fu, Li, and Shi (2013) also explained that exploitative innovation is "a minor, incremental innovation activity, and its intention is to improve the current situation (March, 1991)" (p. 11) and that "[e]nterprise through the use of innovation is to improve existing product designs, expand existing knowledge and skills, expand and enrich existing product lines, improve the efficiency of the existing distribution channels, [and] provide better service to existing customer groups" (p. 11). They further stated that "[e]xploitative innovation relies on the enterprise's existing knowledge foundation for the support and emphasizes existing knowledge to extract, integrate, strengthen and improve (Benner and Tushman, 2003; Jansen et al., 2006)" (p. 11).

Fu, Li, and Shi (2013) concluded that (a) "authoritarianism has a directly negative effect on exploitative innovation and positively moderates the effectiveness of exploitative innovation" (p. 9); (b) "benevolence has a directly positive effect both on exploratory innovation and exploitative innovation" (p. 9); and (c) "benevolence negatively moderates the effectiveness of exploratory innovation and positively moderates the effectiveness of exploitative innovation" (p. 9). They also commented that "If properly used, patriarchal leadership with both authoritarianism and benevolence will effectively enhance innovation performance. Conversely, it may produce negative effects" (p. 9).

The impact of ambidextrous leadership on innovation

Ahlers and Wilms (2017) investigated the relationships between ambidextrous leadership and innovation, considering their opening and closing behaviors with semi structured interviews of a sample of five leaders in diverse positions: senior project coordinator, innovation manager, divisional director of R&D, head of acoustics in research and innovation and head of product development, corresponding to five manufacturing firms in Germany. The results of the study revealed the following:

- Regarding the occurrence of the two leader behaviors through the innovation process: (a) "the cases predominantly use opening leader behaviors in the early stages of the innovation process" (p. 79); (b) "[i]n contrast, closing leader behaviors are rather used in the later phases" (p. 79); and (c) "the findings of the multiple case study indicated that both leader behaviors occur throughout the whole innovation process" (p. 79).
- In order to demonstrate opening leader behaviors, (a) "several cases stressed the enforcement of principles such as an 'error culture' and 'fail faster'" (p. 79); (b) "[f]urthermore, four cases reportedly set up creative workshops or innovation days" (p. 79); (c) "[m]oreover, the cases often take responsibilities for risks and mistakes so their subordinates do not have to worry about possible negative consequences" (p. 79); (d) "[o]n the contrary, the cases described the way they make use of closing leader behaviors more carefully and rather

reluctantly" (p. 79); and (e) "the empirical findings revealed that the effects of closing leader behaviors on subordinates can be restricted by demonstrating opening leader behaviors and vice versa" (p. 79).

Regarding ambidextrous leaders, Zacher and Rosing (2015) explained that they "need to be able to support and encourage both exploration and exploitation behaviors on [the] part of their followers as these are the essential activities in the innovation process" (p. 57). Zacher and Rosing (2015) also explained that the ambidexterity theory of leadership for innovation proposed that "the interaction between two complementary leadership behaviors – opening and closing behaviors – predicts individual and team innovation, such that innovation is highest when both opening and closing leadership behaviors are high (Rosing et al., 2011)" (p. 55) and that "leaders who have the ability to engage in both opening and closing behaviors should be most successful in terms of encouraging innovation among their followers" (p. 55).

Zacher and Rosing (2015) studied the ambidexterity theory of leadership for innovation with a sample of 33 team leaders of 27 architectural and six interior design firms and 90 of their employees in Australia. The results of the study revealed the following:

- "[O]pening leadership behavior (rated by employees) positively predicted team innovation (rated by team leaders), whereas closing leadership behavior did not have a significant main effect" (p. 62).
- "[T]eam innovation was highest when both opening and closing leadership behaviors were high, whereas team innovation was lower when only one of these leadership behaviors was high or when both behaviors were low. This effect was found even after controlling for team leaders' ratings of general team success and employee ratings of leaders' transformational leadership behaviors" (p. 62).
- "These findings suggest that team leaders need to engage in both opening and closing behaviors to produce high levels of team innovation. As can be expected considering the complexity of innovation processes, a combination of these leadership behaviors is more successful in terms of facilitating team innovation than high levels of opening leadership behavior alone or low levels of both opening and closing behaviors" (p. 63).
- "The findings further suggest that leadership behaviors exist that predict team innovation above and beyond transformational leadership which, so far, has generally been considered the most successful type of leadership behavior in terms of facilitating team innovation (Rosing et al., 2011)" (p. 63).

The impact of humorous leadership on innovation

Pundt (2015) studied "the relationship between humorous leadership and innovative behavior and the moderator effects of creative requirement and perceived innovation climate, beyond transformational leadership, and leader-member exchange (LMX)" (p. 878) with a sample of 150 employees of various firms in Germany, and his results revealed that "[e]mployees whose leader used humor more frequently [were] reported to be more innovative, when the employees perceived their tasks to require creativity and innovation" (p. 878) and that a "[p]erceived innovation climate did not moderate the relationship" (p. 878). Pundt (2015) also explained that "[h]umorous leadership is an important element of innovation-relevant leadership behavior" (p. 878) and that "[i]ts use may be integrated in broader leadership development approaches" (p. 878).

Ho, Wang, Huang, and Chen (2011) explained that "[f]or leaders at [the] workplace, humorous leadership may not be the primary criterion for business success but it is very important for building an effective team with high performance" (p. 6675) and that "[q]uite a few studies show that humorous leadership has a direct or indirect influence on the performance of individuals and teams" (p. 6675). Ho, Wang, Huang, and Chen (2011) also described four different humor styles: (a) self-enhancing humor, which is "a positive humor style in favor of oneself" (p. 6676) and "a humorous attitude toward their life" (p. 6676); (b) affiliate humor, which is a "positive humor style in favor of others" (p. 6676) and "spontaneous jocose and also a type of non-hostile humor" (p. 6676); (c) aggressive humor, which is "a negative humor style detrimental to others" (p. 6676) and "unhealthy humor based on the superiority theory that the speaker is better than others" (p. 6676); and (d) self-defeating humor, which is "a negative humor style detrimental to oneself" (p. 6677).

Ho, Wang, Huang, and Chen (2011) evaluated the relationships among humor styles, innovative behavior and leadership effectiveness with a sample of 381subordinated people with leaders or bosses with at least 5subordinated people in corporations in Taiwan. Their results revealed that (a) "self-enhancing humor has a significantly positive influence on leaders' innovative behavior" (p. 6679); (b) "the more leaders can express their self-enhancing humor style, the more likely they have innovative behavior" (p. 6679); (c) "aggressive humor has a significantly negative influence on innovative behavior" (p. 6679); and (d) "[the more] leaders [are] more aggressive in their sense of humor, the more unlikely they will have innovative behavior, only that the degree of influence is not significant" (p. 6679). Finally, Ho, Wang, Huang, and Chen (2011) recommended that (a) "leaders or department heads should deal with the ever-changing and competitive environment by frequently applying self-enhancing humor at [the] workplace and avoiding the use of aggressive humor in interpersonal communications" (p. 6682); (b) "[f]or organizations, a proactive approach is to include self-enhancing humor as one of the criteria in the selection of prospective department heads and to emphasize the development of self-enhancing humor in subsequent trainings" (p. 6682); and (c) "future studies focusing on cross-cultural comparisons between different industries or nationalities may serve as an important reference to humorous leadership at [the] workplace" (p. 6682).

The impact of authentic leadership on innovation

Avolio et al. (2004) perceived authentic leaders as "persons who have achieved high levels of authenticity in that they know who they are, what they believe and value, and they act upon those values and beliefs while transparently interacting with others" (p. 803). Avolio et al. (2004) also considered authentic leadership "a root construct that can incorporate transformational and ethical leadership" (p. 807).

Zhou, Ma, Cheng, and Xia (2014) studied the relationships between authentic leadership (AL), the employees' emotions and employee innovation, with control variables such as gender, age, education level and job tenure (p. 1273). Zhou, Ma, Cheng, and Xia (2014) explained that "[a]uthentic leadership is considered an individual style inherent to the leader, heightening segmented constructs like transformational and ethical leadership (Rego et al., 2012)" (p. 1269) and that "[a]uthentic leaders possess self-awareness and use this knowledge to learn from themselves and to develop their followers (Neider and Schriesheim, 2011)" (p. 1269). Zhou, Ma, Cheng, and Xia (2014) also explained that in the authentic leadership:

> leaders with a high level of self-awareness may influence the followers' thinking, motivation, and choice of behaviors in the following ways: balanced processing allows authentic leaders to practice relatively unbiased information processing from a more holistic perspective; internal moral perspective guides leaders to insist on upholding

moral values and behave in a prosocial and ethical manner in the face of adversity and conflict with tradition; rational transparency refers to leader behaviors of sharing information and creating honest, open, and trustful exchanges with followers (Walumbwa et al., 2008).

(p. 1269)

The results of the study of Zhou, Ma, Cheng, and Xia (2014) were as follows: (a) "leaders using an authentic leadership style encourage employee innovation through evoking positive emotions in their individual team members" (p. 1274); (b) "team AL was positively associated with members' innovation" (p. 1274); (c) "[t]eam AL was positively related to employees' positive emotions" (p. 1274); (d) "the effect of team AL on employee innovation was significant when considering employees' positive emotions" (p. 1274); (e) "employees' positive emotions were positively related to employee innovation" (p. 1274); and (f) "[t]his result implies a partial mediating effect of employees' positive emotions on the cross-level relationship between AL and employee innovation" (p. 1274). Finally, Zhou, Ma, Cheng, and Xia (2014) stated:

Diverse research designs, such as longitudinal or experimental studies, are recommended to examine the relationship between AL and employee innovation more deeply. Because we only identified a partial mediator, other variables that play an important mediating role in the mechanism need to be assessed in future studies.

(p. 1277)

The impact of structuring leadership on innovation

Pei (2017) studied the "influence of structuring leadership on [the] team innovation climate and its subsequent effect on team creativity" (p. 369) with a sample of 54 participant teams working in Chinese high-tech firms (p. 369). Regarding the structuring leadership, Pei (2017) explained that "[t]he behavioral manifestations of structuring leadership include high-performance demands, regulation, and training of team members (Chen, 2011)" (p. 370) and that "[w]hen there is structuring leadership, this involves team members making continual improvement and extra effort in the work environment, while, at the same time, the style of leadership is subordinate-oriented" (p. 370). Pei (2017) also explained "[w]hen challenging team goals are set by structuring leaders this facilitates team creativity (Anderson et al., 2014)" (p. 370).

Regarding team creativity, Pei (2017) stated that this is defined as "the generation of new ideas and valuable solutions that are based on collective efforts and a collaborative exchange of perspectives and information (Carmeli and Paulus, 2015)" (p. 370) and that "[r]esearchers have found that leadership has a major impact on team creativity, with [the] team innovation climate playing a mediating role (Carmeli et al., 2014; Zubair et al., 2015)" (p. 370). Pei (2017) also stated that "[i]n a team innovation climate, individuals abandon their individual agendas and work together to accomplish new and useful outcomes" (p. 370).

The results of the study of Pei (2017) indicated that "structuring leadership was positively related to both [a] team innovation climate and team creativity. In addition, the results supported the role of [a] team innovation climate as a mediator in the relationship between structuring leadership and team creativity" (p. 369). Finally, Pei (2017) explained "[t]heoretical contributions in various cultural contexts are necessary because the majority of mainstream leadership theories were developed within a Western context, and the best practices in a Western context may not apply to a non-Western context" (p. 375).

The impact of entrepreneurial leadership on innovation

Bagheri and Akbari (2018) studied the influence of entrepreneurial leadership on nurses' innovation work behavior and its dimensions using the 10-item Innovation Work Behavior (IWB) Questionnaire and 8-item Entrepreneurial Leadership Questionnaire with a sample of 273 nurses from public and private hospitals in Iran. Bagheri and Akbari (2018) explained:

> Entrepreneurial leadership (EL) has long been suggested to be effective in inspiring innovation and change among nurses (Ballein, 1998). This leadership style also enables leaders to effectively overcome the ever-changing and more serious challenges of healthcare organizations (Guo, 2009). However, empirical research on the impact of leadership style on fostering the IWB of healthcare professionals and particularly nurses is in the early stages of development (Cummings et al., 2010; Malik et al., 2016; Xerri, 2013).
>
> *(p. 29)*

The results of the study of Bagheri and Akbari (2018) revealed that "[e]ntrepreneurial leadership had a significant positive impact on nurses' innovation work behavior and most strongly improved idea exploration, followed by idea generation, idea implementation, and idea championing" (p. 28).

Lope, Asimiran, and Bagheri (2014)studied the relationships among "principals' entrepreneurial leadership practices and school innovativeness through the teacher's perspectives" (p. 1) with a sample of 294 Malaysian secondary school teachers in Selangor, Malaysia. Lope, Asimiran, and Bagheri (2014) stated that "[e]ntrepreneurial leadership, as a distinctive type of leadership required for dealing with challenges and crises of current organizational settings, has increasingly been applied to improve school performance" (p. 1). The results of their study demonstrated that "teachers perceive entrepreneurial leadership as highly important for school [principals]. However, the principals practise it moderately" (p. 1) and that "[f]urthermore, this study found a significant correlation between teachers' perceptions of school principals' entrepreneurial leadership practices and school innovativeness" (p. 1). Finally, Lope, Asimiran, and Bagheri (2014) explained that:

> The findings may be helpful for educators to improve school innovativeness by enhancing school principals' entrepreneurial leadership knowledge and competencies. Moreover, researchers can use the factors examined in this study as a framework to investigate the current schools' entrepreneurial orientation at both leadership and organizational levels.
>
> *(p. 9)*

The impact of developmental leadership on innovation

Kwon and Cho (2016) investigated the relationship between transactive memory systems, the organizational innovation and the mediating effect of the developmental leadership in this relationship (p. 1025) with a sample of 224 participants from an electronics firm in South Korea. The results of the study revealed that (a) "[c]ontrary to previous research results, transactive memory systems were found not to be significantly related to organizational innovation" (p. 1025); (b) "transactive memory systems comprise a statistically significant variable that influences developmental leadership" (p. 1025); and (c) "[s]ubsequently, developmental leadership can be considered to be a valid construct in predicting organizational innovation; it can also be seen to fully mediate the relationship between transactive memory systems and organizational innovation" (p. 1025). Keller, Fehér, Vidra, and Virág (2015) explained the developmental leadership program in Rome as follows:

> In Nádas, interconnected and synergistic projects have been accommodated to an overall developmental framework and helped the coming about of new integrated institutions (minority office, community house, Roma programme leader's status). As a result of these projects, the human and social capital of the Roma developmental leadership has increased and the Roma community's living conditions as well as their relationship to majority society have improved. In Rónakeresztes, on the other hand, in the absence of an independent developmental team and prior developmental projects promoting social integration, the resources of the ongoing project are used within exiting administrative mechanisms of the local government.
>
> (p. 90)

The impact of female leadership on innovation

Flabbi, Piras, and Abrahamst (2016) explained that "[w]omen are an increasingly important resource in the labor market: they participate in the market in higher numbers than at any time in history and they are now acquiring education at a higher rate than men" (p. 2) and that "[t]his is a well-known fact in high-income economies" (p. 2). In this regard, Xie and Pang (2018) explained that "[g]ender diversity represents the organizations' capacity to sustain continuous innovation, competitiveness, and responsiveness to changing workforce demographics" (p. 30) and that "[h]owever, women continue to face barriers and biases when seeking to advance in their organizations, which present subtle, but insidious obstacles to women's leadership" (p. 30). Xie and Pang (2018) cited Chao and Tian (2011), who explained that "people anticipate female leaders who have a transformational leadership style to express more innovation and organizational changes" (p. 32). Xie and Pang (2018) also stated that "[f]emale leaders demonstrate their desire and effort to transcend barriers to leadership" (p. 32). Along those lines, Dezsö and Ross (2012) studied the benefits of female representation in top management with a panel of top management teams of the S&P 1500 firms and found that

- Female representation in top management improves firm performance, but only to the extent that a firm's strategy is focused on innovation, in which context the informational and social benefits of gender diversity and the behaviors associated with women in management are likely to be especially important for managerial task performance. (p. 1072)
- The degree to which innovation activities are distributed throughout a firm's organizational structure, rather than being compartmentalized into specialized units, may also affect the degree to which a firm's focus on innovation moderates the impact of female representation in top management. (p. 1086)

Core competences and innovation

In this section, the concept of core competences, the types of core competences, the reasons for the inclusion of the innovation in the organization's core competences and some studies about the incorporation of the innovation in the core competences for gaining competitive advantages are detailed. Wu (2017) explained that "[t]he enhancement of small and micro enterprises' technological innovation capability not only helps [the] enterprise increase its core competence to adapt to the changeful environment, but also helps our country to increase its national competence" (p. 249). Thus, the incorporation of the innovation in the core competences of the organizations is an urgent need for the growth and the development of the organizations and the countries.

The concept of core competences

Several concepts of core competences have been proposed since 1990 (Prahalad and Hamel, 1990; Cheng and Bennett, 2006; López-Ortega and Ramírez-Hernández, 2007; Schilling, 2013; Xie, Zhan, and Wang, 2014; Rambe and Makhalemele, 2015; Salim, 2015; Agnieszka, 2017). These concepts are both complementary and diverse to provide a better understanding of the management of the organizations.

There are differences between 'competency' and 'competence' because 'competency' is a term relating to people and 'competence' relates organizations (Agnieszka, 2017). Regarding the term 'competency', Agnieszka (2017) explained that it was "first used in management sciences to identify the characteristics which distinguish superior from average managerial performance (Boyatzis, 1982)" (p. 13); that the term "'[c]ompetency' (plural 'competencies') described an underlying characteristic of an individual that is casually related to effective or superior performance in a job" (p. 13); and that "[t]he research gathered that there is a range of factors, not [a] single factor, that differentiated superior from average managers" (p. 13). Agnieszka (2017) also pointed out that "[t]he term 'competence' [. . .] refers to the set of resources held by the organization, related to the performance of activities leading to achieving goals, by the development of adequate capabilities to perform tasks (Guallino and Prevot, 2008)" (p. 13).

Regarding these terms Agnieszka (2017) also stated that (a) both terms are derived from "the Latin word 'competere' which means 'due', 'suitable', 'appropriate' (Nordhaug and Grønhaug, 1994)" (p. 13); (b) "[c]ompetence can be understood as the ability to apply assets in a coordinated way (interaction and integration of capabilities) in order to achieve the key goal" (p. 13); and (c) "[s]kills and capabilities are the basic of competences but capabilities and skills don't always lead to a competence by definition" (p. 13). Agnieszka (2017) also stated that "[t]his is only possible by interaction and integration between them" and that "[t]hus, competence is related to processes and interaction between the assets in an organization and lies generally embedded in cornerstone organizational units (Gimzauskiene and Staliuniene, 2010)" (p. 13). Additionally, Agnieszka (2017) explained:

> There are several criteria for defining core competences (Clardy, 2008). First, the sine qua non condition of core competences is persistent, superior organizational performance. They are based on routines and processes. Core competences are properties of a system and are not generally reducible to or defined by statements of individual task proficiencies. To create their superior effects, core competences are organizationally asymmetric. Core competences cannot, by definition, be common, generic, or universal, because if they are shared, then any organizations can use them to achieve competitive advantage.
>
> *(p. 14)*

Salim (2015) stated that "[c]ore competencies represent special strengths relative to other enterprises in the industry which offer the fundamental foundation for the provision of an added value" (p. 723); that "[c]ore competencies are the shared learning in enterprises, and involve how to organize diverse production skills and incorporate multiple streams of technologies" (p. 723); and that "[i]t is communication, participation and a deep commitment to functioning across enterprise boundaries" (p. 723). Salim (2015) also explained that "[c]ompetencies represent the combined know-how of the firm in commencing or responding to revolutionize, through managerial processes, schemes and procedures, all integrated into manners of deeds, interior networks and interpersonal relations" (p. 723). Additionally, Rambe and Makhalemele (2015) indicated that "core competencies are a complex amalgam of human capital requirements (knowledge, attributes, skills and abilities) and resources and capabilities (innovative capabilities, market management capabilities, resource mobilisation capabilities)" (p. 684).

Xie, Zhan, and Wang (2014) explained that the core competence of companies is "a capacity that companies accumulate for a long time, and is the leader of other abilities" (p. 2273) and that "[a] core competence should be difficult for competitors to imitate, and maintain sustainable competitive advantage for the company, and should make a significant contribution to the perceived customer benefits of the end product" (p. 2273). Xie, Zhan, and Wang (2014) also explained that "[t]he core competence can create value for customers, provide products and services to the market, bring revenue and profits for companies and help companies to maintain a leading position in the market" (p. 2275). Additionally, Xie, Zhan, and Wang (2014) provided some general competences, such as (a) corporate culture, (b) strategic management, (c) innovation, (d) information management, (e) environment adaptation, (f) market development, etc. (p. 2274). Xie, Zhan, and Wang (2014) also explained:

> By analyzing the resources and capabilities possessed by leading companies, the general competences of companies can be got which combines [...]the resources and capabilities. According to the definition of core competence, that if the general competences have characteristics like difficulty to imitate, irreplaceable and rarity, it can be determined that they are the core competences of companies.
>
> *(p. 2275)*

Schilling (2013) indicated that "[a] company's core competencies are typically considered to be those that differentiate it strategically" (p. 118), that "[a] core competency is more than just a core technology" (p. 118), and that "[a] core competency arises from a firm's ability to combine and harmonize multiple primary abilities in which the firm excels into a few key building blocks of specialized expertise" (p. 118). López-Ortega and Ramírez-Hernández (2007) defined core competence as "any means, physical or logical, that are offered to the net of enterprises in order to enhance the overall production capability" (p. 373). Cheng and Bennett (2006) explained that "core competence is an outcome resulting from the acquisition and development of various capabilities and resources by a company" (p. 191).

Originally, the concept of core competence was proposed by Prahalad and Hamel (1990), who defined core competence as "the collective learning in the organization, especially how to coordinate diverse production skills and integrate multiple streams of technologies" (p. 81). Prahalad and Hamel (1990) also indicated that "[i]f core competence is about harmonizing streams of technology, it is also about the organization of work and the delivery of value" (p. 81). Additionally, Prahalad and Hamel (1990) explained that "the force of core competence is felt as decisively in services as in manufacturing" (p. 81).

The types of core competences

Various authors have proposed different types of core competences (Balas, 2015; Hsu, Tan, Jayaram, and Laosirihongthong, 2014; Schilling, 2013; Geraldi, 2009; López-Ortega and Ramírez-Hernández, 2007; Li, 2000). Balas (2015) stated that "[f]rom an economic, competitive and cultural perspective, there are three different types of businesses (Treacy, Wiersema, 1993): product leadership, customer intimacy, and operational excellence" (p. 145). Balas (2015) also explained that "[t]he core competences present distinct clusters of knowledge that differentiate a company strategically from competitors" (p. 145). Balas (2015) further stated that the core competences per each type of business are as follows: (a) "[t]he core competence behind product leadership is product innovation defined as the capacity to conceive attractive new products and services and commercialize them (Hagel, Singer, 1999)" (p. 145); (b) "[t]he core competence behind customer intimacy is customer relationship management defined as the capacity to identify, find, acquire and build relationships with customers" (p. 145); and (c) "[t]he core organizational competence behind operational excellence is infrastructure management defined as the capacity to build and manage facilities for high volume, repetitive operational tasks" (p. 145).

In their research, Hsu, Tan, Jayaram, and Laosirihongthong (2014) operationalized the operations core competency as follows: "a firm's knowledge management, technology management and process management" (p. 5467). In this respect, Schilling (2013) explained that "[c]ompetencies often combine different kinds of abilities, such as abilities in managing the market interface (e.g. advertising, distribution), building and managing an effective infrastructure (e.g. information systems, logistics management), and technological abilities (e.g. applied science, process design)" and that "[t]his combination and harmonization of multiple abilities make core competencies difficult to imitate" (p. 118).

Geraldi (2009) proposed three types of core competences: (a) "core competence on reliability ('we focus on reliability')" (p. 153), (b) core competence "on technological innovation ('we create your future')" (p. 153), and (c) core competence "on interaction ('we make your ideas come true')" (p. 153). López-Ortega and Ramírez-Hernández (2007) also proposed four major classes of core competences: "Product, Resources, Organizations and Processes" (p. 373), and explained that according to this classification, "an Extended Enterprise must be necessarily formed by the appropriate combination of the following: (i) product configuration, (ii) key resources, (iii) organizations, and (iv) manufacturing processes" (p. 373). Additionally, Cheng and Bennett (2006) cited Li (2000) who proposed four types of core competences: "human resources, marketing, product development and manufacturing capabilities" (p. 195).

Reasons for including innovation in the organization's core competences

Balas (2015) explained that "[d]istinct knowledge is hidden and embedded in technical systems, skills of employees, and managerial systems and deeply rooted in values (Leonard Barton, 1992)" (p. 145). Balas (2015) also pointed out that "[t]hese distinct technical systems, skills of employees, and managerial systems and value competitors cannot easily be copied by competitors; therefore they are asymmetric across companies – also referred to as organizational asymmetries – " (p. 145) and that they "thus compose the essence of the competitive advantage (Miller, 2003)" (p. 145).

Stosic and Milutinovic (2014) stated that "[i]nnovation is identified as a key driver for strengthening of competitiveness and the central element of today's knowledge-based economy"

(p. 96). Based on Balas (2015) and Stosic and Milutinovic (2014) it can be concluded that the organizations must include innovation as one of the most important core competences for increasing knowledge that permits them to obtain competitive advantages. Additional related reasons were detailed by the specialists of the British Standards Institution (2008), who indicated that the principal reasons for incorporating innovation into the organization's core competencies are the following:

- To improve the current situation:
  - Reduce costs and raise margins, and hence profitability;
  - Protect market share and survive adverse operating circumstances;
  - Stimulate staff with interesting and challenging work;
  - Provide stability for the workforce.

- To open new horizons:
  - Reposition and alter perceptions of an organization;
  - Exploit avenues with greater potential;
  - Gain competitive advantage and lead the market;
  - Reduce the influence of competitors.

- To reinforce compliance:
  - Comply with legislation (current or anticipated);
  - Fulfill social and environmental responsibilities.

- To enhance the organization's profile:
  - Enhance reputation and raise its market profile;
  - Attract extra funding;
  - Attract those with good ideas and potential alliance partners;
  - Attract and retain higher-caliber staff (p. 20).

Incorporating innovation in the core competences to gain competitive advantages

Some studies about incorporating innovation into the core competences of the organizations to gain competitive advantages were found with samples from (a) Indonesia (Rahab, Anwar, and Priyono, 2016); (b) Spain (Palacios-Marqués, Popa, and Alguacil, 2016); (c) Indonesia, Malaysia, the Philippines, Vietnam and Thailand (Hsu, Tan, Jayaram, and Laosirihongthong, 2014); and (d) Taiwan (Sun, 2013). The details of these studies are provided in the following paragraphs.

Wu (2017) stated that "[i]n order to enhance small and micro enterprises' technological innovation capability, enterprises should build a well technological innovation system, increase the technology innovation input and be active in technological innovation activities" (p. 249). Wu (2017) also explained that "it is essential for the government to play a role of leading, make effective policies and build good environment" (p. 249). Additionally, Kim, Lee, and Cho (2016) pointed out that "sufficient core-technology competence is needed for firms to effectively manage and utilize technological diversification, particularly unrelated one, for their growth" (p. 113).

Rahab, Anwar, and Priyono (2016) studied the relationship among firm core competence, competitive advantage and performance of small and medium enterprises with a sample of 58 owners and managers of Banyumas Batik in Banyunas Region, Central Java, in Indonesia. The results of the study revealed:

- "[R]elationship competence significantly affects competitiveness" (p. 38), which indicates that "the entrepreneur who is responsive with the changes in an environment will be a positive factor for the company" (p. 38).
- "[A]daptation competence has a significant effect on competitiveness" (p. 39), which implies that "the ability to continuously adapt [the]business environment will cause demand for additional investment for keeping up with the technological and market changes" (p. 39).
- "[I]nnovation competence significantly affects competiveness" (p. 39), which means that "[i]nnovation competence will continuously burden the small firm to keep the change of new technology, including new design, batik motif and material" (p. 39).
- "[C]ompetitive advantage significantly influences the business performance" (p. 39), which indicates that "the greater the competitive advantage the better will be the SMEs business performance" (p. 39).

Rahab, Anwar, and Priyono (2016) concluded that "[t]he study has also confirmed that all three dimensions of core competence (relationship competence, adaptation competence and innovation competence) are significant in explaining [a] firm's competitiveness" (p. 40). Finally, Rahab, Anwar, and Priyono (2016) commented that "this study only investigated variables from [the] internal side of a company, while none of the external variables such as business environment and government's support was investigated" (p. 40).

Palacios-Marqués, Popa, and Alguacil (2016) studied the effect of online social networks and competency-based management on innovation capability with a sample of 289 firms from the Spanish biotechnology and telecommunications industries. The results of the study showed that (a) "knowledge transfer mediates relationships between competency-based management, online social network use and innovation capability" (p. 508); (b) "[c]ompetency-based management affects knowledge transfer (0.813) more than online social network use affects knowledge transfer (0.785). Thus, competency-based management and online social network use act as antecedents of knowledge transfer" (p. 508); and (c) "[r]esults also show that in firms that transfer knowledge, it positively and significantly affects innovation capability (0.893)" (p. 508). Finally, Palacios-Marqués, Popa, and Alguacil (2016) explained that "[o]nline social networks should be capable of creating the intensity of the symbiotic relationship between background and foreground knowledge with the aim of creating core-competences that positively affect the creation of competitive advantage for the firm" (p. 508) and recommended that "[o]nline social networks and competency-based management should be incorporated into human resources policies and practices" (p. 508).

Hsu, Tan, Jayaram, and Laosirihongthong (2014) examined the relationships among corporate entrepreneurship, operations core competency and innovation with a sample of automotive OEM (original equipment manufacturer) suppliers from Indonesia, Malaysia, the Philippines, Vietnam and Thailand, such as Ford, General Motors, Chrysler, Toyota, Honda and Nissan. Hsu, Tan, Jayaram, and Laosirihongthong (2014) evaluated the corporate entrepreneurship, operations core competency and innovation as follows: (a) corporate entrepreneurship with corporate culture and leadership; (b) the core competency with knowledge management, technology management and process management; and (c) innovation with process innovation and product innovation (p. 5472). The results of the study demonstrated that (a) "even in the context of developing nations in South-east Asia, investing in corporate entrepreneurship represents an important initial structural mechanism that promotes product and process innovation in firms" (p. 5478), (b) "these three sub-facets of operations core competency are not isolated but are connected via a common higher order facet that has similar nomological content" (p. 5478) and "these facets positively influence innovation performance" (p. 5478), and (c) "a behavioural lens blended with a technical lens contributes to successful innovation activity" (p. 5478).

Sun (2013) stated that "[k]nowledge-sharing within the supply chain could then be used to strengthen the effect of core competences on innovation" (p. 299). Sun (2013) studied the influence of core competences (threshold capabilities, critical capabilities and cutting-edge capabilities) on the innovation of the manufacturing industry in Taiwan with a sample of 139 valid questionnaires of firms of diverse sizes, and the results revealed that (a) "threshold capabilities, critical capabilities, and cutting-edge capabilities positively affect innovation" (p. 299); (b) "the level of knowledge reception among supply chain partners positively affects innovation" (p. 299); (c) "the level of knowledge reception could strength the effect of threshold capability on innovation" (p. 299); and (d) "a high level of knowledge reception could weaken the positive effect of critical capabilities and cutting-edge capabilities on innovation" (p. 299). Finally, Sun (2013) explained that:

> If external information is relied on overly much for corporate development and planning, the firms' innovation will be reduced. In other words, receiving more knowledge does not guarantee positive outcomes. In order to break through the position limitation in a supply chain and achieve innovation, firms should control key capabilities and cutting-edge capabilities. Over-dependency on the partners' information will lead to high risks and prices for future development.
>
> *(p. 322)*

Patents, patent system and innovation

The word *patent* originates from the Latin *litterae patentes*, which means a collection of letters to be laid open or to be made available for public inspection.[1] The ancient use of patents has a more general meaning than the modern use of the term, as it denotes any royal decrees granting exclusive rights to a person. The first patent in the modern sense – a decree that grants rights to an invention – was a license of 20 years granted by King Henry VI in 1449 to John of Utynam for introducing the making of colored glass to England.[2]

Patents were issued by monarchs, who tended to manipulate the system in order to raise royal income. In England, the Statute of Monopolies, which restrained patents to completely novel inventions, was passed in 1624 and began to curb such misuses (Khan and Sokoloff, 2001). Seen as a key moment in the evolution of patent law, the statute was described by Bloxam (1957) as "one of the landmarks in the transition of economy from the feudal to the capitalist". In the United States, the 1787 Constitution authorized the American patent system, and later, in 1790, the first U.S. Patent Act was passed into law.

Patents create legal monopoly. Thus, researchers' initial concern with the patent system was the effects of this kind of legal monopoly on social welfare and technological progress. The discussions and disagreements among researchers on this issue lasted for over 100 years and hence are not negligible. For example, many researchers developed sophisticated models to understand the patent pool and licensing of patents (Shapiro, 1985; Faulí-Oller and Sandonís, 2002; Tauman and Watanabe, 2007; Rudy, McKee, and Bjornstad, 2010). The role of not-for-profit organizations, such as universities, in patenting also draws a great deal of attention (Feller, 1990; Elfenbein, 2007; Hong and Su, 2012). Some country-specific or industry-specific studies also inspire in-depth understandings on patent policy (Hall and Rosemarie Ham, 2001; Chaudhuri, Goldberg, and Jia, 2006; Eom and Lee, 2010). However, this chapter focuses on the relationship between innovation and patent policy. Thus, the following contents will mainly cover the topics on patent protection and antitrust, patent system and technology transfer, patenting behaviors and innovation and patent data and innovation spillover effect.

Patent protection and antitrust

Before the 1850s, researchers were far more often approving than critical of the patent system. For example, Machlup and Penrose (1950) observed that Jeremy Bentham stated a patent system "has nothing in common with monopolies which are so justly decried". Although Adam Smith takes a view that "every derangement of the natural distribution of the stock is necessarily hurtful to the society in which it takes place",[3] he argued that a temporary monopoly granted to the inventor of a new machine could be justified when the inventor undertakes it at his own risk and expense.[4]

The debate on the patent system and monopoly was ignited after antitrust laws were introduced. Trusts, or monopolistic manufacturing conglomerates, suddenly emerged in great numbers after the 1880s. The Sherman Antitrust Act of 1890 trumpeted the antitrust war in the United States and the practice reached its pinnaclein the 1950s and 1960s. It is not surprising that during this period researchers began to be suspicious of whether patent systems brought more benefit than monopolistic costs.[5] According to Smith (1890) many of his contemporaries reflected that "the introduction of modern improvements in the industrial arts has been to injure society and not to improve it". Vaughan (1919) for example, pointed out that "the most efficient and profitable way in which the people can learn of an invention is by using it or the product which it manufactures", and "many patents are purchased in order to prevent the competition of new inventions". This side effect of patent systems is now known as strategic patenting or patent thickets (Galasso and Schankerman, 2010).

If researchers can bear patents' monopolistic cost for speeding up innovation, they certainly cannot keep silent when patents possibly block innovation. Kahn (1940) argued that "the most important – and most fallacious – assumption is its individualistic conception of the process of invention. In fact, invention is a group process, the individual contributions being relatively minor. In modern industrial research this is particularly so. A grant of separate proprietary rights over each inventive contribution thus imposes barriers to further innovation and reduction to practice of the whole". Vaughan, 1948 agreed that "our patent system fails to promote public welfare in many instances because it discourages rather than encourages the inventor". He also suggested a remedy to the patent system, claiming "it would be necessary in some instances to pool the useful patents of the entire industry and to license any prospective manufacturer to use the technology which they cover upon payment of royalties according to his volume of output". Ironically, this remedy of compulsory licensing is no longer practiced in the United States but is in many developing countries (Kingston, 1994). Phillips (1966) argued that the patent system also facilitates a "success breeds success" tendency, because "initial success in an environment of continuously changing technical possibilities tends to make further success by those firms less difficult than is the achievement of similar success by firms which wish to swarm into the new area" and this in turn fosters oligopoly.[6]

However, to many, the patent system and antitrust laws are not mutually exclusive, but rather complementary. As Polanvyi (1944) suggested, the Patent Office would have to continue issuing patents on the basis of the present law, but courts should wield power to reduce the rewards of notorious 'paper patents'. In a historical study of the patent law practice in the UK and United States, Bloxam (1957) found these countries "have powerful safeguards against the misuse of patents and, at any rate so far as the United Kingdom is concerned, the safeguards have but seldom been invoked". Markham (1966) took a similar opinion that "a strong patent policy and a strong antitrust policy should stimulate innovation".

Substantial progress on researchers' understanding of the patent system only occurs after rigorous economic theory is applied to the issue. To reconcile patent-induced monopoly and antitrust consensus, Nordhaus (1969) raised the question on how long the monopolistic protection should be granted to a patent, or in other words, what the optimum life of a patent should be. Some extend Nordhaus' pioneering work by proposing a system that would yield different patent lives for different inventions (Scherer, 1972; Arditti and Sandor, 1973). Although Nordhaus himself was skeptical of this idea, he did maintain a supportive view of the patent system that "too long a patent life is better than too short a patent life" (Nordhaus, 1972).[7]

Competition and imitation among rival firms can also help with diminishing the hazards of patent-induced monopoly of new innovations. Kamien and Schwartz (1974) extended the framework of Nordhaus (1969) by introducing rival competition, which is found to be a key factor that affected invention. Mansfield, Schwartz, and Wagner (1981) followed with an empirical investigation and found about 60 percent of the patented innovations in their sample were imitated within four years. Therefore, they argued that, excluding drugs, patent protection did not seem essential for the development and introduction of most patented innovations.

In terms of studies on competition of rivalries, game theory is a natural tool for thorough analysis. Reinganum (1982) is one of the early applications of game theory to patent system studies. Reinganum found that increased rivalry may accelerate or delay innovation, depending upon the payoff structure. In the case of perfect patent protection, increasing the number of rivals results in an increase in each individual firm's Nash equilibrium rate of investment in R&D. Fudenberg et al. (1983) analyzed patent races as dynamic games. They focus on what determines the possibility that a firm that is behind in the race can leapfrog the competitor and jump ahead.

One implication of these two pioneering works is that the patent system may or may not block technological progress because industry-specific factors may overwrite the effect of patent protection. Empirical studies seem to support this view too. For example, Levin (1986) surveyed 650 R&D executives in 130 industries and found the effectiveness of patent protection is highly nonuniform across the industries. He observed "patents are viewed as an effective instrument for protecting the competitive advantages of new technology in most chemical industries, including the drug industry; however, most other industries judge them ineffective". Waterson (1990) further argued that giving a monopoly right could often prove socially worthwhile – both in terms of encouraging firms to design innovative products and in terms of supplying society with the right number of products. He took a view that the patent system changed the nature of market entry behavior rather than preventing entry entirely.

To sum up, the patent system has been under heated debate since the antitrust campaign began in the 1890s and turned fierce after World War II. It has mainly been criticized for two reasons: the social welfare loss of legalized monopoly and the blocking of competitors' entry, which in turn hampers technology progress. Apart from some radical claims of completely abolishing the patent regime, most studies focused on design of an optimal patent term.[8] The trade-off between the patent policy instruments of length and breadth could be used to provide sufficient incentives to develop inventions with high social value.[9] In addition, an optimal patent system could be based on different degrees of patent protection, and stronger protection would involve higher fees, allowing self-selection by inventors (Encaoua, Guelle, and Martinez, 2006). Meanwhile, patent race models that incorporate game theory framework suggest the patent system may or may not block technological progress (Reinganum, 1982; Fudenberg et al., 1983; Waterson, 1990).[10] Hence, after a century's debate, it becomes clear that no decision can be made to abolish the patent system.[11] Consequently, the researchers' interest was drawn to fields that are concerned with the patent system and technology transfer, understanding patenting behaviors and other patent-related issues.[12]

Patent system and technology transfer

The cause of technology transfer between countries is an important dimension of economic studies. From the aspect of the patent system, the research question can be restated as international differences in national patent laws affecting cross-country technology transfer. Researchers have never achieved an agreement on this issue. For example, Bosworth (1980) argues that the differences in patent laws did not seem to significantly affect patent flows between countries. In contrast, Tebaldi and Elmslie (2013) find that institutional arrangements explain much of the cross-country variations in patent production.

A stylized fact of international differences in national patent laws is that the patent protection is stronger in the North than in the South (Ginarte and Park, 1997).[13] Stronger patent protection means longer patent life, broader patent breadth or higher patent height.[14] Berkowitz and Kotowitz (1982) argued the North–South difference might be caused by different industrial structures, because the Northern countries "which have a significant concentration of imperfectly competitive inventive enterprises have an incentive to maintain a high degree of patent protection". However, the prevailing competitive structure in the South will imply a relatively short period of patent protection.

On the contrary, many scholars believe a weak patent protection regime is intended by policy makers in the South because stronger patent protection may harm the social welfare. Deardorff (1992) showed that while the welfare of the inventing country rose with the extension of patent protection, the welfare of the other country probably fell. In particular, as patent protection is extended to a larger portion of the world, the effect on the welfare of the world as a whole becomes negative.[15] A typical example is the pharmaceutical industry. For instance, Chaudhuri, Goldberg, and Jia (2006) argued that after India granted production patents to drugs according to TRIPs' requirement, the Indian economy suffered substantial welfare losses.[16]

Innovating firms have the choice of licensing a new product at arm's length to a foreign firm, exporting it or licensing it to a subsidiary. The gains of the Southern firms due to the lack of intellectual property right protection may be offset by the strategic behavior of Northern firms, who opt for technology transfer via subsidiary or monopoly production (Vishwasrao, 1994). Smith (2001) also found stronger foreign patent rights increase U.S. affiliate sales and licenses, particularly across countries with strong imitative abilities. In the long run, patent laws may help to determine the direction of technical change and comparative advantage across countries (Moser, 2005).

These controversial results inspire recent researchers to consider whether there is an optimal protection level for technological progress, rather than simply condemning a weak protection regime. For example, Qian (2007) evaluates the effects of patent protection on pharmaceutical innovations for 26 countries that established pharmaceutical patent laws during 1978–2002. He argues that there appears to be an optimal level of intellectual property right regulations above which further enhancement reduces innovative activities.

Furukawa (2010) and Chen and Iyigun (2011) also suggest that the relationship between intellectual property protection and innovation can be an inverted-U shape.[17]

Apart from North–South differences in patent protection levels, discriminatory protection of intellectual property, which provides different levels of protection depending upon where the firm is located, is another tool of concern. Vaughan (1919) stated "it is a contravention of our patent law and an economic injustice to the American manufacturer to allow a foreigner to take out a patent in this country merely for the purpose of reserving the United States as a market for his patented product". Montgomery (1923) pointed out two distinct tendencies of international aspects of patent legislation. In the first instance, "patent laws are used as a means of protecting [the] home industry and of discriminating against the nationals of other countries".[18] In the second instance, he also suggested there could be a gradual tendency toward a unification of patent laws and a generalization of concessions. History has proven that the second path is what has happened. For example, the *Agreement on Trade Related Aspects of Intellectual Property Rights* (TRIPs) established in 1994 explicitly prohibits any such discrimination.[19]

However, the first path predicted in Montgomery 1923 is still under practice in many countries but only in a more disguised way. Such disguised or strategic discriminations can also affect imitation costs (Fosfuri, 2000).[20] Consequently, it can in turn reward or block technological catching-up or even leap-frogging. This kind of "import substitution policy" in technology can improve the domestic technological infrastructure synergistically (Kotabe, 1992). Nevertheless, Aoki and Prusa (1993) showed that discriminatory protection might increase or decrease domestic R&D, which depends on the costs of R&D, the value of the potential innovation and whether the rivals have pre-existing products.

Patenting behaviors and innovation

What determines firms' patenting behavior? On the supply side, it is related to firms' innovative capability. Naturally, patenting is positively associated with the conduct of R&D (Scherer, 1983).[21] A long unresolved question is whether Schumpeter's theory can stand. Schumpeter's theory states big firms are more innovative, or in other words, there are returns to scale in R&D among large firms. Inventive activities seem to increase more than proportionately with firm size (Soete, 1979). However, some empirical findings reject Schumpeter's theory or suggest Schumpeterian patterns of innovation are technology-specific (Doi, 1996; Malerba and Orsenigo, 1996).[22]

Firms' patenting behavior is also strongly affected by the demand factors (Evenson, 1993). For example, cross-border patenting is very likely induced by the possibility of exporting (Schiffel and Kitti, 1978; Yang and Kuo, 2008). Further, the profitability of patent flows is determined by the size of the recipient country's economy, per capita income and the costs of transfer, which will be reduced when donor and recipient countries are linked through trade and the operations of multinational firms (Bosworth, 1984). Strengthening patent rights can spawn patenting too (Hall and Ham, 2001).

Patenting can be used as a strategic tool in competition. The traditional, defensive patenting behavior is to protect firms' technological knowledge base. However, the strategic offensive patenting behavior is also omnipresent.[23] For example, patent disclosure can create prior art that might stop rivals from patenting, as well as set up a high threshold of entry (Baker and Mezzetti, 2005). Firms may even use patents to mislead rivals (Langinier, 2005). Sometimes, certain firms trap R&D-intensive manufacturers in patent infringement situations in order to receive damage awards for the illegitimate use of their technology. This strategy is often referred to as patent trolling (Reitzig, Henkel, and Heath, 2007).

The propensity to patent is very likely affected by environmental factors, such as the strictness of examination in patent offices, completeness of disclosure at patenting and the feasibility of reverse engineering (Scotchmer and Green, 1990).[24] However, patent applicants have some options to choose to minimize the adverse effect of discrimination. For example, a firm can patent only some fraction of its produced innovations (Horstmann, MacDonald, and Slivinski, 1985; Harter, 1994). Firms can also keep an innovation a secret rather than patent it (Arundel, 2001; Schneider, 2008).

Patent data and innovation spillover effect

Empirical studies on patent data have lagged behind theoretical works. As pointed out by Massel (1966), "we need far-reaching empirical analyses of many current policies. Despite a plethora of studies, we have not yet ... advanced much beyond theological doctrine in most of the public discussions of these problems". Before the digital age, patent data are hard to obtain because of the massive volume. Nonetheless, some have tried to capture R&D output by patent counts (Griliches, 1981; Connolly and Hirschey, 1988).[25] After the data became available, patent counts were first used as a measure of technological output. Together with R&D data as technological input, it is possible to estimate knowledge production function. Ramani, El-Aroui, and Carrere (2008) even showed that by using only patent statistics, it is possible to study the dynamics of knowledge generation without having to resort to additional information on the R&D activities of firms. Some tried to construct a composite indicator of innovative performance from various indicators, such as R&D inputs, patent counts and patent citations (Hagedoorn and Cloodt, 2003; Lanjouw and Schankerman, 2004).

However, when patent counts are used as a response variable rather than explanatory variables, a proper econometric model needs to be developed because patent counts are not normally used as continuous data in econometric models but rather as non-negative integers. A seminal work on this econometric foundation was done by Hausman, Hall, and Griliches (1984) who presented two models – Poisson and negative binomial regressions – to analyze patent count data. Based on this work, some further methods are introduced, for example, heterogeneity, to account for unobservable factors. Crépon and Duguet (1997a) employed GMM (Generalized method of moments) to analyze count panel data. Lewbel (1997) discussed two-staged least squares (TSLS) estimation for count data. Blundell, Griffith, and Windmeijer (2002) discussed individual effects and dynamics in count data models. Furthermore, innovation could create important knowledge spillovers due to its imperfect appropriability. To account for this, Blazsek and Escribano (2010) introduce a general dynamic count panel data model with dynamic observable and unobservable spillovers.

Another application of patent data is to measure technological spillover or knowledge diffusion with backward patent citations (Jaffe, 1986; Jaffe, Trajtenberg, and Fogarty, 2000; Henderson, Jaffe, and Trajtenberg, 2005; MacGarvie, 2005).[26] For instance, Jaffe, Trajtenberg, and Fogarty (1993) found location was a key element affecting knowledge spillovers.[27] As a generalization, Picci (2010) introduced a gravity model using patent data to investigate the internationalization of inventive activity. He finds that the amount of bilateral collaboration is positively affected by the presence of a common language, a common border and more similar cultural characteristics, while it is negatively affected by distance.

Forward patent citations can be used to weigh the importance or value of a patent (Trajtenberg, 1990).[28] Hall, Jaffe, and Trajtenberg (2005) explored the usefulness of patent citations as a measure of the importance of a firm's patents, as indicated by the stock market valuation of the firm's intangible stock of knowledge. They found an extra citation per patent boosted market value by 3 percent. Belenzon (2012) distinguishes two types of citations based on whether or not a firm can reabsorb its 'spilled' knowledge in its later inventions. It is shown that citations on which the firm builds in a future period are positively related to market value, whereas citations on which the firm does not build are negatively related to value.

Backward citations as a measure of technological spillovers can be useful to detect the role of FDI (Foreign Direct Investment) or MNCs (Multinational corporations) in knowledge transfer. Multinational companies go abroad to acquire technological knowledge (technology sourcing) and also contribute knowledge locally (Almeida, 1996).[29] Many studies find that technological leaders are a source rather than a destination of knowledge flows (Mancusi, 2008; AlAzzawi, 2011).

Summary

In summary, this section reviewed the main developments of research on patent-related topics. In a century's debate during the 1880s to the 1980s, researchers attempted to understand whether the patent system is beneficial for innovation and technological progress, seeing that this regime creates legal monopolies. This debate has been largely settled after rigid theoretic models and empirical evidence were brought about. Most researchers have achieved agreement on the necessary function of the patent system in promoting innovation. However, with the use of patent data, there is still large space of research work to investigate how the patent system affects innovation.

Entrepreneurship and innovation

Introduction

Those involved in the study of innovation and entrepreneurship largely agreed that these are the two drivers that trigger long-term business success. However, innovation and entrepreneurship have been treated differently in number of sciences with diverse focus for decades. The competiveness of an organization strongly depends on the level of innovativeness at the international frontier (Porter and Stern, 2001). In the study by Audretsch, Keilbach, and Lehmann (2006), they argued that innovation is not considered as the sole factor, but it has a critical role to play economically. It is also an important factor in allowing organizations and nations to compete at all levels of the market spectrum (Beaver and Prince, 2002). The argument is also true when it comes to discussing entrepreneurship, which is also recognized as being one of the useful accelerators of economic growth (Audretsch, Keilbach, and Lehmann, 2006). The two are so critical to the advancement of growth through competition and knowledge creation to meet markets demand (Audretsch, Keilbach, and Lehmann, 2006).

That's why a business's innovative management approach has to play different roles. The main question is how the management process, from the initial stage of ideas to the realization of ideas, will be managed (Porter and Stern, 2001). This means also understanding how the combination of innovative and enterprises tasks will be implemented. Fortunately, how these processes will be managed remain a critical challenge because no defined process on how to manage it is proposed. The reason is that innovation and entrepreneurship in the current context are still being treated differently within the mainstream of social sciences (Beaver and Prince, 2002). This study focuses on the relationship between innovation and entrepreneurship using a micro-level approach.

The review of a paper by Braumerhjelm (2010) argued that there have been considerable advancement and breakthroughs during the previous decades toward the understanding of the relationship between how knowledge stimulates business growth. This remains important because, failing to understand how innovation and growth are interrelated to stimulate welfare and economic expansion poses a great challenge toward identifying innovative ideas that could fit well with the reality of world. Yet there is little evidence that has demonstrated that how entrepreneurship, innovation and knowledge are interlinked and what the implication could be for growth and development. If this is understood, the adoption of innovation by small and medium enterprises (SMEs) toward economic expansion could be seen as an important step in the right direction. This is because many countries in the world have not yet seen evidence of the role of innovation to SMEs' growth and the expansion of economic infrastructure.

In this review, it is noted that although entrepreneurship has been recognized as a driver of innovation, understanding it in a comprehensive way still poses a great challenge to academics and policy makers in terms of the interface of all variables (such as knowledge, innovation and entrepreneurship and growth). In addition, this has not been well analyzed in the literature.

Braumerhjelm (2010) suggested that when entrepreneurship takes root in a conducive environment, it has the potential to drive growth. The growth is directly attributed to the fundamental forces such as an increase in factors of production, efficiency improvement in the allocation of resources across economics or business activities, knowledge and the rates of innovation. In this case where full employment is obtained and resources are allocated in an efficient way, innovation and knowledge will be at the core of growth and development. In another paper by Brown and Mason (2014) they emphasized that when the process of innovation is considered as a function of incentive structure and institutions, it is assumed that access to knowledge exists. In this situation, it implies that a stock of economically useful knowledge will increase. In this context, innovation is therefore seen as a driver that has the potential to diffuse and upgrade already existing knowledge as a condition for spillover of the realization. Initially, this study is going to discuss the importance of innovation and then relate innovation as a key factor in shaping entrepreneurship behavior.

The article by Golibjon (2016) demonstrates that innovation, either at a small or large dimension, has a direct implication on the overall performance of firms and that of the economic growth. Further, Golibjon emphasizes that the positive implication of innovation reduces the effect of market failures by bringing new ideas to support SMEs' development and business success. In this context, governments across the globe have been analyzing how to use innovation specifically for small enterprises to strengthen their entrepreneurship ideas through product improvement and services. Even though governments have expressed this intention, it does not necessarily mean that any state policy aimed at promoting innovation will bring tangible benefits to their employee's skills and growth. However, the question remains to what extent entrepreneurs and governments are willing to go. This question requires a new approach to the way innovation is applied in different contexts. Conversely, by comparing innovation efficiency and the effectiveness of innovation policy, it should be well understood that a comparison is needed to determine the level of spending and ultimate social returns. This will determine if policy needs to be implemented or not and how effective it would be in the perspective of impact. It also requires getting insight on what steps governments could make to improve the situation. In other studies, it is evidenced that a wider margin is observed between social returns which are higher to innovation and it exceeds private returns.

Chaston and Scott (2012) stated that with the advancement of technology and development as shown in the case of Indonesia, information communication technology has supported the expansion of SMEs, and the idea of innovation and development is now becoming a matter of national urgency. However, the key question is that of investment, which most small businesses view as being expensive, and support from the state is therefore required if innovation and development are to be sustained. This highlights that the Indonesia case provides evidence that because SMEs contributed to 97 percent of employment and contributed 55 percent of country's overall GDP, governments are thus obliged to pay particular attention to using innovation to boost enterprises' competiveness and SMEs' productivity. This has led the government through its science, technology and innovation formulated policy to transform its economy into a knowledge-based economy. Brunswicker and Vanhaverbeke (2014) identified this as being an important key determinant toward the wealth and creation of a prosperous society. This has led Indonesia to be ranked 30th on a subindex of global competiveness. This study shows a tremendous achievement among 144 countries (Brunswickerand Ehrenmann, 2013). In terms of the effectiveness of innovation, SMEs, whether large or small (private or state owned), are encouraged to strengthen their collaboration with independent research, think tanks and universities to create a wealth of knowledge for economic growth and welfare of citizens. It is also noted that governments have an interest to improve intellectual property by creating schemes that have led to the increase of patent applications. Although government efforts are being recognized, training and infrastructures still remain weak. This will pose a great challenge to the effectiveness of innovative ideas in many countries, particularly developing countries.

Hossen (2015) argued that SMEs face challenges such as a complex scientific domain, the coordination of the operative functions and accessibility of updated scientific excellence. Despite the fact that SMEs' knowledge is licensed to other institutions or enterprises, knowledge seems to be more beneficial to them, but it does not benefit them in the short term. In this same paper it is highlighted that policy for open innovation appears to be another way of providing SMEs with R&D. Colombo, Piva, and Rossi-Lamastra (2014) highlighted that SMEs have different approaches toward policy perception. For instance, the idea of open innovation is the key to stimulating SMEs' growth internationally; therefore, education is needed for entrepreneurs so that they become encouraged and appreciate the idea of being creative; accept criticism; adopt self-discipline; and strengthen lifelong learning, cooperation and openness. However, for open innovation to be effective, SMEs have to embrace the network of knowledge to foresee innovative opportunities in the long run for their survival and growth.

Similarly, Ndesaulwa and Kikula (2016) examined that link between innovation and firm performance. However, it is also noted that very little empirical studies are evident in the context of developing regions such as Africa. This reflects that innovation and the way it relates to firm performance is not yet well investigated or documented. Some studies have been done, but they are not sufficient to provide convincing evidence at theoretical and practical levels (see Kuswantoro, 2012; Mbizi, 2013; Ngungi, 2013). To understand the link between innovation and SME performance, some important factors have to be well conceptualized and understood, taking into account the environment in which SMEs operate. Such factors could include sales per staff, export per employees, growth rates of sales, total assets, total level of employment, profit ratio and investment returns. These various factors will provide the best way for those innovative SMEs and noninnovative SMEs to measure their own performance and make a decision to either continue to innovate or remain noninnovative in the perspective of performance. Furthermore, the distribution channel of innovations is often positive and relates to the SMEs' overall performance, but specific reasons on why positive results are obtained not clearly explained.

In their empirical studies (see Kuswantoro, 2012; Masood. 2013; Colombo, Piva, and Rossi-Lamastra, 2014), these authors evidenced that in Kenya, for instance, a weak link was observed in relation to SMEs' performance, particularly sales. These results are disputed by the findings by Colombo, Piva, and Rossi-Lamastra (2014) that innovation has the potential to influence SMEs' growth capability by contributing to the overall expansion of knowledge and revenue generation. However, other studies give a different view – that expansion of knowledge will only be effective under conditions of combined knowledge from different SMEs in order to effectively create ideas that fit the societal needs, not business needs. It has also demonstrated that when entrepreneurs' creative ideas are driven by personal beliefs, innovation has a high risk and may not influence the SMEs' growth. Further, it is argued that even though entrepreneurs have been criticized in adopting this approach, it is demonstrated that the finding conducted in Kenya shows that innovation will influence SMEs' growth. Other studies revealed that SME owners had a tendency to engage in radical innovation, such as getting involved in new experimental research to innovate new products or to understand the market trends in this new age of business competiveness. This approach has led them to develop technological processes that are suitable to the business context. Despite the high risk of investment and limited budgets allocated to innovative initiatives, entrepreneurships are still willing to invest and others are still much more hesitant to do so (Kuswantoro, 2012).

It is also demonstrated that innovation is essential both at macro and micro levels because an economy or a firm can benefit, specifically taking into account the dynamism of the markets and business external environmental factors such as political, economy, technology, culture, environmental and legal. The underlining principle as highlighted in the study by Mbizi (2013) is that the main idea driving innovation is that it helps SMEs survive in this turbulent environment, and they must adapt to new ideas and develop the capacity to deal with a high level of complexity and the speed of changes. In the context of adaptation to change, SMEs that have developed full capacity toward innovation will be able to fully respond to the envisaged or faced challenges in a more efficient way than non-SMEs innovators in the long run. In sum, innovation is a key factor for entrepreneurship to drive economic and firm growth. The remaining sections are as follows: The first section provides a discussion on the life cycle stage of entrepreneurs: how an entrepreneur uses innovation in different stages of the life cycle of the business. Then the second section discusses the multiple characteristics of entrepreneurship, using innovation as a key variable. Also, this study presents some evidence related to entrepreneurship characteristics with reference to developed and developing countries. Finally, the empirical literature is provided as it relates to the link between entrepreneurship and innovation.

Entrepreneur life cycle using innovation as key strategy

This section reviews the different stages of an entrepreneur model. It measures time and entrepreneur duration in the life cycle. This is important because time determines the effectiveness of the entrepreneur development cycle in relation to the adoption of innovation and expansion in business activities. By understanding the effectiveness of this cycle, an overall picture will be obtained with regard to opportunities at the end of one period to another until the cycle is fully completed. This period reflects the capability and strengths of an entrepreneur to remain creative through the formulation, design and implementation of the envisaged innovative ideas. Risk associated with the different stages of the cycle will make an entrepreneur see opportunities that present either a lower risk or higher risk in terms of envisaged innovation and select the best options to meet the challenge of linking the implementation of innovative or creative ideas. In this context, the entrepreneur cycle is explained in the following paragraphs.

The preparatory phase is identified as the first phase of the entrepreneur's innovative activities. During this phase, the entrepreneur is considered as passing through a revolutionary change process. It reflects the way the entrepreneur begins the process of work activities to adapt to the changing environment. This will include the period of crisis for the adoption of the envisaged changes. The preparation period allows the entrepreneur to end the previously adopted methods of business creation and adopt new ways, which could lead to efficiency and innovation (Hunter, 2005). This period makes an entrepreneur go through a crisis, which could be linked to management of the innovation and allocation of financial resources to meet the market demand and support new ideas, which could help the business grow. This period of crisis is the strongest determinant of the entrepreneur's commitment and desire to engage in new ways of dealing with previous high failure rates in the adoption or improvement of existing ideas or venturing into new ideas (Thirtle and Rutcan, 1987).

The period of embarkation is also recognized as important due to the fact that the entrepreneur takes time to grow in terms of efficiency and effectiveness of designing high-quality innovation projects or programs. It is also a difficult period in which entrepreneur may fail to improve their organizational procedures. But it is useful for the entrepreneurs to adapt to the conditions of this period and ensure that they implement early a management approach that could make them develop managerial skills in areas such as planning, organization, budgeting and human resources. These areas are of critical importance for entrepreneurs to develop and acquire to meet the current competitive market forces and remain competitive. As evidenced in a study by Dobb (1981), many entrepreneurs lack these skills, and many of them have failed to successfully implement innovative ideas (Hamel and Breen, 2007).

During the period of exploration, although entrepreneurs have developed ideas, the challenge is for them to come up with the best strategy to put in practice their innovative ideas and start their first business. They may also face entry barriers from other competitors with regard to products and services envisaged for the markets. They could also be faced with limited financial resources, which could constrain their expansion in the long run through the reinvestment of profits. At this stage, firms face several challenges, such as to increase trade networks (with customers and suppliers) and knowledge related to the industry. All these challenges could make entrepreneurs to run just a small business initially due to limited resources (Thirtle and Rutcan, 1987).

Also during the period of exploration, the entrepreneur starts to develop new ventures. This stage is mainly characterized by the adoption of innovative ideas, sourcing for new business partners and capital and ensuring that the risk of failure is at a minimum level. It is during this phase, that entrepreneurs ensure that the commercialization of ideas is successful. In addition, entrepreneurs become more focused during their careers and embark on business ventures that would be seen as the most important to their success. They have levels of knowledge, trusts, networks, problem-solving, management and decision-making skills which have been heightened. Developing further business ventures is identified as the most developmental stage in the entrepreneurs' careers, and it is because they began a business venture, then ceased it and started another one before they make up their minds to begin another venture, which could become the most successful. It is important to note that period 2 of the business innovation cycle which reflects the entrepreneurs' distinct developmental stage due to the reason that the delay observed between the two periods is long. This reflects that entrepreneurs are still acquiring experience (Morris, Kuratko, and Covin, 2008).

During the period of expansion, the entrepreneurs acquire the capacity to develop their businesses. This period reflects the entrepreneur's commitment in terms of a long-term business concentration. They have made their businesses, acquired new capital and developed sustainable growth strategies, which have become more evident. This makes the entrepreneurs invest in other new ventures, using a diversification strategy to expand their businesses. In an attempt to continue growing, they have to develop managerial skills to solve problems. Furthermore, whether expansion is implicit or explicit, businesses have to develop a more sustainable business strategy that is sound and has been tested for competiveness (Dodgson, 1993).

The period of transformation reflects the end of the entrepreneur's business career, and it provides a great shift in the entrepreneur's ideas to more organization leadership. It will also lead to a change in the organization structure, and the leadership is then passed to the entrepreneur who originally created the organization. Some specific ventures could also cease to continue. The key of this period is the recapitalization of the organization becomes the main feature of the transformation period. The process of transforming into a new organization could be seen as a structural organization change from the original entrepreneurial vision. The change could make the organization be transformed into a private or limited company or even change the redesign of the business activities from the original nature. However, it is necessary to indicate that the effectiveness of change in taking over the next generational level was identified as complex in terms of the entrepreneur's life cycle. The review indicates that the entrepreneur life cycle needs to be re-evaluated to take into account the present business environment; if this is done, it could allow entrepreneurs to become more efficient through the development of new skills and creative ideas to meet the current skill gaps. How the entrepreneur life cycle model could be sustained is well mentioned in the literature – this poses a great challenge in understanding the effectiveness of the entrepreneurs' business models. Next this chapter will explore the multiple characteristics of entrepreneurship.

Characteristics of entrepreneurship

Entrepreneurs play a vital role in the economic development of a country. As discussed earlier, entrepreneurs provide new ideas to business using innovation. A number of researchers (Kukoc and Regan, 2008; Rangone, 1999) have identified numerous characteristics of entrepreneurs. To begin with, earlier economists such Joseph Schumpeter (1942) argued that entrepreneurs are the ones who introduce new methods of production, search for new markets and drive the production possibility frontier outward by using various (tangible and intangible) resources. After Schumpeter, other researchers (e.g. Kirzner, 1973; Casson, 1982) determined that alertness (discovery and learning) and strong motivation for achieving optimum profits are the key drivers of entrepreneurs. This chapter is going to discuss the entrepreneur's role in terms of driving the firm's innovation output.

According to Burns (2007), "Entrepreneurs use innovation to exploit or create change and opportunity for the purpose of making [a] profit. They do this by shifting economic resources from an area of lower productivity into an area of higher productivity and greater yield, accepting a high degree of risk and uncertainty in doing so". Burns's definition of entrepreneurship singles out innovation, which is a key driver of firms' growth. Through innovation, entrepreneurs accelerate their firms' performance. Additionally, several researchers identified the various characteristics of entrepreneurship such as their risk-taking behavior (Greve and Salaff, 2003); they are motivated by profits (Cantillon, 1775), alertness or proactiveness (Kirzner, 1973; Miller, 1983); their strong conviction on success (Casson, 1982); and their background of marketing knowledge, that is, understanding the product life cycle, market segmentation and positioning of the product they are involved with (Gardner, 1992). Further, an entrepreneur not only brings new ideas to the business but also exploits the commercial opportunities of such creative ideas. Previous studies (Alexandrova, 2004; Entrialgo, Fernandez, and Vazquez, 2001) combined three factors to measure entrepreneurship: (i) innovation, (ii) risk taking and (iii) proactiveness. These three characteristics of entrepreneurship provide new economic knowledge to the business.

Not surprisingly, Braunerhjelm (2010) discussed the major characteristics of entrepreneurs; they have individual and cognitive abilities such as risk acceptance or tolerance. They are considered to be risk takers and proactive in decision-making. A considerable body of literature states that another characteristic of entrepreneurs is their stronger need to achieve self-efficacy, as well as a preference for autonomy (Williamson, 1971; Schere, 1982; van Praag and Cramer, 2001; Sorenson and Singh, 2007; Benz and Frey, 2008). Some past studies suggested that entrepreneurs bring innovative ideas to the business using knowledge, social skills, etc. One of the early views on innovative opportunities is that these are the result of systematic and purposeful efforts to create knowledge and new ideas by investing in R&D (Chandler, 1990; Cohen and Levinthal, 1989). However, some empirical studies have shown that small and entrepreneurial firms could substantially contribute to aggregate innovation even thought they had modest investments in R&D (Feldman and Audretsch, 1999). Meanwhile, there are other authors such as Sutter (2010), who defines the entrepreneur as a person who enjoys life, a person who has an ability to control

Strategic management of innovation

emotions, the ability to create enthusiasm in other people, etc. All these components have been incorporated in the 'psychological capital' index, which is an important determinant of entrepreneurial endeavor (Audretsch, Falck, and Heblich, 2011).

Invention is a new idea manifested, whereas innovation is the successful implementation of this new idea (McKeown, 2008). Successful entrepreneurship is a process that involves planning, implementation and management, as well as cooperation of others in order to exploit an opportunity for profit (Veeraraghavan, 2009). According to George Day (2007), companies can avoid lackluster growth by better understanding the risks inherent in different levels of innovation and achieving a balance between Big-I Innovation and small-i innovation. The 'small-i' definition of innovation is dominant among both the general public and policy makers (Hindle, 2002b), whereas the 'Big-I' school views innovation as a lengthy, detailed, commercial process (Hindle, 2002; Dodgson and Bessant, 1996).

Figure 7.1 supports the broad definition of entrepreneurship, which is considered the *engine of innovation*. Entrepreneurship can push the discovery of opportunities and business and product development, and it can find the necessary resources and ways of funding. New ideas – so-called small-i innovation – are considered the 'endowments' of a discovery. And a successful combination of all the factors mentioned earlier makes the big-I innovation possible.

The bigger question is how developed and developing countries can succeed in initiating the small-i innovation and make the big-I innovation happen. What is their performance, and what is the gap among them? Do the role of entrepreneurs on growth and productivity differ in relation to the countries' level of development?

Entrepreneurship in developed and developing countries

According to the neo-Schumpeterian growth model, innovative entrepreneurship is the mechanism by which productivity growth is introduced in advanced economies. In these economies,

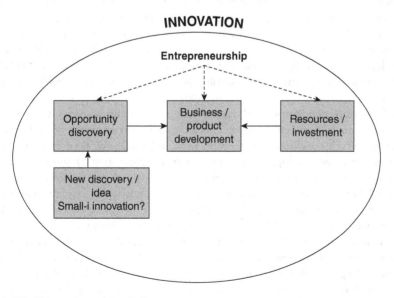

Figure. 7.1 "Big-I" innovation and "small-i" innovation
Source: Hindle and Yencken (2004)

innovation and structural change are more likely to take place through the combined efforts of entrepreneurial small ventures and large innovative firms (Nooteboom, 1994; Baumol, 2002). By merging these two firms, they can complement each other.

Apart from the role of entrepreneurs among developed and developing countries, the focus should be on the size and lifespan of the firms operating in these countries. According to Aldrich and Auster (1986), the larger and older the firm, the less receptive to change the organization becomes. Even though Block et al. (2013) emphasize the positive role of entrepreneurs and small firms in economic growth, again there remain large and unexplained differences across countries.

For a better enlightenment of the conditions needed for an entrepreneurship innovationto take place and the perfomance to affectthe economic growth of a country, the so-called Global Entrepreneuship Monitor (GEM) model needs to be looked at. GEM provides a brief description of how entrepreneurship is allied to economic growth and development and how it is affected by national conditions. Since the beginning, GEM has sought to explore the widely accepted link between entrepreneurship and economic development (Carree and Thurik, 2003; Acs, 2006; Audretsch, 2007) and the way in which the key elements interact. GEM takes a comprehensive socioeconomic approach and considers the degree of involvement in entrepreneurial activity within a country, identifying different types and phases of entrepreneurship (Bosma, Coduras, Litovsky, and Seaman, 2012). Three major components of entrepreneurship are included within the model: attitudes, activity and aspirations.

This diagram, shown in Figure 7.2, emphasizes once again the importance of the general national framework conditions for an established enterprise to thrive (Schwab and Sachs, 1997), and it includes the entrepreneurial framework conditions. According to the GEM model, both frameworks are crucial and support each other. On one side, the institutions (sets of rules), organizational culture, governmental policies, financial markets and external business environment are essential for the establishment of appropriate conditions for innovation. On the other side, the entrepreneur plays an important role in the creation of new technology-based firms and technological innovation with the help of this accumulated knowledge (technological, managerial, risk management, financial, etc.) and culture. Entrepreneurs and small firms exploit existing knowledge through their network and links to other knowledge producers to satisfy their specific needs in the production of goods and services (Braunerhjelm, 2010). However, part of the knowledge is likely to always remain 'tacit' and thus noncodifiable (Polanyi, 1966). All in all, the entrepreneur's background and personality are considered key elements in the process of innovation.

Both framework conditions are directly related to a country'scapacity to provide such a ground and to attract such entrepreneurs. This is the main barrier for the developing countries since the framework conditions are relatively weak, and that's why there is a huge difference betweendeveloped and developing countries concerning innovation. However, the literature is very diverse when we go through the entrepreneur's role in developed and developing countries.

As the GEM model affirms, the better framework conditions that exist, the higher the positive impact on the economy. This model is widely used for the country's performance; however, we can consider the same model for the firm level too. Thus, from a macro-level concept we pass to a micro one. It is extremely important that the firm has the proper framework conditions and has employed such entrepreneurs that are equipped with the necessary tools to discover new entrepreneurial opportunities or to take advantage of existing ones. In furtherance of possessing these conditions, the firms must have the required resources. Related to this, there exists a modern theory of innovation, the so-called resource-based theory of innovation. This theory assumes that companies have access to specific internal resources and competences that interact

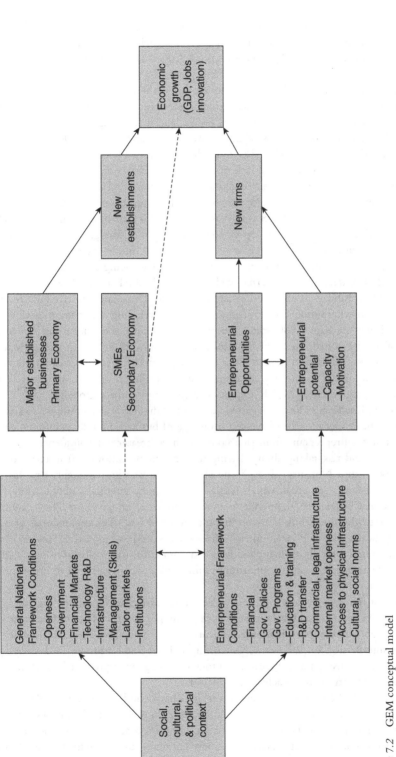

Figure 7.2 GEM conceptual model
Source: Global Entrepreneurship Monitor (2004)

with the environment in which they compete (Hobday, 2005).In this regard, the resource-based theory closely endorses the fundamentals of the GEM model.

Resource-based theory (RBT) is widely acknowledged as one of the most prominent and powerful theories for describing, explaining and predicting organizational relationships (Barney, Ketchen, and Wright, 2011). Usually, resource-based theory assumes a developed country context, with a modern and sophisticated national system of innovation (Hobday, 2005).In the development countries firms draw upon this system, and demanding markets guide decision-making and influence firms' visions of the future (Ansoff and Stewart, 1967). This dynamic Schumpeterian environment hardly exists in developing countries because these countries generally have underdeveloped or a total lack of innovative infrastructure (including all the components of national and entrepreneurial framework conditions). However, while looking at the countries' experience, some developing countries have succeeded in catching up with the innovation. One of the best examples is the case of Korea, for which, according to Kim (1997), the path to catching up was one of step-by-step assimilation of foreign technology, leading to more creative activities. Few works have tried to explain the link between industrial advanced countries' innovation models with the innovation path in developing countries (Hobday, 2005). Examples include Utterback and Abernathy (1975); Kim (1980); Kim and Lee (1987); Lee, Bae, and Choi (1988); Hobday (1995); and Lee and Lim (2001).These authors have built models or improved on each other's models to explain the steps of developing countries in catching up to the advanced ones. As Kim (1980) states, the case of developing countries is just the 'reversed' sequence of the developed ones, which means that they move from a mature to early stage of innovation process. His model is basically a three-stage model for the developing countries: (1) acquisition of foreign technology, (2) assimilation and (3) improvement. But again, there are very few developing countries which have been catching up on these processes.

The study of Koellinger (2008) suggested that most of the innovative entrepreneurs are from developed countries because they have the advantage of business-friendly economic environment. As a result, entrepreneurs from rich countries have greater self-confidence with higher education levels and risk-taking ability driving their creativity (innovation) in terms of establishing a new venture. Not surprisingly, in developing countries entrepreneurs have low levels of income with fewer resources, which results in low entrepreneurial activities (low rate of formation of small businesses).To provide supporting empirical evidence, Acs, Desai, and Hessels (2008) examined the direct link between income level and rate of entrepreneurial firms. This apparently indicates that in poor countries entrepreneurs are less innovative. However, studies suggest that foreign direct investment and large exporter firms may help developing countries in terms of creating new business opportunities for entrepreneurs and lead to innovation and knowledge spillover.

Concerning the data evidence related to entrepreneurship in developed and developing countries, GEM conducted a global survey of entrepreneurial activities.This study analyzed some important variables to compare their entrepreneurial activities in these countries.Tables 7.2 and 7.3 present information on early entrepreneurship behavior and attitudes in developing and developed countries using three indicators: (i) total early stage entrepreneurship, (ii) innovation and (iii) successful entrepreneurs achieving a high status.

Table 7.2 reports the results on entrepreneurship behavior and attitudes in developing countries.The figures are in terms of percentages. In the first column the list of countries is presented. The second column shows the percentage of the population are 18 to 64 who are either a nascent entrepreneur or owner-manager of a new entrepreneurial activity. Overall, Indonesia and Qatar have a low level of tendency towards early-stage entrepreneurial activity. In comparison,Vietnam, Malaysia, Madagascar and Thailand showed a relatively high proportion of (over

Table 7.2 Entrepreneurial behavior and attitudes in developing countries (figures are in percent) in 2007

Countries	TEA*	Innovation**	Successful entrepreneurs***
(1)	(2)	(3)	(4)
China	9.87	25.51	74.57
Egypt	13.25	25.26	82.01
India	9.28	25.60	56.18
Indonesia	7.47	11.58	80.95
Iran	13.32	16.15	79.40
Israel	12.78	26.70	86.07
Kazakhstan	11.32	23.54	80.11
Madagascar	21.76	20.89	77.78
Malaysia	21.60	29.33	69.88
Morocco	8.76	18.68	63.26
Qatar	7.43	37.94	77.32
Saudi Arabia	11.45	27.60	69.25
South Korea	12.98	29.66	68.57
South Africa	10.96	26.35	74.86
Taiwan	8.56	20.19	60.13
Thailand	21.62	29.29	74.48
UAE	8.97	18.67	87.77
Vietnam	23.27	13.86	77.77

* TEA: Total early-stage entrepreneurial activity
** Percentage of those involved in TEA who indicate that their product or service is new to at least some customers and that few/no businesses offer the same product
*** Percentage of population age 18–64 who agree with the statement that in their country, successful entrepreneurs receive high status

21 percent) trend for early-stage entrepreneurial activity. In sum, there is a low level of early-stage entrepreneurial activities in developing countries. On the other hand, column 3 reports the product and process innovation of early-stage entrepreneurs. In China, nearly 26 percent of early-stage entrepreneurs undertake innovation activity, while Indonesia and Iran have overall low levels of innovation activities compared to other countries. To conclude, in developing countries, there is a low level of early-stage entrepreneurial and innovation activities. Interestingly, a large proportion of countries agreed that "successful entrepreneurs achieve high status". This outcome shows that having a successful business in these countries is considered part of a high social status. However, in developing countries starting a new business with an innovative idea requires more physical and financial help from the public and private sectors. This apparently indicates that entrepreneurs in developing countries are more likely to be risk averse in terms of starting a new business or undertaking innovation activities.

Table 7.3 presents the perceptions of entrepreneur behavior and innovation in developed countries. Only Canada and the United States showed a high percentage of early-stage entrepreneurial activities compared to other countries. Approximately 19% of the population age 18 to 64 are new entrepreneurs or owner-managers of the business. But within the nascent entrepreneur category, their level of undertaking innovation activity is high as compared to developing countries. This outcome suggests that entrepreneurs from developed countries view innovation activity as key to the success of the business. Not surprisingly, the majority of the entrepreneurs from developed countries considered being an entrepreneur they could achieve high status.

Table 7.3 Entrepreneurial behavior and attitudes in developed countries (figures are in percent) in 2007

Countries	TEA*	Innovation**	Successful entrepreneurs***
Canada	18.75	43.18	73.96
France	3.92	48.63	74.21
Germany	5.28	23.74	77.9
Ireland	8.93	42.73	81.88
Italy	4.28	28.22	73.21
Japan	4.68	24.68	51.96
Luxembourg	9.05	57.13	69.95
Netherlands	9.92	22.52	67.5
Sweden	7.29	29.05	70.52
Switzerland	8.47	24.93	73.2
United Kingdom	8.4	27.06	75.6
United States	13.64	35.93	75.49

* TEA: Total early-stage entrepreneurial activity
** Percentage of those involved in TEA who indicate that their product or service is new to at least some customers and that few/no businesses offer the same product
*** Percentage of population are 18–64 who agree with the statement that in their country, successful entrepreneurs receive high status

Empirical literature

Concerning the link between entrepreneurial characteristics and firm performance, Madsen (2007) explored the positive association of degree of entrepreneurship (entrepreneurial orientation) with the firms' increasing market share, employment and sales growth by using a panel study of Norwegian SMEs. Similarly, Wiklund and Shepherd (2005) investigated the relationship between entrepreneurial characteristics and firm performance using longitudinal data on 413 Swedish firms. According to Wiklund and Shepherd, entrepreneurial orientation that is, innovativeness, risk taking and proactiveness, positively influence the firms' sales and profitability. Before taking a risk, the entrepreneur must be well aware of the organization strategy, culture and related environmental factors (dynamism and industry characteristics), because information asymmetry on the part of the entrepreneur could affect the firm's performance (Lumpkin and Dess, 1996). To drive innovation at the firm level, the entrepreneur's personality requires multidimensional characteristics such as education (know-how of the business), experience in large firms, management and marketing knowledge (Marcati, Guido, and Peluso, 2008; Capaldo and Landoli, 2003). However, the quality levels of entrepreneurial abilities are different in terms of regions. For instance, studies (e.g. van Stel, Martin, and Thurik, 2005) implied that in developing countries the level of human capital is low, and such countries do not have sufficient number of large firms because large firms usually have a better organizational environment and provide opportunities to workers to display their entrepreneurial skills.

Additionally, others have argued that entrepreneurs not only improve their firms' innovation performance but also enhance competitiveness through internationalization (see Todd and Javalgi, 2007). Interestingly, entrepreneurship plays two major roles in the firms' growth: first they introduce innovation, and second they accelerate the firm's ability to internalize the external knowledge (i.e., absorptive capacity) (Alvarez and Lowell, 2001). In other words, entrepreneurs are multitasking performers. For example, through managerial and entrepreneurial capabilities, they introduce heterogeneous inputs into the firm and then convert these into innovation output as result of their multifaceted role. Another branch of researchers emphasized the social side of the entrepreneurs (see Hashi and Krasniqi, 2008). Entrepreneurs formed business to business, bank to business and intra-inter–firm networks using their social interaction skills. Greve and Salaff (2003) argued that an entrepreneur with social relations would provide the firms access to tangible and intangible resources because entrepreneurs require diverse resources (e.g. capital, technologies and skills) to start the entrepreneurial business. These social relations with family members, friends, colleagues from earlier jobs and others would help entrepreneurs achieve their organizational goals effectively. Similar evidence is provided by Audretsch (2004) related to entrepreneur social interaction with workers from other firms resulting in high innovation performance because social interaction creates knowledge spillovers.

Concerning the other proxies of entrepreneurs, Cuevas and Carrasco's (2007) study on 400 Spanish SMEs (from Seville) found that entrepreneurs' dependence on suppliers, clients and related factors of production (inputs) from the nearest market positively influence growth of SMEs. Leitao and Franco (2008) investigated whether human and organizational capital are important determinants of entrepreneurial performance using multiple regression analysis. Specifically, entrepreneurs' managerial characteristics significantly improve the innovation output. In sum, entrepreneurs contribute more to the national income than nonentrepreneurs because entrepreneurs add economic value to the business (see van Praag and Versloot, 2007). The role of entrepreneurship is not only limited to innovation but also generates employment, increases productivity and enhances the individual utility levels. Entrepreneurs increase the competitive environment and have high job satisfaction with low opportunity costs because of their self-employment.

Conclusion

To sum up, the literature review shows that some of the characteristics of entrepreneurs are inherent and some are developed over time. Inherent characteristics of entrepreneurs are listed as risk takers, proactive in decision making, possessing a stronger need to achieve self-efficacy, preferences for autonomy, social interaction, absorptive capacity, etc. Some of the entrepreneurship characteristics that can be developed over time are the managerial skills, marketing knowledge, awareness of industry characteristics and dynamism, know-how of the business and market, experience in large firms, etc. A thoughtful combination of both characteristics of entrepreneurs, inherent and developed, raises the probability of an innovation taking place. However, most often, the entrepreneurs' characteristics solely are not sufficient to create an innovation. Along with their characteristics, the countries' conditions and environment should be suitable to innovation creation. The OECD, for instance, explicitly includes framework conditions in its review of innovation systems (World Bank, 2010). A strong economy and well-established institutions can be the key determinants of an innovation climate. Meanwhile, an innovation in developing countries may come from abroad or from other users in the same country, or it may be created by public or private R&D labs or firms in the same country. Consequently, because of differences in the national framework conditions, there exist not only differences among developed and developing countries but also differences among similar income-level countries.

Notes

1 The opposite of *litterae patentes* are *litterae clausae*, which are personal in nature and sealed in close so that only the recipient can read their contents. See *Cassell's Latin Dictionary: Latin-English and English-Latin*, James Robert Vernam Marchant and Joseph F Charles, London: Cassell, 1957.
2 www.ipo.gov.uk/p-history.htm

3 Adam Smith, *An Inquiry into the Nature and Causes of the Wealth of Nations*, Edwin Cannan (Ed), Chicago: University of Chicago Press, 2010, Book IV, Chapter VII, Part III, page 148.
4 Ibid., Book V, Chapter I, Part III, page 278.
5 Although it is often presumed that patent and antitrust policies are in conflict, there is no conflict if price discrimination is allowed. Third-degree price discrimination by patent holders can raise static social welfare (Hausmanand MacKie-Mason, 1988; van Dijk, 1995).
6 This theory of the persistence of monopoly is further extended in patent race models, e.g. see Harris and Vickers, 1985, Bental and Fixler, 1988, Leininger, 1991, Denicolò, 1996, Takalo and Kanniainen, 2000, and Denicolò, 2001. Empirical studies on persistence of innovation can be found in Cefis and Orsenigo, 2001, and Cefis, 2003.
7 In fact, it seems not practical in theoretical design of optimal patent terms. As Rafiquzzaman (1987) showed, the optimal patent term is very sensitive to the types of uncertainty and the inventor's attitude toward risk. Judd (1985) proposed that finite-life patents could cause unstable development of innovation in a dynamic general equilibrium. Gilbert and Shapiro (1990) demonstrated that infinitely lived but very narrow patents are optimal, as deadweight losses are minimized and spread through time, but inventors can still recover their R&D expenditures. However, recently researchers show finite-life patents could be the optimal choice under specific conditions (Gallini, 1992). Related studies are reported by Veall (1992); Chouand Shy (1993); Horowitzand Lai (1996); Matutes, Regibeau and Rockett (1996); and Futagami and Iwaisako (2007).
8 Some discussed alternative means of patent systems for public intervention in the research market, for example, compulsory licensing, prizes and direct contracting for research services. See discussions in Wright (1983), Kingston (1994).
9 Patent breadth refers to the flow rate of the profit available to the patentee while the patent is in force (Gilbert and Shapiro, 1990).
10 Some recent studies suggest the patent system is more likely to foster technological progress. For example, Kultti, Takalo and Toikka (2006) demonstrate that a well-designed patent system can induce innovators to patent rather than keep their innovations secret. Similar views are expressed in Mukherjee (2006).
11 Some recent works on the patent system and antitrust refer to patent pools or cross-licensing agreements. Patent pools may be socially beneficial under certain circumstances (Denicolò, 2002; Lerner and Tirole, 2004).
12 The discussions on whether patent protection promotes or blocks innovation keep appearing in the literature. An interesting case study by Selgin and Turner (2011) proposes that monopoly rights of James Watt's 1769steamer patent may actually have hastened the development of the high-pressure steam engine by inspiring Richard Trevithick to revive a supposedly obsolete technology so as to invent around them. Chu et al. (2012)find that strengthening the effect of blocking patents stifles vertical innovation but increases horizontal innovation.
13 Studies show overly weak or overly strong patent protection may hinder technological progress(Diwan and Rodrik, 1991; Mazzoleni and Nelson, 1998). However, more investigation is required on how important patent protection is to affect private returns to R&D (Schankerman, 1998).
14 While patent breadth defines the extent of protection against imitations, the extent of protection against improvements is labeled as patent height (Van Dijk, 1996). Some studies show patent breadth and patent life may have different impacts. For example, Takalo (1998) demonstrated that an increase in patent breadth always discouraged resorting to secrecy, whereas the influence of increased patent life was the opposite with large spillovers. Thus, an increase in patent life can also reduce innovative activity with large spillovers.
15 In addition to the effect of wholesome welfare, a weaker regime seems to affect import (Maskusand Penubarti, 1995; Smith, 1999).
16 The TRIPs agreement achieved in 1994 by the WTO is an effort to harmonize the North–South discrepancy. McCalman (2001) found that this harmonization generated large transfers of income from the South to the North.
17 Chu, A.C., Cozzi, G. and Galli (2012) try to explain this inverted-U effect with a model that features the knowledge-driven or lab-equipment innovation process.
18 He cited two examples, the British law of 1919 and the American Stanley bill, which called for compulsory working of patents under penalty of the patentee being forced to grant compulsory licenses.

19 TRIPs Article 27.1 requires that "patents shall be available and patent rights enjoyable without discrimination as to the place of invention, the field of technology and whether products are imported or locally produced".
20 Other forms of strategic patent policy include government buyout of private patents, which then are placed freely in the public domain (Kremer, 1998). However, this policy is not discriminatory against foreign inventors.
21 Many studies investigate the relationship between R&D and patenting. However, using aggregated R&D may underestimate the productivity of 'R', as mainly 'R' but not 'D' leads to patents. Czarnitzki, Kraft and Thorwarth (2009) show disaggregating 'R' and 'D' show a significant premium of 'R' towards patenting.
22 There are other interesting observations on innovations. For example, Geroski, Van Reenen and Walters (1997) found very few innovative firms are persistently innovative.
23 Blind, Cremers and Mueller (2009) find that companies using patents as a defensive tool tend to receive a higher number of forward citations for their patents, whereas companies using patents as an offensive tool receive fewer citations and less opposition to their patents.
24 Arundel and Kabla (1998) surveyed European firms and found the sector characteristics had a strong influence on product patent propensities. The propensity rates for product innovations average 35.9 percent, varying between 8.1 percent in textiles and 79.2 percent in pharmaceuticals.
25 Still, one must be cautious before taking patent counts as a measure. As demonstrated in Pakes (1986), patents applied for at an early stage in the inventive process are associated with substantial uncertainty. Gradually, the patentees uncover the true value of their patents. Most turn out to be of little value, and only some rare winners are made into further development. Therefore, one would not expect to find a very stable relationship between profits and patent counts for small firms, a view also supported by Basberg (1987).
26 It is noted that patent citations are used to measure technological overlap between firms (Mowery, Oxley and Silverman, 1998).
27 Similar findings are reported in Maurseth and Verspagen (2002) and Bottazzi and Peri (2003).
28 There are some defects of using forward citations to measure the value of patents. For example, citations are added by patent examiners as well as by patent applicants. Thus, it is better to exclude citations added by examiners (Alcácer, Gittelman and Sampat, 2009). Patent citations are also known to be highly skewed; therefore, special statistic models have to be employed (Silverberg and Verspagen, 2007). In addition, "wacky" patents have higher originality, generality and citation lags, suggesting that forward patent citations should be interpreted carefully (Czarnitzki, Hussinger and Schneider, 2011). There are other indicators to measure the importance of a patent, such as the number of years a patent is renewed and the number of countries in which protection for the same invention is sought (Lanjouw, Pakes and Putnam, 1998).
29 Studies on technology sourcing are found in Belderbos (2001), Bas and Sierra (2002) and Iwasa and Odagiri (2004).

References

Abou, N. (2017). The role of corporate parent support for spinoff innovation performance. *International Review of Entrepreneurship*, 15(2), 203–226.

Acs, J. Z., Desai, S. and Hessels, J. (2008). Entrepreneurship, economic development and Institutions. *Journal of Small Business Economics*, 31, 219–234.

Acs, Z. (2006). How is entrepreneurship good for economic growth? *Innovations: Technology, Governance, Globalization*, 1(1), 97–107.

Agnieszka, K. S. (2017). From healthcare manager's competencies to healthcare organization's competences. *Vadyba Journal of Management*, 2(31), 9–15.

Ahlers, M. and Wilms, M. (2017). Ambidextrous Leadership in Innovation: a multiple case study of innovation leaders on the alignment of opening and closing leader behaviors (Master Thesis, Linköping University, Linköping, Sweden).

AlAzzawi, S. (2011). Multinational corporations and knowledge flows: evidence from patent citations. *Economic Development and Cultural Change*, 59(3), 649–680.

Alcácer, J., Gittelman, M. and Sampat, B. (2009). Applicant and examiner citations in U.S. patents: an overview and analysis. *Research Policy*, 38(2), 415–427.

Aldrich, H. and Auster, E. R. (1986). Even dwarfs started small: liabilities of age and size and their strategic implications. *Research in Organizational Behavior*, 8, 165–198.

Alexandrova, M. (2004). Entrepreneurship in a transition economy: the impact of environment on entrepreneurial orientation. *Problems and Perspective in Management*, 2, 140–148.

Almeida, P. (1996). Knowledge sourcing by foreign multinationals: patent citation analysis in the U.S. semiconductor industry. *Strategic Management Journal*, 17, 155–165.

Alvarez, A. S. and Lowell, W. B. (2001). The entrepreneurship of resource based theory. *Journal of Management*, 27(6), 755–775.

Anderson, N., Potočnik, K. and Zhou, J. (2014). Innovation and creativity in organizations: a state-of the-science review, prospective commentary, and guiding framework. *Journal of Management*, 40, 1297–1333.

Ansoff, H. I. and Stewart, J. M. (1967). Strategies for a technology-based business. *Harvard Business Review*, 45(6), 71–83.

Aoki, R. and Prusa, T.J. (1993). International standards for intellectual property protection and R and D incentives. *Journal of International Economics*, 35(3–4), 251–273.

Arditti, F. D. and Sandor, R.L. (1973). A note on variable patent life. *Journal of Industrial Economics*, 21(2), 177–183.

Arundel, A. (2001). The relative effectiveness of patents and secrecy for appropriation. *Research Policy*, 30(4), 611–624.

Arundel, A. and Kabla, I. (1998). What percentage of innovations are patented? Empirical estimates for European firms. *Research Policy*, 27(2), 127–141.

Audretsch, B. D. (2004). Sustaining innovation and growth: public policy support for entrepreneurship. *Industry and Innovation*, 11(3), 167–191.

Audretsch, D.B. (2007). Entrepreneurship capital and economic growth. *Oxford Review of Economic Policy*, 23(1), 63–78.

Audretsch, D. B., Falck, O. and Heblich, S. (Eds.) (2011). *Handbook of research on innovation and entrepreneurship*. Cheltenham: Edward Elgar Publishing.

Audretsch, D.B., Keilbach, M.C. and Lehmann, E. (2006). *Entrepreneurship and Economic*. Oxford: Oxford University Press.

Avolio, B. J., Gardner, W. L., Walumbwa, F. O., Luthans, F. and May, D. R. (2004). Unlocking the mask: a look at the process by which authentic leaders impact follower attitudes and behaviors. *The Leadership Quarterly*, 15(6), 801–823.

Avolio, B. J., Waldman, D. A. and Yammarino, F. J. (1991). Leading in the 1990s: the four i's of transformational leadership. *Journal of European Industrial Training*, 15, 9–16.

Bagheri, A. and Akbari, M. (2018). The impact of entrepreneurial leadership on nurses' innovation behavior. *Journal of Nursing Scholarship*, 50(1), 28–35.

Baker, S. and Mezzetti, C. (2005). Disclosure as a strategy in the patent race. *Journal of Law and Economics*, 48(1), 173–194.

Balas, M. (2015). Competing via creation of distinctive organizational competences: 'How to do it'. *Econviews*, 28(1), 143–159.

Ballein, K. M. (1998). Entrepreneurial leadership characteristics of SNEs emerge as their role develops. *Nursing Administration Quarterly*, 22(2), 60–69.

Barney, J. B., Ketchen, D. J., Jr. and Wright, M. (2011). The future of resource-based theory: revitalization or decline? *Journal of Management*, 37(5), 1299–1315.

Bas, C.L. and Sierra, C. (2002). 'Location Versus Home Country Advantages' in R&D activities: some further results on multinationals' locational strategies. *Research Policy*, 31(4), 589–609.

Basberg, B. L. (1987). Patents and the measurement of technological change: a survey of the literature. *Research Policy*, 16(2–4), 131–131.

Bass, B. M. (1990a). *Bass & Stogdill's handbook of leadership: theory, research, and managerial applications* (3rd ed.). New York: Free Press.

Baumol, W. J. (2002). *The free-market innovation machine: analyzing the growth miracle of capitalism*. Princeton: Princeton University Press.

Beaver, G. and Prince, G. (2002). Innovation, entrepreneurship and competitive advantage in the entrepreneurial venture. *Journal of Small Business and Enterprise Development*, 9(1), 28–37.

Belderbos, R. (2001). Overseas innovations by Japanese firms: an analysis of patent and subsidiary data. *Research Policy*, 30(2), 313–332.

Belenzon, S. (2012). Cumulative innovation and market value: evidence from patent citations. *Economic Journal*, 122(559), 265–285.

Bell, C., Chan, M. and Nel, P.(2014). The impact of participative and directive leadership on organizational culture. *Mediterranean Journal of Social Sciences*, 5(23), 1970–1985.

Benner, M. J. and Tushman, M. L. (2003). Exploitation, exploration, and process management: the productivity dilemma revisited. *Academy of Management Review*, 28(2), 238–256.

Bental, B. and Fixler, D. (1988). Firm behavior and the externalities of technological leadership. *European Economic Review*, 32(9), 1731–1746.

Benz, M. and Frey, B. S. (2008). Being independent is a great thing: subjective evaluations of self employment and hierarchy.*Economica*,75(298), 362–383.

Berkowitz, M.K. and Kotowitz,Y. (1982). Patent policy in an open economy. *Canadian Journal of Economics*, 15(1), 1–17.

Bertrand, O. and Zitouna, H. (2008). Domestic versus cross-border acquisitions: which impact on the target firms' performance? *Applied Economics*, 40(1), 2221–2238.

Blazsek, S. and Escribano,A. (2010). Knowledge spillovers in US patents: a dynamic patent intensity model with secret common innovation factors. *Journal of Econometrics*, 159(1), 14–32.

Blind, K., Cremers, K. and Mueller, E. (2009). The influence of strategic patenting on companies' patent portfolios. *Research Policy*, 38(2), 428–436.

Block, J. H.,Thurik, R. and Zhou, H. (2013).What turns knowledge into innovative products? The role of entrepreneurship and knowledge spillovers. *Journal of Evolutionary Economics*,23(4), 693–718.

Bloxam, G. A. (1957). Letters patent for inventions: their use and misuse. *The Journal of Industrial Economics*, 5(3), 157–179.

Blundell, R., Griffith, R. and Windmeijer, W. (2002). Individual effects and dynamics in count data models. *Journal of Econometrics*, 108(1), 113–131.

Bosma, N., Coduras, A., Litovsky,Y. and Seaman, J. (2012). GEM manual: a report on the design, data and quality control of the Global Entrepreneurship Monitor. *Global Entrepreneurship Monitor*, 1–95.

Bossink, B. A. G. (2004). Effectiveness of innovation leadership styles: a manager's influence on ecological innovation in construction projects. *Construction Innovation*, 4, 211–228.

Bossink, B. A. G. (2007). Leadership for sustainable innovation. *International Journal of Technology Management & Sustainable Development*, 6, 135–149.

Bosworth, D.L. (1980).The transfer of U.S. technology abroad. *Research Policy*, 9(4), 378–388.

Bosworth, D. L. (1984). Foreign patent flows to and from the United Kingdom. *Research Policy*, 13(2), 115–124.

Bottazzi, L. and Peri, G. (2003). Innovation and spillovers in regions: evidence from European patent data. *European Economic Review*, 47(4), 687–710.

Boyatzis, R. E. (1982). *The competent manager – a model for effective performance*. New York: Wiley.

Braumerhjelm, P. (2010). Entrepreneurship, innovation and economic growth: past experiences, current knowledge and policy implications,Working Paper Series 02, Swedish Entrepreneurship.

Breevaart, K., Bakker, A. R., Demerouti, E. and Derks, D. (2016).Who takes the lead? A multi-source diary study on leadership, work engagement, and job performance. *Journal of Organizational Behavior*, 37(1), 309–325.

British Standards Institution (2008). *Design management systems – part 1: guide to managing the innovation*. London: British Standards Institution.

Brown, R. and Mason, C. (2014). Inside the high-tech black box: a critique of technology entrepreneurship policy. *Technovation*, 34(12), 773–784.

Brunswicker, S. and Ehrenmann, F. (2013). Managing open innovation in SMEs: a good practice example of a German software firm. *International Journal of Industrial Engineering and Management*, 4(1), 33–41.

Brunswicker, S. and Vanhaverbeke, W. (2014). Open innovation in small and medium-sized enterprises. *Journal of Small Business Management*. doi:10.1111/jsbm.12120.

Burns, P. (2007). *Entrepreneurship and small business*. Palgrave Macmillan, 2nd Edition.

Cantillon, R. (1755). Essai sur la nature du commerce en général (written c. 1730). Ed. and trans. H. Higgs, London: Macmillan, 1931.

Cantillon, R. (1775). Essai sur la Nature du Commerce en General, edited with an English translation and other material by Henry Higgs, C.B. Reissued for The Royal Economic Society by Frank Cass and Co., LTD., London. 1959.

Capaldo, G. and Landoli, L. (2003). The evaluation of innovation capabilities in small software firms: a methodological approach. *Journal of Small Business of Economics*, 21, 343–354.

Carmeli, A., Sheaffer, Z., Binyamin, G., Reiter-Palmon, R., and Shimoni,T. (2014). Transformational leadership and creative problem-solving: The mediating role of psychological safety and reflexivity. *The Journal of Creative Behavior*, 48, 115–135.

Carmeli, A. and Paulus, P. B. (2015). CEO ideational facilitation leadership and team creativity: the mediating role of knowledge sharing. *The Journal of Creative Behavior*, 49, 53–75.

Carree, M. A. and Thurik, A. R. (2003). The impact of entrepreneurship on economic growth. In *Handbook of entrepreneurship research*. Boston, MA: Springer, pp. 437–471.

Casson, Mark C. (1982). *Basic concepts of the theory' the entrepreneurship, an economic theory*. NJ: Barness and Noble Books, 22–25.

Cefis, E. (2003). Is there persistence in innovative activities? *International Journal of Industrial Organization*, 21(4), 489–515.

Cefis, E. and Orsenigo, L. (2001). The persistence of innovative activities: a cross-countries and cross-sectors comparative analysis. *Research Policy*, 30(7), 1139–1158.

Cefis, E. and Triguero, A. (2016). Make, buy, or both: the innovation sourcing strategy dilemma after M and A. *Growth and Change*, 47(2), 175–196.

Chandler, A. D. (1990). *Strategy and structure: chapters in the history of the industrial enterprise* (Vol. 120). Cambridge, MA: MIT Press.

Chang, Y. (2014). Multilevel transformational leadership and management innovation. *Leadership and Organization Development Journal*, 37(2), 265–288.

Chao, C. C. and Tian, D. (2011). Culturally universal or culturally specific: a comparative study of anticipated female leadership styles in Taiwan and the United States. *Journal of Leadership and Organizational Studies*, 18(1), 64–79.

Chaston, I. and Scott, G. J. (2012). Entrepreneurship and open innovation in an emerging economy. *Management Decision*, 50(7), 1161–1177.

Chaudhuri, S., Goldberg, P. K. and Jia, P. (2006). Estimating the effects of global patent protection in pharmaceuticals: a case study of quinolones in India. *The American Economic Review*, 96(5), 1477–1514.

Chen, T. (2011). Structuring versus autocraticness: exploring a comprehensive model of authoritarian leadership (doctoral dissertation, City University of Hong Kong, Hong Kong SAR, China). Retrieved from http://bit.ly/1SYK89a

Chen, L., Zheng, W., Yang, B. and Bai, S. (2016). Transformational leadership, social capital, and organizational innovation. *Leadership and Organization Development Journal*, 37(7), 843–859.

Chen, M. X. and Iyigun, M. (2011). Patent protection and strategic delays in technology development: implications for economic growth. *Southern Economic Journal*, 78(1), 211–232.

Cheng, J. and Bennett, D. (2006). Strategies for performance improvement in the Chinese Chemical Industry. *Journal of Technology Management in China*, 1(2), 190–207.

Chou, Chien-fu. and Shy, O. (1993). The crowding-out effects of long duration of patents. *The Rand Journal of Economics*, 24(2), 304–312.

Chu, A. C., Cozzi, G. and Galli, S. (2012). Does intellectual monopoly stimulate or stifle innovation? *European Economic Review*, 56(4), 727–746.

Chu, A. C., Pan, S. and Sun, M. (2012). When does elastic labor supply cause an inverted-effect of patents on innovation? *Economics Letters*, 117(1), 211–213.

Clardy, A. (2008). Human resource development and the resource-based model of core competencies: methods for diagnosis and assessment. *Human Resource Development Review*, 7(4), 387–407.

Cohen, W. M. and Levinthal, D. A. (1989). Innovation and learning: the two faces of R and D. *The Economic Journal*, 99(397), 569–596.

Colombo, M. G., Piva, E. and Rossi-Lamastra, C. (2014). Open innovation and within-industry diversification in small and medium enterprises: the case of open source software firms. *Research Policy*, 43(5), 891–902.

Connolly, R. A. and Hirschey, M. (1988). Market value and patents: a Bayesian approach. *Economics Letters*, 27(1), 83–87.

Crépon, B. and Duguet, E. (1997a). Estimating the innovation function from patent numbers: GMM on count panel data. *Journal of Applied Econometrics*, 12(3), 243–263.

Crepon, B. and Duguet, E. (1997b). Research and development, competition and innovation pseudo-maximum likelihood and simulated maximum likelihood methods applied to count data models with heterogeneity. *Journal of Econometrics*, 79(2), 355–378.

Cuevas, J. G. and Caceres-Carrasco, F. R. (2007). Entrepreneurial structure quantitative analysis: the case of Seville (Spain). *International Advance Economic Research*, 13(4), 488–494.

Cummings, G. G., MacGregor, T., Davey, M., Lee, H., Wong, C. A., Lo, E., ... Stafford, E. (2010). Leadership styles and outcome patterns for the nursing workforce and work environment: a systematic review. *International Journal of Nursing Studies*, 47, 363–385.

Curran, D., Van Egeraat, C. and O'Gorman, C. (2016). Inherited competence and spin-off performance. *European Planning Studies*, 24(3), 443–462.

Czarnitzki, D., Hussinger, K. and Schneider, C. (2011). 'Wacky' patents meet economic indicators. *Economics Letters*, 113(2), 131–134.

Czarnitzki, D., Kraft, K. and Thorwarth, S. (2009). The knowledge production of 'R' and 'D'. *Economics Letters*, 105(1), 141–143.

Daft, R. L. (2001). *The leadership experience* (2nd ed.). Fort Worth, TX: Harcourt Publishers Ltd, College Publishers.

Day, G. S. (2007). Closing the growth gap: balancing BIG I and small innovation. *Market Science Institute Reports* (06–121).

Deardorff, A.V. (1992). Welfare effects of global patent protection. *Economica*, 59(233), 35–51.

Deluga, R. J. (1990). The effects of transformational, transactional, and laissez faire leadership characteristics on subordinate influencing behavior. *Basic & Applied Social Psychology*, 11, 191–203.

Denicolò, V. (1996). Patent races and optimal patent breadth and length. *The Journal of Industrial Economics*, 44(3), 249–265.

Denicolò, V. (2001). Growth with non-drastic innovations and the persistence of leadership. *European Economic Review*, 45(8), 1399–1413.

Denicolò, V. (2002). Sequential innovation and the patent-antitrust conflict. *Oxford Economic Papers*, 54(4), 649–668.

Dess, G.G. and Picken, J.C. (2000). Changing roles: leadership in the 21st century. *Organizational Dynamics*, 28(3), 18–34.

Dezsö, C. L. and Ross, D. G. (2012). Does female representation in top management improve firm performance? A panel data investigation. *Strategic Management Journal*, 33(1), 1072–1089.

Diwan, I. and Rodrik, D. (1991). Patents, appropriate technology, and north-south trade. *Journal of International Economics*, 30(1–2), 27–47.

Dobb, M. (1981). *Theories of value and distribution since Adam Smith: ideology and economic theory*. Cambridge: Cambridge University Press.

Dodgson, M. (1993). Organizational learning: a review of some literatures. *Organization Studies*, 14, 375–394.

Dodgson, M. and Bessant, J. R. (1996). *Effective innovation policy*. International Thomson Business Press.

Doğan, E. (2017). A strategic approach to innovation. *Journal of Management, Marketing and Logistics*, 4(3), 290–300.

Doi, N. (1996). Performance of Japanese firms in patented inventions; an analysis of patents granted in the U.S. *Review of Industrial Organization*, 11(1), 49–68.

Eisele, P. (2017). Assessment of leadership for innovation and perceived organizational innovativeness: differences between self-reported individual and social creativity. *International Journal of Organizational Leadership*, 6(1), 470–480.

Eisenbach, R., Watson, K. and Pillai, R. (1999). Transformational leadership in the context of organizational change. *Journal of Organizational Change Management*, 12, 80–89.

Elenkov, D. S., Judge, W. and Wright, P. (2005). Strategic leadership and executive innovation influence: an international multi-cluster comparative study. *Strategic Management Journal*, 26, 665–682.

Elfenbein, D. W. (2007). Publications, patents, and the market for university inventions. *Journal of Economic Behavior and Organization*, 63(4), 688–715.

Encaoua, D., Guellec, D. and Martinez, C. (2006). Patent systems for encouraging innovation: lessons from economic analysis. *Research Policy*, 35(9), 1423–1440.

Entrialgo, M., Fernandez, E. and Vazquez, C. (2001). The effects of the organizational context on SME's entrepreneurship: some Spanish evidence. *Small Business Economics*, 16, 3, 223–236.

Eom, B-Y. and Lee, K. (2010). Determinants of industry – academy linkages and, their impact on firm performance: the case of Korea as a latecomer in knowledge industrialization. *Research Policy*, 39(5), 625–639.

Evenson, R. E. (1993). Patents, R&D, and invention potential: international evidence. *The American Economic Review*, 83(2), 463–468.

Faulí-Oller, R. and Sandonís, J. (2002). Welfare reducing licensing. *Games and Economic Behavior*, 41(2), 192–205.

Feldman, M. P. and Audretsch, D. B. (1999). Innovation in cities: science-based diversity, specialization and localized competition. *European Economic Review*, 43(2), 409–429.

Feller, I. (1990). Universities as engines of R&D-based economic growth: they think they can. *Research Policy*, 19(4), 335–348.

Ferrary, M. (2008). Strategic spin-off: a new incentive contract for managing R&D researchers. *Journal of Technology Transfer*, 33(1), 600–618.

Fiedler, F. E. (1995). Cognitive resources and leadership performance. *Applied Psychology: An International Review*, 44, 5–28.

Finkelstein, S. and Hambrick, D. (1996). *Strategic leadership: top executives and their effects on organizations.* Minneapolis: West Publishing Company.

Flabbi, L., Piras, C. and Abrahams, S. (2016). Female corporate leadership in Latin America and the Caribbean region: representation and firm-level outcomes. IDB Working Paper Series, No. IDB-WP-655, doi:http://dx.doi.org/10.18235/0000249. http://hdl.handle.net/10419/146451.

Fosfuri, A. (2000). Patent protection, imitation and the mode of technology transfer. *International Journal of Industrial Organization*, 18(7), 1129–1149.

Frenkel, A., Israel, E. and Maital, S. (2015). The evolution of innovation networks and spin-off entrepreneurship: the case of RAD. *European Planning Studies*, 23(8), 1646–1670.

Friedrich, T. L., Mumford, M. D., Vessey, B., Beeler, C. K. and Eubanks, D. L. (2010). Leading for innovation: reevaluating leader influences on innovation with regard to innovation type and complexity. *International Studies of Management & Organization*, 40, 6–29.

Fu, X., Li, Y. and Si, Y. (2013). The impact of paternalistic leadership on innovation: an integrated model. *Nankai Business Review*, 4(1), 9–24.

Fudenberg, D., et al. (1983). Preemption, leapfrogging and competition in patent races. *European Economic Review*, 22(1), 3–31.

Furukawa, Y. (2010). Intellectual property protection and innovation: an inverted-U relationship. *Economics Letters*, 109(2), 99–101.

Futagami, K. and Iwaisako, T. (2007). Dynamic analysis of patent policy in an endogenous growth model. *Journal of Economic Theory*, 132(1), 306–334.

Galasso, A. and Schankerman, M. (2010). Patent thickets, courts, and the market for innovation. *The Rand Journal of Economics*, 41(3), 472–503.

Gallini, N. T. (1992). Patent policy and costly imitation. *The Rand Journal of Economics*, 23(1), 52–63.

Gardner, D. M. (1992). Marketing/entrepreneurship interface: a conceptualization. In Hills, E.G. (Ed.), '*Marketing and entrepreneurship', Research ideas and opportunities* (1st ed.). Westport: Quorum Books, pp. 1–5.

Geraldi, J. G. (2009). Reconciling order and chaos in multi-project firms. *International Journal of Managing Projects in Business*, 2(1), 149–156.

Geroski, P. A., Van Reenen, J. and Walters, C. F. (1997). How persistently do firms innovate? *Research Policy*, 26(1), 33–48.

Gilbert, R. and Shapiro, C. (1990). Optimal patent length and breadth. *The Rand Journal of Economics*, 21(1), 106–112.

Gimzauskiene, E. and Staliuniene, J. D. (2010). Model of core competence ranking in audit business. *Engineering Economics*, 21(2), 128–135.

Ginarte, J.C. and Park, W.G. (1997). Determinants of patent rights: a cross-national study. *Research Policy*, 26(3), 283–301.

Golibjon, Y. (2016) Innovation and SME Development: Indonesia Experience in UZBekinstan. *Journal of Entrepreneurship and Organization*, 45, 811–924.

Golla, E. and Johnson, R. (2013). The relationship between transformational and transactional leadership styles and innovation commitment and output at commercial software companies. *The Business Review Cambridge*, 21(1), 337–343.

Grant, R. M. (2010). *Contemporary strategy analysis* (7th ed.). West Sussex: John Wiley & Sons Ltd.

Greve, A. and Salaff, W. J. (2003). Social networks and entrepreneurship. *Journal of Entrepreneurship Theory and Practice*, 28(1), 1–22.

Griliches, Z. (1981). Market value, R&D, and patents. *Economics Letters*, 7(2), 183–187.

Guallino, G. and Prevot F. (2008). Competence-building through organizational recognition or frequency of use: case study of the Lafarge group's development of competence in managing post-merger cultural integration. In Martens, R., Heene, A. and Sanchez, R. (Eds.), *Competence building and leveraging in interorganizational relations*. Oxford: Elsevier Ltd, pp. 65–69.

Guo, K. L. (2009). Core competencies of the entrepreneurial leader in health care organizations. *Health Care Manager*, 28(1), 19–29.

Hagedoorn, J. and Cloodt, M. (2003). Measuring innovative performance: is there an advantage in using multiple indicators? *Research Policy*, 32(8), 1365–1379.

Hagel, J. and Singer, M. (1999). Unbundling the corporation. *Harvard Business Review*, 77(2), 133–141.

Hall, B. H. and Ham, Z.R. (2001). The patent paradox revisited: an empirical study of patenting in the U.S. semiconductor industry, 1979–1995. *The Rand Journal of Economics*, 32(1), 101–128.

Hall, B.H., Jaffe, A. and Trajtenberg, M. (2005). Market value and patent citations. *The Rand Journal of Economics*, 36(1), 16–38.

Hamel, G. and Breen, B. (2007). *Aiming for an evolutionary advantage. Harvard business review.* Boston, MA: Harvard Business School Press.

Harris, A. (2007). Distributed leadership: conceptual confusion and empirical reticence. *International Journal of Leadership in Education*, 10, 315–325.

Harris, C. and Vickers, J. (1985). Patent races and the persistence of monopoly. *The Journal of Industrial Economics*, 33(4), 461–481.

Harter, J.F.R. (1994). The propensity to patent with differentiated products. *Southern Economic Journal*, 61(1), 195–201.

Hashi, I. and Krasniqi, A. B. (2008). Entrepreneurship and SME growth: evidence from advances and laggard transition economies. www.ssrn.com/abstract=1125130, April 25, 2009.

Hausman, J.A., Hall, B.H. and Griliches, Z. (1984). Econometric models for count data with an application to the patents-R&D relationship. *Econometrica*, 52(4), 909–938.

Hausman, J.A. and MacKie-Mason, J.K. (1988). Price discrimination and patent policy. *The Rand Journal of Economics*, 19(2), 253–265.

Henderson, R., Jaffe, A. and Trajtenberg, M. (2005). Patent citations and the geography of knowledge spillovers: a reassessment: comment. *The American Economic Review*, 95(1), 461–464.

Hindle, K. (2002b). Small-I or big-I? How entrepreneurial capacity transforms' small-I' into 'Big-I' innovation: some implications for national policy. *Telecommunications Journal of Australia*, 52(3), 51–63.

Hindle, K. and Yencken, J. (2004). Public research commercialisation, entrepreneurship and new technology based firms: an integrated model. *Technovation*, 24(10), 793–803.

Ho, L., Wang, Y., Huang, H. and Chen, H. (2011). Influence of humorous leadership at workplace on the innovation behavior of leaders and their leadership effectiveness. *African Journal of Business Management*, 5(16), 6674–6683.

Hobday, M. (1995). *Innovation in East Asia: the challenge to Japan.* Aldershot: Edward Elgar Publishing.

Hobday, M. (2005). Firm-level innovation models: perspectives on research in developed and developing countries. *Technology Analysis and Strategic Management*, 17(2), 121–146.

Hoch, J. E. (2013). Shared leadership and innovation: the role of vertical leadership and employee integrity. *Journal of Business and Psychology*, 28(1), 159–174.

Hong, W. and Su, Yu-Sung (2012). The effect of institutional proximity in non-local university – industry collaborations: an analysis based on Chinese patent data. *Research Policy*, In Press, Corrected Proof.

Horowitz, A.W. and Lai, E.L.C. (1996). Patent length and the rate of innovation. *International Economic Review*, 37(4), 785–801.

Horstmann, I., MacDonald, G.M. and Slivinski, A. (1985). Patents as information transfer mechanisms: to patent or (maybe) not to patent. *Journal of Political Economy*, 93(5), 837–858.

Hossen, M.(2015). A review of literature on open innovation in small and medium sized enterprises. *Journal of Global Enterprises Research*, 5–6.

Howaldt, J., Oeij, P. R. A., Dhondt, S. and Fruytier, B. (2016). Workplace innovation and social innovation: an introduction. world review of entrepreneurship. *Management and Sustainable Development*, 12(1), 1–12.

Howell, J. M. and Avolio, B. J. (1993). Transformational leadership, transactional leadership, locus of control, and support for innovation: key predictors of consolidated-business-unit performance. *Journal of Applied Psychology*, 78(6), 891–902.

Hsu, C., Tan, K. C., Jayaram, J. and Laosirihongthong, T. (2014). Corporate entrepreneurship, operations core competency and innovation in emerging economies. *International Journal of Production Research*, 52(18), 5467–5483.

Hunter, I. (2005). Risk, persistence and focus: a life cycle of the entrepreneur. *Australian Economic History Review*, 45(3), 245–268.

Hussain, T., Ali, H. and Arshad, M. (2014). An interactive team leadership: a conceptual model for team based organizational effectiveness in large hierarchical organizations. *International Journal of Innovation and Scientific Research*, 2(1), 59–67.

Ireland, R. D. and Hitt, M. A. (2005). Achieving and maintaining strategic competitiveness in the 21st century: the role of strategic leadership. *Academy of Management Executive*, 19, 63–77.

Iwasa, T. and Odagiri, H. (2004). Overseas R&D, knowledge sourcing, and patenting: an empirical study of Japanese R&D investment in the US. *Research Policy*, 33(5), 807–828.

Jaffe, A.B. (1986). Technological opportunity and spillovers of R&D: evidence from firms' patents, profits, and market value. *The American Economic Review*, 76(5), 984–1001.

Jaffe, A. B., Trajtenberg, M. and Fogarty, M.S. (2000). Knowledge spillovers and patent citations: evidence from a survey of inventors. *American Economic Review*, 90(2), 215–218.

Jaffe, A.B., Trajtenberg, M. and Henderson, R. (1993). Geographic localization of knowledge spillovers as evidenced by patent citations. *The Quarterly Journal of Economics*, 108(3), 577–598.

James, K. and Lahti, K. (2011). Organizational vision and system influences on employee inspiration and organizational performance. *Creativity and Innovation Management*, 20, 108–120.

Jansen, J. J. P., van Den Bosch, F. A. J. and Volberda, H.W. (2006). Exploratory innovation, exploitative innovation, and performance: effects of organizational antecedents and environmental moderators. *Management Science*, 52(11), 1661–1674.

Johnson, G., Scholes, K. and Whittington, R. (2008). *Exploring corporate strategy* (8th ed.). Edinburg Gate: Prentice Hall.

Judd, K.L. (1985). On the performance of patents. *Econometrica*, 53(3), 567–585.

Kahn, A. E. (1940). Fundamental deficiencies of the American patent law. *The American Economic Review*, 30(3), 475–491.

Kamien, M.I. and Schwartz, N.L. (1974). Patent life and R and D rivalry. *American Economic Review*, 64(1), 183–187.

Kao, P., Pai, P., Lin, T. and Zhong, J. (2015). How transformational leadership fuels employees' service innovation behavior. *The Service Industrial Journal*, 35(7), 448–466.

Keller, R. T. (1992). Transformational leadership and the performance of research and development project groups. *Engineering Management Review*, 36, 82–91.

Keller, J., Fehér, K., Vidra, Z. and Virág, T. (2015). Developmental programmes in local communities. *Intersections – East European Journal of Society and Politics*, 1(4), 78–97.

Kern, B. R., Dewenter, R. and Kerber, W. (2016). Empirical analysis of the assessment of innovation effects in U.S. merger cases. *Journal of Industry, Competition, and Trade*, 16(1), 373–402.

Kesting, P., Ulhøi, J. P., Song, L. J. and Niu, H. (2015). The impact of leadership styles on innovation management – a review and a synthesis. *Journal of Innovation Management*, 3(4), 22–41.

Keupp, M. M., Palmié, M. and Gassmann, O. (2012). The strategic management of innovation: a systematic review and paths for future research. *International Journal of Management Reviews*, 14(4), 367–390.

Khalili, A. (2016). Linking transformational leadership, creativity, innovation, and innovation-supportive climate. *Management Decision*, 54(9), 2277–2293.

Khan, B.Z. and Sokoloff, K.L. (2001). History lessons: the early development of intellectual property institutions in the United States. *The Journal of Economic Perspectives*, 15(3), 233–246.

Kim, J., Lee, C. and Cho, Y. (2016). Technological diversification, core-technology competence and firm growth. *Research Policy*, 45(1), 113–124.

Kim, L. (1997). *Imitation to innovation: the dynamics of Korea's technological learning*. Boston, MA: Harvard Business School.

Kim, L. (1980). Stages of development of industrial technology in a developing country: a model. *Research Policy*, 9(3), 254–277.

Kim, L. and Lee, H. (1987). Patterns of technological change in a rapidly developing country: a synthesis. *Technovation*, 6(4), 261–276.

Kingston, W. (1994). Compulsory licensing with capital payments as an alternative to grants of monopoly in intellectual property. *Research Policy*, 23(6), 661–672.

Kirzner, I. M. (1973). *Entrepreneurship in the market process competition and entrepreneurship*. Chicago: University of Chicago Press, pp. 1–20.

Kohl, H., Orth, R., Riebartsch, O. and Hecklau, F. (2016). Integrated evaluation system for the strategic management of innovation initiatives in manufacturing industries. *Procedia CIRP*, 40(1), 335–340.

Kotabe, M. (1992). The impact of foreign patents on national economy: a case of the United States, Japan, Germany and Britain. *Applied Economics*, 24(12), 1335–1343.

Kremer, M. (1998). Patent buyouts: a mechanism for encouraging innovation. *The Quarterly Journal of Economics*, 113(4), 1137–1167.

Kukoc, K. and Regan, D. (2008). 'Measuring entrepreneurship', *Macroeconomic policy*. The Australian Treasury, pp. 15–16.

Kultti, K., Takalo, T. and Toikka, J. (2006). Simultaneous model of innovation, secrecy, and patent policy. *The American Economic Review*, 96(2), 82–86.

Kuswantoro.(2012). Impact of distribution channel innovation on the performance of small and medium enterprises. *International Business and Management*, 15, 50–60.

Kwon, K. and Cho, D. (2016). How transactive memory system relate to organizational innovation: the mediating role of developmental leadership. *Journal of Knowledge Management*, 20(5), 1025–1044.

Langinier, C. (2005). Using patents to mislead rivals. *Canadian Journal of Economics*, 38(2), 520–545.

Lanjouw, J.O., Pakes, A. and Putnam, J. (1998). How to count patents and value intellectual property: the uses of patent renewal and application data. *The Journal of Industrial Economics*, 46(4), 405–432.

Lanjouw, J.O. and Schankerman, M. (2004). Patent quality and research productivity: measuring innovation with multiple indicators. *Economic Journal*, 114(495), 441–465.

Lee, J., Bae, Z. T. and Choi, D. K. (1988). Technology development processes: a model for a developing country with a global perspective. *R&D Management*,18(3), 235–250.

Lee, W. I., Chen, C. C. and Lee, C. C. (2015). The relationship between internal marketing orientation, employee commitment, charismatic leadership and performance. *International Journal of Organizational Innovation*, 8(2), 67–78.

Lee, K. and Lim, C. (2001). Technological regimes, catching-up and leapfrogging: findings from the Korean industries. *Research Policy*,30(3), 459–483.

Leininger, W. (1991). Patent competition, rent dissipation, and the persistence of monopoly: the role of research budgets. *Journal of Economic Theory*, 53(1), 146–172.

Leitao, J. and Franco, M. (2008). Individual entrepreneurship capacity and performance of SMEs, Working Paper No. 8179, 1–13.

Leonard Barton, D. (1992). Core capabilities and core rigidities: a paradox in managing new product development. *Strategic Management Journal*, 13, Special Issue: Strategy Process: Managing Corporate Self-Renewal, 13(S1), 1111–125.

Lerner, J. and Tirole, J. (2004). Efficient patent pools. *The American Economic Review*, 94(3), 691–711.

Levin, R. C. (1986). A new look at the patent system. *The American Economic Review*, 76(2), 199–202.

Lewbel, A. (1997). Constructing instruments for regressions with measurement error when no additional data are available, with an application to patents and R&D. *Econometrica*, 65(5), 1201–1213.

Li, L. X. (2000). An analysis of sources of competitiveness and performance of Chinese manufacturers. *International Journal of Operations and Production Management*, 20(3), 289–315.

Lin, L. (2014). Exploration and exploitation in mergers and acquisitions: an empirical study of the electronics industry in Taiwan. *International Journal of Organizational Analysis*, 22(1), 30–47.

Lin, L. (2015). Innovation performance of Taiwanese information firms: an acquisition-learning-innovation framework. *Total Quality Management*, 26(1), 29–45.

Lodh, S., Nandy, M. and Chen, J. (2014). Innovation and family ownership: empirical evidence from India. *Corporate Governance: An International Review*, 22(1), 4–23.

Lope, Z. A., Asimiran, S. and Bagheri, A. (2014). Entrepreneurial leadership practices and school innovativeness. *South African Journal of Education*, 34(1), 1–11.

López-Ortega, O. and Ramírez-Hernández, M. (2007). A formal framework to integrate express data models in an extended enterprise context. *Journal of Intelligent Manufacturing*, 18(1), 371–381.

Lornikova, N. M., Pearsall, M. J. and Sims Jr., H. P. (2013). Examining the differential longitudinal performance of directive versus empowering leadership in teams. *Academy of Management Journal*, 56, 573–596.

Lumbasi, G. W., K'Aol, G. O. and Ouma, C. A. (2016). The effect of participative leadership style on the performance of COYA senior managers in Kenya. *Research journali's Journal of Management*, 4(5), 2347–8217.

Lumpkin G. T. and Dess G. G. (1996). Clarifying the entrepreneurial orientation construct and linking IT to performance. *Academy of Management Review*, 21, 1, 135–172.

MacGarvie, M. (2005). The determinants of international knowledge diffusion as measured by patent citations. *Economics Letters*, 87(1), 121–126.

Machlup, F. and Penrose, E. (1950). The patent controversy in the nineteenth century. *The Journal of Economic History*, 10(1), 1–29.

Madsen L. E. (2007). The significance of sustained entrepreneurial orientation on performance –a longitudinal analysis. *Entrepreneurship & Regional Development*, 19(2), 185–204.

Makri, M. and Scandura, T. A. (2010). Exploring the effects of creative CEO leadership on innovation in high-technology firms. *The Leadership Quarterly*, 21, 75–88.

Malerba, F. and Orsenigo, L. (1996). Schumpeterian patterns of innovation are technology-specific. *Research Policy*, 25(3), 451–478.

Malik, S. H. (2013). Relationship between leader behaviors and employees' job satisfaction: a path-goal approach. *Pakistan Journal of Commerce and Social Sciences*, 7(1), 209–222.

Malik, N., Lochan, R. and Chander, S. (2016). Authentic leadership and its impact on creativity of nursing staff: a cross sectional questionnaire survey of Indian nurses and their supervisors. *International Journal of Nursing Studies*, 63, 28–36.

Mancusi, M. L. (2008). International spillovers and absorptive capacity: a cross-country cross-sector analysis based on patents and citations. *Journal of International Economics*, 76(2), 155–165.

Mansfield, E., Schwartz, M. and Wagner, S. (1981). Imitation costs and patents: an empirical study. *Economic Journal*, 91(364), 907–918.

Marcati, A. Guido, G. and Peluso, M.A. (2008). The role of SME entrepreneurs innovativeness and personality in the adoption of innovation. *Journal of Research Policy*, 37(9), 1579–1590.

March, J. G. (1991). Exploration and exploitation in organizational learning. *Organization Science*, 2(1), 71–87.

Markham, J.W. (1966). The joint effect of antitrust and patent laws upon innovation. *The American Economic Review*, 56(1/2), 291–300.

Maskus, K.E. and Penubarti, M. (1995). How trade-related are intellectual property rights? *Journal of International Economics*, 39(3–4), 227–248.

Masood.(2013). Innovation and SMEs in Pakistan. *Journal of Accounting Performance*, 4(1), 11–25.

Massel, M. S. (1966). Anniversaries of the patent and Sherman Acts: competitive policies and limited monopolies. *The American Economic Review*, 56(1/2), 284–290.

Matutes, C., Regibeau, P. and Rockett, K. (1996). Optimal patent design and the diffusion of innovations. *The Rand Journal of Economics*, 27(1), 60–83.

Maurseth, P.B. and Verspagen, B. (2002). Knowledge spillovers in Europe: a patent citations analysis. *The Scandinavian Journal of Economics*, 104(4), 531–545.

Mazzoleni, R. and Nelson, R.R. (1998). The benefits and costs of strong patent protection: a contribution to the current debate. *Research Policy*, 27(3), 273–284.

Mbizi.(2013). Effects of innovation types on firm performance. *Journal of Management Accounting Research*, 8(3), 67–82.

McCalman, P. (2001). Reaping what you sow: an empirical analysis of international patent harmonization. *Journal of International Economics*, 55(1), 161–186.

McKeown, M. (2008). *The truth about innovation*. Pearson Education India.

Meier, C., Sachs, S., Stutz, C. and McSorley, V. (2017). Establishing a digital leadership barometer for small and medium enterprises. *Management, Knowledge and Learning, International Conference 2017*, May 17–19, Lublin, Poland.

Michaelis, B., Stegmaier, R. and Sonntag, K. (2009). Affective commitment to change and innovation implementation behavior: the role of charismatic leadership and employees' trust in top management. *Journal of Change Management*, 9, 399–417.

Miller, D. A. (1983). The correlates of entrepreneurship in three types of firm. *Management Science*, 29, 770–791.

Montgomery, R.E. (1923). The international aspects of patent legislation. *Journal of Political Economy*, 31(1), 90–113.

Morris, M., Kuratko, D. and Covin, J. (2008). *Corporate entrepreneurship and innovation* (2nd ed.). Mason, OH: Thomson-Southwestern Publishing Co.

Moser, P. (2005). How do patent laws influence innovation? Evidence from nineteenth-century world's fairs. *The American Economic Review*, 95(4), 1214–1236.

Mowery, D.C., Oxley, J.E. and Silverman, B.S. (1998). Technological overlap and interfirm cooperation: implications for the resource-based view of the firm. *Research Policy*, 27(5), 507–523.

Muethel, M. and Hoegl, M. (2010). Cultural and societal influences on shared leadership in globally dispersed teams. *Journal of International Management*, 16, 234–246.

Mukherjee, A. (2006). Patents and R&D with imitation and licensing. *Economics Letters*, 93(2), 196–201.

Nadler, D. A. and Tushman, M. L. (1990). Beyond the charismatic leader: leadership and organizational change. *California Management Review*, 32, 77–97.

Nam, C. H. and Tatum, C. B. (1989). Toward understanding of product innovation process in construction. *Journal of Construction Engineering and Management*, 115, 517–534.

Ndesaulwa, P.A. and Kikula, J. (2016). The impact of innovation on performance of small and medium enterprises (SMES) in Tanzania: a review of empirical evidence. *Journal of Business and Management Sciences*, 4(1), 1–6.

Neider, L. and Schriesheim, C. (2011). The Authentic Leadership Inventory (ALI): development and empirical tests. *The Leadership Quarterly*, 22, 1146–1164.

Ngungi (2013). Effect of the type of innovation on the growth of small of small and medium enterprises in Kenya: a case of garment enterprises in Jericho, Nairobi. *European Journal of Management Sciences and Economics*, 1(2), 49–57.

Nieto, M. J., Santamaria, L. and Fernandez, Z. (2015). Understanding the innovation behavior of family firms. *Journal of Small Business Management*, 53(2), 382–399.

Nooteboom, B. (1994). Innovation and diffusion in small firms: theory and evidence. *Small Business Economics*, 6(5), 327–347.

Nordhaug, O. and Grønhaug K. (1994). Competences as resources in firms. *The International Journal of Human Resource Management*, 5(1), 89–106.

Nordhaus, W.D. (1969). *Invention, growth, and welfare: a theoretical treatment of tech-nological change*. Cambridge: Cambridge University Press.

Nordhaus, W.D. (1972). The optimum life of a patent: reply. *The American Economic Review*, 62(3), 428–431.

Norrgren, F. and Schaller, J. (1999). Leadership style: its impact on cross-functional product development. *Journal of Product Innovation Management*, 16, 377–384.

OECD and European Commission (2005). *Oslo manual: guidelines for colleting and interpreting innovation data* (3rd ed.). Paris, France: OECD Publishing.

Oladimeji, O. and Ndubuisi, U. (2017). Transformational leadership and organizational culture as predictors of employee creativity and innovation in the Nigerian oil and gas service industry. *IFE Psychologia*, 25(2), 325–349.

Pakes, A. (1986). Patents as options: some estimates of the value of holding European patent stocks. *Econometrica*, 54(4), 755–784.

Palacios-Marqués, D., Popa, S. and Alguacil, M. P.(2016). The effect of online social networks and competency-based management on innovation capability. *Journal of Knowledge Management*, 20(3), 499–511.

Park, W. G. and Sonenshine, R. (2012). Impact of horizontal mergers on research and development and patenting: evidence from merger challenges in the U.S. *Journal of Industry, Competition, and Trade*, 12(1), 143–167.

Paulsen, N., Maldonado, D., Callan, V. J. and Ayoko, O. (2009). Charismatic leadership, change and innovation in an R&D organization. *Journal of Organizational Change Management*, 22, 511–523.

Pearce, C. L. and Manz, C. C. (2005). The new silver bullets of leadership: the importance of self- and shared leadership in knowledge work. *Organizational Dynamics*, 34, 130–140.

Pearce, C. L., Manz, C. C. and Sims, J. R. (2009). Where do we go from here? Is shared leadership the key to team success? *Organizational Dynamics*, 38, 234–238.

Pei, G. (2017). Structuring leadership and team creativity: the mediating role of team innovation climate. *Social Behavior and Personality*, 45(3), 369–376.

Phillips, A. (1966). Patents, potential competition, and technical progress. *The American Economic Review*, 56(1/2), 301–310.

Picci, L. (2010). The internationalization of inventive activity: a gravity model using patent data. *Research Policy*, 39(8), 1070–1081.

Pieterse, A. N., Van Knippenberg, D., Schippers, M. and Stam, D. (2010). Transformational and transactional leadership and innovative behavior: the moderating role of psychological empowerment. *Journal of Organizational Behavior*, 31, 609–623.

Polanvyi, M. (1944). Patent reform. *The Review of Economic Studies*, 11(2), 61–76.

Polanyi, M. (1966). The logic of tacit inference. *Philosophy*, 41(155), 1–18.

Porter, M.E. and Stern, S. (2001). Innovation: location matters. *MIT Sloan Management Review*, 42(4), 28–36.

Prahalad, C. K. and Hamel, G. (1990). The core competence of the corporation. *Harvard Business Review*, May–June, 78–90.

Prasad, B. and Junni, P.(2016). CEO transformational and transactional leadership and organizational innovation – the moderating role of environmental dynamism. *Management Decision*, 54(7), 1542–1568.

Pundt, A. (2015). The relationship between humorous leadership and innovative behavior. *Journal of Managerial Psychology*, 30(8), 878–893.

Qian, Y. (2007). Do national patent laws stimulate domestic innovation in a global patenting environment? A cross-country analysis of pharmaceutical patent protection, 1978–2002. *Review of Economics and Statistics*, 89(3), 436–453.

Rafiquzzaman, M. (1987). The optimal patent term under uncertainty. *International Journal of Industrial Organization*, 5(2), 233–246.

Rahab, R., Anwar, N. and Priyono, R. E. (2016). Effect of core competence on sustainable competitive advantages of batik banyunas small and medium enterprises. *Journal of Comparative International Management*, 19(1), 27–45.

Rajeh, A., Fais, A., Ali, A. and Abdullahi, G. (2017). The moderating effect of government support between gender egalitarianism, assertiveness, future orientation, and female leadership effectiveness: empirical study of public universities in Saudi Arabia. *International Review of Management and Marketing*, 7(2), 390–402.

Ramani, S. V., El-Aroui, M-A. and Carrere, M. (2008). On estimating a knowledge production function at the firm and sector level using patent statistics. *Research Policy*, 37(9), 1568–1578.

Rambe, P. and Makhalemele, N. (2015). Relationship between managerial competencies of owners/managers of emerging technology firms and business performance: a conceptual framework of internet cafés performance in South Africa. *International Business and Economics Research Journal*, 14(4), 677–690.

Rangone, A. (1999). A resource based view approach to strategy analysis in small and medium sized enterprises. *Journal of Small Business Economics*, 12(3), 233–248.

Rego, A., Sousa, F., Marques, C. and Pina e Cunha, M. (2012). Authentic leadership promoting employees' psychological capital and creativity. *Journal of Business Research*, 65, 429–437.

Reinganum, J. F. (1982). A dynamic game of R and D: patent protection and competitive behavior. *Econometrica*, 50(3), 671–688.

Reitzig, M., Henkel, J. and Heath, C. (2007). On sharks, trolls, and their patent prey – unrealistic damage awards and firms' strategies of 'Being Infringed'. *Research Policy*, 36(1), 134–154.

Rosener, J. B. (1990). Ways women lead. *Harvard Business Review*, 68(1), 119–125.

Rosing, K., Frese, M. and Bausch, A. (2011). Explaining the heterogeneity of the leadership innovation relationship: ambidextrous leadership. *Leadership Quarterly*, 22(5), 956–974.

Rudy, S., McKee, M. and Bjornstad, D. (2010). Patent pools as a solution to efficient licensing of complementary patents? Some experimental evidence. *Journal of Law and Economics*, 53(1), 167–183.

Saboo, A. R., Sharma, A., Chakravarty, A. and Kumar, V. (2017). Influencing acquisition performance in high-technology industries: the role of innovation and relational overlap. *Journal of Marketing Research*, 54(1), 219–238.

Sagie, A. (1997). Leader direction and employee participation in decision making: contradictory or compatible practices. *Applied Psychology: An International Review*, 46, 387–416.

Sagnak, M. (2016). Participative leadership and change-oriented organizational citizenship: the mediating effect of intrinsic motivation. *Eurasian Journal of Educational Research*, 62(1), 199–212.

Sagnak, M., Kuruoz, M., Polat, B. and Soylu, A. (2015). Transformational leadership and innovative climate: an examination of the mediating effect of psychological empowerment. *Eurasian Journal of Educational Research*, 60(1), 149–162.

Salim, A. M. (2015). Understanding core competency of small and medium-sized enterprises: a comparative study in Tanzania and China. *International Journal of Innovation and Applied Studies*, 13(3), 722–733.

Schankerman, M. (1998). How valuable is patent protection? Estimates by technology field. *The Rand Journal of Economics*, 29(1), 77–107.

Schere, J. L. (1982). Tolerance of ambiguity as a discriminating variable between entrepreneurs and managers. *Academy of Management Proceedings*, 1982(1), 404–408.

Scherer, F. M. (1972). Nordhaus' theory of optimal patent life: a geometric reinterpretation. *The American Economic Review*, 62(3), 422–427.

Scherer, F. M. (1983). The propensity to patent. *International Journal of Industrial Organization*, 1(1), 107–128.

Schiffel, D. and Carole, K. (1978). Rates of invention: international patent comparisons. *Research Policy*, 7(4), 324–340.

Schumpeter, J. A. (1942). *Capitalism, socialism, and democracy*. New York: George Allen & Uwin, pp. 131–140.

Schilling, M. A. (2013). *Strategic management of technological innovation* (4th ed.). New York: McGraw-Hill.

Schneider, C. (2008). Fences and competition in patent races. *International Journal of Industrial Organization*, 26(6), 1348–1364.

Schwab, K. and Sachs, J. (1997). The global competitiveness report: 1997. Geneva, Switzerland: World Economic Forum, 1997.

Scotchmer, S. and Green, J. (1990). Novelty and disclosure in patent law. *The Rand Journal of Economics*, 21(1), 131–146.

Selgin, G. and Turner, J.L. (2011). Strong steam, weak patents, or the myth of Watt's innovation-blocking monopoly, exploded. *Journal of Law and Economics*, 54(4), 841–861.

Sethibe, T. and Steyn, R. (2015). The relationship between leadership styles, innovation and organizational performance: a systematic review. *SAJEMS NS*, 18(3), 325–337.

Shamir, B., House, R. J. and Arthur, M. B. (1993). The motivational effects of charismatic leadership: a self-concept based theory. *Organization Science*, 4, 577–594.

Shapiro, C. (1985). Patent licensing and R&D rivalry. *The American Economic Review*, 75(2), 25–25.

Sillince, J. A. A. (1994). A management strategy for innovation and organizational design: the case of MRP2/JIT production management systems. *Behavior & Information Technology*, 13, 216–227.

Silverberg, G. and Verspagen, B. (2007). The size distribution of innovations revisited: an application of extreme value statistics to citation and value measures of patent significance. *Journal of Econometrics*, 139(2), 318–339.

Slåtten, T. and Mehmetoglu, M. (2015). The effects of transformational leadership and perceived creativity on innovation behavior in the hospitality industry. *Journal of Human Resources in Hospitality and Tourism*, 14(1), 195–219.

Smith, C. (1890). A century of patent law. *The Quarterly Journal of Economics*, 5(1), 44–69.

Smith, P. J. (1999). Are weak patent rights a barrier to U.S. exports? *Journal of International Economics*, 48(1), 151–177.

Smith, P. J. (2001). How do foreign patent rights affect U.S. exports, affiliate sales, and licenses? *Journal of International Economics*, 55(2), 411–439.

Soete, L. L. G. (1979). Firm size and inventive activity: the evidence reconsidered. *European Economic Review*, 12(4), 319–340.

Somech, A. (2005). Directive versus participative leadership: two complementary approaches to managing school effectiveness. *Educational Administration Quarterly*, 41(5), 777–800.

Somech, A. (2006). The effects of leadership style and team process on performance and innovation in functionally heterogeneous teams. *Journal of Management*, 32(1), 132–157.

Sorenson, O. and Singh, J. (2007). Science, social networks and spillovers. *Industry and Innovation*, 14(2), 219–238.

Spear, S. and Roper, S. (2016). Storytelling in organizations: supporting or subverting corporate strategy? *Corporate Communications: An International Journal*, 21(4), 516–532.

Sternberg, R. J., Kaufman, J. C. and Pretz, J. E. (2004). A propulsion model of creative leadership. *Creativity & Innovation Management*, 13, 145–153.

Stosic, B. and Milutinovic, R. (2014). Innovation projects classification issues. Published at October 24th, 2014. *Economic and Social Development, 7th International Scientific Conference*, New York City.

Sun, L. (2013). Core competences, supply chain partners' knowledge-sharing, and innovation: an empirical study of the manufacturing industry in Taiwan. *International Journal of Business and Information*, 8(2), 299–324.

Sutter, R. C. (2010). *The psychology of entrepreneurship and the technological frontier – a spatial econometric analysis of regional entrepreneurship in the United States*. George Mason University.

Takalo, T. (1998). Innovation and imitation under imperfect patent protection. *Journal of Economics*, 67(3), 229–241.

Takalo, T. and Kanniainen, V. (2000). Do patents slow down technological progress? Real options in research, patenting, and market introduction. *International Journal of Industrial Organization*, 18(7), 1105–1127.

Tauman, Y. and Watanabe, N. (2007). The shapley value of a patent licensing game: the asymptotic equivalence to non-cooperative results. *Economic Theory*, 30(1), 135–149.

Tebaldi, E. and Elmslie, B. (2013). Does institutional quality impact innovation? Evidence from cross-country patent grant data. *Applied Economics*, 45(7), 887–900.

Thirtle, C. G. and Rutcan, V. W. (1987). *The role of demand and supply in the generation and diffusion of technical change*. Harwood: Chur.

Todd, R., P. and Javalgi G. R. (2007). Internationalization of SMEs in India, fostering entrepreneurship by leveraging information technology. *International Journal of Emerging Markets*, 2(2), 166–180.

Tracey, J. B. and Hinkin, T. R. (1998). Transformational leadership or effective managerial practice? *Group & Organization Management*, 23, 220–236.

Trajtenberg, M. (1990). A penny for your quotes: patent citations and the value of innovations. *RAND Journal of Economics*, 21(1), 172–187.

Treacy, M. and Wiersema, F. (1993). Customer intimacy and other value disciplines. *Harvard Business Review*, 71(1), 84–93.

Ullah, M. I., Ab Hamid, K. B. and Shahzad, A. (2016). Impact of transformational leadership on knowledge sharing of employees and innovation capability in the dairy sector of Pakistan. *Pakistan Journal of Social Sciences*, 36(1), 87–98.

Utterback, J. M. and Abernathy, W. J. (1975). A dynamic model of process and product innovation. *Omega*, 3(6), 639–656.

Van Dijk, T. (1995). Innovation incentives through third-degree price discrimination in a model of patent breadth. *Economics Letters*, 47(3–4), 431–435.

Van Dijk, T. (1996). Patent height and competition in product improvements. *The Journal of Industrial Economics*, 44(2), 151–151.

van, Praag, C. M. and Cramer, J. S. (2001). The roots of entrepreneurship and labour demand: individual ability and low risk aversion. *Economica*, 68(269), 45–62.

van, Praag, C. M. and Versloot, P. H. (2007). What is the value of entrepreneurship? A review of recent research. *Small Business Economics*, 29(4), 351–382.

van, Stel A. Carree, Martin and Thurik R. (2005). The effect of entrepreneurial activity on national economic growth. *Small Business Economics*, 24(3), 311–321.

Vaughan, F.L. (1948). Patent policy. *The American Economic Review*, 38(2), 215–234.

Vaughan, F.W. (1919). Suppression and non-working of patents, with special reference to the dye and chemical industries. *The American Economic Review*, 9(4), 693–700.

Veall, M.R. (1992). Brand/product innovation and the optimal length of trademark/patent protection. *Economics Letters*, 40(4), 491–496.

Veeraraghavan, V. (2009). Entrepreneurship and innovation. *Asia Pacific Business Review*, 5(1), 14–20.

Vishwasrao, S. (1994). Intellectual property rights and the mode of technology transfer. *Journal of Development Economics*, 44(2), 381–402.

Walumbwa, F., Avolio, B., Gardner, W., Wernsing, T. and Peterson, S. (2008). Authentic leadership: development and validation of a theory-based measure. *Journal of Management*, 34, 89–126.

Waterson, M. (1990). The economics of product patents. *The American Economic Review*, 80(4), 860–869.

Wiklund, J. and Shepherd, D. (2005). Entrepreneurial orientation and small business performance: a configurational approach. *Journal of Business Venturing*, 20(1), 71–91.

Williamson, O. E. (1971). The vertical integration of production: market failure considerations. *The American Economic Review*, 61(2), 112–123.

Wong, S. K. S. (2013). The role of management involvement in innovation. *Management Decision*, 51, 709–729.

Woolley, J. L. (2017). Origins and outcomes: the roles of spin-off founders and intellectual property in high-technology venture outcomes. *Academy of Management Discoveries*, 3(1), 64–90.

World Bank (2010). *Innovation policy: a guide for developing countries*. Washington, DC: World Bank Group.

Wright, B.D. (1983). The economics of invention incentives: patents, prizes, and research contracts. *The American Economic Review*, 73(4), 691–707.

Wu, S. (2017). Models for evaluating the technological innovation capability of small and micro enterprises with hesitant fuzzy information. *Journal of Intelligent and Fuzzy Systems*, 32(1), 249–256.

Xerri, M. (2013). Workplace relationships and the innovative behavior of nursing employees: s social exchange perspective. *Asia Pacific Journal of Human Resources*, 51, 103–123.

Xie, B., Zhan, W. and Wang, X. (2014). Research of core competence of the leading international engineering constructors. *Applied Mechanics and Materials*, 584–586, 2272–2276.

Xie, M. and Pang, M. (2018). A cross-cultural examination of Chinese and American female leadership in nonprofit organizations. *China Media Research*, 14(1), 30–41.

Yang, C-H. and Nai-F.K. (2008). Trade-related influences, foreign intellectual property rights and outbound international patenting. *Research Policy*, 37(3), 446–459.

Zacher, H. and Rosing, K. (2015). Ambidextrous leadership and team innovation. *Leadership and Organization Development Journal*, 36(1), 54–68.

Zhou, J., Ma, Y., Cheng, W. and Xia, B. (2014). Mediating role of employee emotions in the relationship between authentic leadership and employee innovation. *Social Behavior and Personality*, 42(8), 1267–1278.

Zubair, A., Bashir, M., Abrar, M., Baig, S. A. and Hassan, S. Y. (2015). Employee's participation in decision making and manager's encouragement of creativity: the mediating role of climate for creativity and change. *Journal of Service Science and Management*, 8, 306–321.

8
THE FREE INNOVATION PARADIGM[1]

Eric von Hippel

Introduction and overview

Free innovation involves innovations developed and given away by consumers as a "free good," with resulting improvements in social welfare. I define a free innovation as a functionally novel product, service or process that (1) was developed by consumers at private cost during their unpaid discretionary time (that is, no one paid them to do it) and (2) is not protected by its developers, and so is potentially acquirable by anyone without payment – for free. As we will see, free innovation has very important economic impacts, but from the perspective of participants, it is fundamentally not about money.

Examples of very important free innovation developments by consumers abound. Consider Nightscout, a system that monitors diabetics' blood sugar levels through the night. A series of product innovations and improvements addressing this very important issue are being developed and revealed for free on the Internet by a community of consumers dedicated to addressing problems associated with type 1 diabetes. Many of the participants in this community either have type 1 diabetes themselves or have children who do. The motto of the group, established out of frustration with inadequate products and introduction delays by medical device producers, is "We Are Not Waiting." Nightscout's story, as told by Linebaugh (2014) is as follows:

> Nightscout got its start in the Livonia, N.Y., home of John Costik, a software engineer at the Wegmans supermarket chain. In 2012, his son Evan was diagnosed with Type 1 diabetes at the age of four. The father of two bought a Dexcom continuous glucose monitoring system, which uses a hair's width sensor under the skin to measure blood-sugar levels. He was frustrated that he couldn't see Evan's numbers when he was at work. So he started fiddling around.
>
> On May 14 last year [2013], he tweeted a picture of his solution: a way to upload the Dexcom receiver's data to the Internet using his software, a $4 cable and an Android phone. That tweet caught the eye of other engineers across the country. One was Lane Desborough, an engineer with a background in control systems for oil refineries and chemical plants whose son, 15, has diabetes. Mr. Desborough had designed a home-display system for glucose-monitor data and called it NightScout. But his

system couldn't connect to the Internet, so it was merged with Mr. Costik's software to create the system used today....

Users stay in touch with each other and the developers via a Facebook group set up by Mr. Adams. It now has more than 6,800 members. The developers are making fixes as bugs arise and adding functions such as text-message alarms and access controls via updates.

Free innovation is carried out in the "household sector" of national economies. In contrast to the business or government sector, the household sector is the consuming population of the economy, in a word all of us, all consumers. Free innovation, therefore, is a form of household production.

Nationally representative surveys conducted in six countries document that free innovation is a phenomenon of very significant scale and scope. Tens of millions of consumers annually spend tens of billions of dollars on new product development in these six countries alone (Table 8.1). The scope ranges across all categories of interest to consumers, from medical devices to toys, sports, vehicles, and improvements in dwellings.

How can individual consumers justify investing in the development of free innovations when no one pays them for either their labor or for their freely revealed innovation designs? The answer is that free innovators in the household sector are self-rewarded. When they personally use their own innovations, they are self-rewarded by benefits they derive from that use (von Hippel, 1988, 2005). When they benefit from such things as the fun and learning of developing their innovations or the good feelings that come from altruism, they are also self-rewarded (Raasch and von Hippel, 2013).

The Nightscout project described earlier illustrates several types of self-reward. From the account given, we can see that many participants gain direct self-rewards from personal or family use of the innovation they helped develop. Probably many also gain other forms of highly motivating self-rewards, such as enjoyment and learning, and perhaps also strong altruistic satisfactions from freely giving away their project designs to help many diabetic children.

Table 8.1 The extent of consumer innovation in six countries

Country (n)	UK[a] (1,173)	US[b] (1,992)	Japan[b] (2,000)	Finland[c] (993)	Canada[d] (2,021)	S. Korea[e] (10,821)
% of consumers who engage in consumer innovation	6.1	5.2	3.7	5.4	5.6	1.5
Number of consumer innovators	2.9 mm	16.0 mm	4.7 mm	0.172 mm	1.6 mm	0.54 mm
Amount spent on average project (time + cash in $US)	4.8 days +$125	14.7 days +$1,065	7.3 days +$397	2.6 days +$223	6.7 days +$43	5.9 days +$368
Total annual expenditures per country in $US*	$5.2B	$20.2B	$5.8B	na	na	na
% protected as intellectual property	1.9	8.8	0.0	4.7	2.8	7.0

Source: von Hippel (2017), Tables 2–1, 2.4, 2.5, and 2.7
* Total annual national expenditures include out-of-pocket expenditures for all innovation projects undertaken in a year plus total time investment calculated at average wage rate for each nation.
a. von Hippel, de Jong, and Flowers (2012); b. von Hippel, Ogawa, and de Jong (2011); c. de Jong et al. (2015); d. de Jong (2013); e. Kim (2015).

Survey questions asking about motivations support the conclusion that household-sector innovators are predominantly engaged in free innovation as I defined it earlier. About 90 percent were motivated almost entirely by self-rewards and are not significantly motivated by the prospects of selling or commercially profiting from what they had created. The remaining 10 percent of household-sector innovators, in contrast, were prospective entrepreneurs hoping to profit from what they had created. Most of the innovation protection activity indicated in Table 8.1 was pursued by prospective entrepreneurs, with 36 percent of these individuals protecting their innovations via some form of intellectual property rights (von Hippel, 2017, Chapter 2).

The free innovation and producer innovation paradigms

Due to its self-rewarding nature, free innovation does not require compensated transactions to reward consumers for the time and money they invest to develop their innovations. (Compensated transactions involve explicit, compensated exchanges of property – that is, giving someone specifically this in exchange for specifically that. See Tadelis and Williamson, 2013; Baldwin, 2008). Free innovation therefore differs fundamentally from producer innovation, which has compensated transactions at its very core. Producers cannot profit from their private investments in innovation development unless they can protect their innovations from rivals and can sell copies at a profit via compensated transactions (Schumpeter, 1934; Machlup and Penrose, 1950; Teece, 1986; Gallini and Scotchmer, 2002).

In Figure 8.1, I schematically depict these two paradigms and the interactions between them. Each describes a portion of the innovation activity in national economies. Generally, development activity in the free innovation paradigm is devoted to types of innovative products and services consumed by householders, not businesses. These represent a large fraction of gross domestic product (GDP): In the United States and many other Organisation for Economic Co-operation and Development (OECD) countries, 60 to 70 percent of GDP is devoted to products and services intended for final consumption in the household sector (BEA, 2016; OECD, 2015). In contrast, innovation development activity in the producer innovation paradigm is devoted to addressing both consumer and industrial product and service needs.

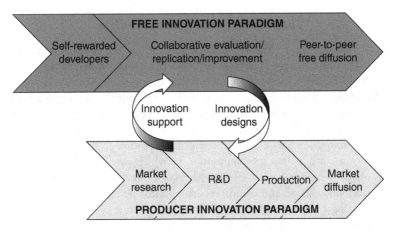

Figure 8.1 The free innovation and the producer innovation paradigms

Eric von Hippel

The free innovation paradigm

The free innovation paradigm is represented by the broad arrow shown in the top half of Figure 8.1. At the left side of the arrow, we see consumers in the household sector spending their unpaid discretionary time developing new products and services. As is implied by the position of the free innovation arrow in Figure 8.1, which starts farther to the left than the producer arrow, individuals or groups of innovators who have a personal use for an innovation with a novel function generally begin development work earlier than producers do – they are pioneers. This is because the extent of general demand for really novel products and services is initially often quite unclear. General demand is irrelevant to individual free innovators, who care only about their own needs and other forms of private self-reward that they understand firsthand. Producers, in contrast, care greatly about the extent and nature of potential markets and, as the rightward positioning of the producer arrow indicates, often wait for market information to emerge before beginning their own development efforts (Baldwin, Hienerth, and von Hippel, 2006).

If there is interest in an innovation beyond the initial developer, some or many other individuals may contribute improvements to the initial design, as is shown at the center of the free innovation paradigm arrow. This pattern is visible in the Nightscout example presented earlier and is familiar in open-source software development projects as well (Raymond, 1999). Thus, in the Nightscout case, many individuals with an interest in helping children with type 1 diabetes came forward to join the efforts of the project's initiators (Nightscout project, 2016).

Finally, free diffusion of unprotected design information via peer-to-peer transfer to free riders may occur, as is shown at the right end of the free innovation paradigm arrow. (Free riders are those who benefit from an innovation but do not contribute to developing it. In that sense they get a "free ride.") Again, a pattern of diffusion to free riders is clearly visible in the Nightscout project.

Note that what is generally being revealed free for the taking by free innovators is design information, not free copies of physical products. In the case of products or services that themselves consist of information, such as software, a design for an innovation can be identical to the usable product itself. In the case of a physical product, such as a wrench or a car, what is being revealed is a design "recipe" that must be converted into a physical form before it can be used. In free peer-to-peer diffusion, this conversion is generally done by individual adopters – each adopter creates a physical implementation of a free design at private expense in order to use it.

The producer innovation paradigm

The long-established producer innovation paradigm centers on development and diffusion activities carried out by producers. The basic sequence of activities in that paradigm is shown on the lower arrow of Figure 8.1. Moving from left to right on that arrow, we see profit-seeking firms first identifying a potentially profitable market opportunity by acquiring information on unfilled needs. They then invest in R&D to design a novel product or service responsive to that opportunity. Next, they produce the innovation and sell it on the market.

The producer innovation paradigm can be traced back to Joseph Schumpeter, who between 1912 and 1945 put forth a theory of innovation in which profit-seeking entrepreneurs and corporations played the central role. Schumpeter argued that "it is . . . the producer who as a rule initiates economic change, and consumers are educated by him if necessary" (1934, p. 65).

The economic logic underlying Schumpeter's argument is that producers generally expect to distribute their costs of developing innovations over many consumers, each of whom purchases one or a few copies. Individual or collaborating free innovators, in contrast, depend only on their own in-house use of their innovation and other types of self-reward to justify their investments in innovation development. On the face of it, therefore, a producer serving many consumers can afford to invest more in developing an innovation than can any single free innovator, and so presumably can do a better job. By this logic, individuals in the household sector must simply be "consumers" who simply select among and purchase innovations that producers elect to create. After all, why would consumers innovate for themselves if producers can do it for them?

Interactions between the paradigms

There are four important interactions between the free innovation paradigm and the producer innovation paradigm (Gambardella, Raasch, and von Hippel, 2017).

First, identical or closely substituting innovation designs can be made available to potential adopters via both paradigms at the same time. For example, Apache open-source web server software is offered free peer-to-peer by the Apache development community, and at the same time a close substitute is offered commercially by Microsoft. In such cases, peer-to-peer diffusion via the free innovation paradigm can compete with products and services that producers are selling on the market. The level of competition can be substantial. In the specific case just mentioned, 38 percent of websites used Apache free web server software in 2015. Microsoft was second, serving 28 percent of sites with its commercial server software (Netcraft.com, 2015). Competition from substitutes diffused for free via peer-to-peer transfers can increase social welfare by forcing producers to lower prices. It can also drive producers to other forms of competitive responses with social value, such as improving quality or increasing investments in innovation development.

Second, innovations available for free via the free innovation paradigm can complement innovations diffused via the producer innovation paradigm. Free complements are very valuable to consumers as well as to producers. They enable producers to focus on selling commercially viable products, while free innovators fill in with designs for valuable or even essential complements. For example, a specialized mountain bike is of little value to a biker who has not learned specialized mountain biking techniques. Producers find it viable to produce and sell the specialized mountain bikes as commercial products, but largely rely on expert bikers innovating within the free paradigm to create and diffuse riding techniques as a free complement. That is, adopters generally learn new mountain biking techniques by a combination of self-practice and informal instruction freely given by more expert peers.

Third, we see from the vertical, downward-pointing arrow toward the right in Figure 8.1 that a design developed by a free innovator may spill over to a producer and become the basis for a valuable commercial product. For example, the design of the mountain bike itself and many further improvements to it were developed by free innovator bikers. These designs were not protected by the free innovator developers and were adopted for free by bike-producing firms (Penning, 1998; Buenstorf, 2003). As we will see, adoption of free innovators' designs can greatly lower producers' in-house development costs (Baldwin, Hienerth, and von Hippel, 2006; Franke and Shah, 2003; Jeppesen and Frederiksen, 2006; Lettl, Herstatt, and Gemuenden, 2006).

Fourth and finally, we see from the vertical, upward-pointing arrow at the left of Figure 8.1 that producers also supply valuable information and support to free innovators. For example, Valve Corporation, a video game development firm, offers Steam Workshop, a company-sponsored website designed to support innovation by gamers (Steam Workshop, 2016). The site contains tools that make it easier for these individuals to develop their own game modifications and improvements and to share them with other players. Investments to support free design, such as the investment in Steam Workshop by Valve, can benefit producers by increasing the supply of commercially valuable designs that free innovators create (Gambardella, Raasch, and von Hippel, 2017; Jeppesen and Frederiksen, 2006; von Hippel and Finkelstein, 1979).

The need for a free innovation paradigm

The Schumpeterian producer innovation paradigm is widely accepted by economists, business people and policy makers today. Thus, Teece (1996, p. 193) echoed Schumpeter: "In market economies, the business firm is clearly the leading player in the development and commercialization of new products and processes." Similarly, Romer (1990, S74) viewed producer innovation as the norm in his model of endogenous growth: "The vast majority of designs result from the research and development activities of private, profit-maximizing firms." And Baumol (2002, 35) placed producer innovation at the center of his theory of oligopolistic competition: "In major sectors of US industry, innovation has increasingly grown in relative importance as an instrument used by firms to battle their competitors."

Why do we need the free innovation paradigm that I proposed earlier? Recall that Thomas Kuhn defined scientific paradigms as "universally recognized scientific achievements that, for a time, provide model problems and solutions for a community of researchers" (1962, viii). Having a paradigm in place that is widely accepted, as in the case of the producer innovation paradigm, can be very helpful to scientific advancement. Once a paradigm is in place, as Kuhn writes, researchers can engage in very productive "normal science," testing and more precisely filling in pieces of a paradigm now assumed to be correct in broad outline. However, as Kuhn also explains, a paradigm never adequately explains "everything" within a field. In fact, observations that do not fit the reigning paradigm commonly emerge during the work of normal science but are often ignored in favor of pursuing productive advances within the paradigm.

In the case of innovation research, empirical evidence related to free innovation in the household sector has been increasing during recent years. However, innovations developed and diffused without compensated transactions lie entirely outside the Schumpeterian producer innovation paradigm – and, indeed, entirely outside the transaction-based framework of economics in general. Ignoring this evidence has allowed researchers to do productive work within the Schumpeterian paradigm while deferring the work of incorporating free innovation into our paradigmatic understanding of innovation processes.

Eventually, Kuhn writes, conflicts between the predictions of a reigning paradigm and real-world observations may become so pervasive or so important that they can no longer be ignored, and at that point, the reigning paradigm may be challenged by a new one (Kuhn, 1962). I propose that this situation has been reached in the case of transaction-free innovation processes developed and utilized by free innovators in the household sector. I therefore frame the free innovation paradigm both as a challenge to the Schumpeterian innovation paradigm and as a useful complement. Both paradigms describe important innovation processes, with the free paradigm codifying important phenomena in the household sector that the producer innovation paradigm does not incorporate.

Recall that I propose that both the free innovation and producer innovation paradigms function in parallel. When Kuhn developed his concept of paradigms to explain how revolutions in understanding occur in the natural sciences, he argued that a new paradigm replaces an existing one in a "scientific revolution." However, today the idea of paradigms has expanded beyond the study of natural sciences to the study of social sciences as well. In the social sciences, Kuhn's observation that new paradigms replace earlier ones is not always followed. Multiple paradigms may coexist as complementary or competing perspectives. (See, e.g. Guba and Lincoln, 1994). It is with that view in mind that I propose the free innovation paradigm as a complement to the

The free innovation paradigm

producer innovation paradigm rather than as a replacement. I am proposing that each usefully frames a portion of extant innovation activity.

Note that by proposing and describing the free innovation paradigm, I by no means claim that research needed to support it is complete. Indeed, I wish to claim precisely the opposite. A new paradigm is most useful when understandings of newly observed phenomena are emergent and when ideas regarding a possible underlying unifying structure are needed to help guide the new research (Kuhn, 1962). This is the role I hope the free innovation paradigm I describe will play. If it is successful, it will usefully frame and support important research questions and findings not encompassed by the existing Schumpeterian producer-centered paradigm, and so provide an improved platform for further advances in innovation research, policy making, and practice.

Major findings from research on free innovation to date

What evidence do we have to date on the value of the free innovation paradigm? First, as I described earlier, we have strong evidence that free innovation is today a large and important type and source of innovations in national economies. We also think that free innovation will only get more important over time. As Baldwin and I explain (2011), the number of innovation opportunities that are viable for individual and collaborative free innovation is increasing rapidly as powerful, easy-to-use design and communication technologies become steadily cheaper. Across many fields, radical reductions in design costs are being driven by advances in computerized design tools suitable for personal use. At the same time, radical reductions in personal communication costs are being driven by advances in the technical capabilities of the Internet. Field-specific tools are following the same trend. For example, inexpensive and easy-to-use tools for genome modification have greatly increased the number of opportunities for biological innovation that are viable for free innovators in the household sector (von Hippel, 2017, Chapter 3).

Second, as was indicated earlier, we know that free innovators play the very important role of often being pioneers with respect to new functions and markets, with producers only following later. Recall that this occurs because free innovators, being self-rewarding, are free to follow their own interests. Unlike producers, they need not restrict their development investments to projects they expect the market to reward. They therefore generally pioneer functionally new applications and markets prior to producers understanding the opportunity. Producer innovators generally enter later, after the nature and the commercial potential of markets have become clear (Riggs and von Hippel, 1994; Baldwin, Hienerth, and von Hippel, 2006).

Not only do producers enter later but they also tend to develop different kinds of innovations when they do enter. Free innovators, when they develop innovations enabling novel capabilities, may create functionality of interest to only subsections of producers' markets. This makes sense because, as was mentioned earlier, free innovators do not care about markets, they only care about their own interests and needs and their related self-rewards. Producers, in contrast, tend to care deeply about the size of markets for the innovations they create, and so tend to develop innovations that every customer will care about, even if only a little. Thus, as is shown in Table 8.2, they tend to focus on developing improvements to "dimensions of merit" that they expect all customers will value, such as improvements to convenience and reliability. As can also be seen in Table 8.2, both free innovators and producers will tend to develop innovations improving devices on performance dimensions such as sensitivity, resolution, and accuracy. These improvements can both enable new functions and improve utility for existing applications

Table 8.2 Sources of scientific equipment innovations by nature of improvements effected

Type of improvement provided by innovation	Innovation developed by		
	User	Producer	Total(n)
New functional capability	82%	18%	17
Sensitivity, resolution, or accuracy improvement	48%	52%	23
Convenience or reliability improvement	13%	87%	24

Source: Riggs and von Hippel (1994), reproduced in von Hippel (2017), Table 4.2.

Third, there are systematic differences between the free and producer paradigms with respect to diffusion – also a very important matter. Consider that the value of free innovation to society comes in part from free innovators' satisfaction of their own needs via the innovations they develop. However, social value can be greatly increased if others also adopt and benefit from those same developments. Of course, to realize this second form of value, free innovations must diffuse from their developers to free adopters.

Investment in diffusion by free innovators can increase social welfare because it is often the case that even relatively small investments can greatly reduce search and adoption costs for many free riders. For example, if I, as a free innovation developer, would invest just a little extra effort to document my open-source software code more fully, I could greatly reduce the time that perhaps thousands of adopters would require to install and use my novel code. Clearly, there would be a net increase in social welfare if I were to expend just that small extra effort.

However, free innovators, unlike producers, do not protect their innovations from free adoption, and they do not sell them. As a result, benefits that free-riding adopters may gain are not systematically shared with free innovators – there is no market link between these parties. For this reason, free innovators may often have too little incentive, from the perspective of social welfare, to invest in actively diffusing their free innovations – in a sense, there is a market failure affecting the free innovation paradigm. In contrast, of course, producers do have a direct market link to consumers, so there should be no similar diffusion incentive shortfall within the producer innovation paradigm. Empirical studies document this effect (de Jong et al., 2015; von Hippel, DeMonaco, and de Jong, 2017).

A proposed division of labor between free and producer innovation

The systematic and important differences between the activities of and incentives affecting free and producer innovators described earlier suggest that a division of innovation development labor between parties in the two paradigms would be of significant benefit both to actors and to social welfare.

Drawing upon modeling by Gambardella, Raasch, and von Hippel (2017), I explain that there is an opportunity for a division of innovation labor between free innovators and producer innovators that simultaneously enhances social welfare and producers' profits.

Most fundamentally, this is because there are important complementarities between the two paradigms. Thus, producers, as my colleagues and I argue, will benefit by not investing in R&D that substitutes for innovations that free innovators develop. Instead, producers will – often but not always – benefit from investing in supporting free innovator design activities. Producers should then focus their own resources on development activities that free innovators do not engage in, such as refinements needed for commercialization. Social welfare, we find, will benefit from public policies that encourage producers to transition from a focus on in-house development to a division of innovation labor with free innovators.

Specific examples of how this could profitably work can be seen from the attributes I described earlier with respect to the attributes of each paradigm and their interactions. First, it makes sense for producers of consumer products to consciously not pioneer new functions, leaving that task instead to free innovators and benefiting from the free designs they create that prove to have commercial promise. Producers will also benefit when complements to the products they commercialize are created and diffused for free to their customers by free innovators.

To illustrate both of these patterns and their value via a concrete example, consider that producers of mountain bikes regularly benefit from commercializing biker-developed free hardware designs – designs for mountain bikes and accessories that mountain bikers regularly pioneer and test in use. Note also that producers profit from the development and diffusion of mountain biking techniques that are an essential complement to mountain bikes themselves. Bike riders develop riding techniques along with novel bike designs – for example, methods of jumping. However, bike producers' ability to profit from diffusing techniques commercially (for example, by founding a mountain biking school) is quite limited. Instead, producers profit indirectly when the biker riders themselves diffuse the innovations for free peer-to-peer as a valuable complement to the mountain bike hardware the producers do sell.

Free innovator peer adopters and producers also benefit when producers adopt free designs and apply the incentives for diffusion that they have via selling and that free innovators, as we saw, themselves lack. For example, mountain bike adopters prefer – even though free designs are available – to buy mountain biking hardware from producers because producers' economies of scale in production (absent in the case of techniques) make that a lower-cost adoption option. Still, free innovators can also keep producer prices in check by being able to turn to the free option if needed. Finally, our modeling shows that it can pay producers to actually support free innovation under many conditions by providing free innovators with design tools and other support, since the benefit to producers from free designs can be quite high.

I conclude this Chapter by again noting that free innovation, free from the need for compensated transactions and intellectual property rights, represents a robust, "grassroots" mode of innovation that differs fundamentally from the prevailing Schumpeterian model of producer-centered innovation. I suggest that the free innovation paradigm described in this Chapter will enable us to understand free innovation more clearly and apply it more effectively, with a resulting increase in social welfare and human flourishing.

Acknowledgments

I wish to thank Professors Prof. Qingrui Xu and Chen Jin for their important contributions to inspiring the work I explore in this chapter.

Note

1 This chapter is based upon the book *Free Innovation* (MIT Press, 2017) by Eric von Hippel. Free eBook copies of the complete book can be downloaded from https://evhippel.mit.edu/

References

Baldwin, C.Y. (2008). Where do transactions come from? Modularity, transactions and the boundaries of firms. *Industrial and Corporate Change*, 17(1), 155–195.

Baldwin, C.Y., Hienerth, C. and Hippel, E. (2006). How user innovations become commercial products: a theoretical investigation and case study. *Research Policy*, 35(9), 1291–1313.

Baldwin, C.Y. and von Hippel, E. (2011). Modeling a paradigm shift: from producer innovation to user and open collaborative innovation. *Organization Science*, 22(6), 1399–1417.

Baumol, W. J. (2002). *The free-market innovation machine: analyzing the growth miracle of capitalism*. Princeton: Princeton University Press.

BEA (Bureau of Economic Analysis, U.S. Department of Commerce). (2016). *Survey of Current Business Online* 96(1), January 2016. January 31, 2016. www.bea.gov/scb/pdf/2015/12%20 December/1215_gdp_and_the_economy.pdf.

Buenstorf, G. (2003). Designing clunkers: demand-side innovation and the early history of the mountain bike. In Metcalfe, J.S., and Cantner, U. (Eds.), *Change, transformation and development*, 53-70. New York: Springer-Verlag.

de Jong, J. P. J. (2013). User innovation by Canadian consumers: analysis of a sample of 2,021 respondents. Unpublished paper commissioned by Industry Canada.

de Jong, J. P. J., von Hippel, E., Gault, F., Kuusisto, J. and Raasch, C. (2015). Market failure in the diffusion of consumer-developed innovations: patterns in Finland. *Research Policy*, 44(10), 1856–1865.

Franke, N. and Shah, S. (2003). How communities support innovative activities: an exploration of assistance and sharing among end-users. *Research Policy*, 32(1), 157–178.

Gallini, N., and Scotchmer, S. (2002). Intellectual property: when is it the best incentive system? In Jaffe, A. B., Lerner, J. and Stern, S. (Eds.), *Innovation policy and the economy*, 2, 51-77. Cambridge, MA: MIT Press.

Gambardella, A., Raasch, C. and von Hippel, E. (2017). The user innovation paradigm: impacts on markets and welfare. *Management Science*, 63(5), 1450–1468.

Guba, E. G., and Lincoln, Y. S. (1994). Competing paradigms in qualitative research. In Denzin, N. K. and Lincoln, Y. S. (Eds.), *Handbook of qualitative research*, 105-117. Thousand Oaks. CA: Sage Publications.

Jeppesen, L. B. and Frederiksen, L. (2006). Why do users contribute to firm hosted user communities? The case of computer-controlled music instruments. *Organization Science*, 17(1), 45–63.

Kim, Y. (2015). Consumer user innovation in Korea: an international comparison and policy implications. *Asian Journal of Technology Innovation*, 23(1), 69–86.

Kuhn, T. S. (1962, 1970). *The structure of scientific revolutions* (2nd ed., enlarged). Chicago: University of Chicago Press.

Lettl, C., Herstatt, C. and Gemuenden, H. G. (2006). Users' contributions to radical innovation: evidence from four cases in the field of medical equipment technology. *R&D Management*, 36(3), 251–272.

Linebaugh, K. (2014). Citizen hackers tinker with medical devices. *Wall Street Journal*, September 26, 2014. December 15, 2015. www.wsj.com/articles/citizen-hackers-concoct-upgrades-for-medical-devices-1411762843.

Machlup, F. and Penrose, E. (1950). The patent controversy in the nineteenth century. *Journal of Economic History*, 10(1), 1–29.

Netcraft.com (2015). March 2015 Web server survey. March 29, 2016. http://news.netcraft.com/archives/2015/03/19/march-2015-web-server-survey.html.

Nightscout Project (2016). *Nightscout*. January 14, 2016. www.nightscout.info.

OECD (2015). National accounts at a glance. Accessed January 30, 2016. www.keepeek.com/Digital-Asset-Management/oecd/economics/national-accounts-at-a-glance-2015/household-final-and-actual-consumption_na_glance-2015-table8-en#page1.

Penning, C. (1998). *Bike history. Die Erfolgsstory des Mountainbikes*. Delius Klasing.

Raasch, C. and von Hippel, E. (2013). Innovation process benefits: the journey as reward. *Sloan Management Review*, 55(1), 33–39.

Raymond, E. A. (1999). *The cathedral and the bazaar: musings on linux and open source by an accidental revolutionary*. Sebastopol, CA: O'Reilly.

Riggs, W. and von Hippel, E. (1994). The impact of scientific and commercial values on the sources of scientific instrument innovation. *Research Policy*, 23(4), 459–469.

Romer, P. M. (1990). Endogenous technological change. *Journal of Political Economy*, 98(5), S71–S102.

Schumpeter, J. A. (1934). *The theory of economic development: an inquiry into profits, capital, credit, interest, and the business cycle*. Cambridge, MA: Harvard University Press. Originally published in German in 1912; first English translation published in 1934.

Steam Workshop (2016). *Steam community: steam workshop*. January 15, 2016. http://steamcommunity.com/workshop/.

Tadelis, S., and Williamson, O. E. (2013). Transaction cost economics. In Gibbons, R., and Roberts, R. (Eds.), *Handbook of organizational economics*, 159-190. Princeton: Princeton University Press.

Teece, D. J. (1986). Profiting from technological innovation: implications for integration, collaboration, licensing and public policy. *Research Policy*, 15(6), 285–305.

Teece, D. J. (1996). Firm organization, industrial structure, and technological innovation. *Journal of Economic Behavior & Organization*, 31(2), 193–224.

von Hippel, E. (1988). *The sources of innovation*. New York: Oxford University Press.

von Hippel, E. (2005). *Democratizing innovation*. Cambridge, MA: MIT Press.

von Hippel, E. (2017). *Free innovation*. Cambridge, MA: MIT Press.

von Hippel, E. and Finkelstein, S. N. (1979). Analysis of innovation in automated clinical chemistry analyzers. *Science and Public Policy*, 6(1), 24–37.

von Hippel, E. A., de Jong, J. P. J. and Flowers, S. (2012). Comparing business and household sector innovation in consumer products: findings from a representative survey in the United Kingdom. *Management Science*, 58(9), 1669–1681.

von Hippel, E. A., DeMonaco, H. J. and de Jong, J. P. J. (2017). Market failure in the diffusion of clinician-developed innovations: the case of off-label drug discoveries. *Science and Public Policy*, 44(1), 121–131.

von Hippel, E., Ogawa, S. and de Jong, J. P. J. (2011). The age of the consumer-innovator. *Sloan Management Review*, 53(1), 27–35.

9
OPEN INNOVATION

Yufen Chen and Wim Vanhaverbeke

Concept and connotation of open innovation

A conceptual comparison of open innovation and several similar innovation models

Open innovation

Chesbrough (2003a) first introduced the open innovation model in 2003. In the model, valuable ideas can be gained from both inside and outside the company, and the commercialization process can take place either inside or outside the company (Chesbrough, 2003b). The open innovation model elevates the importance of external ideas and external commercialization channels to the same level as that of internal ideas and internal commercialization channels (Chesbrough, 2003a). Chesbrough proposed the model mainly in response to the traditional NIH (not invented here) attitude that exists in some large American corporations with strong R&D capabilities.

In the open innovation paradigm, the boundaries of corporates are permeable. Innovative ideas mainly come from R&D and other departments inside a company but may also come from outside the company. Innovative ideas generated inside a company may spread to the outside at any stage of the R&D process through knowledge flow, the movement of personnel, or patent transfer. Some research projects that do not fit in the current business lines of a company may produce tremendous value somewhere else in the market and may be commercialized through external channels. Companies no longer keep their intellectual assets locked in a safe. Instead, they find good uses for them in other companies and gain profits from such assets through licensing agreements, short-term partnerships, and other arrangements (Chesbrough, 2003b).

The open innovation model has changed the NIH mind-set. The model demands that companies make full use of the abundance of external knowledge resources, search for suitable external technologies that will compensate for a lack of internal innovative resources, strive to integrate internal and external technologies, and thereby create new products and services. In the open innovation model, external knowledge complements internal knowledge and plays an equally important role. At the same time, the open innovation model has overcome the prejudice of NSH (not sold here). Companies can commercialize their internal technologies through external channels and thereby maximize returns on R&D investment. The new thinking represented by open innovation has helped us find new approaches to value creation and profit making.

The open innovation model refers to a type of innovation model in which a company in the technology innovation process can simultaneously make use of internal and external complementary resources. The commercialization process of internal technologies can take place inside or outside the company, and the company is engaged in multifaceted and dynamic cooperation with various partners at each stage of the innovation chain. Chesbrough (2006) redefined the concept of open innovation as an innovative paradigm in which companies intentionally make use of inbound and outbound knowledge flows to speed internal innovation or expand knowledge development in external markets.

Open innovation emphasizes the importance to cross organizational boundaries that companies carry out open cooperation with outside organizations and make use of external innovative resources and external marketing channels to improve innovation efficiency. The open innovation model has changed the way in which companies gain the resources necessary for achieving innovation. In the open innovation model, the boundary of a company is permeable. Companies cannot only rely on their own resources and must use the innovative resources of the outside environment, and so a huge knowledge exchange network linking internal company units and various external organizations takes shape. The features of the open innovation model make it possible for a company to be engaged in exploratory and exploitative learning simultaneously.

The concept of open innovation is a microscopic concept of the innovative system of an organization. It is derived from a summary of the innovation modes that result from autonomous adjustments made by companies to adapt their innovative processes to complexity in an innovative and rapidly changing knowledge economy. In an era of knowledge explosion, even companies with the largest knowledge reserves cannot achieve self-sufficiency in all areas of technology, and thus open innovation has become the inevitable choice for effective innovation by individual organizations. Improving the openness of a company's innovation system; enhancing its capabilities in knowledge search, knowledge acquisition, knowledge absorption, and knowledge utilization; and providing feedback to strengthen internal R&D capabilities are the preconditions for achieving independent innovation and collaborative innovation. Open innovation is also the precondition for achieving synergies within the national innovation system.

Collaborative innovation

The concept of collaborative innovation is a macroscopic concept within the processes of the national innovation system. The concept of synergy derives from the synergy theory (Haken, 1978), which is an important branch of complex systems theory. The idea of synergy comes from the study of open systems in physics. The synergistic effect converts a complex system into an orderly system and, in the process, produces a tremendous amount of energy. The concept of collaborative innovation was proposed by Peter Gloor, a researcher at the MIT Sloan Center. According to Gloor, collaborative innovation is a process in which "a networked group of self-motivated people form a collective vision, and then exchange ideas, information and work statuses through the network, and work collaboratively to achieve their common goals" (Chen, 2012). The concept of collaborative innovation leads us to a path through which China can transform itself into an innovative country. To build a vibrant national innovation ecosystem, we must rely on the full collaboration of the government, industries, academia, research institutes, and other innovative entities; build an open network of knowledge generation, knowledge transfer, and knowledge utilization within the national innovation system; and so eventually achieve the strategic goal of independent innovation.

Open innovation in network-based crowdsourcing mode

Network-based crowdsourcing refers to the practice by a company or organization of outsourcing tasks that used to be performed by its own employees to a crowd of nonspecific network users (usually users in a large-scale network) in the form of free and voluntary transactions (Howe, 2006). The network-based crowdsourcing model differs from the traditional outsourcing model in that the traditional model is a mode of transactional cooperation between organizations, in which a company enters into contracts and purchases services from specific organizations. But network-based crowdsourcing is a mode of contractual cooperation between a company and a crowd of network users, in which the objects of cooperation are no longer specific cooperative companies but network users across the globe (and thus the geographic scope of the cooperation expands globally). On the basis of the nature of the tasks, the modes of network-based crowdsourcing can be divided into two categories: information-processing-oriented modes and R&D-and-innovation-oriented modes. These modes are based on the nature of the collaboration among network users and can be divided into cooperative and competitive network-based crowdsourcing.

Open innovation in the network-based crowdsourcing model refers to a mode of operation in which a company takes advantage of the information network shaped by the various online platforms to carry out knowledge search and knowledge matching, collaboration among the many participants, exchange of funds and knowledge, and knowledge absorption and utilization. Simply put, when faced with a technological challenge, the company first formulates a specific technological issue through the technical process and makes an assessment about a reasonable price to pay for resolving the issue. The company then publishes an invitation to bid to network users around the globe through a network-based crowdsourcing platform. Under the supervision of the platform, the company can then choose from among the various solutions submitted. In the process, network users develop solutions through a cooperative or competitive process, so the proposer of the best solution is rewarded and the company obtains the best solution. Given that a network-based crowdsourcing platform can directly access the capabilities of the mass and the various repositories of resources and repositories of ideas, its value and efficiency can greatly exceed those of what can be integrated into any individual company (Schenk and Guittard, 2011). The network-based crowdsourcing model is the most open innovation paradigm for cheaply absorbing high-end innovation resources across all regions, cultures, and technical fields.

In summary, independent innovation is a concept related to the goal of constructing a national innovation system. Collaborative innovation is a macroscopic concept related to the process for constructing a national innovation system, and open innovation is a microscopic concept at the organizational level. In other words, independent innovation is regarded as the strategic objective. Collaborative innovation is the approach for fulfilling the objective, and open innovation is a precondition for fulfilling the objective. Only when a large number of innovation entities attach greater importance to open innovation can we be successful in stimulating a flow of knowledge and promoting the development of synergies among industries, academia, and research institutes – and so enhance our capabilities in independent research to become an innovative nation.

Classification of the modes of open innovation

To distinguish the concept of open innovation from the concepts of innovation network and technology alliance, open innovation is divided into two categories based on the direction of knowledge flow and process direction: inbound open innovation and outbound open innovation (Chesbrough and Growther, 2006). Inbound open innovation refers to the process by which a company absorbs external knowledge and integrates external knowledge, creative ideas, and technologies of value with internal ideas so as to carry out innovation and commercialization inside the company. Outbound open innovation refers to the process through which a company, as the source of innovation, exports its internal knowledge, technology, and creative ideas to external organizations – and the commercialization of such knowledge, technology, and ideas then takes place in external organizations (Wang, 2010).

From the perspective of business processes, Gassmann and Enkel (2004) surveyed 124 companies based on the direction of knowledge flow and proposed three types of open innovation: (1) outside-in open innovation (which emphasizes the integration of suppliers, customers, and other external knowledge sources to expand the knowledge base of the company, improve its internal R&D, and enhance its innovative capabilities); (2) inside-out open innovation (which emphasizes "pioneering" to promote the internal knowledge of an organization to the outside and exporting creative ideas through the sale of intellectual property so as to achieve the external commercialization of internal creative ideas); and (3) coupled open innovation (which emphasizes creating complementary knowledge together with strategic partners and jointly developing and commercializing creative ideas through long-term alliances, cooperation, joint ventures, and other means so as to gain advantages with both inbound and outbound knowledge flows).

Dahlander and Gann (2010) classified open innovation into four types on the basis of the direction of knowledge flow and whether or not economic transactions are involved: inbound sourcing, inbound acquiring, outbound revealing, and outbound selling. Among the four types, the inbound sourcing type of innovation involves economic transaction, and the inbound acquiring type of innovation does not involve economic transaction. The research on outbound innovation revealing mostly concerns the inbound acquiring type of innovation.

Laursen and Salter (2006) were the first to point out that openness should be measured for the inbound acquiring type of innovation and proposed a method for measuring openness, which has been referenced by many scholars. On the basis of their work, Chen and Chen (2008a) expanded on the measurement of inbound openness from the perspectives of technology-driven and experience-driven industries. However, the research on openness mentioned earlier is limited to inbound openness without considering the outside commercialization of the internal knowledge of a company. Henkel, taking embedded Linux as an example, carried out the first initial exploratory study of outbound openness (Wang, 2010). Lichtenthaler (2009a, 2009b) studied open innovation of the outbound selling type. Their study helped them conclude that the external commercialization of a company's internal technology holds great strategic importance to the success of the company.

Essential connotation of technological innovation

Schumpeter was the first to propose innovation theory from the perspective of economics. Schumpeter argues that innovation refers to the introduction of an unprecedented "new combination of production factors" into production systems – and the aim of innovation is to obtain profits (Schumpeter, 1934). What is special about Schumpeter's definition of technological innovation is the emphasis on the effective combination of economic factors and that technological innovation should be regarded as the organic combination of economic factors (such as information, talented people, material capital, and entrepreneurial ability) to produce a unique usefulness. He specifically distinguishes invention from innovation. If an invention has not found its practical application, it is economically ineffective.

From the perspective of business management, technological innovation is a process from the generation of new ideas to research, development, trial production, actual production, and initial commercialization. Technological innovation means the combination of invention, development, and commercialization that turns a creative idea into reality and carries a concept to the market for commercialization.

Technological innovation emphasizes the integration of technology and market

Technological innovation is an economic activity that aims to turn a creative idea into a commercial success. That is to say, it must meet the needs of society and the market. The indication of the success of a technological innovation project is the initial commercialization of the technological invention. Technological innovation is the combination of technology and market, and neither is dispensable. If a company is always pursuing "technical perfection" without fully taking changing market factors into account, even the most advanced technology will fail to produce successful innovation (Chen and Liu, 2006). Technological leadership is no guarantee of successful innovation, and sometimes it even hinders innovation. There is no intrinsic value in technology itself, and value only emerges when we commercialize technology through some business model (Chesbrough, 2003a). An innovative product in any type of business must ultimately be oriented toward its market to meet the needs of users. Only when an invention has been transformed into economic activities and has produced significant profits can it be regarded as a technological innovation.

Technological innovation emphasizes the effective integration of the R&D, manufacturing, and marketing departments

Difficult passages across the Darwinian seas must be successfully navigated in the process of turning an innovative technology into a popular product. The uncertainty of technological innovation is also reflected in market and business strategy. The failures of most technological innovation projects are not caused by failures in technology, but by shortcomings in market research, sales, and organizational management. Therefore, to succeed with technological innovation, we must successfully coordinate R&D, marketing, and production. Technological innovation is not just the work of the R&D department. Instead, innovation must reach deep into the organization and every root and branch of the company.

Technological innovation emphasizes the effective integration of internal and external knowledge

Technological innovation requires knowledge and technologies from an increasing number of fields of study, and the comprehensiveness and complexity of innovation increases day by day. For companies with limited resources, it is not enough to rely on their own resources to enhance innovative capabilities because such resources no longer meet the needs of current technological innovation. Individual companies are not strong enough to internally produce all the knowledge needed, and it is impossible for them to have all the resources and technologies required for innovation (Teece, 1986). An external knowledge source is usually the key element in an innovation process (Cohen and Levinthal, 1990). Therefore, to gain and maintain competitive advantage, the ability to adapt, integrate, and configure internal and external technological resources is important (Teece, Pisano, and Shuen, 1997). The ability to make effective use of external resources has become a key component of a company's innovative capability (Cohen and Levinthal, 1990).

Two modes of technological innovation

Professors Jensen and Lundvall proposed two modes of technological innovation: the STI mode, which is focused on science, technology, and innovation; and the DUI mode, which is based on learning by doing, using, and interacting (Jensen, Johnson, Lorenz, and Lundvall, 2004). At the same time, they pointed out that the perfect combination of STI and DUI modes would greatly enhance innovative capability and that it is insufficient to just focus on one of the two modes.

Innovation mode is based on scientific research or R&D; the innovation process goes from basic research, applied research, experimental development, trial production, actual production, and eventually to commercialization. The successful application of this innovation mode usually requires strong R&D and technology capabilities. With adequate human and material resources for R&D, a company can rely on its own effort to explore and achieve breakthroughs in core technologies. On the basis of such breakthroughs, companies can again rely on their own technological capabilities to complete the development of new products and successfully commercialize such products. Innovation modes based on scientific research are highly dependent on R&D activities. Internal R&D capability is a strategic asset of an enterprise, but innovation modes based on scientific research are not simply technology-driven linear processes. A company in this mode of innovation must still emphasize the integration of scientific research and industrial and market chains – which is dictated by the nature of technological innovation.

The experience-based innovation model refers to a process in which employees and users encounter problems when producing and using the product, and the company, with its existing technological capabilities, implements R&D in collaboration with universities or research institutes to search for solutions to problems – and thereby achieve technological innovation. In the solution searching process, employees or users gain technological knowledge or abilities. If this process is rather complicated, finding solutions will require interactions among members of a team or among members of different teams, and thus there will be many instances of experience sharing and knowledge sharing. The successful application of this innovation mode requires that employees and users have a sense of responsibility and the necessary technical skills, which in turn requires that employees adopting this mode of innovation must be well qualified in terms of scientific training. This innovation mode relies on continued improvements in the practical setting to increase the efficiency of technology, and thus the accumulation of experience plays a key role. The focus of this innovation mode is on users, rather than just products or core technologies. Effective innovation in noncore technology areas can also improve innovation performance and economic competitiveness, and represents an effective approach for technology accumulation.

The combination of STI and DUI modes can increase efficiency in the use of innovative resources and improve innovation performance (Jensen, Johnson, Lorenz, and Lundvall, 2004). Jensen et al., illustrate the importance of combining these two innovation modes with examples of technological innovation in Nordic countries. Innovation in STI mode requires considerable

R&D investment and energetic R&D activities, but it does not mean that DUI mode can be ignored. Similarly, DUI mode must be based on STI mode. Technological opportunities and market conditions are changing rapidly in a global economy, and everything must be considered for achieving innovation: from the development of core technologies to the market, user needs, user experience, and so on. Companies must fully grasp the rules of technological innovation and coordinate internal R&D, technology matching, manufacturing, and external factors such as the market. The combination of STI mode and DUI mode ensures the effective use of national scientific resources to speed up the advancement of science and technology and industrialization. Capabilities in technological innovation can be enhanced by combining internal R&D, searches, and external innovative resources

External source theory of technological innovation

Since the 1980s, the seismic changes in technology and breakneck advancement in telecommunications and intensification of global competition have meant that manufacturers must continuously innovate to maintain competitive advantages (Hage and Alter, 1993; Brown and Eisenhardt, 1998). Highly complex innovations often involve multiple technological fields, particularly in the automotive, electronics, telecommunications, and aeronautics industries. It is usually necessary to combine knowledge from a variety of sources for rapid and continued product development (Hagedoorn, 1993; Chung and Kim, 2003). It is difficult for any individual company to engage in simultaneous research in all key technological areas, and thus few companies can maintain a leading position in every area of technological research. No individual companies are strong enough to internally produce all the knowledge needed for technological innovation, and it is impossible for companies to obtain all the resources and technologies needed for such innovation (Teece, 1986; Caloghirou, Kastelli, and Tsakanikas, 2004). It is therefore worthwhile for companies to interact with external organizations to gain new scientific and technological knowledge (Mowery, Oxley, and Silverman, 1996).

For effective innovation and development, a company must pay more attention to its external environment and place more emphasis on integrating various resources. Most research in innovation management has stressed the importance of learning and technology search for interdisciplinary innovation through interactions between organizations. Nelson and Winter (1982) proposed a decision-making process for new technology searches outside the organization. Teece (1986) pointed to the importance of complementary assets for innovation success and explained why innovative companies often fail to gain the first mover advantage – while fast followers often make enormous profits. Teece pointed out that innovation pioneers lacking in complementary assets must acquire manufacturing and marketing capabilities from the outside through cooperation and integration for the successful commercialization of new products.

Cohen and Levinthal (1989) emphasize that R&D cannot just produce new knowledge and encourage innovation and must also improve a company's capacity to absorb knowledge from the external environment. External knowledge sources represent the key factor in the effort to attain success in innovation (Cohen and Levinthal, 1990). Rosenberg (1990) questioned why companies invest in fundamental research and found that fundamental research can enhance their ability to make good use of external scientific knowledge. Rosenberg sees fundamental research as an "admission ticket" to information networks for monitoring and evaluating external technologies, and he believes that companies that are bad at using external knowledge are at a competitive disadvantage. Innovation sources are greatly varied according to von Hippel (1988), and he specified four external sources of innovation: users and suppliers, universities and research institutes, competitors, and other countries. Rothwell's fifth-generation technological innovation process suggests that integration of the system and expansion of the network model is an innovation process with multiple factors that requires a high degree of integration of both intra- and intercompany resources (Rothwell, 1994). Knowledge base theory emphasizes the importance of knowledge-based and learning-based interactions between internal elements and external elements of an organization. It holds that any important resource that can enhance the innovative capabilities of a company, regardless of whether inside or outside the company, should be incorporated into the company's system of capabilities (Nonaka, 1994). The core competitiveness of a company is increasingly dependent on its capabilities when searching for knowledge, creating knowledge, and making technological innovations (Powell, 1998). Scholars in organizational theory and structural sociology who hold an open system view (Wellman, 1988) have long insisted that the most important part of an organization's environment is the social network of its external links and any economic activity in open systems. Key resources other than those owned by the company itself can be obtained by various forms of links to external entities. Thus, various links of different forms between companies can produce considerable relational rent and competitive advantages (Dyer, 1996). Although these articles do not include the term "open innovation", they nevertheless all contain the idea of "openness".

The idea that a company can facilitate its technological innovation with resources acquired externally has attracted the attention of many experts in innovation management. In the past, outsourcing was regarded as a disadvantage to a company. But with the changes in the competitive environment, resource outsourcing has become a key factor for the successful operation of an intelligent business. The creation of capabilities in new technological areas is a dynamic learning process for a company that requires the combination of external technology acquisition and internal technological activities (Granstrand, Patel, and Pavitt, 1997). The integration of internal and external technological resources is the key dimension of an effective innovation strategy. A successful company, on the basis of its own capabilities, investment, and decision process, can always strive to take advantage of both internal and external technologies to maintain and strengthen its competitive advantages (Wheelwright and Clark, 1992).

Impact of open innovation on innovation performance

Company boundaries are permeable in the open innovation paradigm. Valuable creativity can be obtained from inside and outside a company, and the commercialization of such ideas can take place inside or outside the company. The open innovation system can reduce the uncertainty of technological and market innovation and help the company avoid the dilemma of innovation.

The open innovation mode proposed by Chesbrough has become a popular research field in the international academic community and received recognition from scholars at home and abroad (Gassmann and Enkel, 2004; Christensen, 2005; Vanhaverbeke, 2006; Gassmann, 2006). In addition to being suitable for companies in R&D-intensive high-tech industries, open innovation mode is suitable for mature and low-tech industries (Chesbrough and Crowther, 2006; Vanhaverbeke, 2006; van de Meer, 2007; Spithoven, 2011). In addition to large corporations, open innovation is equally suitable for small and medium-sized enterprises (van de Vrande, Lemmens, and Vanhaverbeke, 2006; van de Vrande et al., 2009; Spithoven, 2011). Open innovation has also been introduced to service-related innovation in areas of business management (Chesbrough, 2011).

How did the open innovation paradigm affect the development of a company's innovative capabilities? And how has it become the focus of both academia and industry? There are three research conclusions about the impact of open innovation on innovation performance.

Positive impact

Lichtenthaler (2009a) pointed out that open innovation has a positive impact on enterprise performance, but patent protection is bad for open innovation. Based on data gathered from Austrian companies, Todtling, Lehner, and Kaufmann (2009) concluded that external cooperation in the innovation process has a significant impact on the performance of new product-related innovation. Yeoh (2009) argues that companies can absorb different types of knowledge through R&D-based cooperation, and companies can be more effective in acquiring technology and knowledge by interacting with external knowledge sources to improve innovation performance. The number of exploratory cooperative alliances has a significant impact on company performance (Yamakawa, Yang, and Lin, 2011). Chiang and Hung (2010) believe that broad openness is good for breakthrough innovation, and the depth of openness helps to improve incremental innovation in a company's performance. By analyzing the impact of both regional and inter-regional R&D cooperation on innovation performance, as well as the moderating role of technology diversification, Sun and Zang (2017) found that both regional R&D cooperation and inter-regional R&D cooperation have a significant positive impact on innovation performance. Regional cooperation helps more in expanding the scale of innovation, while inter-regional cooperation helps more in improving the quality of innovation. Technology diversification always has a significant negative moderator effect.

Negative impact

Costs are associated with implementing open innovation, including costs for knowledge search, coordination, and maintaining confidentiality. Open innovation will cause changes in company culture and organizational structure, inertia in the company's own R&D, leakage of key knowledge, and so on. This may cause the company to become dependent on network embeddedness and weaken its innovative capabilities (Ahuja and Lampert, 2001). In view of the negative impact of open innovation, an increase in openness will slow the development pace of new products and increase product development costs (Knudsen and Mortensen, 2011).

Nonlinear effects

A study by de Man and Duysters (2005) shows that the external cooperation of a company can have different effects on its innovation performance, including positive, negative, and neutral effects. Laursen and Salter (2006, 2014) analyzed the impact of openness on innovation performance and found that there is an "inverted U-shaped" relationship between openness and innovation performance. This finding has also been supported by research (Almirall and Casadesus-Masanell, 2010; Chiang and Hung, 2010). Chen and Chen (2008b) explored the effects of innovation openness on innovation performance in various industries and expanded the conclusions reached by Laursen and Salter (2006). Sofka and Grimpe (2010) pointed out that openness can encourage innovation performance, but companies must be careful about the direction of external search. Lichtenthaler, Hoegl, and Muethel (2011) indicated that the sale and purchase of technology with external entities can achieve the highest return in enterprise innovation – but that it is dangerous for a company to only focus on technology sales. According to the data from Italian manufacturing companies, Berchicci (2013) found that the use of external technology sources becomes detrimental to innovation performance beyond a particular value.

In accordance with the conclusion proposed by Laursen and Salter (2006), Greco, Grimaldi, and Cricelli (2016) analyzed the effects of openness depth and coupled OI on breakthrough innovation and incremental innovation (on the basis of data from 84,919 companies in European innovation). The study shows that there is an "inverted U-shaped" relationship for the breadth of openness with breakthrough innovation and incremental innovation. The depth of open innovation does not have a weakening effect on breakthrough innovation. However, there is an inverted U-shaped relationship between the depth of open innovation and incremental innovation, which is not an obvious relationship. There is also an inverted U-shaped relationship between coupled OI and breakthrough innovation.

Given that the interaction between a company's absorptive capacity and the openness of innovation has not been taken into account and the openness of innovation has not been matched to absorptive capacity, there are conflicts in existing empirical studies. With the same openness, the ability to acquire external knowledge is affected by absorptive capacity. Therefore, absorptive capacity is the key factor in determining the effect of open innovation.

Synergies between internal and external innovation resources in an open innovation environment

For innovation and development, a company should pay attention to the external environment and the integration of internal and external resources. The idea of promoting technological innovation with resources acquired externally has drawn the attention of numerous innovation management experts (Teece, 1986; Cohen and Levinthal, 1990; Mowery, Oxley, and Silverman, 1996; Hagedoorn, 1993, 2000; Brusoni, Prencipe, and Pavitt, 2001; Pavitt, 2002; Coombs, 2003; Powell and Grodal, 2005). Many researchers suggest that internal and external R&D are complementary. Internal R&D can improve a company's capacity to absorb knowledge in the external environment (Cohen and Levinthal, 1990; Rosenberg, 1990). The acquisition and utilization of external knowledge is based on internal R&D capabilities, and the complementarity of internal and external knowledge enhances innovation performance (Teece, 1986; Arora and Gambardella, 1990; Cassiman and Veugelers, 2002; Belderbos, Prencipe, and Pavitt, 2004). Other researchers believe that internal and external R&D are negatively correlated (Basant and Fikkert, 1996; Fernandez-Bagües, 2004) and that there is a substitution effect between them. Finally, some researchers find no significant relationships between them.

What is the relationship between internal R&D and external knowledge search: Are they complementary synergies or alternatives? Does excessive external knowledge search weaken the strategic position of internal R&D and negatively affect the company's sustainable competitive advantage? The key issue in this debate lies in the differences in absorptive capacities. A company must rely on its internal capability to effectively use external technologies. The balance between internal capabilities and the acquisition of external innovative resources has become a key issue. Therefore, it is important to understand the relationship between a company's absorptive capacity and openness activities – and how a dynamic balance between internal and external innovation resources should be maintained. Interaction of the two types of resources enhances a company's innovation performance.

The impact of internal R&D on open innovation

Lichtenthaler (2008a) holds that the internalization of external knowledge is required in open innovation – and that the external management capabilities such as absorptive capacity, learning ability, and dynamic capabilities are needed to retain, exploit, and develop interorganizational knowledge (Lichtenthaler, 2009a). Knowledge management capacities can be grouped into six categories: inventive, absorptive, transformative, connective, innovative, and desorptive

(Lichtenthaler and Lichtenthaler, 2009). From the perspective of absorptive capacity and process, Lichtenthaler also studied the learning process with technology and market knowledge (Lichtenthaler, 2008b). By strengthening cooperation with government, enterprises, industries, universities, research institutes, and public service platforms, the innovation performance of companies can be enhanced. Moreover, interactive learning plays an important role in the open learning process.

Internal R&D enhances the ability of a company to recognize, acquire, digest, and use external knowledge, that is, its absorptive capacity (Cohen and Levinthal, 1990). In a rich external knowledge environment, a company must identify and understand the abundance of external knowledge resources. It can then make selections by building links. Internal and external technologies should be integrated to create complex technology combinations, which further create new systems and frameworks (Chesbrough, 2003a). Absorptive capacity is a function of the company's prior knowledge and prior experience, which can be gradually accumulated through the company's R&D efforts (Cohen and Levinthal, 1989, 1990). The strength of a company's internal R&D capabilities determines its ability to recognize, digest, and use external knowledge. External knowledge and technological skills can be effectively used when a company has engaged in fundamental research and acquired sufficient internal R&D capabilities (Rosenberg, 1990; Cassiman, Perez-Castrillo, and Veugelers, 2002).

Positive effect of external knowledge search on internal R&D

For the effective use of external knowledge, companies with many external technology opportunities have strong incentives to increase investment in internal R&D. External knowledge search may therefore encourage, rather than substitute, internal R&D (Arora and Gambardella, 1990; Veugelers, 1997). In view of the complexity and interdisciplinary nature of technology, even large companies cannot keep up with the pace of development in all technologies (Veugelers, 1997). To encourage innovation, companies often need to use external knowledge to compensate for the lack of internal R&D. Therefore, external knowledge search increases the marginal return rate on internal R&D investment, which not only enhances innovation performance but also boosts the accumulation of internal technological capabilities.

Complementarity and synergy of internal and external knowledge

Gassmann (2006) proposed that companies should balance their ability to unearth internal knowledge resources and their ability to profit from external knowledge resources. Dahlander and Gann (2007) believe that the traditional path, structure, and culture of business innovation are the prerequisites for the identification, acquisition, and absorption of external knowledge.

There is complementariness between internal R&D and external knowledge search (Schneider, 2008; Hagedoorn and Ning, 2012; Chen and Ye, 2013; Sofka and Grimpe, 2010; Chen, Vanhaverbeke, and Du, 2016). The stronger a company's internal R&D capabilities, the more efficient is its external knowledge search. External knowledge search drives a company to enhance its internal R&D and improve the efficiency of its internal R&D.

External knowledge search has an important impact on the improvement of enterprise innovation performance, but different types of external cooperation objects differ in their importance to innovation performance. In business innovation practice, there is a complementary and synergistic relationship between internal R&D and knowledge search in vertical cooperative enterprises as well as horizontal enterprises. However, there is not enough evidence to show a complementary relationship between internal R&D and knowledge search by universities or research institutes. Whether a relationship between internal R&D and external knowledge search is complementary or substitutive is primarily determined by a company's capacity to absorb external knowledge. If a company does not have enough absorptive capacity, its external knowledge search will become inefficient. The interactive relationship between internal R&D and external knowledge search explains why some companies can achieve a high efficiency in external knowledge search and achieve high rates of return on R&D investment.

The mechanism through which open innovation can affect innovation performance

Open innovation induces the free flow of innovative resources, which is an advantage. Open innovation mode provides companies with opportunities to obtain the various resources necessary for innovation, enhance their capabilities in technological innovation, and improve competitiveness. In open innovation, the various elements of innovation and means to acquire technologies influence and complement each other, and thus no innovation elements can be analyzed in isolation from the overall innovation strategy of the company. Why does openness enhance business innovation performance? What are the mechanisms by which the various innovation elements enhance innovation performance?

The mechanism that opens innovation and affects innovation performance has been researched from different perspectives, such as resources, knowledge, and capability.

The resource viewpoint

From the viewpoint of resources, Chen and Chen (2009) made an empirical analysis of the mechanism and action process of open innovation and found that open innovation enhances innovation performance through a process in which market information and technologies are acquired to compensate for the lack of internal R&D.

The knowledge viewpoint

Zheng, Ye, and Xu (2017) constructed a model that shows how the openness of clustered companies affects innovation performance based on the characteristics of the clusters. The research shows that innovation performance is affected by knowledge acquisition. A company's capacity to absorb knowledge affects the innovation performance formation process. The potential absorptive capacity plays a positive role in regulating the effect of openness on knowledge acquisition. The actual absorptive capacity plays a positive role in moderating the transformation from knowledge acquisition to innovation performance. Network centrality plays a positive role in regulating the effect of the breadth of openness in clustered companies on knowledge acquisition.

Jiang and Cai (2014) analyzed the open innovation of Refond Optoelectronics based on a case study and grounded-theory analysis. From the perspective of the point-edge-network of the alliance portfolio, the authors summed six structural characteristics or elements: resource diversity (quantity), resource heterogeneity (quality), breadth of openness (quantity), depth of openness (quality), structural strength, and a coupling mechanism on the three levels of the alliance portfolio – company (point), relationship (edge), and network (network). The authors also examined the mechanism by which the six structural characteristics encourage open innovation performance through enhanced knowledge flow, absorption, transfer, and creation. In the future, comparative studies can be made with large cases and empirical studies can be made to verify the action mechanism by which the structural characteristics of the innovation network affect the performance of open innovation.

The capability viewpoint

Yao, Ouyang, and Zhou (2017) studied the mechanism by which open innovation affects enterprise competitiveness from the internal ability and external environment. Based on the empirical data of 271 Chinese companies, the finding shows that open innovation (including inbound and outbound) positively affects enterprise competitiveness. The dynamic capability of knowledge is the full mediation between open innovation and enterprise competitiveness. Partner opportunism negatively moderates the effects of both inbound and outbound open innovation on enterprise competitiveness.

Based on the action process of open innovation, Zhu and Hao (2014) further divided the technological innovation capability of enterprises into three subcapabilities – absorptive capability, integration capability, and original capability. The authors then proposed the pool-pump mechanism by which enterprise technological capability increases cyclically in an open innovation environment. Combined with the case study on the Neusoft Group, the research analyzed the capability of a company to produce endogenous new knowledge through absorbing and integrating external knowledge and resources in an open innovation environment.

Lv, Shi, and Ji (2017) took the smartphone industry as the research object from the embeddedness perspective of innovation networks and explored the effect of the openness of a company's open innovation process on its ability to achieve incremental innovation. Their research shows that innovation process openness indirectly affects the incremental innovation capability by moderating the interaction between the level of innovation network embeddedness and the capability to achieve incremental innovation. In the preliminary stage of technology development in an industry, innovation process openness positively moderates the effect of innovation network embedding on the incremental innovation capability. In an emerging stage of technology development in an industry, the moderating effect of innovation openness ceases to exist. In the stable stage of technology development in the industry, only the breadth of innovation openness positively moderates the effect of innovation network embeddedness on incremental innovation capability.

Yan and Cai (2014) studied the effect of innovation openness on innovation performance. Innovation openness first affects a company's innovation orientation (exploration-based innovation and development-based innovation) and then affects innovation performance. The innovation orientation and business model act as mediators between innovation openness and innovation performance.

Organizational implementation of open innovation

The implementation of open innovation does not happen automatically. External innovation resources do not flow into companies, and implementations of open innovation in different companies produce different results. Open innovation highlights the entire innovation system. For companies of different characteristics and at different stages of the R&D process, decisions about the openness degree may be different, and this is related to the company's absorptive capacity, choice of cooperation objects, and organizational form. Where should a company search for external knowledge? How do they make best use of open innovation?

Christensen, Olesen, and Kjaer (2005) point out that the dynamic characteristics in open innovation and the mode of open innovation management are related to the company's position and the maturity of the technology. On the basis of the U-A model, Chen and Chen (2009) analyzed the key innovation factors for companies in different industries and stages of technological innovation and constructed the dynamic model of open innovation. Chiaroni, Chiesa, and Frattini (2010, 2011) summarized the changes of the organizational structure and management system from the closed to open state. Bianchi et al. (2011) explored the selections of organizational structure and cooperation partners in open innovation by studying biopharmaceutical industries at different stages of drug discovery and development.

Makri, Michael, and Peter (2010) found that dispersed distribution of knowledge and information affects the search strategy in innovation activities. Argote and Greve (2007) believed that diverse external resources could facilitate innovation. Selective knowledge sharing by customers, competitors, and suppliers could enhance a company's innovative capabilities according to von Hippel and von Krogh (2003, 2006). However, constraints on resource consumption are related to the depth of search. A deep search of external knowledge sources is a resource-consuming process and difficult to implement under strict constraints (Ferru, 2010).

What determines the selection of an open innovation model in companies? For innovation activities, different R&D objects at different stages of the innovation process have different investment needs and risk tolerance. Thus, the innovation mode adopted is closely related to the stage of innovation of the "innovation object" – including technology, product, service, etc. (Laursen and Salter, 2006). The mode is also related to whether an organization constantly makes adjustments to its innovative behaviors to adapt to the needs of different innovation objects at different stages (Chesbrough, Vanhaverbeke, and West, 2006). For organizations with diverse technologies (products or services and so on), adopting different modes of open innovation may be a problem.

In the practice of innovation, there are a number of organizational models for innovation that take different external organizations as the main aims of openness – and different models of innovation have different effects on innovation performance. Walsh, Lee, and Nagaoka (2016) analyzed the impact of cooperation with heterogeneous entities on innovation performance at different stages of the innovation process. The empirical studies show that the cooperation with industries, universities, and research institutes helps improve the quality of the invention or patent at the invention stage. And vertical cooperation with customers and suppliers helps improve the success rate of the commercialization of the invention at the implementation stage. There are interactions between a company's internal capabilities and its mode of openness. Companies should choose the mode of openness that matches their internal capabilities. Companies with strong internal R&D capabilities can improve their innovation performance through cooperation with partners in science. Those with strong internal R&D capabilities but average manufacturing capabilities should seek cooperation with other horizontal companies. Those with average levels of internal R&D capabilities can markedly improve their innovation performance through close cooperation with organizations that are technologically strong and partners on the value chain. Enterprises should not blindly open to external organizations. The core issue in selecting the right target of openness is whether or not the company can obtain complementary resources that benefit the innovation effort.

From the point of the microscopic view of R&D entities, Sun, Wang, Ding, and Wei (2016) studied the selection of factors in the open innovation mode. Cases on China's DEEJ, Inc., and Japan's Sankyu, Inc., showed that there can be multiple modes of open innovation in the same business organization, which is closely related to the core competency corresponding to the innovation object. And the selection of innovation modes is the manifestation of the dynamic shifts in the related core competencies. Organizational core competencies include the competency fulcrum and competency periphery. The core competency periphery is further divided into the exclusive capability periphery and cluster capability periphery. The core competences correspond to a specific innovation mode. The depth of innovation mode and the breadth of innovation mode may be suitable for an exclusive capability periphery (with high entry barriers of entry) and for a cluster capability periphery (with low entry barriers of entry), respectively.

Management implications of open innovation

Open innovation emphasizes the importance of external knowledge sources to innovation. It differs from the traditional closed innovation model that emphasizes vertical integration and strict internal control, differs from imitative innovation that is based on the introduction of external technology, and differs from general cooperative innovation. In the open innovation mode, a company conducts an external search and acquires and uses innovation resources. Through win-win synergistic cooperation and integration of internal and external resources, the commercial value gained from R&D investment can be maximized.

The open innovation model has changed the way in which companies obtain innovative resources. Company boundaries are permeable in the open innovation mode. A company cannot only use its own resources, but must use innovative resources from the external environment, such as users, suppliers, competitors, other companies, universities, research institutes, technology intermediaries, government, trade associations, periodicals, seminars, media, and so on. These are all important sources of technology, knowledge, and other innovative resources for companies.

In the open innovation paradigm, external knowledge sources are crucial, regardless of the level of an innovative entity: state, industry, or enterprise (Cohen and Levinthal, 1990). Therefore, the development and use of external knowledge is an important component of a company's innovative capability and external experience – and ideas are considered to be important tools for corporate learning (Jerez-Gómez, Céspedes-Lorente, and Valle-Cabrera, 2005). Many multinationals continuously establish knowledge absorption centers in different regions around the globe so as to strengthen global search in their respective research areas and technology fields. Learning by imitation, interaction, and spillovers of industry competition are important ways to encourage innovation. The process by which a company follows what other companies are doing in a particular area and adopts the useful technologies or practices can improve its capability in learning technologies.

In an open innovation environment, the internal R&D of a company still plays an important role, but the function has changed. The acquisition of external innovative resources is very important for enhancing the company's innovation performance, but internal innovation resources are still the most essential and critical innovation element. External innovative resources supplement internal innovation resources but can substitute for them. Open innovation does not negate internal innovation. Instead, it could make full use of internal and external knowledge and resources and construct an innovation ecosystem that maximizes R&D efficiency.

In the open innovation environment, the various elements of innovation and various means to acquire technology influence and complement each other, and no innovation elements can be analyzed in isolation from the overall innovation strategy of the company. Therefore, in the practice of innovation, a company must seek to match and integrate internal and external resources based on its internal resources and absorptive capacity. A suitable innovation strategy should be adopted to maximize the synergy of its internal and external innovative resources and enhance its innovative capabilities. To improve innovation performance and enhance innovation capabilities, companies need to simultaneously strengthen internal R&D activities and external knowledge search.

The abundance of external innovative resources adds to the complexity of enterprise innovation management. When a company is accumulating and nurturing internal technological capabilities, it also needs to make use of external resources and improve its innovation performance by integrating its internal and external resources. Given that partners in an innovation effort are not independent, the various elements of innovation and the various means to acquire technologies influence and complement each other, so no innovation elements can be analyzed in isolation from the overall innovation strategy of a company.

Implications of open innovation for business management practice

Implications of open innovation on management practice are mainly related to the interaction between a company and external organizations and the utilization of external innovative resources.

In the practice of innovation, companies acquire complementary innovation resources and encourage innovation through purposefully open interaction with such external organizations

It is not advisable to put open innovation capabilities on developing core technologies that are achieving technological breakthroughs. For innovation and development, enterprises should pay more attention to the external environment and the acquisition and utilization of external resources. The technological innovation modes of most companies in China are relatively closed, the utilization rates of external resources are limited, and R&D capabilities are dispersed, and this results in inefficiency in the innovation process. Open innovation can gather the creative ideas and accelerate the pace of innovation to better use market opportunities.

Business leaders must pay close attention to the construction of the innovation ecosystem, and change the closed mode of internal R&D to an open one, and effectively integrate creativity management, R&D management, manufacturing management, and marketing management systems. R&D efficiency is in this way maximized in an environment of rich external technology resources and free knowledge flows.

External knowledge search has an important impact on the improvement of enterprise innovation performance, but different types of external cooperation objects differ in their importance to innovation performance

For Chinese companies, knowledge acquisition from companies in vertical relationships currently has the greatest effect on enhancing innovation performance. Cooperation with companies in horizontal relationships shows the least effect on enhancing innovation performance, and universities, as well as research institutes, play important roles in innovation practices. To encourage innovation, companies in technology-driven industries need to selectively build cooperative relationships with a small number of external sources of innovation. Companies in experience-driven industries should form effective links with external organizations to encourage innovation.

Internal and external R&D innovation strategies complement each other, but the degree of complementarity is influenced by the choice of external search object and a company's capacity to absorb external knowledge

Close connections between a company and external organizations help improve a company's innovation performance, and a company's internal R&D plays an important moderating role. The company's internal resources and the search for external innovative resources are significantly complementary to each other, and the intensity of internal R&D activities determines the degree of influence exerted by its external knowledge search on its innovation performance. If a company does not have enough absorptive capacity, its external knowledge search will become inefficient. In the practice of innovation, a company must seek to match and integrate its internal and external resources. On the basis of its internal resources and absorptive capacity, a suitable innovation strategy should be adopted to maximize the synergy of its internal and external innovative resources and enhance its innovative capabilities. To improve innovation performance and enhance innovation capabilities, companies need to strengthen their internal R&D activities and external knowledge search simultaneously.

In the practice of open innovation, a number of organizational modes of open innovation take a particular cooperation object as the main target of the openness. Different modes of openness have different effects on innovation performance, and there is an interactive relationship between a company's internal capabilities and the mode of openness it adopts.

In practice, there are four types of organizational modes of innovation with a particular cooperation object as the main target of openness: partners in scientific endeavors, partners in the value chain, companies with horizontal cooperation, and organizations in related technology fields. Different organizational modes of innovation are significantly different in their effects on innovation performance. There is an interactive relationship between a company's internal R&D capabilities and the organizational mode of openness. A company with a given set of characteristics should choose a mode of openness that matches its internal capabilities. Companies with strong internal R&D capabilities can improve their innovation performance through cooperation with scientific partners. Those with strong internal R&D capabilities but average manufacturing capabilities should seek horizontal cooperation with other companies. Those with average internal R&D capabilities can markedly improve their innovation performance by close cooperation with organizations in related technologies and partners on the same value chain. Enterprises should not open themselves to external organizations blindly. The key issue in selecting the right targets of openness is whether the company can obtain complementary resources from the innovation.

In the practice of open innovation, internal R&D and innovation of enterprises become more important and internal R&D capabilities are still the key roles

Open innovation is not a model in which external innovative resources are simply required for innovation. Adopting open innovation does not imply abandoning internal R&D and innovation. Faced with an abundance of external knowledge sources, companies need to be engaged in internal R&D activities to identify, understand, select, and connect to external knowledge sources. Companies can then fill in the gaps in knowledge areas that have not been developed externally, integrate internal and external knowledge to form knowledge combinations of greater complexity, create new systems and architectures, and gain extra revenues and profits from the fruits of their own research being used by other companies (Chesbrough, 2003b). In an environment of open innovation, enterprise internal R&D and innovation hold even greater significance for developing countries. It is the ongoing investment in internal R&D that enables companies to efficiently integrate internal and external innovation resources in an internationalized open innovation setting and achieve maximum synergy between internal and external innovation resources.

An innovative company must develop a good organizational mechanism to encourage the effective implementation of open innovation

Open innovation is not an occasional or accidental event for companies. It is a regular and essential activity built on the foundation of the company's business culture, organizational structure, and processes. A good mechanism of open innovation must be developed to ensure that external innovative resources are fully utilized for the improvement of the integrity, continuity, and efficiency of the innovation process, which will enhance the company's innovation performance and sustained competitiveness.

Reaching open innovation maturity in a business

A considerable number of open innovation projects in companies fail because the management firms are not ready to fully engage in open innovation. As we mentioned already, open innovation has to be managed carefully, and most firms lack knowledge about how to manage it. The development of open innovation maturity – that is, an organization's excellence in conducting open innovation – is a slow process taking many years. An analysis of open innovation maturity shows how firms can get onto higher maturity levels over time. In other words, open innovation maturity describes firms' overall capacity to successfully engage in and make use of open innovation.

Enkel, Bell, and Hogenkamp (2011) have developed a detailed framework for open innovation maturity that allows measuring the effectiveness of open innovation processes. They argue that the effectiveness of firms' open innovation activities is a function of their partnership capacity (Cullen, Johnson, and Sakano, 2000; Kauser and Shaw, 2002; Mora-Valentin, Montoro-Sanchez, and Guerras-Martin, 2004; Lichtenthaler and Lichtenthaler, 2009; Cohen and Levinthal, 1990). Also the creation of a climate that is conducive to innovation and visionary leadership is essential for (open) innovation activities (Tidd and Bessant, 2009; Anderson and West, 1998; Thamhain, 2003). Finally, the availability of the right systems, tools, and processes is are an important enabler for open innovation initiatives (Thamhain, 2003; Dilk et al., 2008; Kauser and Shaw, 2002; Ireland, Hitt, and Vaidyanath, 2002).

These three elements of open innovation – climate for innovation, partnership capacity, and internal processes – are the three dimensions in which companies have to make change over time to become mature in open innovation management. Climate for change is operationalized into variables such as clear strategy, incentives, and mind-set. Partnership capacity is about reputation, partner selection, and training and education. Finally, internal processes can be split up into central coordination, resources, knowledge management process, and the legal and IP systems.

Based on the analysis of five cases Enkel, Bell, and Hogenkamp (2011) make a distinction between five stages of open innovation maturity: initial/arbitrary, repeatable, defined, managed, and optimized. As firms make progress and shift from lower to higher stages of open innovation maturity, the approach becomes more detailed at each phase and the progress is based on the accumulated experiences of companies over time in dealing with open innovation. The major managerial contribution of their publication lies in the translation of the concept of open innovation maturity into an easy-to-use Excel tool leading to a spider web graph that visualizes the companies' open innovation maturity against a benchmark.

Analysis and recommendations of open innovation policy

1Improving the capabilities of independent innovation and gaining the capabilities of key technology development is a complex and lengthy process that includes a long period of technology accumulation and investment. China has reached an advanced international level in some technology areas but is still some distance behind the developed nations. In an environment of open innovation, it is not advisable to place all the effort for strengthening innovative capabilities on developing core technologies and seeking breakthroughs. In an era of economic globalization and rapid technological development, maintaining and continuously strengthening our competitive advantages and improving independent innovation depends on our ability to create, apply, share, and accumulate knowledge. It also depends on our ability to acquire and use global knowledge and technologies, and our ability to effectively integrate technological resources globally.

Strive to improve the scientific competencies and learning abilities of our people

Technological innovation emphasizes the integration of research and industry chains. Strengthening self-dependent innovation capabilities is not just a task for science and technology talents: the practice of innovation is a basic duty of every member of society. The key to enhancing the capabilities of independent innovation is by improving the scientific skills and learning abilities of our people. In an open innovation environment, it is the ability to acquire knowledge, rather than the amount of knowledge possessed, that determines innovation performance. Lundvall (2017) pointed out that the key to achieving good economic performance is promoting learning at every stage of the economic system. Only with organizational changes and the broad elevation of employee skills can the introduction of advanced technologies play a positive role. The mere application of technology in the search for solutions to problems is destined to fail.

In an environment of open innovation, the key to strengthening innovative capabilities is the ability to acquire and use knowledge and technologies globally, as well as the ability to integrate technology resources globally. Learning ability is an important foundation for enhancing the capability to absorb external knowledge and integrate internal and external knowledge. To improve independent innovation capabilities in China, we must build a learning society and nurture and elevate the learning ability and innovation awareness of our people. We must provide lifelong education to the general public so that people can learn technological ideas, knowledge, methods, and skills, and so further strengthen their ability to understand, master, and apply modern science and technology. Finally, if scientific thinking and concepts are embedded into our national spirit, then our innovation capabilities will build an innovative nation.

Strengthen the construction of knowledge infrastructure and encourage the dissemination and sharing of knowledge

Independent innovation in an open environment emphasizes the integration and consolidation of multiple innovation elements, for which the transfer and sharing of knowledge play an important role. The ability to efficiently acquire and use innovation resources globally is the key ability for achieving technological innovation. In the process of knowledge dissemination, sharing, and utilization, information and communication technologies serve as the foundation for the free flow of information. Among the many factors that limit our ability to innovate, a failure to build the knowledge infrastructure and a lack of knowledge resources are significant. According to global statistics, investment by advanced companies in knowledge resource acquisition, knowledge management, and other elements related to building knowledge infrastructure account for nearly 10 percent of overall R&D investment. Investment is above 25 percent for the leading firms. In contrast, investment by Chinese companies is only 0.5 percent. We should elevate knowledge resources to the level of strategic national resources by strengthening the construction of nationwide and regional information and communication systems and other knowledge infrastructure projects. Moreover, we must provide companies and people with a learning platform for public knowledge, achieve effective integration among research entities and technology resources, effectively integrate and use global technology resources, and enhance our capabilities of independent innovation.

Encourage companies to increase investment in R&D and improve absorptive capacity and resource integration

In an open innovation environment, the ability to acquire, absorb, and use external knowledge and effectively integrate internal and external innovative resources is the key to improving technological innovation. However, successful implementation of open innovation in our country still requires that our companies have strong R&D capabilities. Such capabilities are the foundation for developing new products with independent intellectual property rights and serve as the essential guarantee for improving external knowledge search, acquisition, and absorption. China's fiscal investment in science and technology currently accounts for a substantial percentage of R&D investment. Encouraging companies to increase their R&D investment is particularly important for guiding R&D investment in our society. The government should adopt the fiscal and financial measures for an active government procurement system that encourages innovation activities and increases R&D investment by enterprises. The government should also provide clear policy guidance and create a favorable macro- and micro-economic environment for enterprise innovation activities.

Give priority to the construction of innovation platforms for industrial technologies and encourage information exchange and technology transfer

The government should provide companies engaged in independent R&D activities with a policy support environment that is conducive to innovation by enacting appropriate laws and regulations. The government should organize and coordinate the construction of platforms for generic technology innovation, perfect the environment for the cooperative development of generic technologies, ensure the rapid transformation of generic technologies, play a role in the development and diffusion of generic technologies, and encourage the advancement of generic technologies. Government agencies should formulate policies optimizing the environment; improve the social support system; build a platform for technology exchange that is conducive to information flow and information transfer; and construct an effective enterprise technology innovation service that can provide services in areas such as information, talent, financing, technology, and management consulting. The government can then encourage technology and information exchange between companies and research institutes or among companies. By giving full play to the interaction between government and companies, a synergy of market mechanism and government support can improve the efficiency of the national innovation system.

References

Ahuja, G. and Lampert, C. M. (2001). Entrepreneurship in the large corporation: a longitudinal study of how established firms create breakthrough inventions. *Strategic Management Journal*, 22(6), 521–543.

Almirall, E. and Casadesus-Masanell, R. (2010). Open versus closed innovation: a model of discovery and divergence. *Academy of Management Review*, 35(1), 27–47.

Anderson, N.R. & West, M.A., Measuring climate for work group innovation: Development and validation of the team climate inventory. *Journal of Organizational Behavior*, 1998, 19(3), 235–258.

Argote, L. and Greve, H.R. (2007). A behavioral theory of the firm—40 years and counting: introduction and impact. *Organization Science*, 18(3),337–349.

Arora, A. and Gambardella, A. (1990). Complementarity and external linkages: the strategies of the large firms in biotechnology. *The Journal of Industrial Economics*, 38(4), 361–379.

Basant, R. and Fikkert, B. (1996). The effects of R&D, foreign technology purchase, and domestic and international spillovers on Productivity in Indian Firms. *The Review of Economics and Statistics*, 78(2), 187–199.

Belderbos, R., et al. (2004). Heterogeneity in R&D cooperation strategies. *International Journal of Industrial Organization*, 22(8), 1237–1263.

Berchicci, L. (2013). Towards and open R&D system: internal R&D investment, external knowledge acquisition and innovative performance. *Research Policy*, 42(1), 117–127.

Bianchi, M., Cavaliere, A., Chiaroni, D., Frattini, F. and Chiesa, V. (2011). Organisational modes for open innovation in the bio-pharmaceutical industry: an exploratory analysis. *Technovation*, 31(1), 22–33.

Brown, S. L. and Eisenhardt, K. M. (1998). *Competing on the edge*. Boston, MA: Harvard Business School Press.

Brusoni, S., Prencipe, A. and Pavitt, K. (2001). Knowledge specialization, organizational coupling, and boundaries of the firm: why do firms know more than they make. *Administrative Science Quarterly*, 46(4), 597–621.

Cassiman, B. and Veugelers, R. (2002). R&D cooperation and spillovers: some empirical evidence from Belgium. *American Economic Review*, 92(4), 1169–1184.

Caloghirou, Y., Kastelli, I. and Tsakanikas, A. (2004). Internal capabilities and external knowledge sources: complements or substitutes for innovative performance. *Technovation*, 24(1), 29–39.

Chen, H. and Liu, X. (2006). Why some technologically leading enterprises can be lacking in innovative capabilities – a case study of Sony Corporation. *Science of Science and Management of Science and Technology*, 27(6), 58–63.

Chen, J. and Yang, Y. J. (2012). Theoretical foundation and connotation of collaborative innovation. *Studies in Science of Science*, 30(2), 161–164.

Chen, Y. F. and Chen, J. (2007). User participation in innovation: a review of foreign literature related to the subject. *Science of Science and Management of Science and Technology*, 28(2), 52–57.

Chen, Y. F. and Chen, J. (2008a). Effect of the degree of openness on performance of the technological innovation process of a business enterprise. *Studies in Science of Science*, 26(2), 419–426.

Chen, Y. F. and Chen, J. (2008b). *Open innovation: mechanism and mode*. Beijing: Science Press.

Chen, Y. F. and Chen, J. (2009). A study on the mechanism through which open innovation promotes innovation performance. *Scientific Research Management*, 30(4), 1–9.

Chen, Y. F., Vanhaverbeke, W. and Du, J. (2016). The interaction between internal R&D and different types of external knowledge sourcing: an empirical study of Chinese innovative firms. *R&D Management*, 46(Suppl), 1006–1023.

Chen, Y. F. and Ye, W. W. (2013). Interactions between internal R&D and external knowledge search – an analysis of innovation strategies for the STI and DUI industries. *Studies in Science of Science*, 31(2), 266–275, 285.

Chesbrough, H. (2003a). *Open innovation: the new imperative for creating and profiting from technology*. Boston, MA: Harvard Business School Press.

Chesbrough, H. (2003b). The era of open innovation. *MIT Sloan Management Review*, 44(3), 35–41.

Chesbrough, H. (2006). *Open business models: how to thrive in the new innovation landscape*. Boston, MA: Harvard Business School Press.

Chesbrough, H. (2011). Bringing open innovation to services. *MIT Sloan Management Review*, 52(2), 85–90.

Chesbrough, H. and Crowther, A. K. (2006). Beyond high tech: early adopters of open innovation in other industries. *R&D Management*, 36(3), 229–236.

Chesbrough, H., Vanhaverbeke, W. and West, J. (2006). *Open innovation: researching a new paradigm*. Oxford: Oxford University Press, pp. 35–60.

Chiang, Y. H. and Hung, K. P. (2010). Exploring open search strategies and perceived innovation performance from the perspective of inter-organizational knowledge flows. *R&D Management*, 40(3), 292–299.

Chiaroni, D., Chiesa, V. and Frattini, F. (2010). Unravelling the process from closed to open innovation: evidence from mature, asset-intensive industries. *R&D Management*, 40(3), 222–245.

Chiaroni, D., Chiesa, V. and Frattini, F. (2011). The open innovation Journey: how firms dynamically implement the emerging innovation management paradigm. *Technovation*, 31(1), 34–43.

Christensen, J., Olesen, F. and Kjaer, M. H. (2005). The industrial dynamics of open innovation – evidence from the transformation of consumer electronics. *Research Policy*, 34(10), 1533–1549.

Chung, S. A. and Kim, G. M. (2003). Performance effects of partnership between manufacturers and suppliers for new product development: the supplier's standpoint. *Research Policy*, 32(4), 587–603.

Cohen, W. and Levinthal, D. (1990). Absorptive capacity: a new perspective on learning and innovation. *Administrative Science Quarterly*, 35(2), 128–152.

Coombs, R., Harvey, M. and Bruce, S. (2003). Tether. Analysing distributed processes of provision and innovation. *Industrial and Corporate Change*, 12(6), 1125–1155.

Cullen, J. B., Johnson, J. L. and Sakano, T. (2000). Success through commitment and trust: The soft side of strategic alliance management. *Journal of World Business*, 2000, 35(3), 223–238.

Dahlander, L. and Gann, D. M. (2007). Appropriability, proximity, routines and innovation: how open is pen innovation? *Paper Presented at the Druid Summer Conference*, Copenhagen, 2007, 34–39.

Dahlander, L. and Gann, D. M. (2010). How open is innovation? *Research Policy*, 39(6), 699–709.

De Man, A. P. and Duysters, G. (2005). Collaboration and innovation: a review of the effects of mergers, acquisitions and alliances on innovation. *Technovation*, 25(12), 1377–1387.

Dyer, J. H. (1996). Specialized supplier networks as source of competitive advantage: evidence from Auto Industry. *Strategic Management Journal*, 17(4), 271–292.

Enkel, E., Bell, J. & Hogenkamp, H. (2011). Open innovation maturity framework, International Journal of Innovation Management, 2011, 15(6), 1161–1189.

Fernandez-Bagües (2004). Complementarity in innovation strategies: evidence from pharmaceutical dynamic panel data. Paper presented at the 30th EARIE conference, Helsinki.

Ferru, M. and Des, L. G. (2010). Collaborations pour innovation le role des constraintes ressources et de mise en relation. *CRIEF Working Papers*.

Gassmann, O. (2006). Editorial opening up the innovation process: towards an agenda. *R&D Management*, 36(3), 223–228.

Gassmann, O. and Enkel, E. (2004). Towards a theory of open innovation: three core process archetypes. *R&D Management Conference*, 1–18.

Gassmann, O. (2006). Opening up the innovation process: towards an agenda. *R&D Management*, 36(3), 18–27.

Granstrand, O., Patel, P. and Pavitt, K. (1997). Multi-technology corporations: why they have 'Distributed' rather than 'Distinctive Core' competencies. *California Management Review*, 39(4), 8–25.

Grant, R. M. and Baden-Fuller, C. (2004). A knowledge accessing theory of strategic alliances. *Journal of Management Studies*, 41(1), 61–84.

Greco, M., Grimaldi, M. and Cricelli, L. (2016). An analysis of the open innovation effect on firm performance. *European Management Journal*, 34(5), 501–516.

Hage, J. and Alter, C. (1993). Organizations working together. *Clinical Orthopaedics & Related Research*, 187, 228–234.

Hagedoorn, J. (1993). Understanding the rationale of strategic technology partnering: interorganizational modes of cooperation and sector differences. *Strategic Management Journal*, 14(5), 371–385.

Hagedoorn, J., Albert, L. N. and Nicholas, V. S. (2000). Research partnerships. *Research Policy*, 29(4), 567–586.

Hagedoorn, J. and Ning, W. (2012). Is there complementarity or substitutability between internal and external R&D strategies? *Research Policy*, 41(6), 1072–1083.

Haken, H. (1978). Synergetics: some recent trends and developments. *Progress of Theoretical Physics Supplement*, 64(64), 21–34.

Hippel, V. E. and Krogh, V. G. (2003). Open source software and the "Private-collective" innovation model: issues for organization science. *R&D Management*, 33(2), 209–223.

Hippel, V. E. and Krogh, V. G. (2006). Free revealing and the private-collective model for innovation incentives. *R&D Management*, 36(3), 295–306.

Howe, J. (2006). The rise of crowdsourcing. *Wired*, 14(6), 1–5.

Ireland, R. D., Hitt, M. A. & Vaidyanath, D. (2002). Alliance management as a source of competitive advantage. Journal of Management, 2002, 28(3), 413–446.

Jensen, M. B., Johnson, B., Lorenz, E. and Lundvall, B. Å. (2004). Absorptive capacity, forms of knowledge and economic development. *Paper Presented at the Second Globelics Conference in Beijing*, pp. 16–20.

Jerez-Gomez, P., Céspedes-Lorente, J. and Valle-Cabrera, R. (2005). Organizational learning capability: a proposal of measurement. *Journal of Business Research*, 58, 715–725.

Jiang, J. H. and Cai, C. H. (2014). Mechanism by which structural characteristics of alliance portfolios influence open innovation: a case study of Refond Optoelectronics. *Studies in Science of Science*, 32(9), 1396–1404.

Kauser, S. & Shaw V., The influence of behavioural and organizational characteristics on the success of international strategic alliances. International Marketing Review, 2002, 21(1), 17–52.

Knudsen, M. P. and Mortensen, T. B. (2011). Some immediate but negative effects of openness on product development performance. *Technovation*, 31, 54–64.

Laursen, K. and Salter, A. J. (2006). Open for innovation: the role of openness in explaining innovation performance among UK manufacturing firms. *Strategic Management Journal*, 27(2), 131–150.

Laursen, K. and Salter, A. (2014). The paradox of openness: appropriability, external search and collaboration. *Research Policy*, 43(5), 867–878.

Lichtenthaler, U. (2008a). Relative capacity: retaining knowledge outside a firm's boundaries. *Journal of Engineering & Technology Management*, 25(3), 200–212.

Lichtenthaler, U. (2008b). Open innovation in practice: an analysis of strategic approaches to technology transactions. *Engineering Management*, 55(1), 148–157.

Lichtenthaler, U. (2009a). Absorptive capacity, environmental turbulence, and the complementarity of organizational learning processes. *Academy of Management Journal*, 52(4), 822–846.

Lichtenthaler, U. (2009b). Outbound open innovation and its effect on firm performance: examining environmental influences. *R&D Management*, 39(4), 317–330.

Lichtenthaler, U., Hoegl, M. and Muethel, M. (2011). Is your company ready for open innovation? *MIT Sloan Management Review*, 53(1), 45–48.

Lichtenthaler, U. and Lichtenthaler, E. A. (2009). Capability-based framework for open innovation: complementing absorptive capacity. *Journal of Management Studies*, 46(8), 1315–1338.

Lundvall, B-A. (2017). *The learning economy and the economics of hope*. London: Anthem Press.

Lv, Y. B., Shi, X. X. and Ji, R. N. (2017). A study on the effect of open innovation on a company's ability to achieve incremental innovation. *Studies in Science of Science*, 35(2), 289–301.

Makri, M., Michael, A. H. and Peter, J. L. (2010). Complementary technologies, knowledge relatedness, and invention outcomes in high technology mergers and acquisitions. *Strategic Management Journal*, 31(6), 602–628.

Mora-Valentin, E.M., Montoro-Sanchez, A. & Guerras-Martin, L.A. (2004). Determining factors in the success of R&D cooperative agreements between firms and research organizations. *Research Policy*, 33(1), 17–40.

Mowery, D. C., Oxley, J. E. and Silverman, B. S. (1996). Strategic alliance and interfirm knowledge transfer. *Strategic Management Journal*, 4(17), 77–91.

Nelson, R. and Winter, S. (1982). *An evolutionary theory of economic change*. Cambridge, MA: Belknap Harvard Press.

Nonaka, I. (1994). A dynamic theory of organizational knowledge creation. *Organization Science*, 5(1), 14–37.

Pavitt, K. (2002). Innovating routines in the business firm: what corporate tasks should they be accomplishing? *Industrial and Corporate Change*, 11(1), 117–133.

Powell, W. (1998). Learning from collaboration: knowledge and networks in the biotechnology and pharmaceutical industries. *California Management Review*, 40(3), 228–240.

Powell, W. W. and Grodal, S. (2005). Networks of innovators. In Fagerberg, J. Mowery, D. C. and Nelson R. R. (Eds.), *The Oxford handbook of innovation*. Oxford: Oxford University Press, pp. 56–85.

Rosenberg, N. (1990). Why do firms do basic research (with their own money). *Research Policy*, 19(2), 165–174.

Rothwell, R. (1994). Towards the fifth-generation innovation process. *International Marketing Review*, 11(1), 7–31.

Schumpeter, J. A. (1934, 1990). *The theory of economic development*. Cambridge, MA: Harvard University Press.

Schenk, E. and Guittard, C. (2011). Towards a characterization of crowdsourcing practices. *Journal of Innovation Economics*, Vol. 7, 93–107.

Sofka, W. and Grimpe, C. (2010). Specialized search and innovation performance-evidence across Europe. *R&D Management*, 40(3), 310–323.

Spithoven, A., Clarysse, B. and Knockaert, M. (2011). Building absorptive capacity to organize inbound open innovation in traditional industries. *Technovation*, 31(1), 10–21.

Sun, H., Wang, N. N., Ding, R. G. and Wei, K. N. (2016). Open innovation mode selection based on core competencies of the organization. *Scientific Research Management*, 37(11), 35–42.

Sun, Y. T. and Zang, F. (2017). Regional/inter-regional R&D cooperation of a company and its innovation performance: the regulative role of technology diversification. *Scientific Research Management*, 38(3), 52–60.

Teece, D. J. (1986). Profiting from technological innovation: implications for integration, collaboration, licensing and public policy. *Research Policy*, 15(6), 285–305.

Teece, D. J., Pisano, G. and Shuen, A. (1997). Dynamic capabilities and strategic management. *Strategic Management Journal*, 18(7), 509–533.

Thamhain, H. J., Managing innovative R&D teams. R&D Management, 2003, 33(3), 297–311.

Tidd, J. & Bessant, J. (2009). *Managing innovation: integrating technological, market and organizational change* (4th ed.). West Sussex, England: John Wiley and Sons Ltd.

Todtling, F., Lehner, P. and Kaufmann, A. (2009). Do different types of innovation rely on specific kinds of knowledge interactions? *Technovation*, 29(1), 59–71.

van de Meer, H. (2007). Open innovation – the Dutch treat: challenges in thinking in business models, *Creativity and Innovation Management*, 16(2), 192–202.

Vanhaverbeke, W. (2006). The interorganizational context of open innovation. In H. Chesbrough, W. Vanhaverbeke and J. West (Eds.), *Open innovation: researching a new paradigm*, Oxford University Press, 205–219.

Veugelers, R. and Cassiman, B. (2002). Complementarity in the innovation strategy: internal R&D, external technology acquisition, and cooperation in R&D. *IESE Business School Working Paper No. 457*.

Veugelers, R. (1997). Internal R&D expenditures and external technology sourcing. *Research Policy*, 26(3), 303–315.

van de Vrande, V., Jong, D., Jeroen, P., Vanhaverbeke, W. and Maurice, D. R. (2009). Open innovation in SMEs: trends, motives and management challenges. *Technovation*, 29(6), 423–437.

van de Vrande, V., Lemmens, C. and Vanhaverbeke, W. (2006). Choosing governance modes for external technology sourcing. *R&D Management*, 36(3), 347–363.

von Hippel, E. and von Krogh, E. (2003). Open source software and the "private-collective" innovation model: Issues for organization science, *Organization Science*, 14(2), 209–223.

von Hippel, E. and von Krogh, E. (2006). Free revealing and the private-collective model for innovation incentives. *R & D Management*, 36, 295–306.

Walsh, J. P., Lee, Y. N. and Nagaoka, S. (2016). Openness and innovation in the US: collaboration form, idea generation and implementation. *Research Policy*, 45(8), 1660–1671.

Wang, P. F. (2010). A study on the effect of outbound open innovation on innovation performance: a perspective based on network embeddedness. Master's Thesis, Zhejiang University.

Wellman, B. (1988). Structural analysis: From method and metaphor to theory and substance. In Wellman, B. and Berkowitz, S. D. (Eds.), *Social structures: a network approach*. Cambridge: Cambridge University Press, pp. 19–61.

Wheelwright, S. C. and Clark, K. B. (1992). *Revolutionizing product development: quantum leaps in speed, efficiency, and quality*. New York: The Free Press, 1992.

Yamakawa, Y., Yang, H. and Lin, Z. (2011). Exploration versus exploitation in alliance portfolio: performance implications of organizational, strategic, and environmental fit. *Research Policy*, 40(2), 287–296.

Yan, C. and Cai, N. (2014). Mechanism by which degree of openness influences innovation performance in an open innovation environment. *Scientific Research Management*, 35(3), 18–24.

Yao, Y. H., Ouyang, X. and Zhou, H. P. (2017). A study on the relationships among open innovation, dynamic knowledge acquisition and business competitiveness: the regulative role of partner opportunism. *Soft Science*, 31(7), 29–33.

Yeoh, P. L. (2009). Realized and potential absorptive capacity: understanding their antecedents and performance in the sourcing context. *The Journal of Marketing Theory and Practice*, 17(1), 21–36.

Zheng, J. Z., Ye, Z. and Xu, Y. J. (2017). A study on the mechanism by which the degree of openness of an enterprise cluster affects innovation performance. *Scientific Research Management*, 38(4), 19–27.

Zhu, J. M. and Hao, K. N. (2014). Categorization of business technological innovation capabilities in open innovation and analysis of the influencing mechanism. *Journal of Central University of Finance and Economics*, 1(8), 106–112.

10
BRINGING OPEN INNOVATION INTO PRACTICE
Methods and approaches

Frank Piller, Sumit Mitra, and Susanna Ghosh Mitra

Open innovation and innovating with partners

Open innovation partnerships

Open innovation (OI) is an interactive process of knowledge generation, and firms can search for external sources of innovation by collaborating with a variety of external stakeholders or by seeking out specialists with useful knowledge (Nieto and Santamaria, 2007). This includes partnering with suppliers, customers, competitors, complementors, organizations that offer similar products in different markets, organizations that offer different products in similar markets, nonprofit organizations, government organizations, universities, or others (Schilling, 2013). Collaboration can be used for many different purposes, including manufacturing, services, and marketing, as well as technology-based objectives, and involves selective collaboration strategies linking the knowledge content to specific partners to leverage the benefits and limit the costs of knowledge boundary-crossing processes (Bengtsson et al., 2015). Factors that influence the use of external sources of innovation include not only the characteristics of the external source but also internal factors such as R&D capabilities and complementary assets (Ceccagnoli, Graham, Higgins, and Lee, 2010; Teirlinck, Dumont, and Spithoven, 2010). Hence, the selection of appropriate OI partners is essential for the success of open innovation, depending on the specific project's purpose, the innovation process phase, and the required expertise or context factors, such as the confidentiality of knowledge and project results (Bengtsson et al., 2015; Todtling, Lehner, and Kaufmann, 2009).

Researchers have identified universities and research centers as specific sources of external knowledge, particularly in studies of high-technology industries (Cassiman, Di Guardo, and Valentini, 2010; Fabrizio, 2009; Vuola and Hameri, 2006). Drawing on scientific and technological knowledge bases of universities and research organizations, the commercial firms maintain flows of tacit knowledge and informal contacts with academics. Such knowledge transfers take place through a variety of mechanisms ranging from recruitment of university graduates to personnel exchanges, joint research, contract research, consulting, patents and publications, licensing, spin-off companies, industry-funded laboratories, and other facilities and informal contacts, such as meetings and conferences. An example of a collective research organization in the exploration phase is provided by Schilling (2013):

[I]n 2002, six Japanese electronics manufacturers (Fujitsu, Hitachi, Matsushita Electric Industrial, Mitsubishi Electric, NEC, and Toshiba) set up a collective research company called Aspla to develop designs for more advanced computer chips. [...] The collaborative research organization would enable the companies to share the development expense and help the Japanese semiconductor industry retain its competitive edge.

(p. 163)

Incremental innovations and the adoption of new technologies occur often in interaction with partners from the business sector.

Studies by Li and Vanhaverbeke (2009) and Schiele (2010) emphasize the role of key organizational suppliers in bringing forward product innovations, including new product technologies, reduced risks, and increased speed to market or performance advantages, and thereby attain competitive advantage. As highlighted by Chung and Kim (2003) involving suppliers is especially evident in the new product development process with benefits such as reduced lead time, reduced development costs and risks of product development, enhanced flexibility and product quality, and improved market adaptability. Collaborating with suppliers might lead to higher competitiveness due to "innovative workable parts co-developed and provided by the suppliers" (Chung and Kim, 2003, p. 600).

There is a strong focus on competitors in the open innovation literature. Co-creation, or collaborations with competitors, defined by Gnyawali and Park (2011) as "a strategy embodying simultaneous cooperation and competition between firms" (p. 650), has received a lot of attention in the last decades, especially in high-technological industries where product life cycles are shrinking, higher investments are needed, and industries' boundaries are shifting. Miotti and Sachwald (2003) present different reasons why a company might decide to collaborate with competitors, such as R&D cost sharing, resource pooling, and faster market penetration. Malmberg and Maskell (2002) argue that monitoring competitors seems to be a more relevant mechanism for knowledge transfer and innovation than input–output links or cooperation, especially in cases where competitors in local industry clusters stimulate innovations.

Customers, too, are considered potentially valuable partners in the open innovation process. Several studies have highlighted a more active role of customers in innovation (Gassmann, Sandmeier, and Wecht, 2006; von Hippel, 2005; von Hippel & Katz, 2002, von Hippel, Ogawa & De Jong, 2011. Studies have proven that the identification of lead users and use of their information has a positive effect on innovation performance (Chatterji & Fabrizio, 2014; Roberts, Luettgens, and Piller, 2016). There is also attention drawn to the frequency and scope of customer–firm interactions to influence the performance (Gales and Mansourcole, 1995) and also the mode and kind of communication and interaction with customers in the context of innovation (Piller and Ihl, 2013)).

Collaboration arrangements can also take many forms, from very informal alliances to highly structured joint ventures or technology exchange agreements (licensing). Firms may license outside technology or intellectual property to complement their internal innovation activities (Lichtenthaler, 2011). This transfer of knowledge from vendors to clients complements the absorptive capacity generated by internal R&D, as was the case with Apple Computer, which license graphical user interface (GUI) technology from Xerox (Chesbrough, 2003b). Open innovation strategy may be implemented through strategic alliances with suppliers and competitors that allows them to quickly respond to market and technological change by leveraging the core competencies of alliance partners (Xie and Johnston, 2004), as is the case with dedicated biotechnology companies linked to large, integrated pharmaceutical companies (Grant and Baden-Fuller, 2004). A special type of strategic alliance is joint ventures, which entail "significant structure and commitment" and involve "a significant equity investment from each partner and often results in establishment of a new separate entity" (Schilling, 2013, p. 160). Sony Ericsson, established in 2001 between Sony Corporation Japan and Swedish company Ericsson to combine Sony's consumer electronics expertise with Ericsson's technological knowledge regarding mobile communications, is a case in point (Trott and Hartmann, 2009). Firms may also outsource in case they do not possess the competencies or facilities to perform all the activities in the value chain to develop new innovations (Schilling, 2013), as, for instance, Dell buying some of its computer peripherals like the video display unit (VDU) from Sony.

Open innovation in social enterprises

Open innovation has become increasingly relevant recently beyond high-technology commercial industries and is considered to yield promising new entrepreneurial opportunities for diffusing knowledge and inventions, especially in the social sector. Specifically, open collaboration for innovation is emerging in the context of social enterprises (SE), which operate to provide sustainable opportunities to solve society's major problems, including poverty (Svirina, Azbbarova, and Oganisjana, 2016; Yun et al., 2017). Though a fundamental difference exists between social enterprises and commercial enterprises, researchers find open innovation processes highly relevant for social business. Unlike their commercial counterparts, social enterprises take into account social change in addition to profits and return-on-investment as the ultimate goal of their strategy. Hence, it is argued that with lower profit rates than conventional entrepreneurship, they require more sustainable models of longer payback periods but at the same time, more sustainable results and loyal customers (Chesbrough and Di Minin, 2014). Their primary goal is not profit maximization but to address issues of poverty, including education, health, technology access, and environment, that threaten individuals and society (Grameen Creative Lab, 2014). Svirina(2016) states that the rationale behind open innovation is suitable for social enterprise as it protects intellectual property, on the one hand, and seeks opportunities at lower margins, on the other. She argues that such concepts should be efficient for social entrepreneurs as long as they provide more efficient business solutions and better utilize resources, as seen in the example of Grameen-Danone. Grameen-Danone provides fortified yogurt at affordable prices to eradicate malnutrition among children in Bangladesh. It devised innovative methods to produce yogurt using solar power, while local Grameen dairy farms, corn-based biodegradable packs, and local women and cycle rickshaws distribute the yogurt locally. All were innovations in technology, sustainable scale plant, manufacturing, and business processes to meet the social objectives of an enterprise while maintaining financial viability, of which Danone, a global giant in yogurt, was partly aware.

Many scholars have argued that the logic of open innovation holds strong in the case of social enterprises. They contend that innovations in such enterprises are open and occur with an underlying assumption of open knowledge processes with a goal of solving social problems while maintaining financial viability. For instance Newth and Woods (2014) emphasize that the development of innovation in social enterprises is likely to take place in multistakeholder environments that may support or inhibit the success of the innovation. They argue that stakeholders may support the innovation process as long as it provides new knowledge and insights and through it ultimately legitimacy for the innovation, or they may have different, sometimes opposing, values and opinions regarding such innovation and thus be a source of resistance. Kong (2010) highlights the importance of social enterprises to be open to their external environment to develop successful innovations, while at the same time making sure that the development process is controlled and efficient and facilitates better decision-making. Theoretical underpinnings of open innovation have subsequently broadened and shifted from organization-centered theories to systems-based theories to explain social enterprises–related phenomena (George, McGahan, and Prabhu, 2012).

Still, despite existing relationship between social entrepreneurship and open innovation management, the field remains underdeveloped; further studies are required on the importance of open innovation in social business development. Given the unique challenges, mission, and strategy of social enterprises, it may be interesting to compare and contrast the nature of open innovation and partnerships with those of commercial enterprises that primarily differ in the extent of competitive focus and the availability of resources to service financially weak beneficiaries, as opposed to premium pricing for customers. Other dimensions of sustainability of such businesses and demands for scaling up follow to add to the existing challenges of social enterprise and their use of OI.

Methods of open innovation

As introduced in the previous section, open innovation is a strategy in innovation management for integrating external knowledge into the innovation process. Contrary to a classic idea of R&D, the knowledge, abilities and skills of the internal R&D department are not the only ones used here. Rather, open innovation requires companies to interact closely and continuously with their environment in their innovation process. The early image of the innovative entrepreneur according to Schumpeter (1942) thus gives way to a more complex view of the innovation process as a network of different actors (Laursen and Salter, 2006). The ability of companies to innovate thus becomes the ability to establish networks with external actors and to maintain interactive relationships with them.

Based on this understanding, the extraction of external information is at the center of this approach. Basically, information required in the innovation process can be differentiated into two types: information on needs and solutions (Reichwald and Piller, 2009; Thomke, 2006). Both types of information help to reduce uncertainties in the innovation process, which are derived from the original characteristics of an innovation – novelty and complexity.

Need information is information about the preferences, wishes, satisfaction factors and purchase motives of current and potential customers or users of a service. This can be information about both explicit and latent needs. Access to need information is based on an understanding of the customer's usage and application environment and provides information about "what", or what type of customer benefit a product is intended to satisfy. This process is often referred to as recording the "voice of the customer". Improved access to need information therefore stands for an increase in effectiveness in the innovation process. If companies do not have the right need information at the beginning of the development process, the risk of failure in new product development increases drastically, since the process cannot be supported by effective action in the sense of demand-oriented development.

Solution information describes the technological possibilities and necessary potentials to transform (customer) needs into concrete performance. How, for example, does the sensor technology of a smartphone have to be created in order to efficiently address latent customer needs? It is not only necessary to generate the right solution information but also to use existing resources efficiently in finding solutions. The solution information thus determines the way "how" (customer) needs can be met in the context of a new product development. Access to solution information and the way it is procured and implemented determine efficiency in the innovation process. However, companies are often subject to the problem of local search when identifying technical solutions (Jeppesen and Lakhani, 2010). In this case, unconventional approaches and solutions that have already proven themselves in other fields are excluded or overlooked from the manufacturer's point of view. In general, the higher the degree of innovation of the idea pursued, the greater the need for solution information from different knowledge domains.

Need and solution information are important input factors in the innovation process. Their generation and use have a decisive influence on the efficiency and effectiveness of the innovation process. To exploit this potential, however, companies need (1) access to information through appropriate methods and (2) organizational skills and structures in order to use the information profitably in the innovation process (Cassiman and Veugelers, 2006). At this point, various methods of open innovation offer a number of approaches to gain better access to need or solution information.

The innovation process consists of a multitude of activities, which are distributed over the different process phases, from the identification of needs to the market launch. In each phase, knowledge of varying quality from previous process steps is used and new knowledge is generated for subsequent activities. If a company follows an open innovation strategy, external actors can theoretically be integrated in all phases of the innovation process.

Categorization of open innovation methods

As a management approach, open innovation provides certain methods and instruments. To this end, the Internet in particular creates many opportunities to reduce the transaction costs associated with interaction. The involvement of external actors is often not based on formal contracts and agreements (e.g. in the form of traditional R&D cooperation or contract research) but through open and informal network and coordination mechanisms. Innovation processes thus become multilayered, open search and solution processes that run across company boundaries between several previously unknown actors. Open innovation does not replace the classical methods of market research and innovation management but supplements the classical forms of procuring market and technological information with additional channels.

To structure different open innovation methods, we use two dimensions: First, as introduced before, the type of information (need or solution information) acquired from external contributors. Whereas this first dimension is a rather general differentiation of activities in the innovation process, our second dimension is specific to open innovation. We suggest that open innovation (methods) be differentiated according to how external actors are identified and how collaborations are initiated (Diener and Piller, 2013). Following Erat and Krishnan (2012), a distinction can be made between an open call for participation and an open direct search (see Figure 10.1).

Open direct search: By defining openness as a balance between search breadth and depth, Laursen and Salter (2006) integrated open innovation into the search literature. In their understanding, search is directly initiated and then actively pursued: the searcher seeks external knowledge through actively scanning a broad range of possible sources for the requested information. This understanding of search has dominated most of the literature on open innovation (e.g. Laursen, 2012; Salge et al., 2013; Stockstrom et al., 2016). Extending the openness of search means here to search for external input without having made any assumptions in advance regarding the concrete information and the source of information or the collaboration partner itself. Typical examples of open innovation methods in which external actors are selected using an open search are the lead user approach (an active and broad search for lead users in analogue markets), the initialization of partnerships and research networks (as introduced in the previous section), or the netnography method (analysis of customer/user dialogues in online communities).

Bringing open innovation into practice

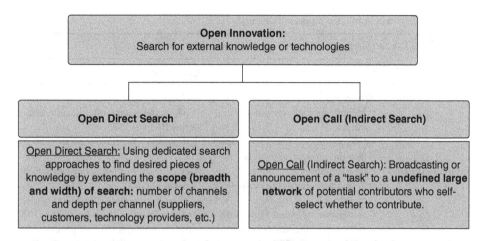

Figure 10.1 Open innovation as a process of search: two approaches

An **open call** or **indirect search** is the second mechanism used to select external actors for open innovation. Here, a problem statement is shared in the form of an open call with a large group of external actors who engage in their own search activities to find a solution and then propose it to the firm (Afuah and Tucci, 2012; Erat and Krishnan, 2012; Terwiesch and Xu, 2008). This later form builds the understanding for the literature on crowdsourcing and innovation contests in open innovation. Open call means in this context that a task to be solved is openly announced to the largest possible external network of potential contributors, who then decide by self-selection whether or not they want to participate in the process of finding a solution (this coordination mechanism also corresponds to the core of the term "crowdsourcing", which can be seen as the central new coordination mechanism of open innovation). Examples of open innovation methods based on the principle of an open call for participation are idea competitions and crowdsourcing for technical.

If one combines the dimensions of the type of information with the way in which the external contributors are identified, and thus cooperation is initiated, the following matrix results (Table 10.1). We will introduce these four methods, which we consider to be the core methods of open innovation, when focusing on methods that go beyond established forms of collaboration like contract research, R&D alliances, or supplier innovation.

Idea competitions to generate need information via an open call

Idea contests cover core activities at the front end of innovation: (1) generating novel concepts and ideas and (2) selecting specific concepts and ideas to be pursued further (O'Hern and Rindfleisch, 2009). Both of these tasks have successfully been handed over to customers by the means of an idea contest (Ebner, Leimeister, and Krcmar, 2009; Piller and Walcher, 2006). In an idea contest, a firm seeking innovation-related information posts a request to a population of independent, competing agents (e.g. customers), asking for solutions to a given task within a given time frame. The firm then provides an award to the participant that generates the best solution. Idea contests thus address a core challenge for firms when opening the innovation process, which is how to incentivize participants to transfer their innovative ideas. A solution reward is important in the early stages of the innovation process because customers are unlikely to benefit

Table 10.1 Differentiation of open innovation methods

External information to be acquired	Identification of external actors and initiation of the collaboration	
	Open direct search	Open call (indirect search)
Need information	*Netnography* • Identification of consumer insights • Integration of the collected ideas into the innovation process	*Idea Contests* • Call for the generation of ideas regarding a question • Integration of selected ideas or concepts
Solution information	*Lead User Method* • Search for solutions in analogue markets • Integration of expert knowledge and cooperation with experts	*Broadcast Search (Crowdsourcing for technical solutions)* • Call to solve a specific technical problem • Integration of problem solving or cooperation with solution providers

directly from their contributions through new product availability within a short time frame, as often occurs in later stages of the innovation process.

Some companies promise cash rewards or licensing contracts for innovative ideas; others build on nonmonetary acknowledgments – promising peer or company (brand) recognition that facilitates a pride-of-authorship effect. Obviously, rewards or recognitions are not given to everyone submitting an idea, but only to those with the "best" submissions. This competitive mechanism is an explicit strategy to foster customer innovation. It should encourage more or better customers to participate, should inspire their creativity, and should increase the quality of the submissions. For instance, over 120,000 individuals around the world served as voluntary members of Boeing's World Design Team, contributing input to the design of its new 787 Dreamliner airplane (www.newairplane.com).

Today we find a broad range of idea contests in practice. A good starting point to explore this field is www.innovation-community.de, a site listing more than 80 idea contests. These are differentiated according to the degree of problem specification, that is, does the problem clearly specify the requirements for the solution sought, or is it more or less an open call for solutions to a vaguely specified problem?

The example of Threadless.com, a company built entirely on a continuous idea contest and user voting process, shows how broadly this kind of co-creation can be used. This company and many others use customers for idea screening and evaluation, that is, customers select submissions with the highest potential. In a successful idea contest a firm might easily end up with hundreds or thousands of ideas generated by customers. They might be evaluated by a panel of experts from the solution-seeking firm and ranked according to a set of evaluation criteria, but we believe that without the integration of users in the idea screening process, large-scale idea contests are not possible. However, Toubia and Flores (2007) also propose that in light of a potentially very large number of ideas, it is unreasonable to ask each consumer to evaluate more than a few ideas. This raises the challenge of efficiently selecting the ideas to be evaluated by each consumer.

Broadcast search or technical crowdsourcing to generate solution information via an open call

In the last decade, crowdsourcing has gained relevance for both scholars and practitioners (Afuah and Tucci, 2012). Many crowdsourcing initiatives are administrated and governed by specialized intermediaries that offer crowdsourcing as a service (Dahlander and Piezunka, 2014; Diener and Piller, 2013; Lopez-Vega et al., 2016). Crowdsourcing intermediaries support the process by engaging large established communities of potential contributors and providing an Internet-enabled communication infrastructure for the effective dissemination of their clients' technology needs.

In the area of technical development and problem solving, dedicated open innovation platforms or intermediaries play a central role. Generating connections between structurally separated fields of knowledge, crowdsourcing intermediaries act as knowledge brokers and help their clients to overcome internal limitations in terms of technical and market knowledge (Howells, 2006; Sieg, Wallin, and von Krogh, 2010). Intermediaries such as NineSigma, InnoCentive, IXC, and Yet2.com broadcast the technology needs of firms ("seekers") to a heterogeneous network of external experts (potential "solvers"), who then self-select to participate and submit solution proposals to the problem at hand (Lopez-Vega and Vanhaverbeke, 2016). So-called requests for proposals (RFPs) or problem statements make the seekers' technology needs understandable for potential contributors from other disciplines, targeting in particular apparently unrelated and distant domains. An RFP originates from a task of a "challenge owner", that is, the individual or unit in a (seeker) organization responsible for finding the respective technical knowledge or putting it into use.

Hence, similar to idea competitions, the "broadcast search" method is also based on an open call. In contrast to the ideas competition, however, the focus here is on access to solution information. The aim is to find existing technical solutions or external experts with good previous knowledge for a precisely defined technical problem (in form of the RFP) within the scope of a development task. Here, too, the problem is advertised broadly and openly, usually by involving an intermediary (Jeppesen and Lakhani, 2010). A cross-industry and international call for solutions (RFP) can usually identify solution providers that the company does not know in advance, which leads to an extension of the range of solution alternatives due to the different knowledge backgrounds of the contributors. Because the development task is not delegated to a supposedly suitable task provider (in the company or by means of classical contract research), potential problem solvers select themselves according to their preferences and abilities. This can lead to a considerable increase in the quality of the solutions, since existing knowledge that is not known to the company can often be used. Knowledge transfer is handled using traditional instruments such as R&D orders, procurement activities, or the acquisition or in-licensing of technical property rights.

Lead-user method for generating solution information via an open search

The lead user method is a qualitative, process-oriented approach that aims at actively integrating individual selected users into the innovation process (von Hippel, 1986). In practice, the lead-user method has proven itself in the search for technical solutions to a given problem, which primarily involves access to solution information. To this end, an open but focused process is used to search for a few highly specialized experts with special market and solution knowledge in analogue markets. An analogue market is similar to the target market in terms of the needs of consumers and/or the technology used, but often belongs to a completely different industry.

Experts from analogue markets have the same basic problem as the searching company, but to a greater extent or under "extreme" conditions that made a solution appear very urgent in the past. However, lead users are usually not customers from the perspective of the focal company. These experts can provide decisive support for the innovation process, as they can be used to combine knowledge from different domains and thus expand the problem-solving space. To this end, the lead users usually work together in the form of innovation workshops to solve specific questions. The success of this method is therefore based on the same basic principle as in "broadcast search": the identification of knowledge of "unknown third parties".

Netnography to generate need information via an open search

Netnography means generating need information in an open search process by observing and analyzing existing contributions from users in online communities. The aim is to identify both explicitly formulated and implicit needs of customers and users of certain products and applications (Kozinets, 2002). The method is based on the idea that users express their needs more openly in the (relative) anonymity of the Internet than in the context of traditional market research measures. It has also been shown that users with lead user properties in particular participate in online communities with innovative contributions. As a result, the contributions are often also more original than in the survey of "representative" customers by market research.

An ethnographic study of online communities offers insights into the usage behavior of customers ("consumer insights") and provides input for the early phases of the innovation process. The core activities of the implementation of a netnography include the identification and selection of suitable online communities, the observation of these communities and the storage of the customer or user dialogue. In the next step, the data obtained are evaluated in terms of content. Today, computer-supported, semi-automatic methods can also be used for this purpose, which permit scalability of the evaluations. Based on the filtered observations, the final step is to guide concrete product concepts.

Putting open innovation into practice: open innovation competences

The management literature sometimes gives the impression that open innovation is already widely applied by most companies today. However, in addition to these success stories, there are examples of companies where the use of open innovation has not led to the expected success, although these are unfortunately documented far less often. These examples show that the implementation and successful use of open innovation is by no means a matter of course, but rather requires new competencies and organizational skills.

> In the course of the "My Pril – My Style" idea competition, which was launched in 2011, Henkel experienced the experience that even simple forms of the ideas competition can lead to implementation difficulties. The design competition, in which customers were asked to generate a draft label for the Pril detergent, ended in a PR debacle for Henkel. The design toolkit provided by the Group contained not only prefabricated design components that could only be rearranged by the participants, but also a freehand drawing function. Disappointed by the limited solution space in the design tool, numerous participants submitted their joke suggestions using the freehand tool. Among them is a scrawly drawing of a grilled chicken with the inscription "Pril: Geschmack lecker nach Chähnchen", which was quickly voted among the top ten entries by the online community. When the company did not want to take into account these contributions favored by the community, the participants in the competition felt betrayed and accused Henkel of manipulation. The result was countless negative press reports.
>
> *(Gatzweiler et al., 2017)*

The cooperation with intermediaries like InnoCentive or NineSigma, an often-quoted prime example of open innovation in the context of network-based solutions to technical problems, is also no unconditional guarantee for success. Lüttgens et al. (2014) report in a qualitative study of companies utilizing NineSigma for technical crowdsourcing that four out of six companies discontinued the broadcast search method after just a few projects and completely broke off contact with the intermediary. The reasons for this were a lack of competence in the area of problem formulation and an inappropriate problem selection, as well as a lack of organizational framework conditions on the part of the tendering companies (for a similar study, Sieg, Wallin, and von Krogh, 2010).

Open innovation competence as an organizational prerequisite

These failures testify to the fact that the implementation of open innovation is not trivial even for established companies. For the innovative company, open innovation means not only focusing on its own solution competence for the R&D process but also training the ability to identify solutions from previously unknown external actors, evaluate them without prejudice, and then integrate the externally generated solution approaches into internal company processes. The literature has so far agreed that the successful implementation and implementation of open innovation requires a set of specific competences (Bogers et al., 2017). These consist of both formal and informal organizational factors.

Structures

Due to their influence on internal communication and knowledge transfer, the organizational structure and processes play a decisive role in building interaction competence. Current research (e.g. Foss, Laursen, and Pedersen, 2011) has shown that central coordination and control on a strategic level in the form of dedicated departments and/or employees significantly support the development of necessary methodological competence through the collection of experience. In addition, routinization of specific open innovation activities through formalized process descriptions promotes the provision of the experience gained across departmental boundaries. This also has positive effects with regard to the use of external knowledge.

Findings from research in fields such as alliances, mergers and acquisitions, and open innovation support the relationship between firms' investment in dedicated resources and capability development for external sourcing. Kale, Dyer, and Singh (2002) find that accumulating a firm's experience with interfirm knowledge transfer in a dedicated function is a powerful predictor of its collaboration performance. The authors suggest that the investment in a dedicated function for external knowledge search provides an important mechanism to enhance firms' ability to generate high returns from interfirm collaboration. This is of particular importance when firms seek to learn from interactions with open innovation platforms and need to align external and internal activities. Here, firms can develop the ability to effectively coordinate external services provided by crowdsourcing intermediaries, by investing in dedicated organizational resources (Rothaermel and Deeds, 2006).

Besides providing the organizational context, dedicated organizational structures have the formal recognition and organizational legitimacy to allocate critical resources to the respective projects (Kale et al., 2002). In providing formal support and leadership, firms may even not face the problems and challenges that are typically resolved via informal roles. The establishment of a formal open innovation department or work group provides legitimacy and internal recognition, signaling to the organization the importance of utilizing external inputs for the innovation process.

Organizational information roles

Extant innovation literature has described informal roles such as champions (Chakrabarti, 1974), gatekeepers (Allen, 1977) and promoters (Gemünden, Salomo, and Hölzle, 2007) who provide informal support for innovation projects based on different sources of power when formal support and leadership are inadequate or missing. Per definition, these roles tend to emerge informally and are usually not delegated. However, research on informal roles in innovation suggested that (key) individuals with characteristics of informal roles can be identified and should be actively searched for, or appointed, to ensure that their valuable contributions are effectively harnessed (Saebi and Foss, 2015). Recently, research on open innovation has discussed distinct informal roles that facilitate the use of external knowledge (Pollok, Lüttgens, and Piller, 2019). Organizational roles such as moderators (Beretta et al., 2017), or idea connectors (Whelan et al., 2011) have been found to contribute to the utilization of knowledge inflows and the development of open innovation–related capabilities at the firm level.

These new roles, however, resemble the traditional roles discussed in the earlier innovation literature. They identify opposition and overcome internal resistance and help to disseminate the application of external knowledge by making use of their own network of internal contacts and their skills in selling ideas to senior management. These key individuals further display high levels of personal involvement, informally secure technical and financial resources for initiatives that are not formally accepted in the respective firm (Markham et al., 2010) and possess the relevant expertise necessary to manage new processes and tasks. In the open innovation context, these characteristics enable individuals who take on informal organizational roles to support the transition process from closed to open innovation and enable the firm to more effectively make use of external knowledge (Saebi and Foss, 2015).

Recent research on crowdsourcing has indicated that the presence of these informal roles is an important success factor. Lüttgens et al. (2014) investigated implementation barriers and sources of resistance in crowdsourcing pilots and found that individuals with promoter characteristics overcome major problems (e.g. communication barriers, insufficient resource commitments, not-invented-here attitudes), which may, if left unresolved, lead to project failure and prevent the repeated application of crowdsourcing in seeker firms.

Preventing not-invented-here

Previous research has demonstrated that open innovation is not an easy task. There is not just a lack of organizational structure and roles, but also organizational inertia and structural rigidities challenge the transfer and utilization of outside knowledge on the level of the organization (Zahra and George, 2002). In most instances, however, knowledge is actually transferred, absorbed and put into practice on an individual level (Rogan and Mors, 2014). Here, previous research has identified multiple heuristic concepts influencing and biasing knowledge utilization and decision-making on the level of the individual, including representativeness, anchoring and availability (Kahneman and Tversky, 1979), or an endowment effect (Plott and Zeiler, 2005). Other literature, especially research in social psychology, has shown that in situations characterized by interactions and exchanges with external entities or external objects, the attitudes of individuals often affect decision-making and lead to biased behavior (Ajzen, 2001).

When it comes to absorbing external knowledge for innovation, the most frequently mentioned bias influencing individual decision-making is the not-Invented-here syndrome (NIH) (Antons and Piller, 2016). It can be best conceived of as a profound attitude-based bias towards knowledge (ideas, technologies) derived from a source or contextual background that is considered "outside" or "external" from the perspective of the individual (Katz and Allen, 1982). There are ample reasons why knowledge in this context is perceived as "external", including a developer talking to a team member who has a different disciplinary background, a colleague from a neighboring department suggesting an idea, an external technology provider offering a technical solution or a customer from a different cultural tradition. Research on NIH postulates that individuals have a generally negative attitude towards such knowledge, ideas or technologies of external origin. When this predisposition holds irrespective of the objective value of an external input, an individual is said to be affected by the NIH syndrome. For an innovating organization, this bias becomes economically damaging when knowledge is rejected or underutilized despite having considerable potential value (Kathoefer and Leker, 2012).

When NIH hinders the reception of knowledge, negative consequences are likely to occur. There are many accounts of closely knit in-groups within companies considering their "insider" knowledge superior to outside knowledge. Apple Computer had such a mind-set in the early 1990s, when managers rejected good external ideas and lived in what was widely known as their own "reality distortion field" (Burrows, 2000). To prevent NIH and overcome the resistance of the organizational members towards external knowledge and input, firms need to work on an adequate *corporate open culture* and implement adequate incentive schemes.

A culture for open innovation

Corporate culture refers to the totality of all norms, values and attitudes within a company. The focus here is on the willingness to learn, the willingness to change, the handling of external knowledge and its significance within the company, as well as the importance of cooperation with internal and external partners. An open corporate culture postulates the inter- and intraorganizational transfer of knowledge as a relevant basis for organizational action. In particular, intraorganizational knowledge transfer, understood as the verbal and nonverbal exchange of information between persons or departments, is cited as a success-relevant factor, especially with regard to the development of network competence (Ritter and Gemünden, 2003). The development of an (open) corporate culture also requires an adjustment of internal incentive systems.

At the same time, the involvement of external actors requires clear rules and mutual respect. More or less arbitrary calls for participation can harm the company in the long term. Companies must be aware that the voluntary use of users and external experts is a valuable and often unique knowledge resource. The understanding of the requirements for cooperation in partnership is increasingly becoming an original success factor with more intensive use of open innovation.

Internal incentive systems include all incentives deliberately set by company management for the purpose of influencing behavior and motivating employees in a targeted manner. Individual motivation plays an essential role in the successful transfer of knowledge. Employees do not per se have a preference for external knowledge (Szulanski, 1996). Therefore, systematic incentives must contribute to overcoming the negative attitudes of one's own employees with regard to the acquisition and use of external knowledge (cf. Chesbrough, 2006). It should be noted that these are set in accordance with the definition of incentives for external contributors. For example, when companies address a broad mass of unknown external actors in the form of an "open call", the motives of these actors are not always known and are not necessarily conflict-free in terms of the goals of the company. The identification and consideration of these motives in the form of special incentive mechanisms are of central importance for the success of interactions between a company and its employees and external knowledge carriers.

Conclusion

Open innovation is a promising complement to existing practices in innovation management. The core of the approach is to improve access to needs and solution information from sources previously unknown to the company, often from other industries or technological domains. However, open innovation does not represent a dominant approach in innovation management. Rather, the use of open innovation should be situational; that is, according to the question or innovation task, individual methods make more or less sense – or even the opening to the outside world itself. There will still be areas where the internal organization and implementation of innovation activities have an advantage over open innovation processes. Examples of this are technologies that fall under the company's core competencies or projects with high confidentiality requirements.

Open innovation also does not want to abolish the internal development department – quite the opposite. The task of internal researchers and developers is changing. Their focus is not so much on solving small technical problems at great expense, but rather on creating application knowledge. They need to coordinate a complex innovation process and absorb, evaluate and reintegrate the contributions of external actors. Above all, however, they must ask the right questions and formulate problems that can then be outsourced by means of crowdsourcing. Similarly, in areas where knowledge is very context specific and based on learning effects, such as in the case of improvement innovations and product modifications, internal handling of product development is often the most efficient and effective approach.

References

Afuah A., Tucci C. L. (2012). Crowdsourcing as a solution to distant search. *Academy of Management Review*. 37(3), 355–375.
Ajzen, I. (2001). Nature and operation of attitudes. Annual Review of Psychology, 52(1), 27–58.
Allen, T. J. (1977). *Managing the flow of technology: Technology transfer and the dissemination of technological information within the R&D organization*. Cambridge, Mass: MIT Press.
Antons, D. and Piller, F. (2015). Opening the black box of "Not Invented Here": Attitudes, decision biases, and behavioral consequences. *Academy of Management Perspectives* 29(2), 193–217.
Bengtsson, L., Lakemond, N., Lazzarotti, V., Manzini, R., Pellegrini, L. and Tell, F. (2015). Open to a select few? Matching partners and knowledge content for open innovation performance. *Creativity and Innovation Management*, 24(1), 72–86.
Beretta, M., Björk, J., & Magnusson, M. (2018). Moderating Ideation in Web-Enabled Ideation Systems. *Journal of Product Innovation Management*, 35(3), 389–409.
Bogers, M. et al. 2017). The open innovation research landscape: Established perspectives and emerging themes across different levels of analysis. *Industry and Innovation*, 24(1), 8–40.
Boudreau, K. and Lakhani, K. (2009). How to manage outside innovation. *MIT Sloan Management Review*, 50(4), 69–76.
Burrows, P. (2000). Apple: Yes, Steve, you fixed it! Congrats! Now what's act two? Business Week, 3692, 102–112.
Cassiman, B., Di Guardo, M. C. and Valentini, G. (2010). Organizing links with science: cooperate or contract? A project-level analysis. *Research Policy*, 39(7), 882–892.
Cassiman, B. and Veugelers, R. (2006). In search of complementarity in innovation strategy: internal R&D and external knowledge acquisition. *Management Science*, 52(1), 68–82.
Ceccagnoli, M., Graham, S. J. H., Higgins, M. J. and Lee, J. (2010). Productivity and the role of complementary assets in firms' demand for technology innovations. *Industrial and Corporate Change*, 19(3), 839–869.

Chakrabarti, A.K. (1974). The Role of Champion in Product Innovation. *California Management Review*, 7(2), 58–62.

Chatterji, A. & Fabrizio, K. (2014). Using users: When does external knowledge enhance corporate innovation? *Strategic Management Journal*, 35 (10), 1427–1445.

Chesbrough, H. (2003a). *Open Innovation: The New Imperative for Creating and Profiting from Technology*. Boston: Harvard Business School Press.

Chesbrough H. (2003b). *The era of open innovation MIT Sloan Management Review*, 44 (3), 35–41.

Chesbrough, H. (2006). Open Business Models: How to Thrive in the New Innovation Landscape. Boston, MA: Harvard Business School Press. Chesbrough, H. and Di Minin, A. (2014). Open social innovation. In Chesbrough, H., Vanhaverbeke, W. and West, J. (Eds.), *New frontiers in open innovation*. Oxford: Oxford University Press, pp. 169–187.

Chung, S. A., & Kim, G. M. (2003). Performance effects of partnership between manufacturers and suppliers for new product development: the supplier's standpoint. Research Policy, 32(4), 587–603

Dahlander L., Piezunka H. (2014). Open to suggestions: How organizations elicit suggestions through proactive and reactive attention. *Research Policy*, 43(5), 812–827.

Diener, K. and Piller, F. (2013). *The market for open innovation* (2nd ed.). Raleigh, NC: Lulu.

Ebner, W., Leimeister, J. M. and Krcmar, H. (2009). Community engineering for innovations: the ideas competition as a method to nurture a virtual community for innovations. *R&D Management*, 39(4), 342–356.

Erat, S. and Krishnan, V. (2012), Managing delegated search over design spaces, Management Science, 58 (3), 606–623.

Fabrizio, K. R. (2009). Absorptive capacity and the search for innovation. *Research Policy*, 38(2), 255–267.

Foss, N. J., K. Laursen, T. Pedersen, Linking Customer Interaction and Innovation: The Mediating Role of New Organizational Practices, in: *Organization Science*, 22. Jg. (2011), S. 980–999.

Gales, L. and Mansourcole, D. (1995). User involvement in innovation projects – toward an information-processing model. *Journal of Engineering and Technology Management*, 12(1–2), 77–109.

Gassmann, O., Sandmeier, P. and Wecht, C. H. (2006). Extreme customer innovation in the front-end: learning from a new software paradigm. *International Journal of Technology Management*, 33(1), 46–66.

Gatzweiler, A.m Blazevic, V. and Piller, F. (2017). Dark Side or Bright Light: Managing Deviant Content in Consumer Ideation Contests. *Journal of Product Innovation Management*, 34(6), 772–789.

George, G., McGahan, A. M. and Prabhu, J. (2012). Innovation for inclusive growth: towards a theoretical framework and a research agenda. *Journal of Management Studies*, 49(4), 661–683.

Gnyawali, D. R., & Park, B. J. R. (2011). Co-opetition between giants: Collaboration with competitors for technological innovation. *Research Policy*, 40(5), 650–663.

Grameen Creative Lab (2014). December 16th. www.grameencreativelab.com/a-concept-toeradicate-poverty/7-principles.html

Grant, R. M. and C. Baden-Fuller (2004). A knowledge accessing theory of strategic alliances. *Journal of Management Studies*, 41 (1), 61–84

Howells, J. (2006) Intermediation and the role of intermediaries in innovation. *Research Policy*, 35(5), 715–728.

Jeppesen, L. and Lakhani, K. (2010). Marginality and problemsolving effectiveness in broadcast search. *Organization Science*, 21 (5): 1016–33.

Kahneman, D., & Tversky, A. (1979). Prospect theory: An analysis of decision under risk. *Econometrica*, 47(2), 263–291.

Kale, P., Dyer, J. and Singh, H. (2002). Alliance capability, stock market response, and long-term alliance success: The role of the alliance function. *Strategic Management J.*, 23(8), 747–767.

Kathoefer, D., & Leker, J. (2012). Knowledge transfer in academia: An exploratory study on the not-invented-here syndrome. *The Journal of Technology Transfer*, 37(5), 658–675.

Katz, R. & Allen, T. (1982). Investigating the Not Invented Here (NIH) Syndrome. *R&D Management*, 12(1): 7–19.

Kong, E. (2010). Innovation processes in social enterprises: an IC perspective. *Journal of Intellectual Capital*, 11(2), 158–178.

Kozinets, R. V. (2002). The field behind the screen: using netnography for marketing research in online communities. *Journal of Marketing Research*, 39(1), 61–72.

Laursen, K. (2012). Keep searching and you'll find: what do we know about variety creation through firms' search activities for innovation? *Industry & Corporate Change*, 21(12), 1181–1220.

Laursen, K. and Salter, A. (2006). Open for innovation: The role of openness in explaining innovation performance among UK manufacturing firms. *Strategic Management J.*, 27(2), 131–150.

Li, Y. and Vanhaverbeke, W. (2009). The effects of inter-industry and country difference in supplier relationships on pioneering innovations. *Technovation*, 29(12), 843–858.

Lichtenthaler, U. (2011). Open innovation: past research, current debates, and future directions. *The Academy of Management Perspectives*, 25(1), 75–93.

Lopez-Vega, H., Tell, F., V. and anhaverbeke W. (2016). Where and how to search? Search paths in open innovation. *Research Policy*, 45(1): 125–136.

Lüttgens, D., Pollok, P., Antons, D., and Piller, F. (2014). Wisdom of the crowd and capabilities of a few: Internal success factors of crowdsourcing for innovation. *Journal of Business Economics*, 84(3): 339–374.

Malmberg, A. and Maskell, P. (2002). The elusive concept of localization economies: towards a knowledge-based theory of spatial clustering. *Environment and Planning A*, 34(3), 429–449.

Markham, S. K., Ward, S., Aiman-Smith, S. and Kingon, A. (2010). The valley of death as context for role theory in product innovation. *Journal of Product Innovation Management*, 27(3), 402–417.

Miotti, L. and Sachwald, F. (2003). Co-operative R&D: why and with whom? an integrated framework of analysis. *Research Policy*, 32(8), 1481–1499.

Newth, J. and Woods, C. (2014). Resistance to social entrepreneurship: how context shapes innovation. *Journal of Social Entrepreneurship*, 5(2), 192–213.

Nieto, M. J. and Santamaría, L. (2007). The importance of diverse collaborative networks for the novelty of product innovation. *Technovation*, 27(6), 367–377.

O'Hern, M. S. and Rindfleisch, A. (2009). Customer co-creation: a typology and research agenda. In Naresh, K. M. (Ed.), *Review of marketing research* (Vol. 6). Armonk, NY: Sharpe, pp. 84–106.

Piller, F. and Ihl, C. (2013). Co-Creation with Customers. In: Leading Open Innovation, edited by A. Huff, K. Möslein & R. Reichwald, Cambridge, MA: MIT Press, 139-155.

Piller, F. T. and Walcher, D. (2006). Toolkits for idea competitions: a novel method to integrate users in new product development. *R&D Management*, 36(3), 307–318.

Plott, C. R., and Zeiler, K. (2005). The Willingness to Pay-Willingness to Accept Gap, the "Endowment Effect," Subject Misconceptions, and Experimental Procedures for Eliciting Valuations. *The American Economic Review*, 95(3), 530–545.

Pollok, P. Lüttgens, D. and Piller, F. (2019). Attracting submissions in crowdsourcing contests: The role of search distance, identity disclosure, and seeker status. *Research Policy*, 48(1): 98–114.

Reichwald, R. and Piller, F. (2009). *Interactive Value Creation*, Wiesbaden: GablerSpringer.

Ritter, T., H.-G. Gemünden (2003). Interorganizational Relationships and Networks: An Overview. *Journal of Business Research*, 59, S. 691–697.

Roberts, D., Luettgens, D. and Piller, F. (2016). Mapping the Impact of Social Media for Innovation: The Role of Social Media in Explaining Innovation Performance. *Journal of Product Innovation Management*, 33 (S1), 117–135.

Rogan, M., and Mors, M. L. (2014). A Network Perspective on Individual-Level Ambidexterity in Organizations. *Organization Science*, 6(12), 1860–1877.

Rothaermel, F. T. and Deeds, D. (2006). Alliance type, alliance experience and alliance management capability in high-technology ventures. *J. Business Venturing*, 21(4), 429–460.

Saebi, T., & Foss, N. J. (2015). Business models for open innovation: Matching heterogeneous open innovation strategies with business model dimensions. *European Management Journal*, 33(3), 201–213.

Salge, T. O., Farchi, T., Barrett, M. I., and S. Dopson (2013) When does search openness really matter? A contingency study of health-care innovation projects. *Journal of Product Innovation Management* 30(4), 659-676.

Schiele, H. (2010). Early supplier integration: the dual role of purchasing in new product development. *R&D Management*, 40(2), 138–153.

Schilling, M. A. (2013). *Strategic management of technological innovation* (4th ed.). New York: McGraw-Hill Irwin.

Schumpeter, J. A. (1942). *Socialism, capitalism and democracy*. New York: Harper and Brothers.

Sieg, J. H., Wallin, M. W. and von Krogh, G. (2010). Managerial challenges in open innovation: innovation intermediation in the chemical industry. *R&D Management*, 40(3), 281–291.

Stockstrom, C. S., Goduscheit, R. C., Lüthje, C. and Jørgensen, J. H. (2016). Identifying valuable users as informants for innovation processes: Comparing the search efficiency of pyramiding and screening. *Research Policy*, 45(2), 507–516.

Svirina, A., Azzbarova, A. and Oganisjana, K. (2016). Implementing open innovation concept in social business. *Journal of Open Innovation: Technology, Market, and Complexity*, 2(20).

Szulanski, G. (1996). Exploring Internal Stickiness: Impediments to the Transfer of Best Practice Within the Firm. *Strategic Management Journal,* 17 (1), 27–43.

Teirlinck, P., Dumont, M. and Spithoven, A. (2010). Corporate decision-making in R&D outsourcing and the impact on internal R&D employment intensity. *Industrial and Corporate Change,* 19(6), 1741–1768.

Terwiesch, C., Xu, Y. (2008) Innovation contests, open innovation, and multi-agent problem solving. *Management Science.* 54(9): 1529–1543.

Thomke, S. H. (2006). Capturing the real value of innovation tools. *MIT Sloan Management Review,* 47(2), 24-32

Todtling, F., Lehner, P. and Kaufmann, A. (2009). Do different types of innovation rely on specific kinds of knowledge interactions?. *Technovation,* 29 (1): 59–71.

Toubia, O., and Florès, L. (2007). Adaptive idea screening using consumers. *Marketing Science, 26*(3), 342–360.

Trott, P. and Hartmann, D. A. P. (2009). Why 'open innovation' is old wine in new bottles. *International Journal of Innovation Management,* 13(4), 715–736.

von Hippel, E. (1986). Lead users: a source of novel product concepts. *Management Science,* 32(6), 791–805.

von Hippel, E. (1988). *The sources of innovation.* Cambridge, MA: MIT Press.

von Hippel, E. (2005). *Democratizing innovation.* Cambridge, MA: MIT Press.

Von Hippel, E., and R. Katz (2002). Shifting innovation to users via toolkits. *Management Science,* 48 (7): 821–33.

Von Hippel, E., S. Ogawa, and J. De Jong (2011). The age of the consumer innovator. *MIT Sloan Management Review,* 53 (1): 21–35.

Vuola, O. and Hameri, A-P. (2006). Mutually benefiting joint innovation process between industry and big science. *Technovation,* 26(1), 3–12.

Whelan, E., Parise, S., de Valk, J., and Aalbers, R. (2011). Creating employee networks that deliver open innovation. *MIT Sloan Management Review,* 53 (1), 37–44.

Xie, F.T. and Johnston, W.J. (2004). Strategic alliances: incorporating the impact of e-business technological innovations. *The Journal of Business Industrial Marketing,* 19(3), 208.

Yun, J. J., Park, K., Im, C., Shin, C. and Xiaofei, Zhao (2017). Dynamics of social enterprises – shift from social innovation to open innovation science. *Technology and Society,* 22(3), 425–439.

Zahra, S. A., & George, G. (2002). Absorptive capacity: A review, reconceptualization, and extension. *Academy of Management Review,* 27(2), 185–203.

11
R&D STRATEGIES FOR DISRUPTIVE INNOVATION

Chang-Chieh Hang and Yi Ruan

Introduction to disruptive innovation

The theory of disruptive innovation, proposed by Christensen in a seminal paper (Bower and Christensen, 1995) and a subsequent book (Christensen, 1997), has attracted the attention of many scholars and appealed widely to practising managers and entrepreneurs. Disruptive innovation (DI) is defined as "a process by which a product or service takes root initially in simpler applications at the bottom of a market or in a new market, and then relentlessly moves 'up market', eventually displacing established competitors." Christensen coined this term to differentiate this type of innovation from the well-known radical, breakthrough type of innovation based on an obviously superior technology (Kostoff, Boylan, and Simons, 2004) and the necessary incremental type of innovation to sustain current business growth by established incumbents.

According to Christensen, a technology can be "disruptive" when it displays two features. One is that it has inferior performance in terms of attributes that the mainstream customers value at the time of product introduction; hence, they are usually dismissed by mainstream incumbent firms. The other is that it has new features appreciated by low-end or new/niche customers (typically cheaper, smaller, easier to use, etc.). But not all technologies that have these "disruptive features" can succeed in the market and disrupt the conventional businesses. There are several essential conditions for that to occur. First is that there exists a performance overshoot, either caused by aggressive sustaining innovation, which makes the performance of the product/service exceed what the mainstream consumers require in the developed economies, or caused by a lack of requirement for the performance or purchasing power when the product/service is introduced to the less developed markets. Second is that the disruptive innovation can be further improved by affordable R&D so that it can reach the "good enough" level for the mainstream customers, given sufficient time, and become a substitute for the mainstream product/service. This allows the disruptive innovation to succeed not only in the initial niche or small, developing markets but also make its way to the conventional and developed markets. Third is that the innovation has to be protected either by intellectual property laws, technology standards and learning curves, or some inabilities of the others to imitate. Some examples of the inabilities of incumbents to imitate DI can be found in Christensen's books and papers (e.g. Christensen, 1997).

Ever since the popularization of disruptive innovation theory, enlightened incumbents have learned the importance of disruptive innovation and are better prepared to exploit DI to avoid potential dethronements from below (Christensen and Raynor, 2003; Inkpen and Ramaswami, 2006). Furthermore, the new market created by DI could grow to become very significant and be worthwhile to pursue by itself (Govindarajan and Kopalle, 2006; Linton, 2009; Utterback and Acee, 2005). Creating potential DI has thus become a purposeful goal of both startups and incumbents seeking new growth.

In a rare attempt (Yu and Hang, 2011), the authors moved upstream to study empirically how one might purposefully create technologies for potential DI in R&D laboratories. They supported their research using cases of successful technological DI across a wide range of industries. These cases were carefully filtered by Govindarajan and Kopalle's four criteria of DI (Govindarajan and Kopalle, 2006). The cases covered five technological categories (e.g. "Industrial/Commercial Computer Hardware and Software") for a deeper study. Their research verified the proposal of four generally applicable R&D strategies for creating disruptive technologies in advanced economies.

In recent years, innovations in emerging economies have increasingly attracted the attention of practitioners and academics. Many papers have discussed the nature and the scale of the potential market – the bottom of the pyramid (Prahalad, 2004) – and how multinational companies (MNCs) should manage overseas R&D centers in emerging economies. One of the distinctive natures of the bottom of the pyramid (BOP) market is that the mass population demands robust products with basic functions at ultra-low prices that match their ultra-low income level and undeveloped harsh living conditions. To meet that need, it would take more than simply downsizing or adapting products developed in the advanced economies (Immelt and Govindarajan, 2009; London and Hart, 2004; Ray and Ray, 2011). Hence, Hart and Christensen (2002) suggested that companies would need to take a "great leap" downwards to exploit the nonconsumption with DI. However, literature on disruptive innovation in emerging economies has remained sparse, especially those developed by local companies. This gap in the literature was addressed recently by Hang and Ruan (2018) who set out to collect relevant DI cases from the two biggest emerging economies in the world – China and India. They analyzed these cases to study if the appropriate R&D strategies were similar to those used in advanced economies, and whether there were any additional generally applicable R&D strategies used in emerging economies.

In the following sections, the appropriate R&D strategies for DI in advanced markets are elaborated and illustrated with representative cases in different industries. This is then followed by the elaboration of the identified R&D strategies for creating DI in the emerging markets, illustrated by several examples from India and China. For both markets, the frequencies of the usage of these strategies are analyzed and the implications for the public and private sectors are discussed.

R&D strategies for developed markets

Yu and Hang's work (2011) succeeded in systematically documenting an intentional approach to incubate technologies for potential DIs in R&D laboratories. Using a qualitative method with an extensive multiple case study approach, they distilled four generally applicable R&D strategies out of 35 DI cases in developed markets, namely *miniaturization, simplification, augmentation, and exploitation*. *Miniaturization* strategy aims to design or construct products with a smaller physical size to create the benefits of portability and convenience with a modest investment of time and resources. *Simplification* strategy looks at ways to reduce redundant features or the degree of performance in certain feature(s) of overly complex products so as to optimize the value for customers at a lower price level. *Augmentation* strategy suggests that firms can augment an existing

Table 11.1 Postulation of the abstracted R&D strategies

Cases/strategies	Miniaturization	Simplification	Augmentation	Exploitation
Transistor Radio	X	X		
2.5-inch Hard Disk Drive	X			
Wii Game Console			X	X
Centrino Chipsets			X	
Tank Gauging Machine		X		
War Games				X
Automated External Defibrillator		X		

product with a disruptive feature. Last but not least, *exploitation* strategy refers to repositioning existing technology and borrowing existing technologies for targeted applications. Illustrations on the use of each strategy are provided in Table 11.1 (Table 9.3 in Yu and Hang, 2011).

The seven selective cases shown in Table 11.1 encompass the four generally applicable R&D strategies for DI. These seven cases also broadly represent the 35 cases in diversity because (i) they cover all five technological categories; (ii) geographic regions include the United States, EU, Japan, Asia except Japan (China), and the Middle East (Israel); and (iii) time periods vary from the 1950s to 2007.

It is noted that Wii game console has applied two strategies. This suggests that the R&D strategies are not mutually exclusive and could be combined as input for the strategy-crafting efforts of firms.

In the following section, each strategy is first defined and two detailed cases are then used to explain how the strategy was applied.

Miniaturization

Many disruptive products have been smaller and lighter than their predecessors (Kostoff and Boylan, 2004). Miniaturization strategy is defined as the strategy to design or construct products on a smaller scale to increase the benefits of portability and convenience. It is important to point out that there are two possible routes to achieve miniaturization. One is by a heavy investment of time and resources to achieve a much superior product with significant reduction in size but without degradation in key performance – this type of breakthrough R&D is adopted in radical innovation (Leifer et al., 2000). The other one is a modest investment of time and resources to achieve a smaller but good enough product to facilitate DI. We are referring to the second route of miniaturization here. Two cases that applied the miniaturization strategy are the transistor radio and hard disk drive, and we use them to explain what we mean by miniaturization.

Transistor radio

The vacuum tube has been replaced by the much smaller, less power-hungry transistor in many applications. But in the 1950s, the early transistor radios were really poor in terms of performance, offering far lower fidelity than the vacuum tube–based tabletop radios. Nevertheless, Sony discovered a new market composed of teenagers who valued the attributes of the pocketability and cheap price of transistor-based radios.

In order to fit the transistors and other electronics components into their small radio, almost every component needs to be miniaturized such as the capacitor, the transformer, the battery, and so on. At that time, most of the components were produced by subcontractors. Therefore, Ibuka, one of the two Sony co-founders, went around to every major component manufacturer in Japan and persuaded them to start to miniaturize every component from scratch, seeding the growth of a prosperous electronics components industry in Japan. With a clear vision and determination to pursue miniaturization and compactness, Sony overcame all technological hurdles within three years to introduce the world's first real portable transistor radio in 1957. It was made with an all-new imaginative design with many purpose-built miniature components.

2.5-inch hard disk drive (HDD)

A more recent example was the 2.5-inch HDD. It has enabled companies such as Seagate to create a new market disruption in mobile computing applications. It is also beginning to encroach on the 3.5-inch HDD in enterprise solutions. Although 3.5-inch HDD outperformed 2.5-inch HDD in primary dimensions such as overall capacity and data transfer rate, the smaller size and lighter weight of the 2.5-inch drives have enabled it to be favored in a niche market of mobile/laptop applications. Of course, 2.5-inch drives have already been a major high-growth business even without the disruption of the 3.5-inch drives. Nevertheless, the 2.5-inch drives may still have the potential to eventually disrupt the 3.5-inch drives in mainstream applications such as desktop computers.

Simplification

The simplification strategy is used to create potentially disruptive products based on the current products' overly high complexity and excess functionality, so that the population that historically lacked the skills to use the current products can become new customers. Simplification is done not only to reduce redundant features or the degree of performance in certain feature(s) but also to focus on the new value proposition that is most delightful to its targeted customers. We shall illustrate this strategy using two cases: a simplified tank gauging machine in the Chinese market and an automated external defibrillator.

Tank gauging machine TSL-2

Tank gauging machines were developed to measure the oil flow that performs the function of inventory control in petrol stations. Traditional tank gauging machines widely adopted in U.S. and European markets in 2000 have highly automated functions and a large capacity – up to 12 tanks – with a premium price of US10,000.

In 2000, a large number of firms in the tank gauging business went to China with their new models of tank gauging machines, and the most successful model was the TLS2, released by Firm A after several episodes of trial and error. Compared with traditional machines, TLS2 was inferior in most dimensions but was good enough to apply in the Chinese market. The new value proposition of "graphic touch screen display" (most operators in Chinese petrol stations did not understand English in 2000) and significant lower cost made the TLS2 a very successful disruption to traditional models in the Chinese market.

Before 2000, the Chinese market was dominated by domestic firms with over 90 percent of market share. In 2001, Firm A captured 52 percent of the Chinese market with its simplified tank gauging machine. Particularly noteworthy, simplification was not limited to high-level features cut-off. It was a new product, not only with reduced redundant features or the degree of performance in certain feature(s) but also with a new value proposition that was most delightful to its targeted customers.

Automated external defibrillator

Early defibrillation is very critical to reviving patients in sudden cardiac arrest (SCA). Manual external defibrillators (MEDs) dominated the defibrillation market until the introduction of the automated external defibrillator (AED). MEDs are full-function defibrillators that support multifunctional operations, making them only suitable for highly skilled medical personnel who have received training in advanced cardiac life support and rhythm recognitions, whereas the AED is a portable defibrillator designed for minimally trained or untrained nonmedical personnel. When compared in terms of traditional performance measures, AEDs are inferior to MEDs. However, its mobility and ease of usage are great attributes well suited for saving lives, as the likelihood for successful resuscitation would decrease by approximately 7 to 10 percent with each minute following the SCA. In addition, the cost of an AED is five to six times cheaper than the hospital-standard MED, which makes it highly attractive to public consumers who are price sensitive and to pre-hospital service, even to same traditional hospital segment.

Philips Medical Systems (PMS) entered the AED market in 2000 with a product that was simplified from the mature and established technology of an existing MED. Recognizing a non-consumption group of 121 million homes in the United States, Philips Medical Systems further simplified the portable AEDs to introduce the first commercial Heartstart OnSite Defibrillator through over-the-counter sales without prescriptions in 2005, successfully extending AED applications to homes, communities, schools, and businesses. A very easy-to-use user interface empowers even ordinary users to save lives.

Augmentation

Augmentation strategy suggests that firms can augment the existing sustaining product with a disruptive feature. This means that the traditional primary performances that mainstream customers historically valued could still be maintained at a satisfactory level of performance, while the R&D could focus on adding new disruptive features. This strategy will be elaborated using two cases: the Nintendo Wii game console and Intel Centrino chipsets.

Wii game console

In 2006, Nintendo launched its new home video game console Wii to compete with Sony's PlayStation 3 and Microsoft's Xbox 360 as the seventh-generation product in the video game industry. The mainstream competitive dimension in the video game market was led by Sony and Microsoft's high-end technologies, such as the synergistic processing elements for higher processing speeds and the superior graphics for resolution and realism. Wii was a surprise entry as it aimed to bring games to nonconventional customers such as females and older folks through the new game interface.

Based largely on the sustaining game console product, the affordable Wii features a new motion-sensitive wireless remote controller, which utilizes a commercially available

Micro-Electro-Mechanical Systems (MEMS) acceleration sensor to enable such actions like racing-game steering and a tennis swing to be done through natural movements of your hands rather than just your thumbs. Wii Sports, packaged with the Wii console, introduces players to these and other experiences. The disruptive feature of the motion-sensing controller has brought huge market success for Nintendo.

Centrino chipsets

Intel Centrino chipsets, developed by Intel R&D Centre in Haifa, Israel, was a huge commercial success. Instead of developing higher-performance microprocessors, which was the R&D goal of Intel headquarters in the United States, Intel Israel R&D management set a completely different goal of transforming laptops into mobile offices as a potential new-market disruption. Its R&D engineers concentrated on adding new features to its existing low-end microprocessors – features which were not yet appreciated in the mainstream market. The result was a hugely successful Centrino chipsets product, which includes an energy-efficient Pentium-M processor (with different architectural features to combine routine instructions and tasks to save time and energy) and a wireless local area network chipset to facilitate mobile Internet access and other wireless applications. The market has demonstrated that eventually the strategy of augmenting existing microprocessors with new features of battery life extension and wireless connectivity enabled Intel to command premium prices.

Exploitation for another application

When attacked by disruptive entrants, incumbents could also think of new applications to reposition their existing products in addition to the option to fight back. On the other hand, entrepreneurial firms could take the initiative to leverage progress of certain sustaining technology that has already created affordable, high-tech products or components to create potential DIs in another targeted application. The strategy of exploitation for another application covers two perspectives: repositioning existing technology and borrowing existing technologies for targeted applications. The two illustrative cases are war game products in the military training industry and the MEMS-enabled controller in the Wii game console.

War games

Due to keen competition in sustaining innovation, product performance would continue to improve substantially over time. But the resultant cost increase could also limit further business growth. The military training simulator market is a good example here. The mainstream simulator product has been revolutionized since the introduction of sophisticated computer technologies. They improved rapidly over time, but the cost has also gone up as more demanding high-end customers could afford it. But subsequently, PC-based games that were developed for the entertainment market were found to be "good enough" as training tools for less demanding customers, especially those who were severely financially constrained. They are also good enough to be used as a recruiting tool for new soldiers. The military simulation is being transformed by PC games. A serial of virtual training devices has been developed particularly for military training. However, with significant performance improvements in gaming consoles such as network playability, local scenario storage, and graphic quality, games like *Spearhead, America's Army* gradually emerged in military training applications.

MEMS in Wii

The successful DI of Nintendo Wii used strategy 3 – Augmentation. The Nintendo Wii also used strategy 4 – Exploitation for another application. The disruptive module of Wii is its controller, called Wii Remote, which is a wireless and motion-sensitive controller.

Wii Remote has an accelerometer, which is the "magic" driver that enables the wireless sensing of 3D movement. The MEMS accelerometer was originally developed as a precision sensor in automobile crash-sensing. Its mass application, coupled with large-scale wafer fab production, has significantly reduced the cost of MEMS sensors. In Wii Remote, an affordable MEMS acceleration sensor is used to enable such actions like racing-game steering and tennis swing to be done through natural movements of your hands rather than just your thumbs, as mentioned earlier. Wii Sports, packaged with the Wii console, introduce players to these and other experiences. Hence, the new application of MEMS sensors in game consoles significantly contributed to Wii's successful disruption.

Discussion

Table 11.2 gives an overview of the application frequencies in each of the five industry categories and also the overall application frequencies of each of the four R&D strategies. For example, it can be seen that "Miniaturization" and "Simplification" strategies are significantly used more frequently than the rest, which reflects the lifestyle trend towards convenience and agility. On the other hand, the relatively less frequent utilization of "Augmentation" and "Exploitation for Another Application" strategies may imply plenty of untapped disruptive opportunities. The potential opportunities will be discussed as follows.

Miniaturization

Miniaturization is the second most frequently used strategy, at 28.6 percent. Furthermore, it is the most frequently used strategy in the "Consumer Electronics" category and the "Healthcare and Medical Equipment" category. This implies that with continuing technology advances in areas such as microelectronics, nanotechnologies, and optimization of architecture designs, there exist many opportunities for firms to miniaturize their products into compact and portable disruptive products, particularly in the consumer electronics and healthcare industry.

Table 11.2 Application frequency of the four R&D strategies

Technological categories	Miniaturization	Simplification	Augmentation	Exploitation for another application
Industrial/commercial computer hardware and software	5	10	3	3
Consumer electronics	4	4	0	1
Communications/networking	1	0	3	1
Healthcare and medical equipment	3	2	0	0
Process and mechanical engineering	1	4	3	1
Overall frequency	14	20	9	6
Relative frequency among all four R&D strategies	28.6%	40.8%	18.4%	12.2%

Simplification

As there exist many high-end sustaining technologies, both incumbents and entrants could proactively simplify them to create potentially disruptive technologies. This strategy was the most frequently used. It is anticipated that companies will find this strategy to be in line with the trend of open innovation (Chesbrough, 2003), as the high-end technology (before simplification) could be sourced externally from universities or other organizations. On the other hand, universities and research institutes have found a lot of difficulties in directly transferring their high-end technologies to small and medium enterprises (SMEs). The Simplification strategy provides a viable solution: if the universities/research institutes proactively simplify their high-end technologies in consultation with the SMEs to better appreciate the "job-to-be-done" market needs (Christensen, 2003), they could create an appropriate technological DI for the SMEs, which will in turn use them in introducing DI.

Augmentation

It is often difficult for firms competing heavily in the traditional value network to set an R&D goal to develop disruptive products that may have high market uncertainty. Augmentation strategy builds on a successful sustaining product to add features that are disruptive – features not appreciative in the mainstream market but appealing to new market segments. The successful use of augmentation by Nintendo demonstrated that it would be very worthwhile to set and realize such an R&D goal.

It is noted that this R&D approach should be more acceptable to incumbent companies, as it will not entail the classical DI route of completely abandoning a sustaining technology. Yet Table 11.2 shows that it was not frequently used. It is thus recommended that companies learn more from successful examples like Intel and Nintendo to gain more awareness of the potential of this strategy.

Exploitation for another application

Finally, there is a possibility of leveraging the sustained progress of certain established products that has already created affordable, high-tech components. The use of the lightweight, good-quality and low-cost head phones in the Walkman (Nayak and Ketteringham, 1994) was one classical example. The literature on text mining (Yoon, Phaal, and Probert, 2008) and patent mapping could be applied here to help search for appropriate product candidates to be borrowed or exploited for potentially disruptive products. From Table 11.2, it is also observed that this approach has been underutilized. This need not be the case if the R&D managers are encouraged to leverage technologies from other fields or other applications to create suitable candidates for disruptive products. It is also anticipated that the trend of open innovation (Chesbrough, 2003) would spur more interest in this R&D strategy for the creation of technological DI.

R&D strategies for emerging markets

The cases used in Yu and Hang (2011) were all from developed economies. This raised the following two questions: (1) Are these four strategies applicable in the emerging economies? and (2) Would the DI cases in the emerging economies add any new strategy to the list? Based on the theory of DI, Hang and Ruan (2018) collected several DI cases in the two biggest emerging economies – India and China – in order to tackle these two research questions.

They carefully selected all the cases according to the original definition of DI in Christensen's theory (1997) and also screened using Govindarajan and Kopalle's four criteria of DI (Govindarajan and Kopalle, 2006). In total, 11 cases – 5 from India and 6 from China – were selected. Their main data sources were academic journals, books, company websites, industry reports, industry yearbooks, and reputable business presses. For data triangulation, they conducted field studies in several of these companies. For each of these companies, they interviewed the CEO, the CTO, the chief engineer, or all of them to find out the details of the relevant R&D processes.

Cases from India

Tata: Nano

Tata Motors set their retail price target at $2,500 before they designed the car. They made their suppliers keep in mind that their target customers were motorcycle and scooter drivers who wanted an enclosed, safer vehicle but could not afford cars already on the market. Tata Motors also provided functional goals for many parts rather than technical specs (i.e. wipe water from windshield vs. windshield wiper must be x mm by y cm and work at z cadence) in the early stage of the design process. By doing this, Tata managed to reorient the basic tenets of efficiency and practicality to meet the cost target.

Both the DI strategy of *miniaturization* and *simplification* were evident in this case, as the car was designed to be smaller and its function was simplified to the most basic level. However, to reach the extremely low price limit set at the beginning, it was almost impossible if all they could do was minimize and simplify an existing car model. It required an overall redesign or re-engineering process, which involved structural changes and reconfiguration of existing or altered components (Ray and Ray, 2011). To create a new altered price-performance package with existing component technologies, they made a series of decisions on what to keep and what to cut based on their knowledge of the low-income Indian families.

Another cost-cutting strategy worth mentioning is its distributed assembly model. Working closely with its suppliers, Tata Motors was able to modularize a lot of parts in Nano and ship them to local manufacturers for final assembly. By doing this, Tata not only reduced its capital cost in inventory, logistics, assembly, etc., but also strengthened its flexibility in adapting the product to the needs of various customers and different regulations in different markets. This unique distribution model could be attributed to the open design platform of Tata Nano and its modular architecture in the initial stage (Ray and Ray, 2011; Sanchez and Hang, 2017).

Godrej: ChotuKool

In 2010, Indian conglomerate Godrej and Boyce launched the world's cheapest super-economical refrigerator "ChotuKool" at the price of $69. The fridge is a portable top-opening unit, weighs only 7.8 kg, uses high-end insulation to stay cool for hours without power, and consumes half the energy used by regular refrigerators. To achieve its efficiency, ChotuKool does not have a compressor; instead, it runs on a cooling chip and a fan similar to those used in computers. So like computers, it can run on batteries. Its engineering credentials are further boosted by the fact that it has only 20 parts, as opposed to more than 200 parts in a normal refrigerator.

It was also evident that *simplification* and *miniaturization* strategies were used in this case. But just like Tata Nano's R&D process, the engineers in Godrej couldn't have achieved this design by only simplifying and minimizing the conventional fridge. Instead, they redesigned the entire product with substitutive components that can perform similar functions but compromise on the effectiveness. Both the design and the materials of the substitutive components were based on the lean resources in rural India. This again showcased the essence of frugal engineering or Gandhian engineering – to exploit more from fewer resources for more people.

Tata: Swach

This water purifier, which was made of rice husk ash, was an initiative undertaken by Tata Research Development and Design Centre. It is a replaceable filter-based product, which is entirely portable and based on low-cost natural ingredients, which safeguards drinking water at a new benchmark of Rs 30 per month for a family of five. It has a 9.5-liters capacity and can filter 3,000 liters until the cartridge has to be replaced, which would last an average family of five 200 days. The purification medium contained inside the cartridge has the capability to kill bacteria and disease-causing organisms.

Priced under Rs 1,000 (US$18), Swach doesn't require electricity or running water to operate. It combines low-cost ingredients such as rice husk ash with nano-silver particles and has been rigorously tested to meet internationally accepted water purification standards. The case of Tata Swach again showcased the power of frugal engineering. By setting the price target so it was affordable to the poor people in India, Tata managed to use the cheap and easily accessible natural resources in India to make the cartridge. But to achieve the functionality of water purification, it also combined such design with its own R&D capabilities in nano-technology. Moreover, it took into consideration the scarcity of electricity in most rural areas in India and designed the machine to be able to run without electricity. All these R&D efforts were based on one idea – to "get more from less for more" – which is the theme of frugal engineering or Gandhian engineering.

Sulzon: Wind turbine

Suzlon wanted to build a vertically integrated business – integrating every process in-house (i.e. R&D, manufacturing, installation, service, etc.) – to better control the cost and collect feedback. It acquired a rotor-blade manufacturer in the Netherlands: Hansen Transmission International – a world-leading manufacturer of gearbox and drive trains for wind turbines; it also acquired Repower Systems AG, a recognized technology leader of multimegawatt wind turbines. Leveraging R&D capabilities in Europe and low-cost manufacturing capabilities in Asia, Suzlon managed to bring down the cost of their wind turbines to 20 percent below their European competitors.

Although Suzlon's products were not suitable for replacing conventional power generation in urban areas, they attracted customers with large manufacturing or other operations in rural areas that had poor or costly access to conventional power supplies.

Suzlon subsequently managed to improve the performance of its wind turbines and quickly expand its manufacturing scale to cut the production cost even further.

Cases from China

BYD: battery core

Since it was founded in 1995, BYD has been determined to develop the battery core business. But it couldn't afford the sophisticated Japanese product line for battery cores. Hence, they chose to rely on their own R&D to design some key manufacturing machines and decompose the assembly line into several procedures that could be operated by people. The decomposed procedures were so simple that the workers could easily operate them after mastering a couple of key skills. Compared with the fully automated Japanese product line with the assistance of robots, BYD's half-automated product line seemed less rigorous but much cheaper. With strict ex-post quality control, BYD batteries achieved equally good quality as its Japanese competitors but reduced the price by one-third. Moreover, the decomposed process enabled BYD to quickly adjust to the changing market demands and to achieve product diversification in a much faster and cheaper manner than its competitors' standardized product lines.

The R&D strategy of BYD's case is more than *simplification* because they redesigned the entire product line based on the limited resources they can leverage (e.g. cheap labor). Although their product line was less sophisticated than the Japanese ones, the basic functions of production were maintained, and they came up with strict quality control to keep up with their competitors in terms of product quality. This strategy shares the same theme as the so-called frugal engineering or Gandhian engineering. In addition, the speedy expansion of their business gave them significant a reward in terms of economy of scale, which was not easily achievable for their competitors.

China's e-bike industry

This industry was born when some companies like Luyuan built their first-generation e-bikes with motors, lead-acid batteries, battery chargers, and controllers, which were all available as key components in the market (Hang and Chen, 2010; Sanchez and Hang, 2017). Due to their affordability and ease of use, e-bikes gradually received the attention of some early customers – older people and mothers who used the bikes to send their young children to school. In the following decade, continuous R&D brought key technology breakthroughs to the industry, which significantly improved the performance of the bikes. The continuous performance upgrading made electric bikes an ideal alternative to motorcycles and manual bicycles.

The case of the e-bike clearly displays several DI features: inferior initial performance, continuous performance improvement, new features that appeal to a niche market, etc. Most companies exploited their own R&D or manufacturing capabilities in their previous businesses, as these companies used to be either suppliers or manufacturers of motorcycles or bicycles. By leveraging their existing capabilities and industry experience, they made the entry into the e-bike business in an easier and cheaper way. Moreover, almost all the e-bike companies used modularized parts provided by mature suppliers in the market.

CIMC: reefer

CIMC started its disrupting journey by quickly acquiring other local container manufacturers during early 1990s. After it established a strong foothold in the domestic Chinese market, it began to look into some high-tech/high-end market segments dominated by foreign companies. In 1995, CIMC decided to enter the refrigerated containers (or "reefers") sector, which was then dominated by Japanese aluminum reefer manufacturers. Instead of the dominant "foaming in situ" technology used by the Japanese incumbents, CIMC chose to buy the less favorable "sandwich foaming" technology from Graaff (a German company). After licensing-in 12 patents, buying a used production line, and getting some key engineers from Graaff to join the newly established subsidiary, Shanghai CIMC Reefer Containers Co. Ltd., CIMC quickly absorbed the German technology and started its own cost reduction R&D. Over the next five years CIMC engineers and technicians fundamentally re-engineered the manufacturing process four times, applying advanced technology borrowed from the auto industry (Zeng and Williamson, 2007).

Furthermore, CIMC found that the expensive aluminum used in the Japanese reefers could be replaced by much cheaper treated steel. In 2003, the sandwich foaming stainless steel reefer container became the new industry standard, CIMC gained 44 percent of the global market share, and all the Japanese incumbents exited the market.

Galanz: microwave oven

When Galanz in China decided to enter the microwave market in 1992, it took on the design and manufacture of its own products for the domestic market created by the newly emerging middle class. Licensing microwave technology from Toshiba, the company built core competence in manufacturing, followed by heavy, sustained investment in R&D and design, to develop a simple, energy-efficient microwave oven that was small and affordable (Hang and Chen, 2010).

By 2000, Galanz dominated the Chinese market with a 70 percent market share. With a strong foothold in the Chinese market, the company lost no time in exporting their disruptive products to other developing markets; simultaneously, it continued its R&D effort, adding features and functionality – first for high-end Chinese customers and then for customers in developed countries. By 2005, more than 50 percent of Galanz's products were manufactured for international export under the Galanz brand. The company has developed many core technologies protected by more than 600 patents.

Haier: mini-washer

In 1996, facing stagnant summer sales of washing machines, Haier decided to try to reach non-consumers by creating new products (Hang and Chen, 2010). The company developed a small washing machine with high, medium, and low water levels that could wash just one pair of underwear or socks. The mini-washer, called Prodigy, used concentric washing technology to operate with high efficiency and low noise, saving water, electricity, weight, and space compared to conventional washers. Consumers embraced the new machine. Urban-dwelling singles who used to tolerate the accumulation of smelly, sweaty summer clothing for a week found that the new Haier product allowed them to do laundry every day.

Based on the success of the Prodigy, Haier developed another product series, the XQBM, a small, high-efficiency washer offering additional features, including 12 different wash modes. Being marketed as the "second washer at home," the XQBM washer has sold about 2 million units and has been exported to 68 countries in Europe, Africa, America, and Asia.

Furthermore, this case is also a classic example from the emerging market that shows how *miniaturization* and *exploitation* were used in the R&D process of DI. By setting the target of washing a small amount of clothes, Haier minimized the traditional washer and continued to improve it with various advanced technologies, and they did so by leveraging their existing R&D capabilities and manufacturing experiences.

GE: ECG and USM

In addition to the cases of companies from China and India, GE's two reverse-innovation cases – the portable electrocardiogram (ECG) machine developed in India and the portable ultrasound machine (USM) developed in China (Inkpen and Ramaswami, 2006) – are important DI cases from these two emerging economies, as they both are from an incumbent firm. In both cases, the local teams of GE redesigned the entire device (ECG or USM) according to the economic and environmental constraints in the rural areas in both countries. They leveraged the global resources in GE and made use of parts like laptops which were easily available on the market at that time. As a result, the cost of these delicate machines was significantly cut down and opened up the mass market in the emerging countries.

In these two GE cases, it is clear that DI strategy *exploitation* was applied during the R&D process, as both the newly designed ECG and USM leveraged the existing technologies and R&D capabilities in GE. However, it is also worth noticing that frugal engineering played a vital role in both cases.

Discussion

The DI cases and the DI strategies in this section for emerging markets are summarized in Table 11.3 (a and b). It is apparent that the four strategies used extensively in developed markets (Yu and Hang, 2011) can also be applied in many cases here, except for *augmentation*. Compared with the cases in Yu and Hang (2011), the distinctive characteristic of the DIs in the emerging markets is that they have to be even cheaper and with less maintenance cost due to an even lower level of consumption and purchasing power. Hence, the R&D teams seemed to have sacrificed a bit more performance for lower cost and affordability and put even more effort on cutting the manufacturing cost. Along with their low purchasing power, people in the rural areas of China and India are also less educated; some are even short of living space, electricity, water, and other resources.

From Table 11.3 (a and b), one could further identify three unique DI strategies particular to the cases in emerging economies, namely *frugal engineering, modularization*, and *drastic manufacturing cost reduction*. Each strategy will be elaborated upon and discussed next.

First, *frugal engineering* refers to the engineering and design processes that provide products with essential features to tap the bottom of the pyramid.[1] Based on this definition, we can see that 7 out of 11 cases showed evidence of this applied strategy in their R&D processes. Originated with the Tata Nano design, this strategy was the theme throughout the R&D process for the cheapest car in the world. For Godrej's ChotuKool and Tata Swach, the key idea of their R&D was also to use as little material as possible to provide the basic functions of a fridge and a water purifier. Both products targeted the mass population in India who are poor and lack access to electricity. In the case of the Galanz microwave oven, the idea was to develop a simple, energy-efficient microwave oven that was small and affordable for most Chinese families, which is essentially frugal engineering and design. BYD's case was slightly different, as the frugal design was not in the final product, but in the production line. Finally, the two medical devices developed by GE India and GE China were also products of frugal engineering. The main idea behind both R&D processes was to use as little as possible to make simple, portable, and cheap machines that have the most basic functions to serve the mass populations in the harsh conditions of rural India and China.

Second, *modularization* refers to building a product on a modular architecture and working with suppliers towards standardized modules so as to achieve the economy of scale based on specialization. Two cases in this chapter display this strategy. In the case of Tata Nano, the car was designed on an open structure, involving part suppliers from all over the world. By setting a price limit in the beginning, letting suppliers bid for the projects and manufacture modularized parts and then having the local manufactures assemble the cars, Tata significantly reduced cost. The other case where this strategy was applied is China's e-bike industry. Based on an open architecture that was standardized by the central government and an existing mature network of part

Table 11.3a Summary of cases and strategies in India

Cases/strategies	Miniaturization	Simplification	Augmentation	Exploitation	Cost innovation Modularization	Frugal engineering	Drastic Manufacturing Cost Reduction
Tata Nano	X	X			X	X	
GE ECG				X		X	
Godrej ChotuKool	X	X		X		X	
Tata Swach		X				X	
Suzlon Wind Turbine				X			X

Table 11.3b Summary of cases and strategies in China

Cases/strategies	Miniaturization	Simplification	Augmentation	Exploitation	Cost innovation Modularization	Frugal engineering	Drastic Manufacturing Cost Reduction
Galanz Microwave Oven				X		X	X
China's E-bike				X	X		
Haier Prodigy Mini-washer	X			X			
GE USM				X		X	
CIMC Reefer				X			X
BYD Battery core						X	X

suppliers for bicycle and motorcycle, China's e-bike companies (i.e. Luyuan, Yadea, Aima, etc.) were able to purchase modularized parts in the market and put together cheap but good enough e-bikes, which slowly become substitutes for bikes and motorcycles for Chinese consumers.

Third, *drastic manufacturing cost reduction* refers to a collection of re-engineering processes that replace sophisticated expensive machinery with self-invented procedures, expensive raw material/parts with slightly lower performance but much lower cost, and fast expansion of business scale to push the cost further down. We observe this strategy being used in many cases in this chapter – one in India (Suzlon wind turbine) and the rest in China (i.e. Galanz microwave oven, CIMC reefer, and BYD battery core). In most of these cases, *drastic manufacturing cost reduction* helped to bring down the cost of the end products to an ultra-low level that made all the incumbents' products uncompetitive and enabled the latecomers to dominate the local and eventually the global markets.

In addition, to meet the needs of these people and stay functional in such a context, some products and services have to be redeveloped from scratch by using the limited resources available in these environments. That is why *frugal engineering* is the most-used DI strategy among all seven strategies in the emerging markets. Furthermore, although most companies in China and India are latecomers in existing industries, they may not necessarily be at a disadvantageous position. The mature supplier networks built on the OEM businesses for the multinational companies in the past few decades now provide opportunities to local firms to pursue *modularization*, which, if used well in an open architectural design, can create humble innovations and generate great disruptive impact on the old industry. Finally, the low cost and cheap price were no longer simply based on cheap labor from these countries. It was the relentless R&D force and the ambitious expanding speed of many businesses that made the *drastic manufacturing cost reduction* possible.

The strategies for emerging markets elaborated on in this section seem to be simple but not necessarily easy to implement. For instance, to be able to apply the three cost innovation DI strategies, a company will need a thorough understanding of the customers, the environment, and the available solutions in the market that are cheap enough and hence can be used to substitute for certain parts in the design.

Conclusion

In this chapter, we have discussed the strategic purpose of developing technology candidates or options to facilitate the creation of potential technological DI. For developed markets, we have discussed four unique R&D strategies distilled from extensive case studies of well-known applications; they could be used either individually or in combination to purposefully create disruptive technology candidates. They are miniaturization, simplification, augmentation, and exploitation for another application. Consciously adopting these four R&D strategies would help more firms to become disruptors. However, the R&D strategies are not intended to be prescriptive, and no "one" or "best" strategy exists. Rather, managers may use them as input for their own strategy-crafting efforts or as tools to benchmark their own efforts.

In addition, policy implications were discussed for the four R&D strategies. For example, firms in consumer electronics and the healthcare industry could apply the miniaturization strategy to create more potential DI by leveraging the progress in microelectronics and nanotechnologies. Universities and research institutes can simplify their high-end technologies and transfer these technologies to SMEs, which may create technological DI and achieve a win-win situation for both universities and industry. Incumbent firms are advised to consider more favorably the augmentation strategy, as they do not need to totally abandon the existing sustaining technology.

Finally, exploitation for another application strategy has been underutilized in the past, yet can be used more frequently with ongoing theory improvement in text mining and patent mapping.

For emerging markets, three out of the four R&D strategies used in advanced markets have been found to be applicable. They are miniaturization, simplification, and exploitation for another market. In addition, another three unique DI strategies have been identified, namely *frugal engineering, modularization*, and *drastic manufacturing cost reduction*. Although these results will need further examination and hence would remain as propositions, we have drawn some implications based on the frequencies of their utilization for practitioners.

When implementing these six R&D strategies for DI in emerging markets, it is also important to pay attention to the full user context, develop local capabilities to ensure an acceptable price/performance ratio, and understand the needed long-term R&D effort to maintain the disruptive advantage. Being sensitive to user context would help to discover the opportunities often associated with an underdeveloped infrastructure in emerging markets.

Through this chapter, we hope to raise further interest from academia, industry, and governments to promote and develop disruptive innovations in both the advanced and the emerging markets.

Note

1 http://en.wikipedia.org/wiki/Frugal_innovation, last accessed on March 11, 2017.

References

Bower, J. L. and Christensen, C. M. (1995). Disruptive technologies: catching the wave. *Harvard Business Review*, 73(1), 43–53.

Chesbrough, H. (2003). *Open innovation: the new imperative for creating and profiting from technology*. Boston, MA: Harvard Business School Press.

Christensen, C. M. (1997). *The innovator's dilemma: when new technologies cause great firms to fail*. Boston, MA: Harvard Business School Press.

Christensen, C. M. and Raynor, M. (2003). *The innovator's solution*. Boston, MA: Harvard Business School Press, 2003.

Govindarajan, V. And Kopalle, P. K. (2006). Disruptiveness of innovations: measurement and assessment of reliability and validity. *Strategic Management Journal*, 27, 189–199.

Hang, C. C., Chen, J. and Subramanian, A. M. (2010). Developing disruptive products for emerging markets: lessons from Asian cases. *Research-Technology Management*, July–August, 21–26.

Hang, C. C. and Ruan, Y. (2018). Disruptive innovation in emerging markets: strategies used in India and China. Accepted for publication by the Special Issue of the *Chinese FEM-Innovation Management Journal*.

Hart, S. L. and Christensen, C. M. (2002). The great leap: driving innovation from the base of the pyramid. *MIT Sloan Management Review*, 51–56.

Immelt, J. R., Govindarajan, V. and Trimble, C. (2009). How GE is disrupting itself. *Harvard Business Review*, 87(10), 56–65.

Inkpen, A. and Ramaswami, K. (2006). *Global strategy: creating and sustaining advantage across borders*. Oxford: Oxford University Press.

Kostoff, R. N., Boylan, R. and Simons, G. R. (2004). Disruptive technology roadmaps. *Technological Forecasting Social Change*, 71(1), 141–159.

Leifer, R., McDermott, C. M., O'Connor, G. C., Perters, L. S. and Rice, M. (2000). *Radical innovation*. Boston, MA: Harvard Business School Press.

Linton, J. D. (2009). De-babelizing the language of innovation. *Technovation*, 29(11), 729–737.

London, T. and Hart, S. (2004). Reinventing strategies for emerging markets: beyond the transnational model. *Journal of International Business Studies*, 35(4), 49–63.

Nayak, R. And Ketteringham, J. M. (1994). *Breakthroughs*. San Diego: Pfeiffer and Co.

Prahalad, C. K. (2004). *The fortune at the bottom of the pyramid: eradicating poverty through profits*. New Jersey: Wharton School Publishing.

Ray, S. and Ray, P. K. (2011). Product innovation for the people's car in an emerging economy. *Technovation*, 31(5–6), 216–227.

Sanchez, R. and Hang, C. C. (2017). Modularity in new market formation: lessons for technology and economic policy and competence-based strategic management. *Research in Competence-based Management*, 8, 131–165.

Utterback, J. M. and Acee, H. J. (2005). Disruptive technologies: an expanded view. *International Journal of Innovation Management*, 9(1), 1–17.

Yoon, B., Phaal, R. and Probert, D. (2008). Morphology analysis for technology roadmapping: application of text mining. *R&D Management*, 38(1), 51–68.

Yu, D. and Hang, C. C. (2011). Creating technology candidates for disruptive innovation: generally applicable R&D strategies. *Technovation*, 31(8), 401–410, 2011.

Zeng, M. and Williamson, J. P. (2007). *Dragons at your door: how Chinese cost innovation is disrupting global competition*. Cambridge, MA: Harvard Business School Press.

12
SMART PROTOTYPING

Fei Yu and Bastian Enste

Introduction

Prototyping, as a central part of the innovation process (Rothwell, 1994), is one of the most critical activities in new product development (NPD) (Wall, Ulrich, and Flowers, 1992). It allows one to assess and to overcome uncertainties of future products (Wang, Guan, and Zhao, 2004; Zhang, Vonderembse, and Cao, 2009), and a good use of prototypes increases the speed to market of the products (Chen, Reilly, and Lynn, 2005). Today, many industries are facing the challenges of increasing competition, shorter product life cycles, changing customer demands and fast technology innovations (Liao and Tu, 2007). In such an environment, a highly efficient prototyping process is crucial to overcoming these challenges that could ensure the speed to market and increase successfulness (Tennyson, McCain, Hatten, and Eggert, 2006).

The modern NPD process is complicated and often requires cross-disciplinary collaboration, especially in prototyping, which contains intensive human-involved activities. It will be important and valuable to have a clearly described prototyping framework to support product design (Menold, Jablokow, and Simpson, 2017). There is often no common understanding of prototyping and the prototyping process. The use of prototypes and prototyping activities can be very different as well (Yu, Pasinelli, and Brem, 2017). The prototyping efforts in design are focused on learning and envisioning solutions (Lim, Stolterman, and Tenenberg, 2008), discovering new opportunities (Dow, Heddleston, and Klemmer, 2009), generating and refining design (Buxton, 2007), experiencing the tangible feeling and discussing with the users (Houde and Hill, 1997), and involving them in the NPD process (Hillgren, Seravalli, and Emilson, 2011). In a technical context, a prototype represents a preliminary version of a product or product component (Warfel, 2009). It focuses more on the product performance and quality, product life cycle, and manufacturability.

Artificial intelligence (AI) technology has gone through dramatic developments in recent years. Several companies have developed and provide platforms and tools for AI applications – for example, Google Tensorflow, Amazon AWS, and Microsoft Azure. The technology barriers have decreased significantly, which makes AI available for nonexperts.

In this chapter, we introduce a smart prototyping concept, which we define as an AI-based approach to support prototyping processes and activities. The chapter presents preliminary AI models to support smart prototyping based on prototyping criteria from previous prototyping literature (Filippi and Barattin, 2014). Four different machine learning algorithms are used in the model for data analysis. Workshops have been designed and used for data collection. By defining and prioritizing the prototyping criteria, the model can generate frameworks and suggestions for the selection of the prototyping process and activities. In the next section, we will present a brief overview of prototyping studies around the following three questions: What is a prototype? What are the materials, tools, and technologies used for prototyping? And what are the efforts related to smart prototyping? Then we introduce the methods used in this study and the development of the AI-based model. Conclusions and future research are presented in the following sections.

Brief overview of the literature

What is a prototype?

Prototypes are used in many fields. To answer this question, we need to know who are we asking of? The definition of a prototype varies among disciplines. The expectation of what a prototype is can be a foam model for industrial designers, a simulation of appearance and behavior for interaction designers, a test program for software developers (Houde and Hill, 1997), and a breadboard circuit for electronic engineers. These different definitions also have different levels of scope. Naumann and Jenkins (1982) state that a prototype system "captures the essential features of a later system" (p. 30). This is based on an engineering perspective that focuses on features and functions. This is in line with the definition by Warfel (2009), who states that a prototype represents a preliminary version of a product or product component. The purpose of a prototype is to gain information about the final product in terms of performance, quality, life cycle, and manufacturability (Warfel, 2009). Houde and Hill (1997) define a prototype as "any representation of a design idea – regardless of medium", and the authors further clarify that "designers are the people who create them – regardless of their job titles" (p. 3). It is a broad definition from the design perspective. Thus, the purpose of a prototype is not limited, but rather focuses on the front end of the process (i.e. represents an idea no matter if the idea leads to any products).

Another definition of a prototype is "an approximation of a product (or system) or its components in some form for a definite purpose in its implementation" (Chua, Leong, and Lim, 2010, p. 2). A prototype is not limited to a physical form. It could be a sketch, a CAD model, a mathematical model, or a functional or physical approximation. The use of a prototype is very flexible, but the authors emphasize that there should be a defined purpose. Prototypes also exist in software development to demonstrate concepts or to find new ways to solve problems (Sommerville, 2011). In contrast, Beaudouin-Lafon and Mackay (2003) define a prototype as "a concrete representation of a part or all of an interactive system" (p. 1007). In this definition, a prototype should be a tangible artifact that is used to envision and reflect on the final system.

Prototyping is then the process of realizing, analyzing, and testing these prototypes (Chua, Leong, and Lim, 2010). In a recent study, Menold, Jablokow, and Simpson (2017) asked 194 design students to define prototyping in their own words, which generated five categories: "Model to Link, Model to Test, Model to Communicate, Model to Decide, and Model to Interact" (p. 82). This reveals the different understandings and uses of a prototype in the same discipline. Thus, we need to understand and respect that prototyping is a complex process and there are differences in the purpose of a prototype.

Prototypes have a variable range of fidelity from low to high (McCurdy et al., 2006). The fidelity normally increases along with the progress of NPD (Exner, Damerau, and Stark, 2016), but there are also pieces of evidence showing the nonlinearity of the process; for example, lower-fidelity prototypes can also be used in the later prototyping phase where a number of high-fidelity prototypes have been developed and tested (Yu, Pasinelli, and Brem, 2017). Ulrich and Eppinger (2011) use alpha and beta prototypes to describe the early prototypes for testing whether the product works as designed and the later prototypes for testing the performance and the reliability, respectively. Depending on the context, prototypes are also called mock-ups, solid images, concepts, or models.

In this chapter, we use the broad definition in that there is no limitation on the form of a prototype, but the purpose of a prototype has to be clear (Chua, Leong, and Lim, 2010). We consider all the artifacts created during the process after the ideation and before the manufacturing (Rothwell, 1994) as prototypes. The study focuses on the development of prototypes for new physical products.

What are the prototyping materials, tools, and technologies?

There can be many different approaches and materials used for prototyping. Different tools and materials can be selected according to different prototyping phases (Yu, Pasinelli, and Brem, 2017). Low-fidelity materials, which are cheap, easy, or faster to handle, are often used in the early prototyping phases. Compared to complex prototypes, simple ones are often more successful (Yang, 2005). Designers are normally open to a wide range of low-fidelity materials (Yu, Pasinelli, and Brem, 2017), for example, clay, foam, or cardboard. They use the materials to quickly demonstrate and verify the physical forms of the prototype. There are a few examples that break the technology barrier between the disciplines. littleBits is a library of discrete electronic components pre-assembled in small circuit boards (Bdeir, 2009). After they were invented and launched in the market by Bdeir (2009), the early-phase prototyping process was disrupted. Developers with or without an electronic background can easily envision electronic features, which are normally developed in a later prototyping phase. This breaks the technology barrier that only engineers can make sophisticated circuits. Developers from other disciplines, and even users, can implement the electronic features in prototypes, and they can do it very quickly in the early phase. This disruptive technology makes it possible to test the features earlier, thus the prototyping speed is increased. Arduino is a well-known electronic platform based on easy-to-use hardware and software. It makes access to an embedded system much easier, although it still requires the developers to have a certain level of skill. For complicated tasks, a more powerful platform (Raspberry Pi) is often used by developers.

Digital tools, such as 3D computer-aided design (CAD) and simulation software, are adopted to flesh out the details and test the features. They are often applied in the middle phase. A virtual prototype is a computer simulation of the prototype in a digital version, which can be used for not only the evaluation of the physical form but also testing the functions (Yang, 2005). It can provide valuable feedback. The failures can be discovered before any expensive and time-intensive process is undertaken. It also helps the cross-disciplinary team members to have a better understanding of the product; thus, it improves the communication, efficiency, and productivity in the development process (Zorriassatine, Wykes, Parkin, and Gindy, 2003). The visual prototype can be used to evaluate the product for the manufacturing process. This can avoid poor planning in design and fabrication, which saves resources and reduces the amount of iterations of physical prototypes (Choi and Chan, 2004; Liu, Campbell, and Pei, 2013)

Generative design is "a designer driven, parametrically constrained design exploration process, operating on top of history based parametric CAD systems structured to support design as an emergent process"(Krish, 2011). It could produce efficient and buildable designs automatically based on the defined targets and constraints. With the adoption of topology optimization, generative designs can significantly reduce the complexity and the weight of the designed object. It frees the designers from the designing process, so they can focus more on creativity, as well as identifying the correct constraints (Jiang, Chen, Sadasivan, and Jiao, 2017). A number of studies have shown the value of a generative design approach in different disciplines. In the biomedical field, Jiang, Chen, Sadasivan, and Jiao (2017) used topology optimization for generative designs of personal aneurysm implants. Krish (2011) demonstrated the applications for consumer products. Troiano and Birtolo (2014) presented the genetic algorithms for supporting the generative design of user interfaces. Shea, Aish, and Gourtovaia (2005) combined a generative structural design system with an associative modeling system and applied it in the civil engineering field of designing an architectural structure. This is one of the first few attempts at generative design in academia. Today generative design functions are available in CAD software (e.g. AutoDesk Fusion 360 and Siemens NX). It becomes much easier to apply this approach in engineering design. Figure 12.1 shows an example of a generative design model. On the left image is an ordinary table we created in AutoDesk Fusion 360. By defining the constraint of the pressure on top and applying a generative design algorithm, the system generated a model as shown in the right image. Compared with the original table, the new one remains the same constraint but reduces the weight significantly. The generative design approach is a great step in smart prototyping with the adoption of computer-aided systems in prototyping activities. Applying it in combination with rapid prototyping technology will create a revolutionary impact on product development, manufacturing, and even changing consumer behavior.

Rapid prototyping (RP) keeps our attention in both the academia and the industry since the first commercial stereolithography was introduced by 3D Systems. It is a prototyping and manufacturing technique that refers to the fabrication of a physical model layer by layer based on a predesigned 3D CAD model. There are several commercially available PR technologies, such as stereolithography apparatus (SLA), laser engineered net shaping (LENS), selective laser sintering (SLS), three-dimensional printing (3DP), fused deposition modeling (FDM), and laminated object manufacturing (LOM) (Vimal, Vinodh, Brajesh, and Muralidharan, 2016). Depending on the technology, different raw materials can be applied for the 3D printing of the model, such as ABS (acrylonitrile butadiene styrene), PLA (polylactic acid), wood-based filaments, metal-filled filaments, and nylon. The form of the raw materials can be wire, powder, liquid, ink, or gas. According to the specification of the selected RP process, the printed prototypes have a variety of properties, and the production speed and cost can be very different as well.

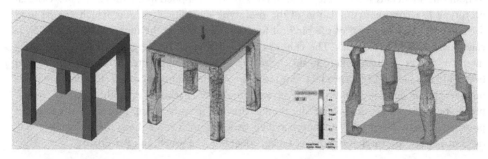

Figure 12.1 From left to right: Original design of the table; define constraint and apply generative design algorithm; generative design model

The RP process is a fast-growing technology that reduces prototyping and tool-making time (Drizo and Pegna, 2006). On one hand, new materials are tested and used for 3D printing. On the other hand, the quality of the models improves, while increasing production speed and lowering production cost. The use of RP is not only for developing prototypes but also as a production technique directly providing end-use products. Additive manufacturing (AM) evolved from RP with the focus on manufacturing and has been adopted by many industrial applications. Although AM is still being researched in most industries, this new processing technology has the potential of bringing a revolutionary change to the traditional manufacturing world due to its ability to build a freeform model – especially those models created by generative design that were not possible to be produced before, or at least at significantly higher cost.

What are the efforts related to smart prototyping?

There are numerous studies about prototyping frameworks, prototyping strategies, and selection of prototyping processes. The goal is to support prototyping processes and activities in terms of situation-based selection of the efficient prototyping process, increasing the effectiveness and efficiency of design teams, and increasing the desirability of products (Menold, Jablokow, and Simpson, 2017). To have a better understanding and holistic description of these efforts, we introduce a smart prototyping concept, defined as an AI-based approach to support prototyping processes and activities. In this section, we select a few outstanding examples that relate to smart prototyping.

Selection of RP process

One of the focused areas is the selection of the RP process. As presented in the previous section, many different RP approaches are available. How to select a proper RP process that fulfills the production requirements has been an interesting research area in prototyping studies for years. Several traditional constraints should be considered, including the use of materials, operating cost, post-processing requirements, speed, surface finish, etc. (Drizo and Pegna, 2006). In addition, environmental criteria like human health, environment, natural energy and resource, such as disposal of the wasted product, the toxicity of material, and energy consumption, are also applied in the selection algorithm (Vimal, Vinodh, Brajesh, and Muralidharan, 2016). A number of AI-based tools are used to select an RP process, for example, modified technique for order preference by similarity to an ideal solution (TOPSIS) (Byun and Lee, 2005), graph theory and matrix approach (Rao and Padmanabhan, 2007), analytic hierarchy process (AHP) (Armillotta, 2008), a rule-based expert system (Masood and Soo, 2002), and a rule-based expert system in combination with a fuzzy inference system (Munguia and Riba, 2008).

Byun and Lee (2006) use three factors to determine the optimal part-oriented RP process: surface quality, build time, and part cost. Surface quality is estimated according to the surface roughness and the contact area of support materials. Build time consists of three elements: data preparation time, part build time, and post-processing time. Part cost is calculated based on the labor time, build time, the volume of both, part material, and support material. Material loss is also considered. The simple additive weighting method is used for decision-making (Byun and Lee, 2006). Rao and Padmanabhan (2007) propose a "rapid prototyping process selection index" and use a matrix-based approach to evaluate and rank the RP processes, including SLA, SLS, FDM, LOM, Quadra, and 3DP. Traditional criteria, including dimensional accuracy of the part, surface roughness of the part, tensile strength, elongation, part cost, and build time, are considered in the algorithm (Rao and Padmanabhan, 2007). In another approach, the adaptive AHP decision model is applied to the RP process selection (Armillotta, 2008). The author provides 16 alternatives to tools and processes and considers 11 factors in the algorithm concerning final prototype properties, system usage, and process cost. In a recent study, Vimal, Vinodh, Brajesh, and Muralidharan (2016) present a conceptual model applying fuzzy analytic network process – TOPSIS-based hybrid methodology to compute criterion weights and use for process ranking. In addition to 16 traditional criteria, the authors select nine environmental criteria for the selection of RP processes. Furthermore, the authors develop a decision support system to save mathematical computation resources.

Prototyping framework

Compared to the numerous efforts on RP process selection, there are much fewer studies supporting general prototyping processes and activities. A possible reason could be the wide range of prototyping processes available – it is fuzzy to have one guideline to support prototyping activities across all disciplines. However, there is extraordinary work that attempts to provide systematic approaches to structure prototyping. Camburn et al. (2015) provide a systematic approach for design prototyping. By identifying the practices that improve prototyping, the authors found six key specific process variables: number of iterations, number of parallel concepts, use of scaling, use of subsystem isolation, use of requirement relaxation, and use of virtual prototypes. The method is correlated with improved outcome assessments, including prototype performance, time to build, cost, and adherence to suggested approach (Camburn et al., 2015). Menold, Jablokow, and Simpson (2017) introduce a holistic prototyping framework, Prototype for X. Based on a systematic review of prototyping research in many disciplines, the authors summarize three major functions of prototypes and four specifications for a holistic and structured prototyping framework. Figure 12.2 shows the Prototype for X structure. The first three goals (i.e. Prototyping for Feasibility, Prototyping for Viability, and Prototyping for Desirability) are designed to integrate human-centered design with a resource-, time-, and function-focused design (Menold, Jablokow, and Simpson, 2017). Filippi and Barattin (2014)

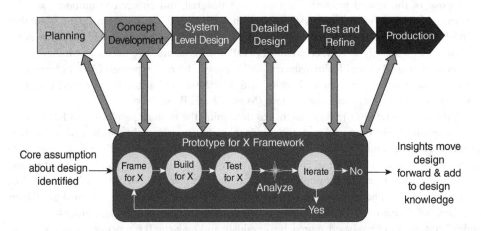

Figure 12.2 Prototyping for X structure and integration into the design process

Source: Menold, Jablokow, and Simpson (2017, p. 86)

classify prototyping activities from a new perspective that five classes of prototyping activities are described in four dimensions (see Figure 12.3). The fifth dimension, time, is not presented in the figure to avoid time-dependent classification. The authors further suggest 11 prototyping situation indices to support the selection of prototyping activities, including direct interaction, physical feedback, total feedback, real environment, error recognition and recovery, functions required, prototype change flexibility, budget, time, human operators, and tolerances (Filippi and Barattin, 2014).

From the overview in the literature, we learn about the complexity of prototyping. The differences across disciplines are the definition of a prototype, the use of a prototype, and the approach and material for prototyping. There have been a lot of efforts to increase effectiveness and decrease uncertainty during the design process. AI-based techniques have been applied to support decision-making for the selection of RP processes, but they are not data-driven approaches, and an AI system is still missing that can support general prototyping processes and activities, even though great efforts have been made to provide holistic and systematic prototyping frameworks. This study attempts to develop an AI-based, data-driven system to support prototyping process and activity selections. In our preliminary setup, we use Filippi and Barattin's (2014) 11 prototyping situation indices as the prototyping parameters to determine the prototyping activities.

Research approach

This study is an attempt to deploy smart prototyping into a professional environment by developing an AI-based system that provides recommendations for selecting the most appropriate prototyping activity based on a given input. To achieve the goal, there are three major steps in the method. First, based on a literature survey, identify the key prototyping variables that can be used as the input to the system. Second, we need to collect data to train and validate the AI model. An experimental research was designed for data collection. 70 percent and 30 percent of the data were used for training and validation, respectively. The next section describes the data collection approach in detail. Then, we selected and applied four different AI models for the smart prototyping system. The performances of each model are analyzed and compared in the fifth section.

Data collection

Theory of experimental research

We chose experimental research as the approach for data collection. The aim of conducting experiments is to find causation, which we can use to predict phenomena in the future. Assuming the hypothesis is based on correct assumptions, a laboratory or artificial experiment makes it possible to carefully observe the effects of chosen independent variables while excluding external unwanted or irrelevant factors (Webster and Sell, 2014). The outcome of the study is thereby replicable and invites other researchers to adopt the research design to gather additional data that further support the research objective.

Further advantages that benefit the research are the ability to create very special environmental conditions while running the tests. This minimizes all eventual environmental variables that could normally influence the measurable outcome. The biggest potential disadvantage of conducting the research in the form of a laboratory experiment is the danger of generalization based on nonprobability samples (Cooper and Schindler, 2003).

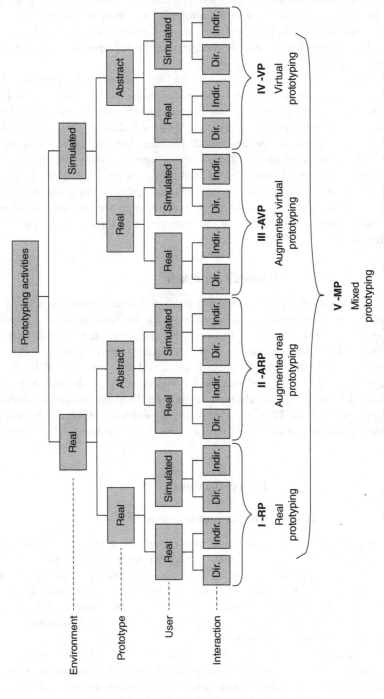

Figure 12.3 Classification of prototyping activities
Source: Filippi and Barattin (2014, p. 3)

Smart prototyping

For the research to capitalize on the advantages and minimize the disadvantages of the chosen method, the experiment must possess certain properties that are crucial to its success. It is necessary to wisely choose the participants for the experiment. While the participating groups should be as homogenous as possible regarding age, background, and education, as this fosters communication within the groups during the experiment, it is also important to eliminate people who are unlikely to contribute towards the discussion or may disrupt other participants (Greenbaum, 1997). Also, the facilities in which the experiment is conducted must be chosen wisely. The chosen room must offer enough space for all participants to work freely, while they must have equal access to given introductions and material (Greenbaum, 1997). This further supports the idea of minimizing the effects of external and environmental factors into the experiment.

To lower the chance of false generalization from the research's findings, randomization in the form of control groups is used to counteract a possible selection bias. Said bias can be entirely removed if the participants are randomly assigned into a treatment group, which is subject to the changing independent variable, and a control group which is not (Duflo, Glennerster, and Kremer, 2008). Doing this will eliminate as many confounding factors within the experiment as possible, that is, the problem of mixing the exposure of interest with other effects of external variables (Van Stralen, Dekker, Zoccali, and Jager, 2010). Lastly, the experiment is meticulously monitored and recorded by the facilitators so that all events can be analyzed by and shared with other researchers who want to comprehend or re-enact the observation.

Taking the previously made points into consideration, a fitting experimental design must be selected. Making an optimal choice here means keeping the balance between factors such as given constraints, making sure that changes in the dependent variables are truly due to changes within independent variables, and strengthening the generalizability of the study's results. Experiments put a further emphasis on matters such as randomization and control groups (Pruzan, 2016), which will highly influence the choice of the design, as can be seen in Figure 12.4.

The idea of the two-group simple randomized design is to randomly assign members of a sample of the population into either an experimental or a control group. The two groups are given different treatments of the chosen independent variable. The benefits can be seen in comparing them to the specifications declared earlier: the chosen design is simple, contains control groups, and therefore allows randomization of the individual differences between members of the sample. The limitations of this method lie mainly in the fact that external factors or influences of those conducting the research are not eliminated, which might influence the result of the experiment (Kothari, 2004).

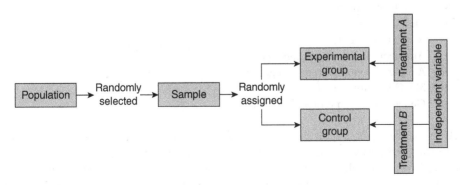

Figure 12.4 Two-group simple randomized experimental design (in diagram form)

The following subsection will explain the final setup of the experiment and how it meets all the previously given requirements.

Experimental setup

The following experimental setup was arranged according to the previously presented two-group simple randomized design. The following requirements must be fulfilled throughout the entire experimental process:

- All relevant results and outcomes must be documented.
- The group of participants is homogeneous and on the same knowledge level regarding the chosen activities.
- Control groups are created, and the experiment is randomized.
- Half of the exercises should be practical, while the other half should be theoretically studied.

The experiment as stated was held in the form of a prototyping workshop that lasted 120 minutes. The period is divided into three steps are described as follows.

1) All participants of the workshop were asked to fill out a questionnaire regarding their previous experiences with prototyping. The selected questions were:

    - How would you describe the experiences you have had regarding prototyping during past or current projects?
    - How much time have you spent on prototyping compared to the whole project duration?
    - Have you ever had problems with deciding on a prototyping activity within your group work?

    The written answers should be given rather quickly and, most importantly, truthfully. The gained information can be used to assess the general experience and knowledge of the contestants regarding prototyping.

2) All participants of the workshop cycle through nine individual stations in which they will experience individual prototyping activities in either a practical or theoretical way. The chosen activities are listed here, while the tasks can be found in the appendix:

    - Paper prototyping
    - Breadboard prototyping
    - Low-fidelity prototyping
    - Quick prototyping
    - Rapid prototyping
    - Augmented real prototyping
    - Augmented virtual prototyping
    - 3D/CAD prototyping
    - Generative design prototyping

After completing each individual task, the participants fill out a form in which they must assess each activity based on 11 descriptive parameters for prototyping activities (Filippi and Barattin, 2014) with values between 0 and 10. Figure 12.5 shows the prototyping activity assessment form. For the participants to rate the prototyping activities as precisely as possible,

Direct interaction between prototype and user	Physical feedback	Additional total feedback (visual, audio, etc.)	Real environment in which the prototype is placed	Error recognition and recovery implemented in the prototype	Functions required in the prototype	Change flexibility	Budget	Time	Human operators required for the prototype to function	Tolerances required in the prototype	Prototyping activity
											Paper prototyping
											Breadboard prototyping
											Low-fidelity prototyping (marshmallow, spaghetti, balloons, etc.)
											Quick prototyping (wood, foam, metal, plastic)
											Rapid prototyping
											Augmented real prototyping
											Augmented virtual prototyping
											CAD/3D prototyping
											Generative prototyping

Figure 12.5 Prototyping activity assessment form

it was necessary to agree on a description of each individual activity to align knowledge and previously gained experience. The initial focus of the chosen prototyping activities was on early product development stages in which the emphasis is on exploring and testing new features or designs. Therefore, the aim of all activities is a quick and easy implementation of ideas into physical or virtual models so that a direct interaction with users can provide valuable insights.

- **Paper prototyping** is an activity commonly used within the field of user-centered design in which the prototype or interface is created solely from painted paper or printed paper, all in 2D.
- **Breadboard prototyping** allows the user to quickly prototype features and functions of electrical systems on a breadboard without permanently tying them to each other.
- **Low-fidelity prototyping** is used in ideation or very early stages of product development to test possible and/or relevant features using cheap and easy-to-access materials. In this case, we provide materials such as balloons, straws, tape, etc.
- **Quick prototyping** is mainly used for design prototypes. Concept ideas or later designs are prototyped using materials such as foam, plastic, or wood, which are easy to form and adapt.
- **Rapid prototyping** utilizes additive manufacturing techniques such as 3D printing to quickly create prototypes previously designed in CAD software.
- **Augmented real prototyping** places an abstract or virtual prototype within a real environment.
- **Augmented virtual prototyping** places a real prototype within a virtual or computer-generated environment.
- **CAD/3D prototyping** creates a purely virtual and computer-generated prototype using CAD software such as Autodesk or Siemens NX.
- **Generative design prototyping** uses simulation abilities within CAD programs to generate designs that satisfy predefined constraints.

A control group that did not previously cycle through the activities was asked to assess the same activities based on 11 parameters. This had the purpose of seeing if the collected data are comparable to that collected during the workshop and if the experiment is transferable to a rather impersonal, survey-based approach for greater data collection. Furthermore, we hereby achieve a certain degree of randomization throughout the experiment, which was one of our requirements.

The second requirement, homogeneity within the participant base, must be fulfilled to minimize the effects of confounding within the experiment. All participants must fulfill the following requirements:

- Same age range
- Same educational background
- Same educational level
- Experience within group and project work

Figure 12.6 presents the general experimental research process. We recruited 17 engineering students with prototyping experience for the experiment. Eleven students were assigned randomly to participate in the workshop, while the remaining four students were in the control group.

Smart prototyping

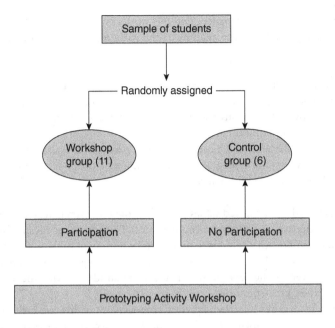

Figure 12.6 Chosen experimental design

Table 12.1 Experiment participant data

	Average age	*Average BIS-11*
Treatment group (11)	25.63	71.72
Control group (6)	22.66	69.33

For an initial assessment of the participant group, all participants were asked to fill out the Barrett Impulsiveness Scale (BIS-11) (Patton, Stanford, and Barratt, 1995) to assess their impulsiveness. Table 12.1 shows the average age and the BIS-11 results of both groups.

Findings

All participants of the study teamed up into smaller groups and accomplished all tasks mentioned in the nine stations of prototyping activity. Complex and abstract prototyping activities such as augmented real prototyping, augmented virtual prototyping, and generative design prototyping were not only hard to teach but also especially hard to understand and assess for the participants without the necessary technical setup and experience. Nevertheless, a mixture of the supplied material and efforts by the facilitator (see appendix) could make it accessible to the participants. Simpler and more practical activities such as paper prototyping, breadboard prototyping, and low-fidelity prototyping were much easier to assess for the participants since they could rely on the previous experiences from other projects or work, but also because the general interaction with the individual activity was more carefree and "fun".

After the workshop, all participants filled out the questionnaire regarding the assessment of prototyping activities. From the analysis of the gathered data, two conclusions could be drawn:

- The assessment of the treatment group and the control group, which was not present during the workshop, gave very similar values to each of the tested parameters of each prototyping activity. This means that upscaling the data collection to a survey is possible to shorten the data collection time.
- Table 12.2 shows all the gathered data from the 17 participants. A dataset of 153 samples was collected. For every prototyping activity, the arithmetic mean and the standard deviation were calculated and added to each row.

The two calculated and extracted values for each of the nine parameters of every prototyping activity are the respective mean and standard deviation. The arithmetic mean of each parameter provides insights into how the different activities differ from each other when examining them on a more in-depth level. This is used to give an understanding of why a certain prototyping activity is chosen over another one in specific cases and an idea of what the machine learning models will base their predictions on.

A small standard deviation hereby expresses homogeneity within the collected data, which will further improve the performance of the models, as rank-breaking values will lower their accuracy and make predictions more random.

Development of the AI-based system

Having the data gathered from the pilot study, the next step is to extract relevant information, insights, and knowledge. We follow the three steps of data science for data examination: exploration, visualization, and prediction.

In the initial step of exploration, it is important to get familiar with the collected data. While accessing the overall amount, it is hereby key to only select features that are beneficial for predicting our outputs. A deeper understanding, especially for external observers and interested parties, is generated and transferred by visualizing the data and their correlations in a graphical way. By doing this, predictions can often already be made with the naked eye. The final step is the application of different machine and/or deep learning algorithms that gradually learn from the data, which gives them the ability to make predictions for future inputs.

Data exploration

The information that can be gathered in the exploration phase is mostly about the data's composition. A sample from the dataset describes an individual prototyping activity using only integer values between 0 and 10. Table 12.2 further tells us that the standard deviation for each of the parameters is small compared to the overall interval of 10. It shows that the gathered data are homogeneous and not entirely random, as we would not have any possibility for prediction based on randomness.

Early in the analysis process, the examination of the correlation between each of the nine parameters can be a very insightful and helpful step. The correlation of two attributes is a measure of their linear relation. A value close to 1 or -1 signalizes a completely positive or negative

Table 12.2 Arithmetic mean and standard deviation of 17 observations after the experiment

	Phy.feedback	Add.feedback	Environment	Error	Functions	Change	Budget	Time	Tolerances	Activity
Mean	1.82	1.59	4.35	1.65	1.82	8.76	0.41	1.94	1.47	Paper Prototyping
StDev	0.95	1.58	3.14	1.22	1.63	0.97	0.51	1.14	1.01	
Mean	7.65	8.06	4.24	6.94	7.94	8.41	3.29	4.00	2.41	Breadboard Prototyping
StDev	2.71	1.64	2.95	3.01	1.14	2.74	2.14	1.94	2.24	
Mean	8.18	2.82	6.47	2.00	2.47	8.82	1.24	1.82	1.18	Low-Fidelity Prototyping
StDev	1.24	1.13	1.33	1.12	1.07	0.95	0.75	1.01	1.01	
Mean	8.24	2.47	7.76	7.00	2.47	7.18	4.82	6.65	5.82	Quick Prototyping
StDev	1.15	1.42	1.20	1.54	1.07	1.33	1.29	1.66	1.74	
Mean	9.06	2.82	8.06	7.88	6.18	7.06	6.59	5.47	8.47	Rapid Prototyping
StDev	0.97	1.70	1.03	1.05	1.24	1.20	1.80	1.18	1.07	
Mean	1.18	4.12	8.82	7.24	2.71	8.06	3.41	4.35	2.41	Augmented Real Prototyping
StDev	1.67	1.36	0.73	1.09	1.21	1.82	1.06	1.22	1.80	
Mean	1.88	3.29	0.88	5.06	6.53	2.76	7.88	7.00	7.06	Augmented Virtual Prototyping
StDev	2.34	1.61	0.78	1.34	1.50	1.25	1.87	1.77	2.41	
Mean	0.94	4.88	0.76	8.35	7.59	9.47	3.47	6.65	9.12	3D/CAD Prototyping
StDev	1.09	2.39	0.90	1.50	1.54	0.87	1.07	1.50	1.90	
Mean	1.41	4.82	1.41	8.82	8.06	9.06	3.76	7.06	9.47	Generative Design Prototyping
StDev	1.23	3.32	1.18	0.95	1.30	1.30	1.15	2.08	0.72	

linear relation, whereas a value close to 0 indicates no linear correlation. A common formula used to calculate the Pearson correlation is given with (Allen, 2018)

$$r = \frac{\sum XY - \frac{\sum X \sum Y}{N}}{\sqrt{\left(\sum X^2 - \frac{(\sum X)^2}{N}\right)\left(\sum Y^2 - \frac{(\sum Y)^2}{N}\right)}}$$

with r being the correlation coefficient, N the number of samples, and X and Y the two variables.

A strong correlation of several parameters can be seen in Table 12.3. With a value of 0.581, the parameters "Budget" and "Time" are highly correlated, which means that higher financial investments in activities cause a direct increase in time investment. Other highly correlated values are:

- Time   <-> Tolerances   0.630
- Additional total feedback   <-> Functions required   −0.489

Higher negative values signalize an inverse correlation between parameters. Looking at "Real environment" and "Functions required", which carry a value of −0.489, shows that putting higher awareness onto a real environment reduces functions required and implemented into the prototype.

Lastly, values around 0 such as for "Physical feedback" and "Additional total feedback" or "Budget" and "Additional total feedback" can imply independency between two parameters, which needs to be explored further.

Data visualization

The second step of visualizing the data is used to make the collected data more understandable and comprehensible for external viewers. Many of the patterns and relationships of the different parameters which will later be used by the machine learning models can be identified with visualization techniques using different chart or graph types. A promising initial approach to a new and unknown dataset is the creation of a pair plot. The result is a grid showing a coordinate system making comparisons of every feature. By color-coding each individual prototyping activity, the observer can recognize features that clearly separate prototyping activities from others. This helps with understanding the decision-making process happening later in the machine learning section.

Figure 12.7 shows an extract of four plots mapping the features "Change flexibility", "Budget", "Physical feedback", and "Additional feedback". Looking at the plot in the top-left corner of "Change flexibility" – "Physical feedback", we can see the separation of the light-grey squares belonging to "Augmented virtual prototyping". The understanding gained from just this step alone would be enough to make the decision for an activity without the use of advanced machine learning models just based on this simple visualization.

A very interesting feature is the "Budget" constraint, as financial investments in the early stages of product development can be crucial. Figure 12.8 shows the distribution plot of the budget feature, which shows how the feature is distributed within the interval of 0 to 10. As the graph shows, the nine chosen prototyping activities were mostly evaluated within the lower half of the spectrum. This further supports that the choice of activities when focusing on early product development stages is backed by the evaluation of the participants. Prototyping activities used so early on should not and cannot produce high financial investments.

Table 12.3 Prototyping data correlation matrix

	Physical feedback	Additional total feedback	Real environment	Error recognition	Functions required	Change flexibility	Budget	Time	Tolerances required
Physical feedback	1.00000	−0.00324	0.41712	−0.03567	−0.09296	−0.04815	0.08272	−0.14829	−0.16270
Additional feedback	−0.00324	1.00000	−0.14845	0.28520	0.45995	0.11186	0.00160	0.14246	0.02679
Real environment	0.41712	−0.14845	1.00000	−0.07759	−0.48874	0.07983	−0.05771	−0.31624	−0.36323
Error recognition	−0.03567	0.28520	−0.07759	1.00000	0.53908	0.06482	0.40622	0.56797	0.59734
Functions required	−0.09296	0.45995	−0.48874	0.53908	1.00000	−0.02957	0.36394	0.43868	0.54121
Change flexibility	−0.05815	0.11186	0.07983	0.06482	−0.02957	1.00000	−0.59031	−0.21991	−0.11504
Budget	0.08272	0.00160	−0.05771	0.40621	0.36394	−0.59031	1.00000	0.58126	0.51576
Time	0.14829	0.14246	−0.31624	0.56797	0.43868	−0.21991	0.58126	1.00000	0.63009
Tolerances required	−0.16270	0.02679	−0.36323	0.59734	0.54121	−0.11504	0.51576	0.63009	1.00000

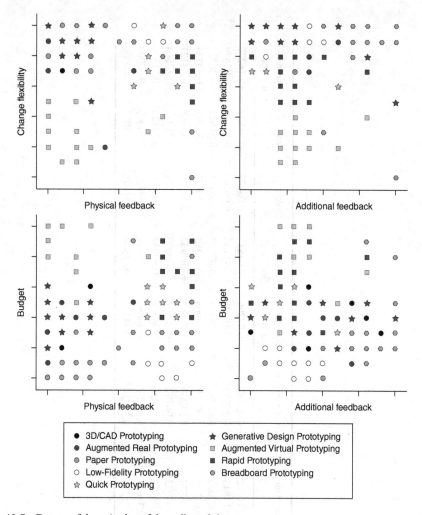

Figure 12.7 Extract of the pair plot of the collected data

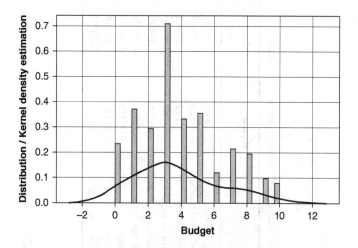

Figure 12.8 Distribution plot of the data

The count plot (Figure 12.9) examines this behavior even more. The count of appearance of every prototyping activity is listed in the graph according to its evaluation based on the "Budget" feature. While the new insights overlap with the ones from the previous graph, it can now be determined which activities were evaluated as outliers in high budget regions and should therefore be excluded from the early development process.

Machine learning algorithms

There is a long list of machine learning algorithms that could be used for this classification problem. With 153 samples gathered, it becomes clear that in particular algorithms that work better with a smaller number of samples such as decision trees or logistic regression might perform very well in the prediction part. To allow an easy approach to the topic, the chosen models are straightforward. The following four algorithms were chosen:

- Decision tree
- K-nearest neighbors
- Logistic regression
- Artificial neural network

Decision trees and K-nearest neighbors models are that are simple to understand and interpret since they resemble the human decision-making process. With them, it is possible to not just view the algorithm as a black box, but rather comprehend how the model performs predictions. Logistic regression utilizes a linear approach by gradually changing variables to model the desired outcome at the best possible rate. Neural networks within the area of deep learning gradually become more and more popular within every application of artificial intelligence, which is why a comparison with traditional algorithms is of interest.

Decision tree

Using the decision tree algorithm for classification purposes is probably one of the most direct approaches in machine learning for labeling data according to its class affiliation. A decision tree consists of several levels, each of which consists of several branches, so-called decision nodes. At each node, the data are split based on certain conditions.

The "smart" component within this algorithm is deciding which parameter is used to split the data. This decision is made based on the information gain that can be acquired from each split. The information gain is a measure of enhancing the entropy or purity of the dataset by splitting and slowly reaching the goal of an accurate prediction (Provost and Fawcett, 2013). The advantages of applying the decision tree algorithm to machine learning problems are diverse. The created models can be applied to classification and regression problems and thus perform well with both small and large datasets (James, Witten, Hastie, and Tibshirani, 2013).

K-nearest neighbors

A secondary simple and intuitive approach is the utilization of the K-nearest neighbors algorithm. K-nearest neighbors is an algorithm that estimates the conditional distribution of all possible classes given the different features and further classifies the observation to the class with the highest probability (James, Witten, Hastie, and Tibshirani, 2013).

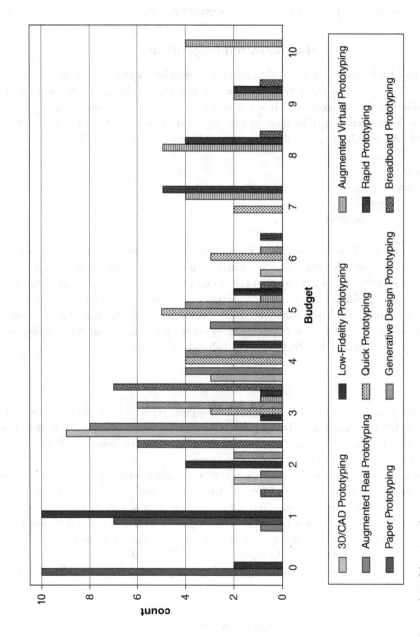

Figure 12.9 Count plot of the given data

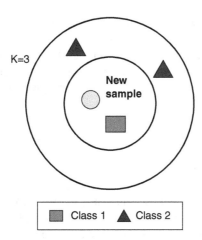

Figure 12.10 K-nearest neighbor classification

After training the model with a chosen integer value for K, the algorithm assigns every new observation O to the class with the biggest resemblance to O. If K is larger than 1, O is assigned to the class that has the most representative data points in the near vicinity, as can be seen in Figure 12.10. It is advisable to iterate through different ascending values for K and choose the value that returns the smallest error on known test data (Cover and Hart, 1967).

Logistic regression

Different from linear regression, in which continuous values are predicted, logistic regression can be used to model the probability of an observation belonging to a particular class. The probability is computed by calculating the log-odds or logit for each observation (Provost and Fawcett, 2013; James, Witten, Hastie, and Tibshirani, 2013):

$$\log\left(\frac{p(X)}{1-p(x)}\right) = \beta_0 + \beta_1 X_1 + \ldots + \beta_n X_n$$

After the beta-coefficients have been computed from the training data, methods such as maximum likelihood analysis can be used so that a new observation will return its class dependency according to the probability given with the formula

$$\hat{p}(X) = \frac{e^{\beta_0 + \beta_1 X_1 + \ldots + \beta_n X_n}}{1 + e^{\beta_0 + \beta_1 X_1 + \ldots + \beta_n X_n}}$$

The graph of the logistic regression curve displays the probability distribution of the data, as the outcome or dependent variable can only take a limited number of possible values between 0 and 1.

Artificial neural network

Artificial neural networks are machine learning models that are modeled after biological neural networks within the human brain. These neural networks consist of several stacked layers with at least one input and output layer and, in the case of deep neural networks, several hidden layers in between, as shown in Figure 12.11.

In each of the individual nodes, all of the input signals are multiplied by individual weights and summed and altered by an activation function such as the sigmoid function to account for nonlinearity (Kröse and Smagt, 1996). The output of a given node for a given input x can hereby be expressed with:

$$O_1 = \sigma(\beta_0 + \beta_1 X_1 + \ldots + \beta_n X_n) = \frac{1}{1 + e^{-(\beta_0 + \beta_1 X_1 + \ldots + \beta_n X_n)}}$$

By using this design, neural networks are able to compute any given function, no matter the complexity (Cybenko, 1989; Hornik, Stinchcombe, and White, 1989). Neural networks learn by using a process called backpropagation (LeCun et al., 1989). As for every given observation the given input and desired output are known, the beta-weights as shown in the equation can be altered and changed, minimizing the error between model output and desired, real output.

The performance of the models

The first step before applying the different machine learning algorithms is splitting the dataset into a training set and a testing set. Seventy percent of the data are randomly selected for training the models, while the model's accuracy is tested on the remaining 30 percent. This is possible since we know the affiliation of each of the samples in the test set.

Applying the first three machine learning algorithms of decision tree, K-nearest neighbors, and logistic regression is simple, as they are part of the scikit-learn library. Importing the relevant model, fitting it to the data, and generating predictions can therefore be achieved with just four lines of code. Figure 12.12 shows an extract of the code for the decision tree classifier.

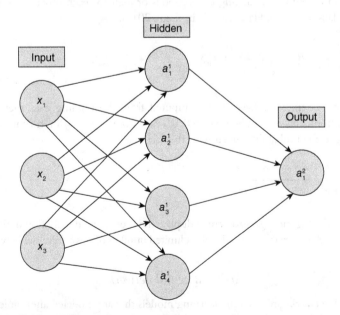

Figure 12.11 Artificial neural network

```
In [8]:  from sklearn.tree import DecisionTreeClassifier

In [9]:  dtree = DecisionTreeClassifier()

In [10]: dtree.fit(X_train,y_train)

Out[10]: DecisionTreeClassifier(class_weight=None, criterion='gini', max_depth=None,
                max_features=None, max_leaf_nodes=None,
                min_impurity_decrease=0.0, min_impurity_split=None,
                min_samples_leaf=1, min_samples_split=2,
                min_weight_fraction_leaf=0.0, presort=False, random_state=None,
                splitter='best')

In [11]: predictions = dtree.predict(X_test)
```

Figure 12.12 Process of importing and fitting the model and generating predictions

The neural network model requires the implementation of additional libraries (Keras and Tensorflow) to make the creation of the network structure more accessible. Keras offers such drastic simplifications that the creation of a multilayer deep network is done by just stacking layer after layer on top of each other. Furthermore, Keras offers tools for hyperparameter optimization, which optimizes the accuracy of the generated predictions.

Certain models even offer an understandable visualization, which helps the human facilitator understand how each individual decision is made. The visualization of the decision tree classifier, shown in Figure 12.13, makes it possible to retrace its decision-making process.

Table 12.4 contains the performance of all four chosen machine learning algorithms. The relevant information is given in a confusion matrix, the classification report and the first five predictions of observations in the testing set.

The tests showed that after applying all four machine learning algorithms, *K*-nearest neighbors performed best on the chosen testing set with precision and recall values of 92 percent and 91 percent, respectively. This good performance is due to the homogeneity of the collected data samples during the workshop. All chosen observations were very close to others of the same class, which explains this behavior.

Having trained several different models, it is now possible to utilize them for prediction purposes. In our case, we can simply create a new list of parameters that we plug into the model. A possible application might be a web application in which the user inputs their desired parameters and the algorithm will suggest the most fitting prototyping activity. Examples are shown in Table 12.5

Discussion and conclusion

Many efforts have focused on the selection of RP processes (Armillotta, 2008; Byun and Lee, 2005; Masood and Soo, 2002; Munguia and Riba, 2008; Rao and Padmanabhan, 2007). Different models have been developed and applied to RP process selection according to predefined criteria. But none of these studies have focused on general prototyping activities. Furthermore, these approaches are not applying data-driven models, that is, the new dataset is not used for training the models to further improve their quality.

Prototyping for X, an outstanding work presented by Menold, Jablokow, and Simpson (2017), is a holistic framework that can help to structure prototyping. It provides different prototyping

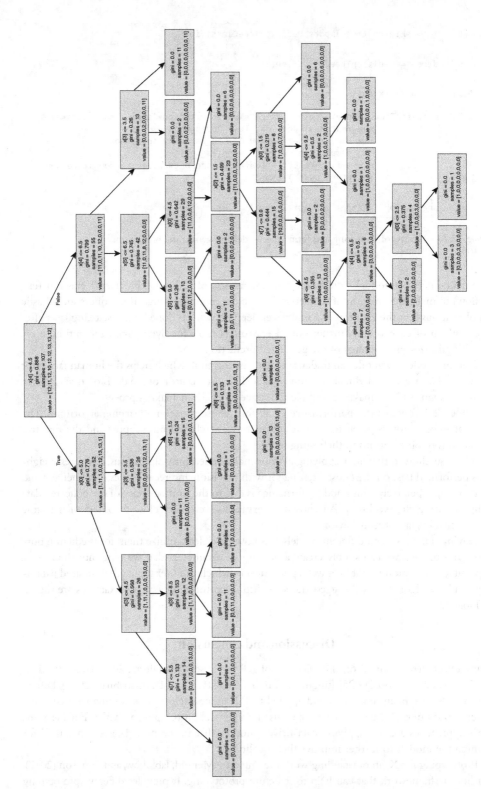

Figure 12.13 Visualization of the decision tree classifier

Table 12.4 Performance of the four machine learning algorithms on the testing set

Machine learning model	Decision trees			K-nearest neighbors (K = 3)			Logistic regression			Neural network		
Confusion matrix	[[4 0 0 0 1 0 0 0 0] [0 4 0 0 0 0 0 1 1] [0 0 4 0 1 0 0 0 0] [0 0 0 6 0 0 0 0 1] [3 0 0 0 2 0 0 0 0] [0 0 0 0 0 5 0 0 0] [0 0 0 0 0 0 3 0 1] [0 0 0 0 0 1 0 3 0] [0 0 0 0 0 0 0 0 5]]			[[3 0 0 0 2 0 0 0 0] [0 5 0 0 0 0 0 1 0] [0 0 5 0 0 0 0 0 0] [0 0 0 7 0 0 0 0 1] [1 0 0 0 4 0 0 0 0] [0 0 0 0 0 5 0 0 0] [0 0 0 0 0 0 4 0 0] [0 0 0 0 0 0 0 4 0] [0 0 0 0 0 0 0 0 5]]			[[1 0 0 0 4 0 0 0 0] [0 5 0 0 0 0 0 1 0] [0 0 4 0 0 0 0 0 1] [0 0 0 7 0 0 0 0 0] [4 0 0 0 1 0 0 0 0] [0 0 0 0 0 5 0 0 0] [0 0 0 0 0 0 4 0 0] [0 0 0 0 0 0 0 4 0] [0 0 0 0 0 0 0 0 1 4]]			[[2 0 0 0 4 0 0 0 0] [0 5 0 0 0 0 0 0 0] [0 0 5 0 0 0 0 0 0] [0 0 0 6 0 0 0 0 0] [3 0 0 0 1 0 0 0 0] [0 0 0 0 0 1 0 5 0 0 0] [0 0 0 0 0 0 4 0 0] [0 1 0 0 0 0 0 3 1] [0 0 0 0 0 0 0 1 4]]		
Classification report		precision	recall		precision	recall		precision	recall		precision	recall
	3D/CAD Prototyping	0.57	0.80	3D/CAD Prototyping	0.75	0.60	3D/CAD Prototyping	0.20	0.20	3D/CAD Prototyping	0.40	0.33
	Augmented Real Prototyping	1.00	0.67	Augmented Real Prototyping	1.00	0.83	Augmented Real Prototyping	1.00	0.83	Augmented Real Prototyping	0.83	1.00
	Augmented Virtual Prototyping	1.00	0.80	Augmented Virtual Prototyping	1.00	1.00	Augmented Virtual Prototyping	1.00	0.80	Augmented Virtual Prototyping	1.00	1.00
	Breadboard Prototyping	1.00	0.86	Breadboard Prototyping	1.00	1.00	Breadboard Prototyping	1.00	1.00	Breadboard Prototyping	0.86	1.00
	Generative Design Prototyping	0.50	0.40	Generative Design Prototyping	0.67	0.80	Generative Design Prototyping	0.20	0.20	Generative Design Prototyping	0.20	0.25
	Low-Fidelity Prototyping	0.83	1.00	Low-Fidelity Prototyping	1.00	1.00	Low-Fidelity Prototyping	1.00	1.00	Low-Fidelity Prototyping	1.00	0.83
	Paper Prototyping	1.00	0.75	Paper Prototyping	1.00	1.00	Paper Prototyping	1.00	1.00	Paper Prototyping	1.00	1.00
	Quick Prototyping	0.75	0.75	Quick Prototyping	0.80	1.00	Quick Prototyping	0.67	1.00	Quick Prototyping	0.75	0.60
	Rapid Prototyping	0.62	1.00	Rapid Prototyping	1.00	1.00	Rapid Prototyping	0.80	0.80	Rapid Prototyping	0.80	0.80
	avg / total	0.82	0.78	avg / total	0.92	0.91	avg / total	0.78	0.76	avg / total	0.77	0.76
First five predictions	• Rapid Prototyping • Generative Design Prototyping • Breadboard Prototyping • 3D/CAD Prototyping • Low-Fidelity Prototyping			• Rapid Prototyping • Generative Design Prototyping • Breadboard Prototyping • Generative Design Prototyping • Low-Fidelity Prototyping			• Rapid Prototyping • Generative Design Prototyping • Breadboard Prototyping • 3D/CAD Prototyping • Low-Fidelity Prototyping			• Rapid Prototyping • Generative Design Prototyping • Breadboard Prototyping • 3D/CAD Prototyping • Low-Fidelity Prototyping		

Table 12.5 Made predictions using the K-nearest neighbors algorithm

Phy. feedback	Add. feedback	Environment	Error	Functions	Change	Budget	Time	Tolerances	Activity
10	3	6	4	3	9	6	6	7	Quick Prototyping
2	4	8	7	2	7	3	3	3	Augmented Real Prototyping
2	2	8	2	2	9	1	2	2	Paper Prototyping

strategies and guiding methods for a variety of purposes. This is in line with our study. The main motivation behind the study is to explain the different uses of prototypes and provide suggestions to support prototyping processes. Instead of creating a holistic framework that covers the overall process, our study aims at developing a smart approach for the selection of prototyping activities.

Camburn et al. (2015) formed a methodology for designing a prototyping strategy based on six key specific process variables that improve prototyping performance. Instead of focusing on the strategy level, our study pays more attention to the best practice of prototyping activities. We chose the criteria suggested by Filippi and Barattin (2014) in our models and further adopted four different AI-based approaches to generate suggestions for prototyping activities. The models are applied and tested for the selection of prototyping activities in the early phase. The beauty of this approach is the improvement of the models with a rising number of applications (i.e. training with new datasets). Our study fills the gap of missing an AI-based system to support the selection of general prototyping activities. More and more efforts on prototyping studies will adopt and benefit from AI technologies.

Limitations and further research

The major limitation of this research effort is the size and quality of the examined dataset. The data exploration, visualization, and predictive modeling discussed earlier is only based on 17 individual observations of engineering students. The participants were mostly subjected to a prior workshop or at least an introductory explanation. The collected dataset was homogenous and from novice engineers, which limits the performance of the model. Further research should investigate a bigger participant group to see if data-gathering efforts based on the questionnaire without a workshop would create comparably good and homogeneous results. Then a much bigger and higher-quality dataset can be collected via questionnaires from more experienced prototype developers. An increased use of the model by experts improves the quality of suggestions provided by the model.

A further approach is the expansion of the dataset with the application of smarter or more effective data mining techniques. By extending the dataset, more complex machine learning models can be applied.

In addition, prototyping activities considered in the pilot study are focused on the early phase of product development. Many more prototyping techniques and activities that were not subject to this study should be included and examined in future studies.

References

Allen, M. (2018). *The SAGE encyclopedia of communication research methods*. Thousand Oaks: SAGE Publications.
Armillotta, A. (2008). Selection of layered manufacturing techniques by an adaptive AHP decision model. *Robotics and Computer-Integrated Manufacturing*, 24, 450–461.

Beaudouin-Lafon, M. and Mackay, W. (2003). Prototyping tools and techniques. In J. A. Jacko and A. Sears (Eds.), *The human-computer interaction handbook*. Hillsdale, NJ: L. Erlbaum Associates Inc., pp. 1006–1031. Retrieved from http://dl.acm.org/citation.cfm?id=772072.772136

Bdeir, A. (2009). Electronics as material. *Proceedings of the 3rd International Conference on Tangible and Embedded Interaction – TEI '09*, 397.

Buxton, B. (2007). *Sketching user experiences getting the design right and the right design*. Morgan Kaufmann.

Byun, H. S. and Lee, K. H. (2005). A decision support system for the selection of a rapid prototyping process using the modified TOPSIS method. *International Journal of Advanced Manufacturing Technology*, 26, 1338–1347.

Byun, H. S. and Lee, K. H. (2006). Determination of the optimal build direction for different rapid prototyping processes using multi-criterion decision making. *Robotics and Computer-Integrated Manufacturing*, 22, 69–80.

Camburn, B., Dunlap, B., Gurjar, T., Hamon, C., Green, M., Jensen, D., Crawford, R., Otto, K. and Wood, K. (2015). A systematic method for design prototyping. *Journal of Mechanical Design*, 137, 081102.

Chen, J., Reilly, R. R. and Lynn, G. S. (2005). The impacts of speed-to-market on new product success: the moderating effects of uncertainty. *IEEE Transactions on Engineering Management*, 52(2), 199–212. https://doi.org/10.1109/TEM.2005.844926

Choi, S. H. and Chan, A. M. M. (2004). A virtual prototyping system for rapid product development. *Computer-Aided Design*, 36(5), 401–412. https://doi.org/10.1016/S0010-4485(03)00110-6

Chua, C. K., Leong, K. F. and Lim, C. S. (2010). Introduction. In *Rapid prototyping: principles and applications*. Singapore: World Scientific Publishing CO. Pte. Ltd, pp. 1–23.

Cooper, D. and Schindler, P. (2003). *Business model research*. New York: McGraw-Hill International.

Cover, T. and Hart, P. (1967). Nearest neighbor pattern classification. *IEEE Transactions on Information Theory*, 13(1), 21–27. https://doi.org/10.1109/TIT.1967.1053964

Cybenko, G. (1989). Approximation by superpositions of a sigmoidal function. *Mathematics of Control, Signals, and Systems*, 2, 303–314. https://doi.org/10.1007/BF02836480

Dow, S. P., Heddleston, K. and Klemmer, S. R. (2009). The efficacy of prototyping under time constraints. In *Proceedings of the Seventh ACM Conference on Creativity and Cognition*. New York: ACM, pp. 165–174.

Drizo, A. and Pegna, J. (2006). Environmental impacts of rapid prototyping: an overview of research to date. *Rapid Prototyping Journal*, 12, 64–71.

Duflo, E., Glennerster, R. and Kremer, M. (2008). Using randomization in development economics research: a toolkit. In T. Schultz and John Strauss (Eds.), *Handbook of development economics* (Vol. 4). Amsterdam and New York: North Holland.

Exner, K., Damerau, T. and Stark, R. (2016). Innovation in product-service system engineering based on early customer integration and prototyping. *Procedia CIRP*, 47, 30–35.

Filippi, S. and Barattin, D. (2014). A Selection algorithm for prototyping activities. *International Journal on Interactive Design and Manufacturing*, 8, 1–11.

Greenbaum, T. (1997). *The handbook of focus group research*. Sage Publication.

Hillgren, P-A., Seravalli, A. and Emilson, A. (2011). Prototyping and infrastructuring in design for social innovation. *CoDesign*, 7, 169–183.

Hornik, K., Stinchcombe, M. and White, H. (1989). Multilayer feedforward networks are universal approximators. *Neural Networks*, 2(5), 359–366. https://doi.org/10.1016/0893-6080(89)90020-8

Houde, S. and Hill, C. (1997). What do prototypes prototype? *Handbook of Human Computer Interaction*, 1–16.

James, G., Witten, D., Hastie, T. and Tibshirani, R. (2013). *An introduction to statistical learning with aplications in R*. New York: Springer. https://doi.org/10.1007/978-1-4614-7138-7

Jiang, L., Chen, S., Sadasivan, C. and Jiao, X. (2017). Structural topology optimization for generative design of personalized aneurysm implants: design, additive manufacturing, and experimental validation. 9–13.

Krish, S. (2011). A practical generative design method. *CAD Computer Aided Design*, 43, 88–100.

Kothari, C. R. (2004). *Research methodology: methods & techniques*. New Delhi: New Age International (P) Ltd.

Kröse, B. and Smagt, P. van der (1996). *Introduction to neural networks* (8th ed.). Amsterdam: The University of Amsterdam.

LeCun, Y., Boser, B., Denker, J. S., Henderson, D., Howard, R. E., Hubbard, W. and Jackel, L. D. (1989). Backpropagation applied to handwritten zip code recognition. *Neural Computation*, 1(4), 541–551. https://doi.org/10.1162/neco.1989.1.4.541

Liao, K. and Tu, Q. (2007). Leveraging automation and integration to improve manufacturing performance under uncertainty: an empirical study. *Journal of Manufacturing Technology Management*, 19(1), 38–51. https://doi.org/10.1108/17410380810843444

Lim, Y-K., Stolterman, E. and Tenenberg, J. (2008). The anatomy of prototypes. *ACM Transactions on Computer-Human Interaction*, 15, 1–27.

Liu, B., Campbell, R. I. and Pei, E. (2013). Real-time integration of prototypes in the product development process. *Assembly Automation*, 33(1), 22–28. https://doi.org/10.1108/01445151311294621

Masood, S. H. and Soo, A. (2002). A rule based expert system for rapid prototyping system selection. *Robotics and Computer-Integrated Manufacturing*, 18, 267–274.

McCurdy, M., Connors, C., Pyrzak, G., Kanefsky, B. and Vera, A. (2006). Breaking the fidelity barrier – an examination of our current characterization of prototypes and an example of a mixed-fidelity success. *Proceedings of the International Conference on Human Factors in Computing Systems (CHI'06)*, Montréal, Canada, 1233–1242.

Menold, J., Jablokow, K. and Simpson, T. (2017). Prototype for X (PFX): a holistic framework for structuring prototyping methods to support engineering design. *Design Studies*, 50, 70–112. https://doi.org/10.1016/j.destud.2017.03.001

Munguia, J. and Riba, C. (2008). A concurrent rapid manufacturing advice system. *4th IEEE Conference on Automation Science and Engineering, CASE 2008*, Washington, DC, 947–952.

Naumann, J. D. and Jenkins, A. M. (1982). Prototyping: the new paradigm for systems development. *MIS Quarterly*, 6, 29.

Patton, J. H., Stanford, M. S. and Barratt, E. S. (1995). Factor structure of the barratt impulsiveness scale. *Journal of Clinical Psychology*, 51(6), 768–774. https://doi.org/10.1002/1097-4679(199511)51:6<768::AID-JCLP2270510607>3.0.CO;2-1

Provost, F. and Fawcett, T. (2013). *Data science for business: what you eed to know about data mining and data-analytic thinking* (1st ed.). Sebastopol, California: O'Reilly Media.

Pruzan, P. (2016). *Research methodology: the aims, practices and ethics of science*. Cham: Springer International Publishing.

Rao, R. V. and Padmanabhan, K. K. (2007). Rapid prototyping process selection using graph theory and matrix approach. *Journal of Materials Processing Technology*, 193, 81–88.

Rothwell, R. (1994). Towards the fifth-generation innovation process. *International Marketing Review*.

Shea, K., Aish, R. and Gourtovaia, M. (2005). Towards integrated performance-driven generative design tools. *Automation in Construction*, 14, 253–264.

Sommerville, I. (2011). *Software Engineering* (9th ed.). Boston: Addison-Wesley. https://doi.org/10.1111/j.1365-2362.2005.01463.x

Tennyson, S., McCain, G., Hatten, S. and Eggert, R. (2006). Case study: promoting design automation by rural manufacturers. *Rapid Prototyping Journal*, 12(5), 304–309. https://doi.org/10.1108/13552540610707068

Troiano, L. and Birtolo, C. (2014). Genetic algorithms supporting generative design of user interfaces: examples. *Information Sciences*, 259, 433–451.

Ulrich, K. T. and Eppinger, S. D. (2011). *Product design and development* (5th ed.). McGraw-Hill.

Van Stralen, K. J., Dekker, F. W., Zoccali, C. and Jager, K. J. (2010). Confounding. *Nephron – Clinical Practice*, 116(2), 143–147. https://doi.org/10.1159/000315883

Vimal, K., Vinodh, S., Brajesh, P. and Muralidharan, R. (2016). Rapid prototyping process selection using multi criteria decision making considering environmental criteria and its decision support system. *Rapid Prototyping Journal*, 22, 225–250.

Wall, M. B., Ulrich, K. T. and Flowers, W. C. (1992). Evaluating prototyping technologies for product design. *Research in Engineering Design*, 3, 163–177.

Wang, G., Li, H., Guan, Y. and Zhao, G. (2004). A rapid design and manufacturing system for product development applications. *Rapid Prototyping Journal*, 10(3), 200–206. https://doi.org/10.1108/13552540410539021

Warfel, T. Z. (2009). *Prototyping*. Rosenfeld Media.

Webster, M. and Sell, J. (2014). *Laboratory experiments in social sciences*. Academic Press.

Yang, M. C. (2005). A study of prototypes, design activity, and design outcome. *Design Studies*, 26(6), 649–669. https://doi.org/10.1016/j.destud.2005.04.005

Yu, F., Pasinelli, M. and Brem, A. (2017). Prototyping in theory and in practice: a study of the similarities and differences between engineers and designers. *Creativity and Innovation Management*, 1–12.

Zhang, Q., Vonderembse, M. A. and Cao, M. (2009). Product concept and prototype flexibility in manufacturing: Implications for customer satisfaction. *European Journal of Operational Research*, 194(1), 143–154. https://doi.org/10.1016/j.ejor.2007.12.013

Zorriassatine, F., Wykes, C., Parkin, R. and Gindy, N. (2003). A survey of virtual prototyping techniques for mechanical product development. *Proceedings of the Institution of Mechanical Engineers, Part B: Journal of Engineering Manufacture*, 217(4), 513–530. https://doi.org/10.1243/095440503321628189

Appendix

Note: Figures, which are used to explain the prototyping activities, are not included here.

Prototyping activity 1

Paper prototyping

You and your design team were instructed to supply a possible design for an app that operates within the topic of a "smart classroom".

During your ideation process, you are asked to supply two designs containing different measured parameters from the classroom and options on how you could display those to the students (energy use, CO_2 level, etc.).

Materials:

- Paper
- Markers

Prototyping activity 2

Breadboard prototyping

For one of your projects, you want to prototype the functionality of one of the components first before implementing it into the final product.

Prototype the following circuit and ensure yourself of its functionality.

Materials:

- Arduino Uno and breadboard
- Cables
- LED
- Button
- 220Ω and 10KΩ resistor

Prototyping activity 3

Low-fidelity prototyping

Using the materials supplied, design a prototype that protects the eggs from breaking when being dropped from a 1-meter height. Be creative!

Materials:

- Balloons
- Straws
- Tape
- Cups
- Toothpicks
- Eggs
- Ribbon

Prototyping activity 4

Quick prototyping

Discuss the intentions of designing and manufacturing prototypes that present a current or future design or a product without actually implementing any further features.

Prototyping activity 5

Rapid prototyping

Assess the steps of design and manufacturing, quality, and tolerances of the provided prototype. Can you notice any limitations or failures of this type of additive manufacturing? If possible, compare it to the prototype examples created earlier.

Materials:

- 3D printed prototypes from previous projects

Prototyping activity 6

Augmented-real prototyping

This prototyping activity involves placing a virtual prototype within a real environment. A very simple implementation of this technique can be achieved with various AR apps available for different smartphones.

Prototyping activity 7

Augmented-virtual prototyping

This prototyping activity involves placing a real prototype within a virtual or computer-generated environment. This technique is especially often used in the automobile industry when cars are exhibited to display weather, aerodynamic behaviour or other influences.

Prototyping activity 8

3D/CAD prototyping

In your first semester and in your semester projects, you should have had some insights into the creation of virtual or 3D prototypes. Discuss possible advantages or disadvantages of these types compared to real prototypes. Also think about what further benefits the virtual aspect brings to the table.

Materials:

- 3D virtual prototype

Prototyping activity 9

Generative design prototyping

Play around with the 3D design on the computer and see what happens to the prototype when you use the slider. Try to describe the generated model compared to a model you might have designed yourself and discuss the advantages of it.

Materials:

- Autodesk simulation showing the design and offering possibilities to make changes

13
FRUGAL INNOVATION
Developing and managing innovations in resource-constrained settings

Eugenia Rosca, Nivedita Agarwal, and Jakob Schlegel

Introduction

> The emerging world, long a source of cheap labor, now rivals the rich countries for business innovation.
>
> *(The Economist, 2010)*

Globalization and lowered trade barriers have led to a deeper integration of emerging markets (EM) in the world economy, making EM a much-sought-after place for businesses globally. The last two decades have propelled the rapid growth of EM, currently contributing around 75 percent of global growth of output and consumption (International Monetary Fund, 2017). While there is demand saturation in developed markets (DM), the EM demand and growth potential are on the rise due to the increasing purchasing power of a large and growing market with an untapped bottom of pyramid (BOP) population comprising more than 4 billion people who live on less than $2 per day with a majority in EM (Prahalad and Hart, 2002). In addition to the market potential, EM offer an ample talent/resource pool, with cost advantages of R&D centers. As a result, the EM are fast turning from "low-cost manufacturing only" to also act as innovation hubs with over 100 Fortune 500 companies setting up local R&D facilities in China and India (Eagar et al., 2011).

In light of these economic developments, frugal innovation emerges as a new innovation paradigm that challenges the traditional, resource-intensive innovation mind-set and strategies. Frugal innovation refers to an inclusive and flexible approach to innovation that maximizes value for the stakeholders while minimizing the use of financial and natural resources. From a more operational perspective, frugal innovation involves the development of affordable, appropriate and accessible solutions for underserved consumers (Agarwal, Grottke, Mishra, and Brem, 2017). While doing so, the main challenges inherent to frugal innovations are to balance opposite extremes of "doing more with less", for example, achieving low cost yet high quality, focusing on localization while keeping up with the global developments, allowing adaptability without comprising efficiency and maximizing profits while enabling societal impact (Agarwal and Brem, 2017, Bhatti, 2013).

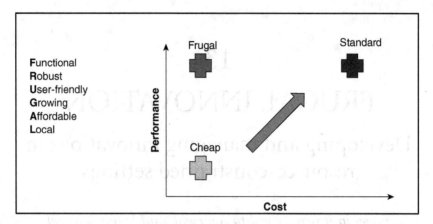

Figure 13.1 Frugal innovation – a simple definition
Source: Adapted from Bhatti (2012)

The original purpose of frugal innovation was not to create new customers, but rather to serve the underserved and to find innovative solutions for pressing social needs. This was accomplished by expanding affordability, availability and acceptability (see Figure 13.1). However, gradually, frugal innovation challenged traditional innovation flows emerging from west to east by pursuing a reverse innovation path from east to west, penetrating DM markets. A survey executed by Ernst and Young (2011) showed that 81 percent of 547 executives agreed that frugal innovation is a major opportunity and has as much relevance in DM as in EM. Even the European Union highlighted that frugal innovation may be applied in developed economies, and India's efforts in this respect can be used as potential learnings for Europe (European Comission, 2014).

Therefore, based on the growing acceptance and relevance of the concept, this chapter discusses the background and emergence of frugal innovation in detail. It explains the phenomenon of frugal innovation following the three-level typological structure suggested by Soni and Krishnan (2014): (1) frugal mind-set, (2) frugal process and (3) frugal outcome.

Untangling the concept of frugal innovation: mind-set, process and outcome

Frugal innovations are created at the intersection of at least two of three key innovation dimensions – technology, society and institutions. One that involves all three elements can be deemed an "ideal" frugal innovation. They can offer a competitive advantage for the pioneering firms and create social as well as business value, with optimal use of resources, and by "doing more with less" in resource-constrained environments (Agarwal and Brem, 2017; Brem and Wolfram, 2014; Bhatti, 2012). Their transformational value offering to the consumer comprises elements of cost efficiency and sustainability without compromising on quality (Radjou and Prabhu, 2015).

Current studies show that frugal innovations can be initiated by a wide range of actors. Figure 13.2 provides an overview of different types of initiators of frugal innovations based on the size of initiative and level of local embeddedness. One can notice that the initiators of frugal innovation range from grassroots and survival entrepreneurs to multinational corporations (MNCs) with medium-sized initiators in between. Depending on the type of initiative, frugal

Frugal innovation

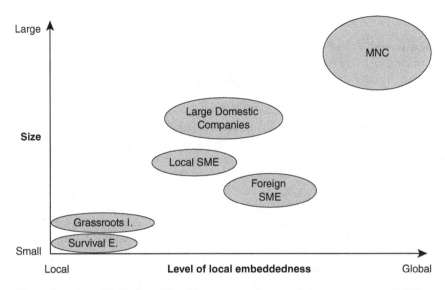

Figure 13.2 Overview of initiatives of frugal innovation – from survival entrepreneurs to MNC

innovation presents different characteristics and potential for social impact. Moreover, the development process also differs depending on the type of initiative. In the next few paragraphs, the concept of frugal innovation will be explained, drawing on the distinction between innovation mind-set, process and outcome. In addition, multiple examples of well-known frugal innovations initiated by various actors will be discussed.

Frugal mind-set

A frugal mind-set is a key factor for successful development of a frugal solution (Radjou and Euchner, 2016). A frugal mind-set develops with a deep understanding of local socioeconomic, institutional and environmental requirements of developing countries and the specific criteria of affordability, acceptability, availability and awareness (Anderson and Markides, 2007). The process of developing such a mind-set starts with a deep understanding of constraints in the local environments related to social norms, cultural aspects, deficient infrastructure, undermined property rights and weak regulatory environment (Prahalad, 2006). These external constraints in the sociocultural and institutional environment internalize in a set of requirements for specific capabilities, knowledge and skills needed to satisfy the external constraints. Developing such a mind-set can be difficult, especially for Western firms, who face challenges in embracing frugal mind-sets due to the lack of frugal thinkers and experience in EM environments (Kroll et al., 2016). Western companies have learned to develop competitive market positions for high-end consumers; however, they have weak to nonexistent positioning in the BOP markets. In order to develop this, Western firms need to develop the necessary skills and capabilities to design and develop frugal products and services. In this sense, developing a frugal mind-set is a pre-requisite. Developing a frugal mind-set is not only beneficial in EM but also in DM, since an increasing amount of customers demand for not only cost-effective but also ecologically friendly products of high quality. Therefore, a developing frugal mind-set can serve as an opportunity for a new type of growth.

The frugal process

The frugal process is "the design innovation process that properly considers the needs and context of citizens [. . .]" (Basu, Banerjee, and Sweeny, 2013). Viewed from a process perspective, the term frugal engineering is often employed to denote actual processes, principles and tools valuable for the development of frugal innovation. Frugal engineering consists of a set of principles and methods used to design and develop low-cost, high-quality products in order to satisfy the needs of customers in developing markets These principles include (1) the essential features valued by the target customers; (2) the optimized design in terms of size, weight and characteristics; (3) the simplification of manufacturing processes through the use of new technologies; and (4) the substitution of expensive materials. While cost discipline is an essential part of frugal engineering, rather than cutting cost from existing products, frugal engineering aims to avoid the unnecessary costs in an initial assessment by identifying the essential features valued by the customer. Moreover, recent studies reveal that the frugal process entails a strong focus on collaborative relationships and local partnerships at the local and global level. Partnerships with local companies and institutions are used to overcome these difficulties by gaining knowledge in the new context through the identification of resources and capabilities in the frugal innovation development process (Kumar and Puranam, 2013). Only by combining top-down and bottom-up approaches and bringing together actors from different stakeholder groups does frugal innovation have real potential to address the multifaceted challenges of poverty and sustainable development in EM (Knorringa, Peša, Leliveld, and van Beers, 2016).

The frugal process comprises three distinct phases: need identification, product/service development and commercialization.

Need identification phase

Due to different living conditions, cultures, value systems and societal relationships in emerging economies compared to the Western world, it can be difficult for product developers to fully understand customer needs in foreign economies without special training or local experiences (Agarwal, Brem, and Grottke, 2018; Zeschky, Widenmayer, and Gassmann, 2011). A proper identification of needs is the basic requirement for the development of innovations, and the mechanism employed for this purpose differs, depending on the owner of the frugal innovation, namely the type of stakeholder (e.g. SME, MNC, small enterprises).

For local companies the process of identifying customer needs is often linked with much less effort than for MNCs, as they are embedded in the local environment and requirements seem natural to them. The case of Grameen Shakti, a company that developed a solar home system for 1 million Bangladeshis who live off the grid, shows that needs can be understood with little effort by local initiatives. A complete national coverage of energy supply has been seen as a futile aspiration, and it was a widespread belief that people in rural areas would experience significant benefits from an electrical light source, which often was not the case. In this case, the problem was more the development of a suitable innovative solution than properly identifying customers' needs (Pansera and Owen, 2015).

International companies sometimes have to pursue a different approach. Both Siemens and Philips built up R&D teams that mainly consisted of local engineers, who collaborated with local institutions and/or doctors in order to identify their needs. They found out that their healthcare innovations needed to be able to handle dirt, provide resistance to power fluctuations, and endure excessive usage (Zeschky, Widenmayer, and Gassmann, 2011). Philips assumed that their products were used in a similar way as in Western economies. They soon found out that their patient monitoring system was additionally used as a writing pad and even carried around. These circumstances were unimaginable for a Western firm (Zeschky, Widenmayer, and Gassmann, 2011). Rehau, a company based in Germany, analyzed the everyday life of their target group, which showed them that numerous families cook with firewood inside their home. The smoke that develops as a consequence can cause respiratory tract diseases. This is how they identified that a healthier sustainable cooking solution was required (Knapp, 2017).

The case of the "lucky iron fish" illustrates a different approach towards understanding customer requirements. After obtaining his undergraduate degree, health professional (now Dr. Christopher Charles) moved to a small village in Cambodia, where his job was to screen people for anemia and to treat parasitic infections. He wanted to quantify how widespread anemia actually was, so he took blood samples of the local population. National estimates predicted that a little over 50 percent of women and children suffer anemia. The results of his blood samples showed rates close to 90 percent. Wherever he went he saw people lying in the shade, adults with no energy to work, children with no energy to study or to play. Children who were raised anemic did not have the ability to concentrate in school – all results caused by iron deficiency – and numerous women suffered hemorrhage during childbirth. As a result, based on his experience, he charged himself to find a cost-effective, sustainable, and accessible solution (Charles, 2014).

The Chinese company Haier identified needs by listening to the consumer. A customer from Sichuan, who was a farmer, complained about his frequently clogged drain. The farmer did not only wash his clothes in this water but also the potatoes he harvested, which was the reason for his problem. They discovered that this is a common procedure among many rural residents. Instead of telling the consumers they should not wash potatoes in the washing machine, Haier developed instructions on how to properly use the washing machine for cleaning vegetables and developed a machine with a larger-diameter drain that was able to wash even larger vegetables (Knapp, 2017).

Other mechanisms include the deployment of local project managers and local R&D centers, setting up local growth teams, and creating rural innovation laboratories. Summarizing the key insights, it can be said that local cooperation or local presence can help firms to reduce the risk and develop a clearer picture of the path towards understanding local customer requirements (Agarwal and Brem, 2012).

Product/service development phase

As the identification of customer needs is closely linked to the development phase, localization is an often-pursued approach, even used by international companies like General Electric, Logitech, or Mettler Toledo. Different examples of frugal product innovations show that during the localized development phase important insights were gained. Logitech, for example, found out that in China fancy packaging is a sign of expensiveness. Hence, they reduced the packing of their frugal computer mouse to a minimum. Siemens developed a computed tomography scanner that was completely designed by Chinese engineers. They achieved frugality by removing unessential features and, most importantly, shifted tasks from hardware to software. Through adding new hardware, the power consumption would have increased, so what the Chinese engineers did was improve the software with new algorithms that took over the job that the hardware had handled before. They even downsized the device with this approach. Through this shift of processing power, they were able to create a faster, more energy-efficient product (Radjou and Euchner, 2016).

The development process of Grameen Shakti was driven by two main factors: providing affordable solutions and offering a flexible, quick, and cheap after-sales service. They achieved affordability through the frugal redesign of existing technologies by using local materials and providers. Most parts of their developed solar home system are produced and assembled locally. Additionally, the price was further reduced by good deals negotiated with providers of the acquired parts (Pansera and Owen, 2015). Companies in the solar industry find it useful to associate their brand with the social initiative Grameen Shakti, which led to the acceptance of lower prices for their products (Pansera and Owen, 2015). The replacement of kerosene lamps and stoves with solar panels and biodigesters has a significant impact on sustainability (Pansera and Sarkar, 2016). An important part in the design phase was the reduction of complexity in order to ease the after-sales services such as repairs. Even the most complex part was designed in such a way that local technicians, trained by Grameen Shakti, can easily repair it. Regarding the biogas digester, they collaborated with a local consultant with extensive experience in biogas digesters and eventually was able to provide a different model of a biodigester – it was later used by Grameen Shakti. Through continuously improving their product and being agile, they made their way from an expensive inefficient solution to a highly efficient quality solution (Pansera and Sarkar, 2016).

The lucky iron fish is an example that shows continuous improvement is essential. The research team developed different prototypes, such as a simple iron bar, which fulfilled the important criteria of affordability, sustainability, and effectivity. Flatness is very important, as flat surfaces release more iron into the substance (Charles, Dewey, Daniell, and Summerlee, 2011). The bar was analyzed in a Canadian lab, where it was shown that by drinking one liter of boiled water in which the iron fish was placed people could meet 75 percent of their daily iron requirements. First trials showed that families used the bar for the wrong purpose: as a door stop, as a paperweight, or for fixing a, but not for cooking. The final design was a fish, which is associated with luck in Cambodia. Understanding the human link was key to solving this problem. The iron fish, which can be used for 10 years and more, is produced in Cambodia from locally available scrap iron – essentially old car parts – to provide sustainability and to improve the local economic development. Each fish contains a tracking number to ensure quality and to keep track of when each batch was produced (Charles, 2014).

The Getinge Groups sterilizer is an example of thinking even further in terms of product development and connecting it with the post-product development phase. In order to open up new distribution channels a product manager demanded further weight reduction. Instead of delivering them to warehouses, lighter sterilizers could be sent directly to consumers, as then one single person could handle and install the sterilizer. Similarly, in the case of defects the customer could use existing delivery services to send the sterilizer back, which would shorten the downtime, leading to overall cost reductions (Altmann and Engberg, 2016).

The development phase of the Dacia Logan, which was designed for developed markets, was based on a price limit. They set themselves the challenge of developing a car for €5000 that fulfilled the need for both quality and affordability. The R&D was based in Romania, where French designers and Romanian engineers were brought together. In the end, they created a car that used 50 percent fewer parts than a regular Renault vehicle and was spacious enough to meet the needs of Romanian families (Radjou and Euchner, 2016).

Commercialization phase

The commercialization phase entails several challenges for all types of firms aiming for self-sufficiency. While in DM settings, the focus of business model design is on identifying new customer segments, unfulfilled needs, and diverse revenue streams, in low-income settings the main challenges related to designing economically viable business efforts include how to transform a social need into a market opportunity and how to design an attractive value proposition aligned with social issues and local needs.

The first step in the commercialization phase includes creating awareness through the promotion of frugal products to BOP consumers. Unilever worked together with doctors as key opinion leaders in order to facilitate the promotion of the Pure-it water filter. They developed its distribution approach from only door-to-door distribution to offering multiple channels like retail and partnership channels. These were continuously analyzed in order to optimize incentives, distribution targets and turnover, and other key performance indicators (Gebauer and Saul, 2014). Regarding the marketing strategy, Unilever built up the brand awareness for their personal care products in a creative way. They saved costs by leveraging the public awareness of street performers in India (magicians, singers, dancers). These people adjusted their scripts and acted based on a clientele requested from the company (Balu, 2001). In 2005, they reached public awareness increases of 8 percent for some of their products (Balu, 2001).

While marketing efforts are easier to pursue for large companies given their financial resources, cases like the lucky iron fish show that acceptance can be reached differently. In order to confirm customer acceptance, the iron fish was distributed to 400 people who were told to use it every day. Analysis showed that an acceptance rate of 90 percent was achieved. To further increase the acceptance and awareness, a team of Cambodian representatives was employed to travel to villages, spreading the word and talking about nutrition, anemia, and health (Charles, 2014). Pure-it and Tata Swatch, both water filters, pursue a similar approach. Their marketing strategy includes promoting awareness of the importance of healthy drinking water (Levänen et al., 2015).

A key aspect related to commercialization and survival in the long run relates to the selection and diversification of revenue streams. Achieving scalability is critical for long-term survival in BOP markets because of the low margins inherent to affordable products and severe affordability constraints. Some ventures are specifically associating their economic success with a revenue model based on high volume (Rosca, Arnold, and Bendul, 2017). Studies show several examples specifically from the healthcare and energy sectors. In the healthcare sector, the revenue models are based on increased standardization, focus, and specialization which dramatically reduce costs. For example, Aravind Eye Care, by relying on standardized processes, were successful in lowering the production and delivery costs of the services and also in reducing morbidity and complications (Angeli and Jaiswal, 2016). In contrast to the healthcare sector, in the energy industry, studies show the emergence of more innovative revenue models, such as pay as you go (PAYG) where customers pay for energy-related services via mobile phones on a daily, weekly, or monthly basis.

Frugal outcome

The frugal outcome of the process includes an appropriate technology or disruptive innovation in the form of a product or service (Soni and Krishnan, 2014). These breakthrough products are 90 percent cheaper than traditional DM products (Gallis and Rall, 2012). For example, use of mosquito net for hernia repair in rural India was one-fifth the price of a standard product (Kingsnorth, Tongaonkar, and Awojobi, 2011). As such, frugal outcomes concentrate on core functionalities and performance, entail a substantial cost reduction in the total cost of ownership, and are robust solutions able to comply with numerous institutional constraints in EM and, in particular, BOP markets. Frugal outcomes need to address social needs in EM and ensure availability, accessibility, affordability, and awareness. Due to its inherent focus on resource constraints, frugal innovation has often been associated with sustainability outcomes. Yet, current empirical work suggests that frugal innovations are not always sustainable and have equal potential for negative environmental impacts (Rosca, Arnold, and Bendul, 2018). Depending on the type of owner for the frugal innovation, the spectrum of potential outcomes can range between positive and negative impacts on local communities and environments. For example, affordable products can lead to increased consumption flows and negative environmental impact, in particular, in areas with weak to nonexistent waste management systems in place. Further research is needed to examine the conditions and mechanisms to be employed by frugal innovation initiatives in order to ensure sustainable outcomes.

Conclusion

In a world of economic austerity and strong concerns for sustainable development, a focus on limited use of resource is of paramount importance for both the public and private sector. In this context, frugal innovation can contribute to addressing pressing societal challenges both in DM and EM. The emergence of frugal innovation along with many other terms in various research streams – inclusive development, responsible innovation, shared value creation, resource stewardship, sustainable innovation, social entrepreneurship, and hybrid business – all point to a paradigm shift from the traditionally economically driven innovation to shared value creation and frugal innovations integrating societal needs and environmental concerns. These innovations are not simply created by redesigning current products and processes; rather, they involve a rethinking of processes and business models (Soni and Krishnan, 2014; The Economist, 2010). Requiring the right mind-set, these innovations go beyond isolated technological or social innovations. Moreover, to reconcile economic, social, and environmental goals, frugal outcomes need the right kind of system created around them – local and global partnerships, embedded operations, diverse revenue streams, and marketing and distribution campaigns.

References

Agarwal, N. and Brem, A. (2012). Frugal and reverse innovation-literature overview and case study insights from a German MNC in India and China. In *Engineering, Technology and Innovation (ICE), 2012 18th International ICE Conference on*, pp. 111, June 18–20, Munich, Germany.

Agarwal, N. and Brem, A. (2017). Frugal innovation-past, present, and future. *IEEE Engineering Management Review*, 45(3), 37–41.

Agarwal, N., Brem, A. and Grottke, M. (2018). Towards a higher socio-economic impact through shared understanding of product requirements in emerging markets: The case of the Indian healthcare innovations. *Technological Forecasting and Social Change*, 135, 91–98.

Agarwal, N., Grottke, M., Mishra, S. and Brem, A. (2017). A systematic literature review of constraint-based innovations: state of the art and future perspectives. *IEEE Transactions on Engineering Management*, 64(1), 1–13.

Altmann, P. and Engberg, R. (2016). Frugal innovation and knowledge transferability. *Research-Technology Management*, 59(1), 48–55.

Anderson, J. and Markides, C. (2007). Strategic innovation at the base of the pyramid. *MIT Sloan Management Review*, 49, 83–88, 93.

Angeli, F. and Jaiswal, A. K. (2016). Business model innovation for inclusive health care delivery at the bottom of the pyramid. *Organization & Environment*, 29(4), 486–507.

Balu, R. (2001). Strategic innovation: Hindustan Lever Ltd. *Fast Company*, 47(May).

Basu, R., Banerjee, P. and Sweeny, E. (2013). Frugal innovation: core competencies to address global sustainability. *Journal of Management for Global Sustainability*, 1(2), 63–82.

Bhatti, Y., Khilji, S. E. and Basu, R. (2013). Frugal innovation. In Shaista K. and Chris R. (Eds.), *Globalization, change and learning in South Asia*. Elsevier, pp. 123–145.

Bhatti, Y. A. (2012). What is frugal, What is innovation? Towards a theory of frugal innovation. *SSRN Electronic Journal*, 1–45. https://doi.org/10.2139/ssrn.2005910.

Brem, A. and Wolfram, P. (2014). Research and development from the bottom up – introduction of terminologies for new product development in emerging markets. *Journal of Innovation and Entrepreneurship*, 3, 1–22.

Charles, C., Dewey, C., Daniell, W. and Summerlee, A. (2011). Iron-deficiency anaemia in rural Cambodia: community trial of a novel iron supplementation technique. *European Journal of Public Health*, 21, 43–48.

Charles, C. V. (2014). How one lucky iron fish can treat anemia. https://youtu.be/0Lf6glgKt3Q

Eagar, R., Oene, F. van, Boulton, C., Roos, D. and Dekeyser, C. (2011). The future of innovation management: the next 10 years. *Arthur D. Little – Publications: Prism Articles*, 1, 20–37.

The Economist (2010). The world turned upside down. www.economist.com/node/15879369.

Ernst and Young (2011). *Innovating for the next three billion*. UK: Ernst & Young Global Limited.

European Commission (2014). *The international dimension of research and innovation cooperation addressing the grand challenges in the global context*. Luxembourg: European Commission.

Gallis, M. and Rall, E. L. (2012). Global development cycles: redefining technological innovation cycles and their impacts within a global perspective. *International Journal of Innovation and Technology Management*, 9(1), 1250008.

Gebauer, H. and Saul, C. J. (2014). Business model innovation in the water sector in developing countries. *Science of the Total Environment*, 488–489, 512–520.

International Monetary Fund (2017). *Chapter 2: roads less traveled: growth in emerging market and developing economies in a complicated external environment*. International Monetary Fund, World Bank.

Kingsnorth, A. N., Tongaonkar, R. R. and Awojobi, O. A. (2011). Commentary on: low-cost mesh for inguinal hernia repair in resource-limited settings. *Hernia*, 15(5), 491–494. www.springerlink.com/index/FR83V0V352627617.pdf.

Knapp, O. (2017). *Frugal: Einfach eine intelligente Lösung*. Munich: Roland Berger GMBH.

Knorringa, P., Peša, I., Leliveld, A. and van Beers, C. (2016). Frugal innovation and development: aides or adversaries? *The European Journal of Development Research*, 28(2), 143–153.

Kroll, H., Gabriel, M., Braun, A., Muller, E., Neuhäusler, P., Schnabl, E. and Zenker, A. (2016). A conceptual analysis of foundations, trends and relevant potentials in the field of frugal innovation (for Europe). Luxembourg: European Commission.

Kumar, N. and Puranam, P. (2013). India inside: the emerging innovation challenge to the west. *Journal of Product & Brand Management*, 22(1), 95–97.

Levänen, J., Hossain, M., Lyytinen, T., Hyvärinen, A., Numminen, S. and Halme, M. (2015). Implications of frugal innovations on sustainable development: evaluating water and energy innovations. *Sustainability*, 8, 4.

Pansera, M. and Owen, R. (2015). Framing resource-constrained innovation at the 'bottom of the pyramid': insights from an ethnographic case study in rural Bangladesh. *Technological Forecasting and Social Change*, 92, 300–311.

Pansera, M. and Sarkar, S. (2016). Crafting sustainable development solutions: frugal innovations of grassroots entrepreneurs. *Sustainability*, 8, 51.

Prahalad, C. K. (2006). The innovation sandbox. *Strategy+Business*, 44, 62–71.

Prahalad, C. K. and Hart, S. (2002). The fortune at the bottom of the pyramid. *Strategy+Business*, 26, 54–67.

Radjou, N. and Euchner, J. (2016). The principles of frugal innovation: an interview with Navi Radjou. *Research-Technology Management*, 59(4), 13–20.

Radjou, N. and Prabhu, J. (2015). *Frugal Innovation: how to do more with less – free e-short*. Profile.

Rosca, E., Arnold, M. and Bendul, J. C. (2017). Business models for sustainable innovation – an empirical analysis of frugal products and services. *Journal of Cleaner Production*, 162, S133–S145.

Rosca, E., Reedy, J. and Bendul, J. C. (2018). Does frugal innovation enable sustainable development? A systematic literature review. *The European Journal of Development Research*, 30(1), 136–157.

Soni, P. and Krishnan, R. T. (2014). Frugal innovation: aligning theory, practice, and public policy. *Journal of Indian Business Research*, 6(1), 29–47.

Zeschky, M., Widenmayer, B. and Gassmann, O. (2011). Frugal innovation in emerging markets. *Research-Technology Management*, 54(4), 38–45. https://doi.org/10.5437/08956308X5404007.

14
INNOVATION IN THE DIGITAL AGE

Michael Dowling, Elisabeth Noll, and Kristina Zisler

Introduction

Today's industrial environment is marked by the increasing use of digital technologies (Yoo et al., 2012) such as artificial intelligence, automation, robotics, additive manufacturing, and human–machine interaction (McKinsey and Company, 2015). Embedded software and sensors are altering classical product characteristics, resulting in "smart products" capable of interacting through the Internet of Things (IoT). The interconnectedness of smart products allows data aggregation (Yoo et al., 2012; Nylén and Holmström, 2015; Porter and Heppelmann, 2014), thereby promoting the importance of "big data" analysis as well as cloud computing technologies (McKinsey and Company, 2015; Nylén and Holmström, 2015; MGI, 2013). In addition to their impact on products, digital technologies are helping to facilitate processes, for example, by accelerating innovation processes through digital simulation (Yoo et al., 2012; Nylén and Holmström, 2015). Integrating digital technologies into products influences competitive structures, blurs industry boundaries, and revolutionizes product as well as service innovation (Yoo et al., 2012; Nylén and Holmström, 2015; Porter and Heppelmann, 2014). New products require expertise from numerous knowledge fields (e.g. IT and manufacturing) that are potentially new to existing firms, which stresses the importance of collaboration across company as well as industry borders. Furthermore, customer focus and agile development methods determine success in today's dynamic industry environment (MIT Technology Review, 2014; Porter and Heppelmann, 2014; Bharadwaj et al., 2013; BMWi, 2016a).

For decades, researchers have been focusing on the innovation process and now conclude that innovation is a prerequisite for corporate success (Brown and Eisenhardt, 1995). However, beyond appreciating that technological innovation can have consequences across industry boundaries (Tushman and Anderson, 1986; Weiber, Kollmann, and Pohl, 1999), there is still little understanding of the role of digitalization as an enabler of significant innovation process changes. Hence, there is a knowledge gap concerning the influence of digitalization on innovation management.

Researchers and managers alike must identify the specific requirements that innovation processes have to fulfill in the future (Bharadwaj et al., 2013). In the innovation management literature, many authors acknowledge the beginning of an "innovation revolution" (Lee Olson and Trimi, 2012, p. 819) and stress the need for research into new types of innovation processes that are enabled by digital technologies and differ from traditional industrial innovation processes (Nylén and Holmström, 2015). Since innovation ecosystems are increasingly important, several authors have called for research into how firms can manage innovation collaboration effectively and how digital resources influence value creation in industrial ecosystems (Bharadwaj et al., 2013; Adner and Kapoor, 2010; Barczak, 2014).

This chapter builds upon the research of Yoo et al. (2012), who identified new requirements for innovation methods in the digital era, for example, that process speed needs to increase. As companies often still rely on classically linear innovation processes such as the stage-gate model (Cooper, 1990), digital technologies and the growing importance of early prototypes, as well as a customer focus, challenge such established methods (Nylén and Holmström, 2015; BMWi, 2016a). In this chapter, we will first discuss the impact of digital technologies on innovation in the automotive industry, which, though known for its innovativeness, still remains a very traditional industry sector (Henfridsson, Mathiassen, and Svahn, 2014). Following this, we will review the impact of digital technologies on innovation in service industries. In order to analyze the consequences of digitalization on the innovation process of the automotive and service industries, we first provide an overview in the second section of the theoretical perspectives that we use in our analysis of the two industries. In the third section, we present the research methods as well as the empirical data and then discuss the results and the ensuing theoretical model in the fourth. We conclude with managerial implications and contributions, as well as limitations of this study and offer suggestions for further research.

Theoretical background

Digital innovation process models in manufacturing

Innovations, defined as "a new technology or combination of technologies introduced commercially to meet a user or a market need" (Utterback and Abernathy, 1975, p. 642), are generated through an innovation process. Gruber and Marquis identify a process with six phases that transport ideas from generation to product launch (Gruber and Marquis, 1969; Cooper, 1976). Building upon their work, Cooper developed the *stage-gate model*, which divides the innovation process into stages and gates to support successful product commercialization. Varying between four and seven stages, a gate controls each stage as the checkpoint for a set of deliverables (Cooper, 1990). The model is often the subject of criticism because of its linearity (Becker, 2006) as well as its lack of agility due to its predefined process steps and early product definition (Bhattacharya, Krishnan, and Mahajan, 1998; MacCormack et al., 2012). Cooper modified the traditional model in 2014 by introducing the *Triple-A System*, which is more adaptive, flexible, and agile (Cooper, 2014).

Having originated in software development research, agile approaches to innovation are gaining importance throughout the industry. As a result of the introduction of the *Manifesto for Agile Software Development* in 2001, characteristics of agile systems such as the value of individuals and interactions, the importance of prototypes, customer collaboration, and a quick response to change (http://agilemanifesto.org) are now incorporated into traditionally linear industrial process models (Cooper, 2014; Sommer et al., 2015). Hybrid processes such as the *Industrial Scrum Framework for New Product Development* support increasing external cooperation and iterative product development by combining stage-gate and Scrum approaches. Scrum is an agile way of developing software based on the principles of transparency, inspection, and adaption. Using quick development intervals, teams are self-organizing and adapt to changes easily (Schwaber and Sutherland, 2016; Schwaber and Beedle, 2002). Using stage-gate and Scrum at different planning levels throughout the project, Sommer et al. (2015) identify company strategies to exploit the advantages of agile systems. While stage-gate mechanisms are often used for strategic management purposes, Scrum supports project execution within development teams. Hence, hybrid models are emerging as an alternative to traditionally linear stage-gate systems in order to succeed in an increasingly complex and dynamic industry environment (Sommer et al., 2015; Cooper, 2014). In addition to the need for a higher degree of agility, the identification of customer needs is gaining importance throughout the innovation process. The design thinking method, which follows the principle "innovation is made by humans for humans" (Brenner, Uebernickel, and Abrell, 2016, p. 8), is also increasingly present in practice. Focusing innovation activities on the human being (e.g. by direct observation), the method emphasizes technological solutions and prototypes to understand and solve customer problems (Brown, 2008; Meinel and Leifer, 2016).

Open innovation and ecosystems

Besides the emerging agile systems and changing classical innovation approaches, the development of the *open innovation* paradigm by Henry Chesbrough in 2003 also had a large impact on the development of formerly closed innovation process models. By developing ideas generated internally as well as externally while following external and internal paths to commercialize them, open innovation enables the exploitation of external knowledge for innovation purposes (Chesbrough, 2003). Numerous forms of open innovation tools have emerged to integrate external expertise, for example, the possibility for companies to solve a specific R&D problem by hosting innovation challenges (Terwiesch and Xu, 2008; Hüsig and Kohn, 2011). Furthermore, crowdsourcing as well as co-creation approaches, both enabled by the Internet and Web 2.0 technologies, actively integrate users into innovation activities (Prahalad and Ramaswamy, 2004; Rayna, Striukova, and Darlington, 2015; Saxton, Oh, and Kishore, 2013). Given the resulting inseparability of producing and consuming products in the digital era, researchers define a *prosumer* as an active user who plays the two roles of an innovator and consumer at the same time (Berthon, Pitt, and Campbell, 2008; Gawer, 2014; Rayna and Striukova, 2016).

In addition to the growing importance of integrating external expertise by collaborating with users and other outside actors, the cooperation between innovation actors also increases. Using a collaboration approach, organizations build long-term networks consisting of suppliers, manufacturers, and competitors (Zineldin, 2004). In the literature, researchers refer to such networks as platforms or innovation ecosystems that enable the offering of customer solutions by combining individual products and services within a collaborative agreement (Adner, 2006; Adner and Kapoor, 2010; Gawer, 2014). Actors in ecosystems collaborate and conduct common innovation activities but are in a competitive relationship at the same time (Lee, Olson, and Trimi, 2012; Gawer, 2014). Given that no single company has the capability to offer the emerging solution individually, an ecosystem is a consortium for complementary product as well as technology and service development (Adner, 2006; Gawer, 2014).

The Apple iPhone with its App Store is an example of an industry platform, where Apple is the platform leader collaborating with its complementors, the app developers. Gawer (2014) argues that the roles played by platform agents evolve over time, and since the interaction between innovation and competition is dynamic, relationships between participants shift. Competitors ally or complementors become rivals, and users as prosumers actively innovate. These multimodal interactions change platform mechanisms, and ecosystems evolve as organizations move along the continuum (Gawer, 2014).

Key new technologies

Data is the most important raw material for digital innovation (Beutner, 2013; BMWi, 2016a). Digital technologies combine information, communication, computer, and network technologies. They offer the potential for new business models and trigger an innovation revolution (Bharadwaj et al., 2013; Lee, Olson, and Trimi, 2012).

New digital technology areas that are particularly relevant include big data analysis, cloud computing, and the Internet of Things (IoT). Big data analysis enables the analysis of vast amounts of generated data in order to draw valuable business conclusions (Bharadwaj et al., 2013). Cloud computing provides online access to IT resources and services (Marston et al., 2011; Porter and Heppelmann, 2014). Companies profit from lower entry barriers due to decreasing investments, and new business models emerge (DaSilva et al., 2013). Furthermore, cloud computing plays an important role with regard to the interconnectedness of products that results from embedded technologies and requires subsequent data processing (Porter and Heppelmann, 2014). The networking of products enabled by a reduction of sensor and technology costs, as well as ubiquitous access to scalable data processing (McKinsey Digital, 2015), has promoted the development of the IoT, which is expected to transform into the Internet of Everything (BITKOM and Fraunhofer, 2014). Since data is a central driver of the digital transformation and all of the earlier-mentioned technologies rely on it, this group is referred to as the *data cluster* of technologies, enabling data generation and processing for innovative purposes (McKinsey Digital, 2015). Furthermore, the data cluster builds the basis for several other important technological concepts like advanced robotics, augmented reality and virtual reality (AR/VR), and 3D printing that are used in products and processes in the digital era (Porter and Heppelmann, 2015; MGI, 2013).

Digital innovation in service industries

Even though services play an increasing role in advanced economies (Mina, Bascavusoglu-Moreau, and Hughes, 2014), the predominant understanding of innovation activities and processes comes mainly from studies focusing on new product development (NPD) in the manufacturing sector (Howells, 2010; Biemans, Griffin, and Moenaert, 2015). The theoretical work of Barras (1986, 1990), the highly influential "reverse product cycle" model, is often regarded as the starting point of service innovation research (Toivonen and Tuominen, 2009). During the last 30 years, the NSD research stream continued to evolve (Biemans, Griffin, and Moenaert, 2015). While some researchers believe that NSD is a mature field of research, the majority have come to the conclusion that the research field is still underdeveloped (Page and Schirr, 2008; den Hertog, van der Aa, and de Jong, 2010; Kuester, Schuhmacher, Gast, and Worgul, 2013; Biemans, Griffin, and Moenaert, 2015). Previous research on service innovation is characterized by different perspectives and priorities (Coombs and Miles, 2000; Droege, Hildebrand, and Forcada, 2009). Authors such as Barras (1986) and Pavitt (1984) focus on technological aspects of service innovation. Moreover, the assimilation view of service tends to disregard the specific features of services and assumes that the concepts and findings from the manufacturing sector can easily be transferred to the service industry (de Brentani and Cooper, 1992; Drejer, 2004). In contrast, the demarcation approach emphasizes the distinctive characteristics of services (den Hertog, 2000; Djellal and Gallouj, 2001) – intangibility, inseparability, heterogeneity, perishability (Parasuraman, Zeithaml, and Berry, 1985; Edgett and Parkinson, 1993; Moeller, 2010) – that make the transfer of knowledge from manufacturing to services difficult (Droege, Hildebrand, and Forcada, 2009). The synthesis stream, in turn, focuses on the increasing convergence between products and services and aims at connecting the findings from both fields of research (Droege,

Hildebrand, and Forcada, 2009; Gallouj and Savona, 2009). Vargo and Lusch (2004, 2008) have argued for an alternative service-dominant (S-D) logic that is increasingly used as a foundation for systemizing innovation in general. Although these theoretical perspectives take up different positions regarding the development of service innovation, consensus exists concerning the importance of ICT in this context (Barrett, Davidson, Prabhu, and Vargo, 2015).

In the past, linear models of service innovation (Bowers, 1989; Scheuing and Johnson, 1989), which divide the NSD process into sequential activities, have been developed based on the NPD model from Booz, Allen, and Hamilton (1982). Typical stages of NSD models include, inter alia, the following: idea generation, screening and evaluation, business case, service development, testing, and launch (Bowers, 1989). Linear NSD processes contributed to the improvement of innovation activities by reducing uncertainty, providing clear guidelines, and eliminating trial-and-error iterations (Lenfle and Loch, 2010). However, they are not suitable for developing new services in the digital age. As the ability to respond to customer needs and market dynamics becomes increasingly important (Carlborg, Kindström, and Kowalkowski, 2014; Weber and Tarba, 2014), more agile methods for developing service innovations gain in significance (Wilson and Doz, 2011; Weber and Tarba, 2014).

Agile methodologies and design thinking

Sambamurthy, Bharadwaj, and Grover (2003) define agility as "the ability to detect and seize market opportunities with speed and surprise" (Sambamurthy, Bharadwaj, and Grover, 2003, p. 238). Although agile development methods have their seeds in the software industry, their principles are widely applicable to any innovation project in a dynamic environment (Lankhorst, 2012). The agile methodology is based on the fundamental assumption that the specifications and requirements of a new service offering are not predictable in advance. Therefore, no (or only a vague) definition of the project objective is necessary. The process is divided into short iterations and starts with the fast development of a first version of the new service product – the so-called "minimum viable product" – which is then discussed with customers. Agile processes are faster, easier, and more customer-focused than traditional NSD processes (Lankhorst, 2012; Link, 2014). Moreover, the design thinking approach, which emerged from design literature, increases in importance and should be integrated into service innovation research (Michel, Brown, and Gallan, 2008; Kimbell, 2011; Barrett, Davidson, Prabhu, and Vargo, 2015). Design thinking is a creative problem-solving approach that highlights the importance of putting the user's needs and preferences at the center of innovation activities (Michel, Brown, and Gallan, 2008; Meinel and Leifer, 2011). Design thinking and agile methodologies have various similarities such as the rapid development of prototypes, an iterative structure, work in small teams, and informal communication (Hirschfeld, Steinert, and Lincke, 2011).

Service innovation ecosystems

Scholars have emphasized the importance of building up ecosystems in order to develop innovations (Yoo et al., 2012; Gawer and Cusumano, 2014). In times of developing digital technology, decreasing communication and coordination costs lead to a geographical diffusion of innovation activities (Maznevski and Chudoba, 2000; Yoo et al., 2012). By utilizing the innovative capabilities of external actors, digital platforms, which support collective value creation and associated innovation ecosystems, enable a dispersion of innovative labor beyond traditional company or supply chain boundaries (Gawer and Cusumano, 2014). According to Lusch and Nambisan (2015), an ecosystem can be defined as a "community of interacting entities – organizations and individuals (including customers) – that coevolve their capabilities and roles and depend on one another for their overall effectiveness and survival" (Lusch and Nambisan, 2015, p. 161). It is becoming increasingly important for the success of service innovation activities to open up the innovation process to external actors and search for knowledge and ideas outside the organizational boundaries (Lopez-Vega, Tell, and Vanhaverbeke, 2016). Such practices include open innovation (Boudreau, 2010), online communities (Faraj, Jarvenpaa, and Majchrzak, 2011), and/or innovation challenges (Boudreau, Lacetera, and Lakhani, 2011).

What these diverse practices have in common is the importance of opening up the innovation process to external actors, as well as the promotion of more flexible and creative approaches towards service innovation. Currently, however, there is no contemporary NSD model integrating agile and creative methodologies as well as innovation ecosystems.

Case study 1: BMW

The automotive industry

The automobile is an example of the dual use of digital technologies. First, such technologies are embedded in the product itself and are increasingly being used throughout the product life cycle (Blümel, 2013). Connected services and location-based technologies alter the characteristics of the car as an enabler of mobility, whereby the combination of software and hardware plays an increasing role for new product development (Bongard, 2015). New competitors like Uber have entered the market for mobility without actually owning cars. Car-sharing business models are on the rise and challenge traditional car manufacturers in the face of digitalization. In this case, we focus on the following: (1) How and why does the innovation process in the automotive industry change in the face of digitalization and transforming product characteristics? (2) How and why do collaborations between OEMs, suppliers, and third parties change – for example, to what extent do innovation ecosystems emerge and how is the innovation process affected?

Company and industry data

The Bayerische Motoren Werke (BMW) AG, with its headquarters in Munich, is the parent enterprise of the BMW Group. The company was founded in 1916 as a manufacturer of aircraft engines before it first began producing cars in 1918. Today, BMW is a premium car manufacturer employing 122,244 people in 150 countries. The company celebrated its 100th anniversary in 2016 (BMW Group, 2015). With the publication "The Next 100," the BMW Group presented a vision for the next 100 years of corporate success in the digital era (BMW Group, 2016a).

After Volkswagen and Daimler, BMW ranks third among German car manufacturers in terms of the number of vehicles produced (Statista, 2017). With 20.6 billion Euro of R&D expenses in 2015, the automotive industry is Germany's strongest industry sector in terms of research investments (BMWi, 2016b). These investments drive product as well as process innovation throughout the economy.

Products and services

Products and services offered by the BMW Group cover the vehicle brands BMW (including the i-series of electric and hybrid models), MINI, and Rolls-Royce as well as BMW motor bikes. In addition, BMW has expanded into a number of services like DriveNow,

ChargeNow, and ParkNow. BMW founded the car-sharing service DriveNow in 2011 as a joint venture with the car rental company Sixt. With ConnectedDrive, BMW offers digital services enabled by the interconnectedness of vehicles, drivers, and their environment through apps and driving assistance services. In 2015, 95 percent of new BMW cars were equipped with embedded technology to form a network. In addition, BMW provides mobility services to business clients, and the company runs a financial services department (BMW Group, 2016b).

Innovation management, process, and culture

At BMW, an independent innovation management department is responsible for the assessment and prioritization of ideas until projects reach the phase of conception. Development projects within innovation management are less cost driven and profit from a high degree of possible exploration by granting space for creativity. Furthermore, BMW has created a digitalization office as a new business unit to promote the development of innovative product-service systems and business models. The company has set up task forces apart from the main organization to address trends like big data and mobility services. Furthermore, the manufacturing unit in Regensburg founded the "InnoLab4," which is dedicated to research focusing on Industry 4.0.

Classically, the development of a new car model follows a linear stage-gate approach assuming a five-year product life cycle. Agile systems are used throughout the company, for example, when developing data services like the self-servicing car. For the development of this product, BMW used a beta version of an app within the UK market in 2016, where car owners of BMW and MINI vehicles tested its functionality. Based on generated user data, the app is designed to inform the driver if the car needs service, like a change of brake pads or oil filter. The system is capable of arranging appointments at the closest service station (based on Google maps) and can transmit data regarding necessary spare parts prior to the appointment in order to minimize waiting times for the customer. Testing user acceptance and behavior of this predictive maintenance concept for cars offers the opportunity to generate real-time feedback during the development process. BMW created the product with a high degree of agility and customer focus to meet user requirements.

In 2015, BMW introduced a new IT strategy (Computerwoche, 2015), which represented a paradigm shift. They replaced the traditional waterfall model with an agile system, thereby accelerating development times from nine to three months. The new concept relies on a questionnaire that identifies the possible rate of agility for each product. Based on individual product requirements, BMW chose one of three predefined development models for the further course of action. First, the possibility of using a classical waterfall model is still available if product characteristics call for a traditional approach. The second option consists of an agile model, and option three offers the opportunity to develop a product using the lean startup development model. The agile method uses a modified business model canvas that covers questions regarding the future customer base of the underlying product. Furthermore, product placement, strategic background, and involved business units are planned. The canvas builds the basis for financial resource allocation in order to develop a proof of concept directed at a dedicated use case. The innovation budget of the group IT is not designed to develop a solution for extensive implementation into the series; rather, it aims at evaluating a technology within a specific field in order to initiate learning processes. Within three months, group IT develops prototypes and finalizes a proof of concept.

In addition, BMW experimented with creativity tools during innovation activities and changed historically implemented rules in order to become more agile. For idea generation purposes, BMW used the design thinking method to iteratively approach user problems. In order to shorten development times, group IT has furthermore changed regulations with regard to the possibility of single sourcings and has implemented rules to facilitate collaboration with startups. Development teams are formed for each project individually, integrating representatives of business units for successful development.

With the existence of these various innovation approaches, BMW aims to satisfy changing requirements for development models. The company identified the need for a higher degree of dynamic reaction to changing user needs as well as volatile environmental and technical developments. Integrating customers into innovation processes is of rising importance for BMW. In addition to solving the problem of differing development cycles of software and hardware, BMW views innovative approaches as a key for future success. Existing vehicle architectures of a historically grown company like BMW have emerged through incremental changes over time. For example, because of the interaction of several dozen engine control units, changes in product architectures are challenging. Due to comparably long hardware life cycles, existing sensors in cars are often outdated and do not meet contemporary technological standards. Carmakers looking back at a long history are therefore currently undergoing a phase of migration, having to exploit technologies in existing models while at the same time developing new architectures that meet future needs.

BMW has traditionally had a strong innovation culture. The company demonstrates a strong innovation focus by using modern technologies such as wearable devices, robotics, and digital assistance systems throughout production processes. Furthermore, innovative technologies like virtual reality, as well as modern 3D printing methods facilitate manufacturing and simulation (BMW Group, 2016c). BMW uses VR and AR technologies for communication purposes (e.g. to consult experts on manufacturing problems that are occurring).

Collaboration partner and networks

To increase innovative capacity and make use of open innovation to integrate external innovation potential, BMW founded the *Startup Garage* in Garching (near Munich) in 2015. Startup companies can apply to participate in a 12-week program that covers four aspects: build, learn, network, and sell (BMW Startup Garage, 2016). Startups get the chance to create an automotive prototype based on their generic idea. The process facilitates learning, connects young entrepreneurs with BMW as well as its suppliers, and offers them an initial client. The car maker aims to create long-term supplier relationships with young entrepreneurs.

In addition to collaborations that emerge from the garage program, BMW organizes hackathons and is engaged in other cooperative structures with startups, one of them being the company nextLAP. Founded in 2014, the startup offers a cloud-based IoT platform and connected hardware for manufacturing and logistics. Having formerly worked for Audi, the two founders highly value close collaboration as well as direct communication with their clients as development partners. Following an agile innovation model, BMW and nextLAP form a common development team whereby engineers of the car manufacturer have the possibility to join the startup team in their lab in Munich.

Despite classical collaboration with suppliers and the growing importance of startup cooperation, BMW is also committed to using co-opetition strategies by working with competitors. In 2015, Nokia sold its maps and location service Here to the car manufacturers BMW, Daimler, and Audi, who all hold an equal share of the mapping business.

Agile process models

Due to the size of BMW as well as its product diversity, it is not possible to identify a single innovation process model that is used throughout all innovation activities. Consequently, product-specific differences in development models exist. Our analysis of the self-servicing car demonstrates that BMW uses agile methods for development purposes. The self-servicing car is enabled by an interplay of embedded intelligence like sensors, connectivity, and data analysis technologies, which is typical of smart products. Moreover, BMW uses a beta version of the app in order to optimize the product in close collaboration with its customers, whereby interaction of numerous knowledge fields is necessary (e.g. IT, after-sales and engineering). BMW uses linear stage-gate models when developing products showing traditional characteristics that require compliance with specific safety standards or meeting high-quality expectations of customers. The innovation process of the BMW group IT follows agile principles as far as underlying product requirements allow. Hence, individual innovation characteristics determine the choice of the process model, whereby smart products as well as software are developed within agile structures. Consequently, innovation process models vary when product characteristics vary. However, in order to construct innovation processes according to the varying individual product requirements, the BMW group IT defined a number of generic process frames that are subsequently optimized with regard to product needs.

The different process models vary, especially with regard to the level of agility in product requirements. Our analysis shows that products that are considered a "digital innovation" are more likely to be developed using agile methods. The need to combine several knowledge fields in order to develop emerging product-service systems by collaborating with customers is typical for digital innovation. Moreover, the use of customer feedback for learning purposes and iterative development steps characterizes these special innovation activities. To meet these requirements, BMW uses proofs of concept and collaborates with customers to achieve fast learning cycles.

Organizational impacts

Our case study results show that working on digital innovation required BMW to design interdisciplinary development teams in order to cover case-specific knowledge requirements. As explained earlier, the group IT unit of the company identifies the relevant individual requirements by using a modified business model canvas for each project. Furthermore, BMW implements interdisciplinary development teams. BMW also uses smaller business units, such as the digitalization office, to offer a higher degree of independence than classically hierarchical business structures allow.

Collaboration

By engaging in car-sharing platforms and offering product-service systems in the context of the digital service brand ConnectedDrive, BMW not only plays the role of a traditional car maker but also of a mobility service provider. Consequently, BMW is dependent on a number of different experts covering knowledge fields like software analysis, who used to play a less important role. Since technology and software know-how, as well as expertise on agile development, is often rooted in startup companies, BMW aims to integrate external knowledge into innovation processes. The establishment of the Startup Garage, as well as the organization of hackathons and the use of other open innovation methods, supports this approach. BMW promotes close collaboration in development activities by conducting explorative research projects with suppliers like nextLAP. As described earlier, BMW engineers are engaged in innovation activities at the startup lab building a joint development team across company borders. In addition to the growing relevance of customer and startup collaboration, co-opetition structures with competitors are gaining importance, as shown by the acquisition of the map service. This engagement on behalf of BMW shows the growing importance of innovation ecosystems consisting of suppliers, customers, and competitors.

BMW is increasingly seeking to gain deep insights into customer needs by using open innovation approaches as well as the design thinking method to identify user problems. Furthermore, close customer collaboration is gaining in importance in order to offer individually optimized mobility services. Direct interaction with the customer is therefore the key to gaining access to user data. Hence, BMW promotes direct user interfaces through ConnectedDrive services in order to generate (real-time) user data. Since ownership patterns are changing, car owners and car users are not always identical. To generate user data, BMW promotes direct customer interaction with digital services, since the identification of customer needs is key for future product success. BMW needs customer feedback in order to pursue agile development approaches. As in the case of the self-servicing car, product iterations developed in an agile way enable quick feedback loops

Case study 2: financial services in Germany

The industry

The financial services industry in Germany is also home to an increasing number of startup companies, so-called FinTechs (for financial technology), that capture niche markets by offering alternative solutions for banking services and by developing new business models. Digital technologies not only offer new opportunities for FinTechs but also for traditional banks (Drummer, Jerenz, Siebelt, and Thaten, 2016). In order to analyze the requirements and success factors of new service development processes in the digital age, we analyzed four companies, their business models, and their approaches to innovation. After describing these cases, we present our overall findings and a cross-case analysis (Eisenhardt, 1989; Yin, 2014).

Company profiles

The first company, which we call "New Entrant A," is a German digital bank that obtained its full banking license in 2009. With the help of the Internet and Web 2.0 technologies, the aim of the firm was to transfer the behaviors and practices that exist in Web 2.0 to the financial services industry. Within the last six years, Entrant A evolved from a small FinTech company into a continuously growing firm with currently about 120,000 retail-banking customers and 30,000 business customers. The firm offers all traditional banking services, including lending and deposit operations. Using the motto "banking with friends," the firm created a much-frequented online forum that allows its members to interact with each other as well as the bank. This forum has become a central element of the firm's innovation activities. Within this community, members discuss ideas for new services and have the opportunity to incorporate their own ideas and requirements. Furthermore, the firm conducts surveys about potential new services, and members of the community are actively integrated into the NSD process, for example, by testing new services.

Entrant B is a German FinTech company founded with the aim of enabling consumers to pay in cash at local retail stores such as supermarkets or drugstores for the products and services they buy online. Like many other FinTechs, the firm does not hold a banking license. Since the company's founding in 2011, the business model has developed further and is no longer limited to online retailers but also offers its services to customers of nine different industries, such as energy suppliers, telecommunications companies, travel portals, and insurance companies. For example, since going online in March 2013, customers can book flights online without a credit card using the payment infrastructure of Entrant B. Moreover, they can pay invoices, such as electricity bills, in cash. If customers decide to use the payment infrastructure of Entrant B, they receive an invoice with a barcode. This barcode can be scanned (and the invoice paid) in about 10,000 retail stores in Germany, such as the supermarket chains "Rewe" and "Penny," or the drugstore chain "dm." For each transaction, Entrant B receives about 1 to 2 percent of the transaction amount. We can identify three user groups: (1) "low-income" earners – this is the largest group – who depend highly on cash payment since they receive their main income in cash (e.g. waiters, taxi drivers, or construction workers) or have a bank account that is overdrawn; (2) people who do not have a credit card and therefore cannot book flights online, or teenagers who get their pocket money in cash and want to spend it on the Internet; and (3) security-conscious people who do not want to disclose their personal data online. Since October 2015, Entrant B – together with the Entrant A bank – has been offering its payment infrastructure to the bank's customers. Supplying customers with cash is a large cost factor for banks. Owning ATMs is expensive, and they do not generate revenue. Moreover, it is less convenient for customers to take a detour in order to find the next ATM than it is to combine their grocery shopping at the supermarket with depositing or withdrawing money. Therefore, the company aims to offer its payment infrastructure to customers of traditional banks. In the long term, the FinTech startup is striving to substitute the traditional bank branch by offering an alternative private payment infrastructure. The company developed a platform that offers a new way to process payments. This platform is increasingly becoming an ecosystem linking diverse actors.

Incumbent Bank A is a traditional bank with about 4 million customers in Germany. The firm has been focusing on the private banking market for more than 90 years. Important distribution channels include branch operations, telephone, Internet, and mobile. Its digital as well as its innovation strategy is part of the overall "omni-channel banking" strategy. The bank incorporates "digital" into the very core of its activities, and usability and customer-centricity are central elements of the innovation activities. The bank does not just create its own innovative solutions but is specifically looking for partners to develop new services.

Incumbent Bank B is one of the largest financial service providers in Germany, serving about 14 million private and corporate clients. The firm has a very dense branch network and is in contact with its customers via branch operations, online, or by telephone. The digitalization activities are comprehensive and embrace several innovation initiatives such as the so-called "campus" – an idea lab that aims to show the firm's employees new methods and tools for being innovative in their everyday lives – or the "idea fabric" – a meeting point for cross-functional teams that work for about four months on innovative tasks and new ideas.

Case study results

Based on our literature analysis, the aspects of acceleration, agility, and customer-centricity (Yoo et al., 2012; Carlborg, Kindström, and Kowalkowski, 2014; Weber and Tarba, 2014; Porter and Heppelmann, 2015) have been identified as the requirements for successful service innovation processes in the digital age. The case of Entrant A shows that the acceleration of innovation activities is a key component of the firm's strategy. Whereas many companies only bring innovations to market that are completely finalized, Entrant A usually introduces products that are "initially incomplete" in order to accelerate the pace of innovation. New features are added later as soon as they are ready for deployment. Entrant B follows the same principle. An accelerated innovation process is necessary for the two established banks as well due to fast and flexible startups that have more financial resources at their disposal than in the past. Banks A and B emphasize the importance of accelerated processes and are trying to deploy new features more often. Entrants A and B both highlight the increasing impact of agility in innovation processes. For them, it is important to continuously reconsider the decisions taken and implement agile development methods as the required pace of innovation can only be realized by agile methodologies. Banks A and B also stress the relevance of agile processes, but for them, the term agility not only describes agile innovation processes but also a specific mind-set. Bank B's manager responsible for digital experience and innovation management states:

> Agility starts in the minds of the firm's employees. It is important to overcome thinking barriers and to encourage them to try various things. This is the basis for agile processes. The evolutionary history has already provided proof that it is not the strongest that is going to survive but the most adaptive.

In contrast to young companies that are digital in nature, established banks struggle with the organizational change. Agility can only be realized when the whole organization is changing. This is in line with Teece (2014), who emphasizes the importance of continuously transforming established behavioral patterns. In his opinion, this ability shows the true value of dynamic capabilities.

Customer-centricity is the third requirement. Entrant A sees customers as the key innovation drivers so that a clear customer focus is important in order to develop innovations that users value. The firm has structured its innovation process in a way that allows the integration of customers into innovation activities. The community forms a central element of the firm's innovation activities and shows the customer-centricity of the firm. Although customers sometimes do not know in advance which products they might value in the future, the analysis of our four cases shows that all firms incorporate customers into innovation processes as they recognize the importance of customer-centricity. The requirements of acceleration, agility, and customer-centricity are equally important for successful NSD processes of entrants and incumbents.

According to the literature, linear innovation processes are less useful in times of technological change so that agile methodologies are gaining in significance (Sethi and Iqbal, 2008; Wilson and Doz, 2011). Entrants A and B designed similar innovation processes that were both a combination of linear and agile proceedings. The so-called "fuzzy front end" of innovation activities, which includes all activities starting with the first impulse for a new idea until the concept is implemented (Menor, Tatikonda, and Sampson, 2002; Alam, 2006), is structured formally and is divided into the stages of idea generation, scoping, and the development of a business case. However, agile elements such as iterations and feedback loops are already established within these three stages. With the start of the development process, a completely agile approach consisting of multiple "sprints" is used. In contrast, Banks A and B use two different innovation processes: a classical linear process for the "back end," and for incremental innovations and a more agile process – equal to the approach of Entrants A and B described earlier – for the development of the "front end" and more radical innovations. In order to realize front-end applications, Bank A often cooperates with partners such as digital design agencies.

The literature also indicates that new forms of innovation practices such as open innovation (Boudreau, 2010), online communities (Faraj, Jarvenpaa, and Majchrzak, 2011), and innovation challenges (Boudreau, Lacetera, and Lakhani, 2011) improve innovation activities. Our cross-case analysis showed that all four companies use all of these approaches. Whereas open innovation, co-creation, and online communities are used to generate new ideas and to discuss and test new services with different stakeholders, innovation challenges are mainly used to find new talent and to build up partnerships with entrepreneurs. Bank B's responsible manager for digital experience and innovation management states: "Hackathons help in the building up of a network of innovators and entrepreneurs. As we want to build up an ecosystem, finding partners is important for us. Innovation challenges help to get in contact with developers and start-ups."

Our literature analysis indicates that the increasing prevalence of digital technology has heightened the role of platforms (Yoo et al., 2012). Entrant A's "community platform," which is described earlier, is the key element of the firm's innovation strategy. The firm is not only using this platform itself but is selling it to other companies. In addition, Entrant A pursues a clear platform strategy. The firm is opening up its banking infrastructure so that other companies can be integrated into the platform and have the possibility to offer their services to Entrant A's customers. The firm therefore not only creates innovations itself but also offers its customers a platform that incorporates the services of other companies. Moreover, Entrant B also focuses on developing a platform with a focus on offering a new way to process payments. Furthermore, Bank B built up a so-called "co-creation platform" in order to integrate customers into innovation activities. About 4,000 persons use the platform, which in addition to customers incorporates noncustomers, FinTechs, and the firm's employees. For Bank B, the "spirit transfer" is of primary importance. Moreover, FinTechs or other stakeholders have the opportunity to use the platform infrastructure (for free) to build or further develop their business. Although Bank A does not focus on platform development, it acknowledges the relevance of digital technology platforms.

Furthermore, ecosystems are an important success factor for the development of innovations in the digital age. Entrant B's co-founder and managing director stated:

> Platforms and ecosystems are the value of the future. They drive innovation. As it is increasingly difficult to develop innovations on one's own, building up ecosystems that promote and foster new ideas is becoming more and more important. The perfect example is Apple: Most of the people do not buy the iPhone because of its hardware but because of the software and the available applications – this means because of the ecosystem around the iPhone. With our infrastructure, we are also building up a platform that brings together diverse actors in an ecosystem.

Moreover, Bank A is currently building an ecosystem around the topic "contactless payment" together with partners from several industries. The firms cooperate in order to realize an innovation based on near field communication technology. Bank A's Chief Marketing Officer states: "In the digital age, diverse players enter the market for financial services so that innovation ecosystems gain in importance because one company alone would not be able to realize some of the innovation projects." In order to create a stable ecosystem, it is important to generate "win-win-win" situations for all stakeholders. Otherwise the cooperation efforts will not be successful.

Innovation in the digital age

A process model for digital innovation

Based on the results of our case studies, we developed the process model shown in Figure 14.1. The figure shows two directions of influence that digitalization exerts in both manufacturing and service industries.

First, digital technologies are used throughout the process while conducting innovation activities. As stated in the proposition in Group 4 in the figure, technologies have the potential to accelerate development activities and can facilitate communication as well as collaboration. These principles build the basis of the generic framework for digital innovation since successful development builds upon the exploitation of this potential.

Second, firms can use digital technologies within products. As explained earlier, firms can alter product characteristics for successful digital innovation. Once firms identify the characteristics, they must choose a suitable process model. Firms can optimize the process according to individual needs, thereby achieving the highest degree of agility possible for the underlying project. Developing digital innovation includes using proofs of concept, early prototypes, and collaborative development structures, if possible. Firms form interdisciplinary teams and sometimes consider the possibility of separating business units. They provide innovation space and promote innovation with new values. Collaboration ecosystems emerge, innovation activities focus on user needs, and close customer cooperation is put into practice. Given the adaptability of innovation activities, the presented framework shows a generic process for digital innovation that is based on the influence of digitalization on products and processes.

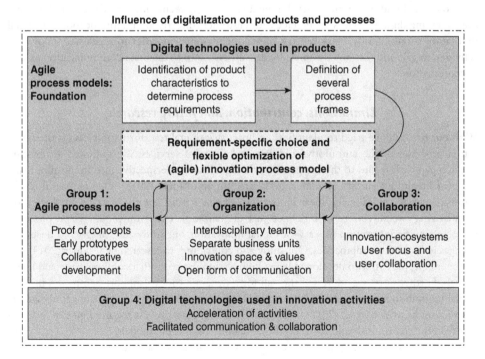

Figure 14.1 The generic innovation process for digital innovation

Conclusion

Managerial recommendations

Internal changes in methods

From our study, we identified several managerial implications as options for future digital innovation success in practice. First, companies should define digital innovation processes individually with regard to the requirements of each project and the possible degree of agility. To facilitate this approach, companies should define a choice of several frame processes that can be individually adapted and optimized according to project needs. Second, companies should develop early prototypes, create proof-of-concept studies, and collaborate with users. Third, firms should critically analyze product portfolios for possible alternative strategies to meet customer needs. Fourth, firms should create development teams individually with regard to project requirements. Fifth, companies should consider the option of temporary as well as permanent organization changes in order to allow space for creativity. Finally, firms must develop values and open communication to promote digital innovation.

External cooperation

For successful cooperative activities for digital innovation, firms must develop a common understanding of innovation when choosing collaboration partners. Innovation success can be promoted by the participation in a digital innovation ecosystem consisting of startups, competitors, and customers. In addition, firms should consider open innovation methods to increase innovation potential. Building interfirm development teams, using techniques like design thinking, and implementing digital services to interact with customers directly are important tools for digital innovation success. Lastly, firms can use digital technologies in order to accelerate innovation activities, to gain insights on customers by data analysis, and to facilitate communication as well as coordination.

Limitations, contribution, and future research

With our research, we tried to identify the impact that digital transformation has on the innovation processes of the automotive industry and financial services. We addressed an existing research gap with regard to the integration of a digitalization perspective into innovation management literature that was identified by Bharadwaj and Noble (2015). Our empirical results show changes to traditionally linear innovation systems arising due to digital technologies. By summarizing two directions of influence that digitalization exerts on products and processes within a generic innovation process for digital innovation, our study adds insights to necessary changes in innovation approaches. Our study also contributes to research by Cooper (2014) and Sommer et al. (2015), who developed hybrid innovation processes that combine agile and linear models. Furthermore, we addressed the call for a dynamic tool to support companies in their digital innovation efforts stated by Nylén and Holmström (2015). By doing so, our study amplifies the results of Yoo et al. (2012), who identified changing process requirements in a digital world. Future research should focus on the development of these models.

In addition to innovation process alterations, we identified organizational success factors for digital innovation with regard to company structure and culture. Analyzing these organizational and cultural changes in more detail is an opportunity for research. Given the complexity of the previously mentioned intertwining research fields, future research projects should be interdisciplinary to generate further valuable insights. Collaboration of science and practice will be necessary to enlarge the existing knowledge base and develop strategies for long-term innovation success in the digital era.

References

Adner, R. (2006). Match your innovation strategy to your innovation ecosystem. *Harvard Business Review*, April, pp. 2–11.
Adner, R. and Kapoor, R. (2010). Value creation in innovation ecosystems: how the structure of technological interdependence affects firm performance in new technology generations. *Strategic Management Journal*, 31(3), 306–333.
Alam, I. (2006). Removing the fuzziness from the fuzzy front-end of service innovations through customer interactions. *Industrial Marketing Management*, 35(4), 468–480.
Barczak, G. (2014). From the editor. *Journal of Product Innovation Management*, 31(4), 640–641.
Barras, R. (1986). Towards a theory of innovation in services. *Research Policy*, 15(4), 161–173.
Barras, R. (1990). Interactive innovation in financial and business services: the vanguard of the service revolution. *Research Policy*, 19(3), 215–237.
Barrett, M., Davidson, E., Prabhu, J. and Vargo, S. L. (2015). Service innovation in the digital age: key contributions and future directions. *MIS Quarterly*, 39(1), 135–154.
Becker, R. (2006). Re-thinking the stage-gate process – a reply to the critics. *Management Roundtable Inc.*, 1–5.
Berthon, P., Pitt, L. and Campbell, C. (2008). Ad lib: when customers create the ad. *California Management Review*, 50(4), 6–30.
Beutner, E. (2013). *Virtuelle Produktentwicklung*. Vogel Industrie Medien/VM.
Bharadwaj, A., et al. (2013). Digital business strategy: toward a next generation of insights. *MIS Quarterly*, 37(2), 471–482.
Bharadwaj, N. and Noble, C. H. (2015). Innovation in data-rich environments. *Journal of Product Innovation Management*, 476–478.
Bhattacharya, S., Krishnan, V. and Mahajan, V. (1998). Managing new product definition in highly dynamic environments. *Management Science*, 44(11, Part 2 of 2), S50–S64.
Biemans, W. G., Griffin, A. and Moenaert, R. K. (2015). New service development: how the field developed, its current status and recommendations for moving the field forward. *Journal of Product Innovation Management* (First Online), August 25, 1–16.
BITKOM, Fraunhofer (2014). Industrie 4.0 – Volkswirtschaftliches Potenzial für Deutschland, December 1st, 2016. www.bitkom.org/noindex/Publikationen/2014/Studien/Studie-Industrie-4-0-Volkswirtschaftliches-Potenzial-fuer-Deutschland/Studie-Industrie-40.pdf.
Blümel, E. (2013). Global challenges and innovative technologies geared toward new markets: prospects for virtual and augmented reality. *Procedia Computer Science*, 25, 4–13.
BMW Group (2015). Annual report 2015. November 7, 2016. www.bmwgroup.com/content/dam/bmw-groupwebsites/bmwgroup_com/ir/downloads/de/2015/12784_GB_2015_dt_Finanzbericht_Online.pdf
BMW Group (2016a). Company homepage: Zukunftsthesen. November 7, 2016. www.bmwgroup.com/content/bmw-groupwebsites/bmwgroup_com/de/next100/zukunftsthesen.html
BMW Group (2016b). Company homepage: Marken und Dienstleistungen. November 7, 2016. www.bmwgroup.com/content/bmw-groupwebsites/bmwgroup_com/de/marken.html
BMW Group (2016c). Company homepage: innovation, www.bmwgroup.com/content/bmw-groupwebsites/bmwgroup_com/de/innovation/unternehmen.html.
BMW Startup Garage (2016). November 7, 2016. www.bmwstartupgarage.com
BMWi (2016a). Digitale strategie 2025. September 1, 2016. www.bmwi.de/BMWi/Redaktion/PDF/Publikationen/digitale-strategie-2025,property=pdf,bereich=bmwi2012,sprache=de,rwb=true.pdf
BMWi (2016b). Automobilindustrie Branchenskizze. November 15, 2016. www.bmwi.de/DE/Themen/Wirtschaft/branchenfokus,did=195924.html
Bongard, A. (2015). From the editor: core competencies. *Automotive IT International*, 3.
Booz, Allen and Hamilton (1982). *New products management for the 1980s*. New York: Booz Allen & Hamilton Inc.

Boudreau, K. (2010). Open platform strategies and innovation: granting access vs. devolving control. *Management Science*, 56(10), 1849–1872.

Boudreau, K. J., Lacetera, N. and Lakhani, K. R. (2011). Incentives and problem uncertainty in innovation contests: an empirical analysis. *Management Science*, 57(5), 843–863.

Bowers, M. R. (1989). Developing new services: improving the process makes it better. *Journal of Services Marketing*, 3(1), 15–20.

Brenner, W., Uebernickel, F. and Abrell, T. (2016). Design thinking as mindset, process, and toolbox. In Brenner, W. and Uebernickel, F. (Eds.), *Design thinking for innovation: research and practice*. Springer International Publishing, pp. 3–24.

Brown, S. L. and Eisenhardt, K. M. (1995). Product development: past research, present findings, and future directions. *The Academy of Management Review*, 20(2), 343–378.

Brown, T. (2008). Design thinking. *Harvard Business Review*, 86(6), 84–92.

Carlborg, P., Kindström, D. and Kowalkowski, C. (2014). The evolution of service innovation research: a critical review and synthesis. *The Service Industries Journal*, 34(5), 373–398.

Chesbrough, H. W. (2003). The era of open innovation. *MIT Sloan Management Review*, 44(3), 35–41.

Computerwoche (2015). Die IT-Strategie von BMW. February 06, 2015. November 8, 2016. www.computerwoche.de/a/die-it-strategie-von-bmw,3102626.

Coombs, R. and Miles, I. (2000). Innovation, measurement and services: the new problematique. In Metcalfe, S. J. and Miles, I. (Eds.), *Innovation systems in the service economy: measurement and case study analysis*. New York: Springer, pp. 85–103.

Cooper, R. G. (1976). Introducing successful new industrial products. *European Journal of Marketing*, 10(6), 301–329.

Cooper, R. G. (1990). Stage-gate systems: a new tool for managing new products. *Business Horizons*, 33(3), 44–54.

Cooper, R. G. (2014). What's next? After stage-gate. *Research Technology Management*, 57(1), 20–31.

DaSilva, C. M., et al. (2013). Disruptive technologies: a business model perspective on cloud computing. *Technology Analysis & Strategic Management*, 25(10), 1161–1173.

De Brentani, U. and Cooper, R. G. (1992). Developing successful new financial services for businesses. *Industrial Marketing Management*, 21(3), 231–241.

den Hertog, P. (2000). Knowledge-intensive business services as co-producers of innovation. *International Journal of Innovation Management*, 4(4), 491–528.

den Hertog, P., van der Aa, W. and de Jong, M. W. (2010). Capabilities for managing service innovation: towards a conceptual framework: den Hertog, Pim; van der Aa, Wietze; de Jong, Mark W. *Journal of Service Management*, 21(4), 490–514.

Djellal, F. and Gallouj, F. (2001). Patterns of innovation organisation in service firms: postal survey results and theoretical models. *Science and Public Policy*, 28(1), 57–67.

Drejer, I. (2004). Identifying innovation in surveys of services: a Schumpeterian perspective. *Research Policy*, 33(3), 551–562.

Droege, H., Hildebrand, D. and Forcada, M. A. H. (2009). Innovation in services: present findings, and future pathways. *Journal of Service Management*, 20(2), 131–155.

Drummer, D., Jerenz, A., Siebelt, P. and Thaten, M. (2016). FinTech – challenges and opportunities: how digitization is transforming the financial sector. Dusseldorf: McKinsey.

Edgett, S. and Parkinson, S. (1993). Marketing for service industries – a review. *The Service Industries Journal*, 13(3), 19–39.

Eisenhardt, K. M. (1989). Building theories from case study research. *Academy of Management Review*, 14(4), 532–550.

Faraj, S., Jarvenpaa, S. L. and Majchrzak, A. (2011). Knowledge collaboration in online communities. *Organization Science*, 22(5), 1224–1239.

Gallouj, F. and Savona, M. (2009). Innovation in services: a review of the debate and a research agenda. *Journal of Evolutionary Economics*, 19(2), 149–172.

Gawer, A. (2014). Bridging differing perspectives on technological platforms: toward an integrative framework. *Research Policy*, 43(7), 1239–1249.

Gawer, A. and Cusumano, M. A. (2014). Industry platforms and ecosystem innovation. *Journal of Product Innovation Management*, 31(3), 417–433.

Gruber, W. H. and Marquis, D. G. (1969). *Factors in the transfer of technology*. Cambridge, MA; London: MIT Press.

Henfridsson, O., Mathiassen, L. and Svahn, F. (2014). Managing technological change in the digital age: the role of architectural frames. *Journal of Information Technology*, 29(1), 27–43.

Hirschfeld, R., Steinert, B. and Lincke, J. (2011). Agile software developpment in virtual collaboration environments. In Plattner, H., Meinel, C. and Leifer, L. (Eds.), *Design thinking: understand, improve, apply* (1st ed.). Berlin, Heidelberg: Springer, [u.a.], pp. 197–218.

Howells, J. (2010). Services and innovation and service innovation: new theoretical directions. In Gallouj, F. and Djellal, F. (Eds.), *The handbook of innovation and services: a multi-disciplinary perspective*. Cheltenham: Edward Elgar, pp. 68–83.

Hüsig, S. and Kohn, S. (2011). 'Open CAI 2.0' – computer aided innovation in the era of open innovation and Web 2.0. *Computers in Industry*, 62(4), 407–413.

Kimbell, L. (2011). Designing for service as one way of designing services. *International Journal of Design*, 5(2), 41–52.

Kuester, S., Schuhmacher, M. C., Gast, B. and Worgul, A. (2013). Sectoral heterogeneity in new service development: an exploratory study of service types and success factors. *Journal of Product Innovation Management*, 30(3), 533–544.

Lankhorst, M. (Ed.) (2012). *Agile service development: combining adaptive methods and flexible solutions*. Berlin, New York: Springer.

Lee, S. M., Olson, D. L. and Trimi, S. (2012). Co-innovation: convergenomics, collaboration, and co-creation for organizational values. *Management Decision*, 50(5), 817–831.

Lenfle, S. and Loch, C. (2010). Lost roots: how project management came to emphasize control over flexibility and novelty. *California Management Review*, 53(1), 32–55.

Link, P. (2014). Agile Methoden im Produkt-Lifecycle-Prozess – Mit agilen Methoden die Komplexität im Innovationsprozess handhaben. In Schoeneberg, K.-P. (Ed.), *Komplexitätsmanagement in Unternehmen*. Wiesbaden: Springer Fachmedien Wiesbaden.

Lopez-Vega, H., Tell, F. and Vanhaverbeke, W. (2016). Where and how to search?: Search paths in open innovation. *Research Policy*, 45(1), 125–136.

Lusch, R. F. and Nambisan, S. (2015). Service innovation: a service-dominant logic perspective. *MIS Quarterly*, 39(1), 155–175.

MacCormack, A., et al. (2012). Do you need a new product-development strategy? *Research Technology Management*, 55(1), 34–43.

Manifesto for Agile Software Development (2001). Manifesto for agile software development. August 4, 2015. www.agilemanifesto.org

Marston, S., et al. (2011). Cloud computing – the business perspective. *Decision Support Systems*, 51(1), 176–189.

Maznevski, M. L. and Chudoba, K. M. (2000). Bridging space over time: global virtual team dynamics and effectiveness. *Organization Science*, 11(5), 473–492.

McKinsey & Company (2015). Digital manufacturing: the revolution will be virtualized. November 15, 2016. www.mckinsey.com/business-functions/operations/our-insights/digitalmanufacturing-the-revolution-will-be-virtualized

McKinsey Digital (2015). Industry 4.0 How to navigate digitization of the manufacturing sector. November 10, 2016. www.mckinsey.de/files/mck_industry_40_report.pdf.

Meinel, C. and Leifer, L. (2011). Design thinking research. In Plattner, H., Meinel, C. and Leifer, L. (Eds.), *Design thinking: understand, improve, apply* (1st ed.). Berlin, Heidelberg: Springer [u.a.], pp. xiii–xxi.

Meinel, C. and Leifer, L. (2016). Design thinking for the twenty-first century organization. In Plattner, H., Meinel, C. and Leifer, L. (Eds.), *Design thinking research: taking breakthrough innovation home*. Springer International Publishing, pp. 1–12.

Menor, L. J., Tatikonda, M. V. and Sampson, S. E. (2002). New service development: areas for exploitation and exploration. *Journal of Operations Management*, 20(2), 135–157.

MGI (2013). Disruptive technologies: advances that will transform life, business, and the global economy. January 14, 2015. www.mckinsey.com/insights/business_technology/disruptive_technologies

Michel, S., Brown, S. W. and Gallan, A. S. (2008). An expanded and strategic view of discontinuous innovations: deploying a service-dominant logic. *Journal of the Academy of Marketing Science*, 36(1), 54–66.

Mina, A., Bascavusoglu-Moreau, E. and Hughes, A. (2014). Open service innovation and the firm's search for external knowledge. *Research Policy*, 43(5), 853–866.

MIT Technology Review (2014). The internet of things. March 31st, 2015. www.technologyreview.com/businessreport/the-internet-of-things/free/.

Moeller, S. (2010). Characteristics of services – a new approach uncovers their value. *Journal of Services Marketing*, 24(5), 359–368.

Nylén, D. and Holmström, J. (2015). Digital innovation strategy: a framework for diagnosing and improving digital product and service innovation. *Business Horizons*, 58(1), 57–67.

Page, A. L. and Schirr, G. R. (2008). Growth and development of a body of knowledge: 16 years of new product development research, 1989–2004. *Journal of Product Innovation Management*, 25(3), 233–248.

Parasuraman, A., Zeithaml, V. A. and Berry, L. L. (1985). A conceptual model of service quality and its implications for future research. *Journal of Marketing*, 49(4), 41–50.

Pavitt, K. (1984). Sectoral patterns of technical change: towards a taxonomy and a theory. *Research Policy*, 13(6), 343–373.

Porter, M. E. and Heppelmann, J. E. (2014). How smart, connected products are transforming competition. *Harvard Business Review*, November, 65–88.

Porter, M. E. and Heppelmann, J. E. (2015). How smart, connected products are transforming companies. *Harvard Business Review*, October, 1–19.

Prahalad, C. K. and Ramaswamy, V. (2004). Co-creation experiences: the next practice in value creation. *Journal of Interactive Marketing*, 18(3), 5–14.

Rayna, T. and Striukova, L. (2016). From rapid prototyping to home fabrication: how 3D printing is changing business model innovation. *Technological Forecasting and Social Change*, 102, 214–224.

Rayna, T., Striukova, L. and Darlington, J. (2015). Co-creation and user innovation: the role of online 3D printing platforms. *Journal of Engineering and Technology Management*, 1–13.

Sambamurthy, V., Bharadwaj, A. and Grover, V. (2003). Shaping agility through digital options: reconceptualizing the role of information technology in contemporary firms. *MIS Quarterly*, 27(2), 237–263.

Saxton, G. D., Oh, O. and Kishore, R. (2013). Rules of crowdsourcing: models, issues, and systems of control. *Information Systems Management*, 30(1), 2–20.

Scheuing, E. E. and Johnson, E. M. (1989). A proposed model for new service development. *Journal of Services Marketing*, 3(2), 25–34.

Schwaber, K. and Beedle, M. (2002). *Agile software development with scrum*. Prentice Hall.

Schwaber, K. and Sutherland, J. (2016). The scrum guide. August 2, 2016. www.scrumguides.org/docs/scrumguide/v2016/2016-Scrum-Guide-US.pdf- zoom=100.

Sethi, R. and Iqbal, Z. (2008). Stage-gate controls, learning failure, and adverse effect on novel new products. *Journal of Marketing*, 72(1), 118–134.

Sommer, A. F., et al. (2015). Improved product development performance through agile/stage-gate hybrids. *Research Technology Management*, 58(1), 34–44.

Statista (2017). Größte Automobilhersteller in Deutschland nach Fahrzeugproduktion 2015. February 14, 2017. https://de.statista.com/statistik/daten/studie/246827/umfrage/automobilproduktion-deutscher-hersteller/.

Teece, D. J. (2014). The foundations of enterprise performance: dynamic and ordinary capabilities in an (economic) theory of firms. *Academy of Management Perspectives*, 28(4), 328–352.

Terwiesch, C. and Xu, Y. (2008). Innovation contests, open innovation, and multiagent problem solving. *Management Science*, 54(9), 1529–1543.

Toivonen, M. and Tuominen, T. (2009). Emergence of innovations in services. *The Service Industries Journal*, 29(7), 887–902.

Tushman, M. L. and Anderson, P. (1986). Technological discontinuities and organizational environments. *Administrative Science Quarterly*, 31(3), 439–465.

Utterback, J. M. and Abernathy, W. J. (1975). A dynamic model of process and product innovation. *Omega*, 3(6), 639–656.

Vargo, S. L. and Lusch, R. F. (2004). Evolving to a new dominant logic for marketing. *Journal of Marketing*, 68(1), 1–17.

Vargo, S. L. and Lusch, R. F. (2008). Service-dominant logic: continuing the evolution. *Journal of the Academy of Marketing Science*, 36(1), 1–10.

Weber, Y. and Tarba, S.Y. (2014). Strategic agility: a state of the art. *California Management Review*, 56(3), 5–12.

Weiber, R., Kollmann, T. and Pohl, A. (1999). Das management technologischer Innovationen. In Kleinaltenkamp, M. and Plinke, W. (Eds.), *Markt- und Produktmanagement*. Springer, pp. 75–179.

Wilson, K. and Doz, Y. L. (2011). Agile innovation: a footprint balancing distance and immersion. *California Management Review*, 53(2), 6–26.

Yin, R. K. (2014). *Case study research: design and methods*, 5. Auflage. Los Angeles: Sage.

Yoo, Y., et al. (2012). Organizing for innovation in the digitized world. *Organization Science*, 23(5), 1398–1408.

Zineldin, M. (2004). Co-opetition: the organisation of the future. *Marketing Intelligence & Planning*, 22(7), 780–790.

15
PERSPECTIVES ON POLICIES TO PROMOTE CONVERGENCE IN INNOVATION

Kong-rae Lee

Introduction

We have seen a myriad of new innovations, including smart cars, drones, 3D printing, smart phones, nanoparticles, Internet of Things (IoT), and biomaterials, emerging almost daily. People are surprised at the amazing functions of smart phones but they alternatively feel confused about the new jargon surrounding all the new technologies and functions. The Schumpeterian prediction (1976) that innovations will routinely emerge as a result of mass R&D activities undertaken in large organizations is now socially recognized in the modern industrial world.

Indeed, almost every class of business entity, including small venture firms, individual entrepreneurs, and medium and large firms, routinely innovates by applying their particular knowledge bases. As we have entered into the twenty-first century, this accelerating trend of innovation promises to continue to shake up and restructure the global economy with both negative and positive outcomes for individuals, business firms and other knowledge-creating organizations such as research institutes and universities.

Some scholars have begun to call this new innovation trajectory the fourth industrial revolution, with the first being water- and steam-powered mechanization, the second electricity-based mass production, and the third the industrial revolution centered on information and electronics technologies. The World Economic Forum (WEF) held in January 2016 in Davos, Switzerland, took *the Fourth Industrial Revolution* as the key discussion agenda. Whereas the third industrial revolution was characterized as the digitalization of the global world via information, communication and telecommunications technology, the fourth industrial revolution is characterized by a convergence of diverse technologies, creating new categories of products such as smart cars, drones, 3D printing, nano-bio and new generations of smarter phones.

The impact of the fourth industrial revolution on the economy and society is expected to be far greater than that of the third industrial revolution in terms of speed and scope. Some people are even scared of changes driven by such a revolution as they foresee negative impacts like job losses and widening disparity of income distribution, whereas many optimists insist that such changes will create plenty of leisure time, thereby enhancing human welfare and convenience.

Technological innovation has been traditionally featured as having a variety of characteristics, from simple learning through imitation to complex interactive learning for more advanced technologies. Modern innovations have had a strong tendency towards convergence, in which information and communication technology (ICT) plays a central role across vast areas of industries, creating a bewildering variety of new products and services. Going beyond ICT, other technologies are also converging or being converged at varying degrees of speed and depth of integration, routinely generating new intellectual property rights issues.

The phenomenon of convergence in innovation is likely to further deepen and widen in the future due to an intense competition among firms in global markets. This applies especially to manufacturing firms in the East and Southeast Asian countries, which have been active in convergence innovation. They are in some respects leading the new global industrial revolution and bringing a center of world economic activities. In this trend, national and regional governments need to be highly keen on responding to the convergence phenomenon. They need various perspectives on policy making to promote convergence.

This chapter briefly summarizes past studies on the principles of convergence in innovation in the second section. In the next few sections, the chapter introduces various perspectives on policy making that promote convergence. The third section presents some policy perspectives at the micro level, including process, collective learning and types of converging, and networks and communications as sources of convergence. The fourth section discusses regional-level perspectives on convergence promoting policies such as scope of clustering, city innovation system, collaboration and globalization of R&D. The fifth section presents such country-level perspectives as institutions, culture and human factors.

Past studies on the principles of convergence in innovation

There has been a group of research topics such as how individuals and firms learn and diffuse knowledge as origins of convergence in innovation, how to navigate the processes of convergence and case investigations into industries and countries so as to discover facts or events happening in reality. The results of the past investigations on convergence and their implications can be briefly summarized as follows.

The term 'convergence' indicates that technological convergence can be defined as a horizontal integration of diverse technologies.[1] Horizontal integration means absorption of diverse fields of technological knowledge for the purpose of creating new functions or products, which often broadens the scope of their technological specialization by interacting with user firms.[2] This phenomenon of technological convergence similarly occurred between machinery industries and electronic industries in 1970 and among a variety of industries, including chemicals, foods, machine tools, and pharmaceuticals (Lee, Kong-rae, and Hwang, Jung-tae, 2005).

Technology convergence increasingly appears in the modern innovation scene. The article on "Technological change in the machine tool industry, 1840–1910" by Rosenberg (1963) explains that, at the end of the nineteenth century, all machines confronted a similar collection of technological problems in dealing with such matters as power transmission, control devices, feed mechanisms, friction reduction and a broad array of problems connected with the properties of metals. These problems became common in the production of a wide range of commodities. They seemed apparently unrelated from the perspective of the nature of the final products. The uses, however, of the final products were very closely related on a technological basis. Rosenberg called this phenomenon technological convergence and argued that the intensive degree of specialization that developed in the second half of the nineteenth century owed its existence to a combination of this technological convergence.

Similar to technological convergence, the term 'technological fusion' has been adopted by some innovation scholars (Kodama, 1986, 1994, 1991; Lee, Kong-Rae, 2005, 2007). Kodama (1986) argued that there are two fundamental types of innovation: one is the technological breakthrough, and the other is technology fusion. According to Kodama, breakthrough innovations are associated with strong leadership in a particular technology, and technology fusion becomes possible through concerted efforts by several different industries. He empirically observed a phenomenon of technology fusion that first occurred between machinery industries and electronic industries in 1970, and later among a variety of industries including chemicals, foods, and pharmaceuticals in 1974.

Recently there has been growing trends of innovation studies on the convergence phenomenon, particularly at the micro level. The processes of convergence begin with individuals so that exploring the processes at the personal level has been of important concern. Lee, Kong-rae (2017b) argues that it starts when a researcher with a cognitive map interacts with another researcher holding another cognitive map. He further states that individuals behave differently in terms of their modes of learning and evolve one after another. Technological learning for convergence has gone beyond the simple mode of learning by doing to the extent of learning by porting via learning by using or learning by integration, producing a synergistic impact on innovation.

In the process of convergence, collective learning can be regarded as an important element for making these processes successful. This is because the interaction between individuals evolves into a collective learning that creates new knowledge and provides a clue for creating an innovation. Under active learning, the applications of a given technology are so diverse that the convergence to create new functions, products or services becomes possible. Managing convergence in innovation is mainly concerned with this collective learning at the firm level (Lee, Kong-rae, 2017b). In particular, large firms are faced with many hardships that have become obstacles in pursuing convergence. To create convergence in innovation, they have to cope with anxiety caused by changes from convergence, objectives and visions for changes, and images that follow changes (Yun, Jong-Yong, and Kim, Changsu, 2017).

To explore the process of convergence, Kim, Euiseok (2014) analyzed the convergence in the innovations of printing and electronic technologies and found that there is a continuous disequilibrium between converging technologies, which are divided into two types: reference technology and matching technology. Two types of converging technologies tend to innovate at differing degrees of speed in such a manner that when one technology (reference technology) is innovated and generates a disequilibrium, the other technology – called matching technology – necessarily innovates to match or adjust an optimal balance between the functions of the two technologies. He stated that the process of tuning involving mutual matching and minute adjustment across disparate technologies to achieve a target performance is one of the most critical attributes in convergence.

As seen in Figure 15.1, Technology A1 and Technology B2 converge to create Technology C1, which is a new innovation creating new functions, new products or new processes. Technology A can be a reference technology or matching technology to match or adjust an optimal balance between the functions of the two technologies. In that sense, both Technology A and Technology B may have a certain degree of tuning capability in the process of matching or adjusting an optimal balance. Tuning capability may imply technological opportunity to make an innovation of an individual technology or a converged innovation of the two technologies involved.

Multiple past studies have also found out that different types of convergence emerge, depending upon firm-specific learning modes and growth strategies (Kodama, Nakata, and Shibata, 2017; Darr, 2017; Kim, Jang-Hyun, and Lee, 2017). The inside-out type of convergence in innovation arises when firms try to utilize their core competence for exploiting business opportunities in other market areas, while the outside-in type prevails when firms are in a booming period

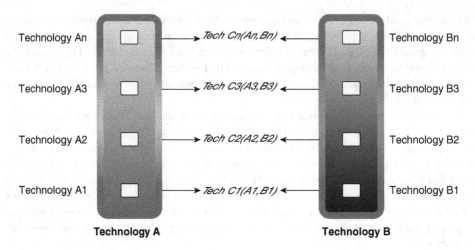

Figure 15.1 Process of convergence between Technology A and Technology B
Source: Lee Kong-rae (2017a)

as they diligently integrate outside technologies into their core competence fields in order to solve their technological problems (Lee, Joseph, and Jeong, 2015).

Regarding sources of convergence, it was argued that networks and communications matter in pursuing convergence since they are likely to be means to diffuse converged knowledge throughout the organizations and societies (Barnett, 2017). He insisted that individuals come up with new innovations through various networks with cognitive processes and communications. Knowledge, information and innovations spread within and between organizations through digital media, such as e-mail and other social network services (SNSs), and are adopted in much the same way as they are from an external source. Networks and communications facilitate and accommodate individual needs, tastes or personal situations, but they also allow dis-adoption due to the dissatisfaction with the innovation or substitution by a newer innovation that better meets the individual's needs or desires, leading to more convergence.

Diversity has also been treated as an important source of convergence in innovation. Steinmueller (2017) stated that diversity is an important enabling factor in navigating convergence in innovation. Diversity presents major steps in creating convergence and often involves generating a space of freedom and opportunities. It is proposed in the context of Asian countries; a transformational change from the legacy of the catching up and competitiveness agenda to the pursuit of diversification has become an important agenda for promoting convergence. In this respect, a strategy of greater diversification remains an option for Asian countries as a response to the risk associated with the current dominance of the catching-up industries and the uneven intersectoral performance.

On the other dimension, a geographic factor in the clustering of firms and professionals appears to be an important element to facilitate convergence in innovation. Wong (2017) found out that a city innovation system matters because it creates a path to convergence. As in the case of Kuala Lumpur and Cyberjaya of Malaysia, a railway company initially assimilated rail technology to attain capability in operation and maintenance (Wong, Chan-Yuan, 2017). As time went by, a group of firms in the railroad industry clustered and learned together, upgrading their level of technology. As a result, convergence in the innovation of companies became evident throughout the period of the 2000s. The knowledge ties among firms clustering in a large city have considerably enabled the emergence of convergence in innovation.

Lastly, intra-industry convergence appeared to be prevailing in contemporary industrial innovation. It has been intensely arising particularly between science-based firms and scale-intensive firms. According to Lee, Kong-rae, 2017b, the specialized suppliers sector showed the highest degree of intra-industry convergence in innovation, implying that it has been the focal point of convergence, integrating forward and backward industries. From the cross-country comparison among China, Japan, Korea and Taiwan, no major differences in the characteristics of convergence in industrial innovation between countries were discovered, implying that the inherent industrial and technological characteristics may play a critical role in convergence activities, regardless of country-specific features (Lee, Kong-rae, 2017b).

As such, the phenomenon of convergence has been observed in many innovations not only in the twentieth century but also today. That is, the convergence between many user sectors and machining technology explored by Rosenberg (1963) is still going on. It is perceived that convergence is a universal phenomenon happening in all technological fields and industrial areas (Rafols and Meyer, 2006; OECD, 1993; Roco and Bainbridge, 2002).

Micro-level perspectives on policies to promote convergence

Diverse viewpoints are required to explore convergence phenomena in innovation. Policies concerned with convergence are generally directed at promoting scientific and technological activities conducive to convergence in innovation so as to increase economic growth and people's welfare. Policies here indicate innovation policies to encourage convergence in innovation. Policy implications at the micro level can be drawn from such perspectives as process, user–supplier and R&D. These perspectives provide better insights for local and central governments in pursuing convergence in innovation.

Looking into the process in which convergence arises and moves seems to be critical for making the right policies to promote it. Learning, particularly collective learning, is vital in managing the processes of convergence at the organizational level. Firms that pursue convergence require policy tools to make institutions well adapted for effective learning. Training and rewarding talented project leaders capable of managing R&D projects will be critical. They are to be well equipped with knowledge and leadership to manage the processes of convergence in order to deal with conflicts or problems arising from the knowledge gap among research personnel and those from the different stages of the process.

In addition to training and rewarding talented project leaders, firms need to have policy tools to play a gate-keeping function. Building up and maintaining linkages between inside and outside organizations through various search activities, forums, regular seminars and so on is a way of facilitating diverse collective learning such as internalization, externalization, socialization and combination and thus managing convergence processes well (Nonaka, 1994).

On the other hand, the user–supplier relationship is one of the key elements to facilitate convergence. The user–supplier interaction is designed to incorporate diverse users' and suppliers' knowledge into the process of convergence in innovation. It emphasizes the downstream side of the innovation process, like early integration of the users' and suppliers' role at the organizational level. The importance of user–supplier interaction has been much emphasized in innovation studies as a source of successful innovation (Lee, Yun, and Jeong, 2015; Lee, 1998; Lundvall, 1988; Sugiura, 1994). It is likely to become even more important in convergence.

Government and corporate policies intended to promote convergence should seriously take users' ideas and viewpoints in addition to those of suppliers. Government-led projects are usually ignorant of user-side ideas so that their results are neither innovative nor sufficient to fulfill originally designed purposes. Therefore, the role of lead users and user–supplier interaction should be considered from the very beginning of a policy designing process and be implemented for the purpose of achieving policy targets.

During the process of convergence in innovation, R&D is a good, powerful instrument for targeting specific convergence in innovation. Planning R&D projects with convergence nature or targets is an effective way of making convergence innovation, assuming that it will be followed by actual implementation. Scientists and engineers generally tend to focus on issues of their own disciplines in conducting R&D. Thus, the portion of R&D projects with a convergence nature is likely to be limited if allowed to run autonomously. One way to promote convergence R&D is to intentionally plan for it.

A substantial portion of government R&D projects and programs today have the characteristics of convergence. This is because they have not only an interdisciplinary nature, but also their objectives require convergence of diverse types of knowledge. Social and technological problems to be solved by governments in reality are so complicated and complex that they need the convergence of diverse knowledge, and so do R&D projects. Government officials in charge of R&D planning therefore need to obtain in-depth knowledge on convergence in innovation.

Last but not least are the human factors determining successful convergence. Human factors include training; general education of people; leaders and their leadership; networks; communications; cooperation and conflict resolution between people; and the credibility, creativity and braveness of people to achieve something complex and complicated. In particular, a university education at the graduate school level needs to be emphasized for making policies to encourage convergence. Through proper education, future professionals are to be well harmonized with each other with respect to diversity and with readiness to carry out convergence projects. The previously mentioned qualities of people conducive to convergence should be cultivated in the education system over a long period. Communications and cooperation among people, both at intra- and interorganizational levels, are critically important for convergence, so they need to be culturally encouraged and strengthened. They are also likely to be amicably accelerated by capable leaders and encourage organizational culture.

Regional-level perspectives on policies to promote convergence

Convergence in innovation can be more clearly observed at the regional level. Diverse players in innovation within a specific region can be easily identified, and so can their innovation activities. This means local government may be able to effectively moderate, facilitate, support and intervene in their innovation activities by using even a small scale of resources. In this regard, regional innovation policies are more effective and efficient than national innovation policies. However, regional governments, especially those with a low level of financial self-reliance, hardly overcome problems arising from a lack of manpower and other resources.

As a way to overcome the limitation of resources at the regional level, innovation policies at the city level can be taken into account. Previous research findings reveal that city and sectoral innovation systems matter in encouraging convergence (Wong, 2017; Pavitt, 1984; Tidd, Bssant, and Pavitt, 2001). Wong's research results (2017) provide a policy implication that such knowledge-creating agents as research institutes, corporate R&D centers, universities, etc., should be geographically clustered as much as possible in city regions to overcome a lack of resources.

Past innovation studies with a cluster approach did not clearly show what scope of geographical area needs to be taken into account in locating knowledge-creating organizations. It is believed that a well-functioning city innovation system effectively creates a path to convergence in innovation. This argument implies that a large city can be a location in clustering them for successful convergence in innovation. This point also needs to be considered when firms globalize their R&D, for instance, sourcing diverse knowledge by locating R&D centers in talented regions.

Collaboration between companies and universities at the city level must be an important element in promoting convergence in innovation. It has been frequently pointed out that both entities are reluctant to collaborate mainly because of cultural differences (Lee, Kong-rae, and Seong, Tae-gyeong, 2009). Companies primarily pursue commercial development and try to achieve relative values of corporate culture, while universities traditionally do early-stage research so as to have a related academic culture. These cultural differences can be overcome by carefully designed policies at the city level. Some universities see their role being extended from teaching and conducting pure research to taking on social challenges and contributing to regional development. Companies also increasingly began to recognize a need to attract the best and brightest talent for meaningful work and social utility (Lutchen, 2018).

Country-level perspectives on policies to promote convergence

At the country level, central government is obviously a core player in developing policies to promote convergence in innovation. It should encourage cooperation among individuals, firms, research institutes and universities. Taking a process perspective means carefully managing each stage of convergence processes. A careful consideration of people and organizations during the convergence processes leads to more frequent cooperation and exchange of knowledge among them, as well as their convergence activities. Governments have so far emphasized competition rather than cooperation among R&D personnel and organizations, which has obviously increased R&D productivity, but they have failed to encourage cooperation for the purpose of generating meaningful innovation. Designing such policies for encouraging cooperation requires more policy research, resources and creative ideas, which requires extra space, time, allowance, margin, etc.

A perspective on the institutional dimension is likely to be also important in making good policies associated with promotion, compensation, protection and co-exploitation of convergence in innovation. A set of institutions enabling people to create or configure convergence that fits into the unique culture of the country or the organization should be identified, formulated and established by policies (Schumpeter, 1976; Tidd, Bssant, and Pavitt, 2001).

Creating convergence in innovation depends greatly upon how many experienced and talented project leaders capable of managing diverse projects are available. Therefore, firms need to have competitive institutions that can select and train such capable project leaders. Not only leaders but also members of organizations and societies require credibility, creativity and braveness to achieve a higher level of convergence innovation. In this regard, the existence of a national innovation system equipped with institutions to nurture human attributes of such leaders is important for fostering convergence in innovation (Lee, Kong-rae, 2017b). Governments should orient their policies towards this end by designing and building up various institutions conducive to convergence in innovation.

The cultural perspective is also a necessary element in making policies to promote convergence. Culture concerns the development of a mind-set such as the creation of community values and social norms, building trust relationship among stakeholders, decision-making of collective agents, and so on. Whether or not organizations or science and technology communities have a culture to adapt to diversity is likely to be critical in promoting convergence in innovation. An autonomous environment is definitely required in R&D communities for convergence to take place, as it helps generate creative ideas.

Likewise, democratic leadership, democratic culture and democratic decision-making rather than authoritative ones are likely to create more convergence. In this respect, people should enjoy freedom as much as possible, both in organizations and communities, unless they exert a negative influence. A liberal working environment should also be respected and regulations should be minimized. A democratic political system is likely to have a higher possibility of developing such a culture than any other regime.

Conclusion

One of the most important features of the current wave of industrialization is the convergence phenomena of different categories or processes of innovation. The concept of 'convergence innovation' put forward helps explain how many diverse knowledge fields are being combined in order to create not only new products but also new functions, processes or services. How can we understand, analyze and interpret modern convergence in innovation? This is not a trivial question. It goes to the very heart of understanding the so-called fourth industrial revolution.

However, until now, we have not had research necessary to understand the processes involved in convergence or its impact on firms, organizations, industries and nations. Moreover, confusion arises when pursuing convergence among policy makers, organizational leaders and business people. They sometimes devise conflictual measures or deepen problems that arise from the conventional ways of doing things. This is because their lack of understanding of the principles of convergence in innovation. Innovation scholars are responsible for solving this situation as they explore the truth in the convergence phenomena today.

There should be more studies so as to create more discussions and new theories, perhaps finally reaching a synthesis on convergence in innovation. It requires bringing together a range of new studies on convergence in innovation so that policy perspectives can be drawn not only for innovation scholars but also for policy makers to promote convergence in innovation. I believe sometime later hypotheses related to convergence will be established as theories, be embedded in innovation theories and contribute to overcoming the problems of the modern capitalist economy through convergence innovation.

The previously mentioned micro-, regional- and country-level perspectives in this chapter provide a clue to developing innovation policies and expanding them across various aspects of convergence. Innovation studies focused on convergence need to refine their research framework and incorporate various perspectives in the future. In-depth research on these perspectives will provide useful insights into the exploration and exploitation of future convergence studies. The suggestions represent useful insights for governments interested in pursuing convergence for the purpose of promoting social welfare and economic growth.

Notes

1 The term 'horizontal integration' in this chapter is not same as that explained by Teece (1976), who used the term as an organizational integration over value chains.
2 Iansiti (1998) stated that technology integration is made up of a set of problem-solving activities that are performed to match a new element of technical knowledge to the complex architecture of established competences.

References

Barnett, G. A. (2017). Innovation and network. In Kong-rae Lee (Ed.), *Managing convergence in innovation*. London: Routledge, Chap 3, pp. 38–50.

Darr, A. (2017). Convergence of service and technical skills: the case of ERP implementation in Israel. In Lee, Kong-rae (Ed.), *Convergence innovation in Asian industries*. New York: Routledge, pp. 40–57.

Iansiti, M. (1998). *Technology integration*. Boston, MA: Harvard Business School Press.

Kim, Euiseok (2014). *Evolutionary patterns and dynamics of technological convergence: the case of printed electronics*, PhD Dissertation, Daejeon: KAIST.

Kim, Jang-Hyun and Lee, Jinsuk (2017). A semantic network analysis of technological innovation in dentistry: a case of CAD/CAM. In Lee, Kong-Rae (Ed.), *Convergence innovation in Asian industries*. New York: Routledge.

Kodama, F. (1986). Inter-disciplinary research: Japanese innovation in mechatronics technology. *Science and Public Policy*, 13(1), 44–51.

Kodama, F. (1991). *Analyzing Japanese high technologies: the techno paradigm shift*. London: Pinter Publishers.

Kodama, F. (1994). *Emerging patterns of innovation*. Boston, MA: Harvard University Press.

Kodama, F., Nakata, Y. and Shibata, T. (2017). Changes in modes of technological learning. In Lee, Kong-Rae (Ed.), *Managing convergence in innovation*. New York: Routledge.

Lee, Kong-Rae (1998). *The sources of capital goods innovation – the roles of user firms in Japan and Korea*. London: Harwood Academic Publishers.

Lee, K-R. (2007). Patterns and processes of contemporary technology fusion: the case of intelligent robots. *Asian Journal of Technology Innovation*, 15(2), 45–65.

Lee, Kong-Rae (Ed.) (2017a). *Convergence innovation in Asian industries*. New York: Routledge.

Lee, Kong-Rae (Ed.) (2017b). *Managing convergence in innovation*. New York: Routledge.

Lee, Kong-Rae and Hwang, Jung-Tae (2005). *A study on innovation system with multi-technology fusion* (in Korean). Seoul: STEPI Policy Study 2005–17.

Lee, Kong-Rae and Seong, Tae-Gyeong (2009). *University-industry collaboration for activating convergence innovation* (in Korean). Seoul: STEPI Policy Report.

Lee, K-R., Joseph, Y. J. and Jeong, E-S. (2015). Convergence innovation of the textile machinery industry in Korea. *Asian Journal of Technology Innovation*, 23(s.1), 58–73.

Lundvall, B. A. (1988). Innovation as an interactive process: from user-producer interaction to the national system of innovation. In Dosi et al. (Eds.), *Technical change and economic theory*. London and New York: Pinter Publishers.

Lutchen, K. R. (2018). Why companies and universities should forge long-term collaborations. *Harvard Business Review*, January 24, 1–10.

Nonaka, I. (1994). A dynamic theory of organizational knowledge creation. *Organizational Science*, 5(1), 14–37.

OECD (1993). *Technology fusion: a path to innovation, the case of optoelectronics*. Paris: OECD.

Pavitt, K. (1984). Sectoral patterns of technical change: towards a taxonomy and a theory. *Research Policy*, 13(6), 343–373.

Rafols, I. and Meyer, M. (2006). *Knowledge-sourcing strategies for cross-disciplinarity in bionanotechnology*. Brighton: SPRU Electronic Working Paper Series: 152.

Roco, M. C. and Bainbridge, W. S. (2002). *Converging technologies for improving human performance*. Arlington, VA: NSF.

Rosenberg, N. (1963). Technological change in the machine tool industry, 1840–1910. *Journal of Economic History*, 23(4), 414–446.

Schumpeter. (1976). *Capitalism, socialism and democracy*. London: George Allen & Unwin.

Steinmueller, W. E. (2017). Convergence and diversity in Korea: moving from catching up to forging ahead. In Lee, Kong-Rae (Ed.), *Managing convergence in innovation*. New York: Routledge, pp. 71–82.

Sugiura, K. (1994). *Technological role of machinery users in economic development: the case of the textile machinery industry in Japan and Korea*. PhD Dissertation, Brighton: University of Sussex.

Teece, D. J. (1976). *Vertical integration and vertical divestiture in the US petroleum industry*. Stanford Institute for Energy Studies, Working Paper No. 300.

Tidd, J., Bssant, J. and Pavitt, K. (2001). *Managing innovation-integrating technological, market and organizational change* (2nd ed.). Chischester: John Wiley & Sons Ltd.

Wong, Chan-Yuan (2017). Convergence innovation in city innovation system: railway technology case in Malaysia. In Lee, Kong-Rae (Ed.), *Managing convergence in innovation*. New York: Routledge.

Yun, Jong-Yong and Kim, Changsu (2017). Convergence innovation in the management of large firms: Samsung Electronics. In Lee, Kong-Rae (Ed.), *Managing convergence innovation*. London: Routledge, pp. 55–70.

16
RESPONSIBLE INNOVATION
Origin, attribution and theoretical framework[1]

Liang Mei and Jin Chen

Introduction

Against the background of new technological developments and a scientific revolution, while many significant innovations, including the internal combustion engine, atomic energy, information technology, and biomedicine technology are driving development (Owen, Baxter, Maynard, and Depledge, 2009), they are also triggering important thoughts on the duality of technological innovations[2](Jonas, 1984). The existing scientific innovation policies and management approaches meet difficulties and limitations when dealing with the issues like moral ethics, environmental protection, social value and sustainable development in technological innovations. Controversial cases on innovation involve the social and ethical crisis with genetically modified organisms and genetic engineering (Grove-White, Macnaghten, and Wynne, 2000), the usage norms of emerging technology (Weart, 1976), the global and regional safety hazards of applying nuclear physics and energy (Groueff, 1967), the safety of flu virus research (Kaiser and Moreno, 2012), the privacy leaks with information and communication technology (Eden, Jirotka, and Stahl, 2013), the institutional risk and fraudulent behaviors in the finance sector and its derivatives (Fratzscher and Imbs, 2009), as well as the environmental negative impacts (e.g. pollution from industrial innovations) of technological advances (Fischer, Parry, and Pizer, 2003). All these trigger the attentions on the negative externality of researches and innovations, as well as the reviews of contractual linear model of a scientific society (scientific freedom should be based on the satisfaction of social needs and social values) (Owen, Baxter, Maynard, and Depledge, 2009) on the research and policy level. The European Union (EU)'s "Horizon 2020" framework program proposed responsible innovation, emphasizing that research and innovation must effectively mirror social needs and social expectations, reflect social value and responsibility, and form the social value wished by all EU nations (Owen, Baxter, Maynard, and Depledge, 2012). In order to meet this target, innovation should be morally acceptable, expected by the society, safe and sustainable (Von Schomberg, 2013). In addition, the "2020 Wise Growth" strategy raised two basic questions while stressing innovation-driving development: (1) Are we able to define the appropriate social result and impact of research and innovation? (2) If we endorse a certain innovation, will we succeed in leading innovation towards the direction satisfactory to the society? The research policy thus increased its focus on the integration of society and technology and was devoted to expanding scientific innovation in terms of the integration of society and moral ethics in the core science and engineering R&D fields so as to lead the innovation path towards society's satisfaction (Rodríguez, Fisher, and Schuurbiers, 2013).

With a focus on the technology advancement and economic effect, the traditional innovation paradigm should borrow from new innovation management paradigms through research and practice on the social crisis that might be brought about by innovative acts or activities, as well as the conflict between the social moral ethics and social expectation satisfaction produced by the innovative activities themselves. As an emerging management paradigm and management ideology, responsible innovation means managing the existing science and innovation collectively in order to explore the future of innovation (Stilgoe, Owen, and Macnaghten, 2013; Mei, Chen, and Sheng, 2014) and make innovation satisfy the social needs and moral and ethical restraints more effectively (Van den Hoven, 2013b). Under the logic that the traditional innovation paradigm focuses on the process from new innovation ideas to the returns by commercialization (Chesbrough, 2003), many topics such as the potential crisis and uncertainty of technology, as well as social harm produced by innovation, have become the focal points of research in responsible innovation. Responsible innovation combines the positive aspects of technological innovation with the drivers of innovation objectives, ethical crisis of the resulting innovation and a mismatch with social needs, as well as uncertainty in innovation (Stilgoe, Owen, and Macnaghten, 2013), to create a paradigm shift that restructures the role and position of technological innovation. This can provide moral, sustainable and effective innovation benefits; realize the in-depth integration of technological innovation and social values (Stilgoe, Owen, and Macnaghten, 2013); and receive a more social response in terms of scientific and technological development, institution and polices (De Saille, 2013). However, on the theoretical level, responsible innovation is still in the construction stage (Gianni and Goujon, 2014), and there is insufficient systematic research on the concept, connotation, attribution and theoretical framework of responsible innovation. In the meantime, as the conceptual product derived from the development situation in Europe shows, the existing theoretical study does not have reflection and discussion of responsible innovation on social and political situations. We must ensure that the theoretical framework of responsible innovation is embedded in the regional situation, culture, practice and all forms of social innovation (Macnaghten et al., 2014). Thought must be given to how to construct a framework of responsible innovation that is applicable to all kinds of situations so that the universality of the theory can be studied (Gianni and Goujon, 2014). Therefore, this chapter conducts a systematic review of the concept, origin and attribution of responsible innovation from a theoretical perspective and constructs the theoretical framework of responsible innovation from the integral view of the responsible innovation framework and institutional situation in order to fill the gap in the research.

Origin, connotation and attribution of responsible innovation

Origin of responsible innovation

Humans' innovation capabilities are far more powerful than innovation itself, and they produce a sustained impact on society (Pandza and Ellwood, 2013). Research is considered the extension of human knowledge as well as the reflection of moral and public interests. With the background of scientific liberation, there is a conflict between scientists' responsibility of creating reliable knowledge and the wider responsibility to society (Stilgoe Owen, and Macnaghten, 2013). The research driven by curiosity can produce new knowledge, but this knowledge only involves what can be done (Beesley, 2003). The possibility that knowledge can bring harm as well as progress was widely ignored (Koepsell, 2010). According to the query of Polanyi's spontaneous order of the scientific community, scientists lack the self-reflection of their social responsibility while innovating and lack the capability to predict the future result of their innovative practice (Glerup and Horst, 2014). This phenomenon gives rise to the focus and discussion of the borders between science and society and science's responsibility to society, and emphasizes that scientists should find the balance between spontaneity and civic responsibility (Douglas, 2003). In the latter half of the 20th century, science and innovation are more interactive in terms of research policy. Technological innovation can bring both benefits and harm (Jonas, 1984). Nanotechnology, genetically modified organisms, electric transportation, stem cell research, online social networks, biology technology, robots, nuclear power, military and safety technology are defined as controversial technological innovations (Eurobarometer, 2005). More emphasis is placed on the responsible innovation by research on the purposive and nonpurposive impact of new knowledge and new technology.

The United States was the first to propose the concept of "responsible development" when it released the 21st-century Nanotechnology Research and Development Act in 2003, focusing on increasing the positive effect of nanotechnology on social progress to the maximum extent and lowering the negative impact of the technological innovation to solve the most urgent social needs of the nation (Owen, Macnaghten, and Stilgoe, 2012). Since then, discussions of "responsible innovation" started to emerge, and over ten years of research and policy discussions followed (Hellstrom, 2003; Owen, Macnaghten, and Stilgoe, 2012). Different from responsible development, which focuses on technology and risk properties, responsible innovation focuses more on the wider innovative policies and scientific governance (Stahl, 2013). It excludes the simple prediction of the future outcome of research and innovation, emphasizes the inherent uncertainty of the future and considers that traditional scientific and research methods cannot handle the scientific innovation and governance model any more (Stahl, 2013). In terms of technological innovation, policy makers and the public, as well as other entities, need to learn about the positive and negative aspects of innovation; understand the direction of science and technology development and future objectives and the challenges of emerging scientific fields; explain the future significance, value and profit of technological innovation (Grunwald, 2014); promote a responsible scientific governance model; and realize the satisfaction of applying technological innovation to social needs and ethical values (Van den Hoven, 2013b).

Connotation of responsible innovation

Traditional studies think that responsible innovation is a contradictory concept. On the one hand, innovation reflects technological development and progress while focusing on the market products and processes; responsibility has multiple meanings and is generally considered to be related to the moral ethics of the potential outcome of innovation, implying a certain degree of restraint on innovation (Gianni and Goujon, 2014). As seen from the perspective of the interaction between moral ethics and technological innovation, technological innovation is often the source of the problem for ethics, not the solution for the moral dilemma; as for technological innovation, moral ethics is often the restraint of technological development instead of the source of innovation (Van den Hoven et al., 2012). The process of innovation commercialization does not fundamentally take into account the complexity in the innovation process and the negative externality produced by the evolution of innovation. At the heart of the traditional innovation paradigm, both past and current experiences cannot bring effective and reasonable guidance to the future of innovation (Adam and Groves, 2011), and this innovation paradigm and research method cannot solve the negative outcome and relevant harms of innovation. Responsibility is created between the subject and object of innovation and directly reflects the orientation of the innovation outcome within the norms and codes (Stahl, 2013). In the meantime, looking at the reaction of innovation to responsibility, studies show that technological innovation can be the impetus of ethical progress, can help solve the so-called problem of moral overload or moral dilemma, can expand options in terms of action and can achieve a value surplus of innovation and morality. Based on this, studies looked at the connotation of responsible innovation, as shown in Table 16.1. This chapter, with its consideration of existing studies, contends that responsible innovation is a dynamic process that contains the joint decisions of multiple stakeholders, evaluates the objectives and outcomes of innovation based on the foresight of existing knowledge and establishes an adaptive institution of scientific governance to guide innovation towards the satisfaction of social needs and the requirement of moral ethics.

Attribution analysis of responsible innovation

Responsible innovation emphasizes socialized responsible projects – the technological innovation and project should serve society to the maximum extent and transform into a norm (Durbin, 2008). The attribution of responsibility can involve things happening in the future: being responsible means that the subject is assigned a certain task or certain duties to learn about the outcome or status to be prevented for a certain object (Doorn, 2012). During the process of technological innovation, responsibility attribution needs to inform the direction of technological development and technological improvement, and apply the method with regard to morality in in research and technological innovation (Doorn, 2012). Existing studies explore the attribution of responsible innovation from the merit-based perspective, rights-based perspective and consequentialist perspective.

The merit-based perspective focuses on the ethical responsibility of innovative acts. The actors (such as the scientists) being ethically responsible and aware of the harms of technological innovation is not equal to being responsible for them in a causal relationship. The responsibility in a causal relationship stresses the objectivity of an act and the relationship between it and the outcome of the act, whereas ethical responsibility emphasizes the reaction and attitude of the actor. This means that the actor is only ethically responsible when the subjective attitude of the actor matches the outcome of the act (Eshleman, 2008). Under the rule of fairness, whether the actor is ethically responsible for the outcome is assessed based on the following conditions: (1) ethics agent, that is, the subject of the act has the motive and is purposive and intentional in the act; (2) spontaneity and freedom, that is, the outcome of the act must happen spontaneously, and the subject of the act is not forced, pressured or hindered beyond his control; (3) the subject of the act has knowledge and judgment regarding the outcome of the act; (4) there is a causal relationship between the act and the outcome; and (5) the outcome breaches/violates the norm, that is, the outcome of the act is wrong under certain norms and situations (Fischer and Ravizza, 1999; Corlett, 2006).

The rights-based perspective is based on the harmless principle of innovative acts. In other words, the outcome of an individual's act does not pose harm to the safety of others' rights, involves the rights' conditions of responsibility and obligation (Miller, 2004) and contains the legality of responsibility (the subject of the act must unconditionally remedy or compensate the damage caused by the individual's act to others, whether he is guilty or at fault) (Zandvoort, 2005); and the right to know of the act (for an act that might cause harm, the potential victim must have the right to know about the act and consent to the condition and possible outcome of the act) (Zandvoort, 2008). This attribution perspective does not care about the fairness of assessing the responsibility of the potential person at fault, but rather cares about the fairness to the potential victim (Doorn, 2012).

Table 16.1 Concept analysis of responsible innovation

Core of concept	Connotation	Focus	Source
Responsible innovation	A better try at the prospective prediction of the issue, that is, considering a wider range of social, moral and environmental topics in the innovation process and creating flexible and adaptive systems to deal with the unknown outcome of innovation	Focus on the assessment of innovation outcomes	Sutcliffe and Director (2011)
Responsible research and innovation	A transparent and interactive process; social actor and innovator take responsibility for each other in order to achieve the (moral) acceptability, sustainability and social satisfaction (with scientific progress properly embedded in social development) of the innovation process and market product	Focus on the governance and communication structure of responsible innovation, as well as the equality of public discussion	Schomberg (2012); Mei and Chen (2014)
Responsible innovation	Explore the future of innovation through the unified management of existing science and innovation	Focus on the governance and prospect of responsible innovation	Stilgoe, Owen, and Macnaghten (2013); Mei, Chen, and Sheng (2014)
Responsible innovation	An activity or process that leads to the expansion of the unknown factors related to the physical, conceptual and institutional world in the innovation process, which in turn increases the options for cognition and acting	Focus on the content description of the concept of responsible innovation	Van den Hoven (2013b)
Responsible research and innovation	Systematically advance research and innovation, enable stakeholders to participate in the research and innovation process at an early stage, acquire information on the possible outcome or research and innovative acts and make an open choice from among the multiple outcomes; conduct effective assessment of the outcome and choice based on social needs and moral ethics; apply these considerations as the functional requirement of new studies and researches	Focus on the assessment principle of responsible innovation	Van den Hovern (2013a)
Responsible innovation	Consider innovation as a future-oriented, uncertain, complex and collective act; the outcome of innovation must satisfy the social needs and moral and ethical requirements more effectively	Focus on the innovative property and assessment principle of responsible innovation	Owen Bessant, and Heintz (2013)

According to the consequentialist perspective, the core of responsibility attribution is not whether the act by the subject triggers the issue of responsibility, but whether the act leads to an expected result, such as achieving improvement in the act of the subject (Eshleman, 2008). Different from the discussions on the fairness of the potential person at fault and potential victims, the consequentialist perspective uses attribution efficacy as the measuring standard, that is, the act by the subject needs to make a contribution to the solution and facilitate improvement of the act itself (Fahlquist, 2009). Unlike the merit-based perspective and the rights-based perspective which stress certain acts themselves, the consequentialist perspective cares more about the status of the outcome of an act (Doorn, 2012).

As a discussion on the responsibility attribution of the technological innovative acts, the merit-based perspective focuses on the assessment after the fact and emphasizes the fairness of the responsibility assessment of the subject and the accountability mechanism. However, the collective act of multiple stakeholders often leads to the inability to conduct a fair assessment of the responsibility of the negative externality of innovation from the individual level in ethics; the innovation process is dispersed to the different stages of the subject's responsibility scope, and the accountability of the outcome of a collective act cannot equal the aggregation of the immorality of individual acts and be punished accordingly (Kutz, 2000); therefore, the merit-based perspective is often limited to the responsibility assessment of innovation on the individual level. For the innovation responsibility attribution from the rights-based perspective, the risk of the irreversible harm of innovation makes it necessary for the act to be approved by all subjects, and the lack of knowledge of the risks by the public or the misleading behaviors of the experts will greatly affect the efficiency and efficacy of innovation, so it is hard to drive innovation in the most efficient way when considering the compensation mechanism and approval mechanism at the same time (Doorn, 2012). The attribution of the consequentialist perspective does not mean the total eradication of any possible threat of innovation, but at the very least all the possible inquiries and outcomes should be discussed during the design and development stage of the technology. By way of careful warning and early analysis, the cost of the potential threat can be controlled and the technology can be recognized (Doorn, 2012), but the consequentialist perspective can hardly induce accountability and compensation for the harm of innovation that has already happened. Based on these points, Table 16.2 summarizes the attribution perspectives of responsible innovation.

Theoretical framework of responsible innovation

Construction elements of responsible innovation

Existing studies have had discussions on the construction elements of the theory of responsible innovation, mainly including inclusion, anticipating, reflexivity and responsiveness (Owen, Macnaghten, and Stilgoe, 2012; Stilgoe, Owen, and Macnaghten, 2013; von Schomberg, 2013; Van den Hoven, 2013a; Gianni and Goujon, 2014).

Inclusion

Responsible innovation deems innovation as a future-oriented, uncertain and complex collective act (Mei, Chen, and Sheng, 2014). Inclusion aims to open up innovative activities for multiple stakeholders to participate and promote discussions in a wider range of innovation subjects other than the scientists in terms of reference, roles, labor distribution and interdisciplinary collaboration (Stilgoe, Owen, and Macnaghten, 2013); listen to the appeals of different subjects towards certain innovations; and realize the opening of technological innovation (Irwin, 2006).

Table 16.2 Comparison and summary of attribution perspectives of responsible innovation

Attribution perspective	Focus	Subject	Purpose of attribution	Analysis object	Analysis method	Principle	Limitation
Merit-based perspective	Who should be responsible for innovation	Potential person at fault	Accountability	Certain actions	Judgment after the fact	Potential person at fault assumes the fairness of ethical responsibility	Hard to define the individual's responsibility in the outcome of a collective act
Rights-based perspective	How to compensate for victims of innovation	Potential victim	Compensation	Certain actions	Assessment after the fact	Compensation to and fairness in right to know by potential victim	Compensation to and guarantee mechanism of rights to know restrain the efficiency of innovation
Consequentialist perspective	Shaping the direction for technological innovation	Not caring	Tool	Status of outcomes	Judgment before the fact	Status and effect achieved by actions	Cannot give accountability and compensation to harm of innovation

The innovation stakeholders involved in existing studies can include the government and policy makers in each level (Stahl, 2013; Sutcliffe and Director, 2011), universities, research institutes and educational organizations (Sutcliffe and Director, 2011; Stilgoe, Owen, and Macnaghten, 2013), commercial organizations, nongovernmental organizations, civil groups (Sutcliffe and Director, 2011), innovation users and independent researchers (Stahl, 2013). These are basically categorized into the following groups of stakeholders: innovation activity experts (including planners of innovation, innovative R&D implementation organizations such as universities and research institutes), the public (including innovation users, social participants of innovation and potential service objects, etc.) and policy makers (including all levels of government and policy institutions, scientific committees and other innovation investment institutions). Studies mostly focus on the reaction of the public, experts and policy makers towards the interaction of science and technology (Devine-Wright, 2014). Experts are considered the actors who have special knowledge and experience of technological innovation, but they are biased in their emotions. For example, they are more focused on their passion towards innovation or their self-interest, or pressured by funds, social status or reputation (Roeser, 2012). In the meantime, experts often have a deeply rooted opinion that the public lacks recognition and risk aversion for technological innovation (Wynne, 2001), and they need to control the deviation of technological innovation while deeming experts themselves as part of the society to be responsible for the potential victims (the public) of innovation (Van der Burg and Van Gorp, 2005). The public has a wider range of emotions towards technological innovation than experts (Roeser, 2012). For a particular technological innovation activity, the public might be more attentive to the issue of procedures, such as the fairness and transparency of procedures (Walker et al., 2010), the distribution of cost and profit and how they learn about and participate in the innovation process (Walker et al., 2010), instead of knowing the technology and harms of this innovation activity (Correljé et al., 2015). This attitude is determined by the interactive process among stakeholders who have different backgrounds, interests, expectations and attitudes towards innovation (Devine-Wright, 2014). In a particular technological innovation activity, experts often stress that the technological innovation threats are unavoidable and question the irrationality of the public's emotion towards the outcome of innovation, as well as the excessive concern over the purpose of the technological innovation. This irrationality and the concern over the negative outcome trigger conflicts between the experts and the public (Roeser, 2012). Policy makers often need to react to the gap between the experts and public, and they are the intermediary between the insights of experts and the public's focus, balancing both sides' emotions towards technological innovation (Roeser, 2012) and seeking solutions of technological innovation in terms of social development by systematic coordination between the subjects of such acts (Roco, 2006). Through integrating research and innovation interest, social values and the participation of stakeholders, policy makers seek viable innovation norm governance between the public and individuals (Wickson and Carew, 2014), take into account the public's emotion towards innovation, coordinate the cognition and emotion gap between the experts and the public and lead friendly discussions and efficient decision making (Roeser, 2012).

Proposition 1: inclusion of responsible innovation is represented in the wider participation of stakeholders in innovative activities. Its three basic subjects of acts include innovators, the public and policy makers.

Anticipating

The anticipating requirement of responsible innovation requests that the moral of new technology and the satisfaction on the social level should be given attention at the early stage of technology development so that innovation can adapt to social needs (van de Poel, 2008; Swierstra and Rip, 2007). This element describes and analyzes potential unknown influences; constructs flexible and self-adaptable systems; effectively deals with the unexpected result of research and innovation while taking into account the social, environmental and moral factors; and forms "governance with foresight" (Sutcliffe, 2011). Under this mechanism, the technological innovators need to conduct discussions on the solutions of the problems driven by the outcome (Davis, 2009). Instead of accountability for the negative outcome of innovation, they are more interested in the premises under which the harms happen or could happen again (Doorn, 2012). The prerequisite to anticipating is to incite technological and social discussions at the early stage of innovation, because the political decision is accustomed to verifying and evaluating the possible outcome of technological innovation through analysis in foresight (Astin, 2012). Take new technology as an example; the technical arguments are in two basic directions: (1) the technology-future outlook can change our way of experiencing the current and future development of technology, just as the social prospect can predict the technology in the future and (2) technology-future exerts a huge influence in the scientific field and pinpoints the technology that will be valuable in the future (Dupuy, 2007). The existing innovation practices have brought in the governance with foresight model in many cases, such as the National Foresight Program in Britain, the Programs of Technology Foresight for Sectors in Brazil, the Foresight Activities in the Canadian government, the Federal Ministry of Education and Research and Research Foresight in Germany, etc. (Wilsdon, 2014). All these programs induced the skills needed in technological innovation in the foresight mechanism, as well as thoughts on the adjustment of culture, processes and organization plans of current policy governance (Wilsdon, 2014), which are supported by methods such as technical assessment, value sensitivity analysis, prospect evaluation and scanning (Schot and Geels, 2008).

Proposition 2: anticipating in responsible innovation needs to rely on the innovation assessment principle to conduct analysis in foresight of the innovation activities' future impact during their early development stage in order to direct the innovation activities towards moral acceptance and social satisfaction control risks in innovation activities.

Reflexivity

Reflexivity in responsible innovation means realizing that there is no standard path to follow in innovation and development; recognizing the cognition limitations of individuals and organizations; and shaping the mirror for the acts, promises, hypotheses and capabilities of individuals and organizations (Wynne, 1993; Mei and Chen, 2014). There is a problem in the premise that technological innovation solves social problems and drives progress. This problem is concerned with the scientists not recognizing their responsibility towards some crises in modern society, their inability to stay detached from the credit issue of scientific achievements and lack of respect for the accountability result for certain innovative acts (Brouwer, 1994). The reflexive rationality declares that scientists have not taken any actions in social governance and that they need to undertake the following challenges to take responsibility: scientists need to focus on the change in the recent scientific situations – good scientific principles and theories need to be reviewed, or the moral and ethical topics should be embedded in the technological innovation culture (Schuurbiers, Sleenhoff, Jacobs, and Osseweijer, 2009). Therefore, scientists as the subjects of technological innovation should review their role as part of the larger society and learn about the impact of their acts on social development in terms of time and location apart from conducting anticipation and innovation activities (Glerup and Horst, 2014). From the perspective of the responsible innovation paradigm, the reflection and cognition structure of the stakeholders is the premise (Gianni and Goujon, 2014); the reflexive warning system can effectively cope with occasional incidents in technological innovation (Gianni, Ikonen, Goujon, and Pearson, 2014) and can manage the innovation promises that come from outside the scientific community or that are wrong (Wilsdon, 2014). As a result, reflexivity reflects the reflexive property of responsible innovation as a "meta-responsibility," that is, responsible innovation needs to consider and repeatedly reflect on the hypotheses, requirements, targets, implementation process and outcome of innovation itself (Stahl, 2013; Mei, Chen, and Sheng, 2014).

Proposition 3: reflexivity in responsible innovation is based on the recognition and review of the issues such as the disparity of recognition of knowledge needed for innovation activities by innovation subjects and the cognition limitations of the evolution of innovation activities and the impact of outcome.

Responsiveness

Responsiveness of responsible innovation is shown in the capability foundation of responsible innovation. It concerns with the adjustment of the act models when the knowledge and control over innovation are insufficient (Collingridge, 1980; Mei, Chen, and Sheng, 2014). In addition, the responsiveness of responsible innovation indicates innovation activities are in the dynamic matching process of technological engineering evolution and social development (Doorn, 2012), coping with uncertainty in innovation through institutional methods. The dynamic process represents an interactive, continuous and flexible adaptive learning process, realizing the institutional coupling of the innovation evolution process with social value response (Owen, Macnaghten, and Stilgoe, 2012; Mei and Chen, 2014). Gilfillan (1935) proposed the idea of embedding social discussions into technology development. Later studies show that technology development itself is a response to the social environment and pressure, and it often has an accumulating effect. New technological innovation is actually the adaptation, adjustment and deepening of old technology and knowledge. Technological innovation itself is a systematic response and structuralization process (Gianni and Goujon, 2014). For social control and governance of technological innovation, the basic conflict of the Collingridge dilemma (the social outcome of a technology cannot be anticipated at the early stage of the technology; when the undesirable outcome does happen, technology has often become part of the whole economic and social structure, and it is very difficult to control and change it) (Gu and Tao, 2014) can be effectively coordinated based on the responsible innovation paradigm under the self-adaptable governance of the response mechanism (Lee and Petts, 2013). For example, the introduction of the interdisciplinary research methods and tools has provided a repeated evolutional method for responsible innovation to respond to issues and situations from multiple perspectives (Wickson, Carew, and Russell, 2006).

Proposition 4: responsiveness in responsible innovation emphasizes that the innovation subject and governance method be based on the interactive, continuous and adaptive process in order to realize the correct guidance and real-time correction of innovation activities.

Institutional situation of responsible innovation

Technological innovation cannot be separated from a particular institutional situation, which concerns two major categories: (1) formal institutions such as laws, standards, rules and contracts and (2) informal institutions such as customs, traditions and norms (Taebi et al., 2014). The institutional situation is essentially the optimization and integration of the divergent values of the innovation process (Correlje and Groenewegen, 2009). Value is not a static entity frozen by technology and institutions, but it exists in the embeddedness and interaction between technological innovation and institutional situations, and extends beyond technology to embed in the interaction between the institutional situation and stakeholders. The researchers' task is to determine the values embedded in the formal and informal institutions and the underlying conflicts of these values (Correljé et al., 2015). The policy formulation is targeted at adaptive mechanism and structures to achieve transition of the role of experts, intermediary institutions and the public (Wilsdon, 2014).

Responsible innovation is proposed against the European development situation with a consideration of the reaction of innovation towards the social environment. In order to ensure that responsible innovation is embedded into other regions, cultures and practices, as well as all types of social innovations (Macnaghten et al., 2014), and to establish a universal theoretical framework (Gianni and Goujon, 2014), the diversity and generality of the institutional situation in the responsible innovation studies should be discussed at the onset of the theory construction stage. Take the comparison of responsible innovation in developed countries and developing countries, for example; the constitution of developed countries such as the EU advocates a "priority sequence of different technological innovation" on top of the social norms and promotes tolerance, fairness and democracy in scientific and social relations (Van Oudheusden, 2014). While developing or underdeveloped countries focus more on the compatibility of innovation development with their own development (Gudynas, 2011), the government plays a more important role in guiding innovation (Fagerberg, Mowery, and Nelson, 2006), and their innovation might include more content that is "borrowed, copied, [and] stolen" (Macnaghten et al., 2014) and properties such as "grassroots, spontaneous innovation, [and] ecological innovation" (Pansera and Owen, 2014). Their innovation paradigm is more simplistic[3] (Zeschky, Widenmayer, and Gassmann, 2011) and inclusive (George, McGahan, and Prabhu, 2012). Therefore, the construction of responsible innovation theory relies on the cross-studies and needs to integrate (1) ethical and moral factors in technology in order to evaluate the value and meaning of innovation; (2) institutional theory, in order to understand the relationship between institution and innovation, as well as their function in value actualization; and (3) policy, in order to achieve the responsible innovation governance (Taebi et al., 2014). Within the discussions of institutional situation of responsible innovation, many multilayered and irregular science and innovation governance structures started to promote the responsibility of anticipating and foresight and to focus on the effective choice of society and policies in order to ensure the stability of certain innovations. New management models such as anticipating governance, construction, authenticity, technical evaluation, upstream participation, value perception design and social technology integration start to emerge and endeavor to open science and innovation to an institutional situation with wider input, public discussion and creativity (Stilgoe, Owen, and Macnaghten, 2013).

The existing theoretical framework of responsible innovation lacks the generalized institutional situation dimensional analysis. A generalized institutional situation element should be an integral part of the theoretical framework of responsible innovation and should contain the following characteristics: first, institution is a controlled collective act, as well as a liberation and expansion of individual acts. It emphasizes the double explanation of both institutional and economic contexts (Commons, 1936), which complies with responsible innovation in expanding the innovators' (such as scientists') acts to the joint act by multiple stakeholders and guiding innovation towards the expected direction based on social satisfaction. Second, institution is a system that establishes and embeds social rules and guides the social interaction process towards structuralization (Hodgson, 2004). This complies with responsible innovation in requiring the innovation outcome to conform to social and ethical requirements and form an anticipative and responsive governance mechanism with interaction among stakeholders. Lastly, the heterogeneous subject acts are influenced by formal and informal institutions. Public value reflects different orientations, competitions, social security systems, safety, fairness, etc. It has not formed a conglomeration and choices because of the market, but is the product of policy and social institution choices (Correljé et al., 2015). This is in line with responsible innovation having social satisfaction and ethical requirements as basic premises, realizing a balance between multiple stakeholders and obtaining innovation returns in the institutional response and self-reflective dynamic evolution. Williamson (1998) provided an effective analysis framework for institutional research from the perspective of "four levels of institutional analysis." Based on the two standards of the core objective of institution and reform frequency, Williamson categorized the institutional situations of human activities into four levels: embeddedness, institutional environment, governance and resource allocation and employment.

Based on the perspective of new institutional economics, economic behaviors are embedded into social norms (Granovetter, 1985); public value is the product of social choice under special political and institutional situations instead of the product of market free choice; the positive and negative effect of the result of technological innovation on the environment, economy and society is affected by local, regional and global social norms (Correljé et al., 2015). Since responsible innovation leads to technological innovation in the end by its institutionalized processes, norms and motives different from those of the traditional paradigm (Veenman, Liefferink, and Arts, 2009), the new institutional economics regards responsible innovation as the endorsement of public value (Taebi et al., 2014). However, the four levels of the institutional analysis theoretical model do not explain the interactive relationship among the levels while emphasizing the embeddedness of acts into institutional situations (Künneke, 2008). The interactive framing theory effectively supplements the interlevel interactive mechanism within the institutions (Gray, Purdy, and Ansari, 2015). Under the top-down lamination mechanism, the institution construction is originated from the single or joint force of high-level institutional situation pressure, and the pressure of the interactive body at the same level exerts influence through core interactive bodies, transmits and extends the efficacy and achieves the normal framework construction within the same level (Munir, 2005). Under the bottom-up amplification mechanism shown in Figure 16.1, with the interaction and synergy of interactive bodies in the same level, the low-level institutional situation accumulates elements to produce an overflow and magnification effect through three mechanisms: (1) absorbing a wider range of stakeholders to expand its scope of framework, (2) optimizing rules and interaction frequency to promote the universality of the framework and (3) enhancing emotions so that it will transform into a higher level of institutional construction and institutional conflict (Gray, Purdy, and Ansari, 2015).

Proposition 5: the institutional situation in responsible innovation stresses that the potential value of innovative activities is embedded in situational elements such as their environment, systems and cultures, and the general framework of responsible innovation theory cannot be discussed detached from the institutional situation element. In the meantime, institution itself as a system contains level classification and dynamic interaction in certain dimensions.

Assessment standards of responsible innovation

The increasing attention to responsibility has redefined the mirroring relationship between science and society in the long traditional development. The traditional linear model is starting to transform (Guston, 2007). For traditional innovation, the process starts with the development of new ideas and ends with commercialization. Market success is regarded as the driving force of innovation, along with the marketized product, system and service reaction (Swann, 2009). Unlike the traditional innovation paradigm, which uses the positive deduction of technological

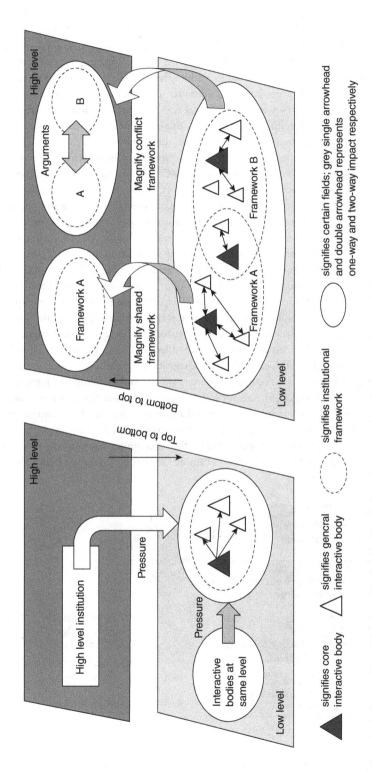

Figure 16.1 Interactive mechanism of institutional levels from the perspective of interactive framework theory

Source: Authors' design, based on Gray, Purdy, and Ansari (2015)

innovation driving economic development as the basic hypothesis, responsible innovation contends that critical discussions should be brought into innovation at an early stage, and technological evaluation of multiple forms should be conducted in order to embed the moral, legal and social factors into the process of technological innovation during the ever-enhancing institutionalization of public engagement and to achieve the modularized integration of society and technology (Wickson and Carew, 2014). Based on the existing basic assessment standards of technological innovation – improvement of technical feasibility and economic efficiency (Van den Hoven, 2013a) – responsible innovation requires the outcome of research and innovation activities to meet two basic standards: (1) acceptability in the moral and ethical level; (2) satisfaction of social needs and social expectation (including economic, social and environmental influences and realizing the goals of social institution norms) (Owen, Macnaghten, and Stilgoe, 2012; Van den Hoven, 2013a; Rodríguez, Fisher, and Schuurbiers, 2013), and in the end realizes public value, as shown in Figure 16.2. The assessment standards of responsible innovation highlight three characteristics: first, the fundamental objective of innovation assessment is the realization of public value. Meynhardt (2009) considers public value as the result of individual, group and society's basic needs influencing public behaviors and relationship interaction as a whole (Meynhardt, 2009). Responsible innovation requires the definition of relevant public value before innovative activities, that is, discussing the possible value conflicts of innovation and choosing acts based on the value assessment of innovation outcome (van de Poel, 2009). As the endorsement of public value (Taebi et al., 2014), responsible innovation contends that the core of social satisfaction and moral acceptability lies in the interaction between stakeholders of innovative activities and their values, the coordination of value conflicts and the embeddedness of value into the technological and institutional situations (Correljé et al., 2015). A diversified stakeholder's value is considered the basis for redesigning the technological innovation system and realizing the integration of divergent values (Correljé et al., 2015). Second is the moral and ethical dimension in innovation assessment. Under the old innovation paradigm, moral and ethics often hinder economic growth (Van den Hoven, 2013a). In the meantime, the innovators represented by engineers face moral and ethical dilemmas in innovation design because they encounter value needs that conflict with those of stakeholders, and the subjects' acts cannot satisfy the value assessment of multiple

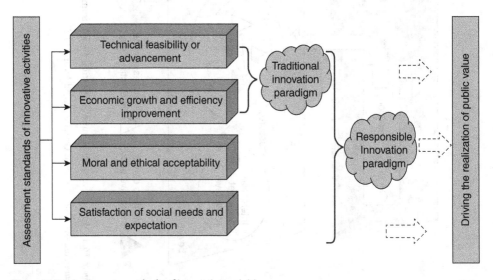

Figure 16.2 Assessment standards of innovative activities

dimensions at the same time; for example, the efficiency, safety guarantee, security and privacy protection of technological innovation cannot be ensured at the same time (van de Poel, 2009). Responsible innovation holds that the essence of technological innovation is to create value surplus and that the subjects of acts can satisfy both the multiple dimensions of innovation assessment and the moral responsibility of innovation at the same time through innovation (Van den Hoven, Lokhorst, and van de Poel, 2012). The basis for innovation to drive moral progress lies in the expansion of the collection of opportunities and choices of innovative acts (van den Hoven, Lokhorst, and van de Poel, 2012). For particular moral restraints in the economic dimension, technological innovation can act as the driving force in the new area of research and the new innovation direction and can lead the economic growth and green innovation in a wider level through creating job opportunities, increasing social security and avoiding the inadequate allocation of research funds (Van den Hoven, 2013a). As for the moral and ethical dilemma faced by innovators, such as engineers at the innovation design stage (that is, the conflicted value needs), responsible innovation advocates support through change in innovation situations (van den Hoven, Lokhorst, and van de Poel, 2012), realizing the balance and coordination of stakeholders' values and driving moral progress from the level of coordinated subjects.[4] The last standard is the social satisfaction dimension in innovation assessment. Responsible innovation contends that the essence of innovation is the satisfaction of social needs (De Saille, 2013). It is not a new concept that science should be responsible for society, which has long required scientists to find the balance between professional autonomy and social and individual needs (Douglas, 2003). The correct evaluation of technological innovation is required to start from the value of social expectation. If a certain technological innovation can be accepted and its potential outcome is beneficial to society, it does not necessarily mean that the crisis is completely avoided, but at least all the possible inquiries and innovation outcomes should be discussed during the technology design and development stage, and the cost of potential crisis should be controlled by carefully designed warning and foresight analysis (Doorn, 2012).

Proposition 6: the assessment of responsible innovation uses the realization of public value as its goal. Based on the standards of the previous innovation paradigm, including technology feasibility or advancement, economic growth and efficiency improvement, the assessment standards of responsible innovation highlight the two dimensions of moral and ethical acceptability, as well as the satisfaction of social needs and expectation.

Theoretical framework of responsible innovation

Responsible innovation is basically oriented by the realization of public value, and the integration of the four levels of institutional analysis theory and interactive framing theory provides a reasonable and effective explanation for the institutional situations of responsible innovation. The institutional situations of innovative activities achieve a top-to-bottom institution construction of the social informal norms with the lamination mechanism from the embeddedness (high level) to the resource allocation and employment (low level), while the activities from the low level aggregate and trigger the institutional restructuring of responsible innovation through a bottom-up amplification mechanism. The interactive system of top-down as well as bottom-up and the rational process have realized the construction and restructuring of institutional situations (Collins, 2004; Gray, Purdy, and Ansari, 2015). The interlevel interaction and cross-level interaction of institutional situations induced by innovative activities, the core interactive bodies and general interactive bodies with the element of inclusion, the objective-oriented and self-reflective principle as basis of anticipating and the influencing factors and frequency of responsiveness display disparity among levels, as shown in Table 16.3. Through the two-way interaction

Table 16.3 Reflection of construction elements of responsible innovation in levels of institutional situations

Levels of institutional situations		Construction dimensions of responsible innovation			
		Inclusion	Anticipation	Reflexivity	Responsiveness
Level 1	Embeddedness	Core interactive actor: public; other interactive actor: innovators (such as scientific community), policy makers, others	Whether innovative activities and their impacts comply with the informal institutions, customs, traditions, norms and religions evolved from national and local history	The target of an act and its premise: acknowledge the national and local historical culture, local customs, norms and respect traditions	Conduct open discussions and summaries on the national and regional levels regarding spiritual values, social traditions, and cultural cores
Interaction of level 1–2	Top-down	Public's value is the fundamental principle (people's interest is above all)			
		Extract and summarize the essence of traditional culture and social core values, promote and implement; have formed basic principle reference for policies and regulations			
	Bottom-up	Policy makers promote democratic development and conduct more discussions engaging the public			
		Explore the universal significance behind the political system and bureaucratic system			
Level 2	Institutional environment	Core interactive actor: policy makers (such as government); other interactive actors: innovators (such as scientific community), public, others	Whether innovative activities and their impacts comply with the formal game rules, including politics, legislation and bureaucratic systems	The target of an act and its premise: obey the national and regional political system principle framework, judicial and bureaucratic rules	Supervision, correction, improvement, optimization, reform and innovation of the political, judicial and bureaucratic systems
Interaction of level 2–3	Top-down	Policy makers make norms for scientific community and their related members in participating science and research			
		Scientific and technological innovation plan, control, management and appraisal under institutional framework and landscape design			
	Bottom-up	Oriented by innovators' advice and influence on policies, such as experts suggestions, think tank reports and tendency analysis			
		The feedback of governance mode and operation management practice pushes for institutional reform and innovation			

Level 3	Governance	Core interactive actor: innovators (such as scientific community), policy makers (such as government); other interactive actors: public, others	Whether innovative activities and their impacts comply with the management and operation rules of a certain field, such as technical contracts, technology expansion and commercialization agreements, industry-university-research cooperation task distribution, etc.	The target of an act and its premise: promote governance under law, strictly obey the rules of organization	Governance methods and management measures make adaptive adjustment for the technology, type, model and industry factors of innovation
Interaction of level 3–4	Top-down	Innovators and policy makers ascertain the subjects of certain innovative activities and the population being influenced by them Innovative activities rules and plans clarify the corresponding resources, labor allocation, distribution of tasks and duties			
	Bottom-up	Practice and studies of innovative activities make appraisal of the duties and performance of innovators and their rule makers, realize the selection of subjects of acts The restraining conditions of the resources and employment of innovative activities have a counter effect on the diversified governance mode, and form a flexible mixed mechanism with marketization and hierarchy			
Level 4	Resource allocation and employment	Core interactive actor: innovator (such as scientific community), public; other interactive actors: policy makers (such as government), others	Whether innovative activities and their impacts match the price and quantity of people, money, property, information and other resources, as well as the incentives for peoples engagement	The target of an act and its premise: obey the reasonable allocation and effective utilization of resources, emphasize on the distribution of people's engagement and benefit allocation	Adjust and coordinate the resource allocation of innovative activities and the engagement mechanism

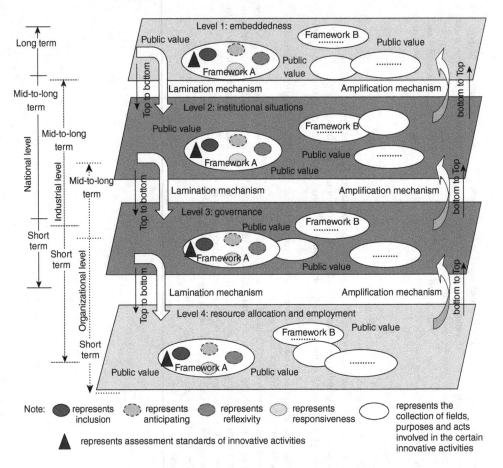

Figure 16.3 Theoretical framework of responsible innovation

of the four levels of construction elements and institutional situations, responsible innovation realizes the satisfaction of the long-term public value in society by innovative activities and drives the coordinated development of innovation and society. Based on this, this chapter forms the theoretical framework of responsible innovation studies as shown in Figure 16.3.

Transnational practice of responsible innovation

Research methods and levels

Based on the theoretical framework, multiple-case method is adopted to proceed the analysis. The case study is based on abundant qualitative data, conducts in-depth description and analysis of a certain phenomenon (Yin, 1994) and is helpful in understanding the complicated mechanism behind the phenomenon (Eisenhardt, 1989). The purposes of the case study include theory verification and theory construction (Yin, 1994). This chapter focuses on the theory verification, that is, the comparison of multiple cases of responsible innovation practices in the United States, EU and China on the national level. The multiple-case study is more effective than a single case study because it can formulate a repeated logic of case experiment to support or refute the research deduction (Yin, 1994; Santos and Eisenhardt, 2009) through data comparison (Eisenhardt, 1991; Ozcan and Eisenhardt, 2009).

The case study focuses on the national level. Responsible innovation is often a dynamic concept and is conducted on different research levels (Stilgoe, Owen, and Macnaghten, 2013). This chapter examines relevant cases on the national level based on the following reasons: (1) the background for proposing the concept of responsible innovation focuses on the discussion of national sustainable development and technological innovation policies, covers the area of important technological innovation and emerging technologies (Fisher, Mahajan, and Mitcham, 2006) and gradually extends to the big challenges of the era – social problems such as climate change, poverty alleviation and an aging society (European Commission, 2011); (2) the fundamental purpose of responsible innovation studies is to reflect on the purpose of science and innovation, the potential motives and plans, so that scientific and technological development, institutions and policies can a receive more social response (Van Oudheusden, 2014), which concerns the strategic demands on the national level and the responsibility embeddedness on the policy level; (3) the core of responsible innovation is the satisfaction of social expectation and moral and ethical requirements, realizing the resolution of important social challenges and innovation with the engagement of multiple stakeholders (Blok, 2014); and (4) many existing national innovation practices already involve many topics on responsibility, such as the discussion of the Manhattan Project over the use of atomic bombs in the Second World War and the scientist research duty triggered from the discussion (Rhodes, 2012), as well as the discussion of the Asilomar conference over the potential risks of DNA restructuring (Glerup and Horst, 2014), as well as the responsible innovation programs and policy plans of developed countries.[5]

Transnational practice of responsible innovation based on nanotechnology

Practice of responsible innovation of nanotechnology in the United States

The practice of responsible innovation in the United States dates back to the parallel studies by the American human genome project over the ethical, legal and societal implications (Rodríguez, Mingyan, and Fisher, 2012), as well as the reflexive assessment implemented in the research process for the first time (Juengst, 1996). With the development of research and policy practice, the consideration and appraisal by scientific research over social factors are incorporated into the evaluation of social funds and the release of the trend of scientific activities by regular institutions as important factors, including scientific moral and ethics, legal and societal implications plan, National Scientific Fund (NSF), social factor evaluation and standard examination of scientific projects by the American Institutional Review Board (Sarewitz and Woodhouse, 2003), global reform and scientific research group human dimension joint program plan (Janssen, Schoon, Ke, and Börner, 2006) and many presidential foundation projects in the bioethical field (Briggle, 2010).

However, what actually took the responsibility factor during the scientific research and innovation process into account to then be issued as formal laws, regulations and policies was the "responsible development" proposed by the American government regarding nano-science and technology. Since then, the social factor was brought into the discussion of scientific and innovation projects for the first time. The United States National Research Council and National Nanotechnology Initiative framework defined the responsible development of nanotechnology as follows: all the innovation stakeholders in the United States increase the positive contributions of nanotechnology innovation to the maximum extent and try to avoid negative implications.

This means that the responsibility of the country over the development and utilization of nanotechnology promises to help fulfill human and social needs and tries its best to anticipate and alleviate any adverse effect that might be produced by nanotechnology (Owen, Macnaghten, and Stilgoe, 2012). In the meantime, the U.S. National Nanotechnology Initiative confirmed that they will define the risks and safety of nanotechnology in detail from two perspectives, including the relevant environmental, health and safety issues, as well as relevant educational and social issues, and use the risk management as a strategy to implement the responsible governance of nanotechnology and its product application, as shown in Figure 16.4. As an important innovation to drive the economic development and scientific advance of the United States, nano-science and technology studies also bring in the societal and moral assessment standards apart from the economic effect and technology advancement standards focused on by the traditional innovation assessment. The American government and National Research Council actively promote the combined policy to facilitate the responsible development of nanotechnology research and innovation (Rodríguez, Mingyan, and Fisher, 2012).

In 2000, the United States included the societal factor into its nano-science research and innovation, and in 2003, the public act for nanotechnology research issued by the federal law clearly stipulated that nano-science and nanotechnology innovation are dedicated to making full use of nanotechnology while recognizing the potential crisis and developing methods to manage nanotechnology. Specific studies, education, collaboration and exchange programs focus on the safety and a wider range of social properties of nanotechnology development and rely on the participation of universities, industries, governmental institutions and social communities (Congress U.S., 2003). The R&D process of nanotechnology needs to consider the moral and ethical, legal, environmental and other social factors, including the potential use of nanotechnology itself

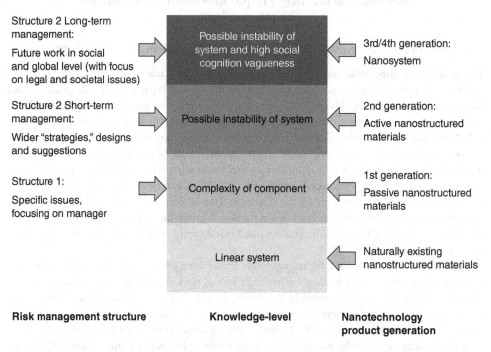

Figure 16.4 Responsible governance of nanotechnology product risk management based on generation

Source: Graph refers to Zhao Y. and Wu S. (2012, p. 9)

to improve human intelligence and develop artificial intelligence that exceeds human capabilities (Congress U.S., 2003). Nano-science and research can integrate moral and ethical, social and environmental implications in order to ensure that nano-science and technology innovation can improve the American public's quality of life (Congress U.S., 2003). The U.S. House of Representatives also issued an act emphasizing that nano-science research programs must integrate the environmental, societal and moral and ethical factors and ensure that the environmental, societal and moral and ethical research can influence the nano-science and technology and its commercialization (U.S. House Committee on Science, 2003). In 2005, the American government released specifically an environmental, health and safety strategic research program of the National Nanotechnology Initiative (Zhao and Wu, 2012). In the same year, the NSF announced that among the authorized institutions for the responsible development of nanotechnology, the nanotechnology social research center of Arizona State University and the St. Barbara Center at the University of California will be the representatives and endorsed the former with US$6.2 million in funds. In 2010, NSF continued to invest in the two research centers to push for the social expectations, moral and ethical, as well as environmental studies of nanotechnology (Rodríguez, Mingyan, and Fisher, 2012).

As a member of the nanotechnology responsible innovation, the nanotechnology social research center of Arizona State University adopts the foresight (anticipating) management model, confirmed the operation rules of strategic anticipation, multiple stakeholder engagement, resource integration and collaborated research based on the characteristics of technological innovation and the qualifications of the research center (Barben. Fisher, Selin, and Guston, 2008), and it uses "reflexivity" as one of the key assessment standards for corporate partners in nanotechnology research and application. The center has built over 20 global research laboratories and brought in humanistic and social researchers. They focus on the nano-research and technology field, how social scholars can be effectively embedded into the highly structured laboratory research and how social factors can effectively help scientific research. This measure has challenged the long-existing norms and customs – scientific research should be independent of the social situations; that is, the research activities of the scientific community should not be influenced by external pressure. Natural scientists usually worry that the integration of external members will affect the scientific research and its industrial application (Brush, 1974). However, with the evolution of research and practice, philosophers and social scientists do more on the basis of observation and analysis, and their issues and perspectives in scientific research are embedded in the negative influence of scientific practice. Meanwhile, after learning about the nanotechnology research topic and basic methods, philosophers and social scientists further extend the value focus and options of feasible solutions of specific research projects from the social, moral, ethical and environmental perspectives. Scientists conduct their daily work based on the evaluation of philosophers and social scientists, including research investigation, conferences and pilot plan tests. This interdisciplinary collaboration has changed the old model of laboratory investigation and practice and extended the options of technical innovation.

With the establishment of over 20 global research laboratories and the engagement of social scientists from nano-laboratories, the nanotechnology social research center of Arizona State University expanded the global resource integration of nanotechnology, extended the common engagement of stakeholders (for example, social ethicists and social scientists all participate in the research topic in the laboratory), realized the responsible research and innovation collaboration of interdisciplinary bodies on a wider scale (including scientists, sociologists, engineers and students from the engineering technology and social humanistic fields) and enabled these research laboratories to become leading institutes of responsible innovation in nanotechnology (Fisher and Maricle, 2014). These 20 and more global research laboratories have gradually combined the social and moral factors into the regular experimental research norms and courses by interdisciplinary collaboration practice and operation management, and realized the synergy effect of the responsible innovation by multiple stakeholders of nanotechnology to the maximum extent under the response of public polices and public value evaluation (Rodríguez, Mingyan, and Fisher, 2012). Fisher described this practice in *Nature* as "triggering reform in scientific experimental research practice – that is, extending the aggregation of the value and issue discussions of scientific research as well as the choice of feasible solutions" (New, 2010). He thinks that the reflexivity and reflection by responsible innovation of nanotechnology has provided new ideas for the topic of nanotechnology research itself and the intelligent structured operation of its research group; the introduction of responsible innovation not only maintained the excellence of research and technology in nano-research in the United States but also enabled the research to better comply with public values. Scientists can ponder over the wider meanings of their research topics while maintaining their technical productivity (New, 2010).

Practice of responsible innovation of nanotechnology in Europe

The practice of responsible innovation in Europe dates back to the discussions of moral, ethical, legal and societal factors in natural science and engineering research by the second framework program of the EU (FP2, 1987–1991) and was gradually applied to bioscience and genetic engineering (the second framework program of the EU), medicine (the third framework program), agriculture, fishery, biotechnology, biomedicine and health, life science and technology (the fourth framework program) (Elizalde, 1998). The fourth framework program (FP4, 1994–1998) officially implemented the parallel studies and reflexive evaluation of moral, ethical, legal and societal factors in natural science and engineering research; requested the importance of interdisciplinary scientific studies; and advocated the engagement of multiple stakeholders, including the scientists, doctors, philosophers, sociologists, jurists, social scientists, technical application clients, industrial members, and the public, into scientific research (Rodríguez, Mingyan, and Fisher, 2012). With the evolution of research, the sixth framework program of the EU (FP6, 2002–2006) has officially added the ethical, legal and societal factors as important links to the application and evaluation approval process of science and engineering research projects (Rodríguez, Mingyan, and Fisher, 2013). The European Commission released a formal paper in 2002 and 2006 offering a legal explanation to promote the integration of science and society. After that, the European technological polices and national strategies have focused more and more on responsible innovation. Evolving from the integration of society and technology to the EU's scientific society plan, responsible innovation carries out discussions on the arguments and limitations of the current technological policies and methods in moral management (Owen, Macnaghten, and Stilgoe, 2012). The "2020 Wise Growth" has clearly defined the core target, value orientation and challenges of the development of Europe; emphasized the social and environmental benefits of innovation and the engagement of a wider group of stakeholders; and confirmed the basic meaning of responsible innovation from the two dimensions of social expectations and moral ethics (Von Schomberg, 2013). In May 2011, the special policies for responsible research and innovation in Europe were released, addressing to define responsible research and innovation, enhance the understanding of the relationship between science and society, and promote the societal satisfied technological innovations (Owen, Macnaghten, and Stilgoe, 2012).

The sixth framework program of the EU was the first to establish responsible innovation in nanotechnology. The "Policy White Book" holds that the existing technology and innovation crisis makes the public doubt the expert-oriented technology policies. The public institutions need to control the harms of nanotechnology advances while coordinating the industrial interest of technology application and the general interest of the public (European Commission, 2001). The European Commission also requires that nanotechnology innovation and the description of its development should enable subjects outside the research community to participate and convey the social meaning of the relevant nanotechnology innovation knowledge (Rodríguez, Mingyan, and Fisher, 2012). The European Commission pointed out that nano-science and technology is the collaboration of the top scientists and policy makers, and can satisfy the value demand of the wider public. Therefore, the European Commission initiated the research and formulated the behavioral norms and principles of nano-science and technology research; discussed the moral norms, research activities, relationships among relevant stakeholders, and governance mechanisms of nanotechnology development; realized the responsible development of nanotechnology; and searched for the possibility of using the nanotechnology and science management norms for the responsible innovation of all emerging technology (Sutcliffe and Director, 2011).

With the evolution of research and policy practice, the European Commission issued the Regulations on Nano-materials, Code of Conduct for Responsible Nano-sciences and Nano-technologies Research and Initiative for Responsible Nano Behavioral Norms successively at the policy level (Zhao and Wu, 2012) and confirmed the codes of conduct for nanoscience and technology research based on meaning, sustainability, preventability, inclusion, excellence, creativity and responsibility (European Commission, 2009). In addition, the European Commission nanoscience and technology responsible research established five application areas of information/communications/electronics, energy/environment, health, textiles and others; built a nano safety colony composed of the European Commission, research and innovation associations and industrial technology groups; and conducted reflexive and anticipatory evaluation over the safety issues of nanotechnology on the national and European Commission levels such as toxicology, eco-toxicology, technical disclosure, technical risks and project standardization studies in order to manage and control all the potential health, environmental and ecological harms of technical applications. In the material field, the European Commission adopted the embedded model of product lifecycle management based on the in-depth investigation of nanoparticles and nano-materials and developed lifecycle management methods to control the potential risks of nano-materials towards consumers, producers and the environment in order to achieve the sustainable development of the nanotechnology industry.[6]

On the laboratory level, which is an important carrier for scientific research and innovation policies, based on the experience of the United States, Europe also promoted the laboratory investigation and research participation by social scientists. The research is divided into three stages of upstream, midstream and downstream. The laboratory scientific research occurs in the midstream, which seeks to balance the interests of public policies and stakeholders so that the nanotechnology responsible innovation laboratory research level can respond institutionally to the social research level based on the integration of interdisciplinary research members (Fisher and Maricle, 2014). This research model transformed the research agenda and priority through the integration of society and technology at the laboratory level, and is beneficial to the research and policy decision-making outside the laboratories (Fisher and Maricle, 2014). Moreover, as the governance foundation for nanotechnology responsible innovation, the EU fully advocates technology transparency evaluation of specific technological innovation to policy makers, innovators and the public; encourages social engagement and transparency of decision-making of policy evaluations; conducts potential crisis analysis from the aspects of physics, health, environment and chemistry; achieves fitness for purpose with target tasks and operation practice; and realizes the institutional coordination of nanotechnology responsible innovation (Borm et al.,

2006). At present, more than 2,000 organizations have joined the responsible innovation and development framework of nanoscience and technology within the EU scope.[7]

Practice of responsible innovation of nanotechnology in China

Compared to the developed countries, the scientific and technological system and innovation policies of China, which is in the rapid economic development and social structure transformation phase, dates back to the decision on scientific and technological system reform made by the Central Committee of the Communist Party of China on March 13, 1985, and has developed in three stages of "scientific and technological work should orient towards economic construction" and "economic construction should rely on scientific and technological work" (1985–1992), "stabilize the major work" and "open up the market" (1993–1998) and "rejuvenate China through science and education" and "build China's innovation system" (1999–present)[8] (Fang and Liu, 2004; Zhu, 2012). In 2006, China proposed the National Mid-to Long-term Scientific and Technological Development Plan, raising the independent innovation capability to the level of national development strategy. The 18th CPC National Congress proposed clearly that "scientific and technological innovation is the strategic foundation for improving the social productivity and comprehensive national strength" and established the "innovation driving development strategy." Xi Jinping (2014) pointed out in the Conference of the Chinese Academy of Sciences and Chinese Academy of Engineering that:

> implementing the innovation driving development strategy is a systematic project; scientific and technological products can achieve their innovative values only when they are combined with the national demand, people's demand and market demand, and completed the triple jump from scientific research, to laboratory development, and to promotion and application.
>
> (Xi, 2014)

However, as a developing country, economic growth is still the leading strategy for China in the current stage. The hypothesis of science, technology and innovation driving economic development rarely triggers reflection, let alone policy research and exploration over the combination of science, technology and innovation, as well as social demand (Rodríguez, Mingyan, and Fisher, 2013). There is no clear discussion or definition of the responsibility topic of scientific research yet, but considerations of the social factor and discussions of the responsibility awareness are burgeoning in scientific innovation on the national level, as shown in Table 16.4.

China's research on nanoscience and technology innovation started rather late – in the 1880s – and the national policy listed "nanomaterial science" as one of the national projects as early as the 8th Five-Year Plan period. From then on, the National Natural Science Foundation of China, Chinese Academy of Sciences and State Education Commission organized eight major projects, assigning relevant scientific personnel to work in the branches of nanomaterials (Yang, Peng, and Zhao, 2012). After about 30 years of development, starting from 2007, the amount of international papers with Science Citation Index published by China in the nanotechnology field has surpassed that of the United States, Japan, and Germany and ranked first, and the number of citations in the SCI papers ranked second. However, as an interdisciplinary science, nanoscience is a potential "double-edged sword," and the risks and uncertainty attached with it have attracted much attention from the scientific, social, ethical, philosophical, management and even judicial fields (Zhao and Wu, 2012). The country has a responsibility to define the harms of nanotechnology based on the regulations made by technological innovation authorities and

Table 16.4 Description of China's science and technology policies based on the responsible innovation perspective

Source of policies	Description
Law of the People's Republic of China on Science and Technology Progress, the 5th rule	China encourages governance agencies, companies, organizations, social groups and citizens to participate in and support scientific and technological advance activities.
Law of the People's Republic of China on Science and Technology Progress, the 6th rule	China encourages the combination of scientific and technological research and development, as well as higher education and industrial development, encourages interdisciplinary fusion and mutual benefit of natural and social science.
Law of the People's Republic of China on Science and Technology Progress, the 29th rule	China forbids any scientific and technological research and development activities that jeopardize national security, damage the social public interest, harm human health or violate morality and ethics.
Declaration on Scientific Ideology by Chinese Academy of Science	While creating huge material and spiritual wealth, science and technology can bring a negative influence to society and challenge the social ethics formed long ago. In the scientific world there exist unfortunate phenomena to different extents, such as apathy in scientific spirit, misconduct and lack of social responsibility.
Declaration on Scientific Ideology by Chinese Academy of Science	In the long-term scientific practice, science boasts of a profound culture and institutional traditions and forms the self-cleansing mechanism and moral codes.
Declaration on Scientific Ideology by Chinese Academy of Science	In terms of the positive and negative influence of modern science and technology and its highly professional and specialized characteristics, scientists are required to spontaneously avoid the negative effect of science and technology, including inspecting and evaluating all possible results of their work; once a drawback or danger is found, they should change or even stop their work; if they cannot make their own choice, they should slow down or pause their research and sound the alarm to the society.
Declaration on Scientific Ideology by Chinese Academy of Science	In terms of the modern science development driving the future of economic and social development, it is required that scientists must have strong historical sense of fate and social responsibility. They are required to regulate scientific conduct from the social, ethical and legal aspects, and strive to make a contribution to the comprehensive and correct understanding of science by the public.
Opinion on Strengthening Scientific and Research Code of Conduct by Chinese Academy of Science	Obeying the moral code of conduct of Chinese citizens, adhering to the rejuvenation of China by science and education, the scientific value outlook of making innovation for the people, promoting a scientific spirit, conforming to the scientific ethics and refusing any immoral scientific research activities.
People's Daily	Scientific and technological products can achieve their innovative values only when they are combined with the national demand, people's demand and market demand and complete the triple jump from scientific research, to laboratory development, to promotion and application.
Annual National Seminar on Ethics of Science and Technology	Transgenic technology ethics seminar in 2011, nanotechnology ethics seminar, stem cell research ethics seminar in 2012, Internet technology development ethics seminar focusing on the ethical issues and scientists' responsibilities in terms of important scientific innovations in 2013.

responsible regulators in order to ensure that the researchers and market operators follow the regulations (Von Schomberg, 2013). In 2001, scientists in the Chinese Academy of Sciences proposed the importance of realizing that the production and manufacturing of nanomaterial has an influence on environmental toxicity and biological toxicity. In 2003, the "Nano Bioeffect and Safety Laboratory" was established by the high-energy physics institute of the Chinese Academy of Sciences. In 2004, academician Bai Chunli summarized the safety and ethicality of nanoscience and technology from five aspects in the Xiangshan Science Conference: (1) the safety of nano-substances, its harms to human health and the environment and ways for it to enter the human body; (2) ethical problems related to nanotechnology; (3) methods to examine the toxicity of nanoparticles; (4) how to formulate national policies, regulations and norms to cope with the safety and ethicality of nanoscience and technology; and (5) how to conduct cooperation on nanotechnology safety and ethicality on a global scale in order to ensure the healthy and sustainable development of nanotechnology (Zhao and Wu, 2012). Later on, China set up the "Joint Laboratory of Nano Bioeffect and Safety" and the "Key Laboratory of Nano Bioeffect and Safety by Chinese Academy of Sciences" to cope with the nanotechnology innovation risks and organized leading industrial scientists to complete a collection of nine books on "nano safety," expanding the practitioners' and the general public's safety response and management over nanoscience and technology innovation based on the results of international nanomaterial safety evaluation research. In addition, since 2009 China has held seminars several times on nano-ethics, with nano-researchers and social scientists participating together, and promoted and advocated responsible innovation in nanoscience through platforms such as journals like the *China Social Science Journal*. However, in general, the integration between science and society in the nanotechnology responsible innovation on the national level and the establishment of relevant systems still lack attention (Rodríguez, Mingyan, and Fisher, 2012); the research on ethics, education and social topics in nanotechnology needs to be strengthened (Fan, 2010; Zhao and Wu, 2012).

Summary and comparison of cross-country practices in nanotechnology responsible innovation

In the United States and Europe, nanotechnology constitutes "the collective capability of emerging technology based on science to reshape the blue print of society, economy and technology" (Van Oudheusden, 2014). Due to its novelty, complexity, uncertainty and public character, nanotechnology has become the representative of "post-normal science" (Funtowicz and Ravetz, 1995) and requires the engagement of potential users and stakeholders in the knowledge production process (Gibbons et al., 1994) in order to achieve the responsible innovation of nanotechnology towards economic growth and social progress. Based on the innovation practice of nanotechnology of the United States, EU and developing countries such as China, Table 16.5 summarizes the national research levels of responsible innovation theory.

Conclusion and outlook

Responsible innovation is a rapidly evolving concept, with ambiguity in its motivation, theoretical framework and practice (Owen, Macnaghten, and Stilgoe, 2012). This chapter conducted a systematic discussion of the origin, connotation and attribution of responsible innovation; integrated the three aspects of construction elements, institutional situations and assessment principles; formed the theoretical framework of responsible innovation research; and demonstrated the feasibility of studying the responsible innovation theory through the practice of nanotechnology responsible innovation in the United States, EU and China.

Table 16.5 Comparison and summary of nanotechnology innovation and governance based on the responsible innovation perspective

Levels of institutional situations	Construction dimensions of responsible innovation			
	Inclusion	Anticipation	Reflexivity	Responsiveness
Embeddedness		α: basic values of U.S. society: individual achievements; work oriented; moral care and humanitarianism; efficiency and utilitarianism; progress and material growth; equality; freedom; nationalism and patriotism; democracy (Williams, 1970). β: basic values of European society: competitive society and market economy; pushing scientific and technological advancement; sustainable development; high qualities of life, health and environment; pushing for social equality, gender equality, solidarity and other basic rights β: core assets of European society's long-term development: economic, industrial and trade strength; respect for democracy, human rights, laws and regulations; healthy partnership among EU member countries; high living standards γ: Prosperity, democracy, civility, harmony, freedom, equality, justice, the rule of law, patriotism, dedication, integrity, friendship			
Interaction of level 1–2	∗: The national core values can be applied to all citizens and all organizations with universal applicability, aim, regulatory effect and binding force. They include the value targets and codes of conduct on the national, social and individual levels. The value targets and codes of conduct from the long-term development of the nation are the principles and foundation for the national political, judicial and bureaucratic administrative system construction. &: The system construction and operation of an institutional environment gives explanation and feedback for the basic values and core assets of the national development and forms the understanding and extension of value orientation and code of conduct.			
Institutional environment	α: Core interactive actor: House of Representatives, Senate, federal government, etc.; other interactive actors: scientific research organizations, industrial sectors and the public β: Core interactive actor: EU Council, each member government; other interactive actors: Europe Policy Research Center, European Commission Research Institute, each member country institute, industrial sectors and the public γ: Core interactive actor: Chinese government, liberal parties and legislature; other interactive actors: public, companies and other general organizations	α: The national nanotechnology plan made a clear definition of technical risks and harms β: EU framework plan (FP2–FP7) gradually started the regulation of project feasibility study and endorsement review of the health, food, energy, nanotechnologies and brought in the relevant dimensions in responsible assessment γ: China's national policy for medium- and long-term scientific development, and Law of the People's Republic of China on Science and Technology Progress and other basic laws and regulations give an explanation of anticipatory control of the development and harms of technical innovation	α: The responsible development initiative of nanoscience and technology; the parallel research integration strategy of scientific projects and moral ethics, law and social influence β: A dedicated policy for responsible innovation was released in 2011 to stress the reflection of policies on innovation harms γ: Explanation and reflection by basic Law of the People's Republic of China on Science and Technology Progress, Declaration on Scientific Ideology by Chinese Academy of Sciences, Opinion on Strengthening Scientific and Research Code of Conduct by Chinese Academy of Sciences	α: In 2003, the federal law made public an act for nanotechnology research, the U.S. House of Representatives issued laws over nanotechnology and scientific research β: The European Commission produced legislation and an announcement over science and society integration; the 2020 Wise Growth plan, social science evolution and EU scientific and social plan γ: Clear explanation by basic regulations such as the Law of the People's Republic of China on Science and Technology Progress, national leader's speech and the promotion by official media such as People's Daily

(Continued)

Table 16.5 (Continued)

Levels of institutional situations	Construction dimensions of responsible innovation			
	Inclusion	Anticipation	Reflexivity	Responsiveness
Interaction of level 2–3	⋆: The United States uses the national nanotechnology plan, nanoresearch federal public act; the EU uses 6th and 7th EU framework program, 2020 Smart Growth Program, legislation on science and society integration; China uses formal regulations and laws such as the national science and technology progress law, a declaration on scientific ideology to regulate responsible innovation in the nano field, proposed references for specific research practices and industrial operation norms and uses them as foundation for management and supervision. &: Expert advice in the nanoscience and technology innovation field, investigating reports in research institutes, industrial trend analysis report guiding policy norms; typical nanotechnology scientific research funds and sponsorship methods and laboratory operation model will supplement and improve the institutional environment.			
Governance	α: Core interactive actor: human genome project committee, national scientific research committee, National Science Fund, American Institute review board, global reform and scientific research group, scientists, etc.; other interactive actors: universities and research institutes (such as Arizona State University), nano-research and technology industrial organization, intermediary institute, nonprofit organizations, public agencies β: core interactive actor: European Commission, nanoscience and technology research institute, experts; other interactive actors: public agencies, industrial organizations	α: The "responsible development" of nanoscience and technology brought in discussions over nanotechnology social harms; Arizona State University nanotechnology social research center promoted the anticipatory technological research and management model; after learning the topics of scientific research and basic methods, philosophers and social scientists further evaluate the value points of certain scientific projects and their feasible solutions from the social, moral, ethical and environmental perspectives β: Conducted foresight evaluation in toxicology, biotoxicology, technical disclosure, technical risks, project standardized research in nanoscience and technology; the sponsorship for feasibility study brought in the anticipatory evaluation of responsible innovation in nanotechnology	α: Moral evaluation of nanoscience and engineering; "reflexivity" evaluation indicator of nanotechnology and industry–university–research cooperation; social scientists supervise the moral, societal and environmental factors involved in the scientists' duties, roles and technical innovation responsibilities β: EU's 6th framework policy white book pointed out that existing technological and innovation crises produced doubt in the public's mind on expert-oriented technical policies; regulations on nano-materials, code of conduct for responsible nanoscience and nanotechnology research, and initiative for responsible nano behavioral norms	α: The double structure of nanotechnology risk management; nano-research and innovation program brought in moral and social reviews, using mixed policy governance; nano-laboratory scientific researchers and social scientific researchers are all involved β: European Commission initiated the research and formulated a code of conduct for nanoscience and nanotechnology research, discussed the moral norms, research activities, relevant stakeholder relations and governance systems of the European nanotechnology development; nanomaterial full lifecycle control; the three-stage response governance mode of nanoscience laboratory platform

		γ: core interactive actor: National Natural Sciences Fund Committee, Chinese Academy of Sciences, National Education Board, Ministry of Science and Technology, National Development and Reform Commission, and other research and policy institutes and scientists; other interactive actors: industrial organizations, scientific service agencies and public agencies	γ: The Xiangshan Science Conference raised attention on the safety and ethicality of nanoscience and technology and held nano-ethics seminars several times to determine the potential harms of nanotechnology in China, implemented anticipatory management; published a collection of nine books on nano-safety	γ: National scientific ethics seminars; opinion on strengthening scientific and research code of conduct by Chinese Academy of Science	γ: In 2003, the high-energy physics research institute of the Chinese Academy of Sciences established the "Nano Bio-effect and Safety Laboratory"; later China established the "Joint Laboratory of Nano Bio-effect and Safety" and the "Key Laboratory of Nano Bio-Effect and Safety" by the Chinese Academy of Sciences
Interaction of level 3–4		⋆. Classified the nano-industrial sector based on specific governance methods; for example, the EU determined five development fields of information/communications/electronics, energy/environment, health, textiles and others; further divided the development plan, personnel and organizational constitution, market scale, organization and labor distribution for each field; and conducted responsible assessment by industrial partners.			
		8. Based on the definition of responsibility and governance mode of innovation subjects of practical experience, such as the classification of American and EU laboratory research, promoted engagement of social scientists in laboratory investigation and achieved the institutional response of nanotechnology responsible innovation from the laboratory research level to the social research level by way of integration of interdisciplinary research members.			
Resource allocation and employment		α: Responsible innovation research bases of nanotechnology were set up with the representatives of the nanotechnology social research center of Arizona State University and nanotechnology social research St. Barbara Center of the University of California, and the former was endorsed with \$US6.2 million in funds. In 2010, the NSF continued to invest in the two research centers. Over 20 global research laboratories were established with the focus of Arizona State University.			
		β: Over 2,000 organizations in Europe participated in the responsible innovation and development framework of nano-science and technology.			
		γ: The number of academic papers and patents of nano-science and technology rank first in the world; over 50 universities, 20 research institutes, 600 companies and 5,000 scholars were dedicated to the nanoscience and technology development (Liu, 2009).			

The research contribution of this chapter primarily involves first inciting new thoughts on the traditional innovation research paradigm and innovation driving development from the perspective of responsible innovation. As the core impetus of economic growth and social development, innovation has always had great importance in terms of national progress, regional polices and corporate development. However, while stressing the logic of innovation driving growth, research and policies do not have sufficient reflection on the negative influence of science and technology (Rodríguez, Mingyan, and Fisher, 2012). The reflection and review of responsible innovation proposes over the positive logic of traditional innovation paradigms. Through the detailed examination of the origin, connotation and attribution of responsible innovation, this chapter holds that responsible innovation recognizes the insufficient cognition by innovation act subjects, anticipates the possible negative results of certain innovation activities, guides innovation towards results accepted by social satisfaction and moral ethics through more engagement from members and the establishment of the response system and achieves the maximum public value output. Traditional sciences and innovation are initiated by researchers and are based on knowledge and disciplines. Modern scientific innovation is driven by situations and focuses on problems (Van Oudheusden, 2014). This evolution and value output of innovation activities cannot be detached from the institutional situations related to the entire process of innovation activities.

Second, by way of introduction and analysis of the institutional situation element, this chapter proposes an important supplement to the responsible innovation research theoretical framework under the European development situation. It holds that the existing responsible innovation research theory (Owen, Macnaghten, and Stilgoe, 2012; Stilgoe, Owen, and Macnaghten, 2013; von Schomberg, 2013; Van den Hoven, 2013a; Gianni and Goujon, 2014) lacks discussions of social and political situations and has deficient in its generalization when dealing with differences in national development level, regional cultural environment and institutional systems. This chapter integrates the four levels of the institutional analysis framework model and interactive framework theory, and holds that responsible innovation and its public value surplus are rooted in the four institutional levels of embeddedness, institutional environment, governance, resource allocation and employment, as well as the interlevel dynamic interaction and evolution process. The core construction elements in the responsible innovation of different institutional levels, as well as the lamination effect from the higher-level institutional situations and amplification effect from the lower-level institutional situations, all lead to the research discussions and public value surplus of innovative activities in the national level, industrial level and organizational level. Therefore, the responsible innovation theoretical framework in this chapter has responded well to the dilemma presented by the requirement that "the theoretical framework of responsible innovation needs to ensure that it is embedded into the regional situation, culture, practice and all forms of social innovation" (Macnaghten et al., 2014) raised by scholars such as Macnaghten, as well as to the urgent theoretical development needs of "how to construct a responsible innovation framework that is applicable in all kinds of situations in order to realize the generality of the theory itself" (Gianni and Goujon, 2014) proposed by Gianni and Goujon.

Third, the responsible innovation theoretical framework makes a contribution to the research in scientific and technological governance. By putting the traditional science governance model into a responsible self-governing management framework (Braun, Moore, Herrmann, and Könninger, 2010; Jasanoff, 2011), responsible innovation achieves scientific governance model innovation (Guston and Sarewitz, 2002). It is considered the response of scientific governance to the legality blank of science and technology topics and the cognition blank of certain authorities (Stilgoe, Owen, and Macnaghten, 2013), so it provides a solution to the "institutional voids" (Hajer, 2003) of emerging technology and management model proposed by Hajer; it achieves the transformation from the old science and innovation governance model to the diversified and open governance model (Stilgoe, Owen, and Macnaghten, 2013) and guides science from the "top-down" model to a more interactive governance process (De Saille, 2013). Therefore, a large amount of multileveled and irregular science and innovation governance starts to adopt the responsible governance with anticipation and foresight, focusing on the social and policy choices to ensure the stability of certain innovations. New science governance models such as anticipating governance (Karinen and Guston, 2010), construction analysis, real-time technology assessment (Guston and Sarewitz, 2002), upstream engagement (Wilsdon and Willis, 2004), value sensitivity design (Van den Hoven, Lokhorst, and van de Poel, 2012) and social technology integration (Schuurbiers, 2011) start to appear, opening science and innovation to a situation with wider input and public discussions and creativity (Stilgoe, Owen, and Macnaghten, 2013).

Lastly, this chapter makes a contribution to China's research on innovation development and science and policy fields. Since the reform and opening up, China has been undergoing a large scale of institutional transformation (Hafsi and Tian, 2005). As a big developing country in economic transformation, economic growth is still considered the major target in the national strategy in the current stage, and the concept of scientific innovation driving economic development is rarely challenged, which is why China lacks the policy reflection over the integration of scientific innovation and social needs (Rodríguez, Fisher, and Schuurbiers, 2013). Responsible innovation holds the target of realizing the country's sustainable development and public value, reveals the nonresponsible acts in the innovation system and anticipates the potential influences of innovation by way of a wider engagement of stakeholders in the innovative acts and continuous interaction of institutional response, so it provides an optional development model and open dialogue platform for the integration of developing countries' innovation strategies and existing policy transformation (Macnaghten et al., 2014) and improves the social response of science and technology innovation, institution and policies (Wynne, 2001). Based on the combination of scientific and technological innovation with social ethics and the close link among public stakeholders, responsible innovation provides effective feedback in terms of national competitiveness and economic fairness (Fisher, Mahajan, and Mitcham, 2006; Guston, 2008), in order to ensure that better social efficacy comes with development, and not just economic growth and technological advances (Wynne, 2001).

Notes

1 From *Management World*, No. 08, Pages 39–57, August 2015.
2 The duality of technological innovation means that technological innovation also creates a crisis when producing benefits.
3 The origin of the term simplistic innovation includes frugal innovation, or Jugaad innovation. It is also translated into Chinese as "节俭式创新."
4 Research by Van den Hoven, Lokhorst, and Van de Poel (2012) indicates that the positive relationship between technological innovation and moral advance needs to exclude two types of special circumstances: (1) technological innovation pushes a moral advance in one value dimension but severely impedes the moral advance in another value dimension (for example, the advancement of technology leads to a surplus of production and an increase in energy consumption); and (2) people often use technological innovation to solve issues that result from the social dimension (for example, the global famine does not come from the lack of food production capacity and innovation, but from the uneven distribution of food resources, such as the imbalance between the waste of food in developed countries and the lack of food in poor countries).
5 The developed countries' responsible innovation plans include the Netherlands' responsible innovation program, UK's engineering and physics research institute nanomedicine public dialogue, Europe's nanoscience and technology management norms, American nanotechnology responsible development plan, UK's engineering logistics science institute responsible innovation framework, Germany's nano plan,

Europe Commission's ETICA program, American "social-technological integrated research" programs, etc. Mei Liang, Chen Jin, and Sheng Weizhong (2014) summarized these.

6 Reference: http://ec.europa.eu/research/industrial_technologies/safety-of-health-and-environment_en.html

7 Source of data: http://ec.europa.eu/research/industrial_technologies/nanoscience-and-technologies_en.html

8 The three milestone events are the Decision over Scientific and Technological System Reform made by the Central Committee of the Communist Party of China on March 13, 1985; the speech given by Deng Xiaoping during his visit to the south of China from January 18 to February 21 in 1992; and the Decision on Strengthening Technological Innovation, Developing High Technology and Achieving Industrialization released in August 1998.

References

Adam, B. and Groves, C. (2011). Futures tended: care and future-oriented responsibility. *Bulletin of Science, Technology & Society*, 31(1), 17–27.

Astin, A. W. (2012). *Assessment for excellence: the philosophy and practice of assessment and evaluation in higher education*. Rowman & Littlefield Publishers.

Barben, D., Fisher, E., Selin, C. and Guston, D. H. (2008). *38 Anticipatory governance of nanotechnology: foresight*. Engagement and Integration.

Beesley, L. G. (2003). Science policy in changing times: are governments poised to take full advantage of an institution in transition. *Research Policy*, 32(8), 1519–1531.

Blok, V. (2014). Look who's talking: responsible innovation, the paradox of dialogue and the voice of the other in communication and negotiation processes. *Journal of Responsible Innovation*, 1(2), 171–190.

Borm, P. J., Robbins, D., Haubold, S., Kuhlbusch, T., Fissan, H., Donaldson and Oberdorster, E. (2006). The potential risks of nanomaterials: a review carried out for ECETOC. *Particle and Fibre Toxicology*, 3, 11, 1–35.

Braun, K., Moore, A., Herrmann, S. L. and Könninger, S. (2010). Science governance and the politics of proper talk: governmental bioethics as a new technology of reflexive government. *Economy and Society*, 39(4), 510–533.

Briggle, A. (2010). *A rich bioethics*. South Bend: University of Notre Dame Press.

Brouwer, W. (1994). Taking responsibility for the implications of science. *Bulletin of Science, Technology & Society*, 14(4), 192–202.

Brush, S. G. (1974). Should the history of science be rated X? The way scientists behave (according to historians) might not be a good model for students. *Science*, 183(4130), 1164–1172.

Chesbrough, H. W. (2003). *Open innovation: the new imperative for creating and profiting from technology*. Harvard Business Press.

Collingridge, D. (1980). *The social control of technology*. London: Pinter.

Collins, R. (2004). *Interaction ritual chains*. Princeton Studies in Cultural Sociology.

Commons, J. R. (1936). Institutional economics. *The American Economic Review*, 237–249.

Congress, U. S. (2003). 21st century nanotechnology research and development act. *Public Law*, 108–153.

Corlett, J. A. (2006). *Responsibility and punishment* (Vol. 9). Dordrecht: Springer.

Correljé, A., Cuppen, E., Dignum, M., Pesch, U. and Taebi, B. (2015). Responsible innovation in energy projects: values in the design of technologies, institutions and stakeholder interactions. *Responsible Innovation*, 2, 183–200.

Correlje, A. F. and Groenewegen, J. P. (2009). Public values in the energy sector: economic perspectives. *International Journal of Public Policy*, 4(5), 395–413.

Davis, M. (2009). *No one here but us chickens. Some thoughts on the professional responsibility of engineers*. Book of Abstracts. Delft, The Netherlands: Delft University of Technology.

De Saille, S. (2013). Innovating innovation: RRI as a guiding principle in the ERA. Available at SSRN 2401076.

Devine-Wright, P. (2014). *Renewable energy and the public: from NIMBY to participation*. London: Routledge.

Doorn, N. (2012). Responsibility ascriptions in technology development and engineering: three perspectives. *Science and Engineering Ethics*, 18(1), 69–90.

Douglas, H. E. (2003). The moral responsibilities of scientists (tensions between autonomy and responsibility). *American Philosophical Quarterly*, 59–68.

Dupuy, J. P. (2007). Complexity and uncertainty: a prudential approach to nanotechnology. *Nanoethics. The Ethical and Social Implications of Nanotechnology*, 119–132.

Durbin, P. T. (2008). Engineering professional ethics in a broader dimension. *Interdisciplinary Science Reviews*, 33(3), 226–233.

Eisenhardt, K. M. (1989). Building theories from case study re-search. *Academy of Management Review*, 14(4), 532–550.

Eisenhardt, K. M. (1991). Better stories and better constructs: the case for rigor and comparative logic. *Academy of Management Re-view*, 16(3), 620–627.

Elizalde, J. (1998). General introduction: ELSA in FP 4. European Commission, e(thical), l(egal) and s(oficial) a(spects) of the life sciences and technologies programmes of framework programme IV. Catalogue of Contracts.

Eshleman, A. (2008). *Moral responsibility.* https://pilotscholars.up.edu/cgi/viewcontent.cgi?article=1001&context=phl_facpubs

Eurobarometer, S. (2005). Social values, science and technology. *Eurobarometer Special Report*, 225.

European Commission (2001). European governance: a white paper, office for official publications of the European communities. http://europa.eu/rapid/press-release_DOC-01-10_en.pdf

European Commission (2009). Commission recommendation on a code of conduct for responsible nanosciences & council conclusions on responsible nanosciences and nanotechnologies research. http://ec.europa.eu/research/science-society/document_library/pdf_06/nanocode-apr09_en.pdf

European Commission (2011). *Horizon 2020 – the framework programme for research and innovation*, Brussels.

Eden, G., Jirotka, M. and Stahl, B. (2013). Responsible research and innovation: critical reflection into the potential social consequences of ICT. In *Research Challenges in Information Science (RCIS), 2013 IEEE Seventh International Conference*, 1–12, Paris, France.

Fagerberg, J., Mowery, D. C. and Nelson, R. R. (2006). *The Oxford handbook of innovation*. Oxford: Oxford Handbooks Online.

Fahlquist, J. N. (2009). Moral responsibility for environmental problems – individual or institutional. *Journal of Agricultural and Environmental Ethics*, 22(2), 109–124.

Fan, C. (2010). *Thoughts on strengthening research on china's nanotechnology social and ethical issues.* Scientific Policy and Management Science Research Institute of the Chinese Academy of Sciences.

Fang, X. and Liu, X. (2014). The review and prospect of the reform of China's science and technology regime. *Qiushi* (求是), 5, 43–45.

Fischer, C., Parry, I. W. and Pizer, W. A. (2003). Instrument choice for environmental protection when technological innovation is endogenous. *Journal of Environmental Economics and Management*, 45(3), 523–545.

Fischer, J. M. and Ravizza, M. (1999). *Responsibility and control: a theory of moral responsibility.* Cambridge: Cambridge University Press.

Fisher, E., Mahajan, R. L. and Mitcham, C. (2006). Midstream modulation of technology: governance from within. *Bulletin of Science, Technology & Society*, 26(6), 485–496.

Fisher, E. and Maricle, G. (2014). Higher-level responsiveness? Socio-technical integration within US and UK nanotechnology research priority setting. *Science and Public Policy*, 017.

Fratzscher, M. and Imbs, J. (2009). Risk sharing, finance and institutions in international portfolios. *Journal of Financial Economics*, 94(3), 428–447.

Funtowicz, S. O. and Ravetz, J. R. (1995). *Science for the post normal age* Netherlands: Springer.

George, G., McGahan, A. M. and Prabhu, J. (2012). Innovation for inclusive growth: towards a theoretical framework and a research agenda. *Journal of Management Studies*, 49(4), 661–683.

Gianni, R. and Goujon, P. (2014). *Governance of responsible innovation.* http://tethys.eaprs.cse.dmu.ac.uk/rri/sites/default/files/obs-design-guideline/GREAT_Del.2.3_final.pdf

Gianni, R., Ikonen, V., Goujon, P. and Pearson, J. (2014). Pan-el-responsible innovation in research: a reflexive governance to scientific development. *Ethics in Science, Technology and Engineering, 2014 IEEE International Symposium on*, pp. 1–3.

Gibbons, M., Limoges, C., Nowotny, H., Schwartzman, S., Scott, P. and Trow, M. (1994). *The new production of knowledge: the dynamics of science and research in contemporary societies.* Thousand Oaks, CA: Sage.

Gilfillan, S. C. (1935). *The sociology of invention.* Chicago: Follett.

Glerup, C. and Horst, M. (2014). Mapping 'Social Responsibility' in science. *Journal of Responsible Innovation*, 1(1), 31–50.

Granovetter, M. (1985). Economic action and social structure: the problem of embeddedness. *American Journal of Sociology*, 481–510.

Gray, B., Purdy, J. and Ansari, S. (2014). From interactions to institutions: micro-processes of framing and mechanisms for the structuring of institutional fields. *Academy of Management Review*, 40(1), 115–143.

Groueff, S. (1967). *Manhattan project: the untold story of the making of the atomic bomb*. Boston, MA: Little, Brown.

Grove-White, R., Macnaghten, P. and Wynne, B. (2000). *Wising up: the public and new technologies, centre for the study of environmental change*. Lancaster: Lancaster University.

Grunwald, A. (2014). The hermeneutic side of responsible research and innovation. *Journal of Responsible Innovation*, 1(3), 274–291.

Gu, Y. and Tao, Y. (2014). The extended actor-network: a new way to solve Collingridge' dilemma. *Studies in Science of Science*, 32(7), 982–986.

Gudynas, E. (2011). Buen Vivir: today's tomorrow. *Development*, 54(4), 441–447.

Guston, D. H. (2007). *Between politics and science: assuring the integrity and productivity of research*. Cambridge: Cambridge University Press.

Guston, D. H. (2008). Innovation policy: not just a jumbo shrimp. *Nature*, 454(7207), 940–941.

Guston, D. H. and Sarewitz, D. (2002). Real-time technology assessment. *Technology in Society*, 24(1), 93–109.

Hafsi, T. and Tian, Z. (2005). Towards a theory of large scale institutional change: the transformation of the Chinese electricity industry. *Long Range Planning*, 38(6), 555–577.

Hajer, M. (2003). Policy without polity? Policy analysis and the institutional void. *Policy Sciences*, 36(2), 175–195.

Hellström, T. (2003). Systemic innovation and risk: technology assessment and the challenge of responsible innovation. *Technology in Society*, 25(3), 369–384.

Hodgson, G. M. (2004). *The evolution of institutional economics*. London: Routledge.

Irwin, A. (2006). The politics of talk coming to terms with the 'New' scientific governance. *Social Studies of Science*, 36(2), 299–320.

Janssen, M. A., Schoon, M. L., Ke, W. and Börner, K. (2006). Scholarly networks on resilience, vulnerability and adaptation within the human dimensions of global environmental change. *Global Environmental Change*, 16(3), 240–252.

Jasanoff, S. (2011). Constitutional moments in governing science and technology. *Science and Engineering Ethics*, 17(4), 621–638.

Jonas, H. (1984). *The imperative of responsibility: in search of an ethics for the technological age*. Chicago: University of Chicago Press.

Juengst, E. T. (1996). Self-critical federal science? The ethics experiment within the US human genome project. *Social Philosophy and Policy*, 13(2), 63–95.

Kaiser, D. and Moreno, J. (2012). Dual-use research: self-censorship is not enough. *Nature*, 492(7429), 345–347.

Karinen, R. and Guston, D. H. (2010). Toward anticipatory governance: the experience with nanotechnology. *Governing Future Technologies*, 217–232.

Koepsell, D. (2010). On genies and bottles: scientists' moral responsibility and dangerous technology R&D. *Science and Engineering Ethics*, 16(1), 119–133.

Künneke, R. W. (2008). Institutional reform and technological practice: the case of electricity. *Industrial and Corporate Change*, 17(2), 233–265.

Kutz, C. (2000). *Complicity: ethics and law for a collective age*. Cambridge University Press.

Lee, R. G. and Petts, J. (2013). Adaptive governance for responsible innovation. *Responsible innovation: managing the responsible emergence of science and innovation in society*, 143–164.

Liu, L. (2009). Nanotechnology and society in China: current position and prospects for development. *Presentation for the 2nd Manchester International Workshop on Nanotechnology, Society and Policy*, pp. 6–8, Manchester, UK.

Macnaghten, P., Owen, R., Stilgoe, J., Wynne, B., Azevedo, A., de Campos, A. and Velho, L. (2014). Responsible innovation across borders: tensions, paradoxes and possibilities. *Journal of Responsible Innovation*, 1(2), 191–199.

Mei, L. and Chen, J. (2014). Reflection and reconstruction of innovation paradigm: the emerging research on responsible innovation. *Science and Management*, 34(3), 3–11.

Mei, L., Chen, J. and Sheng, W. (2014). Responsible innovation: emerging paradigm of research and innovation. *Studies in Dialectics of Nature*, 30(10), 83–89.

Meynhardt, T. (2009). Public value inside: what is public value creation. *International Journal of Public Administration*, 32(3), 192–219.

Miller, D. (2004). Holding nations responsible. *Ethics*, 114(2), 240–268.

Munir, K. A. (2005). The social construction of events: a study of institutional change in the photographic field. *Organization Studies*, 26(1), 93–112.

New, N. M. R. (2010). Research thrives on integration of natural and social sciences. *Nature*, 463, 25.

Owen, R., Baxter, D., Maynard, T. and Depledge, M. (2009). Beyond regulation: risk pricing and responsible innovation. *Environmental Science & Technology*, 43(18), 6902–6906.

Owen, R., Bessant, J. and Heintz, M. (2013). *Responsible innovation: managing the responsible emergence of science and innovation in society.* West Sussex: John Wiley & Sons Ltd.

Owen, R., Macnaghten, P. and Stilgoe, J. (2012). Responsible research and innovation: from science in society to science for society, with society. *Science and Public Policy*, 39(6), 751–760.

Ozcan, P. and Eisenhardt, K. M. (2009). Origin of alliance portfolios: entrepreneurs, network strategies and firm performance. *Academy of Management Journal*, 52(2), 246–279.

Pandza, K. and Ellwood, P. (2013). Strategic and ethical foundations for responsible innovation. *Research Policy*, 42(5), 1112–1125.

Pansera, M. and Owen, R. (2014). *Collaboration for sustainability and innovation: a role for sustainability driven by the global south.* Netherlands: Springer.

Roeser, S. (2012). Moral emotions as guide to acceptable risk. In Roeser, S., Hillerbrand, R., Sandin, P., and Peterson, M. (Eds.), *Handbook of risk theory*. Dordrecht, Netherlands: Springer, pp. 819–832.

Rhodes, R. (2012). *Making of the atomic bomb.* Simon and Schuster.

Roco, M. C. (2006). Progress in governance of converging technologies integrated from the nanoscale. *Annals of the New York Academy of Sciences*, 1093(1), 1–23.

Rodríguez, H., Fisher, E. and Schuurbiers, D. (2013). Integrating science and society in European framework programmes: trends in project-level solicitations. *Research Policy*, 42(5), 1126–1137.

Rodríguez, H., Mingyan, H. and Fisher, E. (2012). *Socio-technical integration: research policies in the United States, European Union and China.* Netherlands: Springer.

Santos, F. M. and Eisenhardt, K. M. (2009). Constructing markets and shaping boundaries: entrepreneurial power in nascent fields. *Academy of Management Journal*, 52(4), 643–671.

Sarewitz, D. and Woodhouse, E. (2003). Small is powerful. In Lightman, A., Sarewitz, D. and Desser, C. (Eds.), *Living with the Genie: essays on technology and the quest for human mastery.* Island Press, pp. 63–83.

Schot, J. and Geels, F. W. (2008). Strategic Niche management and sustainable innovation journeys: theory, findings, research agenda and policy. *Technology Analysis & Strategic Management*, 20(5), 537–554.

Schuurbiers, D. (2011). What happens in the lab: applying mid-stream modulation to enhance critical reflection in the laboratory. *Science and Engineering Ethics*, 17(4), 769–788.

Schuurbiers, D., Sleenhoff, S., Jacobs, J. F. and Osseweijer, P. (2009). Multidisciplinary engagement with nanoethics through education – the nanobio-raise advanced courses as a case study and model. *Nanoethics*, 3(3), 197–211.

Stahl, B. C. (2013). Responsible research and innovation: the role of privacy in an emerging framework. *Science and Public Policy*, 67.

Stilgoe, J., Owen, R. and Macnaghten, P. (2013). Developing a frame-work for responsible innovation. *Research Policy*, 42(9), 1568–1580.

Sutcliffe, H. and Director, M. A. T. T. E. R. (2011). *A report on responsible research and innovation.* Brussels, Belgium: European Commission.

Swann, G. P. (2009). *The economics of innovation: an introduction.* Cheltenham: Edward Elgar Publishing.

Swierstra, T. and Rip, A. (2007). Nano-ethics as NEST-ethics: patterns of moral argumentation about new and emerging science and technology. *Nanoethics*, 1(1), 3–20.

Taebi, B., Correlje, A., Cuppen, E., Dignum, M. and Pesch, U. (2014). Responsible innovation as an endorsement of public values: the need for interdisciplinary research. *Journal of Responsible Innovation*, 1(1), 118–124.

U.S. House Committee on Science (2003). *Hearing on societal implications of nanotechnology, 108th* Congress, House Committee on Science, Washington, DC.

van der Burg, S. and Van Gorp, A. (2005). Understanding moral responsibility in the design of trailers. *Science and Engineering Ethics*, 11(2), 235–256.

van den Hoven, J. (2013a). *Options for strengthening responsible research and innovation: report of the expert group on the state of art in Europe on responsible research and innovation, publications office of the European Union*, Luxembourg.

van den Hoven, J. (2013b). Value sensitive design and responsible innovation. In Owen, R., Bessant, J. and Heintz, M. (Eds.), *Responsible innovation – managing the responsible emergence of science and innovation in society*, pp. 75–84.

van den Hoven, J., Lokhorst, G. J. and van de Poel, I. (2012). Engineering and the problem of moral overload. *Science and Engineering Ethics*, 18(1), 143–155.

van de Poel, I. (2008). How should we do nanoethics? A network approach for discerning ethical issues in nanotechnology. *NanoEthics*, 2(1), 25–38.

van de Poel, I. (2009). Values in engineering design. In Gabbay, D. M., Thagard, P., Woods, J. and Meijers, A. W. (Eds.), *Philosophy of technology and engineering sciences*. Elsevier, pp. 973–1006.

Van Oudheusden, M. (2014). Where are the politics in responsible innovation? European governance, technology assessments and beyond. *Journal of Responsible Innovation*, 1(1), 67–86.

Veenman, S., Liefferink, D. and Arts, B. (2009). A short history of Dutch forest policy: the 'De-institutionalisation' of a policy arrangement. *Forest Policy and Economics*, 11(3), 202–208.

Von Schomberg, R. (2012). *Prospects for technology assessment in a framework of responsible research and innovation.* Charpter of Technikfolgen AbschäTzen Lehren: Springer.

Von Schomberg, R. (2013). A vision of responsible research and innovation. *Responsible Innovation: Managing the Responsible Emergence of Science and Innovation in Society*, 51–74.

Wynne, B. (2001). Creating public alienation: expert cultures of risk and ethics on GMOs. *Science as Culture*, 10(4), 445–481.

Walker, G., Devine-Wright, P., Barnett, J., Burningham, K., Cass, N., Devine-Wright, H. and Theobald, K. (2010). *Symmetries, expectations, dynamics and contexts: a framework for understanding public engagement with renewable energy projects*. London: Earthscan.

Weart, S. R. (1976). Scientists with a secret. *Physics Today*, 29(2), 23–30.

Wickson, F. and Carew, A. L. (2014). Quality criteria and indicators for responsible research and innovation: learning from transdisciplinarity. *Journal of Responsible Innovation*, 1(3), 254–273.

Wickson, F., Carew, A. L. and Russell, A. W. (2006). Transdisciplinary research: characteristics, quandaries and quality. *Futures*, 38(9), 1046–1059.

Williams, R. M. (1970). *American society: a sociological interpretation*. New York: Knopf.

Williamson, O. E. (1998). Transaction cost economics: how it works; where it is headed. *De Economist*, 146(1), 23–58.

Wilsdon, J. (2014). From foresight to hindsight: the promise of history in responsible innovation. *Journal of Responsible Innovation*, 1(1), 109–112.

Wilsdon, J. and Willis, R. (2004). *See-through Science: why public engagement needs to move upstream*. Demos.

Wynne, B. (1993). Public uptake of science: a case for institutional reflexivity. *Public Understanding of Science*, 2(4), 321–337.

Xi, J. (2014). *Report on the 17th Academician Conference in the Chinese Academy of Sciences and the 12th Academician Conference in the Chinese Academy of Engineering.*

Yang, H., Peng, J. and Zhao, H. (2012). *Science and Technology Management Research*, 32(1), 23–26.

Yin, R. (1994). *Case study research: design and methods*. Beverly Hills.

Zandvoort, H. (2005). Knowledge, risk and liability. Analysis of a discussion continuing within science and technology. *Poznan Studies in the Philosophy of the Sciences and the Humanities*, 84(1), 469–498.

Zandvoort, H. (2008). Risk zoning and risk decision making. *International Journal of Risk Assessment and Management*, 8(1), 3–18.

Zeschky, M., Widenmayer, B. and Gassmann, O. (2011). Frugal innovation in emerging markets. *Research-Technology Management*, 54(4), 38–45.

Zhao, Y. and Wu, S. (2012). Risk and rationality: needs orientated nano-science and technology – nano-security in China and the world. *Science and Society*, 2(2), 24–35.

Zhu, X. (2012). "System" and "function" of structural reforms of science and technology. *Studies in Dialectics of Nature*, 28(7), 68–73.

17
SERENDIPITY AND INNOVATION
Beyond planning and experimental-driven exploration

Martin Kamprath and Tassilo Henike

Introduction

Unexpected events are largely treated as unwanted and result from wrong or insufficient planning. Events that do not meet expectations seem to have a negative aura by nature. When unexpected events happen, people fear potential loses more than gains (cf. Kahneman and Tversky, 1984). That is why people prefer to seek expectable events with lower certain gains as well as loses and to avoid unexpectable events with considerably higher uncertain gains or loses. However, according to Peter Drucker (1985), unexpected events are the simplest and easiest source for innovation.

In times of intense competition, along with fast-changing markets and technologies, the key question is not whether to innovate, but rather where do innovations come from and how to systematically leverage these sources. Innovation is, in a broad sense, the creation of a remarkably new mean-end combination and their valuable application (Hauschildt and Salomo, 2011). This encompasses the process of how new things are created as well as the objects that result thereof. Therefore, the sources of innovation are equally relevant for disciplines like technology management, product and service development, business model management, and entrepreneurship. Innovations may originate from demographic changes, changes in perception, new knowledge, incongruities, process needs, industry, and market changes or unexpected occurrences (Drucker, 1985). As innovation activities promise superb benefits, firms and individuals put tremendous engagement in exploring remarkably new, valuable mean-end combinations, although there are no guarantees of rewards (Pisano and Teece, 2007).

In a world of full information and low uncertainty, several innovation alternatives exist that are all characterized by a probability distribution over returns that is initially unknown, yet the distribution is accessible by exploration. Thus, systematic exploration and deterministically planned innovation strategies will lead to the most valuable mean-end combinations (cf. March, 1991).

However, in a world of incomplete information and high uncertainty, the probability distributions and outcomes are unknown and hardly accessible. Savage (1954) called such worlds with imperfect knowledge large worlds. They are distinguished from small worlds with perfect information in that rational models automatically provide the correct answer (Gigerenzer and

Gaissmaier, 2011) and still largely determine innovation practices. Yet, even much engagement in exploration and high costs will not ensure the exploration of certain outcomes. Therefore, in a complex, uncertain and interconnected business world, "there is accumulating evidence that innovation will be just as likely to arise from unexpected serendipitous insights as from deterministically planned innovation strategies" (Loosemore, 2013, p. 1). At this point, unexpected events should not be demonized per se. From a different perspective, an accident may have a positive core that has not been expected by starting the explorative engagement. That is the essence of serendipitous innovation.

This chapter serves to introduce the notion of *serendipity* and has four main objectives: (1) to clarify the origin and relevance of serendipity as a source of innovation, (2) to outline the elements of serendipity and how serendipity is distinguished from other types of exploration, (3) to offer an overview of different patterns of how serendipity unfolds, (4) and to discuss the conditions and managerial aspects of serendipity in innovation processes.

Origin and definition of serendipity

Looking back, we see that serendipitous discoveries contributed significantly to humans' advancement of knowledge and well-being. One of the oldest examples is the discovery of gravity by Isaac Newton. An apple hit Newton's head while he laid in his stepfather's garden. From this occasion, he deduced a connection between the falling apple and the rotation of the moon around the earth (cf. Gaughan, 2011, p. 30). Another well-known example is the discovery of the medicine penicillin by the scientist Alexander Fleming. The landing of the *Penicillium chrysogenum*'s mold on one of Fleming's petri dishes was a result of sheer accident and caused the *Staphylococcus* bacteria to die. This turned out to be the world's first antibiotic substance. Another example is Viagra that was originally intended to cure angina pectoris and later turned out to be an effective treatment for erectile dysfunction. Coca-Cola was also actually designed for medical purposes but is today acknowledged as a refreshing drink. The discovery of X-rays by Wilhelm Conrad Röntgen was also good fortune. Röntgen experimented with a cathode ray tube that he wrapped in black cardboard. Surprisingly, some invisible rays coming from the tube were passing through the cardboard and reflected an object on the fluorescent screen that was coincidentally laid on a table. Other examples include the discovery of nylon, DNA, and gunpowder (cf. Roberts, 1989). As these examples illustrate, serendipity involves in essence the beneficial perception of an unintended outcome that has followed from another activity (cf. Dew, 2009).

Most complex problem-solving tasks require one to think outside of customary ways of reasoning and extensive engagement. These problems are characterized by a given state, a desired goal state, and obstacles between these states. What makes a problem complex is the large number of possibly relevant elements, their high connectivity, possible dynamic changes over time, and the concealment of structure and dynamics (Funke, 2010). Serendipitous discoveries function in such tasks like shortcuts, in that not all elements, interactions, and dynamics need to be understood ex ante. Thus, serendipity creates opportunities for complex problem solving, counterfactual thinking, and exclusive discoveries. These advantages legitimize chance encounters, accidental occurrences, and sheer good fortune as sources of innovation that loom large in business life (Brown, 2005) and give value to serendipitous discoveries within innovation processes (Austin, Devin, and Sullivan, 2012).

Originally, Horace Walpole coined the term in a letter to his friend Horace Mann in 1754. In this letter, Walpole told his friend the ancient tale of "The Three Princes of Serendip". The three princes always discovered things that they were not seeking (Merton and Barber, 2006). For instance, one prince discovered by accident and sagacity that a mule was blind in one eye because the grass was only eaten on one side of the street where the mule had walked. This tale inspired Walport to coin discoveries resulting from accident and sagacity as serendipity:

> The discovery, indeed, is almost of that kind which I call *Serendipity*, a very expressive word, which, as I have nothing better to tell you, I shall endeavour it better by the derivation than by the definition.
>
> *(Merton and Barber, 2006, p. 1f.)*

In this traditional viewpoint, serendipitous findings are accidental findings made when the discoverer is investigating something else (García, 2009). Most authors agree with this general definition. As such, serendipity is described as "search leading to unintended discovery" (Dew, 2009, p. 735), "the art of making an 'unsought finding'" (Van Andel, 1994, p. 643), or "looking for a needle in a haystack and finding the farmer's daughter" (Singh, 2010, p. 67).

Moreover, the accidental discovery is seen as something beneficial, "a certain fortunate coincidence, beneficial accident and positive collision" (Kakko and Inkinen, 2009, p. 540). The concept itself focuses on conducive circumstances and an observer of a lucky accident. It is not limited to technological innovations but also encompasses new strategies and new organizational features (Weisenfeld, 2009).

Aspects and elements of the concept

(1) Surprise and accidental encounter but no luck

The aspect of a sudden occurrence plays a major role when defining serendipity. From the viewpoint of technological innovation, serendipity "means leading an accidental encounter to some invention or discovery, sometimes by interpreting data from a different point of view" (Itaya and Niwa, 2013, p. 74). Yet serendipitous innovation is not a result of pure luck. Pure luck is something that (sometimes) happens and is independent of prior knowledge. In contrast, serendipitous exploration requires preparedness and some sort of engagement (Dew, 2009). It means being active in searching but also being open to findings that are not considered in a linear problem–solution exploration. Serendipitous innovation originates from being aware of multiple problem spaces even in fields outside the intended focus (e.g. outside a specific technical domain, another industry, or a different customer group). The main element of accidental encounter is the absence of intent leading to surprise. The inventor is not aware in advance of the solution that will result. This requires some sort of alertness on the part of the inventor to be able to see applications and benefits outside the intended activity scope that distinguishes serendipity from pure luck.

(2) Intellectual leap

The aspect of an unintended, surprising occurrence plays a major role when defining serendipity. From the perspective of information retrieval, this traditional viewpoint on the process is extended by the aspect of perceiving a certain benefit in this accidental discovery (e.g. Cunha, Clegg, and Mendonça, 2010; Kakko and Inkinen, 2009). While some perceive an accident as a negative collision, others are able to transform this accident into a positive collision and to make use of it (Weisenfeld, 2009). This transformation requires an intellectual leap in that the accident is perceived differently from the former expectations. The intellectual leap may result from minor modifications of the cone of expectation or a complete rejection of it (Austin, Devin, and Sullivan, 2012). Florczak (2015) argues that this surprise and intellectual leap is one of the essential points of qualitative research. Qualitative studies are inherently designed to discover unanticipated occurrences and to put them into perspective with existing knowledge. Through the course of researching, researchers gain more and more insight, connect different dots, and may create new connections. This creation of new connections is an intellectual leap and helps to create a meaningful understanding of unanticipated, serendipitous occurrences.

(3) A beneficial perception as strategic advantage

Serendipity has a dual nature consisting of the accidental process and the perceptual ability of transforming it into a meaningful outcome (McBirnie, 2008). The unexpected emergence of a meaningful outcome makes serendipity a valuable source for exploration and strategic advantages. Strategic advantages ensure firms' positions in the market because these advantages rest on valuable, rare, hardly imitable, and hardly substitutable bundles of resources in relation to the environment (cf. Barney, 1991). Thus, the exploration of these sources of strategic advantage is vital for every firm. In this explorative process, firms are confronted with a high level of uncertainty with regard to the sources' characteristics, sources' locations, and how to attend to these sources. However, uncertainty is a double-edged sword in this explorative process because high uncertainty also impedes competitors' ability to identify these sources. Therefore, firms are challenged to explore these sources with both the help and the handicap of uncertainty.

(4) Prior and follow-up knowledge

To turn unexpected events into a positive outcome, good preparation is essential to work toward the unexpected coincidence and to allow the intellectual leap (de Rond and Morley, 2010a). The searcher's *attitude* is the first important aspect of being prepared. Cunha and colleagues (2010, p. 323) refer to this attitude as "mindfulness". Weisenfeld (2009) similarly points to the motivation that is decisive to being receptive for the observation. As individuals are exposed to various stimuli, they selectively allocate attention to some stimuli while neglecting others (Kahneman, 1973). In other words, attention is a filter to cope with complexity and is driven by searchers' motivations. Thus, the occurrence of an unexpected event should not lead searchers to throw them away, but rather to accept them as potentially meaningful. The accumulation of *relevant knowledge* is a second important aspect. Numerous authors account for the importance of knowledge, yet use different notions: background knowledge (Itaya and Niwa, 2013), expertise (Austin, Devin, and Sullivan, 2012), knowledge of the past (de Rond, 2014; Dew, 2009), or sagacity (Weisenfeld, 2009). Eventually, knowledge is needed to understand the meaning of a discovery (cf. Weisenfeld, 2009) or to create meaning by bringing together different perspectives. This is what happens in scientific teams in that researchers with different background knowledge work together and generate new knowledge (Barnett, 2011). As more and more knowledge is acquired, the benefit from a discovery can be identified (cf. Buckner, 2012). The discovery of the motion center in the brain is an example of how additional knowledge enables serendipitous discoveries. This discovery was not realized for a long time because it was not well understood. The discovery of penicillin is a similar example. Further knowledge was needed to understand what happened during this "accident" (cf. André, Devin, and Sullivan, 2009). "Often, the possibilities afforded by a phenomenon are only appreciated later, after the surprise of the discovery has worn off" (Fabian, 2010, p. 73). Thus, prior and follow-up knowledge extend the possibilities of perceiving the accident's benefit in another context.

Patterns of serendipitous discoveries

In retrospect, innovations occurring as serendipitous discoveries are often rhetorically stylized as a "magic moment" in time (de Rond and Morley, 2010a): the "Eureka" moment signaling a spontaneous inspiration. If this moment actually exists, it is significantly more uncommon than the retrospective tales of serendipitous discoveries suggest. Typically, revolutionary breakthroughs begin as rather normal work and, by telescoping historical development, the tales about these breakthroughs are enriched with far more meaning than they originally possessed (Nickles, 1997). Many serendipitous discoveries resulted from more complex coincidences of factors. Copeland (forthcoming, p. 5) notes that "serendipity in the practice of science is more ubiquitous than momentous". The image of a scientist working in isolation in an ivory tower and having a tabula rasa until the magic moment unfolds does not hold true for the majority of discoveries. A process of discovery is likely to involve participation from multiple persons, experiences from past discoveries, characteristic places, or opportune times. Thus, serendipities' origin and unfolding are manifold and not just magic moments.

Several authors investigated historical cases of serendipitous discoveries and collected classifying patterns to better understand serendipities' origin and unfolding (e.g. van Andel, 1994; Fine and Deegan, 1996; Friedel, 2001; Austin, 2003). A first classification can be made in terms of whether the surprising aspect relates to the process, the outcome, or both. Friedel (2001) describes the first pattern as *someone is looking for something and accidentally discovers it*. The second pattern is described as *discovering something when someone is initially looking for something else*. Based on this logic, the third pattern means that *someone is initially looking for something and accidentally discovers something else*. Thus, this first classification relates to the question: What is the serendipitous aspect in a discovery?

Other authors concentrated on the question: How do serendipitous discoveries emerge and, accordingly, what is the origin of serendipitous discoveries? Van Andel (1994) presents a collection of 17 serendipity patterns that can be related to four overarching dimensions: observation related, environment related, work behavior related, and belief related. *Observation-related patterns* are mainly driven by surprising results of initial activities. Van Andel (1994) distinguishes between serendipitous discoveries that result from surprising observations and the repetition of surprising observations. Moreover, surprising results occur based on turnarounds of initial perceptions because of errors that turn out to be successful, side effects that turn out to be main effects, and by-products that turn out to be main products. *Environment-related patterns* are caused by factors that initially fell outside the field of interest. Analogies are inspiring sources to transfer solutions from one context to another. By watching children scratching with pins on one end of a piece of wood and listening with their ears on the other end, Laennec was inspired to invent the stethoscope (Van Andel, 1994). Unusual groups like children or outsiders serve oftentimes as sources of inspiration for surprising scientific discoveries. *Work behavior–related patterns* cover to a large extent work behaviors that deviate from normal activities. Van Andel (1994) lists jokes, playing, interruption of work, scarcity of resources, and disturbances as factors that enable a breakout from established work routines and thus offer sources for surprising discoveries. The fourth pattern, *beliefs*, also locates the origin of serendipitous discoveries in the realm of individuals. Popular beliefs; wrong, forgotten, or missing hypotheses; and the inversion of beliefs are originating sources for serendipitous discoveries. This shows that the sources of serendipity are manifold and that serendipitous discoveries are only prolonged if the reasons for a surprising moment are understood over time. These reasons can be based on the right timing, being at the right place, or other specific circumstances to make a discovery.

Based on historical examples, we assembled six patterns that answer the question why serendipitous discoveries have been made. The examples show that many discoveries rely on natural laws and through the coincidence of persons and specific circumstances, discoverers were able to unlock these natural laws. That means that the prior described aspects and elements of serendipity are the basic premises, but that there are patterns of the coincidence of specific persons and circumstances that explain different mechanisms for serendipitous discoveries (see Table 17.1).

The first pattern is called *sanctum serendipity* and covers the mechanism that accidental discoveries are made by being at the right place (a figuratively holy place where the magic happens). The discovery of how to measure the volume of irregular solids occurred when Archimedes was getting into a bath and discovered that water displaced as a result (cf. Mirvahedi and Morrish, 2017). The discovery of Kodak's Super Glue is another example of this pattern. Super Glue – also known as cyanoacrylate – was originally discovered in 1942 by Harry Coover who attempted to make clear plastic gun sights to be put on guns. Yet the high adhesiveness of cyanoacrylate impeded its applicability for this case, and Coover let his idea rest until he worked for Eastman Kodak in 1951. While working on a project for developing a heat-resistant acrylate polymer for jet canopies, Cooper realized the great potential of a product that quickly bonds a variety of materials, and Super Glue was commercialized. In contrast to *sanctum serendipity*, *detour serendipity* means discovering something by being accidentally at the right place or by taking another way for an intended solution. Italian Christopher Columbus initially planned to find a quicker route from Europe to Asia, but accidentally was the first European to arrive at the Bahamas. This New World existed without Christopher Columbus' effort, yet it needed his "accidental being at the right (before unknown) place" to transport this discovery to Europe. Both examples show that being at the right place for this event to happen in an unknown place is one reason why serendipitous discoveries are made.

Table 17.1 Patterns of serendipitous discoveries

Patterns	Logic	Examples
Sanctum serendipity	Accidentally discovering something by being in the right place	• Discovery of volume measurement • Discovery of Super Glue
Detour serendipity	Discovering something by being accidentally at the right place	• Discovery of the "New World"
Momentum serendipity	Accidentally observing something because of the right timing	• Discovery of moons around Jupiter • Discovery of bacterium *H. pylori*'s meaning for peptic ulcers • Discovery of cornflakes
Combinatorial serendipity	Discovering something by accidentally combining the right materials	• Vulcanization of rubber • Discovery of X-rays • Discovery of gunpowder
Data serendipity	Accidentally discovering an effect through unknown links and emerging patterns in a data set	• Discovery of Viagra
Communal serendipity	Accidentally discovering something by combining the right people	• Discovery of vitamin C
Aftermath serendipity	Accidentally discovering something after a first discovery occurred	• Discovery of spontaneous radioactivity

The third pattern, *momentum serendipity*, is related to the first two patterns. Momentum serendipity results from accidentally observing something because of the right timing. Time and place are oftentimes strongly interrelated. Galileo Galilei's discovery of four moons around Jupiter that were not sought by him emphasizes that timing plays a more important role than place for momentum serendipity. Some phenomena only occur at a certain time that is especially important for astronomic discoveries. Barry Marshall's and Robin Warren's discovery of *Helicobacter pylori*'s (*H. pylori*) meaning for peptic ulcers is another example for this pattern. For a long time, stress and lifestyle were considered the causes of peptic ulcers. Thagard (1998) documents that attempts to cultivate *H. pylori* repeatedly failed at first and that it was accidentally discovered that the 48 hours given to allow growth was insufficient. Then, the distraction of a busy schedule and the coincidence of a four-day weekend allowed the bacteria five days to cultivate and showed the solution.

Historical examples show that time and place are not always the essential parameters for serendipitous discoveries. The discovery of vitamin C, of the vulcanization of rubber, or of Viagra took place independent of time as well as place and resulted because the right materials or the right people were (accidentally) combined. Wilhelm Röntgen's discovery of x-rays is an example of the pattern resulting from the right combination of materials, what we call *combinatorial serendipity*. Röntgen experimented with a cathode ray tube that he wrapped with a black cardboard. Surprisingly, some invisible rays coming from the tube were passing through the cardboard and reflected an object on the fluorescent screen that coincidentally laid on a table. As he did not know these rays, Röntgen called them x-rays, standing for "unknown rays". The discovery of the vulcanization of rubber was also made by an accidental combination of materials. Charles Goodyear was looking for a method to enable rubber to withstand the cold. However, he had not planned to heat the rubber compound he was working with when it (accidentally) came into contact with a hot stove. The apparently incorrect connection between the rubber and the heat caused the serendipitous discovery of a suitable method.

The next pattern describes a serendipitous discovery of links and emerging patterns in data sets that are unknown. A common example is the discovery of Viagra. Viagra was originally intended to cure angina pectoris, a common precursor to heart attacks. The inventing company Pfizer tried its product with different participants and could not notice a relaxation of blood vessels; instead, male participants reported an increase in erectile functionality. Such unintended discoveries of side effects are often the result of tracking various data points and information. Such discoveries are mostly typical serendipity innovations that lead to an important impact on levels or fields very far from the expected output or result (far outside the cone of expectations according to Austin, Devin, and Sullivan, 2012).

More historical examples show that serendipitous discoveries do not only result from combining the right materials or analyzing data but that also the combination of different people leads to unexpected insights. *Communal serendipity* covers accidental discoveries made by combining the right people. Although Albert Szent-Györgyi von Nagyrápolt may be less known, he and Joseph L. Svirbely discovered one of the most well-known acids: vitamin C. Szent-Györgi isolated a novel substance from plant and tissue extracts that he planned to name "ignose" meaning "I do not know". For a publication, he was forced to call the novel substance hexuronic acid. He showed his discovery to Joseph Svirbely who had previously worked with Charles King, a vitamin researcher at the University of Pittsburgh. Svirbely and Szent-Györgyi conducted a landmark experiment on guinea pigs and found that the novel substance was the long-sought vitamin C. These examples report that social connections can be a main cause of new perspectives resulting in serendipitous discoveries.

The last pattern, *Aftermath serendipity*, is different from the aforementioned patterns, as a serendipitous discovery occurs after a first discovery. That means the first discovery is a necessary precursor. Henri Becquerel's discovery of spontaneous radioactivity is an example of this pattern. Based on the discovery of Röntgen's x-rays, Becquerel was testing the hypothesis that sunlight could excite uranium to emit x-rays and these x-rays would expose photographic films. However, cloudy days disturbed Becquerel's attempts, and he decided to leave it in a closed drawer. After a few days, Becquerel was surprised to see that the film had been exposed in the drawer and concluded that uranium itself was emitting these rays. As summarized in Table 17.1, the patterns document that serendipity does not only happen because of a "magic moment" or "stroke of genius". A more realistic picture is that serendipity is a process in that the general aspects of surprise, an intellectual leap, a beneficial perception, and prior knowledge coincide with more specific aspects like being at the right place, analyzing data, having the right timing, combing the right materials/persons, or leveraging initial discoveries – or sometimes a little of each.

Boundaries of the concept

The aspects, elements, and examples of serendipitous discoveries illustrate that serendipity is one way of exploring new phenomena. In essence, exploration is the act of generating new outcomes with returns that are uncertain, distant, and often negative (March, 1991). The previous examples reflected the inherent uncertainty in the process as well as in the outcomes of serendipitous discoveries. This uncertainty primarily results from the unintended occurrence of these discoveries. Yet not all exploration activities are unintended. Based on the meaning of intention for the process and the outcome, we differentiate between four types of exploration. The four types of exploration – planning, search, experimentation, and serendipity – are shown in Figure 17.1.

Differences in intended outcomes have generally led to the distinction of *effectual* and *causal* exploration logic. Sarasvathy (2001) describes *causation* processes as taking a particular outcome as given and selecting between certain means to create that outcome. The types *search* and *planning* belong to this broad categorization because in both activities a certain outcome is already intended. *Planning* uses given, well-specified goals, well-understood causes, and past histories to create reasonably reliable predictions about the future that can be explored (Sarasvathy, 2003). This type of exploration is the most rational approach in that all possible outcomes and means are well known, the environment is fully understood, and thus an optimal solution can be derived. The process is largely controlled to ensure the adherence of a desired outcome. Different stages and gates along the process are used for evaluating the progress. Failures can

		Process	
		intended	unintended
Outcome	intended	Planned innovation approach	Search innovation approach
	unintended	Experimental innovation approach	Serendipitous innovation approach

Figure 17.1 Typology of exploration

be directly observed and corrected if the actual situation does not meet the planned situation. Exploration plans are necessary for technically complex, high-investment activities like the ExoMars mission (Baglioni et al., 2006). In contrast, *search* differs from planning in that the outcome is intended, yet the process to reach the outcome is uncertain. *Search* is broadly understood as the explorative activity that aims to locate or discover resources in physical, mental, or information spaces (Fu, Hills, and Todd, 2015). Much research on search has focused on the effects of near and distant searches, that is, whether new solutions can be found in more familiar or unfamiliar, specific or unspecific spaces (e.g. Rosenkopf and Nerkar, 2001; Katila and Ahuja, 2002). In the attempt to locate new solutions, searches do not follow a linear flow, yet are iterative. Each result found helps to update information (Nelson and Winter, 1982) and leads to moves backward to initial information and forward to new information (Gavetti and Levinthal, 2000). This moving is a form of net casting (Maggitti et al., 2013) in that searchers gather information both within and outside the domain of interest. Searchers persist and gain perspective by iteratively zooming in and out on details. Afterwards, they categorize the information and integrate ideas from seemingly different disciplines to arrive at their discovery. The central assumption is that knowledge is asymmetrically distributed and new insights can be gained by approaching the right search areas. Therefore, searching is of tremendous interest for technology sourcing (Rothaermel and Alexandre, 2009), product innovations by understanding customers' needs (Taylor and Greve, 2006), and in science contests (Jeppesen and Lakhani, 2010).

In contrast, *effectuation* processes do not focus on a specific intended outcome in advance (Sarasvathy, 2001). The outcomes are contingent on what characterizes both *experimentation* and *serendipity*. *Serendipity* belongs to the effectuation logic because the outcomes of an accidental discovery depend on the positive or negative interpretation of a collision. It is not only the outcome that is unintended but also the way to its discovery because of serendipity's surprising character. *Experimentation* differs from serendipitous discoveries in that the process of discovering is more intended. In uncertain environments, the consequences of certain actions are not foreseeable. Thus, firms engage in experimentation, in that means of the process are controllably modified and their outcomes are tested (Nicholls-Nixon, Cooper, and Woo, 2000). Based on the tests' outcomes, the process is further modified, alternative means are used, and new tests are conducted. Therefore, experimentation is also called trial-and-error learning or a discovery-driven approach (McGrath, 2010). The goal is not to avoid failures but to learn from intelligent failures (Sitkin, 1992). These intelligent failures provide information and the means for further modifications. Experimentation is subject to uncertainty because if outcomes are deterministic, the experienced outcome provides no new information from which to learn (Wildavsky, 1988). The experimental approach has a long tradition in laboratory settings in that hypotheses are generated, tested, and remodified. Due to the introduction of the lean startup approach (Ries, 2011), the experimental approach has gained increased attention in entrepreneurial venturing. The idea of testing hypotheses is called pivoting and depicts how a prototype is rapidly brought to market and the feedback from the market helps to clarify the outcome. Each exploration approach has its strength for innovation projects and activities. Of course, an experimental approach is inappropriate, if, for example, in innovation projects in the aircraft sector or in the health care industry teams are experimenting with technologies and customers, which can cause catastrophic effects.

Table 17.2 summarizes each type's characteristic elements and shows how serendipity is different from other explorative activities.

Table 17.2 Comparison of exploration approaches

	Planned innovation approach	Search innovation approach	Experimental innovation approach	Serendipitous innovation approach
Outcome	intended	intended	unintended	unintended
Process	intended	unintended	intended	unintended
Process flow	sequential	iterative	pivoting	turnaround, upside-down
Process organization elements	stages and gates	net casting (zoom out), categorizing (zoom in), linking	hypothesis generating, testing	preparedness/pre-knowledge and follow-up knowledge
Underlying logic	sense of control	spot unknown areas	insight-driven	unintentional
Focus	technology-push	unknown spots	experimentation	beneficial accident
Expectancy of results/success definition	make-it or break-it (as expected)	solution is located in searchable, yet unknown areas	learn from failure, prototype, measure, learn, improve	find something totally different
Failure culture	avoid failure	balance own lacks	learn from failure, repeat again	turn potential failure in success
Characteristics of innovation projects	technical-complex, high-investment, high-technology uncertainty; B2B markets, medium and high safety standards, low to high technology readiness, complex supply/value chains	knowledge is asymmetrically distributed, sourcing technologies, experts, creating synergies	high market uncertainty, highly saturated markets, B2C markets, high-technology readiness level, scaling business models, low-risk products and services	multi-application technologies, low to medium technology readiness, scientific-grounded discoveries, multiple functions and meanings

Serendipity research in management literature

Given the central role of uncertainty in today's world and firms' need to innovate, the phenomenon of serendipity has only attracted limited attention in business studies (Cunha, Clegg, and Mendonça, 2010). Firms purposefully try to control the uncertainty with vast investments into powerful statistical tools, automation, and novel technologies to squeeze every last drop of success out of scientific discovery programs (de Rond and Morley, 2010a). In other disciplines like natural science or medicine, serendipity has attracted considerably more interest. Weisenfeld (2009) even argues that serendipity plays such a fundamental role in natural science because these journeys of discovery are paved with many unknown yet accepted parameters. Thus, serendipity is intensively discussed in anthropology (Leakey, 2010), biology (Weiss, 2010; Fowke, 2010), chemistry (Spada and Gottarelli, 2004; García, 2009), physics (Friend, 2010), and astronomy (Fabian, 2010). In cosmology, the accidental discovery of the so-called cosmic microwave background radiation helped to formulate the big bang theory (Singh, 2010). Due to the increasing availability of information, serendipity also starts to play a role in information management (McBirnie, 2008; André, Schraefel, Teevan, and Dumais, 2009; Nutefall and Ryder, 2010).

Brown (2005) shows with the help of a historical analysis of cornflakes, Post-It Notes, and Proctor & Gamble that chance, accidental occurrences, and sheer good fortune loom large in many successful and well-known businesses. In management studies, serendipitous discoveries are discussed in entrepreneurship (Bonney, Clark, Collins, and Fearne, 2007; Dew, 2009), organization studies (Graebner, 2004; Cunha, Clegg, and Mendonça, 2010), marketing (Brown, 2005), strategy (Weisenfeld, 2009), and technology management (Itaya and Niwa, 2013) as well as how they relate to creativity (Kakko and Inkinen, 2009; Austin, Devin, and Sullivan, 2012), leadership (Svensson and Wood, 2005), and daily work routines (Eagle, 2004). In entrepreneurship, Bonney and colleagues (2007) document that many entrepreneurial innovations and a great deal of businesses' success in the early stages of development are serendipitous. By studying Houston's Farm, a producer of high-quality bagged salad, the interviewed entrepreneurs were surprised to find so little use of consumer research and stated too much emphasis was spent on existing consumers and their price attitudes in the beginning. However, the serendipitous moment occurred when noticing that most shoppers have not even thought about trying bagged salad. Thus, the problem was not in the price, but rather in shoppers' awareness of this product. Brown (2005) also criticizes the strong focus on experimentation and customer focus in marketing. Instead, he proposes to start taking serendipity seriously because serendipity may explain what is not yet understood. The study by Vasilchenko and Morrish (2011) also supports the assumption that serendipity plays a vivid role in the beginning of new ventures. They studied the role of entrepreneurial networks in the internationalization of high-technology firms and found that social networks can trigger serendipitous encounters. In particular, entrepreneurs used their social networks consisting of serendipitous contacts that were largely influential for the exploration of internationalization opportunities.

Graebner (2004) has revealed that serendipity plays also a role in firm acquisitions. In firm acquisitions, the acquired managers possess knowledge from the old and the new firm that leads to a serendipitous value for the buyer. Serendipitous value refers to windfalls that were not intended by the buyer prior to the deal. However, her study suggests the emergence of serendipitous value mainly in the first few acquisitions that a buyer conducts than from subsequent deals. She relates this result to openness in early acquisitions. Buyers are likely to fill open positions with acquired managers that help with their candid perspectives to identify and exploit serendipitous value. From the viewpoint of technological innovation, serendipity occurs in the research site of technology companies (Itaya and Niwa, 2013, p. 74). In studying six cases in a Japanese technology company, the moment of serendipity propelled the generation of new ideas. Although the researchers have extensively worked with experimentation, they have been stuck in an impasse. The communication with related researchers helped them to open up their minds and that resulted in the moments of serendipity.

Managing serendipity in innovation processes

Common characteristics across all studies are the unfolding of serendipity foremost in the early phases of a process. Austin and colleagues (2012) offer another perspective on the locus of serendipity and explain that the locus of serendipity must not lie necessarily in the early phases of a process when costs of unproductive accidents can be more easily controlled. Serendipitous moments can also occur in the latter stages of a process when novelty or a breakthrough might be particularly valuable. They argue that the locus of serendipity is not time-bounded, but rather related to two factors: (a) the benefit that might result from creating original outcomes and (b) the cost that might be incurred in creating original outcomes. These factors show

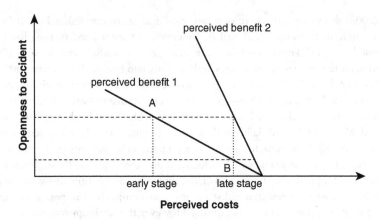

Figure 17.2 Locus of serendipity
Source: (cf. Austin, Devin, and Sullivan, 2012)

that the context for serendipitous discovery is as important as a person's ability to perceive the benefit from accidents (cf. Björneborn, 2017). Austin and colleagues coined these factors *conduciveness to innovation* and *openness to accident*. *Openness to accident* relates to a person's ability to perceive a beneficial nature and to deal with accidents. *Conduciveness to innovation* relates to the context, and in a context where (a) originality was likely to be beneficial and (b) originality was inexpensive to produce, serendipitous outcomes are more likely. Therefore, serendipitous discoveries are likely to happen in earlier stages of a process (see point A in Figure 17.2). However, costs turned out to have a greater influence on openness to accidents. Figure 17.2 displays this relationship and illustrates that the increase in costs leads to a higher decrease in openness to accidents (move from point A to point B). Although costs are higher, serendipitous moments can occur if the perceived benefit significantly exceeds the cost increase. Thus, the perceived benefit of an outcome and the perceived costs of the process determine the locus of serendipity.

This importance of *openness to accident* and *conduciveness to innovation* for enabling serendipitous discoveries was also documented by McBirnie (2008). Although the process cannot be controlled, the conditions and abilities to perceive serendipitous discoveries can be encouraged. An unexpected discovery is only serendipitous if the discovery is perceived as being beneficial. In particular, creating conditions to allow the discovery of unintended yet beneficial accidents lies in the responsibilities of management (McBirnie, 2008). Management can influence the *openness to accident* and *conduciveness to innovation* by various factors lying in the personal as well as social and contextual realm (McCay-Peet and Toms, 2015).

Personal factors

According to Austin and colleagues (2012), the perceived costs and benefits are key for allowing serendipitous discoveries. Thus, a managerial task is to decrease the perceived costs and to increase the perceived benefits. In this regard, expertise, skills, and knowledge are the most important factors. A broad knowledge base is necessary to take other unintended perspectives and make use of them. In the end, knowledge enables essentially the intellectual leap that gives meaning to an observation (Weisenfeld, 2009). Prior knowledge is an essential point that distinguishes serendipity from pure luck (Dew, 2009). This prior knowledge has also helped to build an understanding of the big bang theory:

> However, the serendipitous nature of their discovery was nothing to be ashamed of, because such breakthroughs require not only luck but also considerable experience, knowledge, insight and tenacity.
>
> *(Singh, 2010, p. 71)*

Therefore, a managerial task is to enhance the stock of knowledge by fostering cooperation or offering trainings. At the same time, as the stock of knowledge enables the detection of other values within an outcome, it also can be a hurdle. A fixed concentration on one result based on existing assumptions may lead one to throw away other results. Individuals are exposed to numerous stimuli so that prior knowledge helps to concentrate on the individually perceived, most important stimuli. Thus, the openness to accident also involves a certain mental flexibility and mindfulness (Cunha, Clegg, and Mendonça, 2010). This mindfulness is a personal trait and enables one to assess outcomes from different perspectives. A mind that is also prepared for unexpected results will act emotionally different compared to a mind that expects only one possible outcome. However, mindfulness is also driven from organizational expectations. These expectations create pressure that leads one to favor expected processes and outcomes. A too-rapid convergence prevents the time needed to recognize value in the results of accidents (Austin, Devin, and Sullivan, 2012; Boland, Collopy, Lyytinen, and Yoo, 2008). According to McBirnie (2008), it is important that systems do not filter in too concentrated a fashion because some information may only be appreciated after the discovery has worn off. André and colleagues (2009) suggest alternative presentation formats of search results that permit one to request formerly irrelevant information at later stages. For example, grids instead of rankings enable one to create spatial references between piece of information. These spatial references allow one to store information in reference to each other and creates opportunities for their further processing.

The use of technics is a way to prevent too-rapid convergence and to decrease costs. Costs may be decreased by low-tech methods such as pencil and paper, prototyping with Lego bricks, or using polystyrene. Austin and colleagues (2012) mention that these low-tech methods are more often used because (1) high-tech approaches were more expensive and more difficult to access and (2) (most importantly) low-tech methods seemed to integrate better with expertise and techniques. At the moment, the use of 3D printing is a rather expensive method, yet it enables the rapid creation of prototypes and testing. Software simulation is another method used for testing based on the process of modeling a real phenomenon with a set of mathematical formulas. This allows the user to observe an operation through simulation without actually performing that operation. Simulation software is used widely to design equipment so that the final product will be as close to design specifications as possible without needing expensive process modifications. This digital simulation reduces significantly the costs compared to field tests. With the advancements in machine learning and data analysis, big data analysis is a third technique that is appropriate to detect patterns in information-rich environments. In general, these techniques are used to cope with an overflow of information that significantly decreases costs and increases conduciveness to innovation. Additionally, digital prototypes are easier to test. Therefore, technical solutions are helpful to channel the flow of information and to increase individuals' openness to accidents (André, Schraefel, Teevan, and Dumais, 2009).

Social and contextual factors

Besides the possibilities to further test unexpected outcomes, the culture significantly influences the reaction to serendipitous moments. The culture ought to be receptive to encountering serendipitous discoveries (vgl. Weisenfeld, 2009, p. 140). Therefore, it is essential to create a network that is able to pick up and develop further ideas. Executives must be open to these discoveries, actively consider them as opportunities for innovation, and should provide a framework for action (Cunha, Clegg, and Mendonça, 2010). In other words, they have to provide psychological safety and support for those who want to present their ideas without being dismissed for seemingly inappropriate discoveries. Psychological safety and support ensure a culture of trust, in that it is possible to come up with unusual ideas (Cunha, Clegg, and Mendonça, 2010). Psychological safety suggests neither a careless sense of permissiveness nor an unrelentingly positive affect, but rather a sense of confidence that the team will not embarrass, reject, or punish someone for speaking up (Edmondson, 1999). Personal networks have a similar meaning for identifying different perceptions of an accident that can involve more beneficial perceptions:

> Serendipity travels in good social networks.
> *(Cunha, Clegg, and Mendonça, 2010, p. 324)*

In a social network consisting of interdisciplinary experts, different stocks of knowledge are present. The collation of these stocks of knowledge enables new perspectives to arise. By way of example, André and colleagues (2009) emphasize the coalition of creativity and computer science experts in designing computer systems. In librarianship, Nutefall and Ryder (2010) recommend the collaboration of faculty members and librarians to exchange experiences to improve projects in that serendipity may arise. To explore geographical information, Cartwright (2004) introduced the concept of engineered serendipity to improve cartographic products. In this attempt, designers should collaborate with engineers to increase usability and precision. Also, the direct confrontation and collaboration across industry boundaries provides a fruitful ground to look from different perspectives on insights and potential technologies for cross-industry innovation that might occur by serendipity.

Besides the integration of different backgrounds, the social network's members should meet each other at eye level. If members communicate on the same level, a free flow of information results. This free flow of information may be especially beneficial between persons who have not known each other previously (Cunha, Clegg, and Mendonça, 2010). Therefore, companies should also support informal information and communication channels (cf. Tidd and Bessant, 2013). Graebner (2004) has shown the impact of integrating new persons into a social network and that their perspectives have led to serendipitous values. It is also the case that former contacts may be personally beneficial in later stages. McDonald (2010) revealed that persons who keep in contact with former colleagues had a higher probability of receiving serendipitous job offerings in the future.

Storing and remembering former results is another source of serendipity. This keeps information in mind that can turn out later to be useful in other situations. The participants of Austin and colleagues' study (2012) also attempted to accumulate useful ideas in deliberate disorder. This disorder enabled them to come up with alternative ideas, to look more often into these idea collections, and thus to keep information in mind that could be potentially useful.

Initiatives directed to increase the knowledge base, to create a respectful atmosphere, to enable tests, or to reuse former contacts and results are important levers to react upon unexpected events to increase their perceptions of being beneficial. However, serendipity is – like all other types of exploration – not sustainable in an increasingly complex and competitive environment (Bonney, Clark, Collins, and Fearne, 2007). Serendipity is a valuable extension to other forms of exploration and is one potential source of innovation (cf. Cunha, Clegg, and Mendonça, 2010; Kakko and Inkinen, 2009; McBirnie, 2008; Nutefall and Ryder, 2010). As with all innovation activities, the openminded handling of events is essential. It is important to understand that outcomes can have different benefits depending on the perspective taken. Kakko and Inkinen (2009) propose the serendipity management framework to deal with serendipity in working practice.

This framework is designed to attract curious talent in order to find unexpected, emergent, tacit competence by using facilitation and trust management in very diverse environments. The framework's aim is to reduce the number of inferior unexpected events and to increase the number of valuable unexpected events. To reach valuable benefits from unexpected events, networks could be mixed up and strange connections could be implemented. Fowke (2010) supports this approach based on his own experiences in researching:

> The achievements of my lab were the direct result of my hard working research team, a constantly changing group of bright, dedicated technicians, graduate students, post-doctoral fellows, visiting scientists and collaborators.
> *(Fowke, 2010, p. 443)*

Conclusion

Serendipity complements more well-known types of exploration like searching, experimenting, and planning. Serendipity is neither more nor less important than the other types. Although serendipity is rather neglected as a source for innovation, many well-known and important examples like penicillin, the big bang theory, Coca-Cola, and Vaseline have its origin in serendipitous discoveries. Serendipity is characterized by absent intentions for a specific process or outcome, yet personal as well as social and contextual factors enhance the likelihood of serendipitous discoveries that provide significant competitive advantages. Therefore, managers should consider their visions as a "flexible umbrella" where unexpected events are encouraged and not banned. Serendipity is only possible if people feel safe in their environment and when the conditions allow failures as well as unexpected surprises. In these serendipity-friendly environments, physical and mental spaces are provided to allow different perspectives whenever possible. They also include large stocks of knowledge sources and the active, open collaboration with representatives from other industries or customers to make new discoveries and get inspiration. Scientists, developers, and discoverers can increase their personal openness to accident by the use of cheap prototypes and specifically seeking other work environments, as both solve cognitive fixations. Innovative outcomes result from a variety of sources. Therefore, physical and social conditions need to be prepared to achieve original goals in innovation projects, but at the same time to provide alternative departures for unplanned inventions that arise in the course of the project.

Acknowledgments

We are grateful to Celeste Gianotti for her collaboration in the collection and analysis of relevant literature.

References

André, P., Schraefel, M. C., Teevan, J. and Dumais, S. T. (2009). Discovery is never by chance: designing for unserendipity. *CandC'09, Proceedings of the 7th ACM Conference on Creativity and Cognition*, Berkeley, USA, pp. 305–314.
Austin, J. H. (2003). *Chase, chance, and creativity: the lucky art of novelty.* Cambridge, MA: The MIT Press.
Austin, R. D., Devin, L. and Sullivan, E. E. (2012). Accidental innovation: supporting valuable unpredictability in the creative process. *Organization Science*, 23(5), 1505–1522.
Baglioni, P., Fisackerly, R., Gardini, B., Gianfiglio, G., Pradier, A. L., Santovincenzo, A., Vago, J. L. and Van Winnendael, M. (2006). The Mars exploration plans of ESA. *IEEE Robotics & Automation Magazine*, 13, 83–89.
Barnett, A. H. (2011). Diabetes – science, serendipity and common sense. *Diabetic Medicine*, 28(11), 1289–1299.
Barney, J. (1991). Firm resources and sustained competitive advantage. *Journal of Management*, 17(1), 99–120.
Björneborn, L. (2017). Three key affordances for serendipity: toward a framework connecting environmental and personal factors in serendipitous encounters. *Journal of Documentation*, 73(5), 1053–1081.
Boland, R. J., Collopy, F., Lyytinen, K. J. and Yoo, Y. (2008). Managing as designing: lessons for organization leaders from the design practice of Frank O. Gehry. *Design Issues*, 24(1), 10–25.
Bonney, L., Clark, R., Collins, R. and Fearne, A. (2007). From serendipity to sustainable competitive advantage: insights from Houston's Farm and their journey of co-innovation. *Supply Chain Management: An International Journal*, 12(6), 395–399.
Brown, S. (2005). Science, serendipity and the contemporary marketing condition. *European Journal of Marketing*, 39(11/12), 1229–1234.
Buckner, R. L. (2012). The serendipitous discovery of the brain's default network. *NeuroImage*, 62(2), 1137–1145.
Cartwright, W. (2004). Engineered serendipity: thoughts on the design of conglomerate GIS and geographical new media artifacts. *Transactions in GIS*, 8(1), 1–12.
Copeland, S. (forthcoming). On serendipity in science: discovery at the intersection of chance and wisdom. *Synthese*, 1–22. https://doi.org/10.1007/s11229-017-1544-3.
Cunha, M., Clegg, S. R. and Mendonça, S. (2010). On serendipity and organizing. *European Management Journal*, 28(5), 319–330.
de Rond, M. (2014). The structure of serendipity. *Culture and Organization*, 20(5), 342–358.
de Rond, M. and Morley, I. (2010a). Introduction: fortune and the prepared mind. In de Rond, M. and Morley, I. (Eds.), *Serendipity: fortune and the prepared mind.* Cambridge: Cambridge University Press, pp. 1–9.
de Rond, M. and Morley, I. (Eds.) (2010b). *Serendipity: fortune and the prepared mind.* Cambridge: Cambridge University Press.
Dew, N. (2009). Serendipity in entrepreneurship. *Organization Studies*, 30(7), 735–753.
Drucker, P. F. (1985). *Innovation and entrepreneurship.* New York: Harper & Row.
Eagle, N. (2004). Can serendipity be planned? *MIT Sloan Management Review*, 46(1), 10–14.
Edmondson, A. C. (1999). Psychological safety and learning behavior in work teams. *Administrative Science Quarterly*, 44, 350–383.
Fabian, A. C. (2010). Serendipity in astronomy. In de Rond, M. and Morley, I. (Eds.), *Serendipity: fortune and the prepared mind.* Cambridge: Cambridge University Press, pp. 73–89.
Fine, G. A. and Deegan, J. G. (1996). Three principles of Serendip: insight, chance, and discovery in qualitative research. *Qualitative Studies in Education*, 9(4), 434–447.
Florczak, K. L. (2015). Serendipity. A delightful surprise that requires insight. *Nursing Science Quarterly*, 28(4), 267–271.
Fowke, L. (2010). Creative young minds plus serendipity – a recipe for science. *Botany*, 88(5), 443–451.
Friedel, R. (2001). Serendipity is no accident. *The Kenyon Review*, 23, 36–47.
Friend, R. (2010). Serendipity in physics. In de Rond, M. and Morley, I. (Eds.), *Serendipity: fortune and the prepared mind.* Cambridge: Cambridge University Press, pp. 91–107.
Fu, W. T., Hills, T. and Todd, P. M. (2015). Interfacing mind and environment: the central role of search in cognition. *Topics in Cognitive Science*, 7, 384–390.
Funke, J. (2010). Complex problem solving: a case for complex cognition? *Cognitive Processing*, 11(2), 133–142.

García, P. (2009). Discovery by serendipity: a new context for an old riddle. *Foundations of Chemistry*, 11(1), 33–42.

Gaughan, R. (2011). *Genie aus Versehen: Große Erfindungen und die verblüffenden Geschichten dahinter*. Hamburg: Edel Germany.

Gavetti, G. and Levinthal, D. A. (2000). Looking forward and looking back ward: cognitive and experiential search. *Administrative Science Quarterly*, 45, 113–137.

Gigerenzer, G. and Gaissmaier, W. (2011). Heuristic decision making. *Annual Review of Psychology*, 62, 451–482.

Graebner, M. E. (2004). Momentum and serendipity: how acquired leaders create value in the integration of technology firms. *Strategic Management Journal*, 25(8/9), 751–777.

Hauschildt, J. and Salomo, S. (2011). *Innovationsmanagement* (5th ed.). München: Verlag Franz Vahlen.

Itaya, K. and Niwa, K. (2013). The moment of serendipity in technology companies: study by participant observation. *International Journal of Environment and Sustainable Development*, 12(1), 72–85.

Jeppesen, L. B. and Lakhani, K. R. (2010). Marginality and problem – solving effectiveness in broadcast search. *Organization Science*, 21, 1016–1033.

Kahneman, D. (1973). *Attention and effort*. Englewood Cliffs: Prentice-Hall.

Kahneman, D. and Tversky, A. (1984). Choices, values, and frames. *American Psychologist*, 39(4), 341–350.

Kakko, I. and Inkinen, S. (2009). *Homo creativus*: creativity and serendipity management in third generation science and technology parks. *Science and Public Policy*, 36(7), 537–548.

Katila, R. and Ahuja, G. (2002). Something old, something new: a longitudinal study of search behavior and new product introduction. *Academy of Management Journal*, 45(6), 1183–1194.

Leakey, R. (2010). Understanding humans: serendipity and anthropology. In de Rond, M. and Morley, I. (Eds.), *Serendipity: fortune and the Prepared Mind*. Cambridge: Cambridge University Press, pp. 27–43.

Loosemore, M. (2013). Serendipitous innovation: enablers and barriers in the construction industry. In *Proceedings 29th Annual ARCOM Conference*, September 2–4, 2013, Reading, UK, Association of Researchers in Construction Management, pp. 635–644.

Maggitti, P. G., Smith, K. G. and Katila, R. (2013). The complex search process of invention. *Research Policy*, 42(1), 90–100.

March, J. G. (1991). Exploration and exploitation in organizational learning. *Organization Science*, 2(1), 71–87.

McBirnie, A. (2008). Seeking serendipity: the paradox of control. *Asilib Proceedings: New Information Perspectives*, 60(6), 600–618.

McCay-Peet, L. and Toms, E. G. (2015). Investigating serendipity: how it unfolds and what may influence it. *Journal of the Association for Information Science and Technology*, 66(7), 1463–1476.

McDonald, S. (2010). Right place, right time: serendipity and informal job matching. *Socio-Economic Review*, 8(2), 307–331.

McGrath, R. G. (2010). Business models: a discovery driven approach. *Long Range Planning*, 43(2–3), 247–261.

Merton, R. K. and Barber, E. (2006). *The travels and adventures of serendipity: a study in sociological semantics and the sociology of science* (2nd ed.). Princeton: Princeton University Press.

Mirvahedi, S. and Morrish, S. (2017). The role of serendipity in opportunity exploration. *Journal of Research in Marketing and Entrepreneurship*, 19(2), 182–200.

Nelson, R. R. and Winter, S. G. (1982). *An evolutionary theory of the firm*. Cambridge: Harvard University Press.

Nicholls-Nixon, C. L., Cooper, A. C. and Woo, C. Y. (2000). Strategic experimentation: understanding change and performance in new ventures. *Journal of Business Venturing*, 15(5–6), 493–521.

Nickles, T. (1997). Methods of discovery. *Biology and Philosophy*, 12, 127–140.

Nutefall, J. E. and Ryder, P. M. (2010). The serendipitous research process. *Journal of Academic Librarianship*, 36(3), 228–234.

Pisano, G. P. and Teece, D. J. (2007). How to capture value from innovation: shaping intellectual property and industry architecture. *California Management Review*, 50(1), 278–296.

Ries, E. (2011). *The lean startup: how today's entrepreneurs use continuous innovation to create radically successful businesses*. New York: Crown Publishing Group.

Roberts, R. M. (1989). *Serendipity: accidental discoveries in science* (1st ed.). West Sussex: John Wiley & Sons Ltd.

Rosenkopf, L. and Nerkar, A. (2001). Beyond local search: boundary – spanning, exploration, and impact in the optical disk industry. *Strategic Management Journal*, 22(4), 287–306.

Rothaermel, F. T. and Alexandre, M. T. (2009). Ambidexterity in technology sourcing: the moderating role of absorptive capacity. *Organization Science*, 20, 759–780.

Sarasvathy, S. D. (2001). Causation and effectuation: toward a theoretical shift from economic inevitability to entrepreneurial contingency. *Academy of Management Review*, 26(2), 243–263.

Sarasvathy, S. D. (2003). Entrepreneurship as a science of the artificial. *Journal of Economic Psychology*, 24, 203–220.

Savage, J. L. (1954). *The foundations of statistics*. New York: John Wiley & Sons Ltd.

Singh, S. (2010). Cosmological serendipity. In de Rond, M. and Morley, I. (Eds.), *Serendipity: fortune and the prepared mind*. Cambridge: Cambridge University Press, pp. 65–72.

Sitkin, S. B. (1992). Learning through failure: the strategy of small losses, In Staw, B. M. and Cummings, L. L. (Eds.), *Research in organizational behavior* (14th ed.). Greenwich: JAI Press, pp. 231–266.

Spada, G. P. and Gottarelli, G. (2004). The disclosure of the stepwise supramolecular organization of guanosine derivatives: serendipity or programmed design? *Synlett*, 4, 596–602.

Svensson, G. and Wood, G. (2005). The serendipity of leadership effectiveness in management and business practices. *Management Decision*, 43(7/8), 1001–1009.

Taylor, A. and Greve, H. (2006). Superman or the fantastic four? knowledge combination and experience in innovative teams. *Academy of Management Journal*, 49(4), 723–740.

Tidd, J. and Bessant, J. (2013). *Managing innovation: integrating technological, market and organizational change* (5th ed.). West Sussex: John Wiley & Sons Ltd.

Thagard, P. (1998). Ulcers and bacteria II: instruments, experiments, and social interactions. *Studies in History and Philosophy of Science Part C: Studies in History and Philosophy of Biological and Biomedical Sciences*, 29(2), 317–342.

Van Andel, P. (1994). Anatomy of the unsought finding. Serendipity: origin, history, domains, traditions, appearances, patterns and programmability. *The British Journal for the Philosophy of Science*, 45(2), 631–648.

Vasilchenko, E. and Morrish, S. (2011). The role of entrepreneurial networks in the exploration and exploitation of internationalization opportunities by information and communication technology firms. *Journal of International Marketing*, 19, 88–105.

Weisenfeld, U. (2009). Serendipity as a mechanism of change and its potential for explaining change processes. *Management Revue*, 20(2), 138–148.

Weiss, R. A. (2010). HIV and the naked ape. In de Rond, M. and Morley, I. (Eds.), *Serendipity: fortune and the prepared mind*. Cambridge: Cambridge University Press, pp. 45–64.

Wildavsky, A. (1988). *Searching for safety*. New Brunswick: Transaction Books.

PART III

The organizational perspective of innovation

18
INNOVATION MANAGEMENT WITHIN THE ORGANISATION

Regina Lenart-Gansiniec

Creativity, fuzzy front end, and innovation

In the literature one can see the concept of creativity and innovation being used interchangeably. However, it should be pointed out that these are not identical concepts. The distinction between creativity and innovation is proposed by Amabile et al. (1996): "like other researchers, we define creativity as the production of novel and useful ideas in any domain. We define innovation as the successful implementation of creative ideas within an organization". Innovations include "a process of developing and implementing a new idea" (van de Ven, Angle, and Poole, 1989). The authors believe that "innovation refers to the process of bringing any new problem solving idea into use . . . it is the generation, acceptance, and implementation of new ideas, processes, products, or services". On the other hand, creativity is perceived as the cause of action and creation, as well as the process of communication between innovation and the environment. It is connected with stimulating new thoughts, reformulating the existing knowledge, and analysing assumptions in order to formulate new ideas. It can therefore be concluded that creativity stimulates creating innovations.

Creativity is defined in the literature in different ways. Considering psychology, it should be emphasised that creativity can be understood as a psychological process, part of human intelligence and cognitive ability. In this conceptualisation, the basis of creativity is the emotions, the joy of creating something new, and tolerating ambiguous answers and solutions that translate into readiness and the ability to formulate new problems, communicate, and apply knowledge in different contexts. Thus, creativity in psychological terms is a certain attitude and the result of skills, expert knowledge, intelligence, talent, cognitive and personality processes, cognitive style, internal motivation to undertake tasks, interests, pleasures, a sense of challenge, passion, and external motivators.

In the context of management, creativity is a process that creates or brings to life something new, useful, and generally acceptable. Creativity is a process of developing novel and useful ideas, whether an incremental improvement or a world-changing breakthrough. King and Anderson (1995) consider creativity to be as necessary a characteristic as novelty, that is, the conception must differ significantly from what has gone before. It should also be appropriate to the situation it was created to address, be public in its effect, and deliver a perceived benefit. Creativity is also associated with the domain of exceptional personal influence (Sawyer, 1998), social processes of creating reputation and production, adoption, implementation, diffusion, and commercialisation of innovations (Rogers, 1983; Spence, 1994). For instance, Sternberg and Lobar (1999) define creativity as "the ability to produce work that is both novel (i.e., original, unexpected) and appropriate (i.e., useful, adaptive concerning task constraints)".

The relationship between creativity and innovation seems undisputed. Creativity is a necessary precondition for successful innovation. It is pointed out in the literature that creativity and innovation can be considered determinants of the organisation's performance, its success, and its survival. However, the relationships between creativity and innovation are complex and multi-dimensional, and the benefits gained from this relationship require specific skills. Only then will they allow one to maximise benefits and improve ways of working in the organisation.

Creativity, as the most important feature of human capital, affects the implementation of innovation and is the basis of the innovation process. It is an important feature of all aspects of decision-making in business. It is a phenomenon of stimulating new thoughts, reformulating existing knowledge and analysing assumptions in order to formulate new theories and paradigms or create consciousness. It is a process that involves revealing, selecting, exchanging, and combining facts, ideas, and skills. In practice, this boils down to the fact that organisations are able to use the ideas and suggestions of their employees, which contribute to the generation of new ideas constitute a source of competitive advantage (Anderson, de Drue, and Nijstad, 2004; West, 2002a; Zhou and Shelley, 2003).

It should also be emphasised that it is difficult to indicate at what stage of innovation creativity is important – this is due to the ambiguity and multiplicity of approaches. On the one hand, it is pointed out that creativity is necessary only in the early stages of innovative processes (Oldham and Cummings, 1996; Rank, Pace, and Frese, 2004). It is also debatable that creativity contributes to novelty, while innovations also include the adoption or modification of ideas from other organisations (Anderson, de Drue, and Nijstad, 2004). In addition, creativity has been argued to involve primarily intra-individual cognitive processes, whereas innovation mainly represents interindividual social processes in the workplace (Rank, Pace, and Frees, 2004). However, other authors believe that creativity is necessary during the entire period (Paulus, 2002). They point out that creativity is often seen as the first step of innovation (Mumford and Gustafson, 1988; West, 2002a, 2002b). This is supported by the fact that the innovation process as it unfolds over time is messy, reiterative, and often involves two steps forwards for one step backwards plus several side steps (van de Ven, Angle, and Poole, 1989).

"Fuzzy front-end" (Zhang and Doll, 2001) is another link that can contribute to the success of the entire innovation management process. This term was popularised by Smith and Reinertsen (1991). It denotes all time and activity spent on an idea prior to the first official group meeting to discuss it, or what they call "the start date of team alignment". Another way of thinking about this concept is to highlight the fuzzy front end as that territory leading up to organisational-level absorption of the innovation process (Cohen and Levinthal, 1990). In general, the front end ranges from the generation of an idea to either its approval for development or its termination (Murphy and Kumar, 1997). This is a kind of starting point in which the possibilities of creating innovations are identified.

The "fuzzy front end" of innovation projects includes fostering issues and ideas before the start of the formal project development phase (Koen et al., 2001). It also includes both generating ideas and approving the development or its end (Murphy and Kumar, 1997). In short, "fuzzy front-end" can be defined as a clearly early phase of innovation. This stage precedes the formal process of product development and allows for the acquisition of a multitude of ideas, validation of opportunities, creativity, and making decisions about the resources possessed, as well as seeking and creating value. It includes both generating ideas and approving or ending development

(Murphy and Kumar, 1997). It is not without significance to propose a problem and recognise the possibilities of solving it (Leifer, O'Connor, and Rice, 2001; Urban and Hauser, 1993), gathering information, and exploring it.

In this section, the importance of creativity and "fuzzy front-end" for innovations has been discussed. It also indicates where to start the creativity found in the organisation. In the following sections, the issues of interface management of innovation will be discussed. Interface enhancement tools will be presented, and concurrent engineering and the R&D marketing interface will be discussed.

Interface management of innovation

A review of the literature shows that the process of creating knowledge and innovation resources depends on the cooperation and interaction of many entities. It is also a derivative of the interaction resulting from the cooperation of many departments in the organisation. The marketing, R&D, production, financial, and human resources departments are of great importance here. Their cooperation facilitates interaction – to provide the quality operations of the organisation and the decision-making process with it. Only few authors recognise that to meet the interface requirements, teamwork organisation (Clark and Wheelwright, 1992) and systemic operation are important.

Research into the systemic features of innovation is rooted in two main theoretical currents. One of them focuses on the evolutionary theories of economic and technological changes. According to this conceptualisation, innovation is a derivative of the evolution of various institutions and changes, and it is a process that has its historically conditioned path of development. The second approach draws attention to the role of knowledge and interactive learning in the system. Innovations are considered here as a social process, created by many individuals as well as external and internal factors. Innovation is created by systems of interdependent departments of the organisation that create dependency networks. In particular, the second concept requires proper management.

In essence, the interface management comes down to planning, coordinating, and controlling innovations in cooperation with various units of the organisation. This is particularly important in technological and product-related innovations that require a multifunctional interface. The main goal of interface management is to improve the innovative potential of the organisation and thus facilitate the achievement of success and the implementation of tasks or projects. It is recognised that controlling dynamic interfaces is necessary to achieve goals, schedule, and scope. Moreover, static interfaces should be clearly defined throughout the duration of innovation creation. It also facilitates coordination of work, communication between particular departments, and identification and minimisation of possible problems or threats.

Concurrent engineering and the R&D marketing interface may help in improving interface management. Concurrent engineering comes down to a systematic approach to an integrated, concurrent development of products and accompanying processes, including the production and support system.

It is a method of designing and developing innovations in which individual stages are carried out simultaneously; thus, this requires synchronisation, coordination, quality control, and monitoring. The main task of concurrent engineering is to accelerate and increase the efficiency and quality of product development. Technological and IT solutions that help manage the product's life cycle (idea, design, creation, quality/cost control, use, and reprocessing), shorten the time to create innovations (it reduces the product development time by 30 to 70 percent), and introduce them to the market (time to market 20 to 90 percent.) are helpful here. They also improve the efficiency of the entire innovation creation process (administrative productivity by 20 to 110 percent), contribute to the improvement of the quality of innovations (their application increases the product quality by 200 to 600 percent), reduce the number of necessary changes (number of engineering changes 65 to 90 percent), reduce costs, and match the requirements of construction and technology of innovation in terms of costs, quality, and logistics. They eliminate the need to redesign the project several times, creating a friendly environment for designing products.

A characteristic feature of concurrent engineering is its interdisciplinarity, and its principal task is to collect information necessary to carry out the tasks included in the various phases of innovation creation so that the new product development project can be freely implemented between individual moments of making key decisions for a given project.

Among the IT solutions that make up concurrent engineering, the following are mentioned in the literature:

- Document management systems – they enable collection and classification of documents and facilitate their search and access to them, as well as record the work performed on these documents (e.g. controlling their version, tracking the changes introduced, etc.).
- Workflow systems – they support the implementation of procedures for handling documents; knowledge bases and information extraction mechanisms are included in these systems help to collect materials necessary to create content (e.g. pointing to relevant legal provisions or similar records in previously prepared documents).
- Groupware – facilitates communication between teams and between individuals.
- Intranet – an internal network connecting, for example, computers in one company and its branches, enabling the flow of information within the organisation.
- Corporate portals – allow for combining information from practically all data sources in the organisation (e.g. in the form of e-mails or video recording) in one place. Access to information takes place via a web browser.
- Decision support systems and expert systems – interactive computer systems used in performing planning and decision-making functions. They enable managers to obtain selected, condensed, and already analysed information and facilitate decision-making.

It should be emphasised that the use of IT tools shortens the work cycle of innovations, reduces the number of employees participating in their creation, increases work efficiency, and contributes to creating innovations that are more adapted to the needs of the market. They also allow for effective use and optimal allocation of engineering and production resources; synchronous work and partial overlap of construction, technological, and planning works; team implementation of project work; electronic form of communication between team members; flattening of organisational structures; and high transparency of organisational connections.

Despite its many benefits, the IT tool is recognised as complementary in the literature – it only contributes indirectly to the efficient management of innovations. According to the report of Deloitte (Hagel, Brown, Samoylova, and Lui, 2013), the IT system is not seen as a centre of innovation. They are also not the catalysts of differentiation and competitive advantage. Nevertheless, IT systems are supporting factors because they increase the efficiency of teams working on creating innovations.

The R&D marketing interface constitutes a combination and cooperation of the R&D department with the marketing department. It is defined as an information processing subsystem of the organisation designed to reduce customer, market, and technology uncertainty in the innovation process (Moenaert and Souder, 1990). It should be emphasised that the aim of R&D and marketing is to influence the strategic development of the whole innovation creation process. Cooperation between these departments increases the volume of communication, increases the reliability of the obtained information, and allows for identifying and diagnosing the usefulness of innovations and the fulfilment of market requirements by them. The R&D department should inform the marketing department about new technologies – the purpose of this is to gain knowledge whether their proposals will be accepted by customers. In addition, the marketing department should inform the R&D department about any reservations and expectations of customers regarding new products. Moreover, each of these departments should cooperate with the production department so that the new products are adapted to the company's production capacity and do not generate additional costs. Therefore, individual areas are permeating and numerous feedbacks between them can be observed.

In this section, the importance of concurrent engineering and R&D marketing interface for innovations was discussed. It was explained why cooperation between each department in the organisation is important in the case of creating innovations. In the following section, the problematic aspects of managing new product development processes will be discussed. The term new product development (NPD) will be defined and its course will be discussed.

Management of new product development processes

In 1998 Schilling and Hill stated that "between 33 percent and 60 percent of all new products that reach the market place fail to generate an economic return". Fifteen years later, a similar report is presented by the Nielsen agency in which it was said that more than half of the new products implemented in the world are not able to survive in the market within one year of the introduction date, and out of 100 new products entering the market only 5 will be able to survive. This is also confirmed by the finding of the Product Development Management Association Foundation: new product sales fell from 32 percent of total company sales in 1990 to 28 percent in 2004. This means that the biggest challenge for the organisation is collecting information.

Despite these data, it is emphasised in the literature that new products ensure sales growth, profit, and competitive advantage (Sivadas and Dwyer, 2000). Indeed, they are the key to competitiveness and the driving force of the organisation (Song and Parry, 1997). It is perceived as a strategic priority (Nijssen, Biemans, and de Kort, 2002; Ozer, 2004) and a critical activity. Introducing a new product to the market is a complex and difficult process. It is difficult because at each stage there may be a risk of failure and a threat of the appearance of competitors. Organisations should therefore focus on reducing the number of new product or service failures and shorten the time to introduce new products to the market.

And so the term "new product development" is not only connected with new product development. It also includes developing the concept of new products, as well as using appropriate strategies. This leads to an evaluation of the justification for spending money on new product development (Pisano, 2015). The U.S.-based Product Development and Management Association defines new product development as "a disciplined and defined set of tasks and steps that describe the normal means by which a company repetitively converts embryonic ideas into saleable products or services" (Belliveau, Griffin, and Somermeyer, 2002).

The literature indicates that new product development must be well planned, must be implemented, and should receive support. Moorman and Miner (1998) point out that new product development management should be flexible enough to enable the implementation of any possible necessary changes and adaptation to the changing conditions and new information. It is pointed out in the literature that new product development boils down to ten steps.

First ideas are searched for and generated (Stage 1). It seems that the most important stage is connected with collecting information. Subsequently, these ideas are evaluated in terms of feasibility and efficiency (Stage 2). Testing at the stage of ideas, adaptation to the needs and expectations of customers takes place as part of the next stage (Stage 3). Next, defining the concept of the product, its specification, and testing the concept with the target group (Stage 4). Not without significance is product pricing, cost, and price estimation (Stage 5); the method of implementing the new product and identifying the necessary resources and time to reach this point (Step 6); creation of a project team (Stage 7); and designing the early prototype, its testing, improvement, and modification according to the needs of the users (Stage 8). Next, there is an assessment of the legal regulations and their impact on the new product or service, as well as developing mechanisms for intellectual property protection (Stage 9). The final stage is the development of a marketing strategy oriented on maximising revenues and commercialisation of the new product (Stage 10).

As mentioned, new product development that is efficient and leads to success, as well as reducing production costs, shortening the product implementation cycle, and increasing quality, depends on the adoption of an appropriate strategy for introducing the product to the market. Regardless of the adopted strategy, new product development assumes, among other things, defining an internal process of work on the development of a new product, including developing the concept, design, and prototype of the new product. It is also important to maximise the matching to the needs of customers, which translates into the need to respond to the behaviours of competitors and thus the product's fit, its quality, and accessibility to the requirements and needs of the customers. In addition, it is important to estimate the size of the market, position the product, introduce it into the market at the right time, calculate the price, and determine the methods to promote and advertise the new product.

For the success of the new product development process, various factors that drive the success or failure of the organisation and allow it to achieve the determined effect of implementation and thus affect efficient management are of great importance. Usually, they boil down to four basic factor groups: (1) product strategy and planning; (2) internal knowledge, sharing, and communication; (3) external relationships and cooperation; and (4) use of marketing activities.

Product strategy and planning are the milestones of the new product development (Brown and Eisenhardt, 1995). In particular, it is important to involve the employees in R&D resources and have a flexible and planned strategy, as well as support of the officers enabling its implementation. Cooper and Kleinschmidt (2007) also point to the need for strategic thinking about the new product and its positioning. Ilori, Oke, and Sanni (2000) emphasise the need to allocate resources for R&D and synergy between the product and key competences. Market orientation and technology orientation are also important (Jeong, Pae, and Zhou, 2006).

The second group of factors includes internal knowledge, sharing, and communication. Madhavan and Grover (1998) emphasise the importance of information and knowledge for new product development. In particular, the flow of knowledge in project and innovation teams is important (Moenaert, Caledries, Lievens, and Wauters, 2000); this especially concerns R&D and marketing employees (Gresham, Hafer, and Markowski, 2006). It is because this may increase the involvement of these teams' members (Fredericks, 2005). The knowledge flow and the organisation's relationships with its surroundings are also important (Moenaert, Caledries, Lievens, and Wauters, 2000). For example, the experience of suppliers may contribute to improving the implementation of a specific technology.

The third group of factors is the external connections and cooperation. As was already mentioned, the implementation of a new product must be preceded by collecting information about the needs, expectations, and customer preferences. This information, as well as the customer's involvement, can contribute to improving the success indicators of new product development (Stewart and Martinez, 2002).

And finally the fourth group of factors is the use of marketing activities. Some believe that they are important, whereas others think they are only marginal and rather less important (Rochford and Rudelius, 1997). Certainly, marketing plays a leading role in managing customer relations (Leigh and Marshall, 2001) because it allows for adjusting the product to the customer's needs.

These findings are confirmed by March-Chordà, Gunasekaran, and Lloria-Aramburo (2002). In their opinion, the following are important: market analysis (identification of market trends and requirements and expectations of the customers), planning a new product (creating orders and other formal product development plans, quality management), and the support of top management (setting the strategy direction and working out a systemic approach within its framework, developing a vision of a new product development–oriented organisation, enabling the creation of interdisciplinary project teams and supporting them). In another approach, Brown and Eisenhardt (1995) indicated, in addition to rational planning, additional communication networks and disciplined problem solving. On the other hand, Harmancioglu, Finney, and Joseph (2009) emphasise the importance of a high degree of implementation of project assumptions for a new product, the advantages of the product itself, speed in development and commercialisation, and taking into account the needs and expectations of customers. Marketing activities, appropriate and well-thought-out distribution channels, and financial means necessary to initiate sales as well as R&D are not without significance. In addition, Henard and Szymanski (2001) noticed that environmental factors play an important role.

In this section, NPD for innovation was discussed. It explains how to manage it and the factors that are important for NPD. In the following section, innovation acceleration will be discussed. The differences between acceleration and incubation will be indicated. The notion of an accelerator will be defined. Also, examples of innovation acceleration will be given.

How to accelerate innovation

Acceleration means accelerating the stage related to development and maturation. In this approach, it complements the organisation's innovation strategies, which expect quick results in a short time. It usually includes activities in the areas of market entry, customer relations, promotion and marketing, collaboration with R&D institutions, technology transfer and commercialisation, and networking and building company credibility, as well as raising capital for development. These activities are usually carried out in incubators and technology parks. This includes an attempt to verify the market and support the entrepreneur's business and technological competencies. Acceleration often concerns small and medium-sized companies that introduce new products and develop technological competences. Acceleration of innovative activity complements the innovation strategy or, for entities that expect quick results in a short time, is a kind of "quick path".

There are discussions in the literature about the convergence of the terms acceleration and incubation. This is important because the difference between them is quite open-ended and these terms are often used interchangeably (von Zedtwitz, 2003; Carayannis and von Zedtwitz, 2005; Grimaldi and Grandi, 2001; Pauwels, Clarysse, Wright, and Van Hove, 2015). This linkage is largely because "there is little formal academic literature on the subject and no universally accepted definition of what an accelerator is" (Barrehag et al., 2012). As a result, some researchers seem to even use the accelerator label while actually describing incubators (e.g. Malek, Maine, and McCarthy, 2014). While accelerators have some elements that might resemble incubators, they also have defining characteristics that differentiate them from incubators:

(1) Time horizon: For incubation, it is around three years and for the accelerator it is approximately three months.
(2) Space: Incubators are oriented on diagnosing local potential, while the accelerator only needs an appropriate environment, access to an investor network, and possible partners. However, it is unrelated to a given place.
(3) Required resources: Running an acceleration program requires a team, many years of experience, and networking. However, an incubator needs infrastructure and staff to maintain the tenants at all times.
(4) Work organisation: Incubators operate on a continuous basis, while accelerators are organised periodically, at a specific time and companies are accepted as cohorts.
(5) Forms of support: An incubator offers access to management and other consulting, specialised intellectual property, and networks of experienced entrepreneurs; helps businesses mature to the self-sustaining or high-growth stage; and helps entrepreneurs round out skills and develop a management team and, often, obtain external financing, while the accelerator is a "fast-test" validation of ideas and opportunities to create a functioning beta product and find initial customers, links entrepreneurs to business consulting and experienced entrepreneurs in the Web or mobile app space, and provides assistance in preparing pitches to try to obtain follow-up investment.
(6) Customers: For an incubator, there are all kinds, including science-based businesses (biotech, medical devices, nanotechnology, clean energy, etc.) and nontechnology, all ages and genders; this includes those with previous experience in an industry or sector. For an accelerator, there are web-based mobile apps, social networking, gaming, cloud-based, software, etc.; firms that do not require significant immediate investment or proof of concept; primarily youthful, often male technology enthusiasts, gamers, and hackers.

Accelerators are programs that help entrepreneurs bring their products into the marketplace. They typically operate by inviting a cohort of start-up companies to work intensively on their technologies for a time. Accelerators are organisations offering a suite of professional services, mentoring, and office space in a competitive program format (Fishback et al., 2007). This means that the accelerators:

- are for-profit organisations that receive equity in exchange for the provision of funding to the start-ups.
- do not necessarily provide office space for the start-ups they support, but typically provide meeting space.
- target regional, national, or even global start-ups.

In this section, the problematic aspects of innovation acceleration were discussed. Examples of innovation acceleration were provided. In the following section, the problematic aspects of the chief innovation officer and innovation will be discussed. The skills and competences that should distinguish a chief innovation officer will be provided. Attention will also be focused on proactive leadership.

Chief innovation officer and innovation

A chief innovation officer (CIO) is a person in a company who is primarily responsible for managing the process of innovation and change management in an organisation as well as being in some cases the person who originates new ideas but also recognises innovative ideas generated by other people.

In practice, a CIO's tasks include primarily designing innovation concepts in accordance with the organisation's strategy and the needs of customers. The CIO also monitors the course of innovation, maximises the organisation's potential benefits from innovations and re-education costs, and provides the necessary resources. In addition, he or she is responsible for detecting errors while working on innovations. Moreover, the CIO responsibilities and tasks include supporting best practices, developing the skills of the team working on innovations, motivating the team to generate ideas, supporting business units cooperating in the creation of innovations, identifying new space for creating and implementing innovations, and managing budgets. Due to the wide range of duties, the CIO should have specific skills and competences.

First of all, team management is an important skill. Due to the fact that the CIO is required to support employees and strive for their development, he or she should be able to identify new ideas and insights, encourage and motivate employees, and propose their own ideas and creative thinking. He or she should also create group work opportunities and create open innovations (e.g. by initiating the launch of platforms for generating ideas, organising a hackathon, or using crowdsourcing).

Second, the CIO should update and follow the latest trends and requirements, constantly improve his or her competences and skills, and look for solutions that will contribute to the search for improvements.

Third, the CIO should be an expert in initiating and supporting innovations but also seeking inspiration to create them. He or she should also focus on training managers from other business units in order to educate them about the need to support innovations created by the organisation.

Fourth, the CIO should always look for new opportunities. This includes analysing market trends and seeking opportunities to enter new markets. It is also tracking and analysing the opportunities and threats associated with creating innovation.

The fifth skill is budget management. The CIO has at his or her disposal and manages funds allocated for the creation and implementation of innovations. In addition, he or she is involved in acquiring additional sources of financing, including the inclusion of sponsors.

Analysing the individual requirements and scope of duties of the CIO, it can be considered that he or she should be the so-called "proactive leader". Proactive leadership means behaviour and an attitude in which the officers take the initiative, start some action, initiate, can find the best solution (Seibert, Kraimer, and Crant, 2001), and actively and constantly seek information to increase knowledge resources (Crant, 2000).

A proactive leader focuses also on introducing changes in the organisation as well as his or her behaviour (Parker, Williams, and Turner, 2006). This is connected with identifying the possibilities and willingness to implement these changes (Crant, 1995), effective leadership (Crant and Bateman, 2000), or entrepreneurship (Becherer and Maurer, 1999).

Proactive people have the ability to scan the environment in search of opportunities for change (Bateman and Crant, 1993), to determine effective ways to achieve goals, to anticipate and prevent problems, and to perform tasks in a more effective way. They are also characterised by perseverance, a results orientation, and a vision for the future (Frese and Fay, 2001). Proactive leadership is necessary to create innovative teams, because it focuses on overcoming the old principles of thinking and creating new ones.

In this section, the problematic aspects of the chief innovation officer and innovation were discussed. Examples of skills and competences that a CIO should possess were identified. Moreover, the issue of proactive leadership was discussed. In the following section, focus will be on how to build a high-performance innovation team. Attention will be drawn to the importance of team learning, innovation culture and climate, and trust towards building innovative teams.

How to build a high-performance innovation team

It is pointed out in the literature that most innovations are created through networks – groups of people working in concert. In practice, it comes down to the fact that innovations are born everywhere, in all departments and at all levels of responsibility. Employees constantly share ideas, invent, propose, evaluate, and constantly seek things that can be improved. Innovative teams play an important role. A team in colloquial language means two or more people who interact, but additionally they influence each other in the pursuit of a common goal. It is also referred to as a system that operates through the integration of individuals and work instruments and joint involvement of all members in a matter and acceptance of the resulting obligations. What is important in the team is the discussion, joint determining both individual and group goals, approach to work, and a collective sense of responsibility for the task.

Research suggests that many components contribute to building innovation teams, including team learning, an innovative culture and climate, and trust.

The research has proven the relationships between team learning and building innovative teams. Teamwork fosters innovation, especially at the creating stage, when ideas come to life and initiatives are taken. The team's norms play an important role. They show what is important, what to strive for, and what to avoid. The team's norms are vision, participation, task orientation, risk taking, error tolerance, and speed in action (Anderson and West, 1998). In addition, diversity contributes to the synergy effect. The size of the team is also significant. Teams with not too many members have a mobilising effect on individual participants and ensure efficiency. This leads to the creation of new and unique solutions. In addition, it improves team learning. Team learning is the process of targeting the team and developing its ability to achieve the results that its members desire. It is also joint problem solving that develops the ability of individual groups to take a holistic look that goes beyond individual perception.

This means recognising the team as a carrier of intellectual potential greater than the combined potential of its individual members. The idea of team learning comes from the exercise of dialogue, team members' learning, rejection of predetermined assumptions, and authentic team thinking. Team learning occurs when individuals begin to share information and views in order to obtain or improve the group's efficiency and achieve the set goals. Team members are open to other people's opinions; they accept them or try to understand them, which allows for possible negotiation in matters of interpersonal differences and conflicts – in the case of differences, discrepancies are integrated and patterns of common meaning and agreement are worked out. The most important thing is to achieve the team's goals, which enables synergic learning, and in particular creating knowledge with the possibility of expressing their opinions freely and openly, even if they are different from other team members. Team members in this case are willing to change their views based on internal and external perceptions. The basis is interpersonal relationships, mutual development, good communication, experimentation, expressing "uncomfortable" or ambitious views, and learning. Importantly, team learning takes place on the basis of real work processes, which allows learning new things, but also to observe and experience real work processes. In this approach, team learning, through the synergy effect, enhances the use of the team's potential, its creativity, creative abilities, innovation creation, flow of information and ideas – and by the same token innovation.

Most researchers emphasise the importance of the organisational culture and climate for creating innovations. Stimulating innovative activity requires a specific organisational culture. The climate and innovative culture determine the creative possibilities of the organisation, because from them flows the inclination of employees to take innovative endeavours. Organisational culture is defined as a set of created norms developed on the basis of the assumptions, values, and norms of the models of operation, showing employees how to achieve the company's goals. The basic cultural patterns conducive to innovation are openness to risk, change; willingness to experiment; tolerance of uncertainty; and the use of opportunities, creativity, trust, cooperation, mutual support and error tolerance. What is also important is the autonomy in action, validation, freedom to submit ideas, supporting new ideas, and tolerating discussions on the submitted ideas (Brilman, 2002, p. 172).

Thus, in enterprises with an innovation culture, employees deal with uncertainty themselves, based on their own knowledge, skills, and experiences, and dynamic networks of cooperative ties are created.

The innovative climate is focused on the development of employees, including the assessment of their qualifications, skills, and potential. An organisation with such a climate has a flexible organisational structure, where formalism and strict subjection to regulations and organisational procedures are reduced to a minimum. There is a cult of professionalism, risk tolerance, freedom in action, individualism, and permission to take risks and be innovative. Moreover, there is a large tolerance for errors, because it is thanks to them that the organisation can access new solutions. The goals of the organisation are treated by the employees as challenges (Ekvall and Ryhammar, 1999). The role of the management staff is to encourage and stimulate the employees to submit their own ideas for improving the work or products or services offered by the organisation. Non-formal channels of communication and free flow of information between employees and their superiors are also promoted. This is to enable employees to disclose and exploit their creative potential.

Another factor that may increase the chances of building an efficient innovation team is trust. Trust is defined and interpreted in various ways in the literature. According to a psychological approach, it is a kind of mental state that is related to the willingness to take risks and accepting them. It can also mean being ready to be sensitive to the actions of the other party based on the belief that the other party has done specific actions important to the trusting party, which are independent of the ability to monitor and control. It is also readiness based on the assessment of the other party's credibility in a situation of interdependence and risk.

Trust is a resource of social capital, which means that it is embedded in relationships between people (Nahapiet and Ghoshal, 1998; Misztal, 1996). It is therefore generated and used during social interactions. Additionally, trust is recognised in the literature as a key source of social capital, indispensable for creating a friendly work environment in which ideas are freely generated, evaluated, selected, and transformed into new products and services. Trust is therefore a basic requirement of social integration, organisational efficiency, loyalty of employees, and broadly understood management. This is particularly important in conditions of uncertainty and risk, when it is not possible to check and control the other party.

Conclusion

The chapter focuses on innovation management within the organisation. The meaning of creativity and "fuzzy front end" for innovation were discussed. Then attention was paid to the interface management of innovation. Management of the new product development process was discussed. The answer to the question of how to accelerate innovation was searched for. The role and importance of the chief innovation officer for the innovation process were defined. And finally, the factors or mechanisms that enable building a high-performance innovation team were provided.

Innovation should be treated as a process that should be properly managed. Innovation management is a broad spectrum of activities that focus on motivating employees and inspiring them to think creatively. Systems supporting the processes of creating, collecting, and identifying knowledge are not without significance.

Bibliography

Amabile, T. M., Conti, R., Coon, H., Lazenby, J. and Herron, M. (1996). Assessing the work environment for creativity. *Academy of Management Journal*, 39(5), 1154–1185.

Anderson, N., De Dreu, C. K. W. and Nijstad, B. A. (2004). The routinization of innovation research: a constructively critical review of the state-of-the-science. *Journal of Organizational Behavior*, 25(2), 147–173.

Anderson, N., Potonik, K. and Zhou, J. (2014). Innovation and creativity in organizations: a state-of-the-science review and prospective commentary. *Journal of Management*, 40(5), 1297–1333.

Anderson, N. and West, M. A. (1998). Measuring climate for work group innovation: development and validation of the team climate inventory. *Journal of Organizational Behaviour*, 19, 235–258.

Barrehag, L., Fornell, A., Larsson, G., Mårdström, V., Westergård, V. and Wrackefeldt, S. (2012). Accelerating success: a study of seed accelerators and their defining characteristics. Bachelor Thesis TEKX04–12–10 Chalmers University, Sweden.

Bateman, T. S. and Crant, J. M. (1993). The proactive component of organizational behavior. *Journal of Organizational Behavior*, 14, 103–118.

Becherer, R. C. and Maurer, J. G. (1999). The proactive personality disposition and entrepreneurial behaviour among small company presidents. *Journal of Small Business Management*, 37, 28–36.

Belliveau, P., Griffin, A. and Somermeyer, S. (2002). *The PDMA tool book for new product development*. New York: Product Development and Management Association, p. 450.

Brilman, J. (2002). *Nowoczesne koncepcje i metody zarządzania*. Warszawa: Polskie Wydawnictwo Ekonomiczne.

Brown, S. L. and Eisenhardt, K. M. (1995). Product development: past research, present findings, and future directions. *Academy of Management Review*, 20(April), 343–378.

Carayannis, E. G. and von Zedtwitz, M. (2005). Architecting gloCal (global – local), real-virtual incubator networks (G-RVINs) as catalysts and accelerators of entrepreneurship in transitioning and developing economies: lessons learned and best practices from current development and business incubation practices. *Technovation*, 25(2), 95–110.

Clark, K. B. and Wheelwright, S. C. (1992). *Revolutionizing product development*. New York.

Cohen, W. M. and Levinthal, D. A. (1990). Absorptive capacity: a new perspective on learning and innovation. *Administrative Science Quarterly*, 35(1), 128–152.

Cooper, R. G. (1990). Stage-gate systems: a new tool for managing new products. *Business Horizons* (May–June), 44–55.

Cooper, R. G. and Kleinschmidt, E. J. (1986). An investigation into the new product process: steps, deficiencies, and impact. *Journal of Product Innovation Management*, 3(2), 71–85.

Cooper, R. G. and Kleinschmidt, E. J. (2007). Winning business in product development: the critical success factors. *Research & Technology Management*, 50(3), 52–66.

Crant, J. M. (1995). The proactive personality scale and objective job performance among real estate agents. *Journal of Applied Psychology*, 80(4), 532–537.

Crant, J. M. (2000). Proactive behavior in organizations. *Journal of Management*, 26(3), 435–462.

Crant, J. M. and Bateman, T. S. (2000). Charismatic leadership viewed from above: the impact of proactive personality. *Journal of Organizational Behavior*, 21, 63–75.

Crawford, C. M. (1980). Defining the charter for product innovation. *Sloan Management Review*, 21, 3–12.

Crawford, C. M. and Di Benedetto, A. C. (2003). *New products management* (7th ed.). Burr Ridge, IL: Irwin/McGraw-Hill.

Ekvall, G. and Ryhammar, L. (1999). The creative climate: its determinants and effects at a Swedish University. *Creativity Research Journal*, 12(4), 303–310.

Emerson, R. (1962). Power – dependence relations. *American Sociological Review*, 27(2), 31–41.
Fay, D. and Frese, M. (2001). The concept of personal initiative (PI): an overview of validity studies. *Human Performance*, 14, 97–124.
Fishback, B., Gulbranson, C. A., Litan, R. E., Mitchell, L. and Porzig, M. (2007). Finding business idols: a new model to accelerate start-ups. *Ewing Marion Kauffman Foundation*. 2–8.
Fisher, C. and Schutta, J. T. (2003). *Developing new service incorporating the voice of the customer into strategic service development*. Milwaukee, WI: ASQ Quality Press.
Fredericks, E. (2005). Infusing flexibility into business-to-business firms: a contingency theory and resource-based view perspective and practical implications. *Industrial Marketing Management*, 34, 555–565.
Gresham, G., Hafer, J. and Markowski, E. (2006). Inter-functional market orientation between marketing departments and technical departments in the management of the new product development process. *Journal of Behavioral and Applied Management*, 8(1), 53–65.
Grimaldi, R. and Grandi, A. (2001). The contribution of university business incubators to new knowledge-based ventures: some evidence from Italy. *Industry and Higher Education*, 15(4), 239–250.
Hagel, J., Brown, J. S., Samoylova, T. and Lui, M. (2013). From exponential technologies to exponential innovation. May 9, 2018. https://www2.deloitte.com/content/dam/Deloitte/es/Documents/sector-publico/Deloitte_ES_Sector-Publico_From-exponential-technologies-to-exponential-innovation.pdf
Harmancioglu, N., Finney, R. Z. and Joseph, M. (2009). Impulse purchases of new products: an empirical analysis. *Journal of Product and Brand Management*, 18(1), 27–37. http://dx.doi.org/10.1108/10610420910933344.
Henard, D. H. and Szymanski, D. M. (2001). Why some new products are more successful than others. *Journal of Marketing Research*, 38(3), 362–375.
Ilori, M. O., Oke, J. S. and Sanni, S. A. (2000). Management of new product development in selected food companies in Nigeria. *Technovation*, 20(6), 333–342.
Jeong, I., Pae, J. H. and Zhou, D. (2006). Antecedents and consequences of the strategic orientations in new product development: the case of Chinese manufacturers. *Industrial Marketing Management*, 35(3), 348–358.
King, N. and Anderson, N. (1995). *Innovation and change in organizations*. London: Routledge.
Koen, P. A., Ajamian, G., Burkart, R., Clamen, A., Davidson, J., D'Amoe, R., Elkins, C., Herald, K., Incorvia, M., Johnson, A., Karol, R., Seibert, R., Slavejkov, A. and Wagner, K. (2001). New concept development model: providing clarity and a common language to the 'Fuzzy Front End' of innovation. *Research Technology Management*, 44(2), 46–55.
Leifer, R., O'Connor, G. C. and Rice, M. P. (2001). Creating gamechangers in mature firms: the role of radical innovation hubs. *Academy of Management Executive*, August, 102–113.
Leigh, T. W. and Marshall, G. W. (2001). Research priorities in sales strategy and performance. *Journal of Personal Selling & Sales Management*, 21(2), 83–93.
Lucio, M. M. and Stuart, M. (2002). Assessing partnership: the prospects for, and challenges of, modernisation. *Employee Relations*, 24(3), 252–261.
Lynn, G., Morone, J. and Paulson, A. (1996). Marketing and discontinuous innovation: the probe and learn process. *California Management Review*, 38(3). https://ssrn.com/abstract=2151914.
Madhavan, R. and Grover, R. (1998). From embedded knowledge to embodied knowledge: new product development as knowledge management. *Journal of Marketing*, 62(4), 1–12.
Malek, K., Maine, E. and McCarthy, I. (2014). A typology of clean technology commercialization accelerators. *Journal of Engineering and Technology Management*, 32, 26–39.
March-Chordà, I., Gunasekaran, A., Lloria-Aramburo, B. (2002). Product development process in Spanish SMEs: an empirical research. *Technovation*, 22(5), 301–312.
Misztal, B. A. (1996). *Trust in modern societies: the search for the bases of social order*. Cambridge: Polity.
Moenaert, R. K., Caledries, F., Lievens, A. and Wauters, E. (2000). Communication flows in international product innovation teams. *Journal of Product Innovation Management*, 17, 360–377.
Moenaert, R. K. and Souder, W. E. (1990). An information transfer model for integrating marketing and R&D personnel in new product development projects. *Journal of Product Innovation Management*, 7, 91–107.
Moorman, Ch. and Miner, A. S (1998). Organizational improvisation and organizational memory. *Academy of Management Review*, 23(4), 698–723.
Mumford, M. D. and Gustafson, S. B. (1988). Creativity syndrome: integration, application, and innovation. *Psychological Bulletin*, 103, 27–43.
Murphy, S. A. and Kumar, V. (1997). The front end of new product development: a Canadian survey. *R&D Management*, 27(1), 5ff.

Nahapiet, J. and Ghoshal, S. (1998). Social capital, intellectual capital and the organizational advantage. *Management Review*, 23(2), 242–266.

Nijssen, E. J., Biemans, W. G. and de Kort, J. F. (2002). Involving purchasing in new product development. *R&D Management*, 32(4), 281–289.

Oldham, G. R. and Cummings, A. (1996). Employee creativity: personal and contextual factors at work. *Academy of Management Journal*, 39(3), 607–655.

Ozer, M. (2004). The role of internet in new product performance: a conceptual investigation. *Industrial Marketing Management*, 33(5), 355–369.

Parker, S. K., Williams, H. M. and Turner, N. (2006). Modeling the antecedents of proactive behavior at work. *Journal of Applied Psychology*, 91(3), 636–652.

Paulus, P. B. (2002). Different ponds for different fish: a contrasting perspective on teams innovation. *Applied Psychology: An International Review*, 51(3), 394–398.

Pauwels, C., Clarysse, B., Wright, M. and Van Hove, J. (2015). Understanding a new generation incubation model: the accelerator. *Technovation*, 50–51, 13–24.

Pisano, G. P. (2015). You need an innovation strategy. *Harvard Business Review*, 93(6), 44–54.

Rank, J., Pace, V. L. and Frese, M. (2004). Three avenues for future research on creativity, innovation, and initiative. *Applied Psychology: An International Review*, 53(4), 518–528.

Rochford, L. and Rudelius, W. (1997). New product development process stages and successes in the medical products industry. *Industrial Marketing Management*, 26, 67(18).

Rogers, E. M. (1983). *Diffusion of innovations*. New York: Free Press.

Sawyer, R. K. (1998). The interdisciplinary study of creativity in performance. *Creativity Research Journal*, 11, 11–21.

Schilling, M. A. and Hill, C. W. L. (1998). Managing the new product development process: strategic imperatives. *Academy of Management Executive*, 12(3), 67–81.

Seibert, S. E., Kraimer, M. L. and Crant, J. M. (2001). What do proactive people do? a longitudinal model linking proactive personality and career success. *Personnel Psychology*, 54(4), 845–874.

Sivadas, E. and Dwyer, R. F. (2000). An examination of organizational factors influencing new product development in internal and alliance-based processes. *Journal of Marketing*, 64, 31–40.

Smith, P. G. and Reinertsen, D. G. (1991). *Developing products in half the time*. New York: Van Nostrand Reinhold.

Song, X. M. and Parry, M. E. (1997). A cross-national comparative study of new product development processes: Japan and the United States. *Journal of Marketing*, 61(2), 1–18.

Song, X. M. and Montoya-Weiss, M. M. (1998). Critical development activities for really new versus incremental products. *The Journal of Product Innovation Management*, 15(2), 124–135.

Spencer, W. R. (1994). *Innovation: the communication of change in ideas, practices and products*. London: Chapman & Hall.

Sternberg, R. J. and Lubart, T. I. (1999). The concept of creativity: Prospects and Paradigms. In Sternberg, R. J. (Ed.), *Handbook of creativity*. London: Cambridge University Press, pp. 3–16.

Stewart, H. and Martinez, S. (2002). Innovation by food companies key to growth and profitability. *Food Review*, 25(1), 28–32.

Takeuchi, H. and Nonaka, I. (1986). The new product development game. *Harvard Business Review*, 64, 137–146.

Urban, G. L. and Hauser, J. R. (1993). *Design and marketing of new products* (2nd ed.). Englewood Cliffs, NJ: Prentice-Hall.

van de Ven, A. H., Angle, H. L. and Poole, M. S. (Eds.) (1989). *Research on the management of innovation*. Harper & Row: New York, pp. 31–54.

von Zedtwitz, M. (2003). Classification and management of incubators: aligning strategic objectives and competitive scope for new business facilitation. *International Journal of Entrepreneurship and Innovation Management*, 3.

West, M. A. (2002a). Sparkling fountains or stagnant ponds: an integrative model of creativity and innovation-implementation in work groups. *Applied Psychology: An International Review*, 51, 355–387.

West, M. A. (2002b). Ideas are ten a penny: it's team implementation not idea generation that counts. *Applied Psychology: An International Review*, 51, 411–424.

Zhang, Q. and Doll, J. W. (2001). The fuzzy front end and success of new product development: a causal model. *European Journal of Innovation Management*, 4(2), 95–112.

Zhou, J. and Shalley, C. E. (2003). Research on employee creativity: a critical review and directions for future research. In Martocchio, J. (Ed.), *Research in personnel and human resource management*. Oxford: Elsevier, pp. 165–217.

19
INTERORGANIZATIONAL RELATIONS WITHIN INNOVATION SYSTEMS

Terje Grønning and Parisa Afshin

In this chapter we present and discuss selected works that focus in various ways on the management of interorganizational relations within innovation systems. The insight that corporations innovate more often than not in relation to other organizations draws attention to understanding the need for managing the relations between organizations, in addition to understanding factors enabling or hindering innovation at the corporate level. There are various types of such interorganizational relations, and the chapter is structured into five sections where five predominant types are being presented and discussed in sequence. First, we present research that focuses on modularity-based innovation and innovation through various forms of labor division between client and subsidiary organizations or between collaborating peer organizations. Next we turn to the university as an "engine" for innovation in the case of successful relations between industry and academia. Third, we delve into selected works within the field of strategic alliances for innovation. Whereas in the first three sections we have focused on subfields that discuss interorganizational relations as analyzed at the level of the relations as such (modularity, industry-academia, and alliances), the final two sections look at various relations contextualized within larger systems. Thus we review briefly in the fourth and fifth sections some of the works theorizing the importance of multiple relations between organizations in the context of regional innovation ecosystems and some of the works applying the concept of national innovation systems while theorizing the importance of such systems to corporate innovation within such systems. Each of the sections identifies key perspectives within the subfield, as well as works within the subfield that focus on specific aspects relevant to research on the management of interorganizational relations

Modularity innovation and labor division of innovation

Baldwin and Clark (1997) have drawn attention to the central aspect of modularity being "a strategy for organizing complex products and processes efficiently" (Baldwin and Clark, 1997). Modules compose together a *modular* system, where each module can be designed independently at the same time as the system functions as a whole. It may thus be one solution towards solving the classic dilemma of organizations regarding achieving scale and scope objectives simultaneously.

The literature usually treats modular systems as designed, rather than emergent. This means that organizations consciously strive to both conceive of the purpose and workings of the modules and how these modules are integrated. Baldwin and Clark (1997) refer to this process a design: "Designers achieve modularity by partitioning information into *visible design rules* and *hidden design parameters*" (Baldwin and Clark, 1997 their italics). The partitioning must be both precise and unambiguous, as well as complete, since modularity otherwise will turn out to be unbeneficial. The rules are decisions that have consequences also for later design decisions. There are three types of such rules, where the first is called an architecture. An architecture-type rule determines which modules to include in the system and what their roles should be. The second type is referred to as interfaces and concerns how modules are supposed to interact, fit, connect and communicate with each other. Third, the standards-type of rule concerns measuring whether a module conforms to the design rules presented earlier, as well as each module's performance (Baldwin and Clark, 1997).

Some of the literature on modularity is preoccupied with the relationship between innovativeness on the one hand and the possibility that imitation may occur due to modularity on the other hand. Pil and Cohen (2006) are especially interested in "the dilemma firms face regarding modularity" (Pil and Cohen, 2006, p. 996). They define "modular capability" in terms of two elements, where the first concerns the problem-solving processes which are used in order improve the design of a product. The second element is constituted by the performance criteria that result from these processes. With architectures where there are successful interconnected modules, the possibility of imitation arises. Or, as they state: "The links between product design parameters and performance outcomes are more transparent in modular architectures; this facilitates imitation" (Pil and Cohen, 2006, p. 996). They subsequently propose a series of measures in order to counteract the risk of imitation, including paying attention to product heterogeneity, the nature of innovation within the modular design environment, and implementing decisions at the firm level which are augmenting innovation advantages achievable within the modular environment. Thus, "under certain conditions, the innovation advantages of modularity substantially outweigh the imitation impact on sustained performance" (Pil and Cohen, 2006, p. 996). In a similar vein, Ethiraj, Levinthal, and Roy (2008) examine the relationship between imitation and innovation in the context of modularity and identify at least three different "imitation strategies" it may be worthwhile being aware of, where the first is imitation of the module decisions. Then, the second strategy is imitation of linkages, whereas the third is imitation of both the modules themselves as well as of the linkages (Ethiraj, Levinthal, and Roy, 2008, p. 940).

The advance of modularity has been especially associated with the computer industry. Baldwin and Clark (1997) point to numerous examples where there within this industry were constructed complex products or processes with smaller subsystems which were designed on an independent basis at the same time as these subsystems functioned together with other subsystems. They furthermore claim that such a way of organizing modularity has contributed greatly to the rate of innovation within the industry: "Indeed, it is modularity, more than speedy processing and communication or any other technology, that is responsible for the heightened pace of change that managers in the computer industry now face" (Baldwin and Clark, 1997).

The first modular computer is said to have been the IBM System/360 announced in 1964. Until then, each of the models that IBM produced had been unique, with specific software and parts for each model. This incidentally created a disincentive for consumers to switch machines and systems, since all information had to been rewritten. With the new modular approach, different units within IBM as well as collaborating external companies worked independently on modules. This boosted the rate of innovation in a significant way. One prerequisite for being able to organize in such a way was that there were, after all, "design rules" as explained earlier, which everybody adhered to. However, as long as work and development occurred within the framework of such rules, the participating parties could concentrate on and try out a wide series of different options and hence increase the probability of arriving at workable and ingenious solutions. According to Baldwin and Clarke, "this freedom to experiment with product design is what distinguishes modular suppliers from ordinary subcontractors" (Baldwin and Clark, 1997).

Another industry where modularity has become widespread is the automobile industry. Obviously, decentralized production of components for final assembly at one specific location is a procedure that has got a long history within both the automobile industry and other manufacturing industries. Subsequently, this type of organization should not be referred to as modularity as long as this type of organization is based on subcontracted manufacture of predesigned parts and components, with arm's-length relations between client and suppliers. Whenever suppliers are involved in the design process with a certain amount of "freedom" much in the vein of the citation by Baldwin and Clark (1997) earlier, however, we find a case of modularity.

In modern societies the issue of competitiveness and innovativeness of services is very much in vogue. Baldwin and Clark (1997) tend to apply their framework on modularity in a rather general sense and appear to find few obstacles towards modular organization also within services. They do have some caveats, like the fact that services are intangible; however, like in the case of finances they find the principle applicable. Since "the science of finance is sophisticated and highly developed" (Baldwin and Clark, 1997, p. 3), it is relatively easy to modularize by way of defining, analyzing, and splitting apart these services. This notion has, however, been met with critique (Miozzo and Grimshaw, 2005). Miozzo and Grimshaw (2005) acknowledge that modularity has relevance for services; however, they contend that modularity has its limits, especially in the case of knowledge-intensive business services (KIBS). Based on their own research data, they state that the involvement of external KIBS is "not just a simple substitution of internal services but instead a rather more complex process of knowledge transfer that required reciprocal learning and interaction" (Miozzo and Grimshaw, 2005, p. 1434).

In sum, modularity may be one promising approach towards achieving scale and scope in a simultaneous way, but the principle poses a series of challenges to interorganizational relations. In addition to the dilemma of innovation versus imitation mentioned earlier, the close relationships between organizations involved in a modular system place demands on coordination as well as a high level of trust. In addition, the approach may in some cases turn out to be incongruent with aspirations towards achieving "systemic innovation", since "modularity as a means of coordination involves partitioning activities into those that can take place independent of one another, which does not apply to systemic innovation" (Helfat and Campo-Rembado, 2016, p. 253).

The university as an engine for innovation

Universities have always played a central role in society through education and training of skilled labor as well as conducting basic research. Recently, universities have got an increasingly important additional role in contributing towards innovativeness and economic development, as there is shift in their function from only conducting research and educating skilled labor into a more entrepreneurial role – the third mission of the university. Hence, it has been stated that universities can also improve the economic performance of regional or national innovation systems (Barra and Zotti, 2018; Cooke, Gomez Uranga, and Etxebarria, 1997). As an example of how universities contribute to innovation systems, Motohashi (2005) identified with reference to the case of Japan that this new role of universities can reduce the dependence of the country's innovation system on in-house R&D within large enterprises. It has also been identified that based on their academic research universities create a seed bed for new firms through the formation of firms that can be important in the development of innovation systems (Etzkowitz, Webster, Gebhardt, and Terra, 2000).

Subsequently, university and industry collaboration and relations have been emphasized as an important element for innovativeness and growth in today's knowledge-intensive economy, with the main emphasis on the role of universities as a provider of knowledge to firms, which in turn innovate by bringing science to the market (OECD, 2000). The creation of new knowledge-intensive industries such as nanotechnology and biotechnology underline the significance of this relation that can be in different forms such as joint research and R&D, licensing and intellectual property rights (IPR) transactions, financing, student internships or consultancy.

Therefore, a vastly growing number of studies have been dedicated to understanding the ways that firms in specific sectors benefit from such collaboration, as well as how such collaborations can be encouraged (Liew, Shahdan, and Lim, 2012; Powell, 1998). In this regard, universities are identified as crucial for creating and disseminating knowledge, building skilled human capital, increasing firms' sales and as providing other financial benefits such as cost savings and having a reputation-related benefit (Agrawal, 2001). Another stream of research has focused on the other side of this relationship, looking at how such a relationship can affect and benefit universities (Balconi and Laboranti, 2006; Chapple, Lockett, Siegel, and Wright, 2005; Shattock, 2005) This stream has been gaining popularity, as there is a growing need for understanding the pressure on universities through new policies for creating new knowledge and alternative means for funding (Ankrah and Al-Tabbaa, 2015; Geuna and Muscio, 2009).

In investigating the ways to promote such collaborations, many challenges and issues in managing and increasing the effectiveness of such interorganizational collaboration have been identified that vary depending on the type of the relationships and cooperation, types of science, and the type of industry. For instance, Lin (2017) indicated that excessive collaboration with industry can affect the university's academic innovation negatively, and special attention must thus be paid to collaboration breadth and knowledge capacity strategies of the university when deciding the number and types of such collaborations.

In this section, we will reflect on some selected aspects of university–industry collaboration (UIC) these relations. First, we look at the role of the university in promoting innovativeness in UIC, and second we look at the management of UIC.

One important contribution of universities to innovation is through generating new knowledge that is important for firms, especially within the knowledge-intensive sectors. Firms cannot merely rely on internal knowledge for their progress and innovation – they need to acquire outside knowledge, as innovation is an open mechanism with inflows and outflows of knowledge across boundaries (Chesbrough, 2006). The interaction with science gives firms access to the diversified range of knowledge sources that are important for innovativeness (Kaufmann and Tödtling, 2001). In this regard, it is important to note that the role of the university as a creator and transfer agent of knowledge and technology to the industry is not a new one; nevertheless, the ways that it has been achieved and the institutionalizations collaboration linkages are quite new (Geuna and Muscio, 2009). This new role is fulfilled through various formal and informal models such as research collaborations, recruitment of educated personnel, IPR, spin-offs, licensing and informal or formal networks. Channels for transferring the knowledge can vary depending on the types and stages of the inventions. For instance, early-stage inventions' knowledge transfer can be through scientist and firm interaction, while other transfers will be through patent licensing (Agrawal, 2001).

One of the means of transferring knowledge is through the impact that universities may have on the industry R&D. The impact can be through main channels such as published papers and reports, public conferences and meetings, informal information exchange and consulting (W. M. Cohen, Nelson, and Walsh, 2002). In addition, "degree programmes, in fields useful for local firms, act as a channel for R&D collaborations with universities, public research labs and private firms" (Maietta, 2015, p. 1356).

Universities' joint R&D projects with industries and firms benefit both large enterprises and start-up firms, although it has been stated that large firms benefit more in general from public research (Cohen, Nelson, and Walsh, 2002). These R&D collaborations not only enable firms in the creation of new ideas but also in the completion of ongoing projects (Cohen, Nelson, and Walsh, 2002). Such R&D collaborations can be funded internally by the parties or can be funded through public funding. However, it has been emphasized that when the funding is from a third party – public funding – the result of collaboration is more positive. According to Scandura (2016), having joint R&D efforts with universities through public funding has the benefit of not only obtaining knowledge from the universities research and facilities but also getting access to the pool of employees that are skilled and knowledgeable in that field.

The other key reasons for industry to enter collaboration with the university is to seek opportunities to commercialize university-based technologies for financial gain (Siegel, Waldman, Atwater, and Link, 2003). Such transfer of technology from research to the industry can be through IPR transfers and licensing. It has been claimed that university patents are mostly essential as a source of generic knowledge, as they influence a wide range of technologies rather than creating specific knowledge spillovers (Otsuka, 2011). Universities also have a significant role through the contribution of human capital (Etzkowitz, Webster, Gebhardt, and Terra, 2000; Fukugawa, 2016). In addition to the creation of skilled labor at bachelor, master and even PhD levels, attachment of the researchers and students to the industry by different trainee and internship programs may result in a higher level of engagement and facilitate transfer of knowledge and technology (Liew, Shahdan, and Lim, 2012).

UIC entails a complex interplay between different determinants in different levels, including system, institutional and individual (Muscio and Pozzali, 2013). Promoting this collaboration from the perspective of the university as well as from the firm thus requires considering such interplay and the different system levels, as well as the environmental issues and the nature of different industries that can influence and facilitate or hinder UIC.

The management of the knowledge transfer processes within UICs, including different transfer methods such as IPR, spin-offs and research collaborations, has traditionally been administered through personal relations between people within university, industry and government, whereas recently the processes have been achieved mostly through instruments such as knowledge transfer offices (KTOs), technology transfer offices (TTOs) (Geuna and Muscio, 2009) and research and innovation offices (RIOs) of universities (Liew, Shahdan, and Lim, 2012). These intermediaries can bridge the universities and industries as well as identify the business and focus on the exploitation of IPRs while considering the issues regarding the share of profits, ownership and distribution of responsibilities, whether through licensing or spin-offs, and facilitate UIC (Franco and Haase, 2015; Geuna and Muscio, 2009; Liew, Shahdan, and Lim, 2012). However, the existence of bureaucracy, legal frameworks and weak organizational support may affect the UIC negatively (Franco and Haase, 2015).

At the more micro level, it has been suggested that for bridging offices like TTOs and KTOs to operate optimally, they must have management experienced in knowledge transfer, the ability to hire qualified and expensive staff and be regional rather than for each individual university (Geuna and Muscio, 2009). The university's management is also important in managing the interorganizational relationship by way of improving the interactions, since university leadership can be important in identifying the joint interest between external organizations and their academic counterparts (Etzkowitz, Webster, Gebhardt, and Terra, 2000).

However, the different orientations and procedures of industry and university, respectively, may create TTO-related conflicts that are not easy to alleviate, but can be overcome by way of building strong interorganizational trust through informal reciprocity and exchange based on incentives, procedures and goals (Bruneel, d'Este, and Salter, 2010). The importance of the role of TTOs in facilitating the knowledge transfer of UIC requires more specialized TTOs possessing staff with strong technology backgrounds (Barra and Zotti, 2018).

Another facilitating factor is the role of the individual researcher. It is important that the scientist are involved from the early phases in the case of joint R&D spin-offs or licensing UICs, (Geuna and Muscio, 2009). The network of industry and academic researchers may enhance the productivity of endeavors between firms and universities (Balconi and Laboranti, 2006) (Balconi and Laboranti, 2006). Also, UICs are facilitated when industry hires former academia researchers or when universities hire industry experts in order to seek potential partners (Huang and Chen, 2017). In addition to formal ties, maintaining strong informal ties with industry through scientists in the universities is an important factor in the success of UICs (Liew, Shahdan, and Lim, 2012), as such ties increase the level of trust and mutual understanding (Bruneel,, d'Este, and Salter, 2010). Having informal communication and networking in UICs will increase not only tacit knowledge transfer but also the level of trust in their relationship (Bruneel, d'Este, and Salter, 2010; Liew, Shahdan, and Lim, 2012). Additionally, the presence of highly qualified academics facilitates UICs, since such academics are more engaged in interaction with industries (Franco and Haase, 2015).

At the project level, the research on such collaborations is vast, and different suggestions have been made as a means of improving UICs. For instance, based on their 17-year collaboration in a project between university, industry and government Jones, Scrimgeour, and Tonn (2017) state that several issues must be considered in maintaining a smooth UIC. First, both sides must have engagement early on, as it improves the teams' environment as well as scientific content. Second, defining the roles and responsibilities and expectations prevents conflicts and creates trust, as well as increased financial efficiencies. Third, agreeing on data sharing and standardization leads to cost efficiencies and better management of the collaboration, subsequently treating the project as an experiment that helps understanding the uncertainties as well expecting and resolving setbacks and surprises that in turn leads to faster reactions to unexpected outcomes. Last but not least, defining program success is essential so that all collaborators are aware of what they can expect (Jones, Scrimgeour, and Tonn, 2017).

In addition, Edmondson et al. (2012) list nine main factors in managing the UIC, including the university's leadership abilities, creating selective long-term partnership, having shared visions through assessing the core competences of both sides, putting people that cross boundaries easily in charge of managing the relationship, creating opportunities for people from both sides with the same interests to come together and develop dialogue, developing a "broad overarching framework agreement" (Edmondson et al., 2012, p. 10) for collaboration that does not overemphasize the role of IPR, creating multidisciplinary institutes especially in the university campus and redefining the role of the university research. They state that university leadership can enhance such relations through prioritizing UIC strategies, creating a joint steering group of academics and industry executives and providing resources for keeping basic research while focusing on industry-relevant research. In the case of a long-term relationship, this will ensure that industry knows what is going on in terms of science development in universities and bring the innovations to market (Edmondson et al., 2012).

Strategic alliances for innovation

The literature on strategic alliances encompasses a wide range of diverse issues, for example, who the alliance partners are, as well as the purpose of the alliances (Gulati, 1998). One encompassing definition is that strategic alliances are "trading partnerships and new business forms that enable participating firms to achieve strategic objectives beyond their existing capabilities by providing for mutual resource exchanges (technologies, skills, or products)" (Todeva, 2007). Such alliances thus involve two or more partner firms which, per definition, remain legally independent at the same time, as they in theory share both the benefits and the control of the partnership (Todeva, 2007; Yoshino and Rangan, 1995). Furthermore, partners should continuously contribute to the alliance in order to ensure its survival and success (Todeva, 2007; Yoshino and Rangan, 1995).

Strategic alliances come in various forms, where some may be short term and project based and others may be more long term and involve equity relations (Todeva, 2007). One typology as for why firms attempt to enter into alliances distinguishes between four different types of needs, namely cash needs, the need for increased scale, access to specific markets and the need for specific skills which they assume are available from the partner (Bleeke and Ernst, 1994). It is obviously the fourth type of need which may be most closely associated with issues pertaining to innovation. A similar framework adjusts the perspective from perceived needs to firm motives (Todeva, 2007). Three types of motives correspond overall to the first three types of perceived needs, namely economic motives (e.g. reduction or sharing costs), strategic motives (e.g. cooperating with potential rivals in order to reduce uncertainty) and political motives (e.g. overcoming regulatory barriers). The fourth type of motive, labeled somewhat broadly as "organizational motives" (Todeva, 2007), corresponds roughly to the perceived need for skills and how to possibly satisfy this need by way of one or more strategic alliances aimed at learning, competence building and organizational restructuring (Todeva, 2007).

Related to the theorizing about this latter type of organizational motive, one proposition has been formulated as a "resource-based theory of strategic alliances" (Das and Teng, 2000). In addition to theorizing the individual firm as a set of resources and processes applied in order to acquire these resources, the cases where firms enter into strategic alliances, must according to this view, be analyzed according to resource-based assumptions and concepts. Das and Teng (2000) put forward rationale, formation, structural preferences and performance as four major aspects of strategic alliance, and subsequently propose an analysis of interpartner resource alignments where "resource similarity" and "resource utilization" constitute the two dimensions of the analysis. This results in a typology with four types of alignment: "supplementary", "surplus", "complementary", and "wasteful" (Das and Teng, 2000). They also discuss how particular types of alignment may affect collective strengths and conflicts between allied firms as well as the performance of the alliance.

Research within this tradition thus extends the notion of resource-based firms and the origin of firm innovativeness from the individual firm to its strategic alliance partners (Hagedoorn and Duysters, 2002; Narula and Hagedoorn, 1999). In a similar vein, albeit with an even stronger emphasis on management aspects, there has been a focus recently on the relations between the firms within alliances applying the concept of (dynamic) capabilities, transferring the locus of capabilities management from the individual firm (Teece, 1992; Teece, Pisano, and Shuen, 1997) to the capabilities necessary for the management of strategic alliance-based relations between firms (i.e. "alliance capabilities") (Wang and Rajagopalan, 2015). These capabilities-related issues have, albeit with a different terminology, been the focus also of earlier and ongoing research by Doz (1996) and Oliver and Liebeskind (Oliver, 2009; Oliver and Liebeskind, 1997), focusing on the role of alliance formation on the firm's learning processes. Doz (1996) conducted analyses of learning as occurring along several dimensions (i.e. environment, task, process, skills and goals) and found that successful alliances were evolutionary in the sense that they evolved through a sequence of "interactive cycles of learning, reevaluation and readjustment" (Doz, 1996, p. 55). In contrast, failed projects were inertial. Oliver and Liebeskind (1997) view formalized strategic alliances as but one type of possible relation between firms (i.e. "relationships that operate at the organizational level") and develop a typology which includes two additional types of more informal relations: individual or interpersonal level and interorganizational network relationships that operate at the individual or interpersonal level (Oliver and Liebeskind, 1997). Although strategic alliances are, as introduced earlier, per definition a concept reserved for formalized types of relations, the inclusion of a focus on informal types of relations may be useful, especially in connection with a discussion on interorganizational ties aimed at innovation or learning. Moreover, Oliver (2009) highlights that formal strategic alliances aimed at R&D outputs may in some cases entail delimited transactions in the form of licenses in return for advance investments in successful results of R&D conducted by the other party and are thus not "learning" alliances in the pure sense (Oliver, 2009), whereas other alliances entail various forms of scientific and technological collaboration and warrant the label of learning alliances.

Management of innovation in the context of strategic alliances is thus a field that has taken into consideration a great number of elements, ranging from the original need and subsequent motive for an alliance as perceived from both parties to the question of what type of strategic alliance it is. A special set of challenges may be attached to the type of alliances most conducive to innovation, namely the cases where there is a mutual perception regarding the need for specific skills and hence organizational motives behind alliance formation. Entering into such skills-related alliances may pose particular management challenges, since the alliance must take into consideration issues related to intellectual property rights. In the case of learning alliances the alliance must take into consideration issues such as how to organize collaborative R&D efforts.

Innovation ecosystems

Innovation ecosystem (IE) is a relatively new buzzword in government, industry and academia environments as means of looking at promoting dynamics and affecting innovation (Oh, Phillips, Park, and Lee, 2014). The concept is founded partly on notions such as "business ecosystems" (Moore, 1993) and partly on innovation system conceptualizations. The goal of researchers applying the concept of an ecosystem is to explain the interplay of factors, environment and institutions at different levels that affect and promote innovation in the region, state and organization (Mercan and Götkas, 2011).

Since research in this area is still very limited and very new, there is not a clear cohesive definition of what an IE is. In different definitions that have been offered, the innovation ecosystem concept has encompassed different – yet not that distant – elements (Oh, Phillips, Park, and Lee, 2014). The concept of an ecosystem also has been coupled with other modifiers, such as city-based ecosystem (Cohen and Desarrollo, 2014), industry ecosystem (Tsvetkova and Gustafsson, 2012) and national innovation ecosystem. For instance, while emphasizing the boundary-spanning and networking elements of businesses, Tsvetkova and Gustafsson (2012) highlight in reference to the industry ecosystem that it entails the environment of the industry that the firm is in, including different stakeholders such as customers, partners and suppliers, that affects the firm's business model and business process. Other studies offering a similar definition refer to the ecosystem as the network that firms are connected to providing the required resources, alliance partners and information and are the result of an evolutionary process (Zahra and Nambisan, 2012). While pointing to the importance of an external environment in addition to the internal one in understanding the successful dynamics of innovation, Adner and Kapoor (2010) in their definition of an ecosystem include the external partners of the focal firm that cooperate and compete at the same time in the exchange networks, namely upstream suppliers and downstream customers, as important elements.

Zahra and Nambisan (2012) introduced four models of ecosystems based on the differences and nature of innovation in terms of space and governance: orchestra, creative bazaar, jam central and modification (MOD) station model where communities of innovators can collaborate. An 'orchestra ecosystem model' is a system in which firms are gathered around a key player firm which creates a strong leadership network around itself in order to utilize a market opportunity. In a creative bazaar ecosystem, the key firm obtains innovation through searching the global bazaar and using its infrastructure to realize the values. A 'jam central' ecosystem involves a set of independent entities which collaborate in order to create and develop innovations. And a 'MOD station' ecosystem includes large established firms that smaller newer firms use to enhance their existing and proprietary innovation architecture and products. This perspective mostly looks at the ecosystem in terms of a collection of firms and their relations and networks.

Jackson (2011) defined IE as the complex economic dynamics "between actors or entities whose functional goal is to enable technology development and innovation", in which actors can be material resources, human capital and participating institutions. In this perspective, innovation ecosystem includes two major economies, namely the research economy and the commercial economy (Jackson, 2011). The research economy is driven by basic research, and the latter by the marketplace, and it generates resources, which go back to the research economy in the ecosystem cycle. The spatial element is then an important part of the innovation ecosystem, since entities are geographically localized or strategically linked for implementing a technology and/or business system (Jackson, 2011). Jackson (2011) offers Silicon Valley as an example of such a geographically localized ecosystem, and the European Innovation Initiative as an example of a strategically linked one.

Nevertheless, there have been disagreements as to whether the model is sufficiently defined and constructed and whether there are indeed benefits with adapting this perspective. Oh, Phillips, Park, and Lee (2014) state that the ecosystem phrasing that is mostly used in governmental initiations and industrial papers without peer review is unnecessary and incomplete, and the term "system" would be sufficient in explaining and understanding the developments they actually try to portray. In their paper reviewing the literature on innovation ecosystems, they state that researchers use the term differently; many have used the term loosely and did not have the biological ecosystem as an analogy. One can thus conclude that an "'innovation ecosystem' is identical to 'innovation system,' at present" (Oh, Phillips, Park, and Lee, 2014, p. 2) and although the approach encourages system thinking, which is valuable in itself, the concept itself is not yet a rigorous construct. They further suggest that in order to make the concept into a practical and rigorous construct, there is still a need to define the concept and its precise level and to identify its difference from that of NISs and RISs. Furthermore, there is a need to find ways to measure the system's performance (Oh, Phillips, Park, and Lee, 2014).

Another issue with the current model is that while some use the innovation ecosystem for describing a system at the national level and thus with a macro-perspective (Adner and Kapoor, 2010; Jucevicius, Juceviciene, Gaidelys, and Kalman, 2016; Zahra and Nambisan, 2012), others suggest a micro-perspective of the ecosystem focusing on firm-level strategies of innovation ecosystems (Pellikka and Ali-Vehmas, 2016).

Arguments in favor of the concept and the benefits of using it include, for instance, that unlike in the previous innovation system approaches, the innovation ecosystem approach explains the difference between the innovation events and innovative structure. This is because it includes a focus on the evolutionary and evolving nature of the system, in that it describes both interactions of individual firms and the way the relationships between innovative efforts of firms and the environment can be influenced by institutions through policy (Mercan and Götkas, 2011). In addition, the IE model explains the element of internationalization in a way many of the other innovation system approaches cannot (Mercan and Götkas, 2011).

In attempt to define a more clear IE concept as separate from those of NIS and RIS, Jucevicius, Juceviciene, Gaidelys, and Kalman (2016) define IE, based on the Jackson (2011a) definition, as "a complex network of interactions between the actors from industry, government and academia that underlies the innovative activities and performance in the area" (Jucevicius, Juceviciene, Gaidelys, and Kalman, 2016, p. 430), and although there are some similar key elements in all the well-functioning innovation ecosystems, each IE has its own unique characteristics. This perspective nonetheless seems to be close to that of the triple helix model (Leydesdorff and Etzkowitz, 1998), in which the concept of innovation has been seen as an interplay of the industry, government and academia spheres (Etzkowitz and Leydesdorff, 2000). However, it is claimed that the difference from previous models arises from the "eco" perspective of the new system approach, meaning that the innovation processes are self-organizing and evolutionary, similar to that of the biological ecosystem, and also include the continuous pursuit of balancing the opposite elements of openness and ownership, public and private, short term and long term and supply and demand (Jucevicius, Juceviciene, Gaidelys, and Kalman, 2016). When constructing the model, they emphasize the entrepreneurial value creation role regarding innovation neglected in institutional perspectives such as the triple helix model. The entrepreneurial value creation role is an important factor since it analytically complements the existing regional strengths (Jucevicius, Juceviciene, Gaidelys, and Kalman, 2016). On the whole, the concept aims to address the shortcomings of previous models by way of emphasizing the evolving nature of systems. However, since it is very much in its infancy, it has a long way to go before it can offer a well-constructed and well-distinguished model that can separate itself from the previous institution-focused constructs of NIS and RIS.

However, if, as stated by Jackson (2011a), an IE is a comprise of the two economies (research economy and commercial economy), the important issue in managing within an innovation ecosystem is to address the existing gap between the research economy and commercial economy. This is the gap between the ideas within publicly funded basic research and the commercialization of viable products and services into a marketplace associated with high investments, high risk and high uncertainty (Jackson, 2011a; Jucevicius, Juceviciene, Gaidelys, and Kalman, 2016). This transition of resources from the research economy to the commercial economy is sometimes called the "valley of death" (Butler, 2008, p. 840) and requires the reassessment and reconsideration of the policy at the regional and organizational levels. This means that the regional innovation policy needs to include and consider the specific needs of the emerging innovation ecosystems, while other factors such as entrepreneurial mind-sets, motivation, capabilities and strength are considered at the more organizational levels (Jucevicius, Juceviciene, Gaidelys, and Kalman, 2016).

Additionally, it is important to have a clear and unified vision between the members of an innovation ecosystem, since such unification can result in a more aligned environment and its goals and enhance the collaborations' effectiveness within the system (Pellikka and Ali-Vehmas, 2016). In this respect, Pellikka and Ali-Vehmas (2016) suggest that in an "orchestra innovation ecosystem" (Zahra and Nambisan, 2012), such a vision can be promoted through the core firm in the system. However, this view indicates the role of firms as the main actors in such a system, while it seems to undermine the role of other organizations such as public research institutes and government agencies in the system that can be just as – if not more – influential in how the system functions (Pellikka and Ali-Vehmas, 2016). Thus, in their study of innovation ecosystem "components", Mercan and Götkas (2011) state three components as important elements of the innovation ecosystem, including cluster, university–industry relations and culture. They indicate that strengthening the university and industry relations is the most important aspect of the IE, while culture and clustering, although important, do not affect the innovation output of the system. When considering the university–industry relations in IE, it is important as well to note the role of anchoring entities such as TTOs and PROs (Clarysse, Wright, Bruneel, and Mahajan, 2014). Last but not least, when looking at creating, developing and managing the IE, it is essential to consider that supporting policies must be tailored for each type of ecosystem (Clarysse, Wright, Bruneel, and Mahajan, 2014).

National innovation systems and their importance to corporate innovation

The national innovation systems (NIS) research field has traditionally mostly been preoccupied with a macro level of analysis. In other words, rather than taking corporate innovation as the point of departure for analysis, it is the national system where corporations and their innovative activities are embedded which is being theorized as a context for the innovative activities. The systems are perceived to be composed of actors as well as institutions, and it is the character of the interplay between organizations on the one hand and between these organizations and the systemic institutions on the other hand which are perceived as being conducive towards innovation or functioning as barriers against innovation.

The origins of this approach and its associated concept of NISs are in the works of Freeman (1987) and subsequent theoretical developments by Lundvall (1992) and Nelson (1993). These authors took inspiration from the classical works of List (1789–1846) and his notion of national and systemic contexts for economic activity (Carayannis, Samara, and Bakouros, 2015). Subsequently, the nature and set-up of particular national systems have been theorized while suggesting the kinds of organizations, institutions and policies that are perceived as relevant within the systems based on assumptions that "countries exhibit systematic *differences in terms of economic performance*", that "economic performance depends in large [part] not only on different technological and innovation capabilities but also the *development of institutions*" and "that *innovation and technology policies* are an effective tool for fostering and shaping the performance of countries" (Filippetti and Archibugi, 2011, as cited in Ács, Audretsch, Lehmann, and Licht, 2016. Our italics).

Carayannis, Wright, Bruneel, and Mahajan (2015) provide an overview of these and other central aspects pertaining to the debate on innovations systems as follows. Organizations include businesses, private research facilities, public research centers and universities. It follows that the interaction between various types of organizations is at the center of attention within the approach, be it business-business organization or interaction between business and public research centers. However, one distinguishing feature of the approach is that these interactions are interpreted in view of the constraints and possibilities offered by the institutional framework in which the organizations operate. Institutions relevant for understanding the set-up of a particular innovations systems include, for example, laws, regulations, contracts, rules of market exchange, shared values and codes of conduct (Carayannis, Wright, Bruneel, and Mahajan, 2015, p. 119). More important than organizations as such and their inter-collaboration, as well as the question of institutions as such, is the focus on these two different types of "components" (Carayannis, Wright, Bruneel, and Mahajan, 2015, p. 119) within a system and the inter-relationship which exists between organizations on the one hand and institutions on the other hand. Organizations within the NIS approach are the "players or actors", whereas "institutions may develop simultaneously and are not always characterized by a specific purpose" (Edquist and Johnson, 1997, p. 47).

In addition to the more individually based phenomenon of potential "staff mobility" between organizations Carayannis, Wright, Bruneel, and Mahajan (2015) include in their reflections on the various conceivable types of interactions within NISs the following three types of interorganizational relations. First, *interactions between firms* are potentially crucial. These may be in the form of formal partnerships much in the same vein as the relations reviewed in the sections on modularity and strategic allinaces earlier (i.e. technical cooperation or R&D-related collaboration). More informal relations may also exist between producers and users, for example. The significance of both formal and informal relations between firms may be that it can be a joint usage of technical resources or mutually improved access to human and technical resources (Carayannis, Wright, Bruneel, and Mahajan, 2015, p. 120). Second, *research interactions between the public and private sectors* may be crucial, since such interactions may alleviate improved translational processes between (basic) science and (applied) technology within a system. Such interactions may be divided into different subtypes, with collaboration between industry, universities and reseach centers as the more comprehensive types and cooperation regarding patents or publication activities as more delimited types. In addition, streams of information exchanges, which are a less defined type of relations between the actors, may be conducive towards innovative activities within the NISs (Carayannis, Wright, Bruneel, and Mahajan, 2015, p. 121). Third, interaction may occur through *technology diffusion* by way of the "use of technologies coming from industry and the diffusion of embedded technologies" (Carayannis, Wright, Bruneel, and Mahajan, 2015, p. 122). More speciifically, such diffusion may occur through the transfer of intermediate and capital goods; through embedded technology and the tacit knowledge of people; through access to technology which is codified in the form of documents, databases and patents; and through access to knowledge residing with customers, supliers, competitors and public agencies (Carayannis, Wright, Bruneel, and Mahajan, 2015, p. 122). It may be noted that, as with the other forms of conceivable interactions, these porcceses may occur both within the national system and partners outside, and the relevance of specifying these processes in a context of national innovation systems analysis will subsequently be to reveal and discuss whether there are in particular many or close kinds of such interactions within the national borders.

In recent years, the approach has been supplemented with attempts at theorizing innovation systems at other levels than the national level. The concept of regional innovation systems (RIS) was launched in the early 1990s (Cooke, 1992), partly based on previous research on "the learning region" (Florida, 1995; Morgan, 1997) which had produced empirical results that showed the importance of both interorganizational relations based on an exchange of tacit knowledge and the occasional heavy influence of facilitating agencies at the local level. Also in the early 1990s, the concept and framework of technological systems was introduced in order to highlight the way interactions occur within the processes related to the emergence and further development of specific technologies (Carlsson and Stankiewicz, 1991). The sectoral system of innovation and production concept and framework, defined as "a set of new and established products for specific uses and the set of agents carrying out market and non-market interactions for the creation, production and sale of those products" (Malerba, 2002, p. 248), attempted to highlight the way there may be relations within particular sectors conducive to innovation within such sectors. And the triple helix perspective of innovation systems (Leydesdorff and Etzkowitz, 1998) focuses on the selection environments (i.e., markets, organizations and technological opportunities) and the three networked relations among universities, industries and governments relevant to these environments (i.e. the "carriers" of the system), while assuming that the three selection environments fulfill social functions such as organized knowledge production, wealth creation and control of organizations (Leydesdorff and Zawdie, 2010, p. 789). These additional theoretical developments may at one level be viewed as a critique of the strong emphasis of the national level of analysis within the NIS framework. Taking the recent increased impact of globalizations forces into account, one may argue that the importance of national-level institutions is debilitated and that intercorporate relations at technological and sector levels gain in importance. However, one may also, as in the RIS approach, argue for the continued importance of local processes and relations which are either subnational or may even be supranational in cases where clusters of firms are co-located in regions that geographically span country borders. On the other hand, one may also interpret these additional systems of innovation frameworks as supplementary frameworks rather than fundamental critiques. They take into consideration other sets of indicators and empirical material for use within analysis and highlight additional aspects of the NIS key points without necessarily constituting a fundamental critique or substitute.

One somewhat peculiar feature of the NIS concept and framework is that it has in a much stronger degree than the other four frameworks presented in this chapter been associated with and incorporated within policies at the national and supranational levels. As examples of the former, policies related to innovation and entrepreneurship have been embedded within an NIS framework in Finland (Miettinen, 2002) and Sweden (Bitard, Edquist, Hommen, and Rickne, 2008), and as an example of the latter, the Organisation for Economic Co-operation and Development (OECD) has for a number of years operated with policy formulations heavily inspired by the framework (Lundvall and Borrás, 2005). There are thus several versions of the NIS framework, where some operate within the academic domain striving for theory formulations and empirical analyses, whereas the applications within the policy sphere may be interpreted as more loosely applied guidelines.

Types of critiques that have, however, been posted against both the NIS framework and its supplements include the observation that there may be an overly suppressed role of corporate and individual agency within the frameworks. Perhaps the most vocal proponent of such a critique in recent years is the group suggesting the alternative concept "national systems of entrepreneurship" (Ács, Autio, and Szerb, 2014; cf. also Surie and Groen, 2017) and attempts to align the approach to the "broader ecosystems literature" (Ács, Audretsch, Lehmann, and Licht, 2016, p. 3). They assert that the national innovation systems concept is "mostly about context, how institutions drive knowledge production and application and how countries differ according to their '. . . set of institutions . . . ' but totally overlooks the individual agency" (Ács, Autio, and Szerb, 2014, p. 477). Perhaps there will in coming years be increased efforts at cross-over research where researchers form disciplines focusing on the role of individual and organizational agency, such as management and organization theory, and merge with the economics-oriented researchers hitherto dominating the national systems of the innovation approach.

References

Ács, Z. J., Audretsch, D. B., Lehmann, E. E. and Licht, G. (2016). National systems of innovation. *Journal of Technology Transfer*, 1–12. doi:10.1007/s10961-016-9481-8.

Ács, Z. J., Autio, E. and Szerb, L. (2014). National systems of entrepreneurship: measurement issues and policy implications. *Research Policy*, 43(3), 476–494.

Adner, R. and Kapoor, R. (2010). Value creation in innovation ecosystems: how the structure of technological interdependence affects firm performance in new technology generations. *Strategic Management Journal*, 31, 306–333. doi:10.1002/smj.

Agrawal, A. (2001). Common property institutions and sustainable governance of resources. *World Development*, 29(10), 1649–1672.

Ankrah, S. and Al-Tabbaa, O. (2015). Universities-industry collaboration: a systematic review. *Scandinavian Journal of Management*, 31(3), 387–408. doi:10.1016/j.scaman.2015.02.003.

Balconi, M. and Laboranti, A. (2006). University-industry interactions in applied research: the case of microelectronics. *Research Policy*, 35(10), 1616–1630. doi:10.1016/j.respol.2006.09.018.

Baldwin, C.Y. and Clark, K. B. (1997). Managing in an age of modularity. *Harvard Business Review*. September–October. https://hbr.org/1997/09/managing-in-an-age-of-modularity.

Barra, C. and Zotti, R. (2018). The contribution of university, private and public sector resources to Italian regional innovation system (in)efficiency. *The Journal of Technology Transfer*. doi:10.1007/s10961-016-9539-7.

Bitard, P., Edquist, C., Hommen, L. and Rickne, A. (2008). Reconsidering the paradox of high R&D input and low innovation: Sweden. In Edquist, C. and Hommen, H. (Eds.), *Small country innovation systems: globalization, change and policy in Asia and Europe*. Cheltenham: Edward Elgar Publishing, pp. 237–280.

Bleeke, J. and Ernst, D. (1994). *Collaborating to compete: using strategic alliances and acquisitions in the global marketplace*. New York: John Wiley & Sons Ltd.

Bruneel, J., d'Este, P. and Salter, A. (2010). Investigating the factors that diminish the barriers to university – industry collaboration. *Research Policy*, 39(7), 858–868.

Butler, D. (2008). Crossing the valley of death. *Nature*, 453(7197), 840.

Carayannis, E. G., Samara, E. T. and Bakouros, Y. L. (2015). *Innovation and entrepreneurship: theory, policy and practice*. Zurich: Springer International Publishing.

Carlsson, B. and Stankiewicz, R. (1991). On the nature, function and composition of technological systems. *Journal of Evolutionary Economics*, 1(2), 93–118.

Chapple, W., Lockett, A., Siegel, D. and Wright, M. (2005). Assessing the relative performance of U.K. university technology transfer offices: parametric and non-parametric evidence. *Research Policy*, 34(3), 369–384. doi:10.1016/j.respol.2005.01.007.

Chesbrough, H. (2006). *Open innovation: a new paradigm for understanding industrial innovation*. Oxford: Oxford University Press.

Clarysse, B., Wright, M., Bruneel, J. and Mahajan, A. (2014). Creating value in ecosystems: crossing the chasm between knowledge and business ecosystems. *Research Policy*, 43(7), 1164–1176. doi:10.1016/j.respol.2014.04.014.

Cohen, B. and Desarrollo, U. (2014). Call for papers – The city as a lab: open innovation meets the collaborative economy. *California Management Review*, 3–5.

Cohen, W. M., Nelson, R. R. and Walsh, J. P. (2002). Links and impacts: the influence of public research on industrial R&D. *Management Science*, 48(1), 1–23.

Cooke, P. (1992). Regional innovation systems: competitive regulation in the new Europe. *Geoforum*, 23(3), 365–382.

Cooke, P., Gomez Uranga, M. and Etxebarria, G. (1997). Regional innovation systems: institutional and organisational dimensions. *Research Policy*, 26(4–5), 475–491. doi:10.1016/S0048-7333(97)00025-5.

Das, T. K. and Teng, B-S. (2000). A resource-based theory of strategic alliances. *Journal of management*, 26(1), 31–61.

Doz, Y. L. (1996). The evolution of cooperation in strategic alliances: initial conditions or learning processes? *Strategic Management Journal*, 17(S1), 55–83.

Edmondson, G., Valigra, L., Kenward, M., Hudson, R. L. and Belfield, H. (2012). *Making industry-university partnerships work: lessons from successful collaborations*. Brussels: Science|Business Innovation Board AISBL.

Edquist, C. and Johnson, B. (1997). Institutions and organisations in systems of innovation. In Edquist. C. (Ed.) *Systems of innovation: technologies, institutions and organisations* (pp. 41–63). London: Pinter Publishers.

Ethiraj, S. K., Levinthal, D. and Roy, R. R. (2008). The dual role of modularity: innovation and imitation. *Management Science*, 54(5), 939–955.

Etzkowitz, H. and Leydesdorff, L. (2000). The dynamics of innovation: from National Systems and 'Mode 2' to a Triple Helix of university – industry – government relations. *Research Policy*, 29, 109–123.

Etzkowitz, H., Webster, A., Gebhardt, C. and Terra, B. R. C. (2000). The future of the university and the university of the future: evolution of ivory tower to entrepreneurial paradigm. *Research Policy*, 29(2), 313–330.

Filippetti, A., and Archibugi, D. (2011). Innovation in times of crisis: national systems of innovation, structure, and Demand. *Research Policy* 40(2), 179–192. doi: 10.1016/j.respol.2010.09.001

Florida, R. (1995). Toward the learning region. *Futures*, 27(5), 527–536.

Franco, M. and Haase, H. (2015). University-industry cooperation: researchers' motivations and interaction channels. *Journal of Engineering and Technology Management – JET-M*, 36, 41–51. doi:10.1016/j.jengtecman.2015.05.002.

Freeman, C. (1987). *Technology policy and economic performance: lessons from Japan*. London: Pinter.

Fukugawa, N. (2016). Knowledge spillover from university research before the national innovation system reform in Japan: localisation, mechanisms, and intermediaries. *Asian Journal of Technology Innovation*, 24(1), 100–122. doi:10.1080/19761597.2016.1141058.

Geuna, A. and Muscio, A. (2009). The governance of university knowledge transfer: a critical review of the literature. *Minerva*, 47(1), 93–114. doi:10.1007/s11024-009-9118-2.

Gulati, R. (1998). Alliances and networks. *Strategic Management Journal*, 19(4), 293–317.

Hagedoorn, J. and Duysters, G. (2002). External sources of innovative capabilities: the preferences for strategic alliances or mergers and acquisitions. *Journal of Management Studies*, 39(2), 167–188.

Helfat, C. E. and Campo-Rembado, M. A. (2016). Integrative capabilities, vertical integration, and innovation over successive technology lifecycles. *Organization Science*, 27(2), 249–264.

Huang, M. H. and Chen, D. Z. (2017). How can academic innovation performance in university-industry collaboration be improved? *Technological Forecasting and Social Change*, 123 (October 2017), 210–215. doi:10.1016/j.techfore.2016.03.024.

Jackson, D. J. (2011a). *What is an innovation ecosystem?* Arlington, VA: National Science Foundation.

Jackson, D. J. (2011b). *What is an innovation ecosystem*. Arlington, VA: National Science Foundation.

Jones, N. E., Scrimgeour, G. J. and Tonn, W. M. (2017). Lessons learned from an industry, government and university collaboration to restore stream habitats and mitigate effects. *Environmental Management*, 59(1), 1–9. doi:10.1007/s00267-016-0792-1.

Jucevicius, G., Juceviciene, R., Gaidelys, V. and Kalman, A. (2016). The emerging innovation ecosystems and 'Valley of Death': towards the combination of entrepreneurial and institutional approaches. *Inzinerine Ekonomika-Engineering Economics*, 27(4), 430–438. doi:10.5755/j01.ee.27.4.14403.

Kaufmann, A. and Tödtling, F. (2001). Science-industry interaction in the process of innovation: the importance of boundary-crossing between systems. *Research Policy*, 30(5), 791–804. doi:10.1016/S0048-7333(00)00118-9.

Leydesdorff, L. and Etzkowitz, H. (1998). Triple helix of innovation. *Science and Public Policy*, 25(6), 358–364.

Leydesdorff, L. and Zawdie, G. (2010). The triple helix perspective of innovation systems. *Technology Analysis & Strategic Management*, 22(7), 789–804.

Liew, M. S., Shahdan, T. N. T. and Lim, E. S. (2012). Strategic and tactical approaches on university – industry collaboration. *Procedia – Social and Behavioral Sciences*, 56(Ictlhe), 405–409. doi:10.1016/j.sbspro.2012.09.669.

Lin, J. Y. (2017). Balancing industry collaboration and academic innovation: The contingent role of collaboration-specific attributes. *Technological Forecasting and Social Change*, 123 (October 2017), 216–228. doi:10.1016/j.techfore.2016.03.016.

Lundvall, B. Å. (Ed.) (1992). *National systems of innovation. Towards a theory of innovation and interactive learning*. London: Pinter.

Lundvall, B. Å. and Borrás, S. (2005). Science, technology, and innovation policy. In Fagerberg, J., Mowery, D. C. and Nelson, R. R. (Eds.), *The Oxford handbook of innovation*. Oxford: Oxford University Press.

Maietta, O. W. (2015). Determinants of university – firm R&D collaboration and its impact on innovation: a perspective from a low-tech industry. *Research Policy*, 44(7), 1341–1359.

Malerba, F. (2002). Sectoral systems of innovation and production. *Research Policy*, 31(2), 247–264.

Mercan, B. and Götkas, D. (2011). Components of innovation ecosystems. *International Research Journal of Finance and Economics*, 76(76), 102–112. doi:1450-2887.

Miettinen, R. (2002). *National innovation system: scientific concept or political rhetoric*. Helsinki: Edita.

Miozzo, M. and Grimshaw, D. (2005). Modularity and innovation in knowledge-intensive business services: IT outsourcing in Germany and the UK. *Research Policy*, 34(9), 1419–1439.

Moore, J. F. (1993). Predators and prey: a new ecology of competition. *Harvard Business Review*, 71(3), 75–83.

Morgan, K. (1997). The learning region: institutions, innovation and regional renewal. *Regional Studies*, 31(5), 491–503.

Motohashi, K. (2005). University-industry collaborations in Japan: the role of new technology-based firms in transforming the National Innovation System. *Research Policy*, 34(5), 583–594. doi:10.1016/j.respol.2005.03.001.

Muscio, A. and Pozzali, A. (2013). The effects of cognitive distance in university-industry collaborations: some evidence from Italian universities. *Journal of Technology Transfer*, 38(4), 486–508. doi:10.1007/s10961-012-9262-y.

Narula, R. and Hagedoorn, J. (1999). Innovating through strategic alliances: moving towards international partnerships and contractual agreements. *Technovation*, 19(5), 283–294.

Nelson, R. R. (1993). *National innovation systems: a comparative analysis*. Oxford: Oxford University Press.

OECD (2000). *Benchmarking industry-science relationships*. Paris: OECD.

Oh, D. S., Phillips, F., Park, S. and Lee, E. (2014). Innovation ecosystems: a critical examination. *Technovation*, 54, 3–5. doi:10.1016/j.technovation.2016.02.004.

Oliver, A. L. (2009). *Networks for learning and knowledge creation in biotechnology*. Cambridge: Cambridge University Press.

Oliver, A. L. and Liebeskind, J. P. (1997). Three levels of networking for sourcing intellectual capital in biotechnology: implications for studying interorganizational networks. *International Studies of Management & Organization*, 27(4), 76–103.

Otsuka, K. (2011). University patenting and knowledge spillover in Japan: panel-data analysis with citation data. *Applied Economics Letters*, 19(11), 1045–1049. doi:10.1080/13504851.2011.613743.

Pellikka, J. and Ali-Vehmas, T. (2016). Managing innovation ecosystems to create and capture value in ICT industries. *Technology Innovation Management Review*, 6(10), 17–24.

Pil, F. K. and Cohen, S. K. (2006). Modularity: implications for imitation, innovation, and sustained advantage. *Academy of Management Review*, 31(4), 995–1011.

Powell, W. W. (1998). Learning from collaboration: knowledge and networks in the biotechnology and pharmaceutical industries. *California Management Review*, 40(3), 228–240.

Scandura, A. (2016). University-industry collaboration and firms' R&D effort. *Research Policy*, 45(9), 1907–1922. doi:10.1016/j.respol.2016.06.009.

Shattock, M. (2005). European universities for entrepreneurship: their role in the Europe of knowledge the theoretical context. *Higher Education Management & Policy*, 17(3). doi:10.1111/j.1432-1033.1971.tb01354.x.

Siegel, D. S., Waldman, D. A., Atwater, L. E. and Link, A. N. (2003). Commercial knowledge transfers from universities to firms: improving the effectiveness of university-industry collaboration. *Journal of High Technology Management Research*, 14(1), 111–133. doi:10.1016/S1047-8310(03)00007-5.

Surie, G. and Groen, A. (2017). The importance of social entrepreneurship in national systems of innovation – an introduction. *Technological Forecasting and Social Change*, 121 (August 2017), 181–183. doi:https://doi.org/10.1016/j.techfore.2017.05.010.

Teece, D. J. (1992). Competition, cooperation, and innovation: organizational arrangements for regimes of rapid technological progress. *Journal of Economic Behavior & Organization*, 18(1), 1–25.

Teece, D. J., Pisano, G. and Shuen, A. (1997). Dynamic capabilities and strategic management. *Strategic Management Journal*, 509–533.

Todeva, E. (2007). Strategic alliances. In Clegg, S. and Bailey, J. R. (Eds.), *International encyclopedia of organization studies*. Thousand Oaks, CA: Sage.

Tsvetkova, A. and Gustafsson, M. (2012). Business models for industrial ecosystems: a modular approach. *Journal of Cleaner Production*, 29–30, 246–254. doi:10.1016/j.jclepro.2012.01.017.

Wang, Y. and Rajagopalan, N. (2015). Alliance capabilities: review and research agenda. *Journal of Management*, 41(1), 236–260.

Yoshino, M. Y. and Rangan, S. (1995). *Strategic alliances: an entrepreneurial approach to globalization*. Boston, MA: Harvard Business School Press.

Zahra, S. A. and Nambisan, S. (2012). Entrepreneurship and strategic thinking in business ecosystems. *Business Horizons*, 55(3), 219–229. doi:10.1016/j.bushor.2011.12.004.

20
THE CRUCIAL HUMAN FACTOR IN INNOVATION

Georges Haour

Drawing from learnings gained from practice, as well as from studying the process of innovation, the author concludes that, by far, the success of an innovation project is essentially a function of the talent and motivation of the persons involved. Therefore, management may bring considerable value by taking the time to ensure these two critical requirements. In comparison with this priority, firms should place little importance on "frameworks" and consultants' "models"; instead, managers should trust their collective strength, rather than escaping into hiring external "help".

After looking at the act of creation, the fire of innovative activity, this chapter concentrates on technology-intensive innovations. The latter provides a powerful tool for changing the world and creating wealth. As they represent the key force in this dynamic, technical knowledge workers constitute our focus: their profile and what they require in order to thrive. Attention will then be given to what these requirements mean for management. Lastly, the importance of the human factor will be illustrated with the specific aspect of innovation, which involves the complex transition of "academic" research to commercially successful ventures, following the path called "technology transfer".

Introduction: creation and the essence of innovation

After looking at the act of creation, we'll briefly look at past literature concerned with the human factor in innovation. The dominating drivers for change and innovation in the coming years will then be explored. Finally, the objective of the chapter will be presented.

The mysterious act of creation

The arts and science constitute central elements of the human genius. Ultimate masterpieces, such as Plato's *Republic*, Monteverdi' *Orfeo*, amazing works of art from the Ming dynasty, Leonardo da Vinci's *La Joconde*, Bach's Saint John Passion, Hokusai's wondrous Uki-yoe, Monet's impressionist paintings, Stravinsky's "Rite of Spring", Fleming's discovery of penicillin, because of "his prepared mind" and Berg's *Wozzeck* are a few examples. These superb works are the products of the genius, passion and commitment of individuals. They are most appropriate to depict the great myths of humanity. Carl Jung calls on works of art to illustrate the icons of mankind's mental universe (1968).

In order to evoke the mysteries of the creation process, philosophers have sometimes described creative geniuses as sleepwalkers. Among them, Arthur Koestler (2012) shows how Kepler made two mistakes cancelling each other so that, guided by a mysterious inspiration, he arrived at the proper equation for the elliptic path of the earth. A perspective on scientific discovery is provided by Thomas Kuhn (1962). According to his famed concept of "paradigm shift", a scientific theory goes on as "normal science" until it is progressively challenged to a point of crisis, at which point a new theory takes over. Two theories shift like tectonic plates until they collide, causing an earthquake.

The creative genius of individuals is at the heart of the discovery process, whether in the arts, spice in our lives or in the sciences. It constitutes the essence of the innovation process. By this phrase, we mean going from a novel idea to commercial success. In an attempt to improve their competitive position, firms orchestrate this difficult and unpredictable journey in order to develop differentiated offerings and to make their operations more efficient.

Drivers of change

Because of the digital revolution, the world is undergoing unprecedented, massive change. All sectors of activity are affected by the "digital tsunami". The latter includes 5G, first used on a large scale by Korean Telecom at the 2018 Winter Olympics, allowing a capacity to transmit data roughly 100 times that of 4G. This "digital revolution" includes the Internet of Things (IoT). It is anticipated that 50 billion objects will be connected by 2020, offering an environment that, no doubt, will be exploited by the "hackers". Also coming into play are robotics, big data and analytics, artificial intelligence (AI) and the much-talked-about blockchain.

A special event at the International Institute for Management Development (IMD) in Switzerland, on October 4 and 5, 2018, deals with this panoply of techniques as they affect every sector, turning business models upside down and displacing jobs. The Internet allows cutting out the "middle person", putting consumers in direct contact with suppliers of services. This also makes it possible to accumulate enormous amount of data, which may be valuable to certain organisations. The slogan is: "data is the commodity of the 21st century".

Expected to be particularly affected are the healthcare sector, partly because it has been so slow to move in this area, manufacturing, entertainment and gaming, "fintech" and driverless means of transportation, automobiles in particular. China, the ultimate Internet country, is accelerating its efforts on many fronts with breakneck speed. Shanghai is already the world's capital for "fintech".

On occasion, our societies feel brutalised by the digital revolution. Concerns about cybersecurity are in order. Substantial economic losses are evoked, with estimated figures around $2 trillion worldwide in 2020 as a result of hacking. The annual Def Con cybersecurity conference is always very well attended. This, mitigating risks is in order. Ethical issues should be debated much more. It can be said that algorithms themselves are not "neutral", as they assume a certain set of values.

In dealing with this wild horse, there is sporadic resistance: some people prefer queuing at human cashiers, rather than dealing with charmless machines. For others, "the more digital the world becomes, the more handwritten notes I send". The "lights and shadows" of the digital brave new world should be lucidly evaluated and debated.

Citizens' control of their private data is a central concern. Europe is the first region in the world to take regulatory action in this area – the General Data Protection Regulation (GDPR)

– in full force late May 2018. Indeed, our toxic world demands "smart regulation", in order to protect citizens without stifling economic dynamism.

The digital, geopolitical and ecological changes are prompting consultants and business school types to utter a lot of "gobbledygook" on the managerial attributes required to face these challenges. Words such as "agility, leadership, ecosystems" and "open innovation and cloud sourcing" are uttered *ad nauseam*, but are inadequate to help navigate the resulting rumbustious business environment. The discourse remains at the general macro level and does not articulate any useful wisdom to individuals.

Brief review

Considering how important the motivation and the talent of individuals involved in innovations are, few authors look at the value system and the factors creating strong morale in these individuals. What specific practices and managerial approaches allow and stimulate such individuals to thrive and be productive? Similar considerations apply to public laboratories, nonprofit institutions and university research departments.

Entrepreneurship, or, rather, the entrepreneurial spirit, is necessary, but not sufficient, for innovation to be successful. Its proactive energy constitutes the booster, which catapults innovative offerings into market. In this area, there is much hype about the so-called "entrepreneurial universities".[1]. Many years ago, the private University Babson, in Boston, made entrepreneurship central to its brand. Several Chinese universities are blowing the same trumpet. How does one *effectively* teach entrepreneurship? In the UK, the "Cambridge phenomenon" took place well before anybody was concerned with this question. It happened because there were a few compelling role models, as well as through good practice, such as that at the St John's Innovation Centre, founded in 1987. Its first director, Walter Herriot, well understood the needs of entrepreneurs.

Rather than giving many references to articles, let us highlight a 2012 OECD report reviewing this area.[2] This report lists the components of an "entrepreneurial university". These are: (1) leadership and governance; (2) organisational capacity, people and incentives; (3) entrepreneurship development in teaching and learning; (4) pathways for entrepreneurs; (5) relationships with business; (6) entrepreneurial university as an internationalised institution; and (7) measuring the impact of the entrepreneurial university.

Typically, papers on the human factor and innovation concentrate on the "framework conditions" promoting innovativeness. These are very "macro" considerations, including typologies for the staff. Human resources are taken as an aggregate entity. No consideration is taken as to how to ensure in talented *individuals* the motivation and energy required to make innovation succeed (Christina, 2012; Livesay, 1996). This is also the perspective of the 2014 edition of the annual Global Innovation Index (GII) from the World Intellectual Property Organization (WIPO), a ranking that has put Switzerland on the top place for the last six years. In 2014, the GII focussed on the theme "The Human Factor".[3] By that was meant statistics on the number of graduates, professionals and science parks. These macro-issues do not tell anything about what motivates *individuals*.

Objective of the chapter

In the universe of creativity, innovation and massive change described earlier, this chapter looks at the human factor in the innovation process. We focus on individuals working in companies, including large corporations, small and medium enterprises (SMEs), and start-ups.

Many innovations are non-technical in nature. The example of self-service shows that a major new approach may revolutionise a sector, retail in this case, without involving any technology. On a different level, the European Union constitutes one of the most remarkable innovations (and often a frustrating one) in human history. Our world needs effective conceptual innovations in order to deal with the rapid and massive changes affecting it. In the absence of leadership, these are slow in coming, as the inertia in the system is astounding, likely only to be shaken by the compelling pressure from citizens. There are, however, signs of change. For the first time, the Queen of England has taken a public stand on an environmental issue: "I declare war on plastic", she said on February 12, 2018.[4]

Technical change, particularly in the digital sphere, will continue to be key in solving world's problems and to create wealth for people. This chapter focusses on the human factor in technology-intensive innovations, because they represent the lion's share of the wealth-creation process. We first discuss the characteristics of the key actors in technical innovations (e.g. technical knowledge workers). We will then look at the implications of these characteristics for management. Lastly, we will look at the complex process of technology knowledge transfer.

The technical knowledge worker

Technical knowledge workers are somewhat different from other knowledge workers. Managers of a department for technical development, such as R&D must be sensitive to these differences, discussed next.

Technical content versus process

A student working on the research towards obtaining a PhD in science is likely to consider the world of management very pejoratively: what is paramount to such a student is the *content* of the scientific work and the challenge of progressing knowledge in a very specialised field. Indeed, scientists consider their expertise in a scientific discipline a central part of their identity. With it, scientists characterise themselves: they say "I am a physicist", or "I am a biologist", just like somebody would say: " I am a medical doctor" or "I am a lawyer".

In contrast with the importance of technical *content*, people involved in *processes*, such as managers and consultants, are often considered peripheral. Collective memory confirms the supremacy of content over process. One example is the WWII Manhattan Project, which was set up with a staff of 130,000 persons to develop the nuclear bombs that were dropped on Hiroshima and Nagasaki in August 6 and 9, 1945.[5] History does not recall the name of the project manager, but only the names of the physicists, particularly Robert Oppenheimer, head of the Los Alamos Laboratory, as well as Leo Szilard and Albert Einstein. This recognises the fundamental fact that without expert technical knowledge, there is no project, whereas project management is sort of a commodity.

Our contemporary times sometimes seem to forget this basic fact. Excessive emphasis is often put on the marketing, the financing and managerial practices. Considerable hype surrounds startups, these budding firms that often have a technical innovation at their origin. In Silicon Valley, the proximity of Hollywood seems to encourage the "spin doctors" to hyperbolic exaggeration, when, in fact, the success rate is no better than anywhere in the world: roughly, 75 percent of technical startups die within five years. China seems to be on the same bandwagon, with occasional extravagant story telling on start-ups, incubators, etc. It is nice to see Switzerland remaining true to the quality of content, using a low-key approach and soberness!

The crucial human factor in innovation

Who are the founders of start-ups? Engineers, of course. They bring the technical content, which constitutes the basis for the new business, but they need additional skills to develop it. These skills are often provided by a colleague with a different orientation. Most start-ups have two founders who trust each other: one engineer contributes the technical content, the other one, more extroverted, deals with marketing and business. Technical experts develop management skills and business sense over time, following the path given in the graph in Figure 20.1. A primary responsibility of managers is to help individual staff members develop. Occasionally, timely executive education programmes make it possible to accelerate and amplify this evolution. Thus, management development may truly be an agent of change.

Need for autonomy

Another characteristic of knowledge workers is their high need for autonomy. Since expertise is so important to them, it defines much of their value system and behaviour. They feel that they know best and resent advice or managerial interference. They are difficult to manage in the sense that, in order to be "accepted", a manager must be legitimate in terms of background and track record. In certain cases, technical experts elect to remain technical contributors, growing in seniority without managing any staff. The technical path, parallel to the managerial cursus, constitutes the "dual ladder" system.

Knowledge workers, such as medical doctors, journalists and lawyers, represent a challenge for managers similar to that of technical knowledge workers. It is often said that such staff are fiercely individualistic, just like cats. As is well known, there is no such thing as "corralling a herd of cats".

The expert syndrome

The pride of knowledge workers in their technical competency may be illustrated by a survey of researchers of the contract research organisation Battelle. They were asked: "Why are

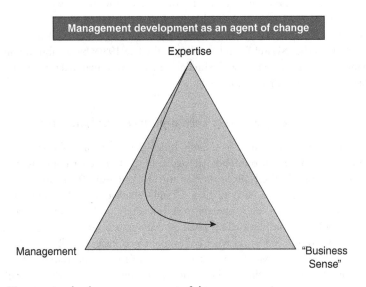

Figure 20.1 Management development as an agent of change

clients funding innovation projects with you as project manager?" More than 80 percent of their answers were "because of my recognized expertise", while the clients' reply was "because we have an issue to resolve".

As a result of their pride, as well as their need for independence, knowledge workers are unlikely to readily engage in collaborations and exchanges with colleagues. Why should they, since they are so good themselves? Furthermore, engaging in a collaboration may expose areas of ignorance, a direct threat to their "prima donna" status. Here again, management must tactfully convince individual experts to engage and collaborate.

In an attempt to seduce experts, start-ups offer a "fun" office space, with colourful coaches, dart games, etc. Instead of such gimmicks, it seems preferable to offer an excellent cafeteria, an efficient nursery for the employees' children, astute advice for personal finances, generous sabbaticals or attractive rotations in other parts of the firm. In-kind advantages provided by certain Chinese firms, such as company cars or low-interest loans for purchasing real estate, are also effective in attracting and retaining staff.

Knowledge inertia

A firm that has outstanding experts in a given discipline, say metallurgical engineering, will want to keep them busy with challenging projects in their specific field. This constraining legacy compels management to continue ploughing the same furrow in comfortable complacency. In fact, these investments should be directed towards more future-oriented projects.

Companies find it difficult to interrupt projects. This is due to a lack of courage and the fear of demotivating the teams. This is an ill-placed concern. The key is to kill projects, not the project members! The reasons, business or otherwise, for stopping a project must be explained to the project team. If done properly, that is, if the management *takes the time* to explain why an activity must be stopped, such interruptions provide an opportunity for a powerful pedagogical message. In most cases, management does not seize this opportunity.

For a company, such inertia often leads to disasters. Examples include Kodak, which failed to manage the advent of digital photography. At the level of an entire industry, in the early 1970s, the senior management of the Swiss watch sector rejected the quartz watch, because it could not resolve itself to abandon the considerable and unique know-how of their staff in precisely making mechanical watches. The Japanese firms then took over the market. The Swiss sector only recovered when the "Swatch" was launched in the late 1980s by combining innovations in design, provided by engineers Mock and Mueller, and advanced manufacturing and marketing,[6] under the leadership of Dr. Ernst Thomke.

Knowledge workers need organisational stability

Uncertainty is at the core of technical research. Indeed, if the results of a project were known, there would no need to carry it out. The daily work of the researcher is a constant battle, more or less acute, depending on the time, against an unclear outcome. With uncertainty central to their work, researchers feel the need to have a stable environment. Management must strive at providing this, in particular, by supporting the researcher and showing empathy when the project goes through difficult phases. This must be done in a positive manner, making relevant suggestions on how to proceed or on what colleagues to contact for help.

Mergers and acquisitions (M&A) represent periods of major uncertainty. These must be as short as possible. The vision of the newly formed entity must be diligently formulated and its organisational structure clarified promptly. Duplications are eliminated, with R&D departments often at the top of the list of activities to be "streamlined" in order to reduce costs. Researchers are unsettled by such uncertainty, so that, during this period, the innovativeness and the research productivity go way down. It is therefore very important to point to the future so that the innovative heart of the firm can start beating again. When Roche acquired the diagnostics company Boehringer Manheim, it decided to manage the merger fully internally, which was the proper thing to do. As a result, the merging process was carried out, retaining the trust from the staff and with due speed, so that the innovation spirit of the development teams was altered relatively little.[7] Roche, admittedly the best pharmaceutical firm in the world, has a history of intelligently handling relationships with new partners, such as Genentech or Chugai.

The richness of diversity in teams

By and large, more diverse teams, or a more multicultural staff, are less conformist and more creative.[8] There is a caveat, however: the desired outcome is obtained *only* if managers see a multicultural staff as a positive asset. Managers who are not at ease with this or do not know how to effectively deal with diversity actually destroy this potential.

Why is diversity an advantage for innovation? People from different genders, social origins, countries, cultures, etc., engage more in debate and dialogue. Robust conversations develop, from which new ideas are more likely to emerge. Coming with different sets of contacts, they have antennas into diverse worlds. In this area, Europe's unique richness of diversity represents a considerable asset. For example, teams involved in projects from the European Union's "framework projects" are the most diverse in the world. Such projects gather people from small and large firms, public and private, from universities and private laboratories, coming from different countries. Managing such teams demands persons who are able to turn this complexity into an asset. When the sophistication of effectively managing highly diverse teams is lacking, however, this complexity is only cumbersome. In most cases, problems encountered in projects are managerial in nature, not technical. Although not a member of the EU, Switzerland fully participates in the EU programmes. This constitutes a testimony to the importance of being part of the European research area. It is probably also because such a multicultural country fully understands the power of diversity.

There are exceptions to the rule: effective innovativeness and market orientation do not absolutely require staff diversity. For example, in Japan in the 1980s, homogeneously Japanese staff belonging to very Japanese companies such as Canon, Sharp or Toyota developed new, winning offerings, which conquered the world. Japan, with a monoculture population and limited global outlook (on boards of Japanese firms, fewer than 1 percent of their members are not Japanese), continues to be a powerhouse for (technical) innovation.

Researchers-entrepreneurs

As a manager of a unit at Battelle in Geneva, the author of this chapter hired a number of researchers from various countries in order to build the diversity mentioned earlier. One phrase used to describe the job was "I need researchers-entrepreneurs". These two words are not usually put together. In fact, common wisdom considers that these two profiles are not found in the same person. This is supported by the fact that, as mentioned earlier, engineers starting new technical ventures find a colleague as an associate, who brings an orientation towards business and entrepreneurship.

Our societies do not want everybody to be an entrepreneur; this would mean chaos. We want somewhat more entrepreneurs; how many more is not clear. Importantly, we want more *effective* entrepreneurs. What firms really want is proactive employees who take initiatives engage with colleagues and move things forward, convince colleagues and focus their energy on worthwhile projects. The terms "intrapreneurship" and "corporate entrepreneurship" refer to an entrepreneurial spirit, which remains within the limits of the corporate system. Corporations seem keen to work with very young companies, in the hope that their entrepreneurial energy will "infect" their corporate bureaucracies. One may be sceptical about the success of such endeavours. Furthermore, the start-ups are uneasy about such encounters, as they fear that their ideas may be stolen by the corporations. On the other hand, the corporate world must definitely learn to deal and interact effectively with start-up companies.

At the macro level, an indication of a country to have an entrepreneurial outlook is given by the ranking of the Global Entrepreneurship Monitor. Its 2017 report may be downloaded from www.gemconsortium.org/report. According to this, the most entrepreneurial countries are Estonia, Israel, the United States, Canada and The Netherlands. In Europe, Switzerland is in the upper range, at the level of the UK. Only 15 to 20 percent of start-ups are led by women. Rankings, however, should not be taken at face value. Their merit is to stimulate debate and discussions in an attempt to better understand the issues.

Implications for management

We have reviewed the characteristics and motivational aspects of technical professionals. We now turn to what these mean for management: what values, management styles and practices are most appropriate to motivate technical knowledge workers.

"Our staff is our most precious asset": often an empty phrase

Annual company reports are replete with motherhood statements on "people empowerment" and "the most important element is our staff". Companies are like individuals: they do not truly practice what they know is good. One example is the level of effort taken by a firm to evaluate a modest investment, say Euros 200,000, while it is often negligent in hiring new staff, which is the most important process in firms. It seems that spending money requires more attention than careful hiring. And yet, a mistake in hiring will cost the company enormously – but there are no "metrics" for this.

An indication of this misplaced priority is given by the generally poor welcome of new hires on their first day at work. This is irresponsible, since the first weeks on a new job strongly influence the motivation of the new recruit for a long time. First-line managers must be particularly attentive. A variation of the following fable, illustrating some of the pitfalls, has been published (Haour, 2004).

After obtaining her doctorate in computer science, Dr Joanne Talent vacationed in Yunnan, China, before starting her new job at Hubritech Corp., in Austin, Texas. On a balmy September morning, Joanne "reports" to work. No, the receptionist is not aware of her arrival; after contacting the personnel department, it turns out that her name is indeed in the roster of the staff. She is therefore allowed in, asking for Joe, her boss in the R&D department. Joe is nowhere to be found and does not answer his cell phone; he does not have an assistant, so Joanne goes from office to office to try to locate either her boss or where she has her desk and computer. Finally, she runs into Isabel, who participated in one of the interviews and who invites Joanne to a cup of coffee at the cafeteria. There, they run into Joe, who seemed to have forgotten all about Joanne's arrival. From then on, things began to get organised for Joanne, but what a disastrous first impression! It is common sense that new hires should be tactfully welcomed and taken care of, with their new office and project work organised.

Contrasting with this calamitous behaviour, Laura, another manager from the same firm, had the habit of having the new hire share her office for a few weeks in order to accelerate the information exchange and integration of new staff. Also, she organised a welcoming party for each new hire as a sign of welcome and to accelerate the introduction to the staff. Laura's colleagues congratulated her for her good practices, but none of them followed her example. Most human organisations do not provide an environment that encourages "borrowing with pride". This is due to insufficient engagement and little encouragement by the higher echelons of management to proactively spread best practices.

More broadly, corporations are generally perceived by young people, particularly in Europe, as treating their staff poorly, largely as a result of the financial tyranny to satisfy shareholders. As a result, much young talent refuses to be salaried and chooses to become freelance professionals. The Internet is a key enabler in this. If an employer only commits to try to make you "employable", to use a common phrase, then many youngsters prefer to take the risk for themselves and be free from the managerial morass. Complacent corporations do not seem to see this a serious problem (e.g. being deprived from having access to a lot good young talent).

The famous "innovation culture"

"Innovation culture" is a catchall phrase. It conveys the idea of risk taking, openness, curiosity, "benefit of the doubt" and a positive, inclusive attitude. It denotes an environment in which novel ways and ideas are welcome and flourish. Such an environment takes a long time to develop; it can be destroyed in a short time. It may be enhanced, but doing so takes sustained and consistent effort over a long time and with the support of top management. In what I call an "innovation journey", I work as an adviser with companies towards that objective.

The region's environment has a role to play. There is the glamourous, much-talked-about Silicon Valley. There is also the region around Cambridge, UK. As indicated, a combination of an ethos of trust, a few powerful role models of successful professors-entrepreneurs and a first-class scientific and technical university, the so-called "Cambridge phenomenon" started with the St John's Innovation Centre in 1987. It developed over a period of 40 years. In 2018, a region in a 30-km radius from Cambridge is home to 4500 firms employing close to 80,000 people. This indicates that the average size of the firms is small. A rare company, the designer of chips ARM, grew to more than 5,000 employees in 2018. It was bought in 2016 by the Japanese company Softbank, for more than £23 billion.

In the 1990s, the company 3M was mentioned as having an "innovation culture". No single fact or policy could be taken as the cause for this. In innovation, as for many managerial matters, there is no panacea, as discussed later.

All policies must support innovation

These days, when asked "what is the most innovative company in the world?" executives are likely to answer "Google". As the largest advertising firm in the world, this company has "deep pockets" and plays with numerous developments; many of them fail, as documented on the Web.[9] The firm Tencent in Shenzhen in the ultimate Internet country, China, is the upcoming leader in this area.

In innovative firms, ways of doing things, practices and policies, incentives, etc., all must be "aligned" to support an innovation-friendly climate. It starts with selecting the new hires. In order to attract more entrepreneurial candidates, a corporation may create an incubator for start-ups. British Telecom did just this, with its "Brightstar" incubator, in Ipswich. Generating and maintaining an "innovative culture" importantly includes personnel policies, rewards and incentives, rules for promotion, etc. Every element must be evaluated and fine-tuned so as to favour innovation. China as a country is obsessed with achieving this at the national, provincial and municipality levels (Soiz, 2017; Haour and von Zedtwitz, 2016). This contributes to accelerate the rapid progress of China towards becoming a main source of innovations for the world.

The walk-around manager

We have seen that technical knowledge workers must deal with the stress of uncertainty. Indeed, there is also considerable uncertainty in the business side of the firm – more than ever in these times of rapid change and global competition. In addition, however, leaders of innovation projects must blaze the trail and face uncertainty in the technical realm.

This situation requires that the direct managers show empathy to the staff. It helps if the manager has been a researcher in the past, preferably a "master of the craft". A non-technical professional is unlikely to be respected by technical knowledge workers over the long term. A positive policy is to rotate the R&D manager to a business job before coming back to the R&D function. Empathy is not enough. The direct manager must be following the progress of the project and bring a positive contribution, with comments and suggestions, in order to help project leaders accelerate the transition towards the markets. This involves suggesting colleagues make use of appropriate publications or conferences, which would help the project leader.

These requirements point to the fact that first-line managers must have daily interaction with project managers. This "walk-around management" is most appropriate to lead and motivate technical knowledge workers. Indeed, one dimension of this perspective is for managers to act as coaches, as discussed next.

Managers-coaches develop project leaders

One widespread scarcity found in companies is the lack of effective leaders of innovation projects. This is unfortunate, since the success of certain projects is key to the well-being of the firm. Developing project leaders requires commitment over the long term, sustained effort and timely rotations, etc. All these things are not well done in our short-term, financially driven corporations. What is needed is that project managers are "mini CEOs" (i.e. individuals with general management capabilities). This is even more acutely needed, as projects increasingly involve many different actors, as discussed later.

As indicated earlier, management often hesitates to stop projects. The result is that companies have too many innovation projects under way. This leaves the real key projects with insufficient resources and managerial "muscle". Furthermore, in recent years, the complexity of innovation projects has dramatically increased, as they must now gather several actors. Figure 20.2 shows the historical trend.

In the OECD countries, at the end of WWII, innovation was centred on science and technology, as implied by the phrase "technology push". At that time corporate laboratories were located "in the woods", away from manufacturing and from customers. Inspiration came from the breakthroughs of an all-powerful science: radar, jet engine and rockets, nuclear energy, advanced materials, etc.

Circa 1960, "marketing" appeared *en force*. Offerings had to satisfy customers in competitive markets. This demanded a more concerted, broadly based effort; hence the multi-functional

The crucial human factor in innovation

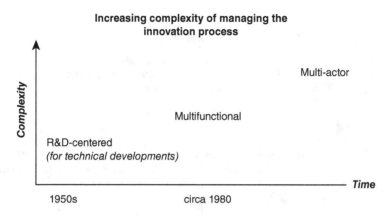

Figure 20.2 Increasing complexity of managing the innovation process

innovation projects. These involved primarily R&D, manufacturing and marketing. It was – and still is – difficult to operate true multi-functional activities. In fact, the innovation process really involves all parts of the firm, including the top executives and the board.

Because of acute competition and the need to be faster, in the late 1980s, it became necessary to increasingly involve partners external to the firm: other companies, SMEs, start-ups, universities and public research laboratories. This was initiated particularly in the area of mobile telecommunications and information and communication technologies (ICT). This is part of what is sometimes called "open innovation", as though innovation had ever been closed. This requires extensive transfer of technology and knowledge, which is a complex process, as will be discussed in the next section. Multi-actor innovation projects constitute an element of the "distributed innovation" approach, first described by Haour (2004) and illustrated in Figure 20.3.

This approach puts the entrepreneurial spirit of the staff in the centre of the firm, that is, a strong orientation towards the market in order to develop so-called "high impact offerings". This means that by proactively anticipating customers, the company comes up with offerings that are differentiating, and, it is hoped, commanding higher prices as a result, as well as slower price erosion. What is sought in this approach is not cheaper, but more *effective*, innovations. Such *high-impact offerings* are defined in the course of internal workshops and mobilising the company staff, who is the best and most knowledgeable to do the job when properly motivated and led. This involves a dynamic of workshops and conversations across various functions of the firm, effectively "facilitated" by managers or the staff. Indeed, a firm should embark on such a process only occasionally (every few years, or so), or it may involve one or two business units. Otherwise, the firm may be "excessively stimulated". In this process, the human factor is indeed key.

As already emphasised, companies lack effective leaders of innovation projects. As the latter increasingly become *multi-actor*, the situation grows even worse. Such leaders require a good knowledge of technical matters, must be business/market literate and good with people in multi-cultural settings. It takes a long time, as well as sustained effort, to develop such profiles of "mini CEOs". Part of their development should include short-term assignments in various functions and locations of the firm. To be effective, this "short-term expatriation" must be carefully prepared by managers on the sending and receiving sides of the traineeship. A good example is the Swiss company Bühler, producer of machinery for the food industry. This company is committed to running an effective international apprentice programme.

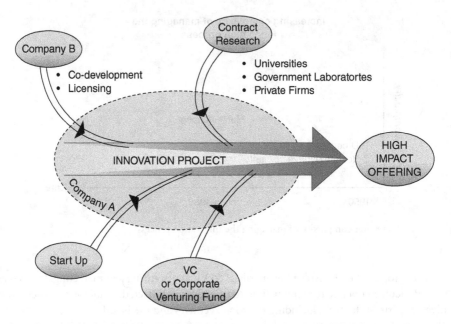

Figure 20.3 Entrepreneurial development of the offering draws on sources of technology distributed inside and outside the firm

The low attention of management for the development of staff beyond the traditional executive development, as well as the high turnover of employees, runs against achieving such long-term development. It is unfortunate, because effective leaders of multi-actor projects are difficult to replicate, giving the firm a clear competitive advantage. An exception is constituted by Japan, where lifetime employment is still largely the rule in large corporations, thus allowing long-term development of project leaders, including their wide rotation in various parts of the firm.

The role of top management in the human factor is candidly described in the book *Science Lessons*, by Gordon Binder (2008), former CEO of the biotech company Amgen. The author draws on his experience to explain his commitment and actions towards building effective teams, as well as hiring and retaining talented people. He also stresses the importance of the company's values and to "walking the talk" about them every day.

We now turn to an element of technical innovations, which consists of transferring knowledge and technology from one institution/public laboratory to a private company, with the objective of enhancing its competitiveness and creating new activities and jobs. In this activity also, much of the success much depends upon the talent and motivation of the staff.

The people-centric process of technology transfer

One vehicle for technical innovation is to transform the results of research carried out in universities or public laboratories into new, job-creating activities. Going from scientific results to business constitutes an extremely complex journey. It requires an understanding of business and markets, in addition to mastering the implications of technical intricacies and IP issues, not to mention the people aspects. In fact, it is one of the most complex processes on earth (Haour and Miéville, 2011).

How central the human factor is in the art of technology transfer is illustrated by the difficulty in turning public laboratories into customer-oriented contract research. Between the 1940s and the late 1980s, the Atomic Energy Research Establishment (AERE) of Harwell, south of Oxford, was the main centre for nuclear research in the UK. At that time, it was decided to open the activities to external clients and the projects appropriately concentrated on R&D/consulting in the environmental sciences. This turned out to be a very challenging transition, as the professionals concerned did not have the skills or the motivation to present their capabilities in ways that would attract firms' funding. Many engineers left until the staff was reduced to fraction of what it was. The decision was then made to invest and turn the site into an innovation centre, with various laboratories and technical activities. In 2012, what was left of AEA was sold to Ricardo, a consulting engineering firm with 2,900 professionals, to become Ricardo – AEA, centred on environmental technologies.

Other examples of this difficult transition are CSIR in both South Africa and India. In the latter case, in the late 1980s, a sustained attempt was made to make government laboratories more relevant to industry and society as a whole. It was hoped that the various laboratories would develop collaborative work and licensing activity with firms, such as Tata or Reliance. In spite of the considerable energy deployed, this transformation did not take place, again, as a result of the staff's insufficient skills and motivation to move down that road. In the best of circumstances, such a transition takes more than five years, such as in the case of CSIR in South Africa.

As a result of the complex nature of the technology transfer process, but also because universities and firms constitute two very different worlds – as it should be, such collaborations between these two worlds are not as extensive and effective as they could be. However, there exists a very broad range of activities connecting these two worlds, as illustrated in Figure 20.4.

The most powerful vehicle for technology transfer is through people (i.e. the hiring of university graduates by firms). As is often said, transfer is best done by moving people. Historically, examples include the forceful transfer of experts in porcelain making from Meissen, near Dresden, to Berlin by Frederick the Great in 1756. The next sections look at the three main channels for technology/knowledge transfer: collaborative research, licensing and spinning out new companies.

University-firm collaborative research

A key channel for a firm to tap into expertise available in universities is to fund R&D projects carried out by a team from that university. Companies use this vehicle more or less intensively. A company like Hewlett Packard routinely has more than 100 collaborations in place with universities; quite a few of these involve Chinese universities. Pharmaceutical companies are practising it the most, because they need to complement their own unproductive drug development pipeline by accessing new molecules and devices found in universities' medical research programmes.

In contrast, SMEs do not use university collaboration much. This is particularly the case in Switzerland. In an attempt to remedy this situation, the Swiss government has created a chain of higher schools (*hautes ecoles*), who are especially tasked to engage with SMEs in order to help them become more competitive over the long term. Again, as stated elsewhere, "helping" SMEs develop their activity by better leveraging global markets is the safest way to create jobs back home.

Research directly funded by firms in universities/public laboratories represents a mere 7 percent of the total research budget in the best research-intensive universities, as shown by the work carried out by the OECD in Paris (2017). Some universities wrongly include in the numbers of

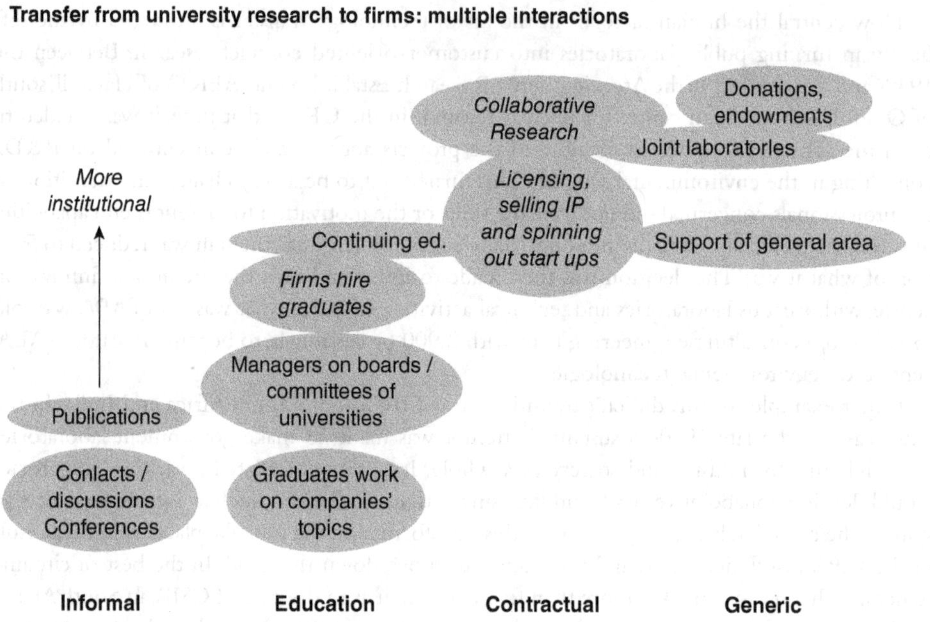

Transfer from university research to firms: multiple interactions

Figure 20.4 Firms engage with universities in many different ways

external funding the matching public monies provided by government grants. The lion's share (93 percent) of university research is funded with taxpayers' money.

Collaborative work

Most frequently, collaborative research is carried out on a one-to-one basis. Often, the technology transfer office (TTO) is putting the two parties in contact; its role of facilitation, as a "middle person", must not be in the way of both sides having a productive dialogue. This will be further discussed later.

The firm and the university team must spend enough time together discussing the issues and the proposed work to address the issue so that they establish a good understanding concerning the business goal, as well as the risks attached to the proposed project. Given that business and university constitute two different worlds, it is important to spend enough time on that phase. This considerably reduces the risks of misunderstandings, thus increasing the chances of success of the project. In the course of these discussions, both parties often *redefine* the issue and objectives as a result of fresh input provided by these conversations. The proposal also results from these discussions. A corresponding contract spells out intellectual property rights, budget and payments, and other administrative matters.

Once the contract is signed and the project begins, it is important that, following the relatively intense period of negotiations, both parties do not excessively reduce their interaction, as it so often happens. The project manager following up on the progress of the work, involving abundant and frequent two-way communication with the client, will avoid many subsequent disappointments and pitfalls. One of the many qualities of a good project manager is that ability to effectively communicate in a timely way.

On the other hand, several firms may join together in funding a project in a university or research lab. Such "multi-client projects" are practised by contract research organisations, such as

Battelle, to investigate a common issue. In this way, the cost of the R&D programme is shared among the participating firms. It may be a good way of assessing the merits of a new process, such as 3D printing or blockchain, for example. If patent material is developed in the course of the project, great care must be taken at the proposal/contractual stage to clearly define the IP rights of each participant. A type of multi-lateral project is carried out as part of the Horizon 2020 programme of the European Union, as discussed earlier, pointing out that such projects are the world's most widely diverse.

Students in firms

Involving graduate students in the R&D activities of a firm constitutes another channel for transferring knowledge and technology. As an example, each year, the German firm Bosch invites roughly 100 students to come to work as trainees in the company. During this period, they are guided so as to provide an effective contribution.

SMEs may well benefit from such internships. Several countries (Holland, Singapore and Switzerland, for example) have instituted *innovation vouchers* in order to jumpstart such collaborations. Small amounts of money (less than 10,000 euros) are put at the disposal of the firm on the basis of a proposal involving work to be carried out by a graduate student. The process is non-bureaucratic and typically Internet-based. Oftentimes, the student is hired by the SME.

Collaboration in non-technical areas

Firms rarely tap into university knowledge in non-technical areas. This is somewhat surprising, since so much of business success depends upon societal, non-business issues, and this is more and more so. Social sciences, such as anthropology and sociology, may well help better understand certain areas, such as the acceptance of new technologies or the person–machine interface. Closer to traditional firms' need to "listen to the customers", *ethnographic marketing* attempts to monitor the behaviour of customers in their interaction with products. This is often at the origin of improved or new designs of the offerings by the firm.

When doing business in China, firms should have a reasonable knowledge of that country's history and culture, which the business partners will appreciate. Universities can provide such knowledge in the course of appropriate educational programmes for managers.

Summary on collaborative R&D

Indeed, the primary missions of universities are excellence in teaching and excellence in research. By transferring their knowledge and technology to firms, however, universities fulfil an additional mission while providing precious input to society. Furthermore, resulting interactions with firms provide healthy stimulation and inputs to university personnel. In fact, it is generally accepted that the better universities are also those which are most active in collaborating with the private sector.

As mentioned, SMEs do not benefit enough from such collaborations. Partly because they are less well prepared to make use of them, mainly due to the lack of understanding and people capabilities to transform technical ideas into useful activities and improvement of operations. In the United States, the small business industrial programme (SBIR) is often presented as a model to force collaboration/business dealings with SMEs. In China, the Torch programme is specifically designed for SMEs. Helping SMEs become more competitive and to better benefit from global trade and markets is probably the safest route for a country to create jobs. This is done with money, of course, but mainly by helping provide them with the proper skills and people, managerial practices and approaches. "Young retirees" may provide such contribution.

Licensing

Research carried out in universities and public laboratories often lead to the filing and sometimes granting of a patent. The strength of the patent is its resilience in defeating the challenge from another patent in a suit, but mainly as the basis for creating new activities and commercial applications. The vehicle for the transfer is patent-based licensing.

Successful licensing demands good knowledge of the industry and of the markets, as well as an ability to dialogue with managers in order to explain the contribution of the contemplated deal. This also requires knowledge of the licensing "mechanics".

Professional associations such as the Association of European Science & Technology Transfer Professionals (ASTP-Proton) and the Association of University Technology Managers (AUTM) in the United States group practitioners in this area. More generally, the Licensing Executives Society (LES), headquartered in London, has members in many countries who regularly meet in order to facilitate exchanges and contacts.

The world's total licensing activity (down payments and royalties) represents more than 200 billion euros per year. The United States has the largest share – more than a third. Paralleling the growth of trade and exchanges, this number has grown in recent decades. There are several years between the granting of a patent and the ramping up of royalties derived from it. The share of university licensing represents a small percentage the total, but is not an insignificant amount.

Having a strong patent constitutes a prerequisite. The rights and ownership of the patent must be clear and straightforward. Otherwise, potential investors will not engage in a negotiation. In the United States, in 1981, the Bayh-Dole Act simplified matters by entrusting the university with the ownership of patents derived in the course of publicly funded research. Universities may then sell rights on the patents in an exclusive or non-exclusive way.

In the (usual) case of a product patent, many elements must be dealt with, starting with scouting for the appropriate company prospect. Then, preparation must be done prior to conducting negotiations on the size of the market concerned, the impact of the innovation proposed, the field of use, the geography concerned, the royalty rate, etc.

University licensing offices must not aim at maximising revenues from licensing deals. They should license to the firm that offers the most chances to best develop its activities as a result of the license. Job and value creation are the criteria for success of the TTO. Indeed, close to 90 percent of university licensing offices do not generate enough revenues to cover their expenses. This should be no problem, as long as the impact to society is substantial.

There are occasional large licensing deals, usually in the life sciences sector. These multi-million "blockbusters" reported in the media give the impression that university licensing is a gold mine. It is, but only for a very small number of deals per year.

University spin-offs

Creating a start-up company constitutes the third channel to bring firms the results of research carried out in universities and public laboratories. This is the most difficult and risky path. All over the world, whether in Cambridge, UK, or in the "glamorous" Silicon Valley, success rates are similar: only 25 percent of technical start-ups survive after five years. Making the transition from technical work to a successful company is highly difficult and complex. Figure 20.5 illustrates the steps along this path. Each step requires a highly competent and up-to-date advisory council.

Spinning out a technical start up company

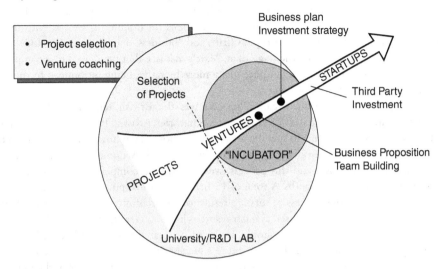

Figure 20.5 Steps in spinning off a technical start-up company

Launching a start-up

The origin of a technical venture is in the laboratories. Typically, university staff is not very knowledgeable about markets and business or management. Therefore, forming a new venture most likely requires a third party be involved who brings the relevant commercial knowledge. Projects carried out there must be steered towards commercial applications. The ventures presenting the most potential are selected by a board of persons familiar with the technical and business aspects of the ventures.

Alumni of the universities may provide such know-how. For example, this is the case of Imperial Innovations in London. This outfit is somewhat unique, in that it is an incubator/accelerator listed on the London Stock Exchange; it concentrates on making money via spinning firms emanating from Imperial College's research, but also from other sources in order to have a sufficiently abundant deal flow.

A key factor for the success of the venture is the quality of its team. Entrepreneurs are like "babies in the wood"; they need advice, guidance, suggestions and, most importantly, they need to be challenged with difficult questions. What is really distinctive in your offering? What is the competition to your approach ? How robust is your business model? How about the intellectual property aspects? Also, business contacts and referrals are suggested to the team. Venture capitalists (VCs) primarily look at the quality of the team, and, when they invest in the venture, contribute business help and support to that team. This is what is called "smart money". Again here, the human factor is a dominating element.

This "coaching" activity is usually done in an "incubator", which aims at accelerating the launch and development of the venture. The value of an incubator is not in the building, laboratories and reception desk. It is in this business coaching and in the learning taking place among the various entrepreneurial teams hosted in the incubator. Indeed, these contacts, as well as discussion forums and informal meetings, must be prompted, catalysed and organised by the coaches.

Over several months, this "on-demand" coaching progresses from managerial issues, value proposition, business model, hiring new staff and IP strategy to looking for financing. The coach helps with formulating the business plan and the requests for funding, as well as with specific sources of financing, such as venture capital firms and "business angels". It may include public funding. The start-up may reach the stage of an "exit", that is, either being sold to a company in a trade sale or, more cumbersome but potentially more lucrative, being introduced to the stock exchange via an initial public offering (IPO).

An example of such a value-creation process was the British Telecom's "Brightstar" in Ipswich, UK. Attached to one of BT's corporate laboratories, Adastral Park, it aimed at exploiting the know-how and patents in specific areas of this laboratory, whose staff was ready to take the challenge to transition from researchers to entrepreneurs. A number of coaches, knowledgeable about the business and this process, were hired to accompany the teams along this transition over a period of months. A total of 15 firms were thus spun off from the laboratory.

Because of the arduous process of turning results of research into commercially viable ventures, the spin-off route must be used as a last resort, when it is clear that it offers the best route for creating value. Also, the company should not be incorporated too early. A key requirement is to have a quality team eager to make the venture a success. If not, licensing out, or collaborative research, must be preferred, and a licensing deal often constitutes the link between the university and the new venture, as the start-up is a licensee of the university.

Universities' business schools should apply their expertise to the commercialisation of knowledge and technology. Indeed, it is not enough to launch start-ups; it is important for them to *grow*. In this area, the United States is performing well, with numerous ICT firms, such as Microsoft, Oracle, Cisco and eBay having rapidly grown to become dominant actors in their industries. China is truly outstanding in its ability to rapidly grow companies. In contrast, Europe's young companies seem to have what this author calls the "Peter Pan syndrome".

China's innovation is relentlessly people-centric

China is rapidly becoming a major source of innovations for the world (Haour and von Zedtwitz, 2016). Its entrepreneurial energy and agility, as well as its relentless business and customer orientation, are remarkable. Chinese entrepreneurs have an uncanny ability to extract value from an activity. Also, the support from the public sector for innovation and entrepreneurship is unfailing at the national, provincial and municipal levels. The large Chinese market, which is highly competitive and demanding, provides a very formative environment for young ventures.

Many practices and policies show that China sharply realises that talent and energy are central to the success of innovation. A first indication is the great effort put in attracting and welcoming the returnees from outside China (about 400,000 each year). Science parks, incubators and business accelerators throw open their arms to them, with staff, guidance, subsidies, tax breaks and services. Second the "Thousand Talent Programme" is a government programme to attract experts in various areas, especially in fields where China has ambitious plans but few professionals, such as the aircraft industry and its maker of civilian planes, COMAC. Third, the extremely vibrant scene is in Shenzhen, where start-ups, SMEs and large firms alike, such as Tencent, Huawei and Foxconn, collaborate and do business alongside the dynamic "makers" movement.

In addition, China puts a lot of attention on education, which demands many improvements, as is the case in numerous countries. There is a strong effort to boost existing universities, as well as to create new ones.

Conclusion on the crucial human factor in innovation

Innovation is not about quantity of input, but about *effectiveness* of output. The amount of R&D investments only constitutes a rough measure of the level of innovation of a firm, or of a country. Companies may invest large budgets and have no useful outcome except for the knowledge acquired in the course of failed projects, which will be useful for the next one. The "innovation crisis" in the pharmaceutical industry illustrates this. Increasing investments are made for drug development, while the number of authorised drugs has been decreasing in recent years.

Ultimately, innovation is a people-centric process. The key determinants of the effectiveness of the innovation process are the talent and the motivation of the people involved. This constitutes the "crucial human factor". To fully focus on the individuals, management must truly engage with technical knowledge workers.

A similar challenge is encountered in a specific element of the innovation process, that is, the transfer of technology/knowledge to turn the results of university research into new activities and jobs. There also, the success of universities' TTOs is predicated upon the quality and competency of its staff along several dimensions. These include technical literacy, business sense and market knowledge, ability to communicate in both "techno speak" and "business speak", and the ease in handling these three channels of technology commercialisation. This means that TTOs must be carefully staffed with sophisticated professionals. Having well understood this, Switzerland acted accordingly and reached the top place in the world for effectiveness in technology transfer in less than 15 years (Haour and Miéville, 2011).

In addition to being very carefully selected, such professionals must receive timely training in IP and technology commercialisation. Specialised, short courses, combined with *apprenticeships*, must be used to accelerate the development of the staff (EPO, 2017).[10] Young TTO officers should occasionally spend time as trainees, just like when they were students. By learning about specific cases from experienced colleagues, they enrich their experience, as well as their confidence to deal with future situations and to communicate with colleagues effectively. A comprehensive manual on technology licensing is given by Cannady (2013).

In our times of financial tyranny, management tends to lose the common-sense notion that low motivation among staff represents a huge cost. Firms focus attention on processes and practices supposed to bring profits, but do not properly consider the crucial human factor. Corporations talk about "brand equity" but no equivalent attention is brought to "staff equity". In listed companies, managers are often *not really engaged* with the staff. They operate in a world of financial "short termism". Hopefully, Chinese companies will not fall in this trap. Family business, private equity firms (i.e. non-listed) and cooperative companies are more detached from such short-term financial pressures, and, as a result, they show more attention to the human factor.

Concerning the process of innovation, there are numerous tools and practices and consultants' recipes pretending to boost its effectiveness. More important than such "old wine in new bottles" is to focus on enhancing the contribution of *individuals*, as well as their ability to work with colleagues effectively. Their talent, motivation and energy are the ingredients that allow innovation to flourish. Through true and sustained attention to these factors, managers bring considerable value to their firm by carefully identifying, selecting, retaining, developing and motivating staff. This time-consuming task demands considerable engagement, while maintaining *trust*. Managers must *take the time* to carry out this task with full commitment.

Notes

1. www.ukspa.org.uk/members/sjic
2. www.oecd.org/site/cfecpr/EC-OECD%20Entrepreneurial%20Universities%20Framework.pdf
3. https://euipo.europa.eu/ohimportal/documents/11370/71142/The+Global+Innovation+Index+2014
4. www.ecowatch.com/plastic-ban-uk-2534089763.html
5. www.history.com/topics/world-war-ii/bombing-of-hiroshima-and-nagasaki. February 2018.
6. *On the Swatch* (checked on February 26, 2018) www.bloomberg.com/news/articles/2017-11-21/how-swatch-started-a-revolution-history-of-fashion-watches.
7. Dr. Moeller, Gerald. private communication.
8. http://onlinelibrary.wiley.com/doi/10.1111/fima.12205/pdf, on line as of January 29, 2018.
9. https://computer.howstuffworks.com/10-failed-google-projects.htm, February 18, 2018.
10. Courses for TTO staff, from ASTP-Proton. www.astp-proton.eu/events/training-courses-2/

References

Binder, Gordon (2008). *Science lessons*. Cambridge, MA: Harvard University Press.
Cannady, Cynthia (2013). *Technology licensing & development agreements*. Oxford: Oxford University Press.
Christina, Mariette di (2012). Human factor in innovation. *Scientific American*, 3017(6), December.
EPO (2017). *Intellectual property course design manual*. European Patent Academy.
Haour, Georges (2004). *Resolving the innovation paradox*. London: Palgrave Macmillan.
Haour, Georges and Miéville, Laurent (2011). *From science to business*, London: Palgrave Macmillan. www.sciencetobusiness.ch
Haour, Georges and von Zedtwitz, Max (2016). *Created in China – how China is becoming a global innovator*. London: Bloomsbury.
Jung, Carl G. (1968). *Der Mensch und seine Symbole*. Olten: Walter Verlag.
Koestler, Arthur (2012). *The sleepwalkers* (first published in 1959). Penguin Arkana.
Kuhn, Thomas (1962). *The structure of scientific revolutions*. Chicago: University of Chicago Press.
Livesay, Howard (1996). Human factors in the innovation process. *Technovation*, 16(4), 173–186.
OECD (2017). *R&D statistics*. Paris: OECD.
Soiz, Ligang (2017). *China's new sources of economic growth: human capital, innovation and technological change*. Australian University Press.

PART IV

Institutions and norms for innovation management

21
INSTITUTIONAL DESIGN OF INNOVATION TOWARDS THE 'ACTIVE INNOVATION PARADIGM'

Dirk Meissner

The understanding of innovation and its overall emergence has changed considerably over the years. Traditionally innovation has been viewed as the 'implementation of a new or significantly improved product (good or service), or process, a new marketing method, or a new organizational method in business practices, workplace organization or external relations'. (OECD, Eurostat, 2005). Innovation practice meanwhile shows that innovation is by nature a value-free term and comprehensively covers the whole spectrum of activities from discovery to first-time practical application of new knowledge. Moreover, innovation aims to fulfill recipients' requirements and goals in a new way, and it stresses that risk and uncertainty are inherent at all stages of innovation processes. This understanding has evolved from innovation concepts, models of innovation and innovation processes over decades (for example, Carlsson, Jacobsson, Holmen, and Rickne, 2002; Godin, 2006).

Meanwhile, there is a broad range of models for innovation processes. All these models share a common understanding that innovation activities can broadly be described and visualized in process models. Some models describe the life cycle of innovation by an S-shaped logistic function, which consists of three separate phases reflecting the application phases of its development: emergence, growth and maturity (Howard and Guile, 1992; Mitrova, Kulagin, Grushevenko, and Grushevenko, 2015; Perani and Sirilli, 2008). Other concepts emphasize the characteristics of innovation, which are defined according to innovation development stages, that is, Maidique (1980) distinguishes the recognition of the invention, development, realization and distribution as phases of the innovation process. In general, linear models of innovation distinguish the discovery (invention), the definition of possible spheres of applications of the results of innovation, its development, design and use as phases of the innovation process (see for example Niosi, 1999; Godin, 2006; Meissner, 2015; Carayannis, Meissner, and Edelkina, 2015 for a simplistic description of innovation processes).

The evolving understanding of innovation as a *process* of activities raises new challenges to innovators and the governance of innovation activities. Although innovation is commonly regarded as the outcome of a process of activities, these are by no means always succeeding in a linear shape, but rather involve several feedback loops. Hence, typical activities and steps are common for many innovation projects, but the uncertainty of achieving results and finishing an activity with the required quality forces innovators to solicit feedback between the activities in order to improve the final solution. These challenges are expressed in the increasing complexity of innovations, which are in turn also determined by the complexity of the surrounding framework conditions. Consequently, the complexity – expressed by the number of information sources, knowledge and application fields for innovation – is rising. In this light, innovators need to analyze and process more information for the same purpose (Carayannis and Campbell, 2011; Carayannis and Turner, 2006; Gokhberg, Kuznetsova, and Roud, 2010; Gault, 2009; Godin, 2010).

Furthermore until recently innovation was considered a process or a sequence of activities and steps, but the surrounding factors such as company culture for innovation and the meaning of human resources for innovation were only partially reflected. The latter is especially relevant for the complexity, which requires unorthodox thinking and must be socially accepted to succeed. Hence, innovation includes new technological, economic, organizational and social solutions, which are not necessarily marketable in an economic sense with direct monetary impact but are applied and used.

The rise of the open innovation paradigm clearly goes beyond the intensification of business R&D internationalization, because innovation is more than R&D, and more opened up processes entail crossing more than geographical borders but also institutional and disciplinary ones. Led by multinational companies, innovation now involves multiple innovation actors, including smaller firms, public research, suppliers and customers. It challenges the adaptiveness of market actors, which must reinvent their business model to survive an increasingly knowledge-based global competition. But it challenges even more corporate management traditional approaches, and instruments may not be fully effective in maximizing benefits from the globalization of innovation markets and networks. The single most important response should be offensive, consisting of the promotion of all forms of international linkages as a way to strengthen the company's innovation ecosystem, with a particular attention to external linkages. Another important objective should be to care even more about the quality of internal framework conditions for innovation, including appropriate specialized infrastructures supporting and servicing innovation, such as central corporate service units, in order to be able to retain or attract increasingly mobile talented people.

In this light governance of innovation becomes an even more important crucial asset of companies with the aim of strengthening economic performance by means of innovation (Tsai and Yang, 2013; Rubera and Kirca, 2012; Hansen, 2014). Furthermore shareholders carefully monitor the company's innovation pipeline thus underlying activities to strengthen the output and economic impact from innovation-related investment. Thus, management is forced to align the corporate governance model continuously to meet shareholders' expectations while at the same time keep the balance with employee motivation.

Other major changes in the innovation activities of companies are switching the focus away from pure product/service innovation towards a more integrated business model innovation, which implies that innovation is more than the product or process in its purest sense; rather, it is accompanied by services and modeled around a business itself. Thus, more attention is given to the overall lifetime of an innovation in the company's portfolio of technologies and innovation, and more freedom to managing these is given.

Governance of innovation

Governance models for innovation have changed over time in line with the development and adjustment of innovation process models. Innovation process models, however, can hardly do more than describe the governance scheme applied within a company, including all different interfaces. Overall, the management adage that 'structure follows strategy' remains in place and valid; for example, a company's organizational model needs to be aligned to allow implementation of strategic decisions. Still it's not about organizational structures only but also about the corporate company cultural dimension and related management models to create and maintain innovativeness. Furthermore, companies are challenged in finding appropriate solutions for the missions, tasks, duties and powers of innovation management inside the company, especially in light of their embeddedness in company operations. When developing a powerful innovation management (IM) scheme, companies are challenged with three overarching questions (Figure 21.1):

- How innovative does the company/Strategic Business Unit (SBU) have to be?
- How efficient is IM in supporting the innovation process?
- Where does IM need to improve?

The ongoing public debate about innovation inherits the danger that companies consider innovation important and develop responses to increasing innovativeness many times over. This obvious reaction to environment, however, might lead to developing and implementing ever different concepts which aren't necessarily in line with the actual challenges the respective company faces. Therefore, in the first instance companies need to find a response to the underlying question *how innovative they need to be*. This requires a profound understanding of the customer and market requirements towards innovation in all facets, for example, frequency of innovation, scope and shape, opportunities and benefits arising from innovation and expected contributions from IM to the company. These are essential to bear in mind when it comes to fine-tuning the company's IM organization and the subsequent processes. The second dimension relates to *determining the current IM performance*, namely the efficiency of IM and the subsequent processes implemented. IM performance measurement is an absolute necessity for companies to employ, but it's also one of the most sensitive and delicate undertakings to develop and implement. The reason is found in the nature of innovation activities, which require substantial human resource investment in the shape of codified and tacit knowledge and social skills. Tacit knowledge and social skills are important assets for teamwork, and it's usually thought that company employees possess such sufficiently. But in order to assess IM performance these skills need to be codified

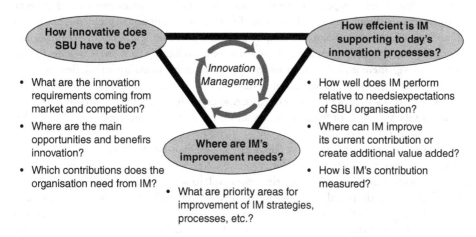

Figure 21.1   Key issues for determining the company's innovation management role

and included in respective indicators, which has been a challenge until recently. Finding appropriate responses to assessing the *efficiency of IM supporting the innovation process* appears equally challenging. This refers especially to assessing the IM performance relative to needs and detecting respective improvement fields and value creation which underlie IM improvement and actions.

These simplistic approaches cannot be treated as real models of the innovation process, but rather as a schematic description. Although genuine models that are more complex were developed in the scientific literature in the second half of the 20th and the early 21st centuries, these models remain idealistic descriptions of innovation generation. Such process models have certain implications for the organization of innovation in companies, research institutes and engineering companies; however, they will change each time a new innovation project is started. One can also argue that there is in fact no definite innovation project, but rather overlapping activities of different kinds and intensities, which form the basis for the next generation of innovation. It is evident that a significant share of the innovation management literature describes the innovation process as somewhat linear, especially in the early works (Usher, 1954, 1955) but also in more recent papers (Kamal, 2006; Baregheh, Rowley, and Sambrook, 2009). The full overview of innovation process models is shown by Kotsemir and Meissner (2013).

The most recent open innovation model emerged when Chesbrough (2003a, 2003b) postulated the open innovation paradigm, which highlights the use of purposive inflows and outflows of knowledge to accelerate internal innovation and expand the markets for external use of innovation, respectively. It assumes that firms can and should use external ideas as well as internal ideas and internal and external paths to market, as they look to advance their technology (Chesbrough, 2006). Innovations are no longer 'just' seen as a process, involving various functions. Rather, it is explained by the participation of a number of different entities, including suppliers, public R&D facilities and (business) external R&D facilities, as well as customers with varying degrees of intensity

Governing innovation under the open innovation paradigm

The management of innovation not only covers traditional methods and instruments of R&D management but strongly emphasizes output/result orientation, regardless of place of generation and origin of innovation. Innovation management hence is the effective and efficient generation of knowledge and competences required to meet customers' requirements and expectations with new or slightly modified solutions for known or unknown problems, challenges, needs and/or requirements. Solutions include products, processes and services, be they either in a commercial or noncommercial sense, as a way of contributing to societal welfare. Second innovation management includes functions to support the implementation of solutions to application in a wide sense be it production introduction, marketing, after-sales services, etc. Hence innovation management is the planning organization controlling and monitoring of innovation processes and the provision of framework conditions conducive to innovation, both internal to the organization and external.

Traditional innovation management puts a special emphasis on the R&D management process as the most important determinant of innovation. Although different sources of innovation such as competitors analysis customer orientation and, to some extent, external collaboration with suppliers, competitors and the public research base is integral to these models, the management of the interfaces to these sources and competences is not stressed. With the occurrence of open innovation, the management process thus is characterized by a strong alignment of institutional (e.g. usually company) internal innovation strategies with external partners and sources.

Figure 21.2 shows a simplified innovation management process highlighting the challenges arising from open innovation.

The basic principles of the innovation management process have not changed considerably over the last decades. R&D still plays the major, if not the utmost, role in the overall process. What has changed and continues to change is the role and meaning of different sources for innovation and the increasing importance of various exploitation paths. It follows that especially the management of interfaces – both company internal interfaces between different departments and functions and interfaces to external organizations – becomes crucial. Additionally shareholder expectations towards the company's overall performance and innovation pipeline especially continue to increase. From this it's obvious that the innovation process takes a more dynamic form involving multiple actors. Though R&D remains one crucial element of the overall process, other subprocess became more and more important and prominent.

Other major changes in companies' innovation activities are a shifting focus away from pure product/service innovation towards a more integrated business model innovation. That implies that innovation is more than the product or process in its narrow sense; rather, it's accompanied by services and modeled around a business itself. Thus, more attention is given to the overall lifetime of an innovation in the company's portfolio of technologies and innovation, and more freedom to managing these is given. As a result, alternative ways to do business with innovation are increasingly important and considered.

Despite the original function of intellectual property schemes as a tool for protecting inventions and markets, open IP practices are more and more the industry standard in the sense that

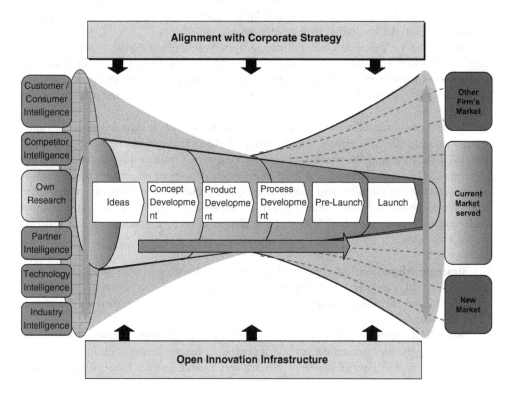

Figure 21.2 Company innovation management in the light of open innovation

open standards are becoming an issue not only in the software industry but in many other industries. Moreover complementary IP (e.g. trademarks, design utilities and trade secrets) are gaining importance in addition to patents and licenses, thus resulting in an increasing complexity of IP management. Also the contribution of the overall IP portfolio of companies is explicitly appreciated by financial investors; thus, more sophisticated valuation standards and methodologies for intangible assets are required/requested.

In line with new business development strategies, companies increasingly either establish new internal venture capital funds or expand their existing venture capital activities which aim at developing promising internal research streams towards market activities and/or are used as strategic investments into upcoming young enterprises which are suited to complement the current product portfolio of the companies. In this respect corporate foresight studies of all types are being applied for emerging technology and detecting business potential as well as increasingly strategic in-licensing. Such tasks are typically being dealt with by internal business development and licensing units and 'search and evaluation' units. In this light selected technology partners are provided with early technology information so they can benefit in their early product development cycles, and partnerships with nonsuppliers in collaborative research projects are searched for; hence, collaborative research is initiated in new fields of research but is still in the precompetitive phases. One major characteristic of such precompetitive R&D collaboration is the objects of cooperation – the majority of cooperation projects turn out to be focused on technology platforms or crosscutting technologies with multiple-application potential.

Eventually the attraction and keeping of talent is considered an ever more important issue for companies. Consequently, most companies are starting to enhance and intensify relationships with academic institutions, as well as designing human resources management and development programs to retain the key staff in their institutions.

Finally it can be concluded that the rise in open innovation still raises significant challenges to all actors. Thus far, the majority of companies are beginning to open their innovation processes towards many different partners and creating innovation networks. However, the big challenge of managing the interfaces between the different actors and sources remains unsolved.

The assumption that innovation equals more or less R&D leads to numerous concepts aiming at increasing the effectiveness and efficiency of R&D, thus generating more and better innovation and increasing shareholder value in the long term. Consequently, the long dominant focus on R&D activities has switched from an internally dominated orientation towards opening up screening and using external sources and capacities that are complementary and in some cases even a substitute for the existing internal competence base. Hence, leading innovators implemented different measures to meet the challenges of rising innovation process management complexity:

- **Strategic Alignment**: Missions of R&D are aligned with corporate strategy and business unit (BU) strategies. This alignment is done frequently – at least biannually. In this case, BU and corporate strategies are changing over time and are designed for continuous adjustment.
- **Inbound Increase:** Diverse access to the ideas of growth opportunities is secured by expanding the idea generation pool. Idea generation for innovation is no longer thought of as a company's internal challenge but includes a much broader range of external idea sources.

- **Effectiveness and Efficiency Increase:** Stock markets and shareholders expect effective and efficient innovation undertakings, which forces management to enhance the hit ratio based on business development capabilities and to streamline processes and interfaces.
- **Outbound Increase:** More attention is given to active commercialization of knowledge and technologies by screening and identifying cross-market opportunities and selling IP in different forms.
- **Open Innovation Infrastructure:** Opening the innovation activities challenges existing innovation monitoring and controlling, requiring new metrics and controlling tools but also an internal culture-related infrastructure that enables open innovation.

The mechanisms behind open innovation often follow similar structures. Measurement of the success and profitability of innovation is not focused on short-term immediate effects only but take a longer perspective. Hence, initiators are often employed in companies that leave enough flexibility to work on open innovation ideas (social science). These companies usually expect a return at a later stage. The rationale behind this is clearly a growing awareness of the meaning of and conditions for purely basic research activities, which by nature allow experiments and free thinking. Although it is widely accepted and expected that the public sector is in charge of financing such early-stage research in public research institutions and higher education institutions, the private sector actors (e.g. innovators) increasingly take the initiative to support these public institutions in many ways. Here companies developed a broad range of models encouraging links of internal innovation (R&D) departments with the pubic science base, including public-private partnerships and industrial PhD programs, among others.

Furthermore large companies often involve small companies in targeted product, process and service development, which allows companies to have a fresh look at their strategic intents, reducing their own risk and resources invested and receiving inspiration. Entrepreneurs increasingly build IP-protected add-on products based on the outcomes of open innovation–related cooperation. The results will further enlarge the spread of open innovation. That trend goes along with the changing behavior of large companies, which often provide a platform for commercial developments by themselves and others (e.g. industry-specific applications often provided by SMEs).

Open innovation remains a fashionable but still ill-defined term. Companies have been engaged in joint R&D efforts with external partners, such as customers, suppliers, universities and third-party companies, for several decades; thus, activities on open innovation have changed little in the last years; only collaborative research with customers has further increased, and in several cases 'triangular' partnerships are set in place with customers and universities. What is more important, however, is that usually few customers are selected for in-depth innovation relationships, and partnerships are built around areas of mutual interest. Often, companies would have not invested without the related customer request and commitment.

The company's focus is increasingly on businesses where technology is a differentiator and offers the opportunity to become a global market leader. Thus, R&D is mainly organized in decentralized structures built around these businesses and not around competencies. Overall technology management might follow a top-down or bottom-up strategy (strategy dimension), formal or informal management processes (process dimension), possess a dedicated infrastructure or networked approach (organization dimension) and dedicate funding significantly or limited from corporate funds (Figure 21.3).

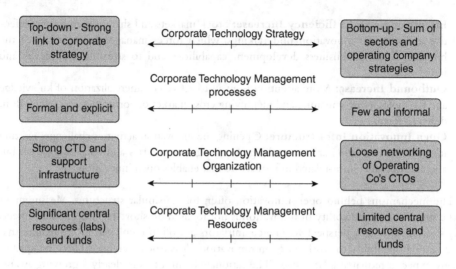

Figure 21.3 Characteristics of an innovation management organization

A significant proportion of the R&D budget is spent on growth (compared to expanding or defending the core) and on longer-term developments. In line with this development, several different paths of R&D can be observed:

1   **R&D with clear aim of business applications:** This part of R&D is in the first instance focused on internal resources with accompanying programs related to joint developments with customers and/or other external partners. Increasingly, the number of joint developments is considered one of the key performance indicators in R&D. Prior engagement into such joint development partners are assessed using standardized criteria in the selection process:

    •   Clear common technical objectives and diversity of opinions.
    •   Agreement on confidentiality and commercial targets. It is common for joint development partners to accept a limitation on exclusivity for up to few months in order to allow for higher investment on the leading partner side.
    •   Visibility in the customer organization at all levels to ensure consistency in case of changes in key relationship people.
    •   Common resources with budget and people. Quite often, the project manager is from the customer and the lead company will provide a dedicated front office engineer to ensure process moderation but also continuous collection of future customer needs.
    •   Complementary skills to build critical mass and reputation of the partner.
        The overall objective is to create a 'virtual circle' of long-term relationship and joint development. The process to start such collaboration is like a 'Trojan horse'. Regardless of a company's experience in joint developments, it's important to create excitement for the customer (e.g. propose ideas for breakthrough innovations) in the starting phase. Moreover projects are often started with modest developments resulting in overdelivery and thus building long-term relationships with engineers.

2   **R&D with the ambition to generate substantial innovation (radical):** This type of R&D is mainly internally driven with limited external support. Such support refers to

cooperation with leading academics, if at all. Usually, two parallel approaches are used: In a bottom-up approach the ideation process is jointly run with clear business orientation in companies' divisions involving all business units and relevant corporate functions with one central coordinator. Top-down approaches stress blue sky thinking to define topics around a business vision. Dedicated teams screen outside competencies and seek creative solutions around product targets and process alternatives.

3   **R&D in incubators or similar institutions:** Incubators usually aim at building and strengthening network relations. Often incubators are accompanied by PhD or master studies programs, which are designed to attract human resources in the long run. The key success factor of incubators is the dedication of people to it. These people will ensure the implementation of research results stemming from incubator activities and ensure the existence of relations even when they leave R&D at a later stage. Results from the incubator are seldom directly measurable but help indirectly in longer-term innovation success.

In total the three types of R&D activities have different weights. R&D with a clear aim of business applications usually accounts for the largest share of the total (typically around 80 to 85 percent), while R&D with the ambition to generate substantial innovation (radical) accounts for 10 percent and incubators are the remaining 5 to 10 percent of the total R&D budget. Such changes in the split of R&D budgets require new organizational approaches. Increasingly pure R&D or technology councils are being replaced by councils with a wider reach, which are often called technology and innovation councils, innovation councils or innovation committees. The objectives of these councils are manifold:

- The definition of core technologies and coordination of activities across the divisions and corporate research and innovation centers
- The definition and review of external partnering strategies, including partnering strategies with academics and public research organizations, as well as other companies
- The systematic screening of surrounding technologies intellectual property rights and businesses
- Company-internal reward systems to build incentives for staff in different functions to contribute to innovation
- The design of an innovation culture in the company
- Proactive public relations work to build respective company images with customers, suppliers, the research community and society

With the increasing pace of innovation-driven competition, companies are constantly reinventing themselves and purposely enter and leave new areas in a life cycle 'wave' in order to always be able to differentiate. In particular high-tech companies focus their activities on businesses, offering value added by technology and knowledge advances and leave the market fields in case of commoditization. With such increasing pace of innovation, the speed of market introductions with widely linked technologies is only partially feasible for one company alone. Thus, companies try to use benefits of economies of scale in building up new markets, which requires multiple market players.

Important innovation activities outside of typical R&D activities focus on market trends, customer relationships (coordination) and safety regulations, but also globalization of internal R&D activities has become a major issue for most companies. While globalization was thought of as relevant for product and process development activities producing incremental innovation adapted to local and regional needs, the same holds true for more substantial research activities.

Thus, R&D facilities are opened around the world to not only serve local customers but also provide a sound technical and technological basis for global companies. Hence, such facilities are settled where the infrastructure and framework conditions meet the companies' requirements most.

This trend is accompanied by the increasing openness of companies to engage in cooperative relationships with the public research base, regardless their location in the world. The quality and availability of research done in public entities count obviously more than related transaction costs associated with the transfer of technology and knowledge. Also it became evident that companies expect and highly appreciate a cooperation culture in the public research entities.

Collaborations with customers, suppliers and academia to achieve innovation has been common in most industries for many years. Thus, open innovation is not considered a new topic in principle. However, some related activities like out-licensing and spinning off are considered more important for the future. Despite the rather widespread diffusion of open innovation, it is not the cooperation and involvement of customers in the innovation process; rather, the challenge lies between different company R&D sites. It has been recognized that knowledge sharing and knowledge management have become the main challenges associated with globalized and decentralized innovation activities, especially when different SBUs are involved and selected partners engaged at different development stages. Therefore, the open innovation model can globally generate inputs from the best sources and share these on a global level. Continuous developments are made to find new opportunities based on new partners, structures (e.g. corporate ventures) and processes (e.g. cross-value chain collaboration). Relevant networks and clusters will become more important to leverage open innovation activities in the future. However, the need for more activities in this field with suppliers, academics and other partners is recognized and actively pursued with different initiatives. The most difficult steps in moving towards open innovation will be the change in culture and identifying appropriate partners.

To engage into lasting relations with external innovation partners, companies increasingly focus on the following factors:

- human resources
- research and innovation excellence
- Innovation culture/awareness for innovation/openness towards risk

The *human resources* dimension involves the availability of qualified staff; related education/further education opportunities; and soft factors such as the ability of systemic thinking, partners' mind-sets and openness, as well as curiosity and empathy paired with dedicated project management and project work skills. In addition, problem identification and formulation capabilities are preconditions for collaborative efforts, and cultural openness is required.

Excellence in research and innovation refers to the reputation of partners, including quality of work and projects, credibility and matching competences. It requires research and innovation staff having dedicated networking capabilities across institutional borders together with systemic thinking and communication skills, as well as interdisciplinary thinking and cross-disciplinary research under broader umbrella topics.

Another important factor is *innovation culture, awareness for innovation* and *openness towards risk*. These include awareness for the application of research, fast responses/quick decisions, the willingness to go in new, unusual ways and openness to experiment. Furthermore, the attitudes of partners in light of acceptance of/openness towards external sources for research and innovation proposals and respective agendas is crucial to match.

Institutional design of innovation

Organization of IM

Different company units are involved in the innovation process to different extents. Figure 21.4 shows the different innovation (e.g. R&D) phases and how the meaning and role of innovation management vary between these stages. During the initial idea screening phase, which is characterized by high uncertainty of completion, innovation management takes a role as a process driver with entrepreneurial behavior. The closer the innovation project gets to prototyping and manufacturing, the less innovation management units are involved. Instead, business units take more active roles in driving the project towards fully taking over with respective profit/loss responsibilities.

'Corporate innovation' often finds it challenging to obtain recognition by companies' operational units because the value generated in these units is frequently longer term and more difficult to measure in the short term. Obviously, business units as a process driver will favor current product improvements to maintain the BU competitive position, which naturally requires a short-term view of BU performance. From this the question emerges which role IM can take and play in the overall company innovation activities. It appears that IM is often part of corporate activities and perceived as a service unit, like many others in the corporate world. In order to empower IM and generate more value and impact from IM it is essential to change the IM role from a pure service provider to an innovation driver (Figure 21.5).

Innovation drivers fulfill different functions in organizations. The innovation service unit is mainly involved in developing new solutions, either on its own initiative or on request by business units. These original duties and functions are extended by an active communication role, which preaches the importance of innovation and provides a communication and information platform inside the company, bringing the different units together by different means. Furthermore, long-term innovation strategic development and external partners relationship management are additional key duties. Eventually, active intellectual property management, in line with

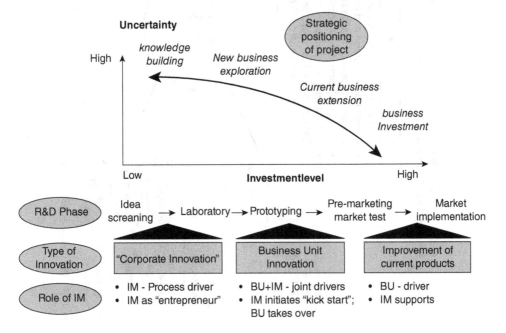

Figure 21.4 Innovation process stages and organizational meaning

425

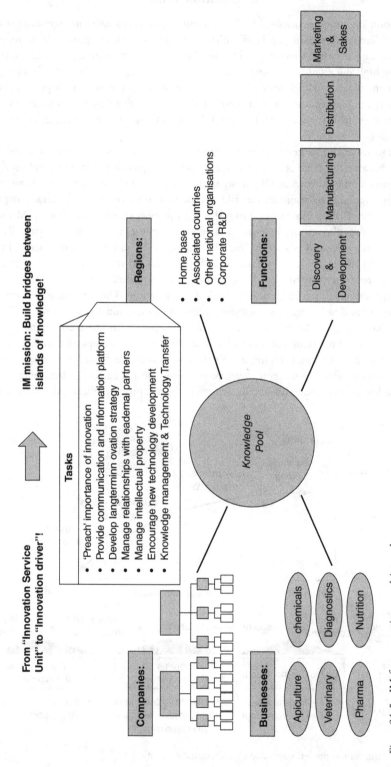

Figure 21.5 IM from a service to a driver role

the legal department and IP office, is also among the duties, in addition to encouraging new technology development and knowledge management, as well as technology transfer.

These duties can be structured along the lines or what and how. With respect to 'what' IM assesses:

- the innovation project portfolio fit with market and competitive conditions;
- portfolio contributions to supporting the corporate strategy;
- the commercial balance of the innovation project portfolio.

Furthermore IM has to enforce:

- the elimination of weak points in the project portfolio;
- the implementation of a seamless company innovation process;
- the coordination of innovation projects with existing resources.

These dimensions relate mainly to achieving the goals set in the company innovation strategy. The second dimension addresses the 'how', for example, always making sure the IM runs smoothly and seamlessly. This includes questions such as:

- Are clear priorities set?
- Is adequate competence available?
- Are the R&D projects handled cost-effectively?
- Are the R&D throughput times as short as possible?
- Are the decision-making processes reliable and fast?
- Are the non-R&D sectors adequately involved?

Innovation programs are managed by a program manager who has authority over members from different units. The program manager has the responsibility for defining the technical strategy of the program (road map of technological goals), the budget responsibility for the program and receives the money after presenting the budget to the corporate chief technology officer and any colleagues. The program manager allocates the money where the resources are, that is, to the laboratories that have a (some) particular area(s) of technical expertise related to the program. Typically the program manager belongs to one of the labs but has line authority over the members of the multinational program team. The program managers work alongside the directors of the laboratories, who have the primary responsibility for the people in their laboratories under a matrix structure.

Eventually, it must be determined if IM is centralized or decentralized. A centralized IM approach enables cross-fertilization of ideas, providing a multidisciplinary pool of resources, which can provide a more innovative environment. Also it enables the company to exploit a commonality of technologies, allows for closer linkage with corporate strategy, maintains a longer-term perspective and provides economies of scale. On the other hand, centralized IM features potentially poor linkage to end-market needs and the threat to engage in research that is interesting rather than useful. It might turn out that return on investment can be very low and linkages with operating units can be weak, resulting in product and process transfers that fail.

In the decentralized IM organization, technology activities are closely linked to the business aims and end markets, and the transfer of products and processes from technology to manufacture is eased. This allows greater accountability for success and failure; thus, this approach is sometimes preferred by shareholders for its business effectiveness. But skills and investments in different competences and capabilities can be duplicated, and a short-term focus fails to safeguard the long-term future, and project continuity is threatened by close linkages to short-term budgetary pressures and putting out fires.

Emerging challenges for IM

Company IM typically has a holistic view of innovation projects, including projects with short-term commercialization potential, for example, one to two years, and the following generation, which can be commercialized in three to five years. The underlying challenge is to fine-tune the sequence of innovation for commercialization to the respective market and customers and design the adequate innovation pipeline across business units. From the corporate level there is hardly a 'one size fits all' solution for all business units under the corporate umbrella. A match in terms of the implementation of performance measures at the corporate and business unit level (e.g. innovation metrics and innovation balanced scorecards) need to account for the market-specific features strongly while also matching them with technology-induced features.

Increasingly companies are establishing IM units with close proximity to markets in a more networked shape by means of stepping back from strong corporate units. Strongly network-oriented IM organizations show that corporate units act more as coordinators between different local units, for example, innovation and technology strategy is orchestrated and implemented by the corporate unit. In this arrangement, the corporate unit is likely to act as a moderator and facilitator of competition between the localized IM units for specific IM projects. A rather new facilitation instrument is that corporate IM launches a call for competitions in technology development that are open to local IM units. Corporate IM takes a role of a coordinator, assuring the innovation project pipeline is in agreement with corporate strategy and budgets are used efficiently. Other positive effects from such an approach are the coordination of IM projects across units, the access to local talent (which is one main driver for establishing dedicated units) and the smaller size of each unit (which allows a more flexible reaction to technological and market changes). Furthermore, technology and market intelligence is strengthened through the local presences. However, this requires a more elaborated internal knowledge management system that takes also account of the competition between local units.

Another challenge comes with the broader and more complex nature of technologies, which are frequently composed of several other technologies, into one solution. The long-term observation of technological development thus is also a more complex undertaking for companies who need to dedicate respective budgets to technology intelligence. Data and information analysis (e.g. most big data approaches) are a means of responding to these challenges but require substantial initial investment. Beyond the actual detection of technological trends IM needs to take a more communicative role inside the organization to ensure timely and targeted diffusion of respective findings and related information.

This is all in line with the coordinated technical support for business units and the transfer of services and core technologies developed by R&D to business units. Furthermore, operation and maintenance (O&M) technologies are undergoing major changes in light of maintenance strategies that are more and more driven by data analysis–based strategic orientation (e.g. preventive maintenance). Here IM is asked to develop respective approaches and instruments for powerful O&M solutions.

Given IM's central position in the corporate organization, the unit is asked to take a more proactive advisory role towards business unit IM entities but also for business units' strategic development units and activities. In addition IM is responsible for developing technology acquisition strategies to achieve business strategy goals, manage outsourced product/technology development and finally manage internal and external technical resources.

Revisiting innovation models towards the 'active innovation' paradigm

The most recent innovation models increasingly postulate external relationships of innovators in many different shapes, including the acquisition and incorporation of knowledge and technology from outside the organization. Such knowledge and technologies can be either publicly accessible or privately owned by other companies, individuals or research institutions. Furthermore, external knowledge and technologies are available either in a codified or personal published, undisclosed form. R&D service providers and public and private research institutions, and increasingly training institutions, contribute much to build, develop and diffuse existing, publicly available 'knowledge and technology pools'. These institutions also provide partners and/or service providers external innovation-related activities (especially R&D activities). Companies' internal R&D activities – as part of the innovation process – are available in the company's knowledge and existing technologies, which are not only a prerequisite for implementing in-house innovation activities but also for the use of external sources for innovation.

The most recent generation of innovation models isn't directly related to earlier ones. Examples of these models include the value chain evolution theory developed by Christensen and Raynor (2003), the strategic innovation process model proposed by Afuah (2002), the 'category-maturity life cycle model' Moore (2005) and the business strategy innovation model Hamel (2000)). Moore's and Hamel's approaches show the potential to incorporate innovation process model thinking. These models cannot really be treated as descendants of sixth-generation models. They draw on some features from the system and evolutionary models. However, they do not apply system or evolutionary models at a micro level, but rather develop third-generation models with new aspects such as network infrastructure or a greater emphasis on outsourcing added. The models discussed in this chapter share a common feature in that they all aim to explain the emergence of innovations from conceptual and process perspectives but don't take account of the side resource of innovation. While the current open innovation paradigm remains dominant in innovation model thinking, even this innovation understanding and model (and thus innovation processes) need to be extended by the human resource dimension and the meaning and impact of organizations' innovation milieus. A company's innovation milieu is strongly interrelated with human resources management and policies for attracting and retaining talent.

Frequently, attracting talent to companies for innovation is less problematic than keeping talent on board and motivating people to perform outstandingly. This is challenging because firms lack staff who have capabilities that are not only directly related to actual innovation activities (e.g. often related to R&D) but also capabilities in management and legal affairs. Firms need these additional competences in light of the increasingly external nature of innovation.

Furthermore, the economic pressure on companies leads to higher expectations by the corporate leadership for the innovation-related activities by all company units. The instruments used for monitoring and assessing innovation projects are improving considerably. Firms' needs for innovation-related competences and corporate management's higher expectations for innovation are very important determinants of current corporate activities, although both carry the risk that innovation is understood a self-fulfilling prophecy. In other words, once companies invest in innovative projects, the corporate leadership expects returns on investment in ever shorter periods to meet externally imposed expectations. Accordingly, it is important to reconsider how innovation and human resource management are organized internally to prepare staff to respond to these challenges.

Equally important is the incorporation of public attitudes and the perception of innovation, which developed into a major driver for the acceptance of innovation by society. Therefore, technology intelligence needs to take a broader perspective, including societal attitudes and perceptions in assessing technologies and technology trend prediction.

Therefore, the current predominantly open innovation paradigm needs to be modified to incorporate a stronger emphasis on the human resources involved in innovation. There are signs that companies are already paying more attention to the human factor for innovation and public perception. Consequently, companies will strive for an 'active innovation' model that builds on the open innovation paradigm.

In this respect, IM governance should employ approaches that combine the open innovation concept with the human factor and public perception, or in other words, the 'company innovation ecosystem' and the 'product innovation ecosystem'. The 'product innovation ecosystem' is understood as a community of users of an innovation which are driven by their specific agendas, which are also embedded in society. Hence, in order to accelerate understanding of the relationship between 'company innovation ecosystems' and 'product innovation ecosystems', more efforts in research are required.

Acknowledgments

The chapter was prepared within the framework of the Basic Research Program at the National Research University Higher School of Economics (HSE) and supported within the framework of the subsidy granted to the HSE by the government of the Russian Federation for the implementation of the Global Competitiveness Program.

Bibliography

Afuah, A. (2002). *Innovation management: strategies, implementation, and profits* (2nd ed.). New York: Oxford University Press.
Aiken, M. and Hage, J. (1971). The organic organization and innovation. *Sociology*, 5(1), 63–82.
Asheim, B. T., Smith, H. L. and Oughton, C. (2011). Regional innovation systems: theory, empirics and policy. *Regional Studies*, 45(7), 875–891.
Baregheh, A., Rowley, J. and Sambrook, S. (2009). Towards a multidisciplinary definition of innovation. *Management Decision*, 47(8), 1323–1339.
Bas, T. G. and Kunc, M. H. (2009). National systems of innovations and natural resources clusters: evidence from Copper Mining Industry Patents. *European Planning Studies*, 17(12), 1861–1879.
Bazalt, M. and Hanush, H. (2004). Recent trends in the research on national innovation systems. *Journal of Evolutionary Economics*, 14(2), 197–210.
Beije, P. (1998). *Technological change in the modern economy*. Cheltenham: Edward Elgar Publishing.
Bessant, J. and Tidd, J. (2007). *Innovation and entrepreneurship*. Chichester: John Wiley & Sons Ltd.
Biondi, L. and Galli, R. (1992). Technological trajectories. *Futures*, 24, 580–592.
Bramanti, A. and Ratti, R. (1997). The multi-faceted dimensions of local development. In Ratti, R., Bramanti, A. and Gordon, R. (Eds.), *The dynamics of innovative regions: the GREMI approach*. Aldershot: Ashgate, pp. 3–44.
Cagnazzo, L., Botarelli, M. and Taticchi, P. (2008). Innovation management models: a literature review, a new framework, a case study. *Proceedings of the 3rd European Conference on Entrepreneurship and Innovation*, pp. 55–69.
Camagni, R. (1991). 'Local Milieu', uncertainty and innovation networks: towards a new dynamic theory of economic space. In Camagni, R. (Ed.), *Innovation networks: spatial perspectives*. London: Belhaven Press, pp. 12–143.

Campodall'Orto, S. and Ghiglione, B. (1997). The technology transfer process within the new innovation models. *Managing Technological Knowledge Transfer* 4.

Carayannis, E. G. and Campbell, D. F. (2011). Open innovation diplomacy and a 21st century fractal research, education and innovation (FREIE) ecosystem: building on the quadruple and quintuple helix innovation concepts and the 'mode 3' knowledge production system. *Journal of the Knowledge Economy*, 2(3), 327–372.

Carayannis, E. G., Meissner, D. and Edelkina, A. (2015). Targeted innovation policy and practice intelligence (TIP2E) Concepts and implications for theory, policy and practice. *The Journal of Technology Transfer*, doi:10.1007/s10961-015-9433-8.

Carayannis, E. G., Provance, M. and Givens, N. (2011). Knowledge arbitrage, serendipity, and acquisition formality: their effects on sustainable entrepreneurial activity in regions. *Engineering Management, IEEE Transactions on*, 58(3), 564–577.

Carayannis, E. G. and Turner, E. (2006). Innovation diffusion and technology acceptance: the case of PKI technology. *Technovation*, 26(7), 847–855.

Carlsson, B., Jacobsson, S., Holmen, M. and Rickne, A. (2002). Innovation systems: analytical and methodological notes. *Research Policy*, 31(2), 233–245.

Carlsson, B., Keane, P. and Martin, J. B. (1976). R and D organizations as learning systems. *Sloan Management Review*, 17(3), 1–15.

Carter, C. and Williams, B. (1957). *Industry and technical progress*. London: Oxford University Press.

Chesbrough, H. W. (2003a). *Open innovation: the new imperative for creating and profiting from technology*. Boston, MA: Harvard Business School Press.

Chesbrough, H. W. (2003b). The era of open innovation. *MIT Sloan Management Review*, 44(3), 35–41.

Chesbrough, H. W. (2006). *Open innovation: researching a new paradigm*. New York: Oxford University Press.

Christensen, C. M. and Raynor, M. E. (2003). *The innovator's solution: using good theory to solve the dilemmas of growth*. Boston, MA: Harvard Business School Press.

Contractor, F. J. and Lorange, P. (1988). *Cooperative strategies in international business*. Lexington, MA: Lexington Books.

Cook, L. G. and Morrison, W. A. (1961). The origins of innovation. *Report No. 61-GP-214*, June, General Electric Company, Research Information Section, New York, NY.

Cooke, P. (1998). Introduction. In Braczyk, H.-J., Cooke, P. and Heidenreich, M. (Eds.), *Regional innovation systems: the role of governance in a globalised world*. London: UCL Press, pp. 2–25.

Coombs, R., Saviotti, P. and Walsh, V. (1987). *Economics and technological change*. London: Palgrave MacMillan.

Cooper, R. G. (1980). Project new prod: factors in new product success. *European Journal Marketing*, 14(5/6).

Docter, J. and Stokman, C. (1987). Innovation strategies of small industrial companies. In Rothwell, R. and Bessant, J. (Eds.), *Innovation: adaptation and growth*. Amsterdam: Elsevier.

Dodgson, M. (1993). *Technological collaboration in industry: strategy, policy and internationalization in innovation*. London: Routledge.

Dosi, G. (1982). Technological paradigms and technological trajectories: a suggested interpretation of the determinants and directions of technical change. *Research Policy*, 11, 147–162.

Dosi, G. (1988). Sources, procedures, and microeconomic effects of innovation. *Journal of Economic Literature*, 26, 1120–1171.

Dosi, G. and Egibi, M. (1991). Substantive and procedural uncertainty: an exploration of human behavior in changing environments. *Journal of Evolutionary Economics*, 1, 145–168.

Dosi, G. and Orsenigo, L. (1994). Macrodynamics and microfoundations: an evolutionary perspective. In Granstrand, O. (Ed.), *Economics of technology*. Amsterdam: North-Holland, pp. 91–123.

Dowrick, S. (Ed.) (1995). *Economic approaches to innovation*. Aldershot: Edward Elgar Publishing.

Eveleens, C. (2010). Innovation management: a literature review of innovation process models and their implications. *Nijmegen, NL*, pp. 1–16.

Feldman, M. (1994). *The geography of innovation*. Dordrecht: Kluwer Academic Publisher.

Florida, R. (1995). Toward the learning region. *Futures*, 27, 527–536.

Freeman, C. (1991). Networks of innovators: a synthesis of research issues. *Research Policy*, 20, 499–514.

Freeman, C. and Perez, C. (1988). Structural crises of adjustment: business cycles and investment behavior. In Dosi, G. et al. (Eds.), *Technical change and economic theory*. London: Pinter, pp. 38–66.

Gackstatter, S., Kotsemir, M., Meissner, D. (2014). Building an innovation-driven economy – The case of BRIC and GCC countries. *Foresight*, 16(4), 293–308.

Gallivan, M. (2001). Organizational adoption and assimilation of complex technological innovations: development and application of a new framework. *ACM SIGMIS Database*, 32(3), 51–85.

Gann, D. (1991). Technological change and the internationalization of construction in Europe. In Freeman, C., Sharp, M. and Walker, W. (Eds.), *Technology and the future of Europe*. London: Pinter, pp. 231–244.

Gann, D. (2000). *Building innovation: complex constructs in a changing world*. London: Thomas Telford.

Gault, F. (2009). Innovatsionnaya strategiya OESR: dostizhenie novykh tsennostey [OECD innovation strategy: delivering value]. *Foresight-Russia*, 3(1), 16–28 (in Russian).

Godin, B. (2006). The linear model of innovation – the historical construction of an analytical framework. *Science Technology & Human Values*, 31(6), 639–667.

Godin, B. (2009). National innovation system the system approach in historical perspective. *Science Technology and Human Values*, 34(4), 476–501.

Godin, B. (2010). Kontseptual'nye osnovy nauchnoy, tekhnologicheskoy i innovatsionnoy politiki [Conceptual frameworks of science, technology and innovation policy]. *Foresight-Russia*, 4(2), 34–43 (in Russian).

Gokhberg, L., Kuznetsova, T. and Roud, V. (2010). Analiz innovatsionnykh rezhimov v rossiyskoy ekonomike: metodologicheskie podkhody i pervye rezul'taty [Analysis of innovation modes in the Russian economy: methodological approaches and first results]. *Foresight-Russia*, 4(3), pp. 18–30 (in Russian).

Gokhberg, L. and Meissner, D. (2013). Innovation: superpowered invention. *Nature*, 501, 313–314.

Hadjimanolis, A. (2003). The barriers approach to innovation. In Shavinina, L. V. (Ed.), *The international handbook on innovation*. Amsterdam: Elsevier, pp. 559–573.

Hagedoorn, J. (1990). Organizational needs of inter-firm cooperation and technology transfer. *Technovation*, 10(1), 17–30.

Hamel, G. (2000). *Leading the revolution*. Boston, MA: Harvard Business School Press.

Hansen, E. (2014). Innovativeness in the face of decline: performance implications. *International Journal of Innovation Management*, 18(5), 1450039.

Hayes, R. and Abernathy, W. J. (1980). Managing our way to economic decline. *Harvard Business Review*, July–August.

Hayvaert, C. H. (1973). *Innovation research and product policy: clinical research in 12 Belgian industrial enterprises*. Belgium: Catholic University of Louvain.

Hodgson, G. (1993). *Economics and evolution: putting life back into economics*. Oxford: Polity Press.

Howard, W. G. and Guile, B. R. (1992). *Profiting from innovation*. New York: The Free Press.

Iammarino, S. (2005). An evolutionary integrated view of regional systems of innovation: concepts, measures and historical perspectives. *European Planning Studies*, 13(4), 497–519.

Jacobs, D. and Snijders, H. (2008). *Innovation routine: how managers can support repeated innovation. Stichting management studies*. Assen: Van Gorcum.

Jarillo, J. (1988). On strategic networks. *Strategic Management Journal*, 19, 31–41.

Kamal, M. M. (2006). IT innovation adoption in the government sector: identifying the critical success factors. *Journal of Enterprise Information Management*, 19(2), 192–222.

Keeble, D. and Wilkinson, F. (2000). SMEs, regional clustering and collective learning: an overview. In Keeble, D. and Wilkinson, F. (Eds.), *High-technology clusters, networking and collective learning in Europe*. Aldershot: Ashgate, pp. 1–20.

Khripunova, A., Vishnevskiy, K., Karasev, O. and Meissner, D. (2014). Corporate foresight for corporate functions: impacts from purchasing functions. *Strategic Change*, 23, 147–160. doi:10.1002/jsc.1967.

Kirat, T. and Lung, Y. (1999). Innovation and proximity: territories as loci of collective learning processes. *European Urban and Regional Studies*, 6, 27–38.

Kline, S. J. and Rosenberg, N. (1986). An overview of innovation. In Landau, R. and Rosenberg, N. (Eds.), *The positive sum strategy*. Washington, DC: National Academy Press, pp. 275–305.

Knight, K. (1967). A descriptive model of the intra-firm innovation process. *The Journal of Business*, 40(4), 478–496.

Kotsemir, M. N. and Meissner, D. (2013). Conceptualizing the innovation process – trends and outlook. *Working Papers by NRU Higher School of Economics. Series WP BRP 'Science, Technology and Innovation'*, 2013. No. 10/STI/2013.

Langrish, J., Gibbons, M., Evans, W. G. and Jevons, F. R. (1972). *Wealth from knowledge*. London: Palgrave Macmillan.

Longhi, C. and Keeble, D. (2000). High-technology clusters and evolutionary trends in the 1990s. In Keeble, D. and Wilkinson, F. (Eds.), *High-technology clusters, networking and collective learning in Europe*. Aldershot: Ashgate, pp. 21–56.

Lundvall, B-A. (1992). *National systems of innovation: towards a theory of innovation and interactive Learning*. London: Pinter.

Macleod, G. (1996). The cult of enterprise in a networked, learning region? Governing business and skills in lowland Scotland. *Regional Studies*, 30, 749–755.

Maidique, M. (1980). Entrepreneurs, champions, and technological innovation. *Sloan Management Review*, 21(2), 59–76.

Mansfield, E. (1995). Contribution of R&D to economic growth in the United States. *Innovation, Technology and the Economy*, I, 255–273.

Marceau, J. (1992). *Reworking the world: organizations, technologies and cultures in comparative perspective*. Berlin: De Gruyter.

Marinova, D. and Phillimore, J. (2003). Innovation models. In Shavinina, L. V. (Ed.), *The international handbook on innovation*. Amsterdam: Elsevier, pp. 44–53.

Marquis, D. G. (1988). *The Anatomy of successful innovations. Readings in the management of innovation*. Ballinger Publishing Company.

Meissner, D. (2014). Approaches for developing national STI strategies. *STI Policy Review*, 5(1), 34–56.

Meissner, D. (2015). Public-private partnership models for science, technology, and innovation cooperation. *Journal of the Knowledge Economy*, 1–21, doi:10.1007/s13132-015-0310-3.

Merrifield, B. D. (1986). Forces of change affecting high technology industries. *A Speech by U.S. Assistant Secretary of Commerce*.

Metcalfe, S. (1995). Technology systems and technology policy in an evolutionary framework. *Cambridge Journal of Economics*, 19, 25–46.

Mitrova, T., Kulagin, V., Grushevenko, D. and Grushevenko, E. (2015). Technology innovation as a factor of demand for energy sources in automotive industry. *Foresight and STI Governance*, 9(4), 18–31. doi:10.17323/1995-459x.2015.4.18.31.

Moore, G. A. (2005). *Dealing with Darwin: how great companies innovate at every phase of their evolution*. New York: Penguin Group.

Mowery, D. and Rosenberg, N. (1979). Influence of market demand upon innovation – critical-review of some recent empirical studies. *Research Policy*, 8(2), 102–153.

Myers, S. and Marquis, D. G. (1969). *Successful industrial innovations: a study of factors underlying innovation in selected firms*. NSF 69–17, Washington, DC: National Science Foundation.

Nelson, R. R. (1993). *National innovation systems: a comparative analysis*. New York: Oxford University Press.

Nelson, R. R. (1995). Recent evolutionary theoritising about economic change. *Journal of Economic Literature*, 33, 48–90.

Nelson, R. R. (2000). National innovation systems. In Acs, Z. (Ed.), *Regional innovation, knowledge and global change*. London: Pinter, pp. 11–26.

Niosi, J. (1999). Fourth-generation R&D: from linear models to flexible innovation. *Journal of Business Research*, 45(2), 111–117.

OECD (1996). *The OECD jobs strategy: technology, production and job creation* (Vol. 2). Paris: OECD.

OECD (1999). *Managing national innovation systems*. Paris: OECD.

OECD, Eurostat. (1997). *Oslo manual – Guidelines for collecting and interpreting innovation data*. Second edition. Paris.

OECD, E. (2005). *Oslo manual – guidelines for collecting and interpreting innovation data* (3rd ed.) Paris: Sp 46.

Pavitt, K., Robson, M., Townsend, J. (1989). Accumulation, diversification and organization of technological activities in U.K. companies, 1945–83. In Dodgson, M. (Ed.), *Technology strategy and the firm: management and public policy*. Harlow: Longman, pp. 38–67.

Perani, G. and Sirilli, S. (2008). Benchmarking innovatsionnoy deyatel'nosti evropeyskikh stran [Benchmarking Innovation in Europe]. *Foresight-Russia*, 2(1), 4–15 (in Russian).

Perez, C. (1983). Structural change and the assimilation of new technologies in the economic system. *Futures*, 15, 357–375.

Peters, T. J. and Waterman, R. W. (1982). *In search of excellence*. New York: Harper and Row.

Pierce, J. and Delbecq, A. (1977). Organizational structure, individual attitudes and innovation. *Academy of Management Review*, 2(1), 26–37.

Proskuryakova, L. N., Meissner, D. and Rudnik, P. B. (2015). The use of technology platforms as a policy tool to address research challenges and technology transfer. *The Journal of Technology Transfer*, 42(1), 206–227.

Rogers, E. M. (1995). *Diffusion of innovations* (4th ed.). New York: Free Press.

Rosenberg, N. (1976). *Perspectives on technology*. Cambridge: Cambridge University Press.

Rosenberg, N. (1982). *Inside the black box: technology and economics*. Cambridge: Cambridge University Press.

Rothwell, R. (1976). Innovation in textile machinery: some significant factors in success and failure. *Science Policy Research Unit, Occasional Paper Series*, No 2, June.

Rothwell, R. (1991). External networking and innovation in small and medium-sized manufacturing firms in Europe. *Technovation*, 11(2), 93–112.

Rothwell, R. (1992). Industrial innovation and environmental regulation: some lessons from the past. *Technovation*, 12(7), 447–458.

Rothwell, R. (1994). Towards the fifth-generation innovation process. *International Marketing Review*, 11(1), 7–31.

Rothwell, R., Freeman, C., Horsley, A., Jervis, V. T. P., Robertson, A. B. and Townsend, J. (1974). SAPPHO updated: project SAPPHO phase II. *Research Policy*, 3(3), 258–291.

Rothwell, R. and Zegveld (1985). *Reindustrialization and technology*. Harlow: Longman.

Rubenstein, A. H. (1957). Looking around. *Harvard Business Review*, 35(3), 133–145.

Rubera, G. and Kirca, A. H. (2012). Firm innovativeness and its performance outcomes: a metaanalytic review and theoretical integration. *Journal of Marketing*, 76(3), 130–147.

Sahal, D. (1981). *Patterns of technological innovation*. New York: Addison-Wesley.

Sako, M. (1992). *Price, quality and trust: how Japanese and British companies manage buyer supplier relations*. Cambridge: Cambridge University Press.

Saviotti, P. P. (1996). *Technological evolution, variety and the economy*. Cheltenham: Edward Elgar Publishing.

Schock, G. (1974). *Innovation processes in Dutch industry*. Apeldoorn: TNO, Policy Studies and Information Group.

Sharif, N. (2006). Emergence and development of the national innovation systems concept. *Research Policy*, 35(5), 745–766.

Solow, R. M. (1957). Technical change and the aggregate production function. *Review of Economics and Statistics*, 39, 312–320.

Szakasitz, G. D. (1974). The adoption of the SAPPHO method in the Hungarian electronics industry. *Research Policy*, 3.

Tisdell, C. (1995). Evolutionary economics and research and development. In Dowrick, S. (Ed.), *Economic approaches to innovation*. Aldershot: Edward Elgar Publishing, pp. 120–144.

Tsai, K. H. and Yang, S. Y. (2013). Firm innovativeness and business performance: the joint moderating effects of market turbulence and competition. *Industrial Marketing Management*, 42(8), 1279–1294.

Usher, A. P. (1954). *A history of mechanical inventions*. Revised edition. New York: McGraw Hill.

Usher, A. P. (1955). *Technical change and capital formation, in National Bureau of Economic Research, capital formation and economic growth*. Princeton: Princeton University Press, 523–550.

Utterback, J. M. (1975). *The process of innovation in five industries in Europe and Japan*. Cambridge, MA: Centre for Policy Alternatives, MIT Press.

Verloop, J. (2004). *Insight in innovation: managing innovation by understanding the laws of innovation*. Amsterdam: Elsevier.

Vishnevskiy, K., Karasev, O. and Meissner, D. (2015). Integrated roadmaps and corporate Foresight as tools of innovation management: the case of Russian companies, *Technological Forecasting and Social Change*, 90, Part B. No. January, 433–443.

Zhang, Y., Robinson, D. K., Porter, A. L., Zhu, D., Zhang, G. and Lu, J. (2015). Technology roadmapping for competitive technical intelligence. *Technological Forecasting and Social Change*, 110, 175–186.

22
ETHICS IN INNOVATION MANAGEMENT AS META-RESPONSIBILITY

The practice of responsible research and innovation in human brain simulation

Bernd Carsten Stahl, Jos Timmermans, Stephen Rainey and Mark Shaw

Introduction

The concept and practice of responsible research and innovation (RRI) are subjects of intense academic scrutiny (Timmermans, 2015). This high level of attention is at least partly due to the support of RRI by research funders such as the European Union, the UK Engineering and Science Research Council (EPSRC), the Netherlands Organisation for Scientific Research (NWO) and others. Much research is being undertaken to clarify conceptual underpinnings and to describe current and future practice. Despite these activities, it is currently not clear how theoretical accounts of RRI can be put into practice to achieve RRI's promise to contribute to the social acceptability and desirability of R&I activities.

In this chapter we fill this gap by developing an account of RRI as a meta-responsibility and providing a high-profile case of how this meta-responsibility can be put into practice. The starting point is the application of theories of responsibility to RRI. We argue that responsibilities are pervasive in R&I environments. Traditional theories of responsibility tend to focus on singular instances of the term and describe why and how a subject is held to be responsible for an object. In social practice, however, responsibilities are always multiple and can be better understood as networks of overlapping and intermingling relationships. Using this idea of networks of responsibility, we propose that the best way of conceptualising RRI is as a meta-responsibility that aims to shape, maintain, develop, coordinate and align existing and novel R&I-related processes, actors and responsibilities with a view to ensuring desirable and acceptable research outcomes (Stahl, 2013).

Using the concept of meta-responsibility, we describe how RRI can be put into practice in the field of human brain simulation. The example of the EU Future Emerging Technology (FET) Flagship Human Brain Project (HBP) shows how the components of RRI can be realised. Drawing on various empirical sources, we trace the development of RRI back to the inception of the HBP. Despite constant attention to principles of RRI, we show that initially the extensive RRI activities had little influence on the overall project. The theory of meta-responsibility allows for an understanding of why the initial setup remained unsatisfactory and points the way towards a resolution. The HBP more recently adopted an approach to ethics management that we reconceptualise as the missing piece required to render RRI as a meta-responsibility successful. We show how the various activities within the ethics management stream affected existing responsibilities and thereby contribute to the broader goals of RRI.

The chapter makes an important theoretical contribution to the debate on RRI by developing the concept of meta-responsibility. This theory builds on traditional accounts of responsibility and demonstrates that they can successfully be used in the complex socio-technical environments of modern large-scale science projects. By using the case of a high-profile live project such as the HBP, the chapter provides practical insights into the unfolding of RRI activities. The conclusions of these insights are spelled out in terms of lessons of interest for both the management of research on a project level and research policy.

Responsible research and innovation as a meta-responsibility

In this section we introduce the discourse on RRI and its current failing to translate its aspiration as an integrative concept to R&I practice. To remedy this gap, we propose conceptualising RRI as a meta-responsibility. Building on traditional theories of responsibility, we argue that in practice responsibility relationships are always embedded in networks. This view of networks of responsibility is the basis for the conceptualisation of RRI as a meta-responsibility.

Responsible research and innovation

RRI has developed into a key concept in the discourses around research governance and research policy. It has been adopted by the European Commission (2013, 2012) as a cross-cutting theme of its 8th research framework programme called Horizon 2020, which means that all research undertaken in this programme, which is worth around €70 billion between 2014 and 2020, will have to adhere to it. Other funders have adopted aspects of RRI as part of their strategy (e.g. the UK Engineering and Physical Science Research Council).[1] Some funding bodies, including the European Commission, the Dutch Research Council, and the Norwegian Research Council, have produced research programmes focusing on RRI. These aim to identify how RRI can play out in practice and be integrated into research policy and governance.

The debate concerning the definition and implementation of RRI is in full swing. A pivotal contribution by von Schomberg (2011) sees RRI as a process that renders societal actors mutually responsive to each other with respect to ensuring the acceptability, desirability and sustainability of research processes and outcomes. Whilst this raises a number of theoretical and practical questions, it can serve as a good starting point for understanding the discourse. Von Schomberg's understanding of RRI can be seen as a recasting of research governance within a long tradition of governance approaches to R&I. These approaches combine the desire to retain the beneficial consequences of research activities while controlling their downsides (Habermas, 1974, p. 268 ff). RRI thus builds on and incorporates long-standing activities such as technology assessment (TA) (Grunwald, 2014, 2009; Joss and Belucci, 2002; Stephan, Wütscher, Decker, and Ladikas, 2004), futures and foresight studies (Adam and Groves, 2011; Cagnin et al., 2008; Markus and Mentzer, 2014; Wilsdon, 2014), public engagement (Bickerstaff, Lorenzoni, Jones, and Pidgeon, 2010; Marris and Rose, 2010; Rowe and Frewer, 2005), science and technology studies (STS) (Coenen and Simakova, 2013; Grunwald, 2011), R&I policy (Auld et al., 2014; Čeičytė and Petraitė, 2014; Hekkert et al., 2007; Smits and Kuhlmann, 2004) and many others that aim to influence the role of R&I in society.

The academic discourse on RRI (Owen, Heintz, and Bessant, 2013; Stilgoe, Owen, and Macnaghten, 2013) has argued that RRI represents a novel contribution to research governance that builds on those prior activities and allows novel insights into R&I practice and policy. It allows the incorporation of particular policy aims, such as those promoted by the European Union (European Commission, 2012), which include gender equality, open access, ethics, public engagement, science education and research governance. Many questions concerning RRI continue to be the subject of investigation and discussion. These include the questions of normative underpinning, that is, how can RRI be justified, in particular, when it intervenes in existing R&I systems (Pandza and Ellwood, 2013). Candidates for such normative underpinnings include human rights (EU, 2010; Ruggie, 2010), philosophical ethics in its various flavours (Gutmann, 2011), established principles and good practice Sutherland et al., 2012) and references to related areas such as corporate social responsibility (Garriga and Melé, 2004; Iatridis and Schroeder, 2015) and the need to account for co-responsibility in increasingly complex societies. Furthermore, discussions cover the question of how RRI is to be implemented given a large array of methodologies and instruments ranging from risk assessment (Owen and Goldberg, 2010) and various impact assessments (Becker, 2001; Wright, Gellert, Gutwirth, and Friedewald, 2011) to deliberative and mode 2 engagement with stakeholders and society (Hankins, 2012; van Est et al., 2012). In order to be successful, RRI will need to be based on capabilities that may be built through various mechanisms, such as education (Technopolis and Fraunhofer ISI, 2012), standards (Sutcliffe, 2011), professional bodies (Gorman, 2001; Wyndham et al., 2015) and others.

In order to integrate this wide range of approaches, methodologies, instruments and theories, RRI has been portrayed as an umbrella term (Grunwald, 2011; Stahl, McBride, Wakunuma, and Flick, 2013; von Schomberg, 2011). It comprises anticipation, reflection, engagement and action (the AREA framework, see [Owen, 2014]). The novelty of RRI lies in the first place in its drawing together of these different theoretical notions, practical approaches and methods that share a concern for ensuring that science, research, technology and innovation have positive, socially acceptable and desirable outcomes. The thread that is suggested to bind all these different components together is the concept of responsibility (Fisher and Rip, 2013; Grinbaum and Groves, 2013; Grunwald, 2011; Jacob et al., 2013; Stilgoe, Owen, and Macnaghten, 2013; van den Hoven, 2013). Responsibility, therefore, is the second major strand of the novelty of RRI, hence the adjective 'responsible'. In addition to enabling integration, the emphasis on responsibility supports the embedding of existing approaches 'in a day-to-day operational context' (Owen and Goldberg, 2010). Responsibility thus functions as a means to bridge the gap between theory and R&I practice that pre-existing reflexive fields such as ethics, STS and TA encounter in their efforts to affect R&I. However, in order for responsibility to fulfil its purpose, it is suggested that the concept needs to be reevaluated (Stilgoe, Owen, and Macnaghten, 2013).

Nevertheless, despite the aspiration of being all-encompassing under the heading of responsibility, thus far the discourse has not managed to produce a substantive conceptualisation of responsibility that achieves this aspiration. Consequently, the discourse still consists of a loosely connected amalgam of approaches and theories. On the one hand, the discourse comprises general discussions on RRI that have not yet determined how the term is to be translated into practice, while on the other hand it covers an ever-expanding multitude of approaches and theories geared towards rendering R&I societally acceptable and desirable without conceptually linking these approaches.

To contribute to meeting the integrative aspiration of RRI as well as closing the gap between theory and practice, this chapter further develops the notion of RRI based on a re-conceptualisation of responsibility.

Dimensions of responsibility

In order to accommodate the breadth and depth of the theories and approaches associated with RRI, our re-conceptualisation of responsibility needs to be as inclusive as possible, while also capturing the intricacies of individual components. For that purpose we build on a procedural account of responsibility that covers several important dimensions of responsibility that have been forwarded by established theories.

Responsibility has its etymological root in 'response', which points to a dialogical understanding of the term. This understanding is dominant in English as well as other languages such as French (Etchegoyen, 1993) or German (Lenk and Maring, 1995). A typical definition of responsibility in this sense is that it means 'liability to answer' (Lewis, 1972, p. 124), which carries a strong legal connotation but, we believe, is equally applicable to most other uses of the term.

These initial considerations provide the basic structure of responsibility (Lenk, 2006). Somebody or something is responsible for something or somebody else. We call the entity that is responsible the subject (S) and the entity that the subject is responsible for the object (O). This basic structure can be represented as shown in Figure 22.1.

Some examples of responsibility can be described like this, for instance, the responsibility of a parent for a child. However, in reality, responsibility always includes more aspects. A key additional component is what we call the authority (A). The authority is the entity to which the subject answers. The authority observes the consequences of the responsibility and is typically in a position to attribute sanctions to the subject. These sanctions can be positive (rewards) or negative (punishments). They can be manifest (e.g. a financial penalty) or more elusive (increase in peer esteem). This relationship could be depicted graphically as shown in Figure 22.2.

This still very simple model allows us to clarify some basic aspects of the theory of responsibility. First, we underline that responsibility in our sense is not a natural phenomenon but socially constructed and supported (Grunwald, 2012). Responsibility is something that is ascribed to the subject, and different social contexts will lead to different ascriptions.

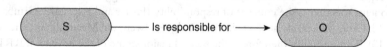

Figure 22.1 Basic structure of responsibility

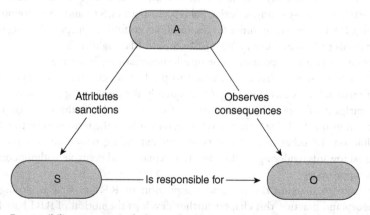

Figure 22.2 Responsibility structure including authority

The next basic point to be made is that responsibility as the social construct of ascription always has a purpose. There are different types of purposes, the most widely accepted of which is the determination of punishments or rewards (French, 1992, p. 18). Others include retribution and revenge, as well as an expression of the prevailing moral sentiment (Hart, 1968). We hold that the purpose of responsibility ascriptions in all of these cases is to reinforce, uphold or promote a particular social outcome. This view aligns the theory of responsibility with RRI that aims to ensure the desirability and acceptability of research processes and outcomes.

Having established that responsibility is a social construct of ascription that has the purpose of establishing a certain social state, we can return to the model of responsibility introduced earlier. All of the three core components, subject, object and authority, raise additional questions. There have been discussions about what constitutes a suitable subject of responsibility, whether it has to be an individual human being or whether it can be a legal person or collective body (Stilgoe, 2014; Velasquez, 1991) or whether technical artefacts may serve as subjects (Anderson and Anderson, 2007; Bechtel, 1985; Coeckelbergh, 2015). The answer to this question hinges on the conditions that a subject is deemed to have to fulfil. The literature on responsibility contains a significant number of such conditions, most of which can be interpreted as requirements that need to be in place for the social consequences of the responsibility ascription to be realised. They include freedom of will and action (Fischer, 1999), knowledge of the relevant aspects of the situation (De George, 2003; Groves, 2009; Weckert and Adeney, 1997) and the wherewithal to act appropriately, which requires a number of further characteristics, including the power or influence to have the desired effect on the object.

The philosophically inclined reader will see that this is a list of highly contentious issues that philosophy has grappled with for millennia. And the questions do not stop with the subject. There are numerous different types of responsibility. The type of responsibility influences what counts as an appropriate authority, how the link between subject and object is construed and which sanctions may be linked to the ascription. Important types of responsibility include legal, moral and role responsibilities (Paul, Miller, and Paul, 1999), as well as capacity, causal, role, outcome, virtue and liability responsibility (Vincente, 2011). These often overlap and mirror each other, but they also differ in important aspects. One of these differences refers to authority. In some cases, such as legal responsibility, the authority is clearly defined (judge, jury) and there are clear ways of attributing sanctions and enforcing them. In the case of moral responsibility, the authority is much less clear and may be one's conscience, one's community or a metaphysical entity. Professional and role responsibility can sit between these, and the authority may be a professional body or a code of conduct with sanctions being less clear.

The mechanisms of ascribing responsibility to the subject differ according to the type of responsibility. The ascription may happen transitively or reflexively, which means that in some cases the subject assumes responsibility voluntarily, whereas in others it is forced upon the subject. Responsibilities can have different temporal horizons; sometimes looking back to past events and objects, sometimes looking to the future, and sometimes covering both aspects (Poel et al., 2012). The type of responsibility and authority furthermore influences what counts as the normative basis of responsibility. This can be the law, philosophical ethics, professional standards, community expectations and many more. Figure 22.3, while not claiming comprehensive coverage, attempts to capture some of the aspects of an individual case of responsibility ascription and reflect its complexity.

Figure 22.3 shows that responsibility is a highly complex term that is laden with difficult concepts and assumptions. The figure is indicative only. Real-life responsibility relationships are invariably even more complex, as the context of ascription potentially influences all of the components and dimensions listed earlier. Despite this complexity, however, responsibility is not

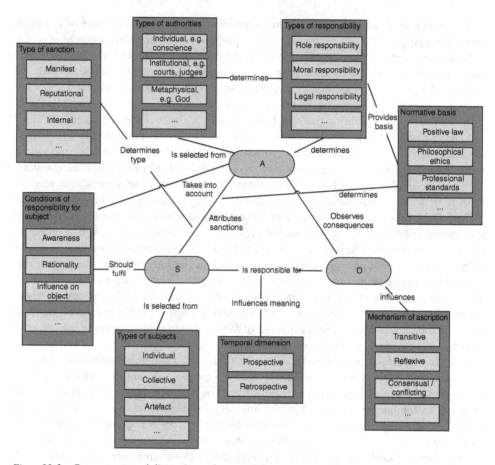

Figure 22.3 Components and dimensions of responsibility

only a theoretically interesting concept but also is practically highly relevant. Most importantly for our argument, it is successful in the sense that the mechanisms of responsibility described earlier actually steer individual and social action and often lead to desired outcomes. It would be difficult to explain this practical relevance of the concept using the description of responsibility offered so far. In order to understand why and how responsibilities are practically relevant, we now move beyond an individual instance of responsibility and introduce the ideas of networks of responsibility and meta-responsibility.

Meta-responsibility for the networks of responsibility

One crucial aspect of responsibility that much of the philosophically informed literature referred to earlier tends to overlook its flexibility and fluidity. The enumeration of key components and their representation in figures such as Figure 22.3 could be misread as meaning that responsibility is fixed and static. In practice, this is far from true. While there are generally agreed instances that one could see as social templates of responsibility, the individual responsibility relationship is socially negotiated and continually open to further re-negotiation. Rather than being static and fixed, responsibilities are dynamic and fluid. Some aspects may remain constant, while others change.

Theoretical accounts of responsibility are not always immediately or clearly action-guiding in a given context. This means that there are always elements of contexts that may influence a particular responsibility ascription that are not clear in advance and that can affect the practical outcome. One of the advantages of the concept of meta-responsibility is that it is tailored to deal with this type of ambiguity. The relationship between the key components can be adjusted according to specific requirements. Practical examples can clarify this point. Let us look at the responsibility of an engineer in an innovation process. The product the engineer works on may have foreseeable social consequences that require the engineer's attention. A change in the technical infrastructure (e.g. widely available social networks) may affect the way in which this knowledge can be gathered. Therefore, the engineer's professional responsibility towards their customers may change. This can happen through an update of guidelines issued by their professional body. If the engineer infringes on these, the professional body as the authority in this particular example can use established mechanisms to determine reasonable expectations and how the engineer should have acted in accordance.

The point here is that responsibility, while potentially infinitely complex, is built in a way to accommodate this flexibility. A meta-responsibility approach circumscribes a normative horizon relevant to the actions of particular actors, such that accountability is possible without resorting to universal moral theories. This is done overtly, and so all parties can be said to know their responsibilities. Where important components of responsibility are unclear and contested, there are normally mechanisms that allow for these questions to be clarified. And, interestingly, these mechanisms are typically also responsibilities, but they are of a different reach and configured differently from the original responsibility.

This leads us to the next point, which is that some literature on responsibility tends to overlook the diversity of views on responsibilities and the connections among them. In social reality, responsibilities never appear in the singular. The context in which they appear is an essential ingredient for understanding what they mean and what they imply among those who they involve. New responsibilities are always placed in a social world full of existing responsibilities.

This networked nature of responsibility is part of the social fabric. It is important to note that there are numerous linkages between different responsibilities. One typical responsibility within R&I, for example, would be to clarify standards and good practice in a particular field. The subject of this responsibility might be a professional body under the authority of a statutory requirement. In our terminology, this means that the definition of an authority (or norm) is the object of a different responsibility. This complex network of interlinking, often overlapping and sometimes even contradicting responsibilities is the background for the introduction of the concept of meta-responsibility.

The behaviour of actors in R&I is governed by a fluctuating and often ambiguous set of interlinking responsibilities. Any approach to research governance has to contend with this complex social structure. We propose that RRI should not be seen as a mechanism that simply adds to the complexity of existing responsibilities by requiring further actions (e.g. public engagement) or setting up additional structures (e.g. ethics review boards), but that it is better conceptualised as taking place on a different level. RRI should look at the overall landscape of intermingling and networked responsibilities and aim to affect the overall constellation of responsibilities with a view towards achieving the acceptable, sustainable and desirable consequences that it stands for.

Accepting this concept of RRI implies seeing RRI activities on a different level from the established networks of responsibility that currently govern research. RRI would then sit above other responsibilities and could be construed as a responsibility to shape, maintain, develop, coordinate and align R&I-related processes, actors and responsibilities, with a view to achieving its aims. To use a legal analogy, in this view RRI could be likened to constitutional law (i.e. the law that determines how other laws and regulations are created). The position of RRI on a higher level than existing responsibilities explains the use of the term meta-responsibility.

We believe that this concept of RRI as a meta-responsibility can make an important contribution to the discussion of RRI and of research governance more generally. It offers a role to RRI that does not conflict with existing governance structures but provides it with a constructive influence on research. It answers the question of whether research prior to RRI was irresponsible by pointing out that despite numerous existing responsibilities, further responsibilities may be required to achieve social aims.

Despite the importance of the idea of RRI as meta-responsibility, we are aware that at present it raises more questions than it answers. If RRI entails new responsibilities that constitute its meta-level nature, then this immediately raises a number of follow-on questions: Who or what is the subject of the meta-responsibility? How are the objects identified and constituted? What are authorities and norms? Which sanctions and consequences arise from it? What are its limitations? These are just some of the more obvious questions. We do not believe that these questions can simply be answered from an abstract point of view, but that they will be subjects of social negotiation. Instead of attempting a top-down theoretical definition of RRI as meta-responsibility, we therefore introduce an example to show how the idea of a meta-responsibility can be put into practice. This example will be drawn from the field of brain simulation and will focus on the activity of ethics management as a way of realising meta-responsibility.

Applying RRI in human brain simulation

RRI is most obviously important in cases where research is complex, multidisciplinary and can raise public concerns, be it over safety, ethics, use of resources or other potentially controversial issues. Our example, the EU-funded HBP fulfils all of these. The project was planned as a 10-year flagship project set to receive funding in the area of €1 billion and bring together more than 100 partner organisations. The fundamental idea behind the HBP is that the use of ICT can offer insights into the human brain that would otherwise be difficult or impossible to gain.

In this section we start by outlining the methodology used to understand the activities of the HBP. We then describe the project itself in more detail, before going into social and ethical concerns. This is the basis of the discussion of RRI in the HBP. The limitations of the original setup of RRI led to the creation of an ethics management activity, which we discuss using the theoretical ideas of meta-responsibility.

Methodology

The data that inform this paper originate from different sources. The description of the original perception of ethical and social issues draws on a set of 20 interviews with the leaders of the HBP's 12 subprojects. These interviews were conducted between January and July 2014. They were tape recorded, transcribed and analysed using principles of thematic qualitative data analysis (Miles and Huberman, 1994). Following the initial round of interviews, the key concerns were tested by sending a quantitative survey to all researchers in the HBP which aimed to find out to which degree researchers shared the view that the issues were relevant – 266/714 (37 per cent) researchers responded. The survey was started in November 2014, and reminders were sent in February 2015. The survey was closed in March 2015.

In addition to these formal data collection methods, the chapter is based on the experience of the authors. The first author was appointed ethics manager of the HBP in April 2015, and the other authors are part of the ethics management team. This means that the chapter can draw on insights gained by participation in senior management meetings, as well as interaction with all parts of the project in the context of ethics management. The research informing this chapter displays characteristics of interpretive case study research (Walsham, 1995), participant observation (Oates, 2005) and (confessional) auto-ethnography (Schultze, 2000). Given the ongoing role in ethics management and the fact that the research informs current and future practices through circles of planning, acting, observing and reflecting, the research furthermore displays characteristics of action research (Argyis and Schon, 1989; Baskerville and Wood-Harper, 1998; Blythe, Grabill, and Riley, 2008). We believe, however, that the question of an appropriate label for the methodology is less important than the insights we have gained into the practice of RRI.

The Human Brain Project

The HBP (www.humanbrainproject.eu/) is an EU FET flagship project funded under the Future and Emerging Technologies research stream. It started in October 2013, and is set to run for 10 years with an overall budget of more than €1 billion, half of which will be provided by the European Commission. The project combines numerous activities related to neuroscience and ICT research, including the provision of strategic mouse and human data required for simulation, cognitive architectures, the development of theory, creation of approaches and technologies to neuroinformatics and simulation, as well as new inputs to high-performance computing, neuromorphic computing and neurorobotics. Following a two-and-a-half-year ramp-up phase, the project moved to its operational phase in April 2016. Its main objectives for the operational phase are to (HBP, 2015, p. 9):

- Create and operate a European scientific research infrastructure for brain research, cognitive neuroscience and other brain-inspired sciences.
- Gather, organise and disseminate data describing the brain and its diseases.
- Simulate the brain.
- Build multi-scale scaffold theories and models of the brain.
- Develop brain-inspired computing, data analytics and robotics.
- Ensure that the HBP's work is undertaken responsibly and that it benefits society.

This list of objectives points towards the complexity of activities undertaken in the project. The proposal for the first two years of the operational phase includes 667 pages, which makes it clear that we cannot do justice to all aspects of the project. The one point we wish to underline is the last objective of undertaking the work responsibly and for the benefit of society. The inclusion of this point into the main objectives demonstrates the commitment of the HBP to RRI and the importance of rendering RRI practically relevant.

Ethical and social concerns

It was clear from the outset that the project would raise significant ethical and social questions (Rose, 2014). These are related to its subject matter, its size and its potential to disrupt the status quo in neuroscience, medicine and ICT, as well as its potential social impact. In order to provide an initial insight into the complexity and multitude of ethical issues, we discuss the findings of the 'researcher awareness' task. This task is part of the ethics and society activities, and communicates with HBP scientists to explore their concerns regarding ethical and social aspects of the project.

Governance of data and platforms

The HBP gathers data to support the development of 'brain signatures' for future medical purposes. The idea is that such brain signatures can provide insights into brain diseases and be linked to 'disease signatures'. Proper management of such data raises many ethical and social issues, particularly with regard to individual privacy.

Data are also gathered about animal and human brains to support the creation of simulations. Encouraging neuroscientists to disclose their experimental data to a repository before journal publication represents a change of practice for this community. The social and ethical concerns about the handling of these scientists' intellectual property are therefore important.

The ICT platforms will be made available not only within but also outside the consortium. This resource needs to be controlled in some way. All of these issues point to the need for sophisticated data and platform governance. Much data are produced within the HBP, but the simulations also require access to available external data. Both the flow of data into the various computing platforms and the use of data and models within and outside the HBP needs to be governed. Ethical issues to be addressed here range from immediate regulatory concerns, such as data protection, to difficult issues concerning incentives for collaboration and community engagement for platform use.

Responsible research practice

The size of the consortium and the diverse backgrounds of its members mean that responsible research conduct needs to be considered, especially as there are a variety of scientific approaches, not only in the consortium but also among external and future partnering projects. Of particular concern are animal experimentation and common standards, as well as the need to be assured of research integrity.

These issues are typically covered by research ethics and are subject to review and approval by research ethics committees. Clinical scientists are typically well aware of the issues and the regulations surrounding them. A difficult issue in this type of large collaborative project is that the various national regulations and requirements are not consistent. Research ethics cultures vary across the EU. While some aspects are regulated via European directives which have to be translated into national law (notably clinical trials and animal experimentation), the exact interpretation by national authorities can diverge. Similarly, the standards of research integrity may vary by country and discipline, rendering it difficult to tell when exactly accepted standards have been breached.

Development of collaboration

The diverse membership of the consortium and possible partnering projects implies that the ability to work together can cause problems. The social and ethical themes raised by creating such a collaboration is considered in four areas: the ability to discuss shared concerns, the tension between individual and common good, the support of multiple ontologies and the handling of intellectual property.

The structure of the HBP during the ramp-up phase reflected the many approaches to neuroscientific research that need to be part of the consortium. Interviewees recognised that this scientific diversity should be embraced and forums provided where there is an opportunity to discuss different positions.

The tension between individual and common good refers to the question of how partners balance their obligation to the project as a whole with their interest in promoting their own research. While collaborative projects generally face this issue, the size and complexity of the HBP exacerbate it. This refers both to the partners within the project and perhaps to a greater extent to the interaction with external user communities who make use of the infrastructure being built.

Furthermore, this complexity of the communities involved raises the question of shared understanding of epistemology and ontology. Little was said directly in the interviews that recognised this as a problem and a potential source of conflict.

The development of trust should extend to ensuring the proper handling of intellectual property with regard to applications resulting from the work of the HBP. This is especially true when those outside the consortium come to use the platforms.

Remote issues

In addition to the mostly practical concerns listed so far, the HBP increases the likelihood of various issues that may arise in the future if the research is successful. Some of these refer to individuals, for example, the question of the consequences of brain-based 'disease signatures' that may be used to classify individuals' disease states. This links to broader concerns about the way in which increased knowledge of the brain and its functions not only determine categorisations and treatment of diseases but also affect individuals' views of themselves and as members of the community.

The outcomes of the HBP may have an effect on many aspects of society. This starts with the way in which neuroscience and neurology are undertaken. The insights gained by the HBP may lead to novel types of individualised treatments and thus contribute to the trend of personal medicine, which raises further questions about accessibility and fairness. In addition, new brain-based computing artefacts may revolutionise the way society uses computers, further accelerating the rate of change brought about by emerging technologies.

Finally, there are rather distant scenarios which can be influenced by the HBP, including questions of machine intelligence and consciousness (Lim, 2013), machine ethics and human–computer confluence, that are currently in the realm of science fiction but may become reality at some point.

HBP-wide survey

Following the senior scholar interviews, we undertook an HBP-wide survey. This survey was sent to all 714 researchers in the HBP, and 266 responded with 5 refusing their consent to continue. The effective response proportion was 261/714 (37 per cent). Of the 261 respondents, 89 per cent (233) were working in a university or an affiliated institution.

Likert scale questions were asked around the themes of data protection, intellectual property and governance of the shared platforms, animal experimentation, research excellence, applications of brain signature research, development of collaboration and responsible R&I. The answers ranged from 'strongly disagree' to 'strongly agree' in seven steps, with neutral being the mid-step. After scoring disagreement in the range -3 (strong) to -1 (some) and agreement from 1 to 3, an average score was calculated.

With regard to data protection, there was agreement (represented by a positive average score) that individual consent should be provided for all human data used in the HBP, that the HBP should share responsibility with the collecting institution for the protection of personal data, that the HBP should appoint a designated officer responsible for privacy and data protection and that it should establish best practices for medical 'big data' research. Respondents were neutral (zero average score) about whether public good outweighed concerns about privacy.

With respect to the medical applications of HBP research, respondents agreed that the social and scientific consequences of identifying brain signatures need to be assessed by research and that the prevalence of brain signatures in the general population should also be assessed. They were neutral about whether it would be possible for a patient to challenge a psychiatric diagnosis based on brain signatures and were against the concept that psychiatric disease can only be defined in terms of brain abnormalities.

These responses are broadly in line with expectations one might have if the respondent were choosing an 'ethical' stance; something that is borne out by analysis of the other themes in the survey. The conclusion is perhaps unsurprising because it is likely that only those who considered it important to express their views on ethical matters responded to the survey. In this light, a response rate of 37 per cent suggests that a substantial minority of HBP staff are concerned about the ethical issues raised by the project and hold broadly conventional views.

Networked responsibilities in the HBP

These various ethical issues link to many responsibilities, some of which are straightforward and clear-cut, while others are more open and ambiguous. In a large and heterogeneous project such as the HBP the attribution of responsibilities is not always straightforward. Let us take the example of animal data. Where the HBP undertakes research on animals, this is done by labs which typically have a lot of experience in such research and have the required infrastructure in place, including relevant approvals. However, it may well be that the simulation of parts of a rodent brain on the brain simulation platform would require additional data, which might be sourced via the neuroinformatics platform from a lab outside the HBP and outside Europe. In this case, it is not immediately obvious who, if anyone, is responsible for ensuring that the original data collection followed acceptable principles and what should happen if this were not the case.

In a project with over 150 tasks and a similar number of task leaders who can all serve as local principal investigators (PIs) drawn from a broad range of disciplines, it becomes clear that the attribution of responsibility for the various ethical issues becomes difficult.

To exacerbate matters, the HBP was subject to intense public scrutiny and controversy. This culminated in an open letter to the European Commission, signed by more than 800 scientists (www.neurofuture.eu/). In particular, parts of the neuroscience community were critical of the approach and the governance of the project (Frégnac and Laurent, 2014). In addition, there were internal tensions between partners related to the external controversy, which led to an external mediation exercise (Marquardt, 2015).

This very brief outline shows that it is appropriate to speak of networks of responsibility within the HBP. The originally planned RRI activities added to this network by introducing ways to better understand social and ethical concerns.

RRI in the HBP

From the outset the HBP realised that it needed to engage with social and ethical concerns and therefore included the ethics and society subproject as part of project's core activities. At inception this subproject covered five work packages, each addressing a different angle of RRI.

The first set of activities was part of technology foresight (Georghiou et al., 2008) and aimed to explore the possible future in the three main areas of activity of the HBP: future medicine, future ICT and future neuroscience. Second, there was a set of philosophical and conceptual investigations that explored questions of relevance to the HBP, such as the concept of simulation (Dudai and Evers, 2014) and issues around consciousness. The third work package included activities related to engagement, with a number of events organised to reach out to an interested audience and the European public at large. Fourth, there was work on researcher awareness that aimed to explore the views and positions of researchers and scientists within the HBP, as reported earlier. Finally, there was a governance aspect that aimed to assemble a research ethics committee and an ethical, legal and social aspects committee to support the HBP, later merged into the ethical advisory board (EAB).

All of these activities are reasonable; they are clearly part of RRI and were carried out competently. Despite this, they had a rather limited effect on the HBP as a whole. The RRI activities included numerous and frequent interactions with the affected researchers of the HBP, but in spite of willingness to engage on both sides, practical exchanges rarely occurred. It remained unclear as to what exactly the ethical issues of the HBP were and how the issues could be assessed and prioritised to allow the RRI activities to focus on those that were most relevant. The overall governance of the HBP was rather complex and underwent changes. As a result, it was not clear as to what degree the highest level of project management and governance supported RRI.

This was the situation the project found itself in when it underwent a technical and ethics review by the European Commission in January 2015. The outcome of this review included significant changes to the project governance structures (Abbott, 2015) and a review of how ethical components were being managed. An ethics management component was added to the RRI activities. We believe that this ethics management component displays the characteristics of a meta-responsibility that was previously missing.

Ethics management as practiced meta-responsibility

Explicit attention to the management of ethical issues was introduced by the HBP's ethics and society subproject in response to the apparent shortcomings of the RRI processes. We now summarise the activities of the ethics management function and explain how it can be understood as a key component of meta-responsibility. This will be followed by discussion of the limitations of this view.

Ethics management plan in the HBP

Ethics management includes a number of interdependent activities and processes. The first one was the decision to have ethics management explicitly and visibly represented in the project structure. This was achieved by creating a work package on ethics management, which is led by the ethics manager. The ethics manager became a non-voting member of the board of directors, the highest decision-making body of the HBP. Furthermore, the ethics manager is responsible for the creation and maintenance of the HBP ethics map (see later for more detail) and the development of standard operating procedures to govern particular issues. The ethics management team sets up and maintains a point of registration (PORE) that allows members of the HBP, as well as external stakeholders, to raise issues they believe to be of importance. A crucial activity with regard to European Commission rules was the redesign of compliance procedures which require all local PIs and task leaders to provide approvals for their research, which are held in a central repository. Ethics management works closely with the European Commission to ensure that mutual expectations are clear. A new ethics advisory board (EAB) was formed from the previous research ethics committee and the ethical, legal and social aspect committee. This board is supported by the ethics management function. Members of the EAB were selected on the basis of their expertise. The members are independent of the HBP and provide expert advice. The interaction between the EAB and the HBP follows various routes, with a key one being the ethics rapporteurs, a concept that was proposed by the EAB members. The ethics rapporteur programme is also supported by the ethics management function. Each subproject nominates one or two individuals as their permanent contact points with regard to ethical and social issues.

All of these activities have project management components. However, instead of seeing them as part of project management, they should be interpreted as a means of improving transparency and communication about social and ethical issues. The guiding idea is that they should provide a social, discursive infrastructure that allows issues to be identified and discussed openly with subject experts and allows appropriate ways of addressing them to be found. Furthermore, the various components of ethics management are meant to provide an audit trail of all of these activities, which partly satisfies funding requirements, but more importantly allows discourse to be picked up where open questions remain and allows external input from within and beyond the project.

Changing networks of responsibility

We argue that these ethics management activities play a key role in transforming RRI from a more research-oriented activity to a meta-responsibility that can shape and align both new and existing responsibilities to ensure that the social acceptability, sustainability and desirability of the project are promoted. In order to make this argument, we discuss the three main components of responsibility and outline how the networks of responsibilities are affected.

The first and most obvious component is that of the objects of responsibility. What are the problems and issues that should be considered? Perhaps even more importantly, what is the relationship between these? The ethics management group went through a number of processes to identify these issues. In addition to drawing on the interviews and the survey mentioned earlier, as well as the work of other parts of the ethics and society subproject, the group arranged meetings with all subproject leaders, managers and ethics rapporteurs. These meetings were used to discuss known issues and raise potential further ones. A further online survey was subsequently sent to all task leaders to ask them about issues.

All of this led to a long list of issues, starting with issues raised by ethics reviewers and including numerous further ones. These range from well-regulated and easily identifiable ones, like the ethics of animal research, to more fluid and contested ones, such as ethical issues arising from big data. At the end of the spectrum there are more distant and speculative issues, such as the changing nature of the medical profession or even the possibility of machine consciousness.

A key task of the ethics management team was to represent these in a way that is accessible to both internal and external users. This was done by developing the 'HBP ethics map'. The idea behind this map is that it is the central repository of all relevant ethical issues that is used to discuss future actions. For this purpose, the map has the form of a spreadsheet. More important in terms of relating various issues and allowing them to be prioritised and discussed is the graphical representation of the issues as shown in Figure 22.4. The figure maps the issues along two axes: one indicating the likelihood that these issues are going to be serious and create problems for the HBP and the other indicating the potential social impact that the issues will have.

Figure 22.4 represents the state of discussion at a particular point in time. It does not claim to be complete nor to be a perfect representation. Whether an issue has a higher or lower likelihood and whether they should be grouped together as indicated is up for further debate. The map should be seen as the starting point for discussion, rather than its definitive outcome.

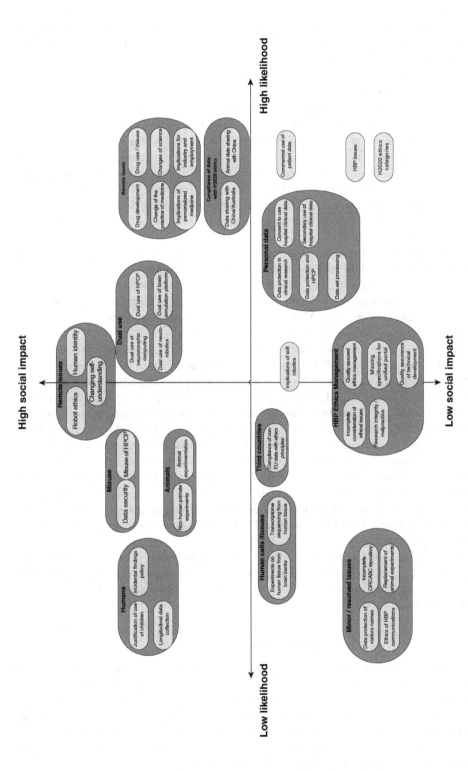

Figure 22.4 Graphical representation of the HBP ethics map

For the argument in this chapter, however, the graphical representation of the ethical issues is of crucial importance. It is a tool that allows us to see the various objects of responsibility in relation to one another. This is necessary for prioritising issues and discussing the relationships between them. It renders it clear, for example, that some of the remote issues, that is, those issues that are unlikely to come to full fruition in the immediate future, have a greater potential impact than many of the issues that have been the focus in the past (e.g. compliance issues of clinical and animal research). Its purpose as a tool is not so much to be a correct representation of reality but to be a stimulus for a debate that allows us to contextualise the various issues.

In addition to gaining an overview of the objects of responsibility, ethics management has also made significant progress in identifying the relevant subjects, i.e. determining who is responsible for the various issues. This was achieved by meeting with the senior scientists, managers and ethics rapporteurs, as well as surveying all PIs. These activities provide the groundwork for the overt circumscription of normative horizons that facilitates the knowledge of role and activity responsibility. It also doubles as an awareness-raising activity for the ethics management procedures that are underway.

The identification of the authority involved in the various aspects that make up the network of responsibilities in the HBP was greatly aided by the publication of a European Commission guide on how to undertake an ethics self-assessment (European Commission, 2014). This document lays out the types of ethical issues that the EC requires to be reflected on (corresponding to the dotted ovals in Figure 22.4). More importantly, it contains references to applicable legislation and the details of meeting ethical and legal requirements.

Arguably the most important work undertaken by the ethics management team in terms of RRI as meta-responsibility was the development of standard operating procedures (SOPs) and ethics action plans. SOPs were developed as general guidance on how to deal with particular issues in the HBP. Action plans for specific ethical issues were developed in collaboration with the affected scientists in order to give specific guidance on topics that fall outside of general guidance. These documents are linked to the HBP ethics map to indicate how the individual issues are to be addressed. Work on these documents is crucial because it allows for an open discussion across the different disciplines, with a view to ensuring that the issues are addressed in accordance with the overall aim of the project and also with a view to broader societal concerns. This is therefore the step that allows for the harmonisation and alignment of different responsibilities and the shaping of new ones where required. This clarifies to whom each of the roles within the HBP are responsible, making accountability transparent.

The various steps of the ethics management function thus live up to the idea of RRI meta-responsibility. They shape, maintain, develop, coordinate and align existing and novel R&I-related processes, actors and responsibilities, with a view to ensuring desirable and acceptable research outcomes.

Limitations of ethics management

Ethics management in the HBP fulfils the criteria of RRI as meta-responsibility. It represents a crucial step from reflection and deliberation to action to ensure that RRI has manifest outcomes. We do not claim, however, that it is perfect or a panacea for all ethical and social issues.

The limitations start with the arguably contradictory term 'ethics management' itself. Ethics as the philosophical reflection of morality (Stahl, 2012) is not and cannot be subject to management. It is, in fact, the relationships between different actors and the overall network of responsibilities that are managed, so the term is somewhat misleading.

Furthermore, there are practical questions. The case of ethics management described earlier is relatively novel and is still very much in development. At this point it is not clear how successful it will be in terms of achieving the societal goals. Furthermore, it is part of a very dynamic project environment that has attracted much public and political attention. It is difficult to foresee how this will affect ethics management.

The practical implementation of ethics management is on its way, but again, it is too early to tell whether scientists will resist it because they feel it is too onerous or whether it can raise questions with regard to enforcement.

However, we believe that these points, while raising caution with regard to the particular example of ethics management in the HBP, actually strengthen the overall argument for RRI as meta-responsibility. The socio-technical environment of R&I activities in societies tends to be fluid and contested. It is difficult to identify the exact actors and their responsibilities. Governance activities are likely to curtail options for some actors and may thus lead to resistance. In this environment a flexible and procedural approach is required that has the potential to see beyond immediate necessity to shape the overall research landscape.

Conclusion

RRI is a key concept of R&I governance and policy. The discourse around RRI is rich and offers numerous competing definitions and components. One aspect that is currently not clear is how RRI goes beyond the numerous well-established activities in science and research governance, such as technology assessment, foresight or science and technology studies. Similarly, on the European policy level it is not clear whether the six pillars (ethics, engagement, science education, gender, open access and governance) are comprehensive or whether addressing them would render research automatically responsible.

In this chapter we propose a different view of RRI as a meta-responsibility that aims to shape, maintain, develop, coordinate and align existing and novel R&I-related processes, actors and responsibilities, with a view to ensuring desirable and acceptable research outcomes. This proposal assigns a fundamentally different role to RRI that encompasses the various components and yet goes beyond them. We believe that this idea contributes to the RRI discourse by providing a focus and offering ways of rendering RRI practically relevant.

The theoretical contribution of the chapter is thus a development of the RRI discourse based on long-established theories of responsibility. The idea of networks of responsibility provides the basis for the re-conceptualisation of RRI as a meta-responsibility.

In addition to this theoretical contribution, we provide empirical evidence of the usefulness of the concept of meta-responsibility. Drawing on the newly established practice of ethics management in the HBP, we demonstrate that meta-responsibility can gain practical relevance and guide work on RRI. This does not replace existing RRI activities, but allows them to move out of isolation to be practically relevant. In terms of the AREA framework of RRI (anticipate, reflect, engage, act [Owen, 2014]) the idea of RRI as a meta-responsibility points towards options of realising the final A, the 'act'. If RRI is to remain an important component of research governance, then this move to practical relevance needs to be established.

Recommendations

Having demonstrated that RRI can be understood as a meta-responsibility and that this interpretation can help put it into practice, we can make some preliminary recommendations to individuals involved in setting research policy, as well as those who put it into practice.

RRI as a meta-responsibility constitutes an instance of responsibility in its own right. This means that the various components need to be defined and the conditions of a successful practice of responsibility should be considered. Most of this chapter spoke about the various objects of responsibility that RRI has to consider, from research ethics and gender equality to technology foresight and public engagement. To be able to align and coordinate these, RRI needs to be linked to a subject of responsibility. At present the RRI discourse shies away from the question of who is responsible for RRI. However, from the theory of responsibility we know that this is a crucial aspect of any successful responsibility ascription. It is therefore advisable to define the need for someone responsible for RRI on a policy and programme level as well as on the level of the individual project.

A second set of recommendations that arise from RRI as meta-responsibility relates to what we have called the authority, that is, the norms, the question of how they are applied and what sanctions are linked to their application. To put it differently, what are the rewards for a successful implementation of RRI, and what are the sanctions for failing to do so? These are important questions which are clear with regard to some aspects of RRI (e.g. failure to comply with research ethics can lead to withdrawal of funding) but are much more open with regard to other aspects such as temporally more remote questions, including the changing nature of the medical profession or the impact of novel neurotechnologies on human identity. In addition, they are generally not addressed with regard to RRI as a whole. Successful implementation of RRI in research policy thus requires attention to be paid to these questions and, at a minimum, a definition of processes that will lead to practical answers.

These recommendations are very preliminary and subject to further discussion. What they show, however, is that the concept of RRI as meta-responsibility not only improves our understanding of the topic but also can provide practical input into research policy development.

Further research

Much research remains to be done. This chapter demonstrates the applicability of the idea of meta-responsibility using one specific example. RRI spans all of R&I, and it is therefore important to explore whether and how meta-responsibility can be instituted in different contexts. It seems likely that ethics management as described here is not the only way of implementing meta-responsibility. Another open question refers to the specifics of discipline and subject. Our example of the HBP is of interest due to the size of the project, its interdisciplinary nature and the intuitive ethical relevance of the subject. It remains open, however, as to whether projects of different sizes or in different fields raise comparable or fundamentally different issues and how the idea of meta-responsibility might be used to address them.

Further work would also be useful in applying different theoretical lenses to reflect on RRI as meta-responsibility. Here we have focused on the theory of responsibility, which is plausible due to the inclusion of this term in 'RRI'. We suspect that similar arguments could be made from other theoretical positions. One strong candidate for such an alternative theory would be that of discourse ethics (Apel, 2002, 1990; Habermas, 1991; Mingers and Walsham, 2010). We believe that the idea of meta-responsibility could be expressed in these terms. If so, it would be interesting to see which practical implications could be drawn from this.

However, despite the clearly recognisable need for further work, both conceptually and empirically, this chapter has provided a much-needed theoretical development of RRI and used one of the biggest and most complex research projects worldwide to demonstrate the importance of this development. The chapter therefore furthers both theory and practice in research governance and policy.

Acknowledgements

The research leading to these results has received funding from the European Community's Seventh Framework Programme (FP7/2007–2013) under grant agreement n° 604102 (HBP Ramp-Up Phase) and from Horizon 2020 under grant agreement n° 720270 (HBP Specific Grant Agreement 1) and grant agreement n° 650003 (HBP Framework Partnership Agreement).

The authors would like to thank members of the ethics advisory board and Subproject 12 for input and discussions. We acknowledge the contributions by Henrik Waltern, Markus Christen, Michael Reinsborough, Christine Aikadi and Colin McKinnon.

The ideas presented in this chapter represent the views of the authors and do not necessarily reflect the position of the Human Brain Project or its of its funder, the European Commission.

Note

1 EPSRC: Framework for Responsible Innovation https://epsrc.ukri.org/research/framework/, accessed November 11, 2018.

References

Abbott, A. (2015). Human Brain Project votes for leadership change. *Nature*. doi:10.1038/nature.2015.17060.
Adam, B. and Groves, C. (2011). Futures tended: care and future-oriented responsibility. *Bulletin of Science, Technology & Society*, 31, 17–27. doi:10.1177/0270467610391237.
Anderson, M. and Anderson, S. L. (2007). Machine ethics: creating an ethical intelligent agent. *AI Magazine*, 28, 15–26.
Apel, K.-O. (1990). *Diskurs und verantwortung.: Das problem des übergangs zur postkonventionellen moral*. Frankfurt a.M., Germany: Suhrkamp Verlag KG.
Apel, K.-O. (2002). *The response of discourse ethics to the moral challenge of the human situation as such and especially today*. Leuven, Belgium: Peeters Publishers.
Argyis, C. and Schon, D. (1989). Participatory action research and action science compared. *American Behavioral Scientist*, 32, 612–623.
Auld, G., Mallett, A., Burlica, B., Nolan-Poupart, F. and Slater, R. (2014). Evaluating the effects of policy innovations: lessons from a systematic review of policies promoting low-carbon technology. *Global Environmental Change*, 29, 444–458. doi:10.1016/j.gloenvcha.2014.03.002.
Baskerville, R. L. and Wood-Harper, T. (1998). Diversity in information systems action research methods. *European Journal of Information Systems*, 7, 90.
Bechtel, W. (1985). Attributing responsibility to computer systems. *Metaphilosophy*, 16, 296–306. doi:10.1111/j.1467-9973.1985.tb00176.x.
Becker, H. A. (2001). Social impact assessment. *European Journal of Operational Research*, 128, 311–321. doi:10.1016/S0377-2217(00)00074-6.
Bickerstaff, K., Lorenzoni, I., Jones, M. and Pidgeon, N. (2010). Locating scientific citizenship: the institutional contexts and cultures of public engagement. *Science Technology and Human Values*, 35, 474–500.
Blythe, S., Grabill, J. T. and Riley, K. (2008). Action research and wicked environmental problems: exploring appropriate roles for researchers in professional communication. *Journal of Business and Technical Communication*, 22, 272–298. doi:10.1177/1050651908315973.
Cagnin, C., Keenan, M., Johnston, R., Scapolo, F. and Barré, R. (Eds.) (2008). *Future-oriented technology analysis*. Berlin & Heidelberg: Springer.
Čeičytė, J. and Petraitė, M. (2014). The concept of responsible innovation. *Public Policy and Administration*, 13, 400–413.
Coeckelbergh, M. (2015). Good healthcare is in the 'how': the quality of care, the role of machines, and the need for new skills. In van Rysewyk, S. P. and Pontier, M. (Eds.), *Machine medical ethics*. Heidelberg: Springer, pp. 33–48.
Coenen, C. and Simakova, E. (2013). STS policy interactions, technology assessment and the governance of technovisionary sciences. *Science, Technology and Innovation Studies*, 9, 3–20.
De George, R. T. (2003). *The ethics of information technology and business*. New York: Wiley-Blackwell.

Dudai, Y. and Evers, K. (2014). To simulate or not to simulate: what are the questions? *Neuron*, 84, 254–261.
Etchegoyen, A. (1993). *Le temps des responsables*. Julliard.
EU (2010). *Charter of fundamental rights of the European Union*.
European Commission (2012). Responsible research and innovation – Europe's ability to respond to societal challenges. European Commission, Publications Office, Brussels.
European Commission (2013). Options for strengthening responsible research and innovation (Report of the Expert Group on the State of Art in Europe on Responsible Research and Innovation). Publications Office of the European Union, Luxembourg.
European Commission (2014). How to complete your ethics Self-Assessment version 1.0. European Commission – DG Research and Innovation.
Fischer, J. M. (1999). Recent work on moral responsibility. *Ethics*, 110, 93–139.
Fisher, E. and Rip, A. (2013). Responsible innovation: multi-level dynamics and soft intervention practices. In Owen, R., Bessant, J. R. and Heintz, M. (Eds.), *Responsible innovation: managing the responsible emergence of science and innovation in society*. Chichester: Wiley, pp. 165–183.
Frégnac, Y. and Laurent, G. (2014). Neuroscience: where is the brain in the Human Brain Project? *Nature*, 513, 27–29. doi:10.1038/513027a.
French, P. A. (1992). *Responsibility matters*. University Press of Kansas.
Garriga, E. and Melé, D. (2004). Corporate social responsibility theories: mapping the territory. *Journal of Business Ethics*, 53, 51–71. doi:10.1023/B:BUSI.0000039399.90587.34.
Georghiou, L., Harper, J. C., Keenan, M., Miles, I. and Popper, R. (2008). *The handbook of technology foresight: concepts and practice*. Cheltenham: Edward Elgar Publishing.
Gorman, M. E. (2001). Turning students into ethical professionals. *IEEE Technology and Society Magazine*, 20, 21–27. doi:10.1109/44.974504.
Grinbaum, A. and Groves, C. (2013). Understanding the ethical issues. In Owen, R., Bessant, J. R. and Heintz, M. (Eds.), *Responsible innovation: managing the responsible emergence of science and innovation in society*. Chichester: Wiley, p. 119.
Groves, C. (2009). Future ethics: risk, care and non-reciprocal responsibility. *Journal of Global Ethics*, 5, 17–31.
Grunwald, A. (2009). Technology assessment: concept and methods. In Gabbay, D. M., Meijers, A. W. M., Woods, J. and Thagard, P. (Eds.), *Philosophy of technology and Engineering sciences: 9*. Amsterdam: North Holland, pp. 1103–1146.
Grunwald, A. (2011). Responsible innovation: bringing together technology assessment, applied ethics, and STS research. *Enterprise and Innovation Management Studies*, 7, 9–31.
Grunwald, A. (2012). Responsible nanotechnology. In *Philosophy and ethics*. Routledge, Taylor & Francis Group, LLC.
Grunwald, A. (2014). The hermeneutic side of responsible research and innovation. *Journal of Responsible Innovation*, 1, 274–291. doi:10.1080/23299460.2014.968437.
Gutmann, A. (2011). The ethics of synthetic biology: guiding principles for emerging technologies. *Hastings Center Report*, 41, 17–22.
Habermas, J. (1974). *Theory and practice*. Boston, MA: Beacon Press.
Habermas, J. (1991). *Erläuterungen zur Diskursethik*. Frankfurt am Main, Germany: Suhrkamp.
Hankins, J. (2012). *A handbook for responsible innovation* (1st ed.). Milan: Fondazione Giannino Bassetti.
Hart, H. L. A. (1968). *Punishment and responsibility: essays in the philosophy of law*. Oxford: Clarendon Press.
HBP (2015). *Human brain project specific grant agreement 1*, Proposal.
Hekkert, M. P., Suurs, R. A. A., Negro, S. O., Kuhlmann, S. and Smits, R. E. H. M. (2007). Functions of innovation systems: a new approach for analysing technological change. *Technological Forecasting and Social Change*, 74, 413–432.
Iatridis, K. and Schroeder, D. (2015). *Responsible research and innovation in industry: the case for corporate responsibility tools*. Heidelberg: Springer.
Jacob, K., Nielsen, L., van den Hoven, M. J., Roure, F., Rudze, L., Stilgoe, J., Blind, K., Guske, A. L. and Martinez Riera, C. (2013). Options for Strengthening Responsible Research and Innovation. Report of the Expert Group on the State of Art in Europe on Responsible Research and Innovation (Expert Group Report No. EUR25766 EN), Research and Innovation. European Commission, Luxembourg.
Joss, S. and Belucci, S. (Eds.) (2002). *Participatory technology assessment: European perspectives*. London: Centre for the Study of Democracy, University of Westminster.
Lenk, H. (2006). What is responsibility? *Philosophy Now*, 56, 29–32.

Lenk, H. and Maring, M. (1995). Wer soll Verantwortung tragen? Probleme der Verantwortungsverteilung in komplexen (soziotechnischen-sozioökonomischen) Systemen. In Bayertz, K. (Ed.), *Verantwortung. Prinzip Oder Problem?* Darmstadt: Wissenschaftliche Buchgesellschaft, pp. 241–286.

Lewis, H. D. (1972). The non-moral notion of collective responsibility. In French, P. (Ed.), *Individual and collective responsibility*. Cambridge, MA: Schenkman, pp. 116–144.

Lim, D. (2013). Brain simulation and personhood: A concern with the Human Brain Project. *Ethics and Information Technology*, 1–13. doi:10.1007/s10676-013-9330-5.

Markus, M. L. and Mentzer, K. (2014). Foresight for a responsible future with ICT. *Information Systems Frontiers*, 1–16. doi:10.1007/s10796-013-9479-9.

Marquardt, W. (2015). *Human Brain Project – Mediation Report*. Juelich: Forschungszentrum Juelich.

Marris, C. and Rose, N. (2010). Open engagement: exploring public participation in the biosciences. *PLoS Biology*, 8, e1000549. doi:10.1371/journal.pbio.1000549.

Miles, M. B. and Huberman, A. M. (1994). *Qualitative data analysis: an expanded sourcebook*. Thousand Oaks, CA: Sage.

Mingers, J. and Walsham, G. (2010). Towards ethical information systems: the contribution of discourse ethics. *MIS Quarterly*, 34, 833–854.

Oates, D. B. J. (2005). *Researching information systems and computing*. Thousand Oaks, CA: Sage.

Owen, R. (2014). The UK engineering and physical sciences research council's commitment to a framework for responsible innovation. *Journal of Responsible Innovation*, 1, 113–117. doi:10.1080/23299460.2014.882065.

Owen, R. and Goldberg, N. (2010). Responsible innovation: a pilot study with the U.K. Engineering and Physical Sciences Research Council. *Risk Analysis: An International-Journal*, 30, 1699–1707. doi:10.1111/j.1539-6924.2010.01517.x.

Owen, R., Heintz, M. and Bessant, J. (Eds.) (2013). *Responsible innovation*. New York: John Wiley & Sons Ltd.

Pandza, K. and Ellwood, P. (2013). Strategic and ethical foundations for responsible innovation. *Research Policy*, 42, 1112–1125. doi:10.1016/j.respol.2013.02.007.

Paul, E. F., Miller, F. D. M. and Paul, J. (Eds.) (1999). *Responsibility*. Cambridge: Cambridge University Press.

Poel, I. van de, Fahlquist, J. N., Doorn, N., Zwart, S. and Royakkers, L. (2012). The problem of many hands: climate change as an example. *Science and Engineering Ethics*, 18, 49–67. doi:10.1007/s11948-011-9276-0.

Rose, N. (2014). The human brain project: social and ethical challenges. *Neuron*, 82, 1212–1215. doi:10.1016/j.neuron.2014.06.001.

Rowe, G. and Frewer, L. J. (2005). A typology of public engagement mechanisms. *Science, Technology, & Human Values*, 30, 251–290. doi:10.1177/0162243904271724.

Ruggie, J. (2010). Business and human rights: further steps toward the operationalization of the 'protect, respect and remedy' framework (Report of the special representative of the secretary-general on the issue of human rights and transnational corporations and other business enterprises, UN Doc A/HRC/11/13). United Nations.

Schultze, U. (2000). A confessional account of an ethnography about knowledge work. *MIS Quarterly*, 24, 3–41.

Smits, R. and Kuhlmann, S. (2004). The rise of systemic instruments in innovation policy. *International Journal of Foresight and Innovation Policy*, 1, 4–32.

Stahl, B. (2012). Morality, ethics, and reflection: a categorization of normative IS research. *Journal of the Association for Information Systems*, 13.

Stahl, B. C. (2013). Responsible research and innovation: the role of privacy in an emerging framework. *Science Public Policy*, 40, 708–716. doi:10.1093/scipol/sct067.

Stahl, B. C., McBride, N., Wakunuma, K. and Flick, C. (2013). The empathic care robot: a prototype of responsible research and innovation. *Technological Forecasting and Social Change*, 84, 74–85. doi:10.1016/j.techfore.2013.08.001.

Stephan, S., Wütscher, F., Decker, M. and Ladikas, M. (2004). *Bridges between science, society and policy: technology assessment – methods and impacts*. Heidelberg/New York: Springer.

Stilgoe, J. (2014). Collective responsibility towards research and innovation's risks and new ethical dilemmas. EuroScientist Webzine. www.euroscientist.com/collective-responsibility-towards-research-innovations-risks-new-ethical-dilemmas/.

Stilgoe, J., Owen, R. and Macnaghten, P. (2013). Developing a framework for responsible innovation. *Research Policy*, 42, 1568–1580. doi:10.1016/j.respol.2013.05.008.

Sutcliffe, H. (2011). A report on responsible research and innovation. https://ec.europa.eu/research/science-society/document_library/pdf_06/rri-report-hilary-sutcliffe_en.pdf

Sutherland, W. J., Bellingan, L., Bellingham, J. R., Blackstock, J. J., Bloomfield, R. M., Bravo, M., Cadman, V. M., Cleevely, D. D., Clements, A., Cohen, A. S., Cope, D. R., Daemmrich, A. A., Devecchi, C., Anadon, L. D., Denegri, S., Doubleday, R., Dusic, N. R., Evans, R. J., Feng, W.Y., Godfray, H. C. J., Harris, P., Hartley, S. E., Hester, A. J., Holmes, J., Hughes, A., Hulme, M., Irwin, C., Jennings, R. C., Kass, G. S., Littlejohns, P., Marteau, T. M., McKee, G., Millstone, E. P., Nuttall, W. J., Owens, S., Parker, M. M., Pearson, S., Petts, J., Ploszek, R., Pullin, A. S., Reid, G., Richards, K. S., Robinson, J. G., Shaxson, L., Sierra, L., Smith, B. G., Spiegelhalter, D. J., Stilgoe, J., Stirling, A., Tyler, C. P., Winickoff, D. E. and Zimmern, R. L. (2012). A collaboratively-derived science-policy research agenda. *PLoS One*, 7, e31824. doi:10.1371/journal.pone.0031824.

Technopolis, Fraunhofer ISI (2012). *Interim evaluation & assessment of future options for Science in Society Actions Assessment of future options*. Brighton, UK: Technopolis group.

Timmermans, J. F. C. (2015). Annual report on RRI 2014 – Landscape of RRI discourse (Deliverable No. D 6.4-b), GREAT project. FP-7 GREAT Project.

van den Hoven, J. (2013). Value sensitive design and responsible innovation. In Owen, R., Bessant, J. R. and Heintz, M. (Eds.), *Responsible innovation: managing the responsible emergence of science and innovation in society*. Chichester: Wiley, pp. 75–83.

van Est, R., Walhout, B., Rerimassie, V., Stemerding, D. and Hanssen, L. (2012). Governance of nanotechnology in the Netherlands, informing and engaging in different social spheres. *Australian Journal of Emerging Technologies and Society*, 10, 6–26.

Velasquez, M. (1991). Why corporations are not morally responsible for anything they do. In May, L. and Hoffman, S. (Eds.), *Collective responsibility: five decades of debate in theoretical and applied ethics*. New York: Rowman & Littlefield Publishers, pp. 111–131.

Vincente, N. (2011). A structured taxonomy of responsibility concepts. In Vincent, N. A., Poel, I. van de, Hoven, J. van den (Eds.), *Moral responsibility: beyond free will and determinism*. Heidelberg/New York: Springer Science & Business Media, pp. 15–35.

Von Schomberg, R. (Ed.) (2011). *Towards responsible research and innovation in the information and communication technologies and security technologies fields*. Luxembourg: Publication Office of the European Union.

Walsham, G. (1995). Interpretive case studies in IS research: nature and method. *European Journal of Information Systems*, 4, 74–81. doi:10.1057/ejis.1995.9.

Weckert, J. and Adeney, D. (Eds.) (1997). *Computer and information ethics, contributions to the study of computer science*. Westport, CT: Greenwood Press.

Wilsdon, J. (2014). From foresight to hindsight: the promise of history in responsible innovation. *Journal of Responsible Innovation*, 1, 109–112. doi:10.1080/23299460.2014.885176.

Wright, D., Gellert, R., Gutwirth, S. and Friedewald, M. (2011). Precaution and privacy impact assessment as modes towards risk governance. In von Schomberg, R. (Ed.), *Towards responsible research and innovation in the information and communication technologies and security technologies fields*. Luxembourg: Publication Office of the European Union, pp. 83–97.

Wyndham, J. M., Albro, R., Ettinger, K., Smith, K., Sabatello, M. and Frankel, M. S. (2015). Social responsibility: a preliminary inquiry into the perspectives of scientists, engineers and health professionals. (Report prepared under the auspices of the AAAS Science and Human Rights Coalition and AAAS Scientific Responsibility, Human Rights and Law Program.) March 2015. doi: 10.1126/srhrl.aaa9798.

23
INTELLECTUAL PROPERTY AND INNOVATION MANAGEMENT

Can Huang and Suli Zheng

Introduction

Intellectual property (IP) refers to an intellectual creation for which the law assigns a monopoly right to designated owners (Markman, Espina, and Phan, 2004). It manifests in various forms, including copyright, trademarks, patents, industrial designs and trade secrets. IP has been defined in and protected by laws for several centuries; however, only in recent decades has IP become the primary locus of value for many organizations (Al-Aali and Teece, 2013). In business practice, IP is usually integrated into organizations' overall business models and innovation activities and plays an increasing role in the contemporary competitive world. In the academic literature, an increasing number of studies from management and economics focus on IP as their central topic and research its implications for business strategy, organizational behavior, innovation, competitiveness and economic development.

The protection of intellectual property rights (IPRs) can provide incentives for innovation (Mazzoleni and Nelson, 1998). Innovators would not have an incentive to invest in R&D if they were unable to appropriate the returns from innovation. Abraham Lincoln's succinct description of IP law – "adding the fuel of interest to the fire of genius" – demonstrates the importance of IP in reaping the benefits of private investment in innovation. However, social welfare can be increased if competitors can imitate and improve on innovations (Levin, Klevorick, Nelson, and Winter, 1987). IP law seeks to resolve this tension between the incentives for innovation and the widespread diffusion of its benefits. For example, the patent laws in most countries offer patent protection for 20 years. Eighteen months after a patent application is filed, many patent offices will disclose the application document, revealing the invention to society. After a patent expires at the end of the 20-year protection period, the patented innovation becomes public knowledge and can be practiced by anyone.

As IPRs become increasingly important in the knowledge economy, a crucial element of formulating a firm's innovation strategy is to determine how to protect its technological innovation through IPRs. Traditionally, economic and strategic studies have emphasized the importance of vigorously protecting an innovation to reap its rewards, but the decision of whether and how to protect an innovation is a more complex issue. Fisher and Oberholzer-Gee (2013) argued that the ways in which a firm can use IP to appropriate returns from innovation depend on the firm's strategy, its position in the marketplace and the rapidly changing IP laws in the countries in which the firm operates.

This chapter analyzes the literature on IP and innovation management in the period 1986–2018. Our primary goal is to review the development of IP and innovation studies and provide a quick reference for researchers interested in technology and innovation management, strategy or entrepreneurship.

In the next section, our literature review shows that scholarly interest in IP has grown considerably over the past 30 years, especially since the 2000s. To paint a broad picture of developments in this field, we identify a set of IP-related articles from 29 premier academic journals. In doing so, we build on Ziedonis (2008), who provided an excellent review of the IP-related literature published from 1986 to 2007 and introduce some extensions: First, we broaden the journal scope to include more innovation journals such as *Technovation, Journal of Product Innovation Management* and several leading business journals such as *Harvard Business Review* and *MIT Sloan Management Review*; second, the time frame for this study extends from 1986 to 2018, and we center our discussion on the articles published after 2000, which were not discussed in detail in Ziedonis's (2008) review. We first describe the overall profile of all the articles retrieved from a comprehensive search and then identify the most-cited 48 management and innovation articles according to the number of average annual citations that they received in the Web of Knowledge database by March 2018. We organize and review these articles according to five themes and discuss the main findings, methodological advances and unanswered questions of these studies.

Methodology

Considering the multidisciplinary nature of IP and innovation studies, we consult a relatively broad literature, searching for works on IP and innovation in the economics, management, business, legal and innovation fields. We select 29 leading academic journals for the search and retrieve a total of 2,081 articles that include the following IP-related terms in their titles, abstracts or keywords: IP, intangible asset, intellectual capital, patent, trademark, copyright or secret (secrecy). Book reviews, research notes and articles in conference proceedings are excluded.

Table 23.1 reports the journals from which the research articles related to IP and innovation are identified. Although far from comprehensive, the list includes prominent peer-reviewed

Table 23.1 Source journals of IP and innovation studies

Journal name	Subject domains	Abbreviation
Academy of Management Journal	Management	AMJ
Administrative Science Quarterly	Management	ASQ
American Economic Review	Economics	AER
California Management Review	Business	CMR
Econometrica	Economics	ECTR
Economics of Innovation and New Technology	Innovation and Economics	EINT
Harvard Business Review	Business	HBR
Industrial and Corporate Change	Innovation and Economics	ICC
International Journal of Industrial Organization	Economics	IJIO
Journal of Finance	Economics	JOF
Journal of Financial Economics	Economics	JFE
Journal of Industrial Economics	Economics	JIE

Journal name	Subject domains	Abbreviation
Journal of Law & Economics	Law and Economics	JLE
Journal of Law Economics & Organization	Law and Economics	JLEO
Journal of Legal Studies	Law	JLS
Journal of Management	Management	JOM
Journal of Management Studies	Management	JMS
Journal of Political Economy	Economics	JPE
Journal of Product Innovation Management	Innovation	JPIM
Management Science	Management	MS
MIT Sloan Management Review	Business	SMR
Organization Science	Management	OS
Quarterly Journal of Economics	Economics	QJE
Rand Journal of Economics	Economics	RJE
Research Policy	Innovation	RP
Review of Economic Studies	Economics	RES
Review of Economics and Statistics	Economics	REAS
Strategic Management Journal	Management	SMJ
Technovation	Innovation	TNV

outlets in management (e.g. *Academy of Management Journal, Strategic Management Journal and Management Science*), economics (e.g. *American Economic Review and Quarterly Journal of Economics*), law and economics (e.g. *the Journal of Law, Economics, and Organization* and *the Journal of Law and Economics*) and innovation (e.g. *Research Policy, Technovation* and *Journal of Product Innovation Management*). Due to their significance as outlets for research on IP and innovation, business journals such as *Harvard Business Review, MIT Sloan Management Review* and *California Management Review* are also included.

General profile of IP-related articles between 1986 and 2018

Figure 23.1 plots the number of IP-related articles according to publication year. Before 1996, the number of IP articles published annually in these journals remained quite stable, at roughly 20 publications per year. Between 1997 and 2006, the number of related articles grew steadily and reached approximately 80 in 2006. During the past decade, however, the number of IP publications has climbed sharply, with over 144 IP-related articles published in 2016 alone. This demonstrates an increasing level of academic interest in the topic.

To demonstrate the impact of these studies on the topic, we further examine the forward citations of these articles. Although several pioneering studies were published before 1996, they have generated few citations in total, and each of these papers had approximately one accumulated citation in the period 1986–1996. Between 1997 and 2006, the annual total citations increased from 341 to 4,011, with an annual growth rate of 120 percent. As the number of publications increased, the citations soared. In 2017, the accumulated number of citations increased to 16,586. As seen in Figures 23.1 and 23.2, the development of IP-related studies has gained momentum since the 2000s, as reflected by the rapidly growing numbers of publications and citations in the period.

Of these 2,081 articles, 342 received more than 100 citations and 49 attracted considerable attention, with more than 500 citations, and the total number of citations for these 49 papers amounted to 42,826, which accounts for 30 percent of the total citations of the 2,081 papers. An

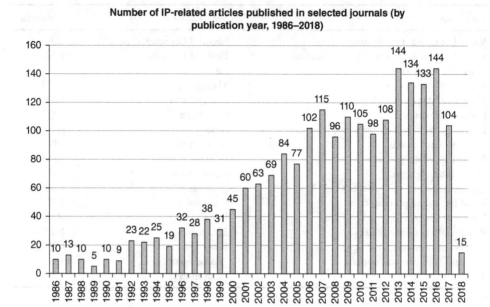

Figure 23.1 Number of IP-related articles published in selected journals

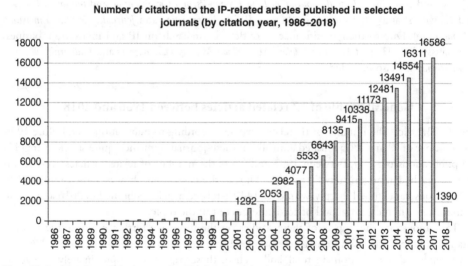

Figure 23.2 Number of citations to the IP-related articles in selected journals

example of a highly cited article is "Geographic localization of knowledge spillovers as evidenced by patent citations" written by Jaffe, Trajtenberg and Henderson and published in 1993. It has been cited 2,498 times and ranks first among all articles by the accumulated number of total citations.

The number of publications broken down by journal indicates that IP-related articles are distributed across a variety of subject domains (Figure 23.3). The leading journal in innovation, *Research Policy*, has published 647 articles in the last three decades, accounting for 31.1 percent

Intellectual property

Figure 23.3 Number of publications in selected journals

of all the publications. Another innovation journal, *Technovation*, ranks second, having published 182 articles, followed by *Harvard Business Review* (136 articles), *Strategic Management Journal* (127 articles), *International Journal of Industrial Organization* (110 articles) and *Industrial and Corporate Change* (104 articles).

Figure 23.4 displays the distribution of citations across different journals. The articles in *Research Policy* received 37,971 citations, which accounts for 26.7 percent of all the citations in our sample. *Strategic Management Journal* and *Management Science* received 18,688 and 10,489 citations, respectively. The average citations per article amounts to 147 for these two journals, demonstrating their leading positions in the field. *Rand Journal of Economics, American Economic Review* and *Academy of Management Journal* all received more than 6,000 citations, demonstrating their considerable impact on IP and innovation research as a whole.

Because of the time lag in citations, many articles published in journals in the 2010s have yet to receive significant numbers of citations. Because Ziedonis (2008) offered a thorough review of the widely cited studies published in the 1980s and 1990s, in the present review, we focus on the management and innovation studies that were published after 2000 and are not discussed in detail in her work.

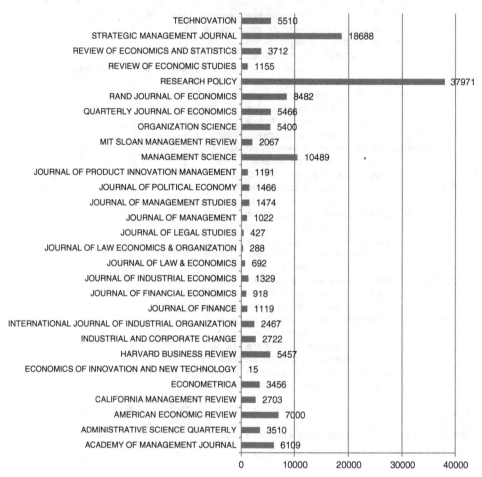

Figure 23.4 Number of citations to publications in selected journals

Table 23.2 lists the 48 most-cited articles published after 2000. As we can see from Table 23.2, 14 of the 48 papers were published in *Research Policy* and 9 papers each were published in *Strategic Management Journal* and *Management Science*. The remaining 16 appear in *Academy of Management Journal, Administrative Science Quarterly, Organization Science, Technovation, Harvard Business Review, Industrial and Corporate Change* and *Journal of Management Studies*.

Teece's article "Explicating dynamic capabilities: The nature and microfoundations of (sustainable) enterprise performance" published in *Strategic Journal of Management* tops the list, with 2,139 total citations and 178 average annual citations since its publication in 2007. Another article by Teece (1986) referenced in Ziedonis's (2008) review, "Profiting from technological innovation: Implications for integration, collaboration, licensing and public policy," ranks first on the list of articles published before 2007. Fleming contributed four papers on this list, and Ahuja and Almeida both have three articles on this list. Hence, these scholars have made the greatest contributions to IP and innovation research in recent decades.

Table 23.2 List of 48 most-cited articles between 2000 and March 2018

Rank[a]	Author	Article title	Journal[b]	Year	# Cites	# Annual Average cites
1	Teece, David J.	Explicating dynamic capabilities: The nature and microfoundations of (sustainable) enterprise performance	SMJ	2007	2139	178.3
2	Ahuja, G	Collaboration networks, structural holes, and innovation: A longitudinal study	ASQ	2000	1501	79.0
3	Subramaniam, M; Youndt, MA	The influence of intellectual capital on the types of innovative capabilities	AMJ	2005	971	69.4
4	Huizingh, Elk K. R. E.	Open innovation: State of the art and future perspectives	TNV	2011	423	52.9
5	Owen-Smith, J; Powell, WW	Knowledge networks as channels and conduits: The effects of spillovers in the Boston biotechnology community	OS	2004	780	52.0
6	Rosenkopf, L; Nerkar, A	Beyond local search: Boundary-spanning, exploration, and impact in the optical disk industry	SMJ	2001	903	50.2
7	Perkmann, Markus; Tartari, Valentina; et al.	Academic engagement and commercialization: A review of the literature on university-industry relations	RP	2013	288	48.0
8	Roberts, PW; Dowling, GR	Corporate reputation and sustained superior financial performance	SMJ	2002	711	41.8
9	Ahuja, G; Katila, R	Technological acquisitions and the innovation performance of acquiring firms: A longitudinal study	SMJ	2001	738	41.0
10	O'Reilly, CA; Tushman, ML	The ambidextrous organization	HBR	2004	607	40.5
11	Stuart, TE	Interorganizational alliances and the performance of firms: A study of growth and innovation rates in a high-technology industry	SMJ	2000	768	40.4
12	von Hippel, E; von Krogh, G	Open source software and the private-collective innovation model: Issues for organization science	OS	2003	636	39.8
13	Furman, JL; Porter, ME; Stern, S	The determinants of national innovative capacity	RP	2002	655	38.5
14	Rothaermel, Frank T.; Agung, Shanti D.; Jiang, Lin	University entrepreneurship: a taxonomy of the literature	ICC	2007	460	38.3
15	Fleming, L	Recombinant uncertainty in technological search	MS	2001	657	36.5
16	Schilling, Melissa A.; Phelps, Corey C.	Interfirm collaboration networks: The impact of large-scale network structure on firm innovation	MS	2007	433	36.1
17	Ahuja, G	The duality of collaboration: Inducements and opportunities in the formation of interfirm linkages	SMJ	2000	643	33.8
18	D'Este, P.; Patel, P.	University-industry linkages in the UK: What are the factors underlying the variety of interactions with industry?	RP	2007	405	33.8
19	Rosenkopf, L; Almeida, P	Overcoming local search through alliances and mobility	MS	2003	516	32.3

(*Continued*)

Table 23.2 (Continued)

Rank[a]	Author	Article title	Journal[b]	Year	# Cites	# Annual Average cites
20	Sampson, Rachelle C.	R&D alliances and firm performance: The impact of technological diversity and alliance organization on innovation	AMJ	2007	381	31.8
21	Sorensen, JB; Stuart, TE	Aging, obsolescence, and organizational innovation	ASQ	2000	603	31.7
22	Lu, JW; Beamish, PW	International diversification and firm performance: The S-CURVE hypothesis	AMJ	2004	476	31.7
23	Shane, S; Stuart, T	Organizational endowments and the performance of university start-ups	MS	2002	517	30.4
24	Acs, ZJ; Anselin, L; Varga, A	Patents and innovation counts as measures of regional production of new knowledge	RP	2002	516	30.4
25	Hitt, MA; Dacin, MT; et al.	Partner selection in emerging and developed market contexts: Resource-based and organizational learning perspectives	AMJ	2000	556	29.3
26	Mowery, DC; Nelson, RR; et al.	The growth of patenting and licensing by US universities: an assessment of the effects of the Bayh-Dole act of 1980	RP	2001	520	28.9
27	Benner, MJ; Tushman, M	Process management and technological innovation: A longitudinal study of the photography and paint industries	ASQ	2002	471	27.7
28	Hagedoorn, J; Cloodt, M	Measuring innovative performance: is there an advantage in using multiple indicators?	RP	2003	442	27.6
29	Di Gregorio, D; Shane, S	Why do some universities generate more start-ups than others?	RP	2003	441	27.6
30	Bozeman, B	Technology transfer and public policy: a review of research and theory	RP	2000	500	26.3
31	Harhoff, D; Scherer, FM; Vopel, K	Citations, family size, opposition and the value of patent rights	RP	2003	397	24.8
32	Fleming, Lee; Mingo, Santiago; Chen, David	Collaborative brokerage, generative creativity, and creative success	ASQ	2007	287	23.9
33	Gans, JS; Stern, S	The product market and the market for ideas: commercialization strategies for technology entrepreneurs	RP	2003	382	23.9
34	Fleming, L; Sorenson, O	Science as a map in technological search	SMJ	2004	357	23.8
35	Agrawal, A; Henderson, R	Putting patents in context: Exploring knowledge transfer from MIT	MS	2002	402	23.7
36	Singh, J	Collaborative networks as determinants of knowledge diffusion patterns	MS	2005	328	23.4
37	Youndt, MA; Subramaniam, M; Snell, SA	Intellectual capital profiles: An examination of investments and returns	JMS	2004	344	22.9
38	Zucker, LG; Darby, MR; Armstrong, JS	Commercializing knowledge: University science, knowledge capture, and firm performance in biotechnology	MS	2002	386	22.7
39	Song, J; Almeida, P; Wu, G	Learning-by-hiring: When is mobility more likely to facilitate interfirm knowledge transfer?	MS	2003	339	21.2
40	Fleming, L; Sorenson, O	Technology as a complex adaptive system: evidence from patent data	RP	2001	375	20.8
41	Lockett, A; Wright, M	Resources, capabilities, risk capital and the creation of university spin-out companies	RP	2005	287	20.5

42	Almeida, P; Phene, A	Subsidiaries and knowledge creation: The influence of the MNC and host country on innovation	SMJ	2004	306	20.4
43	Thursby, JG; Thursby, MC	Who is selling the Ivory Tower? Sources of growth in university licensing	MS	2002	342	20.1
44	Delios, A; Beamish, PW	Survival and profitability: The roles of experience and intangible assets in foreign subsidiary performance	AMJ	2001	329	18.3
45	Romijn, H; Albaladejo, M	Determinants of innovation capability in small electronics and software firms in southeast England	RP	2002	305	17.9
46	Frost, TS	The geographic sources of foreign subsidiaries' innovations	SMJ	2001	306	17.0
47	Cohen, WM; Goto, A; et al.	R&D spillovers, patents and the incentives to innovate in Japan and the United States	RP	2002	288	16.9
48	Bouty, I	Interpersonal and interaction influences on informal resource exchanges between R&D researchers across organizational boundaries	AMJ	2000	294	15.5

Notes:
1. Because the more recent articles have relatively fewer total citations in comparison to the earlier publications, this ranking is based on the average annual citations received by each article.
2. Journal abbreviations are reported in Table 23.1.
3. Insights from highly cited articles.

In this section, we examine the most-cited IP-related articles published after 2000 and group them according to the following five themes:

- Intangible assets and innovation
- Alliance, network and innovation
- Patenting as a proxy for innovation activities
- IP management and innovation
- University technology transfer

These themes reflect the academic community's growing interest in IP-related issues. We will highlight the selected articles, the methodologies that they employ, their main findings and remaining issues in the following discussion.

Intangible assets and innovation

As firms' business activities have become increasingly knowledge-intensive, intangible assets have accounted for a growing share of the total value of public companies. In 1975, only 17 percent of the market value of Standard and Poor's 500 companies was from intangible assets, but this figure had increased to 87 percent by 2015 (Ocean Tomo, 2015). Among the highly cited articles, the following contributions discussed the importance of intangible assets and how companies can better manage them.

As introduced in the previous section, in an influential article, Teece (2007) proposed a framework of dynamic capabilities. He argued that firms that compete in an open economy with rapid innovation need dynamic capabilities to sense the opportunities and threats associated with technological change; to seize these opportunities; and to strengthen their competitiveness through protecting, enhancing and reconfiguring their intangible and tangible assets. According to Teece, to improve its dynamic capabilities, a firm needs to sharpen its skills and improve its process, procedure, organizational structures, decision rules and disciplines to realize firm-level sensing, seizing and reconfiguring capacities. The firm not only needs to adjust itself to business ecosystems but also to shape them through innovating and collaborating with other firms and organizations. Related to the framework of dynamic capabilities, O'Reilly and Tushman (2004) emphasized that established companies need to explore new business opportunities while simultaneously exploiting the potential of existing businesses. Companies need to establish an ambidextrous organization, in which the new and exploratory units are separated from the traditional and exploitative ones, but both units are tightly integrated at the senior executive level.

Roberts and Dowling (2002) demonstrated by analyzing a dynamic model that firms with good reputation, which is an intangible asset, are able to sustain superior financial performance over time. The reputation data came from an annual survey of Fortune 1000 firms, which cover eight scales: asset use, community and environmental friendliness, the ability to develop and keep key people, financial soundness, the degree of innovativeness, investment value, management quality and product quality. The authors decomposed the overall reputation score into a component that can be explained by previous financial performance and another component that can be considered a residual ("left over"). They showed that both components contribute to the persistence of above-average firm financial performance over time.

Based on a longitudinal data set of 1,489 Japanese firms and their internationalization activities from 1986 to 1997, Lu and Beamish (2004) researched the relationship between multinationality and firm performance. They found that the relationship between firms' internationalization activities and performance can be best described as a horizontal S-curve. Specifically, firm performance first declines with increased internationalization activities, which are measured by the number of overseas subsidiaries and the number of countries in which a firm had overseas subsidiaries. Performance then increases with increasing geographical diversification and declines again at a very high level of multinationality. The authors also found that firms investing more heavily in intangible assets, such as technology and advertising, achieved greater profitability from their investment in foreign countries. In a related study, Delios and Beamish (2001) studied how a firm's intangible assets, which are measured by R&D and advertising intensity, and its experience affect subsidiary survival and profitability. The authors suggested that internationalizing firms should adapt their existing intangible asset advantage to compete in new foreign markets. In addition, the host country experience contributes to the positive relationship between a multinational firm's intangible assets and subsidiary profitability.

Studying the international partner selection of firms from emerging and developed markets Hitt et al. (2000) suggested that firms select alliance partners to obtain access to resources and gain organizational learning opportunities. They found that emerging market firms emphasized financial assets, technical capabilities, intangible assets (including technical and managerial capabilities, unique competencies, market knowledge, and access) and willingness to share expertise in the selection of partners. In contrast, developed market firms highlighted unique capabilities and local market knowledge and access in their partner selection. This research demonstrates that both tangible and intangible assets are the critical factors that firms would consider when selecting international alliance partners.

Alliance, network and innovation

Firms establish strategic alliances to exchange and share resources to develop products and services (Hoang and Rothaermel, 2005; Krishnan, Martin, and Noorderhaven, 2006). While alliances are used as a ubiquitous strategic tool in many industries, scholars are interested in their impact on firms' innovation activities or performance. In addition, an alliance relationship connects firms in an industry or a cluster to form a network, the structure, feature and characteristics of which have separate influences on firm performance. The following influential articles represent efforts at examining the relationship among alliances, networks and innovation, and many of them used patent data to construct their network measures. They provide insights into how a firm can leverage its alliances and position in a network to promote innovation activities.

Stuart (2000) researched the relationship between technology alliances and firm performance, which is measured by sales growth and the number of granted patents. He argued that how much a focal firm can benefit from strategic alliance largely depends on the resource of its alliance partners. Large or leading firms are the most valuable partners because of their reliability, reputation and track record of prior accomplishments. For young or small firms, forming an alliance with a large and innovative partner can be regarded as endorsement, because to form such an alliance, young or small firms have to survive the due diligence of their prominent partners.

Studying the relationship between a firm's position in the industry network of interfirm collaborative linkages and its innovation output, Ahuja (2000a) argued that direct ties, indirect ties and structural holes have differential impacts on the firm's subsequent innovation output. The direct and indirect ties both positively influence innovation, and the number of direct ties moderates the relationship between indirect ties and innovation. Increasing structural holes has a negative effect on innovation. In a related study, Ahuja (2000b) argued that linkage formation by firms can be explained by the incentives and opportunities to do so. He drew upon the theories of the resource-based view and social networks to identify three forms of accumulated capital – technical, commercial and social – that can affect a firm's incentives and opportunities to form linkages. Examining the networks of 35,400 collaborative patent inventors, Fleming, Mingo, and Chen (2007) examined the career histories of inventors using data on U.S. patents from 1975 to 2002. They found that collaboration in a cohesive network, in which most individuals have direct ties to one another, only produces marginal benefits for creating novel patent subclass combinations. In addition, the marginal benefits of cohesion are only two-thirds as much as its negative first-order effect on the generation of novel patent subclass combinations. Fleming et al., also found that the novel patent subclass combinations produced by brokered collaboration, in which one person links two or more others who have no direct ties to one another, are less likely to be used in the future.

Intrigued by the questions regarding the extent to which a firm is able to learn from its partners, Sampson (2007) studied the influence of partner technological diversity and the organizational forms of alliances on firm innovation performance. She found that alliances contribute far more to firm innovation when the difference between allied firms' technological capabilities is moderate, rather than low or high, irrespective of the chosen organizational form of the alliance. In terms of the impact of the organizational form of alliances, firms benefit from organizational alliances that take the form of an equity joint venture when the technological diversity between partners is high. The benefits from collaborative activities organized as equity joint ventures are greater than those of collaborations taking the form of a bilateral contract with either a moderate or high level of diversity.

Schilling and Phelps (2007) studied the impact of the structure of alliance networks on their potential for knowledge creation based on a panel of firms operating in 11 industry-level alliance networks. They argued that firms are able to perform better in terms of innovation output in the alliance networks that are characterized by both high clustering and high reach (short average path lengths to a wide range of firms) than in the networks that do not show these characteristics. The reason is that dense connectivity of clusters creates transmission capacity in a network, which enables a large amount of information to diffuse rapidly, while reach ensures that a large quantity and diversity of information can be brought to firms in the network within relatively close range.

Knowledge flow tends to be limited within regional and firm boundaries. Singh (2005) attributed this phenomenon to the distribution of interpersonal networks. He used collaboration information for patents registered with the U.S. Patent and Trademark Office (USPTO) to construct a database of interpersonal relations among all inventors recorded by the USPTO since 1975. He found that knowledge flows, which are measured by patent citations, are stronger within than between regions and firms. However, Singh also found that geographic proximity and firm boundaries have little additional effect on the probability of knowledge flows between inventors who are already closely connected in the collaboration network. The regional and firm boundaries continue to matter more for the knowledge flows between inventors with no or only very indirect ties. Owen-Smith and Powell (2004) studied the human therapeutic biotechnology firms located in the Boston metropolitan area and argued that two features of formal interorganizational networks (i.e., geographic proximity and organizational form) change the flow of information through a network and thus enable a firm to leverage its position within a large network to strengthen its innovation performance.

Patenting as a proxy for innovation activities

Knowledge creation manifests as invention. After being examined by patent examiners at the patent office, invention can be protected through patents. As multiple studies have demonstrated

(Trajtenberg, 1990; Hagedoorn and Cloodt, 2003), patents are valid and robust indicators of knowledge creation. In the following studies, patenting activities are considered a proxy for innovation activities at the firm level and country level, and the information contained in the patent document, such as citations, is often used to study firms' innovation activities.

Sorensen and Stuart (2000) advanced two seemingly contradictory theories for the relationship between the age of companies and their innovations, which are measured by patents. One theory is that firms' innovations increase with age. The other is that firms' innovations decrease with age, as technological leadership is temporal, and the firms at the technological frontier are quickly outcompeted by new rivals. Based on the patent data of firms in the semiconductor and biotechnology industries, they provided evidence that as organizations age, they become better able to generate new innovations (patents). However, the authors also showed that as firms age, they become increasingly likely to exploit existing competences and improve on older areas of technology, and thus, their patents are less likely to be cited by other firms than the patents owned by younger firms.

Researching the relationship between process management and technological innovation, measured by patents, Benner (2002) hypothesized that process management would reduce variance in organizational routines and thereby encourage exploitative innovations but reduce exploratory innovation. The author used ISO 9000 quality program certifications to represent process management activities and developed several measures of exploitation and exploration based on the extent to which a firm's patents cited its own patents or patents that it had previously cited. The empirical evidence supports the hypothesis that firms tend to exploit existing knowledge and capabilities rather than engage in exploratory activities as organizational routines are established and repeated.

Drawing on the resource-based view and the theories of technological innovation and learning, Ahuja and Katila (2001) studied the influence of acquisitions on the subsequent innovation performance of acquiring firms in the chemicals industry. They measured innovation performance by the patenting frequency of the acquiring firms, and they distinguished technological and nontechnological acquisitions according to whether technology was a component of the acquired firm's assets. Ahuja and Katila found that for technological acquisitions, the absolute size of the acquired knowledge base is positively associated with innovation output, while the relative size of the acquired knowledge base is negatively associated with innovation output. The relationship between the relatedness of acquired and acquiring knowledge bases and the innovation output of acquiring firms is nonlinear. As the degree of relatedness increases, the innovation performance of acquiring firms first increases and then decreases.

Studying the patenting activities of engineers who moved from U.S. firms to non-U.S. firms, Song, Almeida, and Wu (2003) argued that firms are able to acquire knowledge beyond their current technological and geographic boundaries by hiring experts from other firms. The authors termed this mechanism "learning-by-hiring" and found that mobility is more likely to result in interfirm knowledge transfer if the hiring firm is less path dependent, if the hired engineers possess technological knowledge that is distant from that of the hiring firm or if the hired engineers work in noncore technological areas in the new firm. In a related study, Rosenkopf and Nerkar (2001) suggested that mobility of inventors and the formation of strategic alliances can enable firms to overcome geographic and technological constraints in searching for new knowledge. They found that mobility of inventors facilitates interfirm knowledge flows, notwithstanding geographical distance. However, when technological distance rises, the usefulness of alliances and mobility also increases.

Examining a sample of U.S. semiconductor firms, Almeida and Phene (2004) found that the knowledge linkages of multinational corporations' (MNCs') subsidiaries to host country firms and the technological diversity within the host country positively influence the innovation of subsidiaries of MNCs. Frost (2001) studied the subsidiaries of foreign companies located in the United States and argued that subsidiary innovations that build on the existing technology of the parent firm are more likely to cite patents originating in the home base of parent firms. The larger the share of company patents generated by the subsidiary is, the more likely these patents are to cite patents originating from the host country. Moreover, subsidiaries are more likely to draw upon knowledge from the host country environment if the parent firm has a greater presence in the host country.

Fleming (2001) synthesized the theories on the sources of technological novelty: invention is a recombination and local search process, and technological uncertainty arises when an inventor searches unfamiliar components and component combinations. By analyzing the 17,264 U.S. patents granted during May and June 1990, Fleming found that experimentation with new components and new combinations produces less useful inventors on average, but it may also result in an increase in the variability that can lead to breakthroughs. In a related study, Fleming and Sorenson (2004) researched how scientific research can increase the rate of technological advance. They argued that science would not have a material impact when inventors work with relatively independent components but can become beneficial when inventors seek to combine highly coupled components.

Advancing the studies on exploitation and exploration activities, Rosenkopf and Nerkar (2001) argued that moving beyond local search requires exploratory activities that cross some boundary. The authors created a typology of exploratory activities by distinguishing organizational and technological boundaries: local exploration spans neither organizational nor technological boundaries, external boundary-spanning exploration spans the organizational boundary only, internal boundary-spanning exploration spans the technological boundary only and radical exploration spans both boundaries. Analyzing the patenting data of optical disk firms, Rosenkopf and Nerkar found that exploration that does not cross either boundary has a smaller impact on subsequent technological development. When exploration spans both boundaries, it has the greatest impact on subsequent technological evolution, even beyond the optical disk domain.

In addition to being used as indicators of innovation activity at the firm level, patents are used as indicators at the country level. Acs, Anselin, and Varga (2002) compared innovation count data and patent count data at the lowest possible levels of geographical aggregation in the United States (i.e. metropolitan statistical areas) and confirmed that the patent data developed by the USPTO is a valid proxy for innovative activity at the regional level. Furman, Porter, and Stern (2002) defined national innovative capacity as the extent to which a country can produce and commercialize new-to-the-world technologies in the long run. National innovative capacity depends on a strong common innovation infrastructure, innovation environments in a country's industry cluster and the connection between the common innovation infrastructure and various clusters. They also found that the estimated level of national innovative capacity affects total factor productivity growth and a nation's share of high-technology exports, and they suggested that a country's international patents are driven by a small number of factors that determine a country's national innovative capacity.

IP management and innovation

Several topics emerge from the highly cited articles on the theme of IP management and innovation, which include how to protect and leverage IP in an open innovation environment (Huizingh, 2011; von Hippel and von Krogh, 2003; Bouty, 2000; Gans and Stern, 2003), how to protect and promote innovation to enhance firm performance (Cohen et al., 2002; Romijn and

Albaladejo, 2002; Youndt, Subramaniam, and Snell, 2004; Subramaniam and Youndt, 2005) and determinants of the value of patents (Harhoff, Scherer, and Vopel, 2003).

Open innovation has become one of the most popular topics in innovation management (Huizingh, 2011) over the past two decades. von Hippel and von Krogh (2003) described two models of innovation. One is the private investment model in which private goods production and effective intellectual property protection brings returns to innovation. The other is the collective action model in which innovators collaborate to produce a public good. They argued that open-source software development is an example of a combined "private-collective" model of innovation that sits in between the private investment and the collective action models. Bouty (2000) studied the paradox of interpersonal exchanges of resources between R&D scientists across organizational boundaries, which can enhance both innovation and the potential risk of intellectual property leaks. She found that social capital is the key success factor in the resource acquisition process and that strategic resources can only be exchanged under conditions of acquaintance and mutual trust. She also revealed that social capital is a major success factor in these particular organizational learning processes and that community is an important conduit for sharing resources and knowledge.

Advocating a synthetic framework for identifying the drivers of start-up commercialization strategy, Gans and Stern (2003) suggested that for many start-up innovators, the collaborators who control complementary assets are most likely the current market players with an incentive to expropriate the start-ups' technology. Therefore, the interaction between start-up innovators and incumbent firms is largely shaped by whether there is a market for the idea in question. The authors' key insights are that when intellectual property protection is effective and important complementary assets are held by incumbent firms, start-up innovators can generate more rents if they pursue cooperation with incumbent firms. In contrast, when intellectual property protection is weak and barriers to entry are low, start-up innovators may pursue competitive commercialization strategies.

To investigate the methods that firms use to protect and promote innovation, Cohen et al. (2002) conducted a survey of the managers of R&D units of manufacturing firms in the United States and Japan. They found that secrecy appears to be the predominant appropriability strategy of the U.S. firms but not of the Japanese firms. In contrast, patents represent the most important channel for information flows in Japan. This may be due to the lower number and narrow claims per patent in Japan, which give rise to greater mutual dependence across the patent portfolios of competing firms and thus promote greater information-sharing among rivals. Romijn and Albaladejo (2002) surveyed 33 small software and electronics manufacturing companies in the UK in 1998. They found that the important internal factors determining innovation performance include the owner's or manager's prior experience in a scientific environment and the staff's science and engineering degrees. The initial support from the science laboratory or university department from which the companies had spun off and public R&D support are the important external factors contributing to the companies' innovation performance.

Youndt, Subramaniam, and Snell (2004) adopted a configural approach to study how investment in human, social and organization capital, which forms intellectual capital, affects firm performance. Human capital refers to the knowledge, skills and abilities of employees. Social capital describes the resources available from the networks of relationships that firms establish. Organizational capital represents a firm's institutionalized knowledge and codified experience stored in media such as patents, databases, manuals and routines. Youndt et al., found that human resource management and IT investment influence intellectual capital formation more than R&D investment does. Moreover, human resource management, IT investment and R&D investment are all high in a small group of high-performing companies with high levels of human, social and organization capital. In a related study, Subramaniam and Youndt (2005) found that human, social and organizational capital differentially influenced the incremental and radical innovative capabilities of firms. Specifically, social capital positively influences both incremental and radical innovative capabilities, while organizational capital only influences incremental innovative capabilities. Subramaniam and Youndt also found that human capital when being interacted with social capital can affect radical innovative capability.

In a survey of all 772 granted patents with 1977 German priority dates that were renewed to full term until 1995, Harhoff, Scherer, and Vopel (2003) found that the backward citations contained in a patent and the forward citations that a patent receives are positively related to its value. Citations to the nonpatent literature can indicate the value of patents in the pharmaceutical and chemical fields, but the authors did not find the similar results in other technical fields. Patents associated with large patent families and patents that are still valid after going through opposition procedure are highly valuable.

University technology transfer

Bozeman (2000) provided a comprehensive literature review on domestic technology transfer from universities and government laboratories. He advocated a contingent effectiveness model of technology transfer, which includes five dimensions that determine effectiveness: (1) transfer agent, (2) transfer media, (3) transfer object, (4) demand environment and (5) transfer recipient. Rothaermel, Agung, and Jiang (2007) reviewed 173 academic articles on the topic of university entrepreneurship and classified them into four areas: entrepreneurial research university; the productivity of technology transfer offices; new firm creation; and the environmental context, including networks of innovation. Specifically, the literature on entrepreneurial university discusses the factors related to the organization designs of universities that may dampen or promote the commercialization of university inventions. The literature on the productivity of technology transfer office regards university entrepreneurship as a function of the productivity of technology transfer offices and discusses the factors that are important to their productivity. The literature on new firm creation discusses the factors inhibiting or enhancing the creation of new ventures as a result of university entrepreneurial activities. The articles on environmental context regard university entrepreneurial activities as being embedded in networks of innovation and influenced by the external environment. In another review, Perkmann et al. (2013) defined "academic engagement" as collaborative research, contract research, consulting and informal relationships for university-industry knowledge transfer and described commercialization as creation of intellectual property and academic entrepreneurship. They analyzed and compared the individual, organizational and institutional antecedents and consequences of academic engagement and commercialization.

Mowery, Nelson, Sampat, and Ziedonis (2001) argued that the Bayh-Dole Act was only one of the several important factors stimulating the rise of university patenting and licensing activity after the 1980s. The act seems to have had little effect on the content of academic research at the three leading universities (i.e., the University of California, Stanford University and Columbia University). They suggested that for universities already active in patenting and licensing, such as University of California and Stanford University, the Bayh-Dole Act led to these universities' expanded efforts to market academic inventions. For universities that were inactive in this area, such as Columbia University, the Act prompted them to change the course of their policies and start large-scale patenting and licensing activities. Thursby and Thursby (2002) echoed Mowery, Nelson, Sampat, and Ziedonis's (2001) arguments and suggested that the increasing licensing activities of U.S. universities after the Bayh-Dole Act were primarily due to an increased willingness of university administrations to license and a growing dependence of industry on external R&D rather than a change of faculty research.

Analyzing the data of 101 U.S. universities over the 1994–1998 period, Di Gregorio and Shane (2003) investigated why some universities are able to generate more start-ups than others. They argued that intellectual prominence and two particular policies, namely, making equity investments in start-ups and maintaining a low inventor's share of royalties, promote new firm formation. Zucker, Darby, and Armstrong (2002) researched the economic value of the knowledge generated at universities and argued that academic science exerts a substantial impact on the success of firms in the biotechnology field. They found that firms whose scientists collaborated with top university scientists produced more patents and more highly cited patents.

Based on the data of 134 firms founded to commercialize technologies licensed from Massachusetts Institute of Technology during the 1980–1996 period, Shane and Stuart (2002) studied how resource endowments, in particular, founders' social capital endowments, affect the incidence of early-life performance milestones. The results show that new ventures with founders that have direct and indirect relationships with venture investors prior to firm founding are the most likely to receive venture funding and thus less likely to fail. In addition, receiving venture funding is the single most important event leading to a successful IPO. Agrawal and Henderson (2002) also studied the technology transfer activities at the Massachusetts Institute of Technology and found that patenting plays a relatively small role in the technology transfer in the Mechanical and Electrical Engineering departments. Most faculty members there estimated that patents only account for less than 10 percent of the knowledge that is transferred from their labs. However, the evidence shows that the number of patents may be a valid indicator of research impact because the numbers of patents and paper citations are positively correlated.

Studying the channels through which UK university researchers interact with industry, D'Este and Patel (2007) found that the individual characteristics of researchers are more important in shaping university-industry linkages than are the characteristics of departments and universities. Lockett and Wright (2005) studied data from two surveys conducted in 2002 and 2003 on UK universities' commercialization activities and found that both the number of spin-off companies created and the number of spin-off companies attracting external equity investment are positively associated with universities' expenditures on intellectual property protection, the business development capabilities of technology transfer offices and universities' royalty regimes.

Conclusion

This chapter reviews the recent advances in the literature on IP and innovation management. Following the methodology used in Ziedonis (2008), we use a set of keywords closely related to IP and innovation management to search for relevant publications in 29 leading academic journals. We retrieve 2,081 articles from these journals published between 1986 and March 2018. Based on a bibliometric analysis of these articles, we demonstrate growing interest in academic community on the topics of IP and innovation management, as reflected by the rapid growth in the number of publications and citations to these publications in the observation period. In particular, the growth of both numbers seems to accelerate in the 2000s. We then rank the retrieved articles by the annual average citations they received and obtain a list of most-cited articles. As the articles highlighted by Ziedonis (2008) were mostly published in the 1980s and 1990s, we focus on reviewing the highly cited articles published after 2000 and regard our effort as an extension of Ziedonis's (2008) work.

Examining these 48 highly cited articles, we group them into five themes, namely, intangible assets and innovation; alliance, network and innovation; patenting as a proxy for innovation activities; IP management and innovation; and university technology transfer. In the streams of literature on intangible assets, alliances, networks and innovation, we observe that scholars investigate how firms can invest, obtain and leverage their intangible assets or alliance networks to boost their innovation activities and firm performance. In particular, scholars often use patent data to construct variables to measure network and firm linkages. The availability of fine-grained patent data in electronic format and innovations in methods of using these data enable scholars to advance in their use of patenting as a proxy for innovation activities and generate novel insights on how to protect and leverage IP in an open innovation environment and how to protect and promote innovation to enhance firm performance. Finally, we identify a set of highly cited articles focusing on the topic of university technology transfer, thereby demonstrating the importance of universities as knowledge generators and transmitters in a national innovation system.

Acknowledgments

The authors are grateful for Ms. Hang Qiu's research assistance. Can Huang acknowledges the financial support by the National Natural Science Foundation of China, Grant No. 71402161, 71874152 and 71732008. Suli Zheng acknowledges the financial support by the National Natural Science Foundation of China, Grant No. 71572187.

References

Acs, Z. J., Anselin, L. and Varga, A. (2002). Patents and innovation counts as measures of regional production of new knowledge. *Research Policy*, 31, 1069–1085.
Agrawal, A. and Henderson, R. (2002). Putting patents in context: exploring knowledge transfer from MIT. *Management Science*, 48, 44–60.
Ahuja, G. (2000a). Collaboration networks, structural holes, and innovation: a longitudinal study. *Administrative Science Quarterly*, 45, 425–455.
Ahuja, G. (2000b). The duality of collaboration: inducements and opportunities in the formation of interfirm linkages. *Strategic Management Journal*, 21, 317–343.
Ahuja, G. and Katila, R. (2001). Technological acquisitions and the innovation performance of acquiring firms: a longitudinal study. *Strategic Management Journal*, 22, 197–220.
AL-Aali, A.Y. and Teece, D. J. (2013). Towards the (strategic) management of intellectual property: retrospective and prospective. *California Management Review*, 55, 15–30.
Almeida, P. and Phene, A. (2004). Subsidiaries and knowledge creation: the influence of the MNC and host country on innovation. *Strategic Management Journal*, 25, 847–864.
Benner, M. J. (2002). Process management and technological innovation: a longitudinal study of the photography and paint industries. *Administrative Science Quarterly*, 47, 676–706.
Bouty, I. (2000). Interpersonal and interaction influences on informal resource exchanges between R&D researchers across organizational boundaries. *Academy of Management Journal*, 43, 50–65.
Bozeman, B. (2000). Technology transfer and public policy: a review of research and theory. *Research Policy*, 29, 627–655.
Cohen, W. M., Goto, A., Nagata, A., Nelson, R. R. and Walsh, J. R. (2002). R&D spillovers, patents and the incentives to innovate in Japan and the United States. *Research Policy*, 31, 1349–1367.
D'este, P. and Patel, P. (2007). University-industry linkages in the UK: what are the factors underlying the variety of interactions with industry? *Research Policy*, 36, 1295–1313.
Delios, A. and Beamish, P. W. (2001). Survival and profitability: the roles of experience and intangible assets in foreign subsidiary performance. *Academy of Management Journal*, 44, 1028–1038.
Di Gregorio, D. and Shane, S. (2003). Why do some universities generate more start-ups than others? *Research Policy*, 32, 209–227.
Fisher, W. W., III. and Oberholzer-Gee, F. (2013). Strategic management of intellectual property: an integrated approach. *California Management Review*, 55, 157–183.
Fleming, L. (2001). Recombinant uncertainty in technological search. *Management Science*, 47, 117–132.

Fleming, L., Mingo, S. and Chen, D. (2007). Collaborative brokerage, generative creativity, and creative success. *Administrative Science Quarterly*, 52, 443–475.

Fleming, L. and Sorenson, O. (2004). Science as a map in technological search. *Strategic Management Journal*, 25, 909–928.

Frost, T. S. (2001). The geographic sources of foreign subsidiaries' innovations. *Strategic Management Journal*, 22, 101–123.

Furman, J. L., Porter, M. E. and Stern, S. (2002). The determinants of national innovative capacity. *Research Policy*, 31, 899–933.

Gans, J. S. and Stern, S. (2003). The product market and the market for 'ideas': commercialization strategies for technology entrepreneurs. *Research Policy*, 32, 333–350.

Hagedoorn, J. and Cloodt, M. (2003). Measuring innovative performance: is there an advantage in using multiple indicators? *Research Policy*, 32, 1365–1379.

Harhoff, D., Scherer, F. M. and Vopel, K. (2003). Citations, family size, opposition and the value of patent rights. *Research Policy*, 32, 1343–1363.

Hitt, M. A., Dacin, M. T., Levitas, E., Arregle, J. L. and Borza, A. (2000). Partner selection in emerging and developed market contexts: resource-based and organizational learning perspectives. *Academy of Management Journal*, 43, 449–467.

Hoang, H. and Rothaermel, F. T. (2005). The effect of general and partner-specific alliance experience on joint R&D project performance. *The Academy of Management Journal*, 48, 332–345.

Huizingh, E. K. R. E. (2011). Open innovation: state of the art and future perspectives. *Technovation*, 31, 2–9.

Jaffe, A. B., Trajtenberg, M. and Henderson, R. (1993). Geographic localization of knowledge spillovers as evidenced by Patent citations. *The Quarterly Journal of Economics*, 108, 577–598.

Krishnan, R., Martin, X. and Noorderhaven, N. G. (2006). When does trust matter to alliance performance? *Academy of Management Journal*, 49, 894–917.

Levin, R. C., Klevorick, A. K., Nelson, R. R. and Winter, S. G. (1987). Appropriating the returns from industrial research and development. *Brookings Papers on Economic Activity*, 783.

Lockett, A. and Wright, M. (2005). Resources, capabilities, risk capital and the creation of university spin-out companies. *Research Policy*, 34, 1043–1057.

Lu, J. W. and Beamish, P. W. (2004). International diversification and firm performance: the S-CURVE hypothesis. *Academy of Management Journal*, 47, 598–609.

Markman, G. D., Espina, M. I. and Phan, P. H. (2004). Patents as surrogates for inimitable and non-substitutable resources. *Journal of Management*, 30, 529–544.

Mazzoleni, R. and Nelson, R. R. (1998). The benefits and costs of strong patent protection: a contribution to the current debate. *Research Policy*, 27, 273–284.

Mowery, D. C., Nelson, R. R., Sampat, B. N. and Ziedonis, A. A. (2001). The growth of patenting and licensing by US universities: an assessment of the effects of the Bayh-Dole act of 1980. *Research Policy*, 30, 99–119.

Ocean Tomo (2015). Annual study of intangible asset market value from Ocean Tomo, LLC, available at http://www.oceantomo.com/2015/03/04/2015-intangible-asset-market-value-study/.

O'Reilly, C. A. and Tushman, M. L. (2004). The ambidextrous organisation. *Harvard Business Review*, 82, 74–81.

Owen-Smith, J. and Powell, W. W. (2004). Knowledge networks as channels and conduits: the effects of spillovers in the Boston biotechnology community. *Organization Science*, 15, 5–21.

Perkmann, M., Tartari, V., Mckelvey, M., Autio, E., Brostr M. A., D'este, P., Fini, R., Geuna, A., Grimaldi, R., Hughes, A., Krabel, S., Kitson, M., Llerena, P., Lissoni, F., Salter, A. and Sobrero, M. (2013). Academic engagement and commercialisation: a review of the literature on university – industry relations. *Research Policy*, 42, 423–442.

Roberts, P. W. and Dowling, G. R. (2002). Corporate reputation and sustained superior financial performance. *Strategic Management Journal*, 23, 1077–1093.

Romijn, H. and Albaladejo, M. (2002). Determinants of innovation capability in small electronics and software firms in southeast England. *Research Policy*, 31, 1053–1067.

Rosenkopf, L. and Nerkar, A. (2001). Beyond local search: boundary-spanning, exploration, and impact in the optical disk industry. *Strategic Management Journal*, 22, 287–306.

Rothaermel, F. T., Agung, S. D. and Jiang, L. (2007). University entrepreneurship: a taxonomy of the literature. *Industrial and Corporate Change*, 16, 691–791.

Sampson, R. C. (2007). R&D alliances and firm performance: the impact of technological diversity and alliance organization on innovation. *Academy of Management Journal*, 50, 364–386.

Schilling, M. A. and Phelps, C. C. (2007). Interfirm collaboration networks: the impact of large-scale network structure on firm innovation. *Management Science*, 53, 1113–1126.

Shane, S. and Stuart, T. (2002). Organizational endowments and the performance of university start-ups. *Management Science*, 48, 154–170.

Singh, J. (2005). Collaborative networks as determinants of knowledge diffusion patterns. *Management Science*, 51, 756–770.

Song, J., Almeida, P. and Wu, G. (2003). Learning-by-hiring: when is mobility more likely to facilitate interfirm knowledge transfer? *Management Science*, 49, 351–365.

Sorensen, J. B. and Stuart, T. E. (2000). Aging, obsolescence, and organizational innovation. *Administrative Science Quarterly*, 45, 81–112.

Stuart, T. E. (2000). Interorganizational alliances and the performance of firms: a study of growth and innovation rates in a high-technology industry. *Strategic Management Journal*, 21, 791–811.

Subramaniam, M. and Youndt, M. A. (2005). The influence of intellectual capital on the types of innovative capabilities. *Academy of Management Journal*, 48, 450–463.

Teece, D. J. (1986). Profiting from technological innovation: implications for integration, collaboration, licensing and public policy. *Research Policy*, 15, 285–305.

Teece, D. J. (2007). Explicating dynamic capabilities: the nature and microfoundations of (sustainable) enterprise performance. *Strategic Management Journal*, 28, 1319–1350.

Thursby, J. G. and Thursby, M. C. (2002). Who is selling the Ivory Tower? Sources of growth in university licensing. *Management Science*, 48, 90–104.

Trajtenberg, M. (1990). A penny for your quotes: patent citations and the value of innovations. *The RAND Journal of Economics*, 21, 172–187.

Von Hippel, E. and von Krogh, G. (2003). Open source software and the 'private-collective' innovation model: issues for organization science. *Organization Science*, 14, 209–223.

Youndt, M. A., Subramaniam, M. and Snell, S. A. (2004). Intellectual capital profiles: an examination of investments and returns. *Journal of Management Studies*, 41, 335–361.

Ziedonis, R. H. (2008). Intellectual property and innovation. In Shane, S. (Ed.), *Handbook of technology and innovation management*. New York: John Wiley & Sons Ltd.

Zucker, L. G., Darby, M. R. and Armstrong, J. S. (2002). Commercializing knowledge: university science, knowledge capture, and firm performance in biotechnology. *Management Science*, 48, 138–153.

PART V

Methodologies for innovation management

24
STANDARDS, MODELS, AND METHODOLOGIES FOR INNOVATION MANAGEMENT

Emigdio Alfaro

Commonly, the innovation processes prioritized creativity (Alfaro, 2017a, p. 35) but not standardization due to the belief of the obstacles presented by standardization for the innovation (Alfaro, 2017b, p. 37; Castillo-Rojas, Karapetrovic, and Heras, 2012, p. 1085); however, in this chapter, the reader will learn that the standards, models, and methodologies for managing the innovations could accelerate the innovations with a real focus on value generation and not prioritizing the creativity processes by themselves, which commonly are not integrated with the strategic planning (Alfaro, 2017b, p. 32) and could be failures of diverse types and not only financial failures. This chapter includes the following themes: (a) problems associated with the lack of standards and methodologies for managing the innovation in the organizations, (b) standards for managing the innovation, and (c) models and methodologies for the innovation management. There are diverse problems related to (a) innovation processes, (b) innovation products, (c) innovative business models, (d) project management problems of the innovative projects, (e) lack of prioritizing of the value generation of the innovations, (f) lack of regulatory framework for norming the innovation processes, and (g) lack of investments for the innovation.

After the literature review, diverse standards for managing innovation of diverse countries were found, such as (a) China, (b) the United States, (c) the United Kingdom, (d) Portugal, (e) Spain, (f) Russia, (g) Germany, (h) Denmark, (i) France, (j) Ireland, (k) Mexico, (l) Brazil, and (m) Colombia; also, standards for managing innovation from Europe were found. Additionally, the following innovation management models were found: (a) Integrated Service Innovation Method (iSIM), (b) Open Innovation Maturity Model for the Government, (c) Innovation Capability Maturity Model (ICMM) of Essmann, (d) Integrated Innovation Maturity Model (I2MM), (e) Model for measuring the Business Model Innovativeness, and (f) the Open Business Model and are presented in this chapter. Finally, the following methodologies were presented: (a) Methodology of Innovation Management for Obtaining the Level 3 of I2MM (MIM3); (b) Methodology for Evaluating the Value Generation of Information Technology (MEVGIT), which could be adapted and applied not just for innovations on information technologies; (c) Lean Product Innovation Management; (d) Lean Startup; (e) Very Lean Startup; (f) Design Thinking; (g) Living Lab Methodology; (h) Goodyear's Business Model Innovation Process; (i) FastWorks Framework; (j) Lean Innovation Model, Seeking Solutions Approach; and (k) 3-Stage Roadmap.

Problems associated with the lack of standards, models, and methodologies for managing innovation in organizations

The problems associated with the lack of standards, models, and methodologies for managing innovation in organizations are explained in this section. For that purpose, it is necessary first to understand the value generation of the standardization of the innovation.

The value generation of the standardization of the innovation

To introduce the problems associated with the lack of standards and methodologies for managing the innovation, it is important to understand the following themes: (a) How do the innovations of the organizations generate value? (b) How do the standardization process and the standards contribute to the value generation of the organizations? (c) How does the standardization of the innovation generate value for the organizations? All of these aspects are treated in the following paragraphs. After the corresponding explanation, a list of problems associated with the lack of standards and methodologies for managing innovation in organizations is exposed.

Regarding the manner in which innovations generate value for organizations, it is important to remember the considerations for the value generation of the organizations. In this respect, Alfaro (2017a) explained that for the cases of for-profit organizations: "the value generation is represented as the improvement of the financial indicators, which require the improvement of the stock value, the improvement of the profitability or the improvement of the net present value of the firms" (p. 132) and indicated that for the cases of nonprofit organizations, "the value generation is represented mainly by the improvement of the value for the target population, and not only by the improvement of the financial indicators." (p. 132). Alfaro (2017a) also explained that "[t]hese considerations must be taken into account for evaluating the value generation of the diverse types of operations and projects in the organizations" (p. 132), including the innovations. In this regard, Caetano (2017) explained: "Innovation management enables organizations to focus on competitiveness and successful performance" (p. 8). Then, the innovations generate value for the organizations introducing significant changes in the processes or products, which will be appreciated by the markets or will improve the effectiveness of the processes or the perceived quality of the products.

Regarding the contribution of the standardization process and standards for the value generation of the organizations, de Casanove, Morel, and Negny (2017) explained: "Organizations set up a framework to support the achievement of the targets of their core businesses and the replicability of the activities. A management system defines this framework with an organization and a set of policies, processes, and procedures." (p. 4), and Caetano (2017) stated that "[s]tandardization can enhance organizational capabilities in order to be aligned with national and international best practices as well as to develop internal competences, routines and processes that can leverage an innovation journey towards excellence" (p. 8). However, due to the complexity of the standardization process, "[d]etermining the value of a standard within a procurement project is complex and likely to require multiple dependent factors to be modelled in a structured and transparent manner" (Revie et al., 2016, p. 4). To that end, Vollebergh and Van der Werf (2014) explained that "[s]tandards and standardization processes play a key role in technological change" (p. 230).

Vollebergh and Van der Werf (2014) indicated that a standard is "a document that specifies characteristics of technical design or rules of behavior." (p. 231) and that a categorization of standards according to their specific role in the society includes (a) standards for measurement and reference, (b) standards for (minimum) quality and safety, and (c) compatibility and interface standards (p. 231). Regarding standardization, Vollebergh and Van der Werf (2014) provide the following definition: "Standardization is 'the action of bringing things to a uniform standard' (David, 1987, p. 212). The process of standardization can be initiated by government, but firms and consumers may also demand uniformity regarding a particular good or service." (p. 232), and David and Greenstein (1990) identified four types of standardization processes: (a) unsponsored standardization, (b) sponsored standardization, (c) agreed through voluntary standards-writing organizations, and (d) initiated or mandated through government intervention (p. 232). Then, the standardization permits organizations and their products into remain in the markets and also permits them to work according to the government rules, avoiding legal and normative problems.

De Casanove, Morel, and Negny (2017) explained that "[w]orking on innovation requires a specific set of tools and methods. This set is different from the ones used in new product/service [development]" (p. 3) and that "[t]here are more uncertainties and more unknowns in innovation than in the development of a new product. Managing an innovation project requires developing the learning curve of the team" (p. 3). To that end, Caetano (2017) stated that "[a]t national and international levels, evidence demonstrates the importance of standardization, as a body of knowledge, to contribute to business innovation and to increase competitiveness and realization of value" (p. 8). Caetano (2017) also explained that "[a]s a voluntary process, standardization is recognized as a potential driver for innovation. Several studies highlighted that it can help companies to demonstrate their innovative products features and to increase business value creation (Swann, 2010)" (p. 8). The standardization of the innovation is considered by various authors as a necessary condition for improving the innovation.

About the use of standards for innovation, de Casanove, Morel, and Negny (2017) pointed out that "[t]hese standards provide best practices to support implementation of the innovation policies as well in Small to Medium Enterprises (SMEs) as in worldwide groups including public institutions, universities, research centers or non-profit organizations" (p. 3). de Casanove, Morel, and Negny (2017) also explained that "[b]y using these documents, organizations can increase their awareness of the value of an Innovation Management, expand their capacity for innovation, and ultimately generate more value for the organization and its stakeholders" (p. 9) and that "[t]he use of a systematic approach to managing innovation is a good stepping stone for any organization aiming to become more innovative" (p. 9). The value generation of the standardization of the innovations of the organizations can be explained due to the fact that the standardization process will permit innovations to be generated and will improve the innovation processes for the organizations continuously. The lack of standardization of the innovation processes would delay this improvement and consequently, would reduce the value generation of the organizations. In this respect, de Casanove (2014) explained the use of standards in the innovation process as follows:

> How do we use standards in our innovation process? First, standards can be considered as the state of the art, the soil of your seed for innovation. Then, when you are developing your innovative project, you need to have partnerships and if you have partnerships, it means that you also need interfaces. Standards will bring you these interfaces. Finally, we come to the valuation of your product. In this case, you also have to organize your market and I think that's one of the key advantages of standardization. Standards can support the organization of a market, meaning that when you have a performance standard, it helps to bring clarity to the market and may eliminate those competitors who have very low-performance products. I have in mind a case where we contributed to the development of a performance standard and our customers used it in their

request for proposals. They can indeed use this standard to say "we want a product with this level of performance". As a result, some of our competitors providing very low-performance products were pushed out of the market.

(p. 95)

There are no contradictions between the standardization and the existence of innovation processes due to the fact that the standardization is not an obstacle to creativity, which is commonly cited as the most important aspect related to innovation. The standardization does not block to creativity; conversely, focusing standardization on innovation could improve the results of the innovation in diverse aspects such as the (a) quantity of innovations, (b) creativity of the innovative solutions, (c) customer satisfaction with the innovations, (d) satisfaction of the people who produce or offer the innovative goods and services, and (e) the financial results of the innovations, which must be the most important aspect to be taken into account in for-profit organizations (Alfaro, 2017a, p. 132).

The problems related to the lack of standards, models, and methodologies for innovation management

Various authors have explained the different problems related to the lack of standardization of the innovation processes (Alfaro, 2017b; Liedtka, 2015; Gupte, 2015; Pinget, Bocquet, and Mothe, 2015; Attia, 2015; Stošić and Milutinović, 2014; Castillo-Rojas, Karapetrovic, and Heras, 2012). Alfaro (2017b) explained the common issues related to the innovation processes of the organizations as follows:

- The lack of integration of the innovation processes to the strategic planning of the organizations. (p. 32)
- The innovation processes obtained good new products (goods or services, or both); however, the solution didn't include the complete business model to which the innovative product would be a part of, and as a consequence, the innovation failed. (p. 33)
- The innovation processes obtained good new products; however, the personnel of the organization don't know which needs of which users will be satisfied or which problems will be solved with the new products, or the costs are very high. (p. 33)
- The project management of the innovative projects has the common type of problems which are presented in the diverse types of projects, related to: integration management, scope management, time management, cost management, quality management, human resources management, communications management, risk management, acquisitions management, and stakeholders management. (p. 33)
- For the innovation processes, the creative processes and not the value generations of the organizations are prioritized. (p. 35)
- The lack of regulatory framework for norming the innovation processes in the organization. There is not a regulatory framework which norms the following aspects: incentives (monetary or non-monetary), roles, committees, intellectual property rights, participation of the benefits after the new products are developed or put in the market, accounting processes for registering the innovation processes and products, etc. Also, the individual contracts commonly did not include anything about the innovation processes or innovative products that the personnel must realize, without the cases of people who have contracts for innovative or intellectual processes or areas, such as: research and development areas in industries, research areas in universities, etc. (p. 35)

- The lack of motivation or incentives to the personnel of the organization, for proposing new ideas or innovative projects. (p. 35)
- The lack of time and opportunities for the personnel of the organization, for presenting new ideas or innovative projects. The personnel of the organization are commonly fighting the daily labors and don't have time in the regular labor time for the innovative processes or the creation of new ideas or products. (p. 35)
- The lack of training and competencies (knowledge, abilities, and attitudes) for creating and developing new ideas or innovative projects. (p. 36)
- The lack of investment or expenses on infrastructure, equipment and other resources, for prototyping and testing the new ideas. The elaboration of prototypes requires investment or expenses in infrastructure, equipment and other resources (materials, personnel, and investment), which commonly is promised but not budgeted or simply is not budgeted or is not sufficiently assigned. (p. 36)
- Absence of a collaborative culture which permits the synergies among the workers of the organization for improving the ideas of innovative projects. Each worker wants to shine by herself or himself, and doesn't want to collaborate with coworkers for improving the ideas of innovative projects. (p. 36)
- Many workers of the organizations feel that the standardized norms and procedures limit them for introducing new ideas of innovative projects. In this sense, many workers are fearful of realizing actions out of the standardized norms and procedures for avoiding the future and negative reactions of their bosses who commonly act in a negative way in front of the presentation of new ideas, considering them as a waste of time, effort, and money. (p. 37)
- The innovation processes are developed without the validation of the satisfaction of the needs to the early adopters or consumers with similar characteristics, with the innovative products (goods, services, or both). (p. 37)
- The introduction of the innovative products into the market doesn't have a previous validation with early adopters with similar characteristics to the target consumers. As a result, the consumers of the target market don't buy the innovative product and the organization fails in its introduction, with the corresponding waste of time, effort, and money. (p. 37)

Liedtka (2015, p. 930) indicated the cognitive biases and their innovation consequences as follows:

- Projection bias (projection of past into future): failure to generate novel ideas
- Egocentric empathy gap (projection of one's own preferences onto others): failure to generate value-creating ideas
- Focusing illusion (overemphasis on particular elements): failure to generate a broad range of ideas
- Hot/cold gap (current state colors assessment of future state): undervaluing or overvaluing ideas
- Say/do gap (inability to accurately describe one's own preferences): inability to accurately articulate and assess future wants and needs
- Planning fallacy (overoptimism): overcommitment to inferior ideas
- Hypothesis confirmation bias (look for confirmation of hypothesis): disconfirming data missed
- Endowment effect (attachment to first solutions): reduction in options considered
- Availability bias (preference for what can be easily imagined): undervaluing of more novel ideas

Gupte (2015) explained that "[i]n reality, focusing on customers before a product idea is difficult, because most entrepreneurs and innovators work from passion first – they have an idea and they then try to make a business of it" (p. 52). Gupte (2015) also indicated that:

> In some cases they may not have an idea, but their experience, skills and interests determine what kind of products they are inclined to make. In fact, that last sentence carries the germ of success for the initial idea – experience and interest will often point an Entrepreneur to the problems that need to be solved in order to have a real business with real customers.
>
> (p. 52)

Pinget, Bocquet, and Mothe (2015) studied the perceptions of barriers to environmental innovation (EI) in small and medium-sized enterprises (SMEs) with a sample of 435 chief executive officers of French SMEs and concluded the following:

- First, with regard to perceived barriers, SMEs engaged in EI believe that they face more barriers than other SMEs (those that pursue "dirty" TIs and noninnovators). They also perceive those barriers as more intense than the other two groups of SMEs do. Only the intensities of financial and market-related barriers do not differ between environmentally innovative and technologically innovative SMEs. These results indicate a key distinction of environmentally innovative SMEs: because of the complexity of EI, they must deal with many more dimensions than technologically innovative SMEs. (p. 147)
- Second, environmentally innovative SMEs perceive knowledge barriers as more intense and more numerous than technologically innovative SMEs, possibly due to the higher level of complexity and novelty of the knowledge required to innovate (De Marchi, 2012; Petruzzelli, Dangelico, Rotolo, and Albino, 2011), but also because EI is more knowledge- and information-intensive (Horbach, Oltra, and Belin, 2013). EI often relies on knowledge and competences that are not core to firms (De Marchi, 2012; Marin, Marzucchi, and Zoboli, 2014). (p. 148)
- Third, regarding the antecedents of EI, we confirm the effect of regulation, in that firms in polluting sectors tend to introduce more EIs. Beyond these regulatory aspects, firms that have the highest probability of introducing EIs are those that are the most mature in their environmental strategy. Three major antecedents relate to firms' strategies: belonging to a cluster, R&D cooperation, and environmental monitoring. (p. 148)

Attia (2015) indicated that "[t]here are two main general barriers to collaboration between university and industry" (p. 116) and explained each of the barriers as follows:

> The first one is orientation-related barriers, which we focused on measuring three elements directly related to the orientation of university research and researchers. These three elements are: university research is extremely orientated towards pure science, long-term orientation of university research (concerns over lower sense of urgency of university researchers compared to industry researchers) and mutual lack of understanding about expectations and working practices (Bruneel, d'Este, and Salter, 2010).
>
> The second barrier is transaction-related barriers, which are related to conflicts over intellectual property, and dealing with university administration. The measurement of transaction-related-barriers includes the following four elements from the question on barriers: industrial liaison offices tend to oversell research or have

unrealistic expectations, potential conflicts with university regarding royalty payments from patents or other intellectual property rights and concerns about confidentiality, rules and regulations imposed by universities or government funding agencies and absence or low profile of industrial liaison offices in the university (Bruneel, d'Este, and Salter, 2010).

(p. 116)

Pinget, Bocquet, and Mothe (2015) stated the limitations of their study as follows: "We did not separate product and process EIs, so further research should delineate whether barriers differ with changes in the type of EI (process/product) or its beneficiary (firm/client)" (p. 148). Pinget, Bocquet, and Mothe (2015) also stated "[n]or did we distinguish incremental from radical innovations; incremental innovation is much less resource- and competency-demanding than radical innovation is, which destroys previous products and skills" (p. 148). Additionally, Stošić and Milutinović (2014) identified four levels of uncertainty for innovation projects according to the industrial sector: (a) low technological uncertainty for low-tech projects, (b) medium technological uncertainty for medium-tech projects, (c) uncertainty for high-tech projects for high technological projects, and (d) super high technological uncertainty for super high technological projects (p. 100). Based on Stošić (2013) and Keegan and Turner (2002), Stošić and Milutinović (2014) indicated some characteristics for comparing innovation and conventional projects as follows:

- as opposite to the conventional projects, innovation projects start with poorly defined and sometimes ambiguous objectives, which become more specific in the following phases of the project;
- since the failure is one of the possible outcomes, innovation teams are more involved in management of project risk, in sense of being proactive about it. They must quickly overcome failures and orient on the new, more attractive options.
- project teams have to be made up of different people among whom exist high level of confidence (their work does not always result in success);
- ideas presented in innovation projects have to be sold to sponsors (function in project teams for innovation), which is not characteristics for conventional projects. (p. 99)

Castillo-Rojas, Karapetrovic, and Heras (2012) explained that "[t]here is conflicting evidence in the academic literature about the relationship between the utilisation of such MSSs and organisational performance in general" (p. 1076). Castillo-Rojas, Karapetrovic, and Heras (2012) also indicated that "[t]here is also doubt about the more specific question of whether the implementation of MSSs promotes or hinders a firm's development of innovative products and processes" (p. 1076). Previously, Castillo-Rojas, Karapetrovic, and Heras (2012) named MSSs for "management system standards" (p. 1075). Additionally, Castillo-Rojas, Karapetrovic, and Heras (2012) pointed out that "[w]hile a number of new MSSs for innovation are emerging, such as UNE 166002: 2006 and CWA 15899: 2008, the question of whether MSSs promote or hinder innovation processes in an organisation remains unresolved" (p. 1078). Finally, after their study with 249 Spanish organizations registered to both ISO 9001 and ISO 14001, Castillo-Rojas, Karapetrovic, and Heras (2012) concluded that "[o]n the contrary, the more the organisations had been pushed by their external stakeholders to implement these standards, the more prevalent is the perception that MSSs are a barrier to innovation" (p. 1085) and that "[t]hus, when the decision of MSSs implementation was made under external pressures, namely 'External Requirements', the perception of them as innovation inhibitors arises" (p. 1086). As a summary, the problems discovered are detailed with their respective authors in Table 24.1.

Table 24.1 Identified problems associated with the lack of standards, models, and methodologies for managing organizational innovation

Problem	Authors who commented about the problem
Working on innovation requires a specific set of tools and methods	(De Casanove, Morel, and Negny, 2017, p. 3)
Managing an innovation project requires developing the learning curve of the team	(De Casanove, Morel, and Negny, 2017, p. 3)
Lack of training and competencies (knowledge, abilities, and attitudes) for creating and developing new ideas or innovative projects; projection of past into future; failure to generate a broad range of ideas; reduction in options considered; environmentally innovative SMEs perceive knowledge barriers as more intense and more numerous than technologically innovative SMEs	(Alfaro, 2017b, p. 36; Liedtka, 2015; p. 930; Liedtka, 2015, p. 930; Liedtka, 2015, p. 930; Pinget, Bocquet, and Mothe, 2015, p. 148)
Projection of own preferences onto others	(Liedtka, 2015, p. 930)
Lack of integration of the innovation processes to the strategic planning of the organizations	(Alfaro, 2017b, p. 32)
The innovative solution did not include the complete business model to which the innovative product would be a part of; most entrepreneurs and innovators work from passion first – they have an idea and they then try to make a business of it	(Alfaro, 2017b, p. 33; Gupte, 2015, p. 52)
The personnel of the organization don't know which needs of which users will be satisfied or which problems will be solved with the new products, or the costs are very high; they may not have an idea, but their experience, skills, and interests determine what kind of products they are inclined to make	(Alfaro, 2017b, p. 33; Gupte, 2015, p. 52)
Existence of common project management problems in the innovation projects: integration, scope, time, cost, quality, communication, human resources, risk, acquisition, and stakeholders related problems; innovation projects start with poorly defined and sometimes ambiguous objectives, which become more specific in the following phases of the project; innovation teams are more involved in the management of project risk in the sense of being proactive about it; project teams have to be made up of different people among whom exist a high level of confidence; ideas presented in innovation projects have to be sold to sponsors	(Alfaro, 2017b, p. 33; Stošić and Milutinovic, 2014, p. 99; Stošić and Milutinović, 2014, p. 99; Stošić and Milutinović, 2014, p. 99; Stošić and Milutinović, 2014, p. 99)
For the innovation processes, the creative processes and not the value generations of the organizations are prioritized	(Alfaro, 2017b, p. 35)
Lack of regulatory framework for norming the innovation processes in the organization; transaction-related barriers, which are related to conflicts over intellectual property, and dealing with university administration	(Alfaro, 2017b, p. 35; Attia, 2015, p. 116)
The effect of regulation, in that firms in polluting sectors tend to introduce more EIs; when the decision of MSSs implementation was made under external pressures, namely "external requirements", the perception of them as innovation inhibitors arises	(Pinget, Bocquet, and Mothe, 2015, p. 148; Castillo-Rojas, Karapetrovic and Heras, 2012, p. 1086)

Problem	Authors who commented about the problem
Lack of motivation or incentives to the personnel of the organization for proposing new ideas or innovative projects	(Alfaro, 2017b, p. 35)
Many workers of the organizations feel that the standardized norms and procedures limit them from introducing new ideas of innovative projects; the more prevalent is the perception that MSSs are a barrier to innovation	(Alfaro, 2017b, p. 37; Castillo-Rojas, Karapetrovic, and Heras, 2012, p. 1085)
The innovation processes are developed without validating the satisfaction of the needs to the early adopters or consumers with similar characteristics, with the innovative products	(Alfaro, 2017b, p. 37)
The introduction of the innovative products into the market doesn't have a previous validation with early adopters with similar characteristics to the target consumers; inability to accurately articulate and assess future wants and needs; hypothesis confirmation bias	(Alfaro, 2017b, p. 37; Liedtka, 2015, p. 930; Liedtka, 2015, p. 930)
The lack of the evaluation of the value generation of innovations; undervaluing or overvaluing ideas; overcommitment to inferior ideas; undervaluing of more novel ideas	(Alfaro, 2017a, p. 132; Liedtka, 2015, p. 930; Liedtka, 2015, p. 930; Liedtka, 2015, p. 930)
SMEs engaged in EI believe that they face more barriers than other SMEs	(Pinget, Bocquet, and Mothe, 2015, p. 147)
Orientation-related barriers in universities: orientation to pure science, lower sense of urgency of university researchers compared with industry researchers, and mutual lack of understanding about expectations and working practices;	(Attia, 2015, p. 116)
Four levels of uncertainty for innovation projects in the industrial sector: low, high, super, and super-high technological uncertainty for high-technological projects	(Stošić and Milutinović, 2014, p. 100)

Standards for managing innovation

Diverse standards for managing innovation have been developed in various parts of the world. Table 24.2 shows the standards identified for managing innovation. Some of these standards are explained in this section.

ISO 50500 Series of Innovation Management

De Casanove, Morel, and Negny (2017) explained the ISO 50500 series as an international standard on innovation management and indicated that the ISO 50500 series "would [start] being published in 2018 and will provide best practices to support implementation of innovation policies as well in Small to Medium Enterprises (SMEs) as in worldwide groups including public institutions, universities, research centers or non-profit organizations" (p. 6). de Casanove, Morel, and Negny (2017) also explained:

> To achieve this goal, the work is focused in particular on a management system for innovation and all the tools and methods associated to this system (such as but not limited to open innovation, design innovation, strategic intelligence, creativity management and also self-assessment of innovation management).
>
> *(p. 6)*

Table 24.2 Identified standards for managing innovation

Standard	Country/region	Authors who commented on the standard
GB/T 29490:2013 Enterprise Intellectual Property Management	China	(De Casanove, Morel, and Negny, 2017, p. 5)
GB/T 33250:2016 Intellectual Property Management for Research and development organizations	China	(De Casanove, Morel, and Negny, 2017, p. 5)
GB/T 33251:2016 Intellectual Property Management for higher education institutions	China	(De Casanove, Morel, and Negny, 2017, p. 5)
ISO 50500 Series for Innovation Management (in development)	United States	(De Casanove, Morel, and Negny, 2017, p. 5)
ISO/TC 279 Innovation Management	United States	(De Casanove, Morel, and Negny, 2017, p. 4; ISO, 2013)
CEN/TS 16555 Innovation Management	Europe	(Caetano, 2017, p. 10)
CWA 15899:2008 Standardization of an innovation capability rating for SMEs	Europe	(Mir and Casadesús, 2011b, p. 53)
EFQM Framework for Innovation	Europe	(Mir and Casadesús, 2011b, p. 53)
BS 7000 Design Management Systems	United Kingdom	(British Standards Institute, 2008)
NP Series of R&D&I Management	Portugal	(Mir and Casadesús, 2011b, p. 53)
UNE 166002 R&D&I Management	Spain	(AENOR, 2014; Gil, Varela, and González, 2008)
GOST R 54147:2010 – Strategic and innovation management – Terms and definitions	Russia	(Mir, Casadesús, and Petnji, 2016, p. 27).
DIN 77100:2001 – Patent Valuation – General principles for monetary patent valuation	Germany	(De Casanove, Morel, and Negny, 2017)
DS-hæfte 36:2010 – User oriented innovation management	Denmark	(Mir, Casadesús, and Petnji, 2016, p. 27)
FD X50–271:2013 – Innovation management – Guide for innovation management implementation	France	(Mir, Casadesús, and Petnji, 2016, p. 27)
FD X50–272:2014 – Guidelines for the implementation of open innovation	France	(De Casanove, Morel, and Negny, 2017, p. 5)
FD X50–273 – Implementation of sustainable development in the innovation process	France	(De Casanove, Morel, and Negny, 2017, p. 5)
FD X50–274:2015 – Innovation Management – Creativity management	France	(De Casanove, Morel, and Negny, 2017, p. 5)
FD X50–146:2010 Innovation Management – Intellectual Property Management	France	(De Casanove, Morel, and Negny, 2017, p. 5)
NWA 1:2009 – Guide to good practice in innovation and product development processes	Ireland	(Mir, Casadesús, and Petnji, 2016, p. 27)
NMX-GT-003-IMNC-2008 – Technology Management System Requirements	Mexico	(De Casanove, Morel, and Negny, 2017; Mir, Casadesús, and Petnji, 2016, p. 27)

Standard	Country/region	Authors who commented on the standard
ABNT NBR 16501:2011 – Guidance for the research, development and Innovation (R&D&I) management system	Brazil	(Mir, Casadesús, and Petnji, 2016, p. 27; de Casanove, Morel, and Negny, 2017, p. 5)
NTC 5801:2008 – R&D&I Management: Requirements of the R&D&I management system	Colombia	(Mir, Casadesús, and Petnji, 2016, p. 27)

About the structure of the ISO 50500 series, de Casanove, Morel, and Negny (2017) indicated the following parts:

ISO 50500 Innovation Management – Fundamentals and Vocabulary

This document will contain a standard vocabulary and will address the innovation management principles, such as: (a) realization of value, (b) future-focused leaders, (c) purposeful direction, (d) innovation culture, (e) exploitable insights, (f) mastering uncertainty, (g) adaptability, and (h) transformation of the organization. (p. 6)

ISO 50501 Innovation Management – Innovation Management System – Guidance

This document will contain the following mandatory chapters: (a) introduction, (b) scope, (c) normative references, (d) terms and definitions, (e) context of the organization, (f) leadership, (g) planning, (h) support, (i) operation, (j) performance evaluation, and (k) improvement. (p. 7)

ISO 50502 Innovation Management – Assessment – Guidance

ISO 50502 is based on the following innovation management principles: (a) add value to the organization, (b) challenge the organization's objectives and strategy, (c) motivate and mobilize for organizational development, (d) be timely and encourage a focus on the future, (e) allow for context and promote the adoption of best practice, (f) be flexible and holistic, and (g) be an effective and reliable process (p. 7). ISO 50502 will include: (a) existence (to check if a system is present and what is its level of maturity), (b) efficiency (does it produce results in a timely and cost-effective manner?), and (c) effectiveness (does it help the organization learn and achieve more/better results?) (p. 8). ISO 50502 will point out the different lacks or gaps in their organizations, policies, and process (p. 8). Once the gaps or lacks have been identified, organizations can set up an action plan (p. 8).

ISO 50503 Innovation Management – Tools and Methods for Innovation Partnership

ISO 50503 will provide guidance on methods and tools that the collaborating partners can use to achieve a successful interaction and outcome. Indeed, partnership is becoming increasingly widespread in innovation. Organizations can achieve much more as a result of partnership than acting alone. However, failure to manage it correctly can result in a waste of time and resources. To improve the governance of the partnership, all stakeholders should be aware of the parameters that must be addressed to increase the chances of success and reduce the waste resulting from failure. Innovation partnerships are developed to create value for each partner working together towards an innovative outcome. (p. 8)

ISO 50504 Strategic Intelligence Management

This standard will provide guidelines to facilitate the scanning and analyzing process of the organization environment in order to support decision making at all levels within the organization, fostering the implementation of stable strategic intelligence management practices. (p. 8)

ISO 50505 Intellectual Property Management

An efficient management of intellectual property creates an interesting backbone to protect and increase the competitiveness of an innovation project. This standard will propose guidelines for supporting the intellectual property within innovation management. It aims at addressing the following topics of IP management at strategic and operational levels. (p. 8)

UNE 166002 R&D&I Management

Gil, Varela, and González (2008) indicated that the UNE 166000 had the following components:

- UNE 166000:2006 Management of R&D&I: Terms and definitions of the activities of R&D&I
- UNE 166000:2006 Management of R&D&I: Requirements of a R&D&I project (certifiable)
- UNE 166000:2006 Management of R&D&I: Requirements of the R&D&I Management System (certifiable)
- UNE 166000:2006 Ex Management of R&D&I: System of Technological Surveillance
- UNE 166000:2006 Ex Management of R&D&I: Competences and evaluation of auditors of R&D&I Management System

The term R&D&I means research and development and innovation. AENOR (2014) detailed the parts of the UNE 166002:2014- R&D&I Management: Requirements of the R&D&I Management System as follows:

1 Context of the organization. It included:

- Knowledge of the organization and its context. The organization must determine the internal and external aspects which are pertinent to its purpose and that affects to its capacity for obtaining the expected results of the management system of the R&D&I. (p. 7)
- Comprehension of the needs and expectations of the stakeholders. The organization must determine which interested parts are relevant in relation with the system and to identify its needs, expectations and requirements. (p. 7)
- Management system of the R&D&I. The organization must establish, document, implement and maintain a management system of the R&D&I and improve continuously its effectiveness according to the requirements of this norm. The organization also must determine the limits and the applicability of the system for establishing and for documenting its scope. (p. 8)

2   Leadership

- Vision and strategy of the R&D&I. The vision of the R&D&I begins commonly of the organizational vision, which is a declaration about the organizational purposes, concretely in terms of R&D&I for the purposes of this norm. (p. 8)
- R&D&I Policy. The policy of R&D&I must be documented and communicated into the organization and to be available for the interested parts which were defined by the Direction. (p. 9)
- Leadership and commitment of the management. The Direction must demonstrate its leadership and the commitment in relation to the management system of R&D&I. (p. 9)
- Promotion of an innovation culture. The Direction must promote a culture which supports the innovation. That culture is understood as a mentality and all the members of the organization are responsible for contributing to its growth. (p. 9)
- Roles, responsibilities, and organizational authorities. The Direction must assure that the responsibilities and authorities for the pertinent roles are assigned and communicated inside the organization. (p. 10)

3   Planning

- Risks and opportunities. To plan the system, the organization must take into account the internal and external analysis, the needs, the expectations, the requirements, and the innovation policy of this norm, and must determine the risks and opportunities for assuring that the system obtains the expected results, for preventing or reducing the undesirable effects, and to get the continuous improvement. (p. 10)
- Purposes of the R&D&I and plan for obtaining them. The organization must establish the R&D&I purposes for the pertinent functions and levels. The organization also must conserve documented information about the purposes of R&D&I. The plan for obtaining the R&D&I purposes must determine the activities, resources, responsibilities, duration times, and indicators for measuring the accomplishment of purposes. (p. 10)

4   Support of the R&D&I

- Organization of the roles and responsibilities. The organization must define the responsibilities of the management unit of R&D&I (for the whole management of the R&D&I) and if applies, the units of R&D&I for specific R&D&I projects. (p. 11)
- Resources. The organization must determine and provide the required tangible and intangible resources for the development, implementation, maintenance and continuous improvement of the system. (p. 12)
- Competencies. The organization must determine the required competencies of people which develop and work in R&D&I activities, to assure that people have or obtain the required competencies, and improve continuously the required capacities for increasing the R&D&I performance, and maintain the records of education, formation, skills and experience. (p. 12)
- Awareness. The personnel of the organization should be conscious and motivated about the importance of the R&D&I for the organization, the R&D&I policy, and the importance of their personal contribution to the effectiveness of the system, including the benefits of a better performance of the R&D&I, and the implications of the lack of accomplishment of the requirements of the system. All these aspects should be obtained through a solid innovation culture. (p. 12)
- Communication. The organization must establish the relevant internal and external communications for the system, taking into account aspects as what communicate,

when, to who and by part of who, and to provide adequate channels for the communication and the expected feedback. (p. 13)
- Documented information. The system must include the required documented information of this norm and the organization as necessary for the effectiveness of the system and for contributing with evidences about its performance, as is derivate of the application of this norm. This documentation must be created, identified, shared, updated, stored, controlled, and protected in a right manner. (p. 13)
- Intellectual and industrial property, and knowledge management. The organization must define guidelines for the management of intangible assets (including the knowledge and the know-how) and its intellectual and industrial property. (p. 13)
- Collaboration. The organization must define guidelines for the internal and external collaboration which promote to share ideas and knowledge among different people, groups, and units. The organization must assure that the possible outsourcings or acquired products accomplish the specified requirements of the R&D&I management system. (p. 13)
- Technological surveillance and competitive intelligence. The R&D&I management system must include a process of technological surveillance and competitive intelligence. The technological surveillance permits to realize the capture, the analysis, the diffusion and the exploitation of useful information of diverse types: scientific, technical, legislative, normative, economic, market, social, etc., in a systematic manner. The information of the technological surveillance is fundamental for the knowledge of the environment of the organization and for the competitive intelligence. The competitive intelligence includes analysis, interpretation, and communication of the information with strategic value, which is transmitted to the responsible people of the decision making in the organization, including the decisions which are related to the R&D&I management system. (p. 14)

5 Operating Processes of R&D&I

- Generalities. According with its strategy, policy and purposes of R&D&I, the organization must establish the operating processes of R&D&I which include all the relevant activities, since the information acquisition about a problem or opportunity (ideas) until the exploitation of the results of the R&D&I. The common aspects that integrate the R&D&I cycle are the management of ideas, the development of R&D&I projects, the protection and the exploitation of the results. (p. 14)
- Management of ideas. The management of ideas includes generation, collection, evaluation and selection. (p. 15)
- Development of R&D&I projects. The R&D&I projects must be developed with a documented methodology. The main advantage of the use of a methodology is the discipline that it imposes due to [its] established clear project plan, purposes and deliverables which are supervised with the advance of development of the project. (p. 15)
- Protection and exploitation of the results. The protection and exploitation of the results of the R&D&I activities must be realized according to the corresponding guidelines, applying the best option for protecting each step and following the mechanisms and the defined exploitation agreements, such as cession of intangible assets, concession of licenses of intangible assets, and securitization of intangible assets. (p. 16)
- Introduction to the market. For considering the existence of a success of an innovation, it should produce a return to the organization through the introduction of the

results to the market or through an internal improvement of processes. For introducing a product, process or service to the market, the organization must plan the actions considering: to identify the environment of the intellectual and industrial property in the destination markets, to develop a marketing and sales plan, to assure available funds and resources for introducing it into the market and for the expansion or implantation of the new process, and to establish the production, the supply chain, the client attention, the mechanisms for knowing its acceptance level and the formation of the involved agents, according to the needs. (p. 16)

- Results of the operating processes of the R&D&I. These results vary in function to the developed activities and the associated processes. The monitoring of the operating processes of the R&D&I is realized over the basis of the established indicators. The evaluation of the results in respect to these indicators should provide information about the success or the failure of the R&D&I and the learning for the improvement of the operating processes of the R&D&I. (p. 17)

6 Performance Evaluation of the R&D&I Management System

- Monitoring, measuring, analysis and evaluation. The organization must determine the methods for monitoring, measuring, analyzing and evaluating the performance and the effectiveness of the R&D&I Management System considering the following processes: R&D&I strategic processes, R&D&I operating processes, and R&D&I support processes. The results of this evaluation must permit to obtain information about the contribution of the R&D&I Management System such as: growth rate of benefits, growth rate of sales, growth rate of the operating margin, market share, scientific impact of the research results, generated intangible assets (number of registers of intellectual or industrial property, knowledge, recognition indexes, brand reputation, relationships, etc.), and the impact in social and environmental sustainability (reduction of emissions, reduction of energy consumption, material efficiency, improvement of the environment and work conditions, etc.). (p. 17)
- Internal Audit. The organization must realize documented procedures for internal audits periodically for determining the conformity of the effectiveness of the R&D&I management system with the requirements of this norm and the organization; also, for informing about the results and the corresponding records. (p. 17)
- Evaluation by the Direction. The Direction must review the R&D&I management system periodically for assuring its continuous convenience, adequation, and effectiveness. The evaluation of the Direction must include considerations about: the state of the actions of previous evaluations, the changes of internal and external conditions which can affect to the R&D&I management system, the information about the performance of the R&D&I management system (including nonconformities and corrective actions, monitoring and results of the measurements, and the results of the audits), and the opportunities of continuous improvement. (p. 18)

7 Improvement of the R&D&I Management System

The organization must improve continuously the suitability and the effectiveness of the system through the R&D&I strategy and policy, the leadership, the purposes, the planning, the R&D&I support processes and the performance evaluation. The organization must identify the deviations and nonconformities and to establish adequate corrective actions for eliminating the causes or to establish actions for improving the effectiveness and the results of the R&D&I Management System. (p. 18)

Mir and Casadesús (2011a) described the case of a Spanish manufacturing firm that implemented UNE 166002:2006 standard, which was "the first in the world to offer a certifiable standardized management system for innovation" (p. 171). Mir and Casadesús (2011a) also pointed out: "It is apparent from this case study that the standard encourages innovation and improvement in procedures for internal transfer and assimilation of technology, as well as facilitating improved results in terms of innovative products and services" (p. 184) and indicated the benefits after the implementation of the standard as follows: "the case company now has the capacity to detect emerging technologies (or existing technologies not yet applied in its sector), and to assimilate and develop these technologies to strengthen its future innovation activities and enhance its competitiveness". (p. 184)

Regarding the problems with implementing the UNE 166002:2006 standard, Mir and Casadesús (2011a) explained: "In particular, the quantity of documentation required for implementation was sometimes onerous, and some personnel (especially those with a low level of 'innovation culture') experienced difficulties in adapting to the new management system" (p. 184) and stated "[i]f the company in this case had not had prior experience with other management system standards (ISO 9001:2000, ISO 14001:2004, ISO -TS 16949:2002, and EMAS), these difficulties would certainly have been more significant". (p. 184) This adaptation could be more difficult for innovative people in particular.

CEN/TS 16555 Innovation Management

Caetano (2017) stated that "[t]he main objective of the CEN 'Family' of Technical Specifications (TS) is to guide European organizations to be aware and to develop innovation as a driver for competitiveness and value creation" (p. 10). Caetano (2017) also summarized the parts of the CEN/TS 16555 standard as follows:

- CEN/TS 16555–1:2013, Innovation Management System: This Technical Specification aims to present a framework, integrating activities crucial to generate innovations as a "routine" process and to target specific innovation determinants that include Organization Context, Leadership, Planning, Innovation Enablers, Innovation Process and Results, Innovation Management Techniques and Innovation, Performance assessment. (p. 10)
- CEN/TS 16555–2:2014, Strategic intelligence management: As innovation management depends on organizational capabilities to translate strategic signals and emerging trends into valuable inputs to innovation strategy and projects, this TS can be used to ensure intelligence and foresight can support innovation management. (p. 11)
- CEN/TS 16555–3:2014, Innovation Thinking: Based on a structured approach, that can be complemented by other methods and tools to promote innovation, Innovation Thinking aims to capture information, insights and experiences to maximize opportunities and problem solving in order to accelerate time to market and to create value-added innovations. (p. 11)
- CEN/TS 16555–4:2014, Intellectual Property Management (IP) Organizations must consider IPR as a strategic asset that can be linked to competitiveness, especially when considering value creation. Innovation management must consider IP as an enhancer and a tool to increase temporary market advantages and to use it as a knowledge management method that can capture information about competitors scientific and technological competences and assets. (p. 11)
- CEN/TS 16555–5:2014, Collaboration Management: Innovation management has been evolving towards an open and collaborative model. This TS targets collaboration as a new

domain that needs strategic guidance and management processes capable to enable organizations with internal tools to address issues that include "Why", "When", "How" and "With whom". (p. 12)

- CEN/TS 16555–6:2014, Creativity Management: Ideas are at the heart of the innovation process. By that reason, it was considered crucial to identify conditions necessary to nurture and develop ideas generation, collection, selection and implementation. (p. 12)
- CEN/TS 16555–7:2015, Innovation Management Assessment: Evaluation and assessment of innovation contribution to firms performance, competitiveness and sustainability are powerful instruments. Among other reasons, learning and improvement can illustrate why innovation assessment is gaining relevance at micro and macro levels. Through this TS, organizations can identify which tools can be used, from simple check lists to more complex models as the maturity or benchmarking instruments, and which results can be obtained. (p. 12)

ISO/TC 279 Innovation Management

De Casanove, Morel, and Negny (2017) explained that "[t]he charter of this group (ISO/TC279 business plan, 2014) has been defined at the creation the committee in 2013" (p. 6) and "aims at defining 'Standards on innovation management will allow organizations to share their best practices in innovation management. This will facilitate collaboration and also develop the capability to innovate and to bring innovations successfully to market.'" (p. 6) de Casanove (2014) also stated:

> That's what we do in ISO/TC 279 on innovation management. This is a new technical committee and the goal is to develop tools and methods that support the development of this innovation culture. We are quite young. The committee was created last year. For the moment, we have agreed on the work structure, that's a good achievement. We have four working groups. One will work on an innovation management system; the second on terminology, to ensure that we share the same definition of innovation and that we differentiate between innovation and innovation process.
>
> *(p. 98)*

The scope of this standard is consistency in the terminology tools, methods, and interactions among the relevant parties to enable innovation in the organizations (ISO, 2013). This standard has the following structure: (a) ISO/TC 2791/WG 1Innovation Management System, (b) ISO/TC 2791/WG 2 Terminology, terms and definitions, (c) ISO/TC 2791/WG 3 Tools and methods, and (d) ISO/TC 2791/WG 4 Innovation Management Assessment (ISO, 2013).

BS 7000 Design Management Systems

The British Standards Institution (2008) indicated that BS 7000 Design Management Systems includes the following components:

- Part 1: Guide to managing innovation (this part);
- Part 2: Guide to managing the design of manufactured products;
- Part 3: Guide to managing service design;
- Part 4: Guide to managing design in construction;

- Part 6: Guide to managing inclusive design;
- Part 10: Vocabulary of terms used in design management.

Other parts might be added. (p. v)

The British Standards Institution (2008) also indicated the following phases and stages of the Guide to Management Innovation:

Phase 1: Explore the Potential/Set the Context

Stage 1: Review the current innovation practices to determine the potential for improvement

It is necessary to review: current situation (quantified wherever possible) of the diverse aspects of the innovation in the organization, market information, projections of financial performance, intellectual property to be exploited, strengths, weaknesses, opportunities and threats, and comparisons with competitors and the best organizations of the industry (p. 32). All the information will be integrated in a business case with the assistance of experts and lead users of products (p. 32).

Stage 2: Create future vision

The creation of a future innovation vision should be clear and should guide and motivate to the improvement of capabilities for the innovation and the development of long term products (p. 33).

Stage 3: Draw up mission statement related to innovation

The organization's innovation mission should articulate organization's general stance, or philosophy, towards innovation, the prime reasons for promoting innovation, and its contribution to overall performance. The innovation mission of the organization joined to the objectives and strategies are determinants for investing in innovative activities. (p. 33)

Stage 4: Distill innovation objectives and strategies from the organization's objectives and strategies

The innovation objectives and strategies must be formulated from the organization's objectives and strategies, coordinating all the disciplines and elaborating documented key plans. (p. 33)

Phase 2: Establish foundation

Stage 5: Determine the innovation highway

The innovation highway sets the direction an organization takes to develop its next three product generations. It should illustrate how market demand, specific customer needs, technological advances, etc. can be brought together in the range of products offered by the organization. (p. 33)

Stage 6: Plan introduction of organization's new approach to innovation

The introduction of a new approach to innovation should encompass: (a) setting the context, (b) establishing mechanisms, (c) knowing what has been done, and (d) refining for the future. (p. 34)

Stage 7: Communicate essence of innovation mission, objectives and strategies

The innovation highway must include the rules, terrain and plans for improving innovation management issues, including the stakeholders outside the organization, using the appropriate language and terms to the targeted audiences, including informal communication alongside formal channels, and reducing the burden of bureaucratic paperwork. (p. 35)

Stage 8: Promote innovation nurturing culture

The leaders should evolve the organizational identity and the organizational culture to an innovative culture characterized by: (a) the foundations, (b) acknowledgement and leading from the top, (c) involvement of staff, (d) enlightened systems and rigorous application, and (e) making to most of experience. (p. 37)

Stage 9: Reinforce infrastructure and expertise to manage innovation

It includes: (a) need for rigorous innovation management system, and (b) augment internal competencies with external expertise. (p. 37)

Phase 3: Implement changes

Stage 10: Draw up master innovation programme

All innovative activities (long- and short-term) should be co-ordinated within a master innovation programme that details work on each potential product, technology or process broken down into stages (with deliverables, budgets, schedules and reviews). (p. 38)

Stage 11: Implement programme and support new approach to innovation

An innovation highway must be focused considering the projects in the master innovation programme to develop thinking, get closer to target audiences, gain greater insights into requirements and conceive options; also, innovation leaders should maintain the energy of the teams and remain properly informed of the progress of innovation projects. (p. 39)

Stage 12: Evaluate progress and contribution of master innovation programme

Principals are responsible for overseeing and evaluating the innovative work undertaken by, or on behalf of, their organizations. Regular reviews should be scheduled into the master innovation programme. Investments in innovation should be evaluated by means of a formal procedure that is documented, transparent and familiar to a wide range of personnel within the organization. (p. 41)

Phase 4: Build on expertise and enhanced reputation

Stage 13: Build distinctive competencies and competitive advantage through innovation

Organizations that develop distinctive competencies in innovation are likely to be at a competitive advantage where sustained performance in constantly changing circumstances is at a premium. (p. 42)

Stage 14: Document, share, publicize and celebrate achievements through innovation

It is essential to capture the essence of innovative work through documentation and rigorous analysis due to that such references help to make contributions to corporate performance more tangible in the short and medium terms. (p. 43)

Stage 15: Enhance organization's reputation through innovation

The value of innovation could be enhanced further by building it into a core component of an organization's reputation; a key driver and highly visible deliverer of corporate performance. Showing that innovation makes a valuable contribution to sustainability and the communities where facilities are located also helps. (p. 43)

Stage 16: Review and refine overall approach to innovation.

Principals should also reinforce the regime of continually improving their organizations' approaches and innovation management systems with more substantial longer-term reviews that reflect increased confidence and credibility as a result of mounting quantified achievements. (p. 44)

NP Series of R&D&I Management

Mir and Casadesús (2011b) detailed the documents of the NP Series of R&D&I Management as follows:

- NP 4457:2007 *Requisitos do sistema de gestão de IDI* (Requirements of the R&D&I Management System)
- NP 4456:2007 *Terminologia e definições das actividades de IDI* (Terms and definitions of the R&D&I activities)
- NP 4458:2007 *Requisitos de um projecto de IDI* (Requirements of a R&D&I Project)
- NP 4461:2007 *Competência e avaliação dos auditores de sistemas de gestão da IDI e dos auditores de proyectos de IDI* (Competences and availability of the auditors of R&D&I Management System and of the auditors of R&D&I Projects)

Models and methodologies for innovation management

Many authors have developed diverse models and methodologies for managing innovation in organizations. In this section, some of the models and methodologies which were found in the literature review are presented.

Innovation management models

Some of the innovation management models that were found in the literature review are in Table 24.3 with their respective authors.

iSIM: Integrated Service Innovation Method

Chew (2016) proposed the model of iSIM (Integrated Service Innovation Method) with the following components: (a) strategy, (b) service architecture, (c) monetization, (d) customer value proposition, (e) service concept, (f) service system, and (g) customer experience (p. 463). Chew (2016) also described the iSIM end-to-end design processes as follows:

- **Service business strategy design**

    Strategy (step 1) is designed (by C-level leadership team) to fulfill the firm's vision and mission. To that end, it defines the firm's business logic, its platform choice, and corresponding m-sided market model. Service strategy defines the overarching directional guide for all design process elements in iSIM. (p. 465)

- **Customer type and value proposition design**

    Step 2 customer-type and value proposition (CVP) design and step 7 monetization design are co-dependent factors of business model design. They are analyzed and chosen by using competitive game theory and contingency theory. These steps are typically marketing-led in collaboration with IT and finance executives. Customer type and value proposition (CVP) design process element defines the external fitness requirements for all other design process elements. (p. 465)

- **Service concept design**

    A marketing-led practice (supported by IT and operations executives), step 3 service concept design process element designs the service logic (e.g. Dell's Build-to-order^ logic [McGrath, 2010]) in line with the business logic and strategic intent defined in step 1 in order to fulfill the high-level customer value proposition designed in step 2. (p. 465)

- **Service system design**

    Service system design (step 4) at service delivery level is an IT/operations-led cross-disciplinary endeavor. It starts with the customer/user and defines how the service will be performed using human-centered and user-participatory methods to model the service performance (Patricio et al., 2011; Holmlid and Evenson, 2008). Service

Table 24.3 Identified models for innovation management

Name	Authors who commented on the standard
iSIM: Integrated Service Innovation Method	(Chew, 2016)
Open Innovation Maturity Model for the Government	(Ham, Lee, Kim, and Choi, 2015)
Innovation Capability Maturity Model (ICMM v2) of Essmann	(Knoke, 2013)
I2MM: Integrated Innovation Maturity Model	(Müller-Prothmann and Stein, 2011)
Model for Measuring the Business Model Innovativeness	(Spieth and Schneider, 2016)
The Open Business Model	(Khumalo and Van der Lingen, 2017)

innovation, and thus the step 4 service system design process element, could be exploratory requiring comprehensive service system radical redesign. (p. 466)

- **Customer experience design**

    Service design excellence strives to achieve superior customer experience (step 5), which is defined by the usability and pleasurability of the service interactions (Stickdorn and Schneider, 2010, p. 84). Service organizations are increasingly managing customer experiences to promote differentiation and customer loyalty. Due to its strategic significance as a competitive differentiator, this specialist practice of service encounter design, whilst an integral part of service system design, is factored out as a crucial step deserving special attention in the overall integrated design method. Customer experience is the outcome of the co-created customer value fulfilled by the service (delivery) system design in line with the CVP of the customer type in question. The desired customer experience envisioned by the CVP for each service type is analyzed as the (outside-in) objectives of service encounter blueprinting design (Bitner et al., 2008; Patricio et al., 2008, 2011). (p. 467)

- **Service architecture design**

    Service architecture is designed to systematize service design and innovation by providing a common language across different views on service design and a systematic way to operationalize and measure the degree of service architecture modularity (Voss and Hsuan, 2009). It is designed in accordance with the principle of modularity (Baldwin and Clark, 1997) comprising five dimensions: components, the interfaces, degree of coupling, and commonality sharing between components, and platform as the overarching configuration of components and interfaces that make up the service architecture (Fixson, 2005; Tiwana et al., 2010; Yoo et al., 2010; Gawer and Cusumano, 2014). (p. 467)

- **Monetization design**

    Step 7 monetization design is interlinked with customer type design choice in Step 1. Customer types can be chosen (Eisenmann et al., 2006) by the business model as: (a) one-sided – where the end-user customers pay to use the service offered; (b) two-sided – where the end-user customers use the service offered free, which is actually subsidized by the advertiser customers who pay the focal firm to target-advertise to the firm's huge captive audience of end-user customers according to their service usage behaviors – an end-user co-created value offered to the advertisers as a value proposition; or (c) multi-sided – often found in B2B business model context, where different roles played by different actors: service usage by end-users, authorization of service contract by senior executive, and payment for service used by finance officer. Monetization service experience (influenced by monetization intensity) can be further refined and customized by deciding when, what and how money is raised. (p. 468)

Open Innovation Maturity Model for the Government

Ham, Lee, Kim, and Choi (2015) described the components of the Open System Framework for Open Innovation in the Government and the fundamental structure of the Open Innovation Maturity Model for the Government. Ham, Lee, Kim, and Choi (2015) indicated the components of the Open System Framework for Open Innovation in the Government as follows:

- **Input**
  - Legal needs: open data–related law
  - Political needs: open data use for political activities
  - Social needs: transparent government
  - Economical needs: open data–related business
  - Institutional needs: open data–related institution
  - Operational needs: efficiency of data and information
  - Technical needs: open linked data

- **Transformation**
  - Management subsystem: exploitation/exploration
  - Supportive subsystem: exploitation/exploration
  - Production subsystem: exploitation/exploration
  - Maintenance subsystem: exploitation/exploration
  - Distribution subsystem: exploitation/exploration
  - Adaptive subsystem: exploitation/exploration
  - Value generating mechanism:
    i. Transparency
    ii. Participation
    iii. Efficiency
    iv. Innovation

- **Outputs**
  - Social value (Impacts)

    i. OECD: BLI (Better Life Index)
       www.oecdbetterlifeindex.org
       - Housing, Income, Job, Community
       - Education, Environment
       - Civic Engagement
       - Health, Life Satisfaction, Safety
       - Work-Life Balance

    ii. NEF: HPI (Happy Planet Index)

  - Economic Value (Impacts)

    i. GNP (Gross National Product)
    ii. GDP (Gross Domestic Product)
    iii. GNI (Gross National Income)
    iv. GDI (Gross Domestic Income)

  - Competitive Value (Impacts)

    i. WEF: GCI (Global Competitiveness Index)
       - Basic Requirements
       - Efficiency Enhancers
       - Innovation and Sophistication

- **External Environment**
  - Environmental condition: Legal, political, social, economical, institutional, operational, and technical environment

Ham, Lee, Kim, and Choi (2015) considered that the model proposed in their study is "the best means not only to assess the current maturity level of the open innovation of a government but also to provide the government with appropriate future directions and guidelines to increase the maturity level" (p. 5). Ham, Lee, Kim, and Choi (2015) also stated that the procedures of the development processes of the Open Innovation Maturity Model for the Government as follows: (a) problem identification, (b) comparison of existing maturity models and determination of a development strategy, and (c) iterative maturity model development (p. 5). Ham, Lee, Kim, and Choi (2015) also explained the fundamental structure of the Open Innovation Maturity Model for the Government as follows: (a) the generic and specific processes of each system are extracted from the literature review on open data, open innovation and maturity model research, (b) the definitions of the measurements are extracted from the literature review on open data, open innovation and maturity model research, (c) the capability scores are extracted from the calculation based on the evaluated points of each measurement, (d) the capability types of each subsystem are extracted from the results of capability scores, and (e) the capability level of each subsystem is extracted from the mapping results of capability types (p. 6).

Innovation Capability Maturity Model (ICMM v2) of Essmann

Knoke (2013) explained the five maturity levels of the Innovation Capability Maturity Model ICMM v2 of Essmann, as follows:

- Ad-hoc innovation: consumed with day-to-day operations; outputs are inconsistent and unpredictable
- Defined innovation: need to innovate identified and defined; outputs are inconsistent but traceable
- Supported innovation: practices, procedures and tools implemented; consistent outputs maintain market share
- Aligned innovation: integrated and aligned activities and resources; outputs are a source of consistent differentiation
- Synergized innovation: synchronization of activities and resources; outputs provide sustained competitive advantage. (p. 8)

Integrated Innovation Maturity Model (I2MM)

Müller-Prothmann and Stein (2011) described the I2MM process areas and the I2MM capability levels. Müller-Prothmann and Stein (2011) detailed the I2MM process areas as follows: (a) Ideation and Product Development, which "concentrates on activities with regard to seeking, analysing, and evaluating ideas" (p. 6); (b) Innovation Management, which "covers among other aspects the innovation strategy, its documentation, and transparency to employees as well as the degree of its realisation" (p. 6); (c) Requirements Engineering, which "deals with development, definition, documentation, planning, and improvement of requirements" (p. 6); and (d) Quality Management, which "is characterised by the necessity for quality processes and products. Therefore, both processes and products need to be continuously improved to reduce bugs, problems, costs, and risks" (p. 6). Müller-Prothmann and Stein (2011, p. 6) also described the I2MM Capacity Levels as follows:

- **Capability Level 1:** Chaotic. Chaotic organization, ad-hoc managed, structure processes with unpredictable outcomes, disorganized, unregulated, unknown and undocumented requirements for products and processes, projects frequently exceed schedule and budget, without integration with stakeholders, conservative, firefighter behavior without the idea of the complexity and interconnectedness of problems, strongly conservative towards improvements, innovations and external knowledge and experts, nonintegrated and limited communication, and not documented innovation-related knowledge, which is not seen as relevant for quality and risk management.
- **Capability Level 2:** Organized. Documented processes and subprocesses, although not harmonized in every single division, rudimentary quality management results in quality guidelines, some claims of management processes and customer feedback, some feedback loops are converted into lessons learned, upper management communicates innovation objectives, innovative ideas and solutions are rejected as unworkable, identification of stakeholders, and the transfer of knowledge or cooperation with other areas is not considered as important.
- **Capability Level 3:** Standardized. Documented and harmonized processes in all divisions of the organization, standardized company-wide innovation process with embedded requirements engineering and permanent feedback to relevant staff members, minimized risks in checked projects, knowledge is shared and broadcasted, learning culture is constant, knowledge management tools are available to management and individual staff members only, cooperation with stakeholders has been improved but remains an exception, the stakeholders and their ideas and expectations are identified systematically, the ideas are evaluated and rewarded with incentives, quality management is implemented and harmonized in all divisions to evaluate processes and to achieve customer satisfaction, and benchmarking of markets is developed and is used to optimize processes and products.
- **Capability Level 4:** Predictable. Stakeholders are integrated into ideation and product development with continuous feedback, creativity workshops, cross-organizational cooperation inside and outside of networks, innovation process and its documentation are permanently assessed and adjusted if required, continuous usage of termination criteria throughout the process ("kill early, kill cheap" mentality), lessons learned are registered and reviewed, planned and evaluated processes through indicators and expected results, the tools and techniques are accessible to each employee, the knowledge management stimulates the process improvement and is deeply integrated in corporate processes, and continuous examination of consumer satisfaction, time to market, adherence to schedules, costs, product, and process quality.
- **Capability Level 5:** Innovation "Black Belt". Defined to respond to changing project conditions, processes and products are improved continuously, permanent benchmarking of markets for determining the best practices, organizational culture can be easily adjusted to changing requirements, organization realizes strategic foresight with knowledge networks inside and outside the organization, innovation methods are suggested by stakeholders, innovations are planned and generated systematically, open innovation methods inspire new products, processes and technologies, requirements are classified according to the phases of the product lifecycle, employee creativity is fostered, and financial incentives and time to help to employees for realizing the ideas.

Statistical Model for Measuring the Business Model Innovativeness

Spieth and Schneider (2016, p. 686) evaluated a Statistical Model for Measuring the Business Model Innovativeness with the following dimensions, elements, and indicators:

1. Value Offering Innovation: The value proposition towards the customer has changed

    - Target customers: Target customers have changed
    - Positioning: The product and service offering has changed
    - Product and service offering: The firm's positioning in the market has changed

2. Value Architecture Innovation: The value creation architecture has changed

    - Core competencies and resources: The firm's core competences and resources have changed
    - Internal value creation: Internal value creation activities have changed
    - Partners in value creation (external value creation): The role and involvement of partners into the value creation process has changed
    - Distribution: Distribution has changed

3. Revenue Model Innovation: The logic how revenues are generated has changed

    - Revenue mechanisms: Revenue mechanisms have changed
    - Cost mechanisms: Cost mechanisms have changed

The Open Business Model

Khumalo and Van der Lingen (2017) stated that the concept of Open Business Model originated from the intersection of open innovation and the business model (p. 149). Khumalo and Van der Lingen (2017) also stated that open innovation is best understood as "a paradigm that assumes that organisations can and should use external and internal ideas, as well as internal and external paths to market, as they look to advance their technology" (p. 149) and detailed the open innovation practices as follows:

- Inbound: alliances, purchase of scientific services, in-licensing, institutional collaboration, venture capital, acquisition, customer involvement, and external networking – including conferences, fairs, knowledge clusters, and crowdsourcing (p. 150).
- Outbound: spinoff, supply of scientific services, out-licensing, external technology commercialization, knowledge exploitation, venturing out, industry groups, and institutional collaboration/partnerships (p. 150).

Khumalo and Van der Lingen (2017) explained that the Business Model Canvas includes (a) key partners, (b) key activities, (c) value proposition, (d) customer relationships, (e) customer segments, (f) key resources, (g) channels, (h) cost structure, and (i) revenue streams (p. 151). Khumalo and Van der Lingen (2017) also explained that "[m]ultiple studies tend to recommend openness" (p. 156) and that "there is no explicit directive about what managers have to deal with or how they should overcome the challenges brought about by openness" (p. 156). Additionally, Khumalo and Van der Lingen (2017) pointed out: "A strategic and operating management model, or rather a toolkit, is necessary" (p. 156). Khumalo and Van der Lingen (2017) also stated:

> In more progressive organisations, business model change is not necessarily motivated by poor organisational performance, but can even occur while the organisation is

thriving [97]. Such proactiveness could anticipate a decline in performance, or offer foresight into better returns with a new configuration. The development of new organisational routines, such as evaluation procedures and metrics of performance [74], could be considered to be the foundation of business model archetypes. Furthermore, the literature generally agrees that enterprises, when operating under uncertainty, should experiment with a range of business models [98]. Through experimentation, the initial value proposition evolves into a viable business model by using a series of trial-and-error changes that are pursued along various dimensions [99].

(p. 156)

Khumalo and Van der Lingen (2017) pointed out: "An open business model archetype does not need to digress from existing knowledge. Only a new configuration of existing elements is necessary" (p. 156) and proposed the features of the Open Business Model as follows: (a) Iteration (consists of decision gates and feedback loops), (b) Value calculation mechanism, (c) Strategic agility/flexibility, (d) Managerial assumptions (effort on proximity to fact), (e) Organizational dynamic capability, and (f) Boundary-spanning concept (p. 156).

Innovation management methodologies

After the literature review, diverse methodologies for innovation management were found. A short list of these innovation management methodologies is in Table 24.4.

MIM3

Alfaro (2017b) developed "MIM3: Methodology of Innovation Management for Obtaining the Level 3 of I2MM", which is a holistic methodology for the obtaining level 3 of the Integrated Innovation Maturity Model. Alfaro (2017b) stated that MIM3 is "an integrated methodological approach which includes the good management practices of

Table 24.4 Identified methodologies for innovation management

Methodology	Authors who commented on the methodology
MIM3: Methodology of Innovation Management for Obtaining the Level 3 of I2MM	(Alfaro, 2017b)
MEVGIT: Methodology for Evaluating the Value Generation of Information Technology	(Alfaro, 2017a)
Lean Product Innovation Management	(Wang, Ming, You, Kong, and Li, 2011)
Lean Startup	(Ciobanu and Nastase, 2015).
Very Lean Startup	(Gupte, 2015)
Design Thinking	(Coleman, 2016; Liedtka, 2015; Joyce, Ching, Wong, and Huang-Yao, 2015; Brown, 2008)
Living Lab Methodology	(Schuurman, de Marez, and Ballon, 2016)
Goodyear's Business Model Innovation Process	(Euchner and Ganguly, 2014)
FastWorks Framework	(Merfeld, 2014)
Lean Innovation Model	(Frederic, Lam, and Martin, 2014)
Seeking Solutions Approach	(Deutsch, 2013)
3-Stage Roadmap	(Belkhir, 2015).

the following management areas: (a) strategic management, (b) project management, (c) innovation models and innovation methods, (d) standards for innovation management, (e) knowledge management, and (f) financial management" (p. 31). Alfaro (2017b) also explained that

> The proposed MIM3 methodology integrates the generation of ideas of innovative projects in an aligned manner with the strategic planning of the organizations through the concordance with the organizational purposes and goals of the organizations and the areas or processes of the organizations joined to the manner in which the innovative project idea will contribute to the goals searching the quantification of the impact. MIM3 also includes the knowledge areas (integration management, scope management, time management, cost management, quality management, human resources management, communications management, risk management, acquisitions management and stakeholders management) of the project management according to Project Management Body of Knowledge (Project Management Institute, 2013) in a summarized manner and the use of the Critical Chain (Goldratt, 1997), with the processes of some of the main innovation models and innovation methods which were found in the literature review, considering the good practices of the standards of innovation management. MIM3 also includes some knowledge management good practices, such as the yellow pages and the evaluation of the value generation of the innovative projects with a procedure based on the MEVGIT methodology (Alfaro, 2017a), which is also based on free cash flow, total cost of ownership and the direct costing.
>
> (p. 32)

Additionally, Alfaro (2017b) indicated the policies of the MIM3 as follows:

The general policies which are necessary for the application of the methodological proposal are the following:

- This methodological proposal is applicable to all the innovative projects which the personnel want to present in each one of the processes or areas of the organization.
- The innovation area will maintain a service vocation for all the personnel of the processes or areas, all the time. In this way, the innovation area will support with the corresponding technical knowledge to the diverse proposals of innovation projects.
- The innovation area will consider "Idea of an Innovative Project" to an idea of project which would generate value and would have a creative or new component for the reality of the process of the organization.
- The innovation area must receive and evaluate all the ideas of innovative projects which each worker of the organization or its stakeholders consider innovative project. (p. 56)

Alfaro (2017b, p. 57) described the processes of the MIM3 as follows:

1. To generate and to evaluate the "Idea of Innovative Project".
2. To prepare the "Innovative Project Charter" and "Plan for the Management of Innovative Project".
3. To determine the technical feasibility of the innovative project.
4. To determine the financial feasibility of the innovative project.

Is feasible technical and financially?
Then
5   To plan, implement and evaluate the "Proof of Concept".
    Was the "Proof of Concept" a success?
    Then
6   To plan, implement, and evaluate the pilot project.
    Was the "Pilot Project" a success?
    Then
7   To implement the innovative project.
8   To record "Learned Lessons", to update "Yellow Pages", and to realize the "Closure of the Project"
9   To select the successful and culminated innovative projects and apply for national and international awards or competitions.
10 To register copyright or inventions, as determined by the Chief Executive Officer or the Board of Directors.
    Go to process 1.
Otherwise
    Go to process 8.
Otherwise
    Go to process 8.
Otherwise
    Go to process 8.
    Go to process 1.

Each one of the processes of MIM3 with its respective forms are detailed (Alfaro, 2017b). The forms of MIM3 are the following: (a) FR-MIM3–001–001 Idea of Innovative Project, (b) FR-MIM3–002–001 Innovative Project Charter, (c) FR-MIM3–003–001 Template of the Project Management Plan – Table of Contents, (d) FR-MIM3–004–001 Technical Evaluation of the Project, (e) FR-MIM3–005–001 Risks Management of the Innovative Project, (f) FR-MIM3–006–001 Financial Evaluation of the Project, (g) FR-MIM3–007–001 Registration of Innovative Project's Learned Lessons, (h) FR-MIM3–008–001 Form of Project Closure, (i) FR-MIM3–009–001 Budget of Outflows of the Innovative Project, (j) FR-MIM3–010–001 Schedule of the Project, (k) FR-MIM3–011–001 Control of Changes of the Innovative Project, (l) FR-MIM3–012–001 Communications Management of the Innovative Project, and (m) FR-MIM3–013–001 Yellow Pages of the Project (Alfaro, 2017b).

MEVGIT

Alfaro (2017a, p. 170) described MEVGIT (Methodology for Evaluating the Value Generation of Information Technology) as a methodology for evaluating the financial value generation of investments in information technology innovation and outlined its steps as follows:

1   To calculate the additional inflow which will be collected by the product or result of the project.

    • To calculate the additional contribution margin (in the case of firms) or the additional gross domestic product (in the case of nonprofit governmental entities) due to the product or result of the project

For firms:

- To calculate the additional contribution margin due to the increase of sales to the current clients.
- To calculate the additional contribution margin due to the increase of sales to new clients.
- To calculate the additional contribution margin due to the organization would avoid the loss of sales.
- To calculate the additional contribution margin due to the reduction of the variable cost of sales.

For nonprofit governmental organizations:

- To analyze how to convert the nonfinancial benefits with the goods or services of the nonprofit governmental entities, to amounts of gross domestic product.
- To calculate the amount of gross domestic product which will be increased through the product or result of the project.

- To calculate the savings due to the product or result of the project
- To calculate the savings due to the reduction of investments.
- To calculate the savings due to the reduction of expenses.

2   To calculate the additional outflows which will be collected by the product or result of the project.
- To calculate the additional investments: hardware acquisition, software acquisition, installation, infrastructure, furniture and equipment, and others.
- To calculate the additional expenses: personnel, advertising, training, support, maintenance, inactivated time, space and energy, and others.

3   To calculate the net flow. The calculation of the net flow is the difference of the additional inflows and the additional outflows.

4   To estimate the discount rate.

The discount rate must consider the following criteria: (a) to be higher than the risk free rate, (b) to be higher than the average return on investment of the firms of the economic sector of the country or region, (c) to be higher than weighted average cost of capital, and (d) to be equal or greater than a minimum discount rate that the board of directors determined.

5   To calculate the net present value.

For calculating the net present value, the discount rate and the net flow must be considered. Each one of the net flow at the end of each period must be discounted dividing (1 + discount rate)i, where "i" is each one of the periods. The sum of the discounted net flows of each period will be the net present value.

Lean Product Innovation Management

Wang et al. (2011, p. 2076) explained the five steps of an approach toward Lean Product Innovation Management as follows:

- Adopt lean. Adopt a lean paradigm: prepare in advance
- Specify value. Rapid response to market and customer demands; customers define value by new product and form of service

- Identify current value stream. Data collection: record current value stream status of product innovation; show the product and information
- Create future value stream. Analyze the current-state value stream based in the definition; eliminate nonvalue-added activities and get a new value stream
- Implement flow. Actualized innovation process; continuous; control and standardize the process of innovation

Wang et al. (2011) also explained the roadmap to transition to Lean Product Innovation Management as follows:

1. Pre-innovation plan.

    The company's senior leadership committed to product innovation lean organization and implementation of the reform process. Prevent the blind development of new products in mobile phone development process examining options to be sure to prepare adequately and to handset development teams focus on the project from the beginning.

2. The definition of value.

    Collect and analyze data from the fact of consumer, at the same time market researcher studies the competitor's product as comprehensive as possible to accurate understanding of consumer needs.

3. Value stream.

    According to company the prior product development process, the numbers of development team proposed development process milestone, the actual delivery time, and the number and impact of project changes. Through this accurate data collection and rigorous data analysis, the waste in project is definite.

4. The future value stream.

    In order to reduce the occurrence of changes and rework the final detailed schedule and work plan, the tools which can identify and eliminate waste such as mass matrix, causal analysis, brainstorming and other methods to be used, and then implementation of resources is allocated in a new mobile phone development process.

5. Implementation Process.

    To become learning-oriented enterprises, Staff training Lean thinking and suppliers attend new product development. (p. 207)

Lean Startup

The concept of Lean Startup was introduced by the entrepreneur Eric Ries in 2011 in his book: *The Lean Startup, How Today's Entrepreneurs Use Continuous Innovation to Create Radically Successful Businesses*" (Ciobanu and Nastase, 2015, p. 81). Ciobanu and Nastase (2015) stated that the Lean Startup method "is based on a different kind of thinking and asks from the entrepreneurs to see productivity differently" (p. 83) and "builds sustainable and effective companies because it allows businesses into the startup phase to test and recognize when it is time to change strategy, without consuming resources irresponsible relying on predefined and pre-accepted strategies"

(p. 83). Additionally, Ciobanu and Nastase (2015, p. 83) explained their interpretation of the five principles of the Lean Startup method as follows:

- Entrepreneurs can be found everywhere and can be anyone from novices to intrapreneurs.
- Entrepreneurship means new management adjusted to an environment of maximum uncertainty.
- Validating learning by empirical research of their own entrepreneurial vision.
- Transforming ideas into products through the loop Construct–Evaluate–Learn.
- Measuring results and entrepreneurial progress through accounting for innovation.

Finally, Ciobanu and Nastase (2015, p. 84) described the following characteristics of the Lean Startup:

- Empirical research of the market by creating a minimum viable product (MVP);
- Low initial production, avoiding wasting resources on a product that is likely to be unsaleable;
- Reduced time of execution of the first versions of the product/service that come on the market;
- Use continuous innovation for improving the quality of the product as a function of early customer feedback;
- The failure of the product/service can be determined earlier through testing, when production is reduced in quantity. In this way the risk of bankruptcy is also reduced;
- The focus is on the quality and value offered to the customer according to his needs by involving him in the design process to the final product.

The Very Lean Startup Method

Gupte (2015) stated that "[t]he Very Lean Startup Method© or perhaps the Really Lean Startup Method© is but a natural extension of the Lean Startup Method." (p. 52) and that "[t]he Very Lean Startup Method focuses on identifying customers before an entrepreneur builds or perhaps even defines a product" (p. 52). Gupte (2015) also proposed the processes of the Very Lean Startup Method as follows:

- Conduct brainstorming and informal "research".
- Identify possible customer demographics.
- Make the collateral.
- Send out the collateral.
- Send out variations with different pricing or offers.
- Find out why the nonresponses didn't respond.
- Ask the responding customers to pay.
- Do the math on the cost of customer acquisition and pricing.
- Adjust the cost of feature development in the business model.
- Modify the offering – product/price/placement/target customer.
- Repeat until you have a viable business model.

Design Thinking

Joyce, Ching, Wong, and Huang-Yao (2015) described design thinking as follows: "Design thinking is implicit in intentional acts that lead to the creation or improvement of products, services, and experiences" (p. 537). Design thinking is "a discipline that uses the designer's sensibility and methods to match people's needs with what is technologically feasible and what a viable business strategy can convert into customer value and market opportunity" (Brown, 2008, p. 96). Coleman (2016) explained that Tim Brown, president and CEO of IDEO, describes design thinking as "a methodology that imbues the full spectrum of innovation activities with a human-centered design ethos" (p. 63). Coleman (2016) also stated:

> By this I mean that innovation is powered by a thorough understanding, through direct observation, of what people want and need in their lives and what they like or dislike about the way particular products are made, packaged, marketed, sold and supported (Brown, 2008, p. 86).
>
> *(p. 63)*

Regarding the design thinking process, Coleman (2016) explained that "[t]he Institute of Design at Stanford University (a.k.a., the d School) lists five steps in the design thinking process" (p. 64) as follows:

> Step one is to understand or empathize. In this step the design team focuses on observing and interviewing their subjects and learning as much as possible about their audience. The team will be looking to answer questions such as "Who is the user?" and "What matters to this person?"
> Step two is to define the issue and the needs of the user. What is the audience's point of view and what are the needs of the end user?
> Step three is the ideate stage. The team brainstorms as many creative solutions as possible. "Crazy ideas" are encouraged!
> Step four is the prototype stage. This stage involves creating or building a rough representation of one or more ideas to show to the end user.
> Step five is to test the product, sharing ideas and prototypes with end users and a larger audience to garner feedback. (p. 64)

Liedtka (2015, p. 928) described the common design thinking tools as follows: (a) visualization: use of imaginary, either visual or narrative; (b) ethnography techniques: participant observation, interviewing, journey mapping, and job-to-be-done analysis; (c) structured collaborative sense-making techniques: mind mapping, collaborative ideation techniques (brainstorming and concept development techniques); (d) assumption surfacing; (e) prototyping techniques; (f) cocreation; and (g) field experiments. As can be appreciated, the design thinking tools are very diverse and promote the collaborative work. Liedtka (2015, p. 928) also described the models of design thinking in practice from IDEO, Continuum, Stanford Design School, Rotman Business School, and Darden Business School, as follows:

- **IDEO**
  - Stage I – Data gathering about user needs: Discovery and interpretation
  - Stage II – Idea generation: Ideation
  - Stage III – Testing: Experimentation and evolution

- **Continuum**
  - Stage I – Data gathering about user needs: Discover deep insights
  - Stage II – Idea generation: Create
  - Stage III – Testing: Make it real: prototype, test and deploy

- **Stanford Design School**
  - Stage I – Data gathering about user needs: Empathize and define
  - Stage II – Idea generation: Ideation
  - Stage III – Testing: Prototype and test

- **Rotman Business School**
  - Stage I – Data gathering about user needs: Empathy
  - Stage II – Idea generation: Ideation
  - Stage III – Testing: Prototyping and experimentation

- **Darden Business School**
  - Stage I – Data gathering about user needs: What is?
  - Stage II – Idea generation: What if?
  - Stage III – Testing: What wows? and What works?

Living Lab Methodology

Schuurman, de Marez, and Ballon (2016) explained the Living Lab Methodology as an alternative to quasi-experimental design. Schuurman, de Marez, and Ballon (2016) explained that quasi-experimental design includes the following processes: (a) Pre-Test, (b) Intervention, and (c) Post-Test. Schuurman, de Marez, and Ballon (2016) also explained the processes of the living lab methodology inside each one of the processes of the quasi-experimental design as follows: (a) in Pre-Test: contextualization, selection, and concretization; (b) in Intervention: implementation; and (c) in Post-Test: feedback (p. 9). Additionally, Schuurman, de Marez, and Ballon (2016) indicated the three types of living lab projects with the six stages of new product development: (a) exploration: idea and concept; (b) experimentation: prototype; and (c) evaluation: pre-launch, launch, and post-launch (p. 10). Finally, after the application to 27 innovation projects from Flemish startups and small and medium-sized enterprises (SMEs) carried out within the iMinds Living Labs constellation, Schuurman, de Marez, and Ballon (2016) concluded:

> We summarize and translate our findings in three propositions. First, the discussed living lab projects are aimed at opening up the company boundaries towards user contributions, thus facilitating outside-in open innovation. Moreover, in terms of the collaboration typology of Pisano and Verganti (2008), the projects can be labelled as hierarchical and shifting between open and closed participation. The user contributions were successful for almost two-thirds of the projects, leading to modifications of the innovation during or after the project based on user contributions. Moreover, for two-thirds of projects, this innovation resulted in a market introduction or in further development. These findings show that living lab projects are a means to successfully facilitate open innovation in startups and SMEs.
>
> (p. 13)

InnoCamp model

Kaski, Alamäki, and Moisio (2014) presented the InnoCamp model, which is really a method that "comprises the typical participatory open innovation approach with the concept of rapid innovation and coaching" (p. 163). Kaski, Alamäki, and Moisio (2014) stated that "[t]his way it compresses the key phases of the innovation process into two working days" (p. 163). It was tested at the Vierumäki Sport Institute for two days with sport firms. Kaski, Alamäki, and Moisio (2014) explained the InnoCamp processes as follows: (a) Pre-Assignments: Pre-understanding); (b) First Day: company task sharing, idea creation – several methods-, and evaluations; and (c) Second Day: selection, improvement, concept creation, selling, and pitch (p. 167).

As was mentioned, the standards, models, and methodologies for managing the innovation could accelerate the value generation of the innovations and avoid various types of failures, and not only financial failures. The learning and the application of the standards, models, and methodologies for innovation management, with previous adaptations to the realities of the organization, should be necessary to obtain the expected results of the investments in innovation.

References

AENOR (2014). *Gestión de la I+D+i: Requisitos del Sistema de Gestión de la I+D+i* [R&D&i Management: R&D&i Management System Requirements]. Madrid, Spain: AENOR.

Alfaro, E. (2017a). Urgent! . . . To reward the innovation in information technologies with a real focus on value generation. In Brem, A. and Viardot, E. (Eds.), *Revolution in innovation management*. Heidelberg/New York: Palgrave Macmillan/Springer.

Alfaro, E. A. (2017b). MIM3: methodology of innovation management for obtaining the level 3 of I2MM. *ICPE Public Enterprise Half-Yearly Journal*, 23(1), 31–83.

Attia, A. M. (2015). National innovation systems in developing countries: barriers to university-industry collaboration in Egypt. *International Journal of Technology Management & Sustainable Development*, 14(2), 113–124.

Belkhir, L. (2015). The innovation levers to sustainable management: entrepreneurship, design and policy. *Journal of Management and Sustainability*, 5(1), 10–19.

Baldwin, C. Y. and Clark, K. B. (1997). Managing in an age of modularity. *Harvard Business Review*, 75(5), 84–93.

Bitner, M. J., Ostrom, A. J., and Morgan, F. N. (2008). Service blueprinting: a practical technique for service innovation. *California Management Review*, 50(3), 66–94.

British Standards Institution (2008). *Design management systems – part 1: guide to managing the innovation*. London: British Standards Institution.

Brown, T. (2008). Design thinking. *Harvard Business Review*, June, 84–92.

Bruneel, J., d'Este, P. and Salter, A. (2010). Investigating the factors that diminish the barriers to university-industry collaboration. *Research Policy*, 39(7), 858–868.

Caetano, I. (2017). Standardization and innovation management. *Journal of Innovation Management*, 5(2), 8–14.

Castillo-Rojas, C., Karapetrovic, C. and Heras, M. (2012). Is implementing multiple management system standards a hindrance to innovation? *Total Quality Management*, 23(9), 1075–1088.

Chew, E. K. (2016). iSIM: an integrated design method for commercializing service innovation. *Information Systems Frontiers*, 18(1), 457–478.

Ciobanu, O. G. and Nastase, C. E. (2015). The coordinates of a sustainable economic development strategy by reconfiguring the Romanian entrepreneurship – generation Y and Lean startup method. *Economic Insights – Trends and Challenges*, 4(67), 75–86.

Coleman, M. C. (2016). Design thinking and the school library. *Knowledge Quest*, 44(5), 62–68.

David, P. A. (1987). Some new standards for the economics of standardization in the information age. In P. Dasgupta, and P. Stoneman (Eds.), *Economic policy and technological performance*. Cambridge: Cambridge University Press.

David, P. A. and Greenstein, S. (1990). The economics of compatibility standards: an introduction to recent research. *Economics of Innovation and New Technology*, 1(1/2), 3–41.

De Casanove, A. (2014). Standardization and innovation – Standards, an innovation booster? *ISO-CERN Conference Proceedings*, November 13–14, 2014. www.iso.org/files/live/sites/isoorg/files/archive/pdf/en/standardization_and_innovation.pdf.

De Casanove, A., Morel, L. and Negny, S. (2017). *ISO 50500 series innovation management: overview and potential usages in organizations*. https://hal.univ-lorraine.fr/hal-01624970.

De Marchi, V. (2012). Environmental Innovation and R&D Cooperation: empirical Evidence from Spanish manufacturing firms. *Research Policy*, 41(3), 614–623.

Deutsch, C. (2013). The seeking solutions approach: solving challenging business problems with local open innovation. *Technology Innovation Management Review*, 3(3), 6–13.

Eisenmann, T., Parker, G. and van Alstyne, M. W. (2006). Strategies for 2-sided markets. *Harvard Business Review*, 84(10), 92–101.

Euchner, J. and Ganguly, A. (2014). Business model innovation in practice: a systematic approach to business model innovation can help capture value and reduce risks. *Research-Technology Management*, November–December, 33–39.

Fixson, S. K. (2005). Product architecture assessment: a tool to link product, process, and supply chain design decisions. *Journal of Operations Management*, 23(3/4), 345–369.

Frederic, T., Lam, T. and Martin, V. (2014). A lean innovation model to help organizations leverage innovation for economic value: a proposal. *International Journal of Management & Information Systems*, 18(2), 99–108.

Gawer, A. and Cusumano, M. A. (2014). Industry platforms and ecosystem innovation. *Journal of Product Innovation Management*, 31(3), 417–433.

Gil, A. M., Varela, G. and González, A. (2008). Guía Práctica para la Implantación de la Norma 'UNE 166002:2006 Gestión de la I+D+I: Requisitos del Sistema de Gestión de la I+D+I' en Empresas del Sector de la Edificación Residencial. Published at 2008. www.euskadi.eus/r41-18971/es/contenidos/informacion/guia_innova/es_innova/adjuntos/tomo2cast.pdf.

Goldratt, E. (1997). *Cadena Crítica [Critical Chain]*. Mexico D. F.: Ediciones Castillo.

Gupte, A. (2015). The very lean startup model. *Journal for Contemporary Research in Management*, 2(2), 52–56.

Ham, J., Lee, J-N., Kim, D. J. and Choi, B. (2015). Open innovation maturity model for the government: an open system perspective – research-in-progress. *Thirty Sixth International Conference on Information Systems*, Fort Worth 2015. https://pdfs.semanticscholar.org/8633/35ff33f617d0de6d9203204e5c6d30b25ae6.pdf.

Holmlid S. and Evenson, S. (2008). Bringing service design to service sciences, management and engineering. In B. Hefley and W. Murphy (Eds.), *Service science, management and engineering education for the 21st Century*. Springer, pp. 341–345.

Horbach, J., Oltra, V. and Belin, J. (2013). Determinants and specificities of eco-innovations compared to other innovations – an econometric analysis for the French and German industry based on the community innovation survey. *Industry and Innovation*, 20(6), 523–543.

ISO (2013). ISO/TC 279 Innovation management. www.iso.org/iso/iso_technical_committee%3Fcommid%3D4587737.

Joyce, H. L. K., Ching, S. C., Wong, B. and Huang-Yao, H. (2015). Technological Pedagogical Content Knowledge (TPACK) and design thinking: a framework to support ICT lesson design for 21st century learning. *The Asia-Pacific Education Researcher*, 24(3), 535–543.

Kaski, T., Alamäki, A. and Moisio, A. (2014). A multi-discipline rapid innovation method. *Interdisciplinary Studies Journal*, 3(4), 163–170.

Keegan, A. and Turner, J. R. (2002). The management of innovation in project-based firms. *Long Range Planning*, 35(4), 367–388.

Khumalo, M. and Van der Lingen, E. (2017). The open business model in a dynamic business environment: a literature review. *South African Journal of Industrial Engineering*, 28(3), 147–160.

Knoke, B. (2013). A short paper on innovation capability maturity within collaborations. CEUR Workshop Proceedings. 1006.

Liedtka, J. (2015). Perspective: linking design thinking with innovation outcomes through cognitive bias reduction. *Journal of Product Innovation Management*, 32(6), 925–938.

Marin, G., Marzucchi, A. and Zoboli, R. (2014). *SMEs and Barriers to Eco-Innovation in EU: A Diverse Palette of Greens*, Working Paper No.° 2014–04, Ingenio, Valencia, Spain.

McGrath, R. G. (2010). Business models: a discovery driven approach. *Long Range Planning*, 43(1), 247–261.

Merfeld, D. (2014). GE is in a startup state of mind. *Research-Technology Management*, November–December, 26–31.

Mir, M., Casadesús, M. and Petnji, L. H. (2016). The impact of standardized innovation management systems on innovation capability and business performance: an empirical study. *Journal of Engineering and Technology Management*, 41(2016), 26–44.

Mir, M. and Casadesús, M. (2011a). Standardised innovation management systems: a case study of the Spanish Standard UNE 166002:2006. *Innovar*, 21(40), 171–187.

Mir, M. and Casadesús, M. (2011b). Innovation management standards: a comparative analysis. *Dyna*, 86(1), 49–58.

Müller-Prothmann, T. and Stein, A. (2011). I2MM – integrated innovation maturity model for lean assessment of innovation capability. *XXII ISPIM Conference 2011: sustainability in Innovation*.

Patricio, L., Fisk, R. P., and Cunba, J. F. (2008). Designing multi-interface service experiences: the service experience blueprint. *Journal of Service Research*, 12(5), 318–334.

Patricio, L., Fisk, R.P., Falcao e Cunha, J. and Constantine, L. (2011). Multilevel service design: from customer value constellation to service experience blueprinting. *Journal of Service Research*, 14(2), 180–200.

Petruzzelli, A.M., Dangelico, R.M., Rotolo, D. and Albino, V. (2011). Organizational factors and technological features in the development of green innovations: evidence from patent analysis. *Innovation*, 13(3), 291–310.

Pinget, A., Bocquet, R. and Mothe, C. (2015). Barriers to environmental innovation in SMEs: empirical evidence from French firms. *M@n@gement*, 18(2), 132–155.

Pisano, G. P. and Verganti, R. (2008). Which kind of collaboration is right for you? *Harvard Business Review*, 86(12), 78–86.

Project Management Institute (2013). Project management body of knowledge (5th ed.). Pennsylvania, USA: PMI Publications.

Revie, M., Bedford, T., Walls, L., Shimell, J. and Baldwin, T. (2016). What is the value of a standard? *Risk, Reliability and Safety*. https://strathprints.strath.ac.uk/58768/1/Revie_etal_ESREL2016_What_is_the_value_of_a_standard.pdf.

Schuurman, D., de Marez, L. and Ballon, P. (2016). The impact of living lab methodology on open innovation contributions and outcomes. *Technology Innovation Management Review*, 6(1), 7–16.

Spieth, P. and Schneider, S. (2016). Business model innovativeness: designing a formative measure for business model innovation. *Journal of Business Economics*, 86(1), 671–696.

Stickdorn, M. and Schneider, J. (2010). *This is service design thinking*. The Netherlands: BIS Publishers.

Stošić, B. (2013). *Innovation management – innovation projects, models and methods*. Belgrade, Serbia: FON.

Stošić, B. and Milutinović, R. (2014). Innovation projects classification issues. *Published at October 24, 2014. Economic and Social Development, 7 International Scientific Conference*, New York City.

Swann, G. M. P. (2010). The economics of standardization: an update. *Published at May 27, 2010*. http://citeseerx.ist.psu.edu/viewdoc/download?doi=10.1.1.618.5922&rep=rep1&type=pdf.

Tiwana, A., Konsynski, B., and Bush, A. A. (2010). Platform evolution: coevolution of platform architecture, governance, and environmental dynamics. *Information Systems Research*, 21(4), 675–687.

Vollebergh, H. R. J. and Van der Werf, E. (2014). The role of standards in eco-innovation: lessons for policymakers. *Review of Environmental Economics and Policy*, 8(2), 230–248.

Voss, C. A. and Hsuan, J. (2009). Service architecture and modularity. *Decision Sciences*, 40(3), 541–569.

Voss, C. and Hsuan, J. (2011). Service science: the opportunity to rethink what we know about service design. In H. Demirkan, J. C. Spohrer, and V. Krishna (Eds.), *Science of service systems, service science: research and innovations in the service economy*. Boston: Springer, pp. 231–244.

Wang, L., Ming, X., You, J., Kong, F. and Li, D. (2011). An approach for lean product innovation management. *Applied Mechanics and Materials*, 55–57(1), 2075–2079.

Yoo, Y., Henfridsson, O., and Lyytinen, K. (2010). The new organizing logic of digital innovation: the agenda for information systems research. *Information Systems Research*, 21(4), 724–735.

25
TECHNOLOGICAL INNOVATION AUDIT

Xuesong Geng

As a new concept emerging in recent years, the technological innovation audit (TIA) is borrowed from the financial concept of an audit. In essence, TIA covers but is not limited to the measurement and assessment of technological innovation in every aspect. In this chapter, TIA is examined systemically. The underlying theoretical logics for TIA will be introduced first, followed by the development of a system of indicators for process and performance audit, as well as the metrics designed based on empirical results. Although this section focuses on the analysis of process audit, it is complementary to a performance audit, and the combination of both process audit and performance audit has significant importance for applying TIA to the innovation management of a firm.

Background of TIA

Chiesa, Coughlan, and Voss (1996) described a technological innovation audit as using the innovation audit metrics to examine the current status of innovation management of a firm against the ideal status, identify the problems and issues in need of improvement and collect the necessary empirical information so as to implement the plan to enhance the innovation management. Put differently, TIA can be used to improve innovation management of a firm through the measurement and assessment of innovation activities by firms themselves or third parties. Chiesa, Coughlan, and Voss (1996) pointed out that a technical innovation audit is an important and practical method to improve technological innovation management. TIA has several special features in terms of its theoretical and methodological foundations:

TIA is based on a management audit

Auditing in modern society is an authentication activity carried out by appointed and authorized independent entities or persons on the economic activities of commercial entities. It is highly independent, systematic and authoritarian (i.e. endorsed by governmental bodies). Auditing essentially is a monitoring and evaluating process that provides an evidence-based assessment to ensure the professional and legal compliance of target organization's activities. For example, a finance audit involves the examination and evaluation, as well as necessary corrective suggestions, performed by independent auditors (e.g. accounting firms or certified public accountants) of a firm's accounting reports and financial statements. Besides finance audit, other forms of auditing include production audit, management audit, performance audit and social audit.

A management audit is deemed to be a measure of managerial performance. It encompasses planning, organization, leadership, controls, etc., in many management functions like marketing, production, HR, information system, etc. It is performed primarily through a standardized questionnaire. One of its earlier forms was developed by Jackson Martindell, the founder of the American Institute of Management, back in 1962. The survey consisted of 301 questions on various managerial aspects of a firm, including economic functions, organizational structure, remuneration system, R&D, leadership, production, sales, etc. Notably, it highlighted the fact that effective management can lead to generally good outcomes. Other scholars, such as William Greenwood (1967) and William P. Leonard (1962), also developed management audit questionnaires, laying the groundwork for future research.

A management audit differs from a financial audit in the sense that a financial audit focuses on the end results, whereas a management audit focuses more proactively and forward-looking on processes leading to results. Through a financial audit, the causes are inferred, making it challenging to implement any preemptive measures. Instead, a management audit allows managers to discover loopholes in the management process which can be addressed through the implementation of preventive measures, helping managers achieve organizational goals more effectively. A management audit sets the standards and guidance for effective management.

Benchmarking is the methodological support for TIA

In the modern industrial society, it is nearly impossible for any firm to develop knowledge and R&D all by itself to gain competitive advantages without the use of external knowledge sources and information. The firm must be adept at monitoring and learning advanced technologies from its competitors and integrating them into their own core competencies. As an effective management tool, benchmarking helps firms to achieve this goal. A firm benchmarks itself against the best managerial practices of the most competitive rivals or prominent industry leaders in order to analyze the causes contributing to their outstanding performance and to identify areas for improvement.

MIT and APQC statistics have shown that the vast majority of large American corporations had carried out various benchmarking programs by 1995. Recent research has revealed that benchmarking initiatives have been the main management practice engaged in by the majority of large American companies (collectively accounting for one-fourth of the states' GDP in total) – it is the only management practice that managers in these companies want to continue to strengthen in the future. Xerox Corporation, the original developer of this practice, has seen its productivity increased by 8 to 10 percent since the practice was introduced into its logistics and warehousing sectors. Thirty to fifty percent of this improvement is said to be directly attributed to the benchmarking programs.

A benchmarking program can be divided into five stages. The first stage is the planning stage whereby the firm decides on the relevant departments and specific program components. The key is to find out the core elements contributing to corporate competitiveness. The second stage is to analyze the gaps between the firm and the target benchmarked firms in terms of performance and practice. The third stage is to communicate and share the methodology and philosophy among the employees. The fourth stage is the implementation. The final fifth stage is institutionalization, in which the benchmark program, once proven successful, will be institutionalized as a key activity into organizational routines and procedures. Benchmarking helps the firm to set a credible and practicable goal, making improvement in its competitiveness feasible.

Since the firm always keeps the references to the best-performing firms, benchmarking becomes a dynamic and adaptable process when the external environment changes.

Benchmarking therefore becomes the foundations for the effective management auditing that allows the firm to identify its weaknesses and shortcomings. The quality of benchmarking directly affects the quality and effectiveness of the management audit.

Technological innovation survey provides metrics for TIA

Technological innovation measurement is a critical part of technological innovation management. Measurement is the numerical quantification of a state. Technological innovation measurement uses statistical and empirical data to quantify technological innovation. It involves a comprehensive and systematic analysis of technological innovation activities based on a large amount of empirical data and empirical analysis.

Early innovation research basically revolves around the analysis of factors contributing to success or failure. Examples include a 1969 U.S. research study on 500 innovations across a variety of industries, a 1968 survey by Mansfield on the determinants of American industrial technology changes and a research by Utterback on the successful scientific instrument industry in the United States. In 1976, Lebbenstein studied the purpose of 176 innovations from 13 American companies. Lastly, Project SAPPHO by the University of Sussex, after studying about 40 cases, found six fundamental features of successful innovation.

The corporate innovation survey was first introduced by Germany in 1979 as an annual undertaking. From 1979 to 1989, the technological innovation survey diffused to Canada, the United States, France, the UK, Spain, Italy, Finland, Norway, Sweden and Australia. Among them, the surveys made by Germany and Italy were the most influential.

The Oslo Manual, compiled by the OECD and published in 1992, is the official technological innovation measurement indicator system. It collects the innovation survey experience of OECD countries, and has become the basic guideline for the collection and analysis of technological innovation data. In 1993, the EC Harmonized Innovation Survey 1992/1993 was compiled based on the Oslo Manual. In 1995, 16 Italian manufacturers were chosen for an interview survey and to advise on the Oslo Manual amendment. As new developments of the technological innovation measurement initiative, the OECD S&T indicators experts proposed an amended version in 1997, which incorporated many indicators that reflected characteristics of technological innovation in a knowledge-based economy.

These technological innovation surveys provide reference standards for the evaluation of the process, behavior and performance of technological innovation. The measurement systems developed and adopted by many governmental and professional authorities have made quantitative measurement and auditing of technological innovation possible.

Overall, TIA is based on the development of a management audit, benchmarking and technological innovation survey. However, it integrates these developments in a more systematic and comprehensive manner.

TIA modeling

In general, technological innovation covers the process from the ideation to the commercialization of a technology, involving various functions of a company over a long period, including R&D, production, marketing, strategy and financing. Technological innovation has very high risk and complexity. One of the most common models used to define technological innovation is the chain model (Figure 25.1), which identifies stages of the innovation process and emphasizes the strong interdependence and links between different stages.

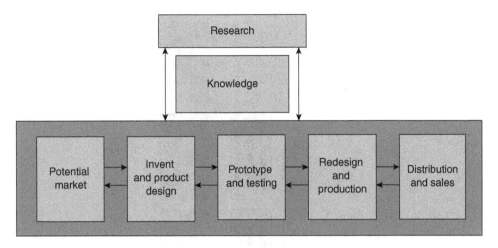

Figure 25.1 The chain model of technological innovation

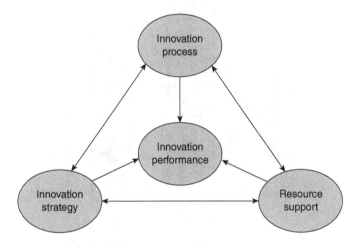

Figure 25.2 The new product performance triangle

The chain model is basically a descriptive model with limitations in practical applications. The model has no clear indication of which links are crucial to innovation performance. In addition, it does not take into account the interplay between technological innovation and other functions in a company such as strategy, structure, culture and HR. With the development of benchmarking, a model of technological innovation success factors has emerged. The model highlights the fact that the outstanding performance of technological innovation is a result of the confluence of five factors: product development process, organizational form, technological strategy, innovation atmosphere and senior management support. Further, based on these five successful drivers, three key organizational factors have been identified as the "new product performance triangle" (see Figure 25.2). The model breaks down the stereotype of a sequential technological innovation model by identifying the key factors for success.

The OECD's Oslo Manual for technological innovation uses the characteristics of technological innovation to divide the basic innovation process into several aspects, as shown in Figure 25.3.

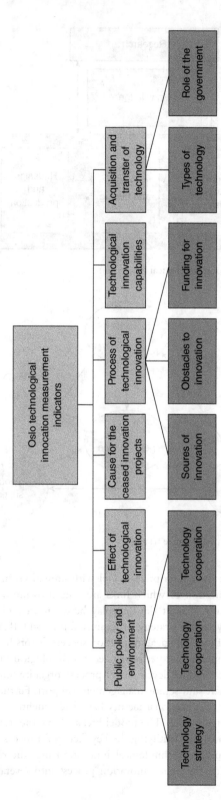

Figure 25.3 Technological innovation measurement indicator system in the Oslo Manual

Innovation process measurement framework	Input measure	Tangible factor	• R&D investment • Non-R&D input • Equipment level
		Intangible factor	• Innovation goal • Innovation strategy • Source of ideas
	Implementation measure	Success factor	
		Failure factor	
		Interface management	
	Output measure	Quantitative direct output	
		Quantitative indirect output	
		Qualitative direct output	
		Qualitative indirect output	
	Non-phase factor	Obstacles	
		Incentive factor	
		Governmental factor	

Figure 25.4 The stage-based technological innovation process measurement framework

Chinese academia and firms have proposed various theories and approaches regarding the measurement of technological innovation. In terms of applicability, the stage-based technology innovation process measurement model proposed by Professor Gao Jian of Tsinghua University has been influential in the development of the TIA in China. As shown in Figure 25.4, the model takes into account the situation of the Chinese firms.

Combining these different models, we believe the technological innovation process can be analyzed from two perspectives. One perspective is based on the sequential thinking of input, implementation and final output, in accordance with the nature of the technological innovation process itself. The other perspective is to view technological innovation as embedded in the company context, examining its interplay with other corporate functions. Based on these two perspectives, this chapter proposes a new technological innovation audit model as shown in Figure 25.5.

First, this model adopts the systematic and dynamic view of the entire technological innovation process. The model is systematic because it not only reflects the components of technological innovation but also the interplay among these components in the organizational context. The entire system consists of the core processes and the supporting systems. There is a mutually dependent relationship between the core processes and the supporting systems; neither can function optimally without the support of the other. Technological innovation has to be contextualized in a specific corporate environment. As different firms have different corporate cultures and organizational structures, they may form different strategies (including corporate strategy and technology strategy, which can influence each other), in different developmental stages and market environments. The model shows that the organizational internal environment interacts with the core innovation processes through the supporting system, as shown in Figure 25.5.

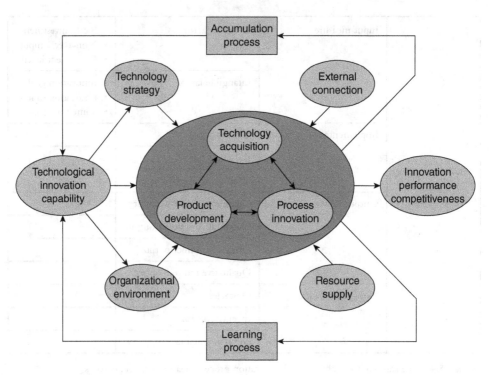

Figure 25.5 The TIA theoretical model

In addition, the model reflects the complex interaction between various components. In the core processes, there are interactions between technology acquisition, product development and process innovation. For example, successful technology acquisition can improve the technological capabilities of the company, which can further promote product development or process innovation. If the company has high product innovation capabilities, it can easily assimilate the external technology knowledge, facilitating technology acquisition. If the company has high capability in process innovation, it can facilitate the acquisition of product innovation as well. The reinforcing effect is also evident between product innovation and process innovation, as suggested by the combinative innovation theory. Second, the supporting system interacts with the core process as mentioned previously. Third, there are interplays among components in the supporting system. For instance, different strategies will directly affect resource supply, and senior managers' support will affect cultural and employee incentives. Moreover, an effective and stable organizational structure is important for the reliability of resource supply.

Moreover, the model reflects the dynamic nature of technology innovation that involves the learning process and path dependence. A learning organization can grow quickly, and its potential resides in the accumulation of knowledge. The difference between firms' creativity can be due to primarily the difference in firms' knowledge stock, which is dependent on firms' learning capabilities. In contrast to tangible resources (e.g. capital, machinery and equipment), intangible resources like knowledge and skills are hard to imitate. Therefore, the difference in technology accumulation can result in a substantial gap in resource possession between firms. As a result, sufficient technology accumulation helps the firm gain an advantage in the race for technological innovation. Knowledge and skill accumulation underlies each step of a technological innovation process, which, conversely, forms a supportive environment for technology accumulation.

Learning and accumulation enable the firm to improve on its technological and innovation capability. This is the heart of sustainable corporate technological innovation.

Another feature of the model is its easy implementation that facilitates senior managers to assign responsibilities to different departments of the firm and conduct management audits effectively. The strategy department can be responsible for strategy matters, the HR or logistics departments for resource supply and the technical or internal auditing department for performance assessment.

Based on the TIA theoretical framework, the firm needs to develop the specific TIA indicator system as illustrated in the following sections. TIA evaluates not only the innovation performance but also the entire process of the technological innovation. A process audit reviews whether fundamental technological innovation processes are being carried out and how optimal implementation plans are being performed, whereas a performance audit reviews the achievements of the various innovation processes and their impact on the firm's market competitiveness.

Process audit of technological innovation

The process audit of technological innovation encompasses the systematic analysis of primarily the core process, supporting system and technological capability accumulation, as well as the corresponding indicator system.

Core process

The core process encompasses primarily technology acquisition, product development and process innovation.

Technology acquisition

The technology acquisition audit focuses on the effective external connections, reasonable technology acquisition strategy and implementation of acquisition.

To acquire technology effectively, a firm must establish broad and reliable external connections, which include other firms (whether competitors or noncompetitors), universities, research bodies, the government, etc. External connections lay the foundation for an innovation network which, as one of the main sources of technology acquisition, links upstream product/equipment suppliers and downstream wholesalers and users, thereby expanding the external connections for technological innovation. External connections are believed to facilitate the technology acquisition to improve technology capability. Besides, the innovation network requires the firm to maintain close relations with the external connections that can only built up over a long time. A firm with an innovation network can acquire or transfer technology in the network with greater ease, thanks to the trust it maintains with long-time partners, hence reducing transaction costs significantly. Therefore, a broad network of connections is indispensable to successful technology acquisition. External connections normally go through key employees, like technology gatekeepers and project managers. Such close personal relationships form an indispensable part of a firm's external connections.

Technology acquisition can be accomplished in many forms, including technology rental, license, cooperation, strategic partnership and joint venture. An appropriate technology acquisition strategy must consider multiple factors such as technology trends, technological features and corporate conditions, as well as their impact on the firm's core capabilities. It is also important to systematically monitor the technology trends by identifying upcoming new technology, acquiring technology information, monitoring competitors and examining internal technology capabilities to determine the best avenue for technology acquisition.

Product development

The product development process refers to the identification of consumer demand, the development of new products using the existing technology or the improvement of the existing product line to meet such demand. Primarily, it encompasses three parts: innovative idea generation (i.e. identification of consumer demand to generate new ideas); product innovation planning (i.e. drafting of product innovation strategy, scope and level of the innovation, and the timeline to commercialization); and product innovation (i.e. the entire process of a product development from planning, to prototyping, to production, and finally to sales and distribution).

In product development, the first activity is the identification of the source of innovative ideas. The source of innovation is not limited only to technical workers but can be from consumers and suppliers as well. As successful innovations are invariably those that can meet consumer demand the best, the role of the consumers or end users is essential. The key is to examine to what extent market demand and new opportunities can be discovered, especially from those departments (e.g. sales, service, etc.) that deal directly with the consumer, and to what extent the creative customers can be identified and how their roles can be integrated in the development, testing and improvement of new products. The end user as the source of innovation ideas serves a dual role. First, as the user of an innovation, he or she is the ultimate motivation for innovation. Second, the end user can guide and assist the product innovation by getting involved in ideation and new product development. A survey shows that user-driven innovations are important in many industries in China, such as textile, printing, metal products, electrical equipment manufacturing, electronics and communications equipment, instruments and meters, etc.

Other external sources of innovation include technological breakthroughs, emulation of competitors, government-backed innovation policies, conferences and exhibitions, science and technological literature, patents, licensing and technology assimilation, as well as guidance in the form of laws, regulations and standards.

The second activity is innovation planning. One example is the product innovation scorecard, which is used to detail the target markets, innovation goals and specific action plans. The routinized product innovation planning can help managers to organize and coordinate activities in product innovation. Moreover, innovation planning facilitates the optimal decision-making under limited resources among various market opportunities, innovation levels and market entry timings.

The third activity is innovation itself, during which the new concept materializes into successful products through development, test and production. Product development covers primarily four components: project management, teamwork and organizational structure, conversion of design to production and sales and industrial design.

Process innovation

Process innovation is a critical process due to its impact on product innovation and its role as the direct source of competitive advantages. According to the Oslo Manual, product innovation revolves around products, while process innovation revolves around manufacturing. Process innovation refers to the adoption of new or significantly improved production methods in order to manufacture products or improve productivity that otherwise could not be possible using current production methods. Process innovation primarily has four modules: production strategy, process innovation, new process implementation and sustainable process innovation.

Technological renovation should be paid special consideration in formulating the production strategy in Chinese companies. Technological renovation refers to the replacement of outdated processes and equipment with advanced processes and equipment to increase production efficiency and improve product quality, improving the technological capabilities as a result. Since the majority of its goals are primarily related to the process innovation, technological renovation bears the closest relationship with process innovation in China. In making a technological renovation plan, proactive and preempting consideration should be given to the future technological potential as well as the existing technological capacities and technological base. Technological renovation is as risky as technological innovation, which makes it very important to conduct a scientific assessment.

Special attention must be paid to the relationship between product innovation and process innovation. According to a finding by the MIT Commission on Industrial Productivity, one of main reasons why America lost its competitiveness and economic development momentum in many industries is because American companies focus too much on product innovation but too little on process innovation. In contrast, the economic development accomplished by Japan and Germany is inseparable from their emphasis on the coordinated development in both product innovation and process innovation. This is particularly important for China as well, because for long time, the dominance of product innovation has led to a biased perception that process innovation is only secondary to product innovation.

Effective implementation of innovative processes is a critical component of process innovation. It depends on the use of cross-functional teams, technology supply and the supporting manufacturing and organizational capabilities. A firm has to manage the inherent risk based on the assessment of the complexity of the process.

Sustainable process innovation is reflected in continuous incremental innovations. To promote sustainable innovation, firms can, for example, set up a special task force to identify new opportunities for sustainable innovation to analyze the process control data, consumer feedback and market competition information so as to continuously improve on the existing processes.

Supporting system

A supporting system for technological innovation includes technical strategy, organizational environment, resource supply and effective external connection. The external connection has been discussed previously as a mechanism that ensures the supporting system enables the core process in the technological innovation.

Technology strategy

The technology strategy consists of strategic formulation, strategy content and strategy implementation. The formulation of technology strategy is based on the correct assessment of the organizational environment. A firm must systematically monitor the changes in the market, in the consumer demand and in the evolution of potential markets. It must also monitor the trends of both existing and future technologies. If possible, the firm should monitor and forecast their competitors' technology and competitive advantages.

In monitoring the external environment, the use of technology-market joint analysis is important for the technology strategy. Technology and market influence each other. As shown in Figure 25.6, in different technology-market spaces, firms need to adopt different innovation

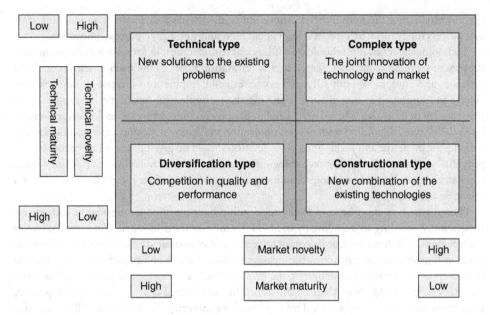

Figure 25.6 The effect of technical and market maturity on technology innovation

strategies. When both the technology and market are mature, the innovation strategy should be designed to improve incrementally based on the existing technology and product platform to meet the needs of users. In performing such a diversification strategy, the traditional market research methods can be effective. Constructive strategy is the new combination of existing technologies. It applies existing technologies to new markets. The driving force for this strategy is customers. The technical strategy is driven by technological developers. It develops and promotes new products according to the needs of users in the existing markets. The complex strategy means that the technology and market are in an uncertain and unpredictable state. For an extremely original or complex one, end users often fail to realize its emergence. Therefore, the firms must develop new technologies and new markets through cooperation between technology developers and leading users.

The formulation of a technology strategy must rely on a firm's own capabilities. The best strategy is the one that can help establish the core competitiveness of a firm. Therefore, in formulating a technology strategy a firm needs to determine the following two issues: first, the positioning of the firm that includes what kind of national innovation system and foreign innovation system it follows, how competitive it is, etc.; and second, the technical development path of the company. Although it is necessary to build the development path on the existing technology, it is important to gradually form some unique core capability that will be difficult for others to imitate.

The technology strategy must satisfy several requirements. It must clearly contribute to the overall corporate strategy. A consensus on the importance of the innovation strategy must be reached within the firm and supported by all its employees. Moreover, the strategy must have emphasis. Also, it must have a long-term goal. Finally, it must effectively satisfy the needs of users and foresee potential future technologies.

Finally, the implementation of the technology strategy must rely on the support of senior leaders as well as the support of employees. Moreover, the firm must strengthen organizational learning capabilities and constantly adapt their organizational forms and management models to a changing environment through benchmarking. The firm needs to formulate appropriate implementation plans based on the corporate strategy and use feedback mechanisms to continuously adjust the existing strategy.

Organizational environment

The organizational environment includes four aspects: top leadership support, cross-functionality, innovation atmosphere and innovation incentives. It examines the internal environment of an organization and the interaction between innovation and other functions.

Top leadership support is one of the key drivers of technological innovation success. The support is reflected in four aspects: top leaders having a great sense of responsibility for technical innovation, assuring the resource supply necessary for technical innovation, playing an important role in decision-making for suspension/continuation of technical innovation projects and providing suitable personnel for technical innovation.

Cross-functionality relies on the integration of technological innovation and other functions, as well as the establishment and operation of cross-functional teams. The impact of cross-functionality is more apparent than that of top leadership support. The SAPPHO Project shows that a major factor in the success of innovation is the functional integration of R&D, manufacturing and marketing. According to a survey on the technical innovation of Chinese manufacturing enterprises, the cooperation between the R&D department and marketing and production is the number two decisive factor to the success of innovation. In order to promote such integration, a cross-functional team is often used in the management of technological innovation projects.

The innovative atmosphere is also a driving force for innovation. A good innovation atmosphere can stimulate employees to create new product ideas, to support spontaneous trial prototyping, to exchange ideas for new products and to adopt pioneering and innovative behaviors. Such an atmosphere can promote the formation of "intrapreneurs". In an innovative organization, individuals with good innovation ability will have the opportunity to fully realize their talent and have the opportunity to put their ideas into practice.

Innovation incentive is an important way to stimulate the enthusiasm and creativity of technical workers by rewarding innovative behavior. There are many ways of incentivizing innovation. One example is the "double career ladder" incentive system that recognizes and promotes the innovative technical employees without necessarily promoting them to management positions.

Resource supply

The resource supply includes the supply of human resources, capital supply and supply of systems and methods.

Human resources are the key resource for successful innovation. The SAPPHO Project states that the senior innovators in a company (so-called technical leaders) are experienced and authoritative, acting as a key to the success of technical innovation. The technical innovation analysis of China's manufacturing enterprises also shows that the technical leaders and senior technicians are important factors.

Capital supply includes financial support for product development, R&D, process innovation, technical renovation and technology acquisition. Funds have been shown to be a bottleneck to many enterprises and one of the reasons for the poor performance of many innovation projects. Therefore, it is particularly important to ensure sufficient funds for technical innovation. The supply of funds requires certain stability (total amount stability) and flexibility (suitable for some short-term projects).

Systems and methods refer to those approaches, systems and methods that support any innovation process. The range of systems and methods is broad. Each firm should establish a set of systems and methods that specifically serve the core process, for example, the communication systems between different functional departments, management methods for efficient product development, management methods for quality control and self-analysis methods for innovation processes.

Technical capacity accumulation

The technical capability of a firm represents the sum of all internal knowledge stocks residing in the personnel, organizations, information and equipment within the firm. The accumulation of technical capabilities will inevitably lead to the improvement of technical innovation, manufacturing, marketing and decision-making capabilities. It relies on the accumulation of technical knowledge stocks and organizational learning. First, technical accumulation is essentially the accumulation of knowledge and experience, specifically residing in the accumulation of individual capabilities. Therefore, a company should ensure stability of a technical team. The key is the stability of the technical leader. After the development and design of a product family are completed, the technical leader should be tasked with similar designs. Second, as the accumulation and improvement of technical capabilities is firm-specific with continuity, it is costly to break the existing technical knowledge structure to re-establish a new knowledge structure. Therefore, the single product development should be expanded to a product family (platform) that is based on the same core technology, making it the most effective way to continuously improve on the product. Finally, a company should pay attention to the accumulation of tacit knowledge. Tacit knowledge is based on the lessons of past successes and failures accumulated over the long period of the innovation process. It is firm-specific and is a valuable asset of the company because it is more difficult to be imitated by other companies. The success rate for innovation is generally about 15 percent. It is unrealistic to expect success without the accumulation of the lessons from failed projects.

Technical accumulation can be achieved through recruitment, training and self-learning of technical personnel; the establishment and improvement of information networks; and the improvement of organizational structure. It can also be achieved through technical cooperation in which different partners can complement each other's technical capabilities. The firm needs to capture the "codifiable knowledge" as well as "sticky information" and tacit knowledge.

The key to improving a company's technical capabilities is to strengthen its learning ability. There are three major learning modes in technical innovation, namely learning by doing, learning by using and learning by R&D. For example, in Chinese enterprises' technology development, employees need the learning by doing when technology imitation is the main task. In this stage, the level of skilled workers is of crucial importance. Learning by using is the dominant model for technical acquisition and assimilation. In independent innovation, learning by R&D is the most important of all. Therefore, different learning mechanisms should be used for different purposes.

Organizational learning is related to personal learning. Blending individual knowledge can facilitate the interaction and recombination of different knowledge, forming new knowledge. In order to allow more knowledge recombination, it is better to have different individuals within a team so as to have different knowledge backgrounds and knowledge structures but also a certain degree of knowledge overlap between them. Different R&D teams can also achieve this interteam learning. The key to successful learning is to establish an effective information exchange mechanism.

Based on the discussion of the technological innovation processes earlier, we propose the audit metric (indicator) system for TIA in Table 25.1. For various indicators, the assessment metrics take the Likert scales 1 to 5.

Table 25.1 Technological innovation process audit metrics

1 Product Innovation
1.1 Innovation Source
- ★ Systematic survey on market demand
- ★ Wide market information network
- ★ Set up departments that respond to customer demands
- ★ Fully utilize feedback from departments that deal with customer demands
- ★ Build long-term relations with consumers, especially core consumers
- ★ Multifunctional perspective assessment on new product design
- ★ Meet market demand through technological improvement

1.2 Product innovation plan
- ★ Integrate product innovation plan into company plan
- ★ Market-oriented planning process
- ★ Prioritize projects in product development
- ★ New product plan portfolio (long-, medium- and short-term plan integrated)
- ★ Selection mechanism for new or improved products
- ★ Plan for idea generation and product innovation
- ★ Centralized control of all processes in new product development

1.3 Independent invention and creation
- ★ Incentive and motivation of employees for product innovation
- ★ Incentive for innovative behaviors
- ★ Support for spontaneous product innovation
- ★ Promote new product innovation
- ★ Organization and structure conducive for independent invention and creation
- ★ Appropriate personnel arrangement for key independent innovation and research

1.4 Product innovation process
- ★ Management of the product development process (from ideation to product)
- ★ Clarity in the scope, phases, milestone, assessment scope, procedure, etc.
- ★ Periodical feedback and improvement in technological development
- ★ Summarization and reflection of completed projects
- ★ Project management system
- ★ Balance the parallel and sequential relations among procedures
- ★ Control the interdependence of projects
- ★ Reduce and control the conflicts among different projects (regarding resource and personnel allocation)
- ★ Set up project process assessment principles
- ★ Set up project priority assessment standard and corresponding measures

1.5 Organization and coordination
- ★ Integrated control and coordination of related functions in the product development
- ★ Make timely communication with other departments and external organizations
- ★ Communicate with varied organizations in product development process
- ★ Utilize cross-functional teams
- ★ Set up project manager–responsible system
- ★ Clear responsibilities and rights of project managers
- ★ Project manager can get support from other functional departments
- ★ Centralized decision making in early phases

1.6 Transition to production
- ★ Coordination among product design, production and sales
- ★ Effective adjustment of development plan (with corresponding system and organization)
- ★ Timely feedback from production to design
- ★ Guarantee in-time delivery through production and design coordination

(*Continued*)

Table 25.1 (Continued)

1.7 Industrial design
- ⋆ Integrate industrial design into product development
- ⋆ Utilize consulting and advisory teams
- ⋆ Set up mechanism to reflect consumer demand in the design
- ⋆ Take industrial design into consideration in the beginning of product design

2 Process innovation

2.1 Production strategy
- ⋆ Objective assessment on present production capacity
- ⋆ Formal procedures for making production plan
- ⋆ Set up production capacity to meet the market demand
- ⋆ Effective technological renovation procedure and strategy
- ⋆ Technological renovation to meet the requirement of products innovation
- ⋆ Technological renovation according to international standards
- ⋆ Flexibility and adaptability of technological renovation
- ⋆ Process innovation promoted by technological renovation

2.2 Process innovation
- ⋆ Connect process innovation to product innovation
- ⋆ Allocate sufficient resources (human and capital) to develop new process
- ⋆ Multiple sources for process innovation (independent, purchased, cooperative)
- ⋆ Periodical control and improvement of process innovation

2.3 New process implementation
- ⋆ Technological complexity within carrying capacity
- ⋆ Effective coordination between production and design
- ⋆ Identify the typical process
- ⋆ Appropriate adjustment on organizational structure to facilitate process innovation
- ⋆ Improve performance assessment standard to better reflect the impact of process on performance

2.4 Sustainable development
- ⋆ Proactive process improvement
- ⋆ Integrate process improvement and quality control
- ⋆ Set up process assessment standard
- ⋆ Continuous monitoring after the adoption of new process
- ⋆ Have a prototyping process development (or process development backup plan)

3 Technology acquisition

3.1 External connection
- ⋆ Senior managers' attention to external connection
- ⋆ Maintain a wide external connection
- ⋆ Build a long-term and stable relation with suppliers and leading users
- ⋆ Build long-term and stable external connection

3.2 Technological acquisition strategy
- ⋆ Systematically monitor present and future technology
- ⋆ Assess rivals' technological capacity
- ⋆ Predict emerging technology
- ⋆ Understand the firm's technology capability and competitiveness
- ⋆ Set up core competence based on technological capability
- ⋆ Integrate technology with business strategy
- ⋆ Portfolio of technological acquisition methods
- ⋆ Integrate acquired technology to firm's existing technology
- ⋆ Set up core competence in technology with the help of external technology

3.3 Technological resource selection
- ★ Qualitative and quantitative assessment on technological resources
- ★ Has formal procedure for project selection
- ★ Time control in project management
- ★ Encourage communication and interaction between R&D and other departments
- Fully utilize the corporate resource

4 Technical capability accumulation
- ★ Monitor the trend in technology development
- ★ Allocate resource for preparatory research for future technology
- ★ Set up learning organization to accumulate experience
- ★ Learn from failed projects
- ★ Build formal technological documentation system
- ★ Emphasize on improvement on each R&D employee's capability
- ★ Embody technological capability improvement in technology strategy

5 Innovation strategy
5.1 Strategy formulation
- ★ Monitor market and technology
- ★ Market-oriented technological strategy
- ★ Organizational structure to ensure innovation strategy formulation
- ★ Technology strategy is a key part in the corporate strategy
- ★ Technology strategy supports the corporate strategy
- ★ Technology strategy aims to improve core competitiveness
- ★ Clear assessment and selection mechanism
- ★ Use venture investment to enter new field
- ★ Assess the impact of innovation on core competitiveness
- ★ Utilize all available financial capital

5.2 Strategy characteristics
- ★ Specific and clear technological and innovation target
- ★ Core competitiveness embodied in technology strategy
- ★ The strategy has emphases and phases
- ★ Combination of short-, medium- and long-term strategies
- ★ Consensus and support of technology strategy in the entire company
- ★ Technology strategy supported by specific plans

5.3 Strategy implementation
- ★ A specific task force is used to implement the strategy according to the plan
- ★ Constant adjustment based on environment and market feedback
- ★ Supported by every functional department
- ★ Be entrepreneurial in technology strategy formulation and implementation

6 Organizational environment
6.1 Support of top management
- ★ Technological innovation is a KPI for senior managers
- ★ Proactive management to ensure the effective implementation of technological innovation
- ★ Proactive insurance of the sufficient resource for technological innovation
- ★ Conduct effective assessment of technological innovation with corresponding award or penalty
- ★ Improve the innovation process against the industrial best practices

6.2 Innovation atmosphere
- ★ Encourage new idea, risk taking and exploration
- ★ Shared understanding of the importance of innovation

(Continued)

Table 25.1 (Continued)

- ★ Set up KPI system for innovation performance
- ★ Provide promising career path for technical personnel (dual ladder mechanism, international development, cross-department development)

7 Resource supply

7.1 Human resource
- ★ Have specific human resource expansion plan
- ★ Have long-term plan for future talent accumulation
- ★ Have long-term employee training and recruitment plan
- ★ Human resource support from other departments
- ★ Arrange proper personnel to key positions of technological innovation

7.2 Fund
- ★ Stable capital supply for R&D activities
- ★ R&D investment higher than the industrial average
- ★ Flexibility in allocating funds for process innovation and product innovation
- ★ Reduce risk and cost through cooperation
- ★ Raise funds for technological innovation through multiple channels

7.3 System
- ★ Information system used in product development process
- ★ Information sharing and communication system in innovation

7.4 Methods
- ★ Use new product design methods (CAD, CAM)
- ★ Use other advanced product design methods (roadmap, quick prototyping system, K-J analysis, etc.)

7.5 Quality assurance
- ★ Design quality control (ISO9001, etc.)
- ★ Total quality control in innovation process (TQM)
- ★ Integrate process and product innovation into quality control

Performance audit of technological innovation

The performance audit includes three parts: (1) a firm's overall technological innovation performance, which is mainly according to the OSLO Manual; (2) the performance of each process of technological innovation; and (3) the influence of the innovation process on corporate competitiveness, which is according to Chiesa's auditing questionnaire. The overall performance audit indicators are shown in Table 25.2, the audit indicators of the innovation process are detailed in Table 25.3 and the audit indicators of market competitiveness are shown in Table 25.4.

Applications of TIA

The following several steps are recommended for the application of TIA. The first step is to establish an audit model and framework by an expert panel in the firm. The second step is to use the benchmarking method to determine the indicators. The indicator system should be designed according to the specific strategic goals of the company. The third step is to test and modify the audit model and indicator system. The firm can select the representative department/business unit/project team to conduct the auditing in order to discover the limitations and shortcomings of the original system and to make adjustments. The fourth step is to implement the audit within the entire enterprise. The company can establish an audit task force to carry out the audit in the entire organization. The task force should collect data to analyze the gaps in the technological innovation and propose recommendations for improvement. It is noteworthy that these

Table 25.2 Overall technological innovation performances audit for an enterprise

(A) Main economic indicators	(E) Innovation investment
• Industrial gross value • Profit • Product sales revenue • New product revenue/total revenue ratio • New product profitability **(B) Existing production equipment level** **(C) Number of technological innovations** **(D) Technological innovation frequency**	• Research and development cost • Technological acquisition cost • Technological renovation cost • R&D intensity **(F) Total R&D fund** • Government funding • Enterprise self-raised fund • Bank loan • Others

Table 25.3 Innovation process performance assessment indicators

Product development

Innovation process efficiency
- Number of new products in the past three years
- Number of renovated products in the past three years
- Number of independently innovated products in the past three years
- Number of projects for new products investment in the past five years
- Number of patents
- Consumer satisfaction (product design that meets consumer need; product scope and type)
- Product plan period (yearly or generation-based products upgrade)
- Average product cycle

Innovation speed:
- Average duration from ideation to product
- Time of each phase (concept generation, design, prototyping, production)
- Average overtime
- Average time for product renovation
- Average time for redesign

Product property:
- Cost (unit cost, production cost, development cost)
- Technical indicators (e.g. usability, operation cost, equipment property)
- Quality

Advantage and disadvantage of design and plan
- Resulted production cost
- Production feasibility
- Test feasibility
- Proportion of redesigned products
- Sustainable development
- Number of innovation proposals per employee
- Ratio of proposals adopted

Improvement in the production level after process innovation
- Quality cost
- Production speed
- Workload
- Reliability
- Technological capacity

Technology acquisition
- Average R&D or technology acquisition cost per each new product
- R&D projects of new products innovation or renovated products, process innovation, licenses and patents (proportion in the overall project and overall cost)
- Number of licenses in the past three years
- Number of cooperation in the past three years
- Profitability of finished R&D project/ technology acquisition

Organization and coordination
- Number or proportion of personnel with technological or product development background in the main or secondary departments (branch offices)
- Proportion of employees who can realize and understand innovation policy and value
- Proportion of innovation and technology issues in the annual report

(Continued)

Table 25.3 (Continued)

Process innovation	Resource supply
• Numbers of new products and significantly renovated products each year • Speed • Installation time (with assurance of no failure in operation) • Development cost	• Proportion of projects delayed or canceled due to fund shortage • R&D investment capacity • Non-R&D investment capacity • Proportion of projects delayed or canceled due to human resource shortage • Personnel qualification and quantity • Proportion of design personnel with training of mass production design • Proportion of team leaders with training in innovation • Proportion of design and drawing personnel using CAD • Number of products based on CAD data

Table 25.4 Performance indicators measuring competitiveness

Types of competitiveness impact	Measuring indicators
Single innovation impact on enterprise competitiveness (compared with competitors and/or expectation)	Sales: local market, regional market, international market Market share: local market, regional market, international market
Single innovation impact on enterprise products series	Profit: sales and profit before/after product innovation
Impact of series innovation on enterprise competitiveness	Sales, market share, profit from innovation
Innovation impact on enterprise competitiveness in a certain period	Sales/profit ratio after innovation products introduced three to five years ago Sales/profit ratio after major renovation products introduced three to five years ago

steps are not unidirectional. In the course of implementing the TIA, a company must undergo multiple reiterations and episodes of trial and error to determine the final indicator system. In addition, the company should continuously revise the auditing indicator system to adjust to the ever-changing environment.

Bibliography

Alvarez, H. R. L. and Rune, S. (2001). Adoption of uncertain multi-stage technology projects: a real option approach. *Journal of Mathematical Economics*, 35(1), February, 71–97.

Anschuetz, Ned F. (1996). Evaluating ideas and concepts for new consumer products. *PDMA Handbook*, 195–206.

Arman, M. and Kulatilaka, N. (1999). *Real options: managing strategic investment in an uncertain world*. Boston, MA: Harvard Business School Press.

Bogan, C. E. and English, M. J. (1994). *Benchmarking for best practices: winning through innovation adaptation*. New York: McGraw-Hill Inc.

Burglman, R. A., Kosnik, T. J. and Van Den Poel, M. (1988). Toward an innovative capability audit framework. In Burgelman, Robert A. and Maidique, Modesto A. (Eds.), *Strategic management of technology and innovation*. Homewood, IL: Irwin, pp. 31–44.

Chen, J. (2001). *Eternal and sustainable development*. Beijing: China Science Publishing & Media Ltd. (CSPM).

Chen, J. (2002). *Best innovation company*. Beijing: Tsinghua University Press.

Chen, J. (2004). *Project R&D management*. Beijing: China Machine Press.

Chen, J., Geng, X., and Smith, R, S. (1998). Technical innovation audit: framework and Sino-Canada comparison. *Science Research Management*, (6): 21–28.

Chen, J., (2001). A new exploration on technological innovation information source: leading user research. *China Soft Science*, 2001(1).

Chiesa, V., Coughlan, P. and Voss, C. (1996). Development of a technical innovation audit. *Journal of Product Innovation Management*, 13(2), 105–136.

Chung, K-J. and Ching-Shih, T. (1998). Analysis and algorithm for the optimal investment times of the manufacturing technologies in a Duopoly. *European Journal of Operational Research*, 109(3), 632–645.

Cooper, R. G. (1975). Why new products fail. *Industrial Marketing Management*, (4), 315–326.

Cooper, R. G. (1979). Identifying industrial new product success. *Industrial Marketing Management*, 1979a(8), 136–144.

Cooper, R. G. (1980). New product project: factors in new product success. *European Journal of Marketing*, 14, 277–292.

Cooper, R. G. (1981). An empirical derived new product project selection model. *IEEE Transactions on Engineering Management*, (28), 54–61.

Cooper, R. G. (1988). Predevelopment activities determine new product success. *Industrial Marketing Management*, 1988(18), 237–247.

Cooper, R. G. (1990). Stage-gate systems: a new tool for managing new products. *Business Horizons*, May–June, 45–54.

Cooper, R. G. (1997). Fixing the fuzzy front end of the new product process: building the business case. *CMA-The Management Accounting Magazine*, (8), 21–23.

Cooper, R. G. and Kleinschmidt, E. J. (1987a). New products: what separates winners from losers. *Journal of Product Innovation Management*, 4, 169–184.

Cooper, R. G. and Kleinschmidt, E. J. (1987b). Success factors in product innovation. *Industrial Marketing Management*, 16, 215–223.

Cooper, R. G. and Kleinschmidt, E. J. (1987c). What makes a new product a winner: success Factors at the project level. *R&D Management*, 17, 175–189.

Cooper, R. G. and Kleinschmidt, E. J. (1995a). Benchmarking the firm's critical success factors in new product development. *Journal of Product Innovation Management*, (12), 374–391.

Cooper, R. G. and Kleinschmidt, E. J. (1995b). New product performance: keys to success, profitability & cycle time reduction. *Journal of Marketing Management*, 24, 315–337.

Dai, C. and Li, J. (1996). *Benchmark targeting: new method for enterprises pursuing excellence*. Tianjin: Tianjin People's Publishing House.

Dewar, R. D. and Dutton, J. E. (1984). The adoption of radical and incremental innovation: an empirical analysis. *Management Science*, (30), 682–696.

Dixit, A. and Pindyck, R. (1995). The options approach to capital investment. *Harvard Business Review*, May–June, 105–115.

Dixit, K. A. and Robert, P. S. (1994). *Investment under uncertainty*. Princeton: Princeton University Press.

Eric, von Hippel. (2001). Innovation by user communities: learning from open-source software. *MIT Sloan Management Review*, Summer.

Fan, W., Li, T. and Xiong, G. (2004). *The theory and implementation of products data management* (PDM). Beijing: China Machine Press, 1.

Faulkner, T. W. (1996). Applying options thinking to R&D valuation. *Research Technology Management*, May/June, 39(3), 50–56.

Gao, J. (2005). *Influential elements studies on new product Fuzzy Front End (FFE)*. Zhejiang University.

Galvin, R. (2004). Roadmapping: a practitioner's update. *Technological Forecasting & Social Change*, (71), 101–103.

Gang, G. (2002). *New product digital design and management*. Chongqing: Publishing House of Chongqing University, 3.

Georghiou, L. and Keenan, M. (2004). Toward a typology for evaluating foresight exercises. *Proceedings of New Technology Foresight, Forecasting & Assessment Methods-Seville*, Washington, DC, 15–32.

Greenwood, W. T. (1967). *Business policy: a management audit approach*, New York: The Macmillan Company.
Greg, M. Ajamian and Koen, Peter A. Technology stage-gate: a structured process for managing high-risk new technology projects. www.stevens-tech.edu/cce/NEW/publ.htm.
Griffen, A. and Page, A. L. (1996). PDMA success measurement project: recommended measures for product development success and failure. *Journal of Product Innovation Management*, (13), 478–496.
Groenveld, P. (1997). Roadmapping integrates business and technology. *Research-Technology Management*, 40(5), 48–55.
Gu, Q. (2005). The application of TRIZ in DFSS. *China Quality*, April, 40–42.
Hao, Y. and Jin, C. (1999). Leading user research in technical innovation. *Science Research Management*, 1999(3).
Herath, H. S. B. and Park Chan, S. (1999). Economic analysis of R&D projects: an options approach. *The Engineering Economist*, 44(3), 271–287.
Holmes, C. and Ferrill, M. (2005). The application of operation and technology roadmapping to aid Singaporean SMEs identify and select emerging technologies. *Technological Forecasting & Social Change*, 72, 349–357.
Huang, X., and Wang, Q. (2003). Fundamental theory and practice of TRIZ. *Machinery Design & Manufacture*, 3(5), October, 128–130.
Huiman, J. M. K. (2001). *Technology investment: a game theoretic real options approach*. Boston, MA: Kluwer Academic Publishers.
Jagle, A. J. (1999). Shareholder value, real options, and innovation in technology-intensive companies. *R&D Management*, 29(3), July, 271–287.
Jennings, K. and Westfall, F. (1992). Benchmarking for strategic action. *Journal of Business Strategy*, 13(3), 22–25.
Jian, G. (1997). *An analysis on Chinese enterprise technical innovation*. Beijing: Tsinghua University Press.
Jones, H. and Twiss B. (1984). *Technical prediction used for plan and decision*. Shanghai: Fudan University Press.
Kappel, T. A. (2001). Perspectives on roadmaps: how organizations talk about the future. *Journal of Product Innovation Management*, 18, 39–50.
Keenan, M. (2003). Using expert and stakeholder panels in technology foresight-principles and practice. *Technology Foresight for Organizers*, Ankara, Turkey, F1–F22.
Khurana, A. and Rosenthal, S. R. (1997). Integrating the fuzzy front end of new product development. *Sloan Management Review*, (2), 103–120.
Khurana, A. and Rosenthal, S. R. (1998). Towards holistic "Front Ends" in new product development. *Journal of Product Innovation Management*, (15), 57–75.
Kim, J. and David, W. (2002). Strategic issues in managing innovation's fuzzy front end. *European Journal of Innovation Management*, (5), 27–39.
Koen, P., et al. (2001). Providing clarity and a common language to the 'fuzzy front end'. *Research Technology Management*, March–April, 46–55.
Koen, P., et al. (2002). Fuzzy-front end: effective methods, tools and techniques. Toolbook, 2002.
Koen, Peter, Gideon, M., Robert, B. and Richard, R. (2002). Cognitive skills in the Furry-front end: which ones allow corporate teams to obtain start-up funding? In *PDMA Research Conference Proceedings*, Orlando, 87–108.
Lan, M. (2003). Ten years of UK foresight. *Paper Presented at NISTEP International Conference on Technology Foresight*, Tokyo, Japan.
Lan, M. and Keenan, M. (2003). Overview of methods used in foresight. *Technology Foresight for Organizers*, Ankara, Turkey, E1–E16.
Lee, J. and Dean, P. A. (2001). Valuation of R&D: real American sequential exchange options. *R&D Management*, 45(10), 1359–1377.
Leifer, R., et al. (2000). *Radical innovation: how mature companies can outsmart upstarts*. Boston, MA: Harvard Business School Press, 62–98.
Leonard, W. P. (1962). *The management audit*. Englewood Cliffs, NJ: Prentice-Hall.
Liam, F. and Randall, R. M. (1998). *Learning from the future: competitive foresight scenarios*. New York: John Wiley & Sons Ltd.
Linstone, H. A. (1984). *Multiple perspectives for decision making*. New York: North-Holland.
Lint, O. and Pennings, E. (1998). R&D as an option on market introduction. *R&D Management*, 28(4), 279–287.

Li J. (2002). *Global technique foresight trend*. Shanghai: Shanghai Scientific & Technical Publishers.

Li, J. (2003). Time and thoughts on shanghai's technical foresight. *World Science*, 2003(4).

Li, J. and Dai, C. (1996). *Benchmark targeting*. Tianjin: Tianjin People's Publishing House.

Lynn, G. S., Abel, K. D., Valentine, W. S. and Wright, R. C. (1999) Key factors in increasing speed to market and improving new product success rates. *Industrial Marketing Management*, (28), 319–326.

Lynn, G. S. and Akgun, A. E. (1998). Innovation strategies under uncertainty: a contingency approach for new product development. *Engineering Management Journal*, 1998(10), 11–17.

Management Science School of Shanghai Railway Institute (Ed.) (1985). *Technique development and technique prediction*. Shanghai: Shanghai Jiaotong University Press.

Martin, B. and Johnston, R. (1999). Technology foresight for wiring up the national innovation system. *Technological Forecasting and Social Change*, (60), 37–54.

Martino, J. P. (1993). *Technological forecasting for decision making* (3rd ed.) New York: McGraw-Hill.

Mats, L. and Bandhold, H. (2003). *Scenario planning: the link between future and* strategy. Palgrave.

McGrath, R. G. (2000). Assessing technology projects using real options reasoning. *Research Technology Management*, 43(4), July/August, 35–50.

Michelle Jones, L. and Pitts, Barbara M. (2004). Successfully implementing the stage-gate NPD system. Stage-Gate Inc. Working Paper No., 18.

Mitchell, G. R. and Hamilton, W. F. (1988). Managing R&D as a strategic option. *Research Technology Management*, May/June, 15–22.

Moenaert, R. K., et al. (1995). R&D/marketing communication during the fuzzy front-end. *IEEE Transactions on Engineering Management*, 42(3), S243–S259.

Mu, R. (2003). Beijing's technique foresight: practice and thoughts. *World Science* 2003(4).

O'Connor, P. (1994). Implementing a stage-gate process: a multi-company perspective. *Journal of Product Innovation Management*, 11, 183–200.

OECD Statistical Office of the European Communities (1997). *OSLO manual – proposed guidelines for collecting and interpreting technological innovation data*. OECD/Eurostat.

Panayi, S. and Trigeorgis, L. (1998). Multi-stage real options: the cases of information technology infrastructure and international bank expasion. *The Quarterly Review of Economics and Finance*, 38, Special Issue, 675–692.

Perlitz, M., Thorsten, P. and Randolf, S. (1999). Real option valuation: the new frontier in R&D project evaluation? *R&D Management*, 29(3), 255–269.

Petricka, I. J. and Echols, A. E. (2004). Technology roadmapping in review: a tool for making sustainable new product development decisions. *Technological Forecasting & Social Change*, (71), 81–100.

Phaal, R., Farrukh, C. and Mitchell, R. and Robert, D. (2003). Starting-up roadmapping fast. *Research Technology Management*, March–April, 52–58.

Phaal, R., Farrukh, C. and Probert, D. (2001a). *Technology roadmapping: linking technology resources to business objectives*. Cambridge: University of Cambridge.

Phaal, R., Farrukh, C. and Probert, D. (2001b). *The fast start to technology roadmapping: planning your route to success*. Institute for Manufacturing, Cambridge: University of Cambridge, Mill Lane, ISBN: 1-902546-09-01.

Phaal, R., Farrukh, C. and Probert, D. (2004). Customizing roadmapping. *Research Technology Management*, March–April, 26–37.

Pu, X. (2002). Definition of technique foresight and its relations with technique prediction. *Science & Technology Review*, 2002(7).

Rachel, C. and Wootton, A. B. (1998). Requirements capture: Theory and practice. *Technovation*, 18(8/9), August/September.

Richy, J. M. and Grinnell, M. (2004). Evolution of roadmapping at Motorola. *Research Technology Management*, March–April, 37–41.

Rinne, M. (2004). Technology roadmaps: infrastructure for innovation. *Technological Forecasting & Social Change*, 71, 67–80.

Robert, G. (2000). Cooper, doing it right: winning with new products. *Ivey Business Journal*, July/August.

Robert, G. C. (1994). Third-generation new product processes. *Journal of Product Innovation Management*, 11(3), 14.

Robert, G. Cooper, Edgett, Scott J. and Kleinschmidt, E. J. (2002). Optimizing the stage-Gate process: what best-practice companies do. *Research Technology Management*, September/October, 45, 5.

Robert, G. Cooper and Kleinschmidt, Elko J. (1995). Benchmarking firms' new product performance & practices. *European Management Review*, Fall, 112–120.

Robert, J. T. (1980). Management auditing. AMACOM, a division of American Management Associations, New York.

Russ, M. (2003). Control fuzzy front end. *PM World Today*, Translated by Yan Yongmei, July–August 2003.

Samuelson, N. (1998). translated by Xiao Chen, etc. *Economics* (V16). Beijing: Huaxia Publishing House.

Sandia National Laboratories. Fundamentals of technology roadmapping. www.sandia.gov/Roadmap/home.htm#what02.

Scarso, E. (1996). Timing the adoption of a new technology: an option-based approach. *Management Decision*, 34(3), 41–46.

Science Directorate. (2002). *Defra: Defra's horizon scanning strategy for science*. London: British.

Science and Technology Office of National Bureau of Statistics of China (Ed.) (1993). *A handbook of technical innovation statistics*. Beijing: China Statistics Press.

Shao, J. (2004). *Quality function deployment*. Beijing: China Machine Press, 2004.

Smith, J. E. and Robert, F. N. (1995). Valuing risky projects: option pricing theory and decision analysis. *Management Science*, 41(5), 795–816.

Study Team of Technical Prediction and National Key Technique Choice (2001). *From foresight to choice*. Beijing: Beijing Publishing House.

Sun, Z. (2002). Technique foresight in Japan. *World Science*, 2002(7), 41–42.

Tan, R. (2003). Research progress of several questions on product innovation design. *Chinese Journal of Mechanical Engineering*, 2003(9).

Tong, B., and Li, J. *Product Data Management (PDM) technique*. Beijing: Tsinghua University Press, 11.

von Hippel, E., Thomke, S., and Sonnack, M. (1999). Creating breakthroughs at 3M. *Harvard Bussiness Review*, September–October, 47–57.

von Hippel, E. (2005). *The source of technical innovation*. Translated by Liu Xielin, etc. Beijing: intellectual Property Publishing House.2005.

Walsh, S. T. (2004). Roadmapping a disruptive technology: a case study – the emerging microsystems and top-down nanosystems industry. *Technological Forecasting & Social Change*, (71), 161–185.

Wang, G. (2002). Technique foresight in South Korea. *World Science*, 2002(11), 39–40.

Wang, J. (2003). Computer-facilitated innovation design system tesearch based on TRIZ.

Wang, R. and Mu, R. (2003). From technique prediction to technique foresight: theory and practice. *World Science*, 2003(4).

Wang, Y. and Chen, J. (2002). Research on enterprise core capacity high-standard positioning. *Journal of Industrial Engineering and Engineering Management*, (4).

Xu, L., et al. (1989). Technique foresight on hyper quantum intervene device via Delphi method. *Studies in Science of Science*, January.(Ed.) (1986). *Research and development management*. Beijing: Higher Education Press.

Xu, Q. (Ed.) (2000). *Research, development and technique innovation management*. Beijing: Higher Education Press.

Yanger, C. (赤尾洋二). (1990). *An introduction of quality deployment*. Tokyo: Japanese Science and Technology Press.

Yang, C. (2003). *Real option and its application*. Shanghai: Fudan University Press.

Yang, X., Yang, M. and Lu, X. (2005). Innovative design of home-made cellphone based on TRIZ theory. *Packaging Engineering*, 26(2), 140–141.

Zhang, W., Zhang, G., He, H., et al. (2005). Solution to complicated mechanic and electric products innovation design via TRIZ theory. *Machine Design & Research*, 21(3), 15–18.

Zhang, X. (2002). Start with Chinese Translation of QFD names. *China Quality*.

Zhao, X. (2004). *Technical Innovation Theory (TRIZ) and application*. Beijing: Chemical Industry Press.

Zhang, H, Chen, J. and Gao, J. (2004). Research on fuzzy front end management of radical product innovation. *R&D Management*, 16(6), 48–53.

26
INNOVATION MANAGEMENT SIMULATIONS USING AGENT-BASED MODELLING

Petra Ahrweiler

This chapter introduces the methodological approach of innovation management modelling following the advent of digitalisation, big data and computational simulation. It highlights how especially agent-based modelling has become an increasing appropriate innovation management tool for addressing the "what if" questions of organisational interventions, providing managers with insights from realistic scenario modelling in order to test and assess strategic options before the implementation phase. These new experimental methods are not only about identifying potential, chances and options of innovation management strategies but can also be used for avoiding undesirable outcomes in terms of an early-warning system. The computational methods are scalable: they apply to assessing innovation strategies of single firms, to clusters and to industry associations.

Starting from some general considerations of computational modelling in the social sciences, the chapter will introduce the field of agent-based modelling in innovation studies, will illustrate the potential of these new methodologies with five examples relevant to innovation managers from an existing simulation platform and will close with some recommendations for future utility in managerial practice.

Computational modelling in the social sciences

What is a simulation?

Simulations belong to the methodological repertoire of many scientific disciplines; they are used for multiple purposes, where the artificial representation of real-world systems on the computer for experimentation with parameter variations is only one (cf. Gilbert and Troitzsch, 2005).

> We wish to acquire knowledge about a target entity T. But T is not easy to study directly. So we proceed indirectly. Instead of T we construct another entity M, the "model", which is sufficiently similar to T that we are confident that some of what we learn about M will also be true of T. [...] At a moment in time the model has structure. With the passage of time the structure changes and that is behaviour. [...] Clearly we wish to know the behaviour of the model. How? We may set the model running (possibly in special sets of circumstances of our choice) and watch what it

does. It is this that we refer to as "simulation" of the target. As will appear, if the model is a computational process within a computer, then simulation is a matter of executing that process and we speak of computer "simulation"

(Doran and Gilbert, 1994, p. 4f).

There is a high degree of methodological and technical diversification in applying simulation across scientific fields: for the social sciences only, Gilbert and Troitzsch report in "Simulation for the Social Scientist" (2005) advantages and disadvantages of seven common simulation techniques illustrated by examples – among them the well-known equation-based system dynamic models, micro-simulations, queuing models from engineering, cellular automata and multi-agent systems. The latter rely on the approach of agent-based modelling (ABM).

What is ABM?

Agent-based modelling is used to model complex systems of interacting agents (cf. Gilbert, 2008; Epstein and Axtell, 1996; Bonabeau, 2001; North and Macal, 2007; Macal and North, 2009). Every agent in an ABM is an autonomous computer program with properties (variables, context of variables) and behaviours (algorithms, "rules"). Within multi-agent systems, various agent programmes interact with one another and with an environment represented in the model. An agent can be any unit with properties and behaviour ascribed by an observer, be it a human individual, collective actors such organisations, households or countries – everything with "agency" according to the research question under investigation (e.g. cars as agents in a traffic simulation).

With ABM, it can be observed how the structure and dynamics of a system emerge from the properties and behaviours of individual agents. This modelling approach is useful for analysing the relations between the micro and macro level of a system. It enables one to analyse the sequence of decisions leading to particular system behaviour as well as the feedback from changes at the system level for individual action.

There are ABM with simple, homogeneous agents: while every single agent has only few properties and is limited mostly to reactive behavioural options, interaction effects can, however, lead to quite complex system behaviour (an example is the famous Schelling model about segregation in American cities, cf. Schelling, 1971).

However, there are also models with more "intelligent"[1] agents in the wake of artificial intelligence approaches and the so-called "expert systems" featuring many heterogeneous agent types with a broad range of properties – among them anticipation, learning and individual dynamic knowledge bases – and a multitude of behavioural options (cf. concerning agent architectures Wooldridge, 2000; Balke and Gilbert, 2014). These heterogeneous complex agent types interact in dynamic environments.

This second approach is the best choice for representing human or organisation behaviour as realistic and detailed as possible – for example, while aiming at changing these strategies: only if we understand where and how properties and behaviours of agents change system features can we identify where changes at the agent level can lead to desired changes the system level. Though ABM are used for many purposes in a variety of disciplines, mainly the ones with "intelligent" agents are used for modelling complex human and social behaviour; in the social sciences, these are called "social simulations".

The relation between model and empirical data

To represent empirically observable actors and their behaviours in a simulation, agents need to be informed (calibrated) by empirical data. The better the data, the better the scientific theories and empirical knowledge about a certain phenomenon, and the better the simulation. In the simulation, software is used to build "artificial societies" (Doran and Gilbert, 1994) following empirical knowledge available for this world; social simulation crucially depends on sound social science theories and sufficient empirical social research (cf. for the relation between model and empirical reality Gilbert et al., 2018; Ahrweiler, 2017a, 2017b; Ahrweiler and Gilbert, 2005; Gilbert and Ahrweiler, 2009).

If there is enough similarity between empirical and computational models in terms of a qualitative correspondence (comparable dynamics, isomorphic structures), simulation experiments deserve the term "history-friendly":

> History-friendly models are formal models which aim to capture – in stylised form – qualitative theories about mechanisms and factors (. . .). They present empirical evidence and suggest powerful explanations. Usually these 'histories' (. . .) are so rich and complex that only a simulation model can capture (at least in part) the substance, above all when verbal explanations imply non-linear dynamics.
> (Malerba, Nelson, Orsenigo, and Winter, 1999, pp. 3–4)

The more empirical knowledge is used to calibrate a simulation, the more the computational worlds resemble the real-world context. The quality of a simulation can be measured by its "recognition value" for relevant stakeholders: recognising essential aspects of their daily experience settings in a simulation, stakeholders are confident in assessing the chance to learn from and with the simulation and in gaining useful knowledge and advice for interventions into the empirical system (cf., Ahrweiler and Gilbert, 2005).

For this, the calibrated model should be able to show some similarity to an empirical system at a defined point in time, reproducing the "history" of the system that has led to this state. Letting the simulation further run into the future following that same dynamics without any interventions within a "nothing ever changes" scenario (zero hypothesis) can then serve as a benchmark, as the baseline scenario, to conduct experiments with interventions.

Agent-based modelling in innovation studies

Innovation – the creation of new, technologically feasible, commercially realisable products, processes and organisational structures (Schumpeter, 1912; Fagerberg, Mowery, and Nelson, 2006) – is emerging from an ongoing interaction process of innovative organisations such as universities, research institutes, firms, government agencies, venture capitalists and others. These organisations generate and exchange knowledge, financial capital and other resources in networks of relationships, which are embedded in institutional frameworks on the local, regional, national and international level (cf. Pyka and Kueppers, 2003; Ahrweiler, 2010). Innovation is an emergent property from these interactions on the micro level – if the combination of actors and organisations, their compatible capabilities and their cooperative behaviours match. No equation will predict this match or warn of a mismatch beforehand.

Policy makers and managers of firms, universities and other participating organisations try to find out as much as possible about the structures and processes responsible for innovation. The managers want to know how to position their organisation optimally in these networks; the policy makers are concerned with the bird´s-eye perspective on the wellbeing and competitiveness of the overall network on the different policy levels. Those practitioners turn to science for insights into the mechanisms and processes producing these network structures and for guidance how to optimise their performance. What can scientists tell them?

Network analysis and ABM

To provide descriptions and explanations for why and how innovation happens, we need to analyse its structures and processes. The structural "hardware" consists of inter-organisational innovation networks. Innovation happens in networks. Ultimately, innovation performance is dependent on a complex interaction pattern at the micro level of innovative actors: it is "all about new knowledge, and networks are central to how it is produced and generated" (European Commission Workshop Report "Using Network Analysis to Assess Systemic Impacts of Research", March 2009). This is why we have to investigate the role of collaborative R&D arrangements in innovation. Since collaborative innovation has become the dominant and most promising way to produce high-quality output (Bozeman and Lee, 2005), these collaboration structures are the target for policy formation and evaluation.

Network analysis of innovation networks is one of the most vibrant interdisciplinary research activities we can observe in the moment. All parts of innovation networks have been of interest so far: there are studies concerning the binary combinations of involved actors (university-university, university-SME, university-MNE, SME-MNE, SME-SME, etc.) and about all possible links between these actors – R&D alliances (e.g. Siegel, Waldman, Atwater, and Link, 2003), spin-off activity (e.g. Smith and Ho, 2006), licencing (e.g. Thursby and Kemp, 2002) and all other possible link types. We find studies on university-industry links (cf. Ahrweiler, Pyka, and Gilbert, 2011) and all sorts of work on inter-firm networks (e.g. Schilling and Phelps, 2005; Porter, Whittington, and Powell, 2005).

Most of these studies have been carried out by economists or other social scientists. However, due to a rising interest in physics in the past ten years concerning complex networks, there has been much overlap and co-publication between physics and the social sciences from hybrid backgrounds such as econophysics or sociophysics.

> Research by physicists interested in networks has ranged widely from the cellular level, a network of chemicals connected by pathways of chemical reactions, to scientific collaboration networks, linked by co-authorships and co-citations, to the world-wide web, an immense virtual network of websites connected by hyperlinks.
>
> *(Powell, White, Koput, and Owen-Smith, 2005, p. 1132)*

Networks consisting of nodes and edges (or actors and relations, or units and links, etc.) are a ubiquitous phenomenon, where general insights apply to their topologies, structural properties and measures (Albert and Barábasi, 2002; Newman, 2003). Network analysis methods (Wasserman and Faust, 1994) have profited immensely from progress in physics concerning the field of graph theory and complex networks.

On a general level, innovation networks show features both, of so-called scale-free networks (Barábasi and Albert, 1999) and of small worlds (Watts and Strogatz, 1998; Watts, 1999). We have already studied some aspects concerning these two general features in more detail (Pyka, Ahrweiler, and Gilbert, 2009; Ahrweiler, Pyka, and Gilbert, 2011). This area connects to interesting debates, that is, whether strong ties – such as friendship, contracts, face-to-face interaction – or weak ties (such as access to information through loose contacts) are good for innovation (Granovetter, 1973; Uzzi, 1997; Burt, 1992, 2004; Ahuja, 2000; Walker, Kogut, and Shan, 1997; Verspagen and Duysters, 2004). What special network topologies do or do not do for knowledge flows has been widely discussed in this research area (Cowan, Jonard, and Zimmermann, 2007; Gloor, 2006; Sorensen, Rivkin, and Fleming, 2006) occupied both by physicists and social scientists, often in interdisciplinary co-authorship relations. Can we be satisfied with this contribution of science to describe and explain the innovation process?

There is an issue with some deficiencies of network analysis.

> Network analysis is a powerful tool to gather information (...) and can be used to define the properties of variables which may be useful for further investigation. At present, network analysts cannot give an understanding of the dynamic behaviour of the system; it only takes static snapshots of the databases and therefore lacks the time evolution perspectives (...). One may say that the system is far too complex to be modelled, but other scientific fields have shown that dealing with very large and complex systems may be possible with simplified models, capable of very good qualitative and semi-quantitative descriptions of those systems. This is true for economics, thermodynamics, epidemiology and even for the study of social behaviour.
>
> *(European Commission Workshop Report "Using Network Analysis to Assess Systemic Impacts of Research", March 2009, p. 15f)*

Network analysis focuses on structures and states. However, what happens between the states we capture (causal mechanisms/processes producing the structures) and states we analyse? What about innovation behaviour? What about the "production algorithms" for the structures we observe? Network analysis does not address the "agency dimension" of innovation networks (cf. Ahrweiler, 2010) where innovative individuals and/or organisations move in an action space, which is co-evolving with them. The agency dimension, that is, the possibility of actors to move intentionally in the action space, provides the processes and mechanisms for network formation and development: it is what actors do and do not do that matters. Starting to address this dimension by network analysis would imply more complex node properties and/or more heterogeneous link types for each node – be they people or organisations. A real-world actor moves in an action space, which consists of many dimensions (actors are even permanently inventing, constructing, anticipating, changing, developing, etc. their action space, not just moving around in a given world). The notion of "actor" is tale-telling in this respect: it is originally used for being on the stage in a theatre performing multiple roles. Actors in different roles would need rich node descriptions concerning properties, behaviours and states and/or a richer link structure, which manifests what the actor does in relation to others. In network analyses, instead, the dimensions of nodes are rather limited – if an organisation is part of an EU R&D network under investigation, its relevant property is that it is doing funded EU research with other organisations – whatever roles it performs besides does not matter, nor how these different roles provide feedback on the respective R&D network tie. In the moment, multi-level networks are a research challenge for people interested in complex networks.

Furthermore, network analysis does not capture the particularities of knowledge generation and distribution. Network analyses deal with knowledge as "flow substance" in a way which does not discriminate knowledge very much from what flows in other types of networks, such as energy or information. It is structure that matters – not the particularities of the flow substance (i.e. knowledge). One consequence of this focus is that most network analyses address knowledge/innovation diffusion issues but do not provide many insights on the processes of the emergence of the new (knowledge generation, innovation). However, this is exactly what is required to describe innovation processes adequately and help practitioners to deal with their problems.

Adding a procedural perspective to the analyses will provide important insights. Here, an inter-disciplinary, or, even better, a trans-disciplinary, initiative offers a conceptual framework to help. This is complexity science (Bar-Yam, 1997, 2004; Braha, Minai, and Bar-Yam, 2008; Casti, 1995; Flake, 1999; Stewart, 1989; Waldrop, 1992). Business studies and management science have already taken this up: areas such as strategic organisational design (e.g. Anderson, 1999; Brown and Eisenhardt, 1998; Dooley and van de Ven, 1999; Eisenhardt and Bhatia, 2002; McKelvey, 1999) and innovation management (e.g. Buijs, 2003; Chiva-Gomez, 2004; Cunha and Comes, 2003) have applied key concepts of complexity science to innovation issues addressing procedural aspects and qualitative properties of knowledge and agency, rather than merely quantitative features of certain structures.

Complexity science perspectives locate innovation processes in turbulent environments with high uncertainty and ambiguity: they assign to innovation processes characteristics such as multi-scale dynamics with high contingency and non-linearity, emergence, pattern formation, path dependency, recursive closure and self-organisation (Frenken, 2006; Lane, van der Leeuw, Pumain, and West, 2009). Such concepts (cf. Arthur, 1989, 1998) are of rising importance to describe and explain innovation processes, building on mathematical concepts for systems analysis originating from physics and engineering science (Gell-Mann, 1994; Kauffman, 1993, 1995; Prigogine and Stengers, 1984; Holland, 1995). Representing knowledge flows in innovation networks means to follow agents who invent, learn and interact. To capture the dynamics of these learning activities, agent-based modelling is increasingly applied for research (see e.g. Windrum, 2007; Gilbert, Ahrweiler, and Pyka, 2010).

ABM in innovation studies of computational economics

The advantages of using ABM in innovation studies have been confirmed by a growing number of models (cf. Ahrweiler, 2010, pp. 233–315). These models implement, for example, the interaction of knowledge and actors, of outputs and organisations, of network formation and evolution. They simulate the interdependencies of existing innovation policies and funding strategies, of future innovation policy scenarios and alternative technology paths to improve innovation performance. ABM in innovation studies gain more and more prominence, where simulation is increasingly used for innovation policy advice and management support (cf. Dawid and Neugart, 2011). Policy is already very interested in innovation studies in general due to the important role of innovation for economy and society (cf. Martin, 2012); this is increased by the options of ABM to provide answers to what-if questions and ex-ante evaluation for policy interventions (Ahrweiler, Gilbert, and Pyka, 2016).

Herbert Dawid (2006) investigates the potential of the agent-based computational economics (ACE; cf. Tesfatsion, 2003, 2006) approach for the analysis of innovation processes. One of his conclusions is that ABM is particularly appropriate for studying genuine properties of innovation such as the strong substantive uncertainty involved or the special characteristics of knowledge. Furthermore, ABM have proven to be quite successful in explaining sets of stylised facts in innovation which could not be explained by alternative approaches. Dawid also presents the results of a systematic survey on ACE models of innovation and discusses their contribution to the field.

Central insights from an evolutionary economics approach are introduced and models categorised according to their contributions to them. For example, the heterogeneity of agents and their innovation strategies are the focus of models by Dawid, Reimann, and Bullnheimer (2001), Dawid and Reimann (2003, 2004), as well as Llerena and Oltra (2002). Uncertainty of innovation processes is central in models of Birchenhall (1995), Windrum and Birchenhall (1998), Cooper (2000), Ebeling, Molgedey, and Reimann (2000), Yildizoglu (2001), Natter et al. (2001) or Silverberg and Verspagen (2005). Following the early model of Grabowski and

Vernon (1987) for micro-founded insights into the structure of industries Dawid lists models such as Dosi, Marsili, Orsenigo, and Salvatore (1995); Klepper (1996); Winter, Kaniowski, and Dosi (2000, 2003); Malerba, Nelson, Orsenigo, and Winter (1999, 2001); or Malerba and Orsenigo (2002).

Many contributions are listed under the heading "agent-based economic growth model with a focus on innovation" (Dawid, 2006, p. 26) to combine a strong micro-foundation with the reproduction of a number of stylised facts about economic growth. Among them are Silverberg and Verspagen (1994, 1995, 1996); Chiaromonte and Dosi (1993); Chiaromonte, Dosi, and Orsenigo (1993); Kwasnicki (2001); Fagiolo and Dosi (2003); Dosi, Fabiani, Aversi, and Meacci (1994); and Dosi, Marsili, Orsenigo, and Salvatore (1995). More detailed reviews for this field can be found in Silverberg and Verspagen (2005), Pyka and Fagiolo (2005) or Windrum (2007). The analysis of Dawid suggests that we can expect a strong structuring effect of relevant author communities from different disciplines and contexts for shaping the field.

Furthermore, Dawid emphasises the role of knowledge as the "most important input factor for the 'production' of innovation" (Dawid, 2006, p. 1235f). In his section about knowledge accumulation, knowledge structures and spillovers, Dawid introduces knowledge stock with units of knowledge and knowledge structures as the most relevant targets for knowledge representation, where "the stock of knowledge of a firm is not uniform and has a lot of structure" (Dawid, 2006, p. 1236). Representation can be done by a single variable, where "knowledge accumulation is treated either implicitly, by assuming that all current knowledge is embodied in the technology currently used, or by considering a simple R&D stock variable, which is increased by investments over time" (Dawid, 2006, p. 15), or a more complex construct such as a vector in a multi-dimensional space. In the latter case, "models of knowledge are represented with abstract vectors made of topics with a more or less complicated structure" (Barreteau and Le Page, 2011, p. 3.4). Though Dawid (2006) only lists four models in this section of his review: Cantner and Pyka (1998); Ballot and Taymaz (1997, 1999), Gilbert, Pyka, and Ahrweiler (2001) and Meagher and Rogers (2004), his discussion suggests that we can expect a strong structuring effect of different approaches to knowledge modelling for shaping the field.

Central issues in simulating innovation

This expectation is strongly supported by the recent overview and critical discussion of existing computational innovation models with a focus on ABM provided by the book by Christopher Watts and Nigel Gilbert (Watts and Gilbert, 2014). The book reviews model types, general model requirements, techniques and prototypes, rather than aiming at a review of the existing publication landscape. In their chapter on technological evolution and innovation networks, Watts and Gilbert (2014) compare ten existing models for their representations of knowledge, technologies, strategies or rules (p. 232). For most of them, they find a bit string knowledge representation (March, 1991; Lazer and Friedman, 2007; Axelrod, 1997; Lindgren, 1992), for others a representation through cell locations/states in a grid (Silverberg and Verspagen, 2005, 2007), numerical variables (Cowan, Jonard, and Zimmermann, 2007), combinations of logical gates (Arthur and Polak, 2006) or multi-dimensional vectors (Ahrweiler, Gilbert, and Pyka, 2004). Watts and Gilbert discuss the advantages and limitations of these different modes of knowledge representation in detail (pp. 192–238). In this chapter, models are described, which incorporate generation, diffusion and impact of innovation.

Previous chapters discuss models that only cover one or two of these three processes, for example, diffusion models (cf. Rogers, 2003, Abrahamson and Rosenkopf, 1997, Valente, 1996). Of course, knowledge modelling is also crucial for issues around innovation diffusion:

> [R]epresentation of knowledge flows across this boundary is still a difficult question. Several works have already tried to represent pieces of knowledge as specific entities in the modelling of a system and its dynamics. The representation of knowledge flow processes has been developed in the field of innovation diffusions in the context of corporate businesses.
>
> *(Barreteau and Le Page, 2011, p. 3.1)*

Here, another relevant author community comes to attention: the scholars from business studies concerned with knowledge management issues. Their influence will also contribute to the structuring of the field.

Here comes yet another important driver for the field: "ABM in innovation studies". As Watts and Gilbert (2014) state,

> [O]rganisations need to consider their markets and their competitors' behaviour. They also need to reflect on their own sources of innovation and learning, and be prepared to adjust those sources in response to changes in the market (...) computer simulation models of innovation within organisations have demonstrated how problem-solving and learning performance is sensitive to a variety of factors.
>
> *(Watts and Gilbert, 2014, p. 132)*

As can be checked, for example, for the Special Issue "Agent-based Modelling of Innovation Diffusion" of the *Journal of Product Innovation Management* (edited by Garcia and Jager, 2011), most papers on ABM in innovation studies end up with "managerial implications" (Broekhuizen, Delre, and Torres, 2011, p. 214). These statements suggest that the intent of their model is "to provide practical insights (...) to governmental policymakers" (Zhang, Gensler, and Garcia, 2011, p. 164) or that their model is "an effective means for making useful (...) policies and managing the processes (...) under different policy scenarios" (Zhang and Nuttall, 2011, p. 185). We can expect a strong structuring effect from this orientation towards management and policy practice for shaping the field.

In the wake of combining innovation generation and innovation diffusion, these authors introduce important concepts for knowledge modelling to the field, for example, the exploration-exploitation dichotomy, which Watts and Gilbert (2014) discuss in their Chapter 4 in detail: March (1991) uses this distinction in his ABM on organisational learning (Argyris and Schön, 1996), which became one of the influential models in the field and was revisited, for example, by Rodan (2005) and further interpreted by Fagiolo and Dosi (2003). We can expect to find more of such little communities and model trajectories while assessing the publication database. As Watts and Gilbert state: "March's distinction between exploration and exploitation has been much cited, and his computer model has seen some attempts at replication and extensions. (A special issue on March's paper appeared in the Academy of Management Journal 49/4, 2006)" (Watts and Gilbert, 2014, p. 104). Models of organisational learning concern innovation within organisations, which suggests that we can expect not only a strong community looking at systemic interactions between technology, economy and society at large (see earlier) but also an at least similar-sized community looking at innovation on the firm level from a management and business studies perspective. Of course, there are all kind of brokers and bridges between these two communities around the topic of learning and spillovers such as Pyka and Cantner (1998) or Pyka, Ahrweiler, and Gilbert (2009).

Another dichotomy introduced by Watts and Gilbert (2014) in the context of learning and incremental vs. radical innovation is relevant for modelling learning and innovation by searching a knowledge/technology landscape looking for peaks as areas of novelty and success – either in small step changes (incremental) or by jumps into completely different areas of the landscape (radical). Here, models are introduced in the wake of Kauffman's NK fitness landscape (Kauffman, 1995) such as Frenken (2001, 2006) or Lazer and Friedman (2007). Innovation generation has been dealt with by various models, some with a stronger focus on the knowledge side, that is, the evolution of new technologies (Silverberg and Verspagen, 2005, 2007), others with a focus on the actor side, that is, the emergence of innovation networks (Cowan, Jonard, and Zimmermann, 2007).

In summary, there seem to be heterogeneous scientific communities involved with different reasons for using ABM for analysing innovation. In the general innovation literature, there are two poles,

> one of which focuses on innovation in firms, and is popular with scholars in business and management, the other emphasises the role played by technology and innovation in economic and social change more generally. The latter is particularly influential among scholars with a background in economics and other social sciences.
>
> *(Fagerberg, Fosaas, and Sapprasert, 2012, p. 1141)*

Another central issue again centres around the requirements for knowledge modelling in the field. In innovation, new knowledge (scientific discoveries, emergent technologies and disruptive innovations) is involved as the main component and the radical game-changer (cf. Bhupatiraju, Nomaler, Triulzi, and Verspagen, 2012; Loasby, 1999). Knowledge dynamics, that is, how knowledge is generated, shared, distributed, learnt, combined and recombined, forgotten or applied, are the key dynamics on the micro level, which produce innovation performance on the system level measurable using knowledge and innovation output indicators for assessing and tuning desirable system outcomes. It seems as if the conceptual landscape is mainly structured by thematic contributions to issues of knowledge representation.

The last issue we want to follow up on from insights of the previous review literature is that there seems to be a specific dedication of the field to produce impact outside academia. Many papers end up with policy recommendations or management advice stemming from research results. Of course, innovation plays an important role for economy and society, and ABM can provide answers to what-if questions and ex-ante evaluation for policy and management interventions. Models seem to be increasingly used for innovation policy advice and management support. Again, knowledge modelling seems to be a critical issue here. We might assume that the more policy-driven a model is, the stronger the focus on realistic knowledge representation, because knowledge is a key driver for innovation and the first target for policy and management interventions. Therefore, the quality of decision support models might crucially depend on how knowledge is represented.

Firm perspectives on innovation modelling with ABM

For a firm, it is always a risky enterprise to change the innovation strategy: changes can concern technological focus or prioritisation, cooperation or partner choice mechanisms, investment or funding strategies, tech transfer models, entrepreneurship strategy, location, network position and many other dimensions. In most cases, these changes concern highly specialised organisations acting in a complex environment characterised by many actors, competition, resource scarcity, etc. Pressure to be successful is usually high. Change would mean to leave or at least to question the current profile of the organisation and the – possibly very successful – status quo. It often implies a redistribution of financial and human resources and attention; existing priorities have to be changed or reduced for new ones.

Change will only be fully justified by future success, which is, by its nature, uncertain as an outcome, and therefore risky. How to reduce uncertainty and risk by increasing the predictive power of ex-ante evaluation concerning intended changes? Innovation managers need complexity-adapted tools to support their change decisions: the true uncertainty (Knight, 1921) of knowledge availability, access and transfer; of technology absorption; of financial risk; of regulatory barriers and institutional impediments; of market access and profitability counteracts all predictability (Pyka and Ahrweiler, 2008). The characteristics of firm innovation in complex social systems – be it for big multinationals (cf. Narula and Michel, 2010; Heidenreich, Barmeyer, and Koschatzky, 2010) or for small and medium businesses (cf. Asheim, 2010) – leave much remaining uncertainty on the shoulders of innovation managers.

Agent-based modelling of innovation processes can advise innovation management in a way which makes innovation indeed computable (cf. "The Economy Needs Agent-Based Modelling", *Nature* 460, 06.08.2009, p. 685f). An adequate ABM of the innovation landscape will not only allow one to investigate micro-macro links for innovation performance on the system level but will also allow for tracking single agents such as firms of a certain type through the simulation to assess how successful they are with what (combination of) strategies and with what type of managerial interventions. This way, it will be possible to evaluate where a firm sits with its profit model, with its products, with its service and engagement model, etc., in comparison to others and how it can navigate best to improve its position in the innovation ecosystem. In the following, five examples for strategically relevant innovation management questions have been chosen to illustrate the application context of ABM for firm perspectives: they stem from studies using the open-source Creative Commons simulation platform SKIN (cf. Watts and Gilbert, 2014, pp. 228–237).

The SKIN model

The agent-based simulation platform SKIN (acronym for *S*imulating *K*nowledge Dynamics in *I*nnovation *N*etworks) works with heterogeneous, "intelligent" and complex agent types, which act and interact in a computational world resembling the empirical world as much as possible. There is a close relationship between theory, empirical data and simulation. Due to this, SKIN claims to be relevant for providing innovation management advice. SKIN reproduces the research and innovation worlds of empirical actors on the computer. By calibrating the model with empirical data sets, it allows realistic and detailed experiments to answer "what if" questions of innovation management.

The SKIN model is concerned with simulating knowledge profiles, science and research landscapes and innovation networks on different scales. The "basic SKIN model" has been presented elsewhere (cf. Pyka, Gilbert, and Ahrweiler, 2007; Gilbert, Ahrweiler, and Pyka, 2007; Ahrweiler, Gilbert, and Pyka, 2011). On its most general level, SKIN is an ABM with knowledge-intensive organisations as agents, which try to produce new basic or applied knowledge and/or which try to produce new products and processes via innovation. Agents are located in permanently changing, complex social environments where their efforts need to find approval, for example, in the market if they target innovation, or in the scientific community if they try to publish their research results.

SKIN agents are knowledge-intensive, learning organisations. Each agent owns an individual dynamic knowledge profile. In the model, an agent's individual knowledge base – a vector in a multi-dimensional space – is called its "kene" (Gilbert, 1997), which the agent uses as the source and object for its research and innovation activities. The abstract knowledge profile can be "fed" (i.e. calibrated or informed) by empirical data. "Data points" are "units of knowledge" (e.g. core competences, capabilities, codified and tacit knowledge, explicit and implicit knowledge) which are produced, used and made available.

For example, we can directly work here with publication and patent or other source data for specific actors and contexts. Using methods from bibliometrics, scientometrics, patent analysis, etc., structural knowledge profiles of organisations can be collected, analysed and evaluated. Interpretative social science can furthermore contribute to shedding light on knowledge profiles by making the context of meaning and the connectivity to actions accessible and "understandable" via interviews with actors, case studies and document/discourse analysis. Using this modelling approach, SKIN represents and simulates the knowledge profiles of organisations active in research and innovation where, in aggregation and extrapolation, knowledge profiles of countries, regions, municipalities and clusters can be reconstructed and simulated. Simulating knowledge profiles belongs to every SKIN application. The kene is dynamic: an agent can learn – either alone by incremental or radical research, or together with other agents by exchanging and improving knowledge in partnerships and networks (following learning mechanisms from Organisational Learning according to March and Olsen, 1975; Argyris and Schön, 1996).

Within these collaborative arrangements, SKIN agents have a large number of strategies and mechanisms available, for example, to choose partners (following empirical partner choice mechanisms as elaborated by Powell, White, Koput, and Owen-Smith, 2005), to engage in partnerships, to initiate knowledge exchange, to generate collaborative knowledge outputs or to distribute innovation rewards. These interactions and the resulting social structures can be calibrated by empirical data as well. Information on the structures and dynamics of the science and research landscape on the actor and system level is broadly provided for countries, regions, sectors and clusters. "Data points" are actors, interactions and networks in research and innovation. Social network analysis (SNA) is a common tool to analyse this type of empirical data identifying and visualising central actors (hubs), clusters, the position and role of new entries in the research and innovation landscape, etc. However, it only addresses the structural aspects of the science and research landscape. Actors, processes and causal chains producing these network structures are in between "snapshots" of two network states following each other. Information on actors, their expectations, objectives, competences, strategies, cooperation behaviour, etc., and about their action contexts, the processes, cultures and institutional frameworks they are embedded in must be made transparent, accessible and "understandable" again with the help of complementary qualitative methods such as interviews with actors, case studies and document or discourse analysis.

Summarising, agents in any SKIN application interact on both the knowledge level and the social level. Both levels are inter-linked in many different ways. SKIN is all about actors, knowledge and networks. This general architecture is quite flexible, which is why the SKIN model has been called a "platform" (cf. Ahrweiler, Pyka, and Gilbert, 2014). It features applications as different as modelling the Vienna biotech cluster (Korber and Paier, 2014), the simulation of Irish university-industry networks (Ahrweiler, Pyka, and Gilbert, 2011) and also the ex-ante evaluation of EU-funded research projects and the research landscape they produce (Ahrweiler, Schilperoord, Pyka, and Gilbert, 2015).

Petra Ahrweiler

Five examples: SKIN for innovation management

Are R&D alliances and partnerships better than go-it-alone strategies?

This question is quite familiar in innovation management: it addresses the benefits and worries around open innovation (Chesbrough, 2003). The SKIN application investigating this question concerned the biotechnology-based pharmaceutical industry in Europe as a sector *par excellence* of a knowledge-intensive industry. The simulation was about assessing the effects of different learning activities of firms in this sector (go-it-alone strategies such as incremental and radical learning, as well as learning through R&D partnerships and innovation networks). The simulation tested the trade-off between go-it-alone strategies and different cooperation strategies and evaluated what combination of strategies worked best for which type of agent.

The results of this application (Gilbert, Ahrweiler, and Pyka, 2007, 2010; Ahrweiler, Gilbert, and Pyka, 2006) were closely observed by a large multi-national corporation in the UK pharma industry, which at that point in time was concentrating on go-it-alone strategies, because this company's management was about to decide on the future cooperation and embeddedness strategies of their enterprise within the surrounding industry. Tracking the performance of an agent through the simulation that had similar properties as the company but applied different combinations of learning and cooperation strategies provided interesting policy and management insights in how to navigate in complex innovation networks and how to improve its position in the network to exploit its resources to the best advantage. For this company, which was and still is a big player in the field, the simulation showed good results for their then prevalent go-it-alone strategies but demonstrated better results for specific combinations of learning strategies, including cooperation.

Is including SME in big-scale technological innovation projects indeed beneficial?

The European Commission was expecting to spend around €77 billion on research and innovation through its Horizon 2020 programme between 2014 and 2020. It is the successor to the previous, rather smaller programme, called Framework 7. When Horizon 2020 was being designed, the Commission wanted to understand how the rules for Framework 7 could be adapted for Horizon 2020 to optimise it for current policy goals, such as increasing the involvement of small and medium enterprises (SMEs).

The application INFSO-SKIN was built to evaluate possible funding policies. The model was set up to reproduce the funding rules, the funded organisations and projects and the resulting network structures of the Framework 7 programme. Among the tested questions was what would happen if the Commission would manage to increase SME participation (Ahrweiler, Schilperoord, Pyka, and Gilbert, 2015).

The objective to integrate innovative research-intensive SME in EU-funded research is a long-standing one and highly motivated:

> Through their flexibility and agility, SMEs play a pivotal role in developing novel products and services. Outstanding and fast growing SMEs have the potential to transform the structure of Europe's economy by growing into tomorrow's multinational companies (...) although particular attention has been paid to increasing SME involvement throughout FP7, SMEs are still finding it challenging to participate.
> *(Green Paper on a Common Strategic Framework for EU Research and Innovation Funding: Analysis of public consultation, 2011, S. 10)*

The European Commission (EC) had already issued a few studies to find out about the reasons for the "policy failure", why EU funding was not as attractive as expected for SMEs and why the measures taken had not been as successful as expected. However, a discussion had also started among the policy analysts, whether the policy efforts and costly incentive structures to draw SMEs into EU research were really worthwhile and would pay off in the way expected.

Is including SME in big-scale technological innovation projects indeed beneficial? This was not only an interesting question for EU policy but would also be of interest for MNE or industry associations. The related simulation experiments using INFSO-SKIN started with considerably more research-intensive and highly specialised SMEs in the starting population than could be seen in the empirical distribution. The simulation showed that these "additional" SME over-proportionally participated in proposals and, especially, in successful project consortia. Furthermore, they had positive effects on knowledge and network parameters. This result supported the SME policy advocates in the EC stakeholder group who represented the Green Paper position and argued against the critics of these policies within the group.

Do innovation projects need "new actors" such as civil society organisations to become responsive to societal values and act responsible in innovation?

This is another well-known debate in innovation management: What are the advantages of user-driven innovation (von Hippel, 2006)? The SKIN application GREAT-SKIN (Ahrweiler, 2016) was created to test some assumptions of the approach to "responsible research and innovation" (RRI).

> Responsible research and innovation is an approach that anticipates and assesses potential implications and societal expectations with regard to research and innovation, with the aim to foster the design of inclusive and sustainable research and innovation. Responsible Research and Innovation (RRI) implies that societal actors (researchers, citizens, policymakers, business, third sector organisations, etc.) work together during the whole research and innovation process in order to better align both the process and its outcomes with the values, needs and expectations of society. In practice, RRI is implemented as a package that includes multi-actor and public engagement in research and innovation, enabling easier access to scientific results, the take up of gender and ethics in the research and innovation content and process, and formal and informal science education.
>
> *(http://ec.europa.eu/programmes/horizon2020/en/h2020-section/responsible-research-innovation)*

In particular, the involvement of civil society on the individual level as interested citizens and on the organisational level of civil society organisations (CSOs) is supposed to change the research and innovation system towards RRI functions by anticipation and foresight (e.g. to prevent harmful consequences); by permanent accompanying reflection concerning responsibility aspects in research and innovation; by discursive, deliberative and participative opinion formation and decision making embedded in value discussions; and by responsive behaviour of all participants. Quality and accountability of research results will be assigned to the research and innovation process, and especially to the producers (i.e. the societal actors participating in research and innovation).

Empirical findings had indicated, however, that other agent types (universities, research organisations, SMEs, MNEs, etc.) were likewise active in promoting RRI in European research and innovation: these other agent types carried RRI capabilities as well and were major players for RRI diffusion. CSOs, in turn, were involved in projects not only as society representatives but also – and sometimes rather – for their domain and knowledge expertise in specific areas of research. The empirical findings indicated this with data and correlations. They did not, however, offer the full causal explanation, because, of course, in empirical reality it is impossible to observe processes such as "RRI learning" of and between different agent types; it is impossible to observe and measure knowledge exchange, knowledge flows, knowledge diffusion, etc.

This has been the task of the GREAT-SKIN simulation model. It allowed checking for the empirical "un-observables": in a simulation, it is possible to observe and measure "RRI capabilities" of agent types and "RRI learning/diffusion" between them. Simulation experiments were conducted that changed the level of CSOs' involvement in projects. They showed that the number, identity and role of CSOs are *not critical* to the simulation outcomes. Diffusion patterns of RRI showed that special RRI capabilities of CSOs are increasingly adopted and then contributed by other agent types and via the same learning mechanisms, CSOs increasingly adopt and then contribute scientific capabilities. All in all, simulation results confirmed and explained the insights from the empirical data sets, that is, that CSO are not more active than industry to implement institutional mechanisms for anticipation, reflection, deliberation and responsiveness, even hinting that SMEs were the front runners in that activity.

What are the benefits of multi-nationals embedded in industry structures of their host countries?

In this SKIN application, the effects of the presence and embeddedness of multi-national enterprises (MNE) in networks of innovation are investigated (Ahrweiler, Schilperoord, Gilbert, and Pyka, 2012). By looking at knowledge flows and capital stocks, the study aimed at investigating whether the mere presence of MNE is beneficial for innovation networks and whether there is an additional advantage if these MNE are engaged in collaborative R&D with other players in the network. The role of MNE for innovation networks was analysed from the perspective of their subsidiaries' host countries. The simulation was grounded in the empirical example of Ireland, enabling one to analyse the role of MNE in the Irish indigenous industry.

Scenario modelling of the role of MNE for host countries is highly firm relevant: in Ireland, there has been a growth in the high-technology industry sectors, but this has only been fostered by foreign-owned MNE. The MNE were still poorly integrated into Irish networks, clusters and innovation centres.

For the experiments, we operationalised the policy questions in relation to the Irish economy: How important is the knowledge integration function of MNCs as knowledge hubs and financial magnets for regional innovation networks? Does a firm population containing MNCs perform better in terms of knowledge diffusion and innovation performance than a uniform-size population of small and medium firms? What are the effects of MNC presence and activities on the knowledge level of the firm population?

Our results strongly confirmed the current Irish MNC policy strategies. Just attracting and retaining MNCs provides increasing capital availability and innovation performance for the indigenous industry. Surprisingly, even the mere presence of MNCs in the indigenous economy raises the knowledge flows in the host country's industry because firms can more safely engage in R&D and market activities. This is intensified when MNCs engage in local learning activities and embed themselves into the R&D network of regional innovation. The agent-based simulation confirmed that MNCs in R&D collaboration with the indigenous innovation network improve the knowledge and competence level of the whole industry and the innovation diffusion and collaborative arrangements in the host country.

How do entrepreneurs decide on venue and evaluate opportunities for their start-up?

The Irish-funded research programme "Innovation Policy Simulation for the Smart Economy" (IPSE) analysed innovation potentials and innovation strategies in and for Ireland. For example, Ireland currently prioritises its research funding thematically, technologically and sectorally concentrating on areas with high innovation potential. What are the effects and impacts of this strategy? What type of innovation landscape will be created by this prioritisation? Furthermore, in 2013 Ireland established a public-sector–driven centralised technology transfer organisation (cTTO) to work alongside numerous incubators (e.g. NovaUCD) and low-institutionalised tech transfer models. What are the effects and impacts of the different TTO models on innovation performance? Finally, there are only few publicly financed intermediaries between academia and industry such as the Fraunhofer institutes in Germany. What if there were more of these institutions? The IPSE programme investigates these questions using empirically informed simulations (cf. Ahrweiler, Gilbert, and Pyka, 2016).

An important part of the activity was to model entrepreneurship behaviour in Ireland by describing how entrepreneurs discover and evaluate new start-up opportunities. For this, a process was developed following empirical data gathered on the Dublin regional innovation network showing how entrepreneurs create start-ups at fertile locations after testing the viability of the start-up opportunity in general – sometimes in partnership with a technology transfer office and possibly other stakeholders – while being part of a competitive system where they navigate between competitors to survive and even grow in international market environments. The simulation (Schilperoord, 2016) enabled the early identification of high-potential start-ups, tested Irish policy instruments for entrepreneurship and explored the supporting roles of entrepreneurial networks and the decision rules for start-up financing in Ireland.

Utility in managerial practice: summary and outlook

What is the utility of the new methodologies for the future development of innovation management? ABM can shed light into the darkness of the future helping to cope with the challenges of complexity, to understand the dynamics of innovation and to identify potential access points for successful interventions. Simulation results can inform about likely future effects of managerial interventions; some of these effects can be surprising and counter-intuitive. New managerial knowledge is generated: complex contexts are made available and accessible via experimentation. Simulations can help and provide practice how to deal with them.

With the new simulation methodologies, counter-factual analysis is possible: they offer a benchmark, including measurable indicators for impact assessment, appraisal and ex-ante evaluation of managerial interventions. Simulation is a tool for "changing history", that is, testing the impact of past interventions by sensitivity analysis, and for "looking into the future" by exploring what-if questions.

For innovation managers, asking what-if questions (ex-ante evaluation) is an option that is normally not easily available in the management world. They can use scenario modelling as a worksite for their job. Experiments can be used to give an indication of the likely effect of a wide variety of management measures: empirical "un-observables", such as knowledge flows in innovation or learning of agents, can be measured.

However, for reliable results that decision-making can be based on, the evidence must be valid – just a "toy model" without any roots in empirical data will not suffice. A "realistic" ABM such as the one presented earlier gets into contact with empirical data in at least three ways: (i) both quantitative and qualitative empirical data are used to calibrate the model; (ii) data are processed in simulation experiments for producing particular scenarios (sensitivity analyses, ex-ante evaluation); and (iii) the simulations produce artificial data, which need to be analysed and interpreted, and which need to be validated against empirical data.

Simulation models are evaluated and validated by their users (cf. Ahrweiler and Gilbert, 2005, 2015), in this case by innovation managers. To trust the model and its results, they need to understand the mechanisms represented in the model, feel that they have had an input in the design of the agent rules and characteristics and agree that the dynamics of the model are sufficiently close to what they observed had actually happened. As these are relatively new methodologies for practical use, which are not yet part of the regular curricular in international business studies, training and capacity building is required for enabling innovation managers to use agent-based modelling for innovation management simulations.

Note

1 Intelligent"does not necessarily equal, rational", but means that agents display decision-making and strategies for action that have also been observed and analysed by empirical research.

References

Abrahamson, E. and Rosenkopf, L. (1997). Social network effects on the extent of innovation diffusion: a computer simulation. *Organization Science*, 8(3), 289–309.
Ahrweiler, P. (Ed.) (2010). *Innovation in complex social systems*. London: Routledge.
Ahrweiler, P. (2016). Research can be more responsible with the right Partner. *Euroscientist*, January 2016. www.euroscientist.com/research-can-be-more-responsible-with-the-right-partner/.
Ahrweiler, P. (2017a). Agent-based simulation for science, technology, and innovation policy. *Scientometrics*, 110(1), 391–415.
Ahrweiler, P. (2017b). Simulationsexperimente realexperimenteller Politik – der Gewinn der Zukunftsdimension im Computerlabor. In Böschen, S., Gross, M. and Krohn, W. (Eds.), *Experimentelle Gesellschaft*. Nomos Verlagsgesellschaft, edition sigma: Baden-Baden, pp. 199–237.
Ahrweiler, P. and Gilbert, N. (2005). Caffe Nero: the evaluation of social simulation. *Journal of Artificial Societies and Social Simulation*, 8(4).
Ahrweiler, P., Gilbert, N. and Pyka, A. (2004). Simulating knowledge dynamics in innovation networks. In Leombruni, R. and Richiardi, M. (Eds.), *Industry and labor dynamics: the agent-based computational economics approach*. Singapore: World Scientific Press, pp. 284–296.
Ahrweiler, P., Gilbert, N. and Pyka, A. (2006). Institutions matter but . . . organisational alignment in knowledge-based industries. *Science, Technology & Innovation Studies*, 2(1), 39–58.
Ahrweiler, P., Gilbert, N. and Pyka, A. (2011). Agency and structure. A social simulation of knowledge-intensive industries. *Computational & Mathematical Organization Theory (CMOT)*, 17(1), 59–76.
Ahrweiler, P., Gilbert, N. and Pyka, A. (Eds.) (2016). *Joining complexity science and social simulation for innovation policy. Agent-based modelling using the SKIN platform*. Cambridge: Cambridge Scholars Publishing.
Ahrweiler, P., Pyka, A. and Gilbert, N. (2011). A new model for university-industry links in knowledge-based economies. *Journal of Product Innovation Management (JPIM)*, 28, 218–235.
Ahrweiler, P., Pyka, A. and Gilbert, N. (2014). Simulating knowledge dynamics in innovation networks: an introduction. In Gilbert, N., Ahrweiler, P. and Pyka, A. (Eds.), *Simulating knowledge dynamics in innovation networks*. Heidelberg/New York: Springer, pp. 1–14.
Ahrweiler, P., Schilperoord, M., Gilbert, N. and Pyka, A. (2012). Simulating the role of MNCs for knowledge and capital dynamics in networks of innovation. In Heidenreich, M (Ed.), *Innovation and institutional embeddedness of multinational companies*. Edward Elgar: Cheltenham, UK, pp. 141–168.

Ahrweiler, P., Schilperoord, M., Pyka, A. and Gilbert, N. (2015). Modelling research policy – Ex-ante evaluation of complex policy instruments. *Journal of Artificial Societies and Social Simulation (JASSS)*, 18(4), 5.

Ahuja, G. (2000). Collaboration networks, structural holes, and innovation. *Administrative Science Quarterly*, 45, 425–455.

Albert, R. and Barabási, A.-L. (2002). Statistical mechanics of complex networks. *Reviews of Modern Physics T4*, 1, 47–97.

Anderson, P. (1999). Complexity theory and organization science. *Organization Science*, 10(3), 216–232.

Argyris, C. and Schön, D. A. (1996). *Organizational learning: a theory of action perspective*. Reading, MA: Addison-Wesley.

Arthur, B. (1989). Competing technologies, increasing returns, and lock-in by historical events. *Economic Journal*, 99, 116–131.

Arthur, B. (1998). *Increasing returns and path dependence in the economy*. Ann Arbor: University of Michigan Press.

Arthur, W. B. and Polak, W. (2006). The evolution of technology within a simple computer model. *Complexity*, 11(5), 23–31.

Asheim, B. (2010). Innovation is small: SMEs as knowledge explorers and exploiters. In Ahrweiler, P. (Ed.), *Innovation in complex social systems*. London: Routledge, pp. 110–121.

Axelrod, R. M. (1997). *The complexity of cooperation: agent-based models of competition and collaboration*. Princeton: Princeton University Press.

Balke, T. and Gilbert, N. (2014). How do agents make decisions? A survey. *Journal of Artificial Societies and Social Simulation*, 17(4), 13.

Ballot, G. and Taymaz, E. (1997). The dynamics of norms in a micro-to-macro model: the role of training, learning and innovation. *Journal of Evolutionary Economics*, 7, 435–457.

Ballot, G. and Taymaz, E. (1999). Technological change, learning and macro-economic coordination: an evolutionary model. *Journal of Artificial Societies and Social Simulation*, 2. www.soc.surrey.ac.uk/JASSS/2/2/3.html.

Bar-Yam, Y. (1997). *Dynamics of complex systems*. Reading: Addison Wesley.

Bar-Yam, Y. (2004). *Making things work: solving complex problems in a complex world*. Cambridge: Knowledge Press.

Barabási, A-L. and Albert, R. (1999). Emergence of scaling in random networks. *Science*, 286, 509–512.

Barreteau, O. and Le Page, C. (2011). Using social simulation to explore the dynamics at stake in participatory research. *Journal of Artificial Societies and Social Simulation*, April 14.

Bhupatiraju, S., Nomaler, Ö., Triulzi, G. and Verspagen, B. (2012). Knowledge flows – analyzing the core literature of innovation, entrepreneurship and science and technology studies. *Research Policy*, 41(7), 1205–1218.

Birchenhall, C. (1995). Modular technical change and genetic algorithms. *Computational Economics*, 8, 233–253.

Bonabeau, E. (2001). Control mechanisms for distributed autonomous systems: insights from the social insects. In Segal, L. and Cohen, I. R. (Hg.) *Design principles for the immune system and other distributed autonomous systems*. Oxford, pp. 281–292.

Bozeman, B. and Lee, S. (2005). The impact of research collaboration on scientific productivity. *Social Science Studies*, 35(5), 673–702.

Braha, D., Minai, A. and Bar-Yam, Y. (Eds.) (2008). *Complex engineered systems: science meets technology*. New York: Springer.

Broekhuizen, T. L. J., Delre, S. A. and Torres, A. (2011). Simulating the cinema market: how cross-cultural differences in social influence explain box office distributions. *Journal of Product Innovation Management*, 28, 204–217.

Brown, S. L. and Eisenhardt, K. M. (1998). *Competing on the edge: strategy as structured chaos*. Boston, MA: Harvard Business School Press.

Buijs, J. (2003). Modelling product innovation processes, from linear logic to circular chaos. *Creativity & Innovation Management*, 12(2), 76–93.

Burt, R. S. (1992). *Structural holes*. Cambridge, MA: Harvard University Press.

Burt, R. S. (2004). Structural holes and good ideas. *American Journal of Sociology*, 110(2), 349–399.

Cantner, U. and Pyka, A. (1998). Absorbing technological spillovers: simulations in an evolutionary framework. *Industrial and Corporate Change*, 7, 369–397.

Casti, J. (1995). *Complexification. Explaining a paradoxical world through the science of surprise*. New York: Harper Collins.

Chesbrough, H. (2003). *Open innovation: the new Imperative for creating and profiting from Technology*. Boston, MA: Harvard Business School Press.

Chiaromonte, F. and Dosi, G. (1993). Heterogeneity, competition and macroeconomic dynamics. *Structural Change and Economic Dynamics*, 4, 39–63.

Chiaromonte, F., Dosi, G. and Orsenigo, L. (1993). Innovative learning and institutions in the process of development: on the foundations of growth regimes. In Thompson, R. (Ed.), *Learning and technological change*. Macmillan Press, 117–149.

Chiva-Gomez, R. (2004). Repercussions of complex adaptive systems on product design management. *Technovation*, 24(9), 707–711.

Cooper, B. (2000). Modelling research and development: how do firms solve design problems? *Journal of Evolutionary Economics*, 10, 395–413.

Cowan, R., Jonard, N. and Zimmermann, J.-B. (2007). Bilateral collaboration and the emergence of innovation networks. *Management Science*, 53, 1051–1067.

Cunha, M. P. and Comes, J. E. S. (2003). Order and disorder in product innovation models. *Creativity & Innovation Management*, 12(3), 174–187.

Dawid, H. (2006). Agent – based models of innovation and technological change. In Tesfatsion, L. and K. Judd (Eds.), *Handbook of computational economics II: agent-based computational economics*. North – Holland, pp. 1235–1272.

Dawid, H. and Neugart, M. (2011). Agent-based models for economic policy design. *Eastern Economic Journal*, 37(1), 44–50.

Dawid, H. and Reimann, M. (2003). Diversification: a road to inefficiency in product innovations? CEM Working Paper 2003/63, University of Bielefeld.

Dawid, H. and Reimann, M. (2004). Evaluating market attractiveness: individual incentives vs. industrial profitability, to be published in *Computational Economics*.

Dawid, H., Reimann, M. and Bullnheimer, B. (2001). To innovate or not to innovate? *IEEE Transactions on Evolutionary Computation*, 5, 471–481.

Dooley, K. and van de Ven, A. (1999). Explaining complex organizational dynamics. *Organization Science*, 10(3), 358–372.

Doran, J. and Gilbert, G. N. (1994). Simulating societies: an introduction. In Doran, J. and Gilbert, G. N. (Eds.), *Simulating Societies: the computer simulation of social phenomena*. London.

Dosi, G., Fabiani, S., Aversi, R. and Meacci, M. (1994). The dynamics of international differentiation: a multi-country evolutionary model. *Industrial and Corporate Change*, 3, 225–242.

Dosi, G., Marsili, O., Orsenigo, L. and Salvatore, R. (1995). Learning, market selection and the evolution of industrial structures. *Small Business Economics*, 7, 411–436.

Ebeling, W., Molgedey, L. and Reimann, A. (2000). Stochastic urn models of innovation and search dynamics. *Physica A*, 287, 599–612.

Eisenhardt, K. M. and Bhatia, M. M. (2002). Organizational complexity and computation. In Baum, J. A. C. (Ed.), *Companion to organizations*. Oxford: Blackwell.

Epstein, J. M. and Axtell, R. (1996). *Growing artificial societies: social science from the bottom up*. Cambridge, MA: MIT Press.

European Commission (Ed.) (2009). Directorate-general infso: European commission workshop report: using network analysis to assess systemic impacts of research. Brussels, Belgium.

Fagerberg, J., Fosaas, M. and Sappraser, K. (2012). Innovation: exploring the knowledge base. *Research Policy*, 41(7), 1132–1153.

Fagerberg, J., Mowery, D. and Nelson, R. R. (2006). *The Oxford handbook of innovation*. Oxford: Oxford University Press.

Fagiolo, G. and Dosi, G. (2003). Exploitation, exploration and innovation in a model of endogenous growth with locally interacting agents. *Structural Change and Economic Dynamics*, 14, 237–273.

Flake, G. W. (1999). *The computational beauty of nature*. Cambridge, MA: MIT Press.

Frenken, K. (2001). Fitness landscapes, heuristics and technological paradigms: a critique on random search models in evolutionary economics. In Dubois, D. M. (Ed.), *Computing anticipatory systems* (Vol. 573). Melville, NY: American Institute of Physics, pp. 558–565.

Frenken, K. (2006). *Innovation, evolution and complexity theory*. Cheltenham: Edward Elgar Publishing.

Garcia, R. and Jager, W. (2011). Agent-based modeling of innovation diffusion, special issue. *Journal of Product Innovation Management*, 28(2).

Gell-Mann, M. (1994). *The quark and the Jaguar*. New York: Freeman & Co.

Gilbert, N. (2008). *Agent-based models*. Thousand Oaks, CA: Sage Publications.

Gilbert, N. and Ahrweiler, P. (2009). The epistemologies of social simulation research. In Squazzoni, F. (Ed.), *Epistemological aspects of computer simulation in the social sciences*. Berlin/New York: Springer, pp. 12–28.

Gilbert, N., Ahrweiler, P., Barbrook-Johnson, P., Narasimhan, K. and Wilkinson, H. (2018). Computational modelling of public policy: reflections on practice. *Journal of Artificial Societies and Social Simulation (JASSS)*, 21(1), 14.

Gilbert, N., Ahrweiler, P. and Pyka, A. (2007). Learning in innovation networks – some simulation experiments. *Physica A: Statistical Mechanics and Its Applications*, 378(1) 667–693.

Gilbert, N., Ahrweiler, P. and Pyka, A. (2010). Learning in innovation networks – some simulation experiments. Re-Print. In Ahrweiler, P. (Ed.), *Innovation in complex social systems*. London: Routledge, pp. 235–249.

Gilbert, N. (1997). A simulation of the structure of academic science. *Sociological Research Online*, 2(2). www.socresonline.org.uk/2/2/3.html.

Gilbert, N., Pyka, A. and Ahrweiler, P. (2001). Innovation networks-a simulation approach. *Journal of Artificial Societies and Social Simulation*, 4. www.soc.surrey.ac.uk/JASSS/4/3/8.html.

Gilbert, N. and Troitzsch, K.G. (2005). *Simulation for the social scientist*. (2nd. ed.), Maidenhead: Milton Keynes.

Gloor, P. (2006). *Swarm creativity – competitive advantage through collaborative innovation networks*. Oxford: Oxford University Press.

Grabowski, H. G. and Vernon, J. M. (1987). Pioneers, imitators, and generics ? A simulation model of Schumpeterian competition. *Quarterly Journal of Economics*, 102, 491–525.

Granovetter, M. (1973). The strength of weak ties. *American Journal of Sociology*, 78(6), 1360–1380.

Heidenreich, M., Barmeyer, C. and Koschatzky, K. (2010). Product development in multinational companies: the limits for the internationalization of R&D projects. In Ahrweiler, P. (Ed.), *Innovation in complex social systems*. London: Routledge, pp. 137–149.

Holland, J. H. (1995). *Hidden order: how adaptation builds complexity*. Reading, MA: Addison-Wesley.

Kauffman, S. (1995). *At home in the universe. The search for laws of self-organization and complexity*. Oxford: Oxford University Press.

Kauffman, S. A. (1993). *The origins of order: self-organization and selection in evolution*. New York: Oxford University Press.

Klepper, S. (1996). Entry, exit, growth, and innovation over the product life cycle. *American Economic Review*, 86, 562–583.

Korber, M. and Paier, M. (2014). Simulating the effects of public funding on research in life sciences: direct research funds versus tax incentives. In Gilbert, N., Ahrweiler, P. and Pyka, A. (Eds.), *Simulating knowledge dynamics in innovation networks*. Heidelberg/New York: Springer, pp. 99–130.

Knight, F. H. (1921). *Risk, uncertainty and profit*. Boston, MA: Hart, Schaffner & Marx.

Kwasnicki, W. (2001). Firms decision making process in an evolutionary model of industrial dynamics. *Advances in Complex Systems*, 1, 1–25.

Lane, D., van der Leeuw, S., Pumain, D. and West, G. (Eds.) (2009). *Complexity perspectives in innovation and social change*. Berlin/New York: Springer.

Lazer, D. and Friedman, A. (2007). The network structure of exploration and exploitation. *Administrative Science Quarterly*, 52(4), 667–694.

Lindgren, K. (1992). *Evolutionary phenomena in simple dynamics. Vol. 10*. Reading: Addison-Wesley.

Llerena, P. and Oltra, V. (2002). Diversity of innovative strategy as a source of technological performance. *Structural Change and Economic Dynamics*, 13, 179–201.

Loasby, B. J. (1999). *Knowledge, institutions and evolution in economics*. London: Routledge.

Macal, Ch. M. and North, M.J. (2009). Agent-based modeling and simulation. In Rossetti, M.D., Hill, R.R., Johansson, B., Dunkin, A. and Ingalls, R.G. (Hg.) *Proceedings of the 2009 Winter Simulation Conference*. Austin, TX, 86–98.

Malerba, F., Nelson, R., Orsenigo, L. and Winter, S. (1999). 'History-friendly' models of industry evolution: the computer industry. *Industrial and Corporate Change*, 8, 3–40.

Malerba, F., Nelson, R., Orsenigo, L. and Winter, S. (2001). Competition and industrial policies in a 'history-friendly' model of the evolution of the computer industry. *International Journal of Industrial Organization*, 19, 635–664.

Malerba, F. and Orsenigo, L. (2002). Innovation and market structure in the dynamics of the pharmaceutical industry and biotechnology: towards a history-friendly model. *Industrial and Corporate Change*, 11, 667–703.

March, J. G. (1991). Exploration and exploitation in organizational learning. *Organization Science*, 2(1), 71–87.

March, J. G. and Olsen, J. P. (1975). The uncertainty of the past: organizational learning under ambiguity. *European Journal of Political Research*, 3, 147–171.

Martin, B. R. (2012). The evolution of science policy and innovation studies. *Research Policy*, 41(7), 1219–1239.

McKelvey, B. (1999). Self-organization, complexity, catastrophe, and microstate models at the edge of chaos. In Baum, J. A. C. and McKelvey, B. (Eds.), *Variations in organization science – in honor of Donald T. Campbell*. Thousand Oaks, CA: Sage Publications.

Meagher, K. and Rogers, M. (2004). Network density and R&D spillovers. *Journal of Economic Behavior and Organization*, 53, 237–260.

Narula, R. and Michel, J. (2010). Reverse knowledge transfer and its implications for European policy. In Ahrweiler, P. (Ed.), *Innovation in complex social systems*. London: Routledge, pp. 122–136.

Natter, M., Mild, A., Feuerstein, M., Dorffner, G. and Taudes, A. (2001). The effect of incentive schemes and organizational arrangements on the new product development process. *Management Science*, 47, 1029–1045.

Newman, M. (2003). The structure and function of complex networks. *SIAM Review*, 45, 167–256.

North, M. J. and Macal, C. M. (2007). *Managing business complexity: discovering strategic solutions with agent-based modeling and simulation*. Oxford: Oxford University Press.

Porter, K. A., Bunker Whittington, K. C. and Powell, W. W. (2005). The institutional embeddedness of high-tech regions: relational foundations of the Boston biotechnology community. In Breschi, S. and Malerba, F. (Eds.), *Clusters, networks, and innovation*, Oxford: Oxford University Press.

Powell, W. W., White, D. R., Koput, K. W. and Owen-Smith, J. (2005). Network dynamics and field evolution: the growth of inter-organizational collaboration in the life sciences. *American Journal of Sociology*, 110(4), 1132–1205.

Prigogine, I. and Stengers, I. (1984). *Order out of chaos*. New York: Bantam Books.

Pyka, A. and Cantner, U. (1998). Absorbing technological spillovers: simulations in an evolutionary framework. *Industrial and Corporate Change*, 7(2), 369–397.

Pyka, A. and Kueppers, G. (Eds.) (2003). *Innovation networks. Theory and practice*. Cheltenham: Edward Elgar Publishing.

Pyka, A. and Fagiolo, G. (2005). Agent-based modelling: a methodology for neo-Schumpeterian economics. In Hanusch, H. and Pyka, A. (Eds.), *The Elgar companion to neo-Schumpeterian economics*. Cheltenham: Edward Elgar Publishing.

Pyka, A., Gilbert, N. and Ahrweiler, P. (2007). Simulating knowledge generation and distribution processes in innovation collaborations and networks. *Cybernetics and Systems*, 38(7), 667–693.

Pyka, A. and Ahrweiler, P. (2008). Innovation networks – an introduction. *International Journal of Foresight and Innovation Policy*, 4(3/4), 1–8.

Pyka, A., Ahrweiler, P. and Gilbert, N. (2009). Agent-based modelling of innovation networks – the fairy tale of spillovers. In Pyka, A. and Scharnhorst, A. (Eds.), *Innovation networks. New approaches in modeling and analyzing*. Berlin/New York: Springer, pp. 101–126.

Rodan, S. (2005). Exploration and exploitation revisited: extending March's model of mutual learning. *Scandinavian Journal of Management*, 21(4), 407–428.

Rogers, E. M. (2003). *Diffusion of innovations* (5th ed.). New York: Free Press.

Schelling, T. C. (1971). Dynamic models of segregation. *Journal of Mathematical Sociology*, 1, 143–186.

Schilling, M. A. and Phelps, C. C. (2005). Interfirm collaboration networks: the impact of small world connectivity on firm innovation. *Management Science*, 53(7), 1113–1126.

Schilperoord, M. (2016). Start-ups when and where? Using the SKIN platform for modelling the birth of new firms. In Ahrweiler, P., Gilbert, N. and Pyka, A. (Eds.), *Joining complexity science and social simulation for innovation policy. Agent-based modelling using the SKIN platform*. Cambridge Scholars Publishing, pp. 326–348.

Schumpeter, J. (1912). *The theory of economic development*. Oxford: Oxford University Press.

Siegel, D. S., Waldman, D., Atwater, L. and Link, A. N. (2003). Commercial knowledge transfers from universities to firms: improving the effectiveness of university-industry collaboration. *Journal of High Technology Management Research*, 14, 111–133.

Silverberg, G. and Verspagen, B. (1994). Collective learning, innovation and growth in a boundedly rational, evolutionary world. *Journal of Evolutionary Economics*, 4, 207–226.

Silverberg, G. and Verspagen, B. (1995). An evolutionary model of long term cyclical variations of catching up and falling behind. *Journal of Evolutionary Economics*, 5, 209–227.

Silverberg, G. and Verspagen, B. (1996). From the artificial to the endogenous: modeling evolutionary adaptation and economic growth. In Helmstädter, E. and Perlman, M. (Eds.), *Behavioral norms, technological progress, and economic dynamics*. Ann Arbor: The University of Michigan Press.

Silverberg, G. and Verspagen, B. (2005). A percolation model of innovation in complex technology spaces. *Journal of Economic Dynamics & Control*, 29(1–2), 225–244.

Silverberg, G. and Verspagen, B. (2007). Self-organization of R&D search in complex technology spaces. *Journal of Economic Interaction and Coordination*, 2(2), 195–210.

Sorenson, O., Rivkin, J. and Fleming, L. (2006). Complexity, networks and knowledge flow. *Research Policy*, 35(7), 994–1017.

Smith, H. L. and Ho, K. (2006). Measuring the performance of Oxford University, Oxford Brookes University and the government laboratories' spin-off companies. *Research Policy*, 35, 1554–1568.

Stewart, I. (1989). *Does God play dice? The mathematics of chaos*. Cambridge, MA: Blackwell.

Tesfatsion, L. (2003). Agent-based computational economics. Economics Working Papers (2002–2016). Iowa State University.

Tesfatsion, L. (2006). Agent-based computational economics: a constructive approach to economic theory. In Tesfatsion, L. and Judd, K. (Eds.), *Handbook of computational economics II: agent-based computational economics*. North–Holland, Elsevier.

Thursby, J. and Kemp, S. (2002). Growth and productive efficiency of university intellectual property licensing. *Research Policy*, 31, 109–124.

Uzzi, B. (1997). Social structure and competition in inter-firm networks: the paradox of embeddedness. *Administrative Science Quarterly*, 42, 35–67.

Valente, T. W. (1996). *Network models of the diffusion of innovations*. Cresskill: Hampton Press.

Verspagen, B. and Duysters, G. (2004). The small worlds of strategic technology alliances. *Technovation*, 24, 563–571.

Von Hippel, E. (2006). *Democratizing innovation*. Cambridge, MA: MIT Press.

Waldrop, M. M. (1992). *Complexity: the emerging science at the edge of order and chaos*. New York: Simon & Schuster.

Walker, G., Kogut, B. and Shan, W. (1997). Social capital, structural holes and the formation of an industry network. *Organization Science*, 8, 108–125.

Wasserman, S. and Faust, K. (1994). *Social network analysis: methods and applications*. Cambridge: Cambridge University Press.

Watts, D. (1999). *Small worlds*. Princeton: Princeton University Press.

Watts, D. and Strogatz, S. (1998). Collective dynamics of 'small-world' networks. *Nature*, 393, 440–442.

Watts, C. and Gilbert, N. (2014). *Simulating innovation. Computer-based tools for rethinking innovation*. Cheltenham: Edward Elgar Publishing.

Windrum, P. (2007). Neo-Schumpeterian simulation models. In Hanusch, H. and Pyka, A. (Eds.), *The Edward Elgar companion to Neo-Schumpeterian economics*. Cheltenham: Edward Elgar Publishing, 405–439.

Windrum, P. and Birchenhall, C. (1998). Is product life cycle theory a special case? dominant designs and the emergence of market niches through coevolutionary-learning. *Structural Change and Economic Dynamics*, 9, 109–134.

Winter, S. G., Kaniowski, Y. M. and G. Dosi (2000). Modelling industrial dynamics with innovative entrants. *Structural Change and Economic Dynamics*, 11(3), 255–293.

Winter, S. G., Kaniowski, Y. M. and G. Dosi (2003). A baseline model of industry evolution. *Journal of Evolutionary Economics* 13(4), 355–383.

Wooldridge, M. (2000). *Reasoning about rational agents*. Cambridge, MA: MIT Press.

Yildizoglu, M. (2001). Connecting adaptive behavior and expectations in models of innovation: the potential role of artificial neural networks. *European Journal of Economic and Social Systems*, 15, 203–220.

Zhang, T., Gensler, S. and Garcia, R. (2011). A study of the diffusion of alternative fuel vehicles: an agent-based modeling approach. *Journal of Product Innovation Management*, 28, 152–168.

Zhang, T. and Nuttall, W. J. (2011). Evaluating government's policies on promoting smart metering diffusion in retail electricity markets via agent-based simulation. *Journal of Product Innovation Management*, 28, 169–186.

27
TECHNOLOGY INNOVATION INVESTMENT PORTFOLIO PLANNING
A systems approach with application examples

Oliver Yu

Introduction

Technology innovations have been the driving forces for human civilization and economic developments. Effective technology innovation investment portfolio planning is essential for economic growth and competitiveness of not only a corporation but also a country.

This chapter introduces a *systems* approach for technology innovation investment portfolio planning that has been *successfully applied to large corporations as well as government agencies around the world*. In addition to the basic approach and the overall planning process, we will use applications to technology innovation investments by an Asian government as examples throughout the chapter.

The systems approach

The *systems* approach views technology innovation investment portfolio planning as a *total-system decision process* that involves:

- A *systematic decision framework* for *optimally* allocating limited financial, technical, and human resources of an organization *among* alternative technology innovation portfolios.
- A *holistic understanding of a decision-maker's values*.
- An *organized identification of technology innovation alternatives*.
- A *synergy of methods, including scenario analysis for forecasting the relationships* between alternatives and values.
- The use of simple management tools to generate *strategic insights*.
- A *modern portfolio theory-based investment planning process* for the optimal portfolio by balancing the perceived expected returns and risks of long-term technology innovation investments.

Methodology emphasis

Planning is *both a rational and a creative* **decision process**. The systematic approach emphasizes a *structured framework* to systematically and iteratively *integrate* reasoned and informed judgments and build consensus among diverse, intelligent, and knowledgeable professionals to provide a *systematic and supportable* basis to the technology investment decision-maker. Specifically, it strives to:

- Reduce bias, broaden perspective, and stimulate creativity through *diversity*
- Develop logical and structured reasoning and informed judgments through *intelligent and knowledgeable professional interactions and in-depth technical analysis*
- Provide *transparency and accountability* through an open and iterative process

Technology innovation investment planning decision: a systematic framework

A systematic technology innovation investment portfolio planning decision framework includes the following six key steps:

1. Understand and identify the *planning values* of the decision-maker, which are the motivation for decision making and the basis for evaluating alternatives.
2. Identify major available *alternative portfolios*.
3. Forecast the *relationships between alternatives and values*.
4. Generate *strategic insights*.
5. Find the *optimal portfolio*.
6. Explore *policy implications* for plan implementation.

The planning process is depicted in Figure 27.1.

Step 1. Understand and identify planning values based on a new model of human needs

The first step of the planning process is to understand and identify the planning values, which are based on human needs.

The traditional approach to understanding human needs is the well-known Maslowian hierarchical model (Maslow, 1943) shown in Figure 27.2.

The two major characteristics of the Maslowian model are:

1. There are five types of basic needs: physiological, safety, love, esteem, and self-actualization.
2. These basic types of needs are related to each other, "being arranged in a hierarchy of prepotency," in which when a lower level of needs is satisfied, the next level of needs emerges.

Although widely known, the model has largely been criticized for the impractically of the hierarchical structure and for the ambiguity in the characterization of "self-actualization" (Wabha and Bridwell, 1976; Neher, 1991). Specifically, based on anecdotal evidence, many people have been observed to forsake physiological and safety needs to satisfy love and esteem needs, such as sacrificing their lives for love or risking their health for achievements. Moreover, many people have been observed to not strive to fulfill the self-actualization needs even if their love and esteem needs have been satisfied, such as some of the nouveau riches. On the other hand, people who have satisfied their love and esteem needs have often been observed to exhibit strong needs for legacy, altruism, spirituality, and meaningfulness of life, especially during old age, as witnessed by the philanthropic activities of many wealthy individuals.

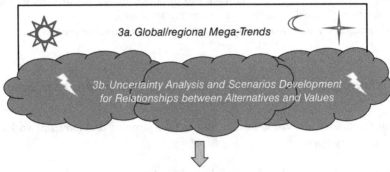

Figure 27.1 A systematic planning process

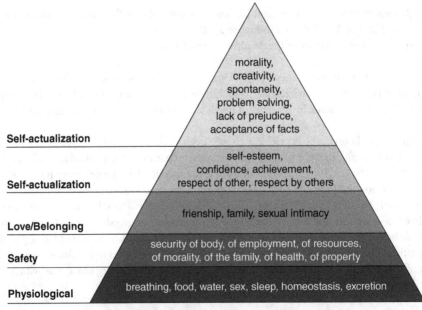

Figure 27.2 The traditional Maslowian hierarchical model of human needs

In sum, Maslow's model describes well the physiological needs for survival and safety and the emotional needs for love and esteem, as well as the needs for psychological growth in the form of self-actualization, but is deficient in explaining the commonly observed counterexamples of the strict hierarchical progress of needs. Furthermore, it appears to have neglected a major category of human needs for recreation and entertainment.

A new model of human needs

Given the deficiencies of the Maslowian model, it may be useful to develop a more comprehensive new model of human needs by reviewing other major theories and exploring the underlying determinants of human needs.

A review of recent literature shows that other major theories of human needs, such as the Existence-Relatedness-Growth Theory of Clayton Alderfer(1969), the Achievement-Authority-Affiliation Theory of David McClelland (1988), and the Autonomy-Competence-Relatedness Theory of James Adie, Duda, and Ntoumanis (1988), are largely variants and refinements of the Maslowian model. Only the categorization by Manfred Max-Neef, Elizalde, and Hopenhayn (1991) includes needs of understanding, idleness, and leisure, which are not directly related to the needs of security or growth in the other theories. Combining these major theories with direct observations of human behaviors provides the following insights on human needs:

1 In addition to security and growth needs, there are needs for idleness, relaxation, recreation, entertainment, and leisure, as well as needs for sensory gratifications, such as tasty foods, beautiful sceneries, and exciting adventures.
2 While self-actualization may be the epitome of human needs, lesser needs in this category would include the needs for tranquility, spirituality, caring for other people and living organisms as well as the environment, and meaningfulness of life.
3 Instead of being strictly hierarchical, human needs tend to move in diverse directions after the satisfaction of the physiological survival needs. Some people may strive for achievement and fulfillment needs, while others may settle with stability and entertainment needs. Furthermore, these moves may change with different circumstances at different times for different people. For example, a person may feel the needs for legacy at old age or for altruism by voluntarily sacrificing oneself to save others.
4 The move of needs from one category to another is affected by available resources. These resources are not simply physical or financial resources, such as energy, materials, and financial wealth that provide means and capabilities for managing the physical environment. They also include psychological resources, such as education and knowledge, as well as intellectual and emotional maturity that provide understanding and tools for managing oneself, as well as the interactions with the physical environment and the emotional relationships with other people and living organisms in the world.

Based on these insights, a new model of human needs can be developed with the following characteristics:

1 The needs can be classified into two broad dimensions: the dimension of physical/physiological vs. psychological and the dimension of safety/security-oriented vs. stimulation/growth-oriented.
2 The physical-security needs for survival and subsistence are the most basic.

3   As more physical, financial, intellectual, and emotional resources become available, the needs can move in diverse ways into other needs, even with different combinations of satisfaction for different people at different times.

A broad categorization of human needs is given in Figure 27.3.

Details of the human needs of each category are discussed next with examples given in Figure 27.4.

For the Physical-Security category, the needs start at the lowest level with the survival or subsistence needs of air, water, food, sleep, and shelter and move to needs for physical safety and health and financial viability. With the increasing availability of mainly physical and financial resources, they then move to the needs for financial viability and stability, physical comfort, and conveniences.

For the Psychological-Security category, the needs are more complex. They start with the needs to avoid the unknown, which include the needs of superstitious and even religious beliefs if they are due to the fear of the potential existence of an undesirable afterlife. They expand into the needs for social interactions with others for affinity, relatedness, love, and affection. They then move to the needs for ego protection and/or submission to others to maintain social order and stability. With increasing availability of mainly intellectual and emotional resources, they move to the needs for power, possessiveness, and control of resources and relationships, and finally to the needs of harmony in the social environment.

For the Physical-Stimulation category, the needs start with sensory stimulations and pleasures, such as sex, tasty foods, recreation, entertainment, beautiful sceneries, and exciting adventures.

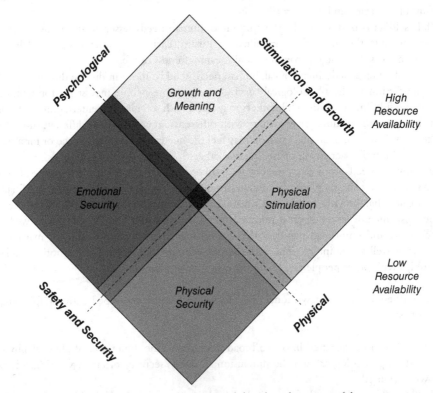

Figure 27.3 Broad categorization of human needs based on the new model

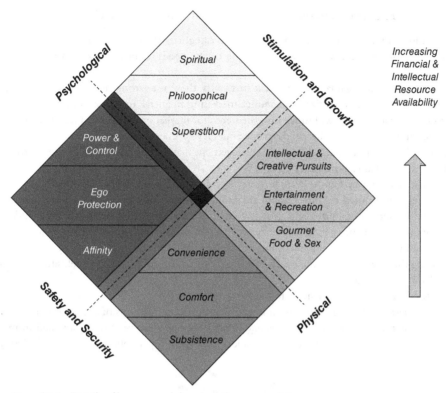

Figure 27.4 Details of human needs based on the new model

They then move with increasing availability of mainly intellectual resources to knowledge acquisition and artistic and other creative pursuits. Interestingly, this category also includes the needs for idleness and relaxation for the pleasures of physiological recovery from stimulations.

Finally, for the Psychological-Stimulation category, the needs start with self-esteem, which is more than ego satisfaction but a sense of value. They then move with increasing availability of mainly emotional resources to empathy and altruism not only for other humans and living organisms but also for the environment as a whole, and eventually to spirituality, morality, and meaningfulness of life.

It is important to note that this categorization of needs is by no means absolute. Many needs can cross over from one category to another. For example, the need for creative pursuits can be a part of the need for self-esteem, and the need for ego protection can also be the beginning of the need for self-esteem. Similarly, the need for harmony in the social environment can also be the need to feel empathetic and altruistic to others.

Furthermore, with increasing resources, the move of needs among the categories can be quite diverse. For example, as financial and intellectual resources increase, a person moves from those in the Physical-Security category to a combination of needs in the other three categories. Moreover, the move may not even be hierarchical. For example, with increasing financial resources, a person may even sacrifice the needs of physical safety and health in the Physical-Security category to satisfy the needs for recreational excitement in the Physical-Stimulation category. Similarly, with increasing emotional maturity, a person may also transcend needs in the Physical-Security category to the needs for spirituality and meaningfulness of life in the Psychological-Stimulation category.

Extensions to the needs of an organization or a society

The new model of human needs can also be used to categorize the collected needs of an organization and the society as a whole. The extension to the needs of an organization is shown in Figure 27.5.

Specifically, for an organization, when it first starts, there is a strong need for financial survival and growth. As the organization acquires increasing financial, technical, and management resources and capabilities, it will move into the needs for market expansion and dominance, and at the same time, it will have the needs to continue development and innovation. Finally, when it achieves a level of financial stability and management maturity, it starts to have the needs for social and even global responsibility.

Similarly, as shown in Figure 27.6, for a society as a whole, when it is at an early stage of development with limited resources, there are strong needs for political stability and economic growth. As the society stabilizes and grows, it then has the increasing needs for independent sovereignty, national security, local influence, and even dominance. Then with further increase in resources and maturity, it has the needs for social equity and international harmony.

Applying the new model to the needs of a society of a small Asian country yields the following results shown in Figure 27.7.

Details of the societal needs are as follows:

For *government* technology innovation investment portfolio decisions of a small Asian democratic country *as an example, Societal Planning Values for the next five years* were obtained from a large group of about 60 societal opinion leaders, including top public officials, key industry

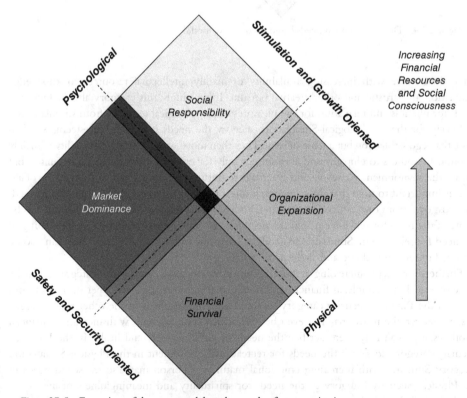

Figure 27.5 Extension of the new model to the needs of an organization

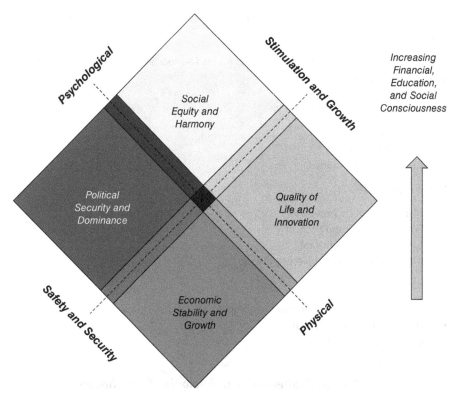

Figure 27.6 Extension of the new model to the needs of a society

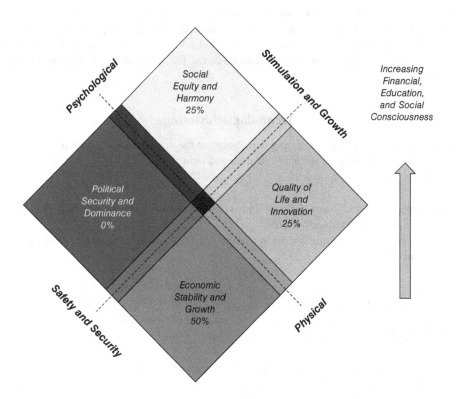

Figure 27.7 Application of the new model to a small Asian country

and business executives, senior technology researchers and social scientists, major educators, top media representatives and artists:

- Economic prosperity (50%)
    - Economic growth
    - Economic stability
    - Increase in value added
- Social equity (25%)
    - Narrowing of income gaps
    - Social welfare improvement
    - Low unemployment rate
    - Care of aged and disabled population
- Life quality (25%)
    - Environmental quality and sustainability
    - Balance of work and leisure
    - General quality of life

Step 2. Identify alternative technologies: form clusters and portfolios

There are generally a large number of alternative technologies available for consideration, which are often difficult to differentiate and compare. Thus, a useful step is to group these alternative technologies into manageable number of clusters and portfolios (i.e. complementary combinations), which once selected can be decomposed in the future to yield individual technologies for further evaluation.

Technology clustering

The objective of technology clustering is to integrate the large number of potential individual technologies into *meaningful, insightful, and manageable* clusters.

There are two basic approaches:

Top-down: The participants, through their knowledge and experience, identify the relevant and important technology clusters.

Bottom-up: The participants are given a large list of technologies to be integrated into various major clusters.

In the application to the small Asian country, the bottom-up approach was used.

To initiate cluster formation, we first divided the list of technologies into major areas: biotech, materials, energy, semiconductors, and information and communications.

To further facilitate clustering, we asked the experts to sort technologies by:

- Shared technology root or developmental processes
- Common practical application or market demand
- Integrated support to societal values and visions

In the actual application, over 250 technologies were initially sorted into six bins:

- Biotech
- Materials Technology
- Energy Technology
- Semiconductor Technology
- Information and Communications Technology
- Other

Each bin yielded multiple clusters (groupings of several technologies).

The initial technology clusters were reviewed again by technology experts to ensure definition clarity and content agreement. Through iterative discussion, differences of expert judgments were reduced and unified. Finally, the process resulted in a total of 42 technology clusters, with the 29 top clusters appearing to be particularly attractive to the societal values of the country.

Step 3. Forecast relationships

In the next step, we need to forecast the perceived future expected values and risks of these major technology clusters. Table 27.1 summarizes the underlying assumptions, representative examples, advantages, pitfalls, and general applicability of six major types of forecasting techniques.

A synergy of forecasting techniques

Technology investments generally have a 3- to 10-year time horizon, which is fraught with uncertainty due to technological advances, economic fluctuations, and socio-political upheavals. A synergy of methods for technology forecasting include:

- Reasoned expert judgments and structural relations as the backbone, due to a lack of credible models and reliable data for the more quantitative methods.
- The experts must be diverse and should include experienced technologists, marketing specialists, business executives, senior government officials, seasoned economists, and sociopolitical researchers.
- Supplementary applications of the more quantitative methods with reasonable assumptions and data research.
- Scenario analysis will be used to manage the uncertainty in highly importance yet highly uncertain relationships.

Scenario analysis

Because of future uncertainties, the scenario analysis method will be discussed in further details.

Many factors in the external business environment, such as global and local socio-economic, technological, and ecological trends, industry structure, government policies, and international relations, can significantly affect the relationships between alternatives and their values to the decision-maker.

Long-term future changes and uncertainties of these factors are generally difficult to forecast. Systematic construction of *decision-focused planning scenarios* can provide:

- an effective envelope for these changes and uncertainties
- the basis for a robust technology investment strategy.

Table 27.1 Summary of major forecasting techniques

	Power of collective wisdom	Potential leading indicators	Continuation of historical patterns	Analogies to well-known phenomena	Structural relations	Causal methods
Underlying assumption	There is power in collective wisdom about the technology development and adoption process	There are potential signs or leading indicators about the technology development and adoption process	Historical patterns or trends will continue due to inherent nature or momentum of the process	The technology development and adoption process is analogous to some well-known phenomena	Technology development and adoption follows a plausible set of structural relations	Causal relations can be mapped for technology development and adoption
Examples	• Delphi – expert opinions • Executive judgments	• Patent analysis • Citation and innovation search	• Trend extrapolation • Growth models • Substitutions	• Technology life cycle • Growth models • Diffusion models	• Relevance tree • Cross-impact matrix	• Techno-economic models • Simulation
Advantages	Good credibility Low cost	Plausibility Relatively low cost	Empirical Short-term momentum	General acceptability and credibility	Systematic and logical	Sophisticated and impressive
Pitfalls	Inherent bias, blind leading the blind	Indicators may be misleading, may miss isolated development	Patterns or trends may not continue as assumed	May be different with the well-known phenomena	Difficult to include feedback loops	Complex, often incomplete and incorrect
Applicability	Far-out technologies with little knowledge	Early warning signs for gradual technology developments	Short-term forecasting with ample data to support validity	Wide applications to forecasting of technology development	Longer-term technology forecasting	An idealistic goal for technology forecasting

Constructing planning scenarios is *conceptually different* from traditional forecast or sensitivity analysis for managing future uncertainties. Strictly speaking, it does *not* develop a single forecast, but rather a set of *structurally different but plausible alternative* scenarios that provides an *envelope to uncertainty* in the future environment.

Specifically, *decision-focused planning scenarios are not*

- Predictions
- Variations around a midpoint/base case
- Generalized views of feared or desired futures
- Products of outside futurists

Rather, they are

- Descriptions of alternative plausible futures
- Significantly, often structurally different views of the future
- Specific decision-focused views of the future
- The result of management insight and perceptions

In a complex and dynamic business environment, the construction of decision-focused planning scenarios can be an effective technology forecasting technique with the following advantages:

- Focus on decision objectives
- A total system view of the decision
- Rich context of alternative futures
- Effective management of uncertainty

On the other hand, a local system-oriented, single realization point forecast, even with sensitivity analysis, is almost always not only wrong but also misleading.

The major iterative steps for scenarios analysis are shown in Figure 27.8.

An application of scenario analysis

The application of scenario analysis for technology portfolio planning for the small Asian country is described in the following sections.

Decision factors

Decision focus and elements pinpoint the *choices* we need to make. We initially assume that our decision will *not* significantly affect external environment, which is the focus of the scenario development process.

Key decision factors are the *key issues in the external environment* that directly affect our decision and that we want to forecast. They often include:

- Technology development
- Market demand growth
- Industry structure
- Government regulations
- Resource requirements
- International relations

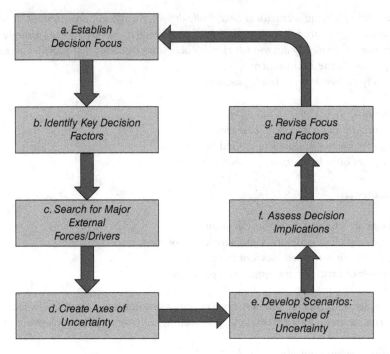

Figure 27.8 Scenario analysis process

Micro and macro forces are *major drivers of changes* in the external environment and the basic causes of future uncertainty, based on which we develop scenarios. Scenario implications are *preliminary assessment of the general impacts* of the scenarios on key decision factors and eventually our decision. Finally, scenarios of the external environment may be refined by our decision through *iterations* of the scenario development process.

External forces

A list of external forces affecting the decision is provided in Figure 27.9 in accordance with their impacts and uncertainties.

We further use global mega-trends as the basis for uncertainty assessment, which include:

- Society:
  - Knowledge society
  - Aging population
  - Continued urbanization
  - Urban crowding
  - Income polarization

- Politics:
  - Regional competition and cooperation
  - International organizations
  - Terrorism

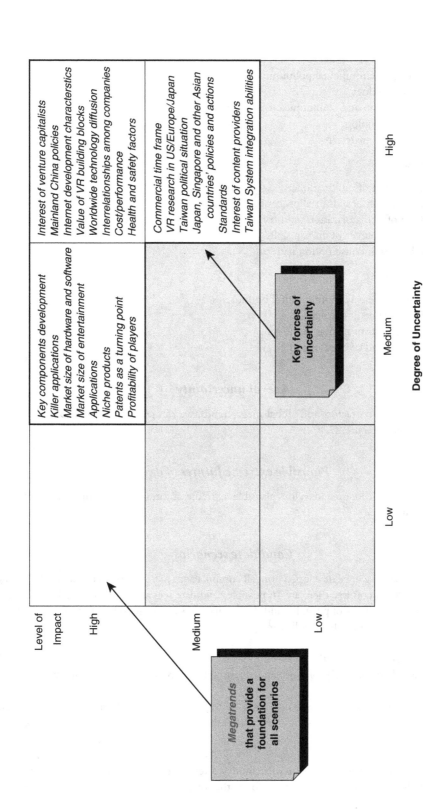

Figure 27.9 Example of external forces

- Technology:
  - Global environmental pollution
  - Biotechnology
  - Information and communications technology
  - Nanotechnology
  - Intelligent materials

- Economy:
  - Expansion of multinationals
  - Revolution of industrial processes
  - Rise of miniaturization industry
  - Shifting sources of human skills
  - Changes in consumption patterns

- Environment:
  - Environment without political boundaries
  - Global climatic changes
  - Limitations of natural resources
  - Widespread of diseases and plagues

Axes of uncertainty

Based on the decision factors and global mega-trends, we can create the major axes of uncertainty as shown in Figure 27.10.

Plausible extreme futures of axes

For each axis, we can then develop plausible extreme futures. Two examples are given in Tables 27.2 and 27.3.

Candidate scenarios

Candidate scenarios can be developed from all combinations of the extreme futures of these axes. For the small Asian country, there are 16 possible candidate scenarios as shown in Table 27.4.

However, the number of possible candidate scenarios is too large to be of practical use. They need to be reduced through the following guidelines:

- Each should be *"structurally" different*.
- Each should be *internally consistent* and a natural fit of components into a "story line."
- Each should be *plausible*.
- Each must have *decision making utility* as a "test bed" for assessing alternative future actions.
- Together, the cases selected should span the realm of plausible future worlds, or the "*envelope of uncertainty.*"

For the application to the small Asian country, after eliminating redundancy and inconsistency and being responsive to the decision focus, the following final scenarios in Table 27.5 were selected.

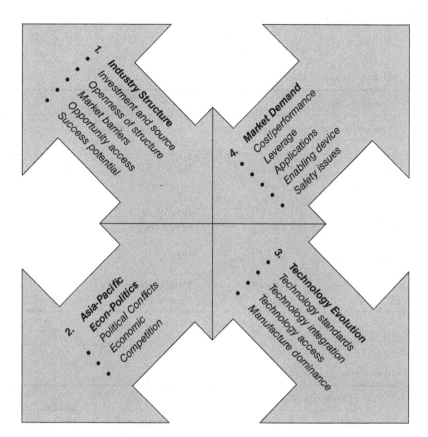

Figure 27.10 Axes of uncertainty

Table 27.2 Example of plausible extreme futures of an axis

Virtual reality industry structure axis	
Alternative	Rationale
Combative fragmented	• Low investment mainly from corporations • Protective structure with high market barriers • Limited access to opportunities
Cooperative integrated	• Heavy investments and many from venture capitalists • Open structure with international cooperation • Full access to opportunities and many small companies have major successes

Table 27.3 Another example of plausible extreme futures of an axis

Technology evolution axis	
Alternative	Rationale
Stuck/disjointed	• Fragmented development • No standards • Disjoint development • Dominance by component manufacturers and patent barriers
Breakthrough	• Coordinated development • Standards achieved • System integration works • Easy access to technology

Table 27.4 Candidate scenarios

Candidate scenario	Uncertainty axes			
	1 Industry structure	2 Asia-Pacific econ-politics	3 Technology evolution	4 Market demand
1	Combative fragmented	Closed	Stuck disjointed	Expensive specialized
2	C/F	Closed	S/D	Cheap mass market
3	C/F	Closed	Breakthrough	E/S
4	C/F	Closed	Breakthrough	MM
...	...	...	...	...
14	Cooperative integrated	Open	S/D	MM
15	C/I	Open	Breakthrough	E/S
16	C/I	Open	Breakthrough	CMM

Table 27.5 Final scenarios

Scenario	Uncertainty axis			
	1 Industry structure	2 Asia-Pacific econo-politics	3 Technology evolution	4 Market demand
(5) Life in hell	Combative fragmented	Closed	Stuck disjointed	Expensive specialized
(12) left behind	Cooperative integrated	Closed	Breakthrough	Cheap Mass Market
(14) Waiting for technology spring	Cooperative integrated	Open	Stuck disjointed	Cheap mass market

Step 4. Strategic insights from factor analysis and strategy maps

The next step is to generate strategic insights from factor analysis. Again using the application to the small Asian country as an example, a set of important attributes of an alternative was selected as *factors*. Using a technology cluster as an example, the major factors may include the following:

Value/importance related:

- Strategic Importance
- Commercial Value
- Commercial Timing

Risk related:

- Risks – Business and Technical
- Current Position in Technology Competition
- Technology Availability

Technology innovation investment

These factors can be expanded and customized for individual applications. They will eventually be integrated and quantified into combined expected importance and combined expected risk through multi-factor evaluation methods, such as the analytic hierarchy process (Saaty, 2008).

For each factor, there needs to be initially a *clear definition*, albeit a qualitative one. Again using the technology cluster as an example:

- *Strategic Importance* – Importance of the technology development as a sustained competitive advantage to the business area
- *Commercial Value* – Size of the financial impact to the company if the technology is successful
- *Commercial Timing* – Time at which the market will adopt or buy this technology at an acceptable business level and at which the competitor will use it commercially
- *Risks* – Likelihood that the technology will fail to accomplish its technical objectives and that, if technically successful, it will fail commercially
- *Current Position* – Strength and ability of the company versus competitors in developing the technology today
- *Technology Availability* – Availability of technology from any source for commercialization

Based on these definitions, we can develop for each factor a set of measures. Again using the technology cluster as an example, typical measures include the following:

- *Strategic Importance* – Degree of impact based on market share, product differentiation, cost efficiency, and market entry speed
- *Commercial Value* – Net present value, return on investment, revenue from increased sales, and other financial measures
- *Commercial Timing* – Calendar time in years with estimated probability
- *Risks* – Probabilities of technical and commercial failures based on internal capability and resource availability and external market size, position, and future uncertainty
- *Current Position* – Degree of strength based on past experience, existing patents, and current capability of the company versus competitors
- *Technology Availability* – Number of sources and their willingness to license

Table 27.6 provides an example of these measures.
These strategic factors are graphically represented in Figure 27.11.

Table 27.6 Example of factor measures

Factors							
Measure	Importance (market impact)	Value (NPV)	Timing (years)	Inverse risks (probability of success)	Position	Availability
High	Major, broad	>$500 M	0–2	>60%	World leader	Readily
Medium	Significant in some key segments	$50-$500 M	3–7	30–60%	Credible follower	Limited
Low	Minor or isolated	<$50 M	>8	<30%	Not Competitive	None

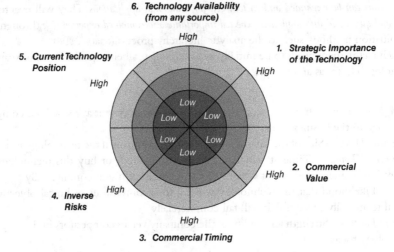

Figure 27.11 Graphical representation of factors

Effective factor analysis has the following emphases:

- To avoid double-counting of their effects, the factors should be as *uncorrelated* with each other as possible.
- To be strategic, the definitions should be made with the perspective of the overall *corporate objective, market conditions, and competitive environment*.
- To avoid ambiguity but without undue effort, the measure should be specified *as clear and quantifiable as practical*.
- Factor analysis should be applied to evaluate each alternative *in a given scenario*.
- The analytic hierarchy process can be applied if *more precision* is desired.

Generate insights from strategic maps

A strategy map is a useful tool for examining the *interactions and balances* between two factors for each alternative in a given scenario. These interactions and balances can provide strategic directions for technology development. Figures 27.12 to 27.16 present a number of illustrative examples based on technology clusters.

Integrated factor analysis can reveal the *robustness* of technology clusters across scenarios and the *strength* of the portfolio within each scenario.

Example: Factor #1 – Strategic Importance of the Technology

Technology	Scenario			Overall
Cluster	A	B	C	Rating
1	MH	MM	MH	MH
2	HL	LH	MH	MM
3	LM	LM	LM	LM
4	MH	ML	LH	ML
Etc.				
Overall portfolio	MM	LH	ML	ML

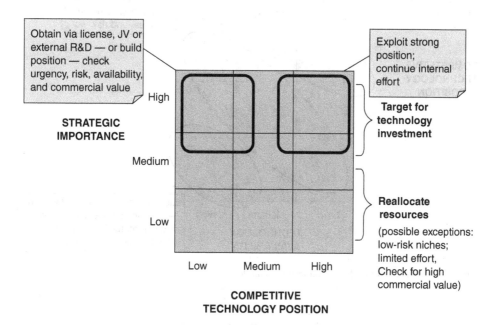

Figure 27.12 STRATEGY MAP: Illustrative example 1

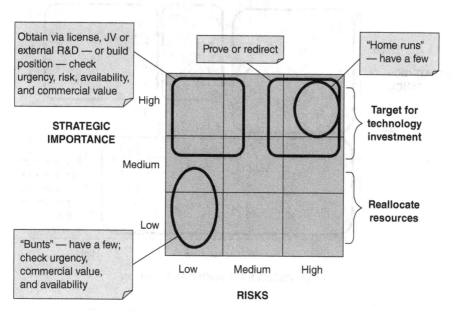

Figure 27.13 STRATEGY MAP: Illustrative example 2

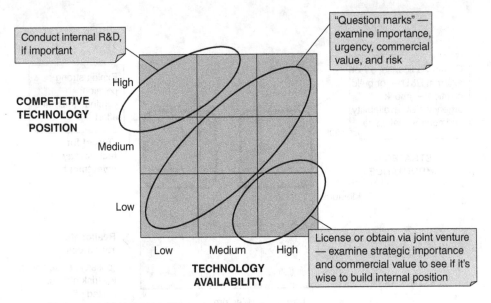

Figure 27.14 STRATEGY MAP: Illustrative example 3

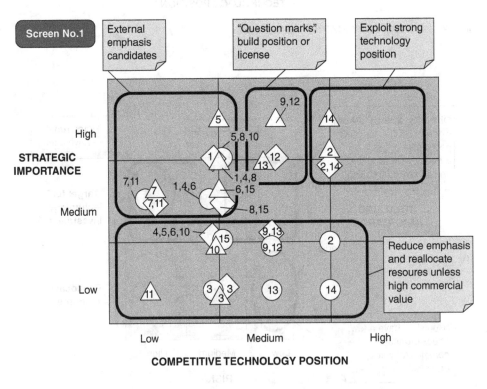

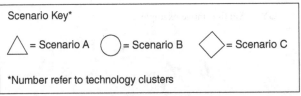

Figure 27.15 STRATEGY MAP: Illustrative example 1 for qualitative portfolio evaluation

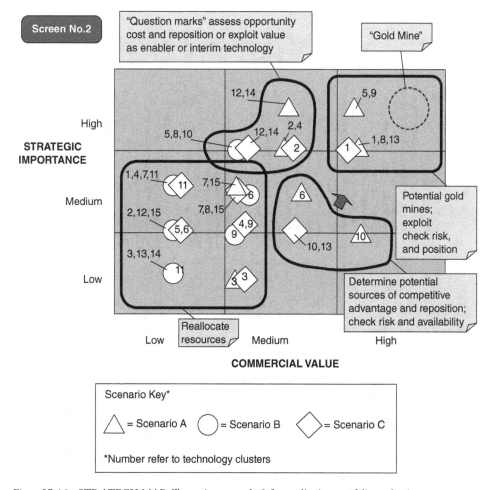

Figure 27.16 STRATEGY MAP: Illustrative example 2 for qualitative portfolio evaluation

The strategy maps can also provide insights about how the portfolio may be *strengthened and improved*.

For the application to the small Asian country, a summary strategic map for combined value and risk is shown in Figure 27.17.

Step 5. Find the optimal portfolio using modern portfolio theory

Based on modern portfolio theory(Markowitz, 1952), all feasible investment portfolios in terms of perceived expected returns (values) and risks are collectively shown as the green region in Figure 27.18. The efficient frontier is the envelope of the best investment portfolios, that is, the collection of portfolios that have the highest returns for a given level of risk, or equivalently, those have the lowest risks for a given level of return. The efficient frontier has been proven to be concave in nature. However, the efficient frontier has a potentially infinite number of best portfolios. For a specific investor, the optimal portfolio will also be determined by the indifference or equal-preference curves of the investor shown by label I in Figure 27.18. An indifference

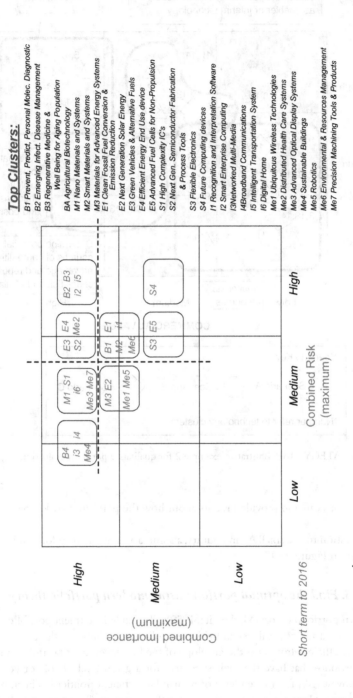

Figure 27.17 STRATEGY MAP: Combined importance vs. combined risk

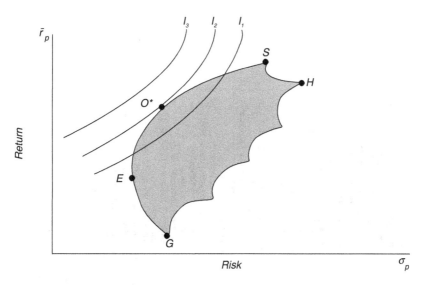

Figure 27.18 Modern portfolio theory

or equal-preference curve is a curve on which the investment portfolios with different returns and risks are indifferent or of equal degree of preference to the investor. The indifference curves of an investor are necessarily parallel to one another (to avoid the contradiction that if two curves should cross each other, then the portfolio at the crossing point would have two different degrees of preference to the investor), proven to be convex in nature, and the more northwestern a curve lies in Figure 27.18, the higher degree of preference to the investor. However, investment portfolios on an indifference curve lying above the efficient frontier are infeasible, and those on a curve lying below the efficient frontier are clearly suboptimal. Thus, the optimal investment portfolio for a specific investor occurs at the *tangential point of the convex indifference curves and the concave efficient frontier* as shown by the point "O" in Figure 27.18.

For the application to the small Asian country, the positions of the technology innovation investments for various technology clusters and the efficient frontier are shown in Figure 27.19. The portfolio the with the lowest risk (i.e., B4, i3, i4, and Me4) in Figure 27.18 has been adjusted for the government investor to have a lower return so that the higher-return portion of the portfolio will be taken by private industry investors.

Dependent on the government indifference curve, or degree of risk tolerance, the best investment portfolio will be one of those on the efficient frontier. Additionally, selection of an optimal portfolio will consider:

- The *robustness* under different scenarios
- The *risk tolerance* of the decision-maker for different time horizons

Step 6. Explore implementation policy implications

Finally, Figure 27.20 provides the government implementation policy implications for the technology innovation investments portfolio. For each of the three areas of the investment portfolio, the policy levers are further depicted in Figures 27.21–27.23.

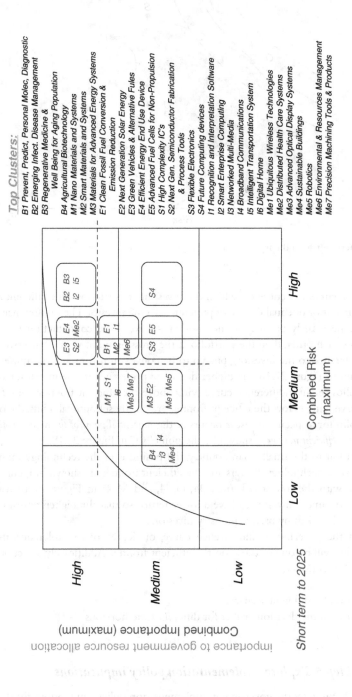

Figure 27.19 Portfolio revised for government investment

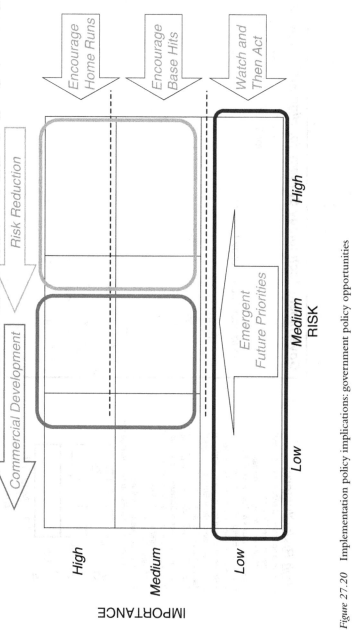

Figure 27.20 Implementation policy implications: government policy opportunities

Risk Reduction Portfolio (16 Clusters)

High Risk Clusters:
B2 Emerging Infect. Disease Management
B3 Regenerative Medicine &
   Well Being for Aging Population
E3 Green Vehicles & Alternative Fuels
E4 Efficient Energy End use Device
S2 Next Gen. Semiconductor Fabrication Process Tools
I1 Recognition and Interpretation Software
I2 Next generation Solar Energy
Me2 Distributed Health Care Systems
B1 Prevent, Predict, Personal Molec. Diagnostic
E1 Clean Fossil Fuel Conversion & Emission Reduction
E5 Advanced Fuel Cells for Non-Propulsion
M2 Smart Materials & Systems
S3 Flexible Electronics
S4 Future Computing Devices
Me6 Environmental & Resources Management

Government Technology Strategy for High Risk Clusters

| | Support Innovator Vision | Support Integrator Vision |

Top Impact Tech. Policy Levers:

- Recruit foreign talent

- Government Support/
  sponsored R&D/
  Center of Excellence/
  National R&D center

- Internatioanl Joint
  Research & Cooperation

- Market Intelligence/
  Technology Foresight

- IP Planning & Development

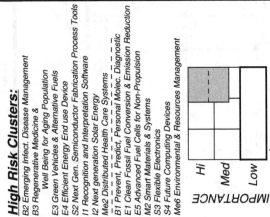

Figure 27.21 Policy levers: risk reductions for high-risk clusters

Commercial Development Portfolio (15 Clusters)

Medium Risk Clusters:

B4 Agricultural Biotechnology
M1 Nano Materials and Systems
S1 High Complexity IC's
I3 Networked Multi-Media
I4 Broadband Communications
I6 Digital Home
Me3 Advanced Optical Display Systems
Me4 Sustainable Buildings
Me7 Precision machining Tools & Products
M3 Materials for Advanced Energy Systems
E2 Next Generation Solar Energy
I2 Smart Enterprise Computing
I5 Intelligent Transportation System
Me1 Ubiquitous Wireless Technologies
Me5 Robotics

Government Technology Strategy for Medium Risk Clusters

Support Innovator Vision   *Support Integrator Vision*

Top Impact Tech. Policy Levers:

- Infrastructure building
- Regulation/Deregulation
- Active Incubators
- Tax incentives/Tax holidays
- Promote local industry alliance
- Grant to enterprise for R&D or technology transfer

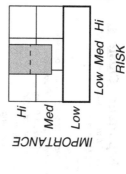

Figure 27.22 Policy levers: commercialization of medium-risk clusters

Emergent Opportunities Portfolio (11 Clusters)

Low Importance Clusters:

B5 Implant. & Min. Invasive Medical Devices
M5 Medica Materials
M6 Fibers
M7 Catalysts
E6 Advanced Batteries for Non-Propulsion
E7 Alternative Liquid Fuel Production
E8 Wind and Ocean Power
S5 Energy Semiconductor
S6 Trusted System
I7 Pervasive Learning
Me7 Exotiv Transportation

Government Technology Strategy for Emergent Clusters

Support *Innovator Vision* Support *Integrator Vision*

Top Impact Tech. Policy Levers:

- Market Intelligence/ Technology Foresight
- Public education sites/ Public awareness (K-12 Curriculum & Teacher development & Science education for Public)
- Support for small business start-ups
- International Cooperation
- Recruit foreign talent

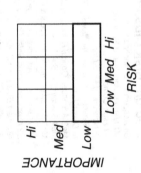

Figure 27.23 Policy levers: observing and assisting low-importance clusters

Summary

A *systems approach* has been used to develop a step-by-step technology investment portfolio planning process that has been successfully applied to large corporations and government agencies around the world.

The major advantages of the process include:

- *Systematic and transparent* approach.
- *Holistic* approach to understand values of the decision-maker.
- *Expert-based* identification and formation of alternative technology clusters and portfolios.
- *Scenario-based* assessment of the uncertain relationships between alternative portfolios and values.
- *Use of simple management tools* for strategic insights.
- *Modern portfolio theory-based* selection of the optimal portfolio.

Potential future extensions include *simplified* processes for:

- VC investment planning and due diligence analysis
- Personal technology purchase planning.

References

Adie, J., Duda, J. L. and Ntoumanis, N. (1988). Autonomy support, basic need satisfaction and the optimal functioning of adult male and female sport participants: a test of basic needs theory. *Motivation & Emotion*, 32, 189–199.

Alderfer, C. P. (1969). An empirical test of a new theory of human needs. *Organizational Behavior and Human Performance*, 4, 142–175.

Markowitz, H. M. (1952). Portfolio selection. *The Journal of Finance*, 7, 77–91.

Maslow, A. H. (1943). A theory of human motivation. *Psychological Review*, 50, 370–396.

Max-Neef, Manfred A., Elizalde, A. and Hopenhayn, M. (1991). *Human scale development*. The Apex Press.

McClelland, D. (1988). *Human motivation*. Cambridge University Press.

Neher, A. (1991). Maslow's theory of motivation: a critique. *Journal of Humanistic Psychology*, 31, 89–112.

Saaty, T. L. (2008). *Decision making for leaders: the analytic hierarchy process for decisions in a complex world*. RWS Publications.

Wabha, M. A. and Bridwell, L. G. (1976). Maslow reconsidered: a review of research on the need hierarchy theory. *Organization Behavior and Human Performance*, 15, 212–240.

INDEX

Note: *Italicized* page numbers indicate a figure on the corresponding page. Page numbers in **bold** indicate a table on the corresponding page.

2.5-inch hard disk drive (HDD) 223
3D computer-aided design (CAD) 239–240
3D printing 297, 355
3M Company 12, 15

absence of ownership in service innovation 39–40
accidental encounter in serendipity 345
accountability in innovation 315
Achievement-Authority-Affiliation Theory 563
active innovation 429–430
adaptive systems 75–76
added value 131
Adie, James 563
aftermath serendipity 349–350
agent-based modelling: computational economics 544–545; computational modelling in social sciences 539–541; defined 540; empirical data 540–541; firm perspectives 547–554; in innovation studies 541, 544–545; introduction to 539; IPSE programme 553; multinational corporations 552–553; network analysis 542–544; responsible research and innovation 551–552; simulations 539–540, 545–547; SKIN model 548–553; small and medium enterprises 550–551; user-driven innovation 551–552; utility in managerial practice 553–554
Agreement on Trade Related Aspects of Intellectual Property Rights (TRIPs) 138, 139
Alderfer, Clayton 563
alignment, defined 116
ambidextrous leadership 124–125
analytic hierarchy process (AHP) 241
Annual Global R&D Funding Forecast (2017) 6
Ant Financial 34

anticipating requirement of responsible innovation 314–315
antitrust and patent protection 136–137
Apache open-source web server 173
Apple iPhone 280
architectural innovation 35
Arizona State University 327
articulation and knowledge 62
artificial intelligent (AI) technology *see* smart prototyping
artificial neural network 257–258
assessment standards of responsible innovation 318–321, *319*, *320*
Association of European Science & Technology Transfer Professionals (ASTP-Proton) 408
Association of University Technology Managers (AUTM) 408
Atomic Energy Research Establishment (AERE) 405
attention and knowledge 59
augmentation strategy in disruptive innovation 224–225, 227
augmented real prototyping 246, 248, 267
augmented virtual prototyping 246, 248, 267
authentic leadership 126–127
authoritarianism 124
AutoDesk Fusion 360 software 240
auto-ethnography 443
automated external defibrillator (AED) 224
automotive industry case study 283–287
Autonomy-Competence-Relatedness Theory 563
autonomy of technical knowledge workers 397

Index

Bai Chunli 332
battery core development 229–230
Bayerische Motoren Werke (BMW): agile process models 286; collaboration 286–287; collaboration partner/networks 285; company/industry data 283; innovation management 284–285; introduction to 283; organizational impacts 286; products and services 283–284
Bayh-Dole Act (1981) 408, 472–473
Becquerel, Henri 350
Bentham, Jeremy 136
big data 92
Big Future of Management (Hamel) 50
Binder, Gordon 404
Bloomberg Innovation Index (2018) 6
BMW Group 12
Boeing 210
boom-recession-depression-recovery cycle 26
Boston Consulting Group (BCG) 7, 82
bottom of pyramid (BOP) 221, 269, 271, 275
breadboard prototyping 246, 248, 249, 266
breakthrough innovation 42, 43–47, *44*, *45*, **46**
British Standards Institute (BSI) 81, 133, 495–498
British Telecom (BT) 410
broadcast search 211
BS 7000 Design Management Systems 495–498
business management practices 195–197
business maturity 197–198
business model innovation 41–42
business R&D internationalization 416
Buurtzorg organization 23–24
BYD company 229–230

CAD/3D prototyping 246, 248, 268
candidate scenarios in technology innovations 574–576, *575*, **575–576**
Cantillon, Richard 30–31
capability viewpoint of open innovation 192
Carson, Shelley 22
case study research methods 324–325
causal exploration of logic 350
causation processes 350
Center for Innovation Management Studies (CIMS) 80
Center for Research in Security Prices (CRSP) 109, 110
Centrino chipsets (Intel) 225
CEN/TS 16555 standard 494–495
ceveloped/developing countires and entrepreneurship *147*, 147–151, *149*, **151**, **152**
change-oriented organizational behavior 115
characteristic leadership 116–117
Chesbrough, Henry 280
chief innovation officer (CIO) 371–372
China: battery core development 229–230; corporate development lag 8, 9; digital revolution 394, 395; disruptive innovation R&D strategies 229–232; e-bike industry 230; economic reforms 94; electrocardiogram 231–232; innovation term 11, 12–13; innovative culture 401–402; microwave market 231; mini-washer market 231; nanotechnology in 330–332, **331**; people-centric innovation 410; product development phase 273–274; R&D facilities in 269; refrigerated containers sector 230–231; technological innovation audit 521; ultrasound machine 231–232
China Credit Information Service 111
China International Marine Containers (Group) Co., Ltd. 12
Chinese Academy of Engineering 330
Chinese Academy of Sciences 330, 332
ChotuKool refrigerator 228–229
Christensen, Clayton M. 45
CIMC company 230–231
city innovation system 300–301
co-creation in open innovation 205
cognition and knowledge 59–60
cognitive disinhibition (CD): associated concepts 20–22, **21**, **22**; defined 19–20; introduction to 17–19; people management implications 23–24; research study findings 22–23
collaboration in open innovation 205
collaborative work 406–407
collective identity 117
collective learning 131
collective-level constructs 55
collective-level creativity 62
collective memory 396–397
commercialization efforts 32
commercialization phase 274–275
commitment, defined 116
communal serendipity 349
Communist Party of China 330
competency-based management 134
competing for the future 76
competitive advantages 129–130, 133–135
component innovation 34–35
Compustat 109, 110
computational economics 544–545
computational modelling in social sciences 539–541
computer-aided manufacturing (CAM) 37
computerized numerical control (CNC) 36
concurrent engineering 365–366
conduciveness to innovation 354
Confucian culture 14
connectome 17
contextual factors in serendipity 356–357
continuous innovation 47
convergence innovation: country-level perspectives on 303–304; introduction to 50, 297–298; micro-level perspectives on 301–302; past

studies on 298–301, *300*; regional-level perspectives on 302–303; summary of 304
CoPS innovation 35–36, **36**
core competencies: competitive advantages 133–135; concept of 130–131; introduction to 129–130; reasons for including 132–133; strategic management of innovation 129–135; types of 132
corporate competitiveness 6–7, *7*
corporate culture 215
corporate entrepreneurship 134
corporate innovation management 7–10, **8**, **9**, **10**, 387–389
corporate portals 366
corporate strategy 109–113
Costik, John 169
cost structure 42
CPC National Congress 330
creation and innovation 30
Creative Flow Test 22
Creative Mindsets Questionnaire 22
creative potential of brain 18–19
creativity and knowledge 61–62
creativity in innovation management 363–365
crowdsourcing 210–211
customer relationships 42, 132
customers in accelerators 370

Dacia Logan 274
Day, George 147
decision factors in technology innovations 571–574, *572*, *573*
decision-making power 115, 186
decision process 560–561
decision support systems 366
decision tree algorithm 255
Def Con cybersecurity conference 394
deliberate–spontaneous conflict 20
Department of Justice (DOJ) 110
Department of Trade and Industry (UK) 9
design thinking 510–512
detour serendipity 348
developed markets (DM) 269–271, 274
developmental leadership 128–129
digital age innovation: agile methodologies and design thinking 282; automotive industry case study 283–287; external cooperation 292; financial services industry case study 287–290; internal changes in methods 292; introduction to 278–279; key new technologies 281; open innovation and ecosystems 280; process model for 291, *291*; Scrum framework 279–280; in service industries 281–282; service innovation ecosystems 282–283; stage-gate model 279; summary of 292–293; theoretical background 279–283; Triple-A System 279
digital revolution 394

dimensions of merit 175
direction for innovation activities 85
directive leadership 114–115
discontinuous innovation 45, 47–49, *48*
discovery-driven planning 76
disruptive innovation R&D strategies: augmentation strategy 224–225, 227; in China 229–232; for developed markets 221–227, **222**, **226**; for emerging markets 227–234; exploitation strategy 225–226, 227; in India 228–229, **233**; introduction to 45, 220–221; miniaturization strategy 222–223, 226, 228; simplification strategy 223–224, 227, 228; summary of 234–235
Disruptive Technologies: Advances That Will Transform Life, Business and the Global Economy by 2025 report 4
distributed leadership 122
distribution channels 42
diversity 300, 317, 399
document management systems 366
drastic manufacturing cost reduction 232, 234
Dreamliner airplane 210
Drucker, Peter 41, 343
DUI mode of technological innovation 185–186
Dutch Research Council 436

early-stage entrepreneurs 150–151
Eastern wisdom and innovation 50–51
e-bike industry, China 230
econometric foundation 140
economic and technological development zone (ETDZ) 28
economic globalization/competition 8
economic growth 6
ecosystems 66–67, 280, 384–387
effectiveness/efficiency increase 421
effectual exploration of logic 350–351
electrocardiogram (ECG) 231–232
emerging markets (EM) 269–272, 275–276
end-to-end processes 73
Engineering and Science Research Council (EPSRC) 435
entrepreneurial leadership 128
Entrepreneurial Leadership Questionnaire 128
entrepreneurial spirit 14
entrepreneurship: characteristics of 146–147; developed/developing countires *147*, 147–151, *149*, **151**, **152**; empirical literature 152–153; innovation and 30–31; introduction to 141–144; life-cycle strategy 144–146; strategic management of innovation 141–153
environmental innovation (EI) 94–98, *95*, **96**, **99**, 484–485
environmental-related patterns of serendipity 347
Ericsson company 206
ethical advisory board (EAB) 447–448

Index

ethical responsibility 310
"Eureka" moment 347
European Commission (EC) 108, 328, 329, 436, 551
European Committee for Standardization (CEN) 81
European Foundation for Quality Management (EFQM) 82
European nanotechnology 328–330
European Union (EU) 307–308, 328–329, 435
Existence-Relatedness-Growth Theory 563
experimental research in smart prototyping 243–246, *244*, *245*
experimental setup in smart prototyping 246–249, *247*, **249**, *249*
experimentation, defined 351
expert syndrome 397–398
explicit knowledge 64
exploitation strategy in disruptive innovation 225–226, 227
external forces in technology innovations 572–573, *573*
external innovation 189–191
externalization of tacit knowledge 64
external knowledge 186, 204
external source theory of technological innovation 186–187
extremity 93
extrinsic motivation 57, 58

false generalization risks 245
family leadership 122–123
Federal Trade Commission (FTC) 110
female leadership 129
financial services industry case study 287–290
FinTechs (financial technology) start-ups 287–288, 290
firm-level innovation 56–57, *57*, 62–63
firm perspectives on agent-based modelling 547–554
Foege, Alec 3
follow-up knowledge in serendipity 346
forecasting relationships in technology innovations 569–571, **570**
for-profit organisations 370
Fortune 500 companies 269
Fortune's Annual Change the World List (2017) 34
free innovation paradigm: introduction to 169–171, **170**; major research findings 175–176, **176**; need for 174–175; producer innovation paradigms *171*, 171–174, 176–177
Freeman, Christophe 27
frugal engineering 232, 234
frugal innovation: commercialization phase 274–275; introduction to 269–270, *270*; mind-set 271, *271*; need identification phase 272–273; outcome of 275–276; process of 272–275; product/service development phase 273–274; summary of 276
fused deposition modeling (FDM) 240
Future Emerging Technology (FET) Flagship Human Brain Project (HBP) 435–436
fuzzy front end in innovation management 363–365

Galanz company 231
General Data Protection Regulation (GDPR) 394–395
General Electric (GE) 231–232
General Motors (GM) 34
generative design *240*, 240–241, 246, 248, 268
German financial services industry case study 287–290
Getinge Groups 274
Gilbert, Nigel 545–547
Global Entrepreneurship Monitor (GEM) 148
Global Innovation Index (GII) 395
globalization 269, 298
Gloor, Peter 181
governance of innovation 98, 416–424, *417*, *419*, *422*
government-led projects 301–302
government technology innovation 566
Grameen Shakti company 272, 273–274
graphical user interface (GUI) technology 205
GREAT-SKIN app 551–552
green innovation management 94–98, **99**
gross domestic product (GDP) 35, 39, 171
groupware 366

Haier Group 12, 14, 231, 273
Hamel, Gary 50
Hansen Transmission International 229
harmless principle of innovation 310
Helicobacter pylori (H. pylori) discovery 349
heterogeneity in service innovation 38
hidden design parameters 378
high-impact offerings 403
high-performance innovation teams 372–373
holistic innovation (HI) **49**, 49–52, *52*
holistic innovation management (HIM) 51
horizontal integration 298
Human Brain Project (HBP): changing networks of responsibility 448–450, *449*; development of collaboration 444–445; ethical and social concerns 443–446; ethics management 447–448, 450–451; governance of data and platforms 444; introduction to 443; networked responsibilities 446; remote issues 445; responsible research and innovation 446–447; responsible research practice 444; survey 445–446
human brain stimulation 442–451

Index

human development and innovation management 3–4, **4**
human factor in innovation: autonomy 397; brief review 395; collaborative work 406–408; content *vs.* process 396–397; drivers of change 394–395; expert syndrome 397–398; implication for management 400–404, *403, 404*; innovation culture 401; introduction to 393–396; mysteries of creation 393–394; organisational stability 398–399; people-centric technology transfer 404–411; project leaders 402–404; researchers-entrepreneurs 399–400; summary of 411; team diversity 399; technical knowledge workers 396–400; university-firm collaborative research 405–407, *406*; walk-around manager 402
human needs model 563–565, *564, 565*
human resource (HR) systems 14
human resource management (HRM) 114
humorous leadership 125–126

IBM computer systems 378
idea contests 209–210, **210**, 212
implementation policy implications 583, *584–588*
improvement of R&D&I Management 493–494
inbound increase 420
inclusion element in responsible innovation 312–314, **313**
incremental innovation 42, 43, 44, **44**, *45*, **46**, 205
India: ChotuKool refrigerator 228–229; disruptive innovation R&D strategies 228–229, **233**; Suzlon 229; Tata Motors 228; Tata Research Development and Design Centre 229
industrial environment 278
Industrial Internet 51
industrial research reports 81–82
industrial revolution 3
Industrial Scrum Framework for New Product Development (Scrum framework) 279–280
information and communication technologies (ICT) 403
information and communication technology (ICT) 298
INFSO-SKIN app 550–551
initial public offering (IPO) 410
InnoCamp model 512–513
innovation: active innovation 429–430; architectural innovation 35; basic types 33–38; breakthrough innovation 42, 43–47, **44**, *45*, **46**; business model innovation 41–42; categorization matrix 37, *37*; component innovation 34–35; continuous innovation 47; CoPS innovation 35–36, **36**; creation and 30; defined 26–28; discontinuous innovation 47–49, *48*; entrepreneurship and 30–31; governance of 98, 416–424, *417, 419, 422*; holistic innovation **49**, 49–52, *52*; incremental innovation 42, 43; invention and 30; levels of 42–47, *44, 45*, **46**; nature of **32**, 32–33, *33*; process innovation 36–37; product innovation 33–36; R&D and 31–32, 418–424; relevant concepts 30–32; research and development 12–13; responsible innovation 99–103, **100, 101**, *102, 103*; service innovation 37–41, **39**; servitization of manufacturing 40; success factors in **29**, 29–30; technological changes and 28, 28–29; technology leadership 29; value of 3–15
Innovation Capability Maturity Model (ICMM v2) 502
Innovation Compass framework 82
innovation culture 401
innovation ecosystems (IE) 384–387
innovation management (IM): articulation and knowledge 62; attention and knowledge 59; BMW case study 284–285; cognition and knowledge 59–60; corporate competitiveness 6–7, *7*; corporate management 7–10, **8, 9**, *10*; creativity and knowledge 61–62; culture of 14–15; ecosystem growth 66–67; emerging challenges 428–429; firm-level innovation 56–57, *57*, 62–63; green innovation management 94–98, **99**; human development and 3–4, **4**; implications for 65; importance of 9–10, *10*; institutional design of innovation 417–418, *425*, 425–428, *426*; integration framework *11*, 11–15; Internet+ age 91–94, **92**; knowledge-based view of 63–64; learning systems 65–66; management systems 66; memory and knowledge 60–61; micro foundations of 55–63; motivation and knowledge 57–59, **58**, 62; national/regional competitiveness 4–6, **5**; organizational learning 64–65; organization of 12–13; of resources 13–14; value of innovation 3–15
Innovation Policy Simulation for the Smart Economy (IPSE) 553
Innovation Work Behavior (IWB) Questionnaire 128
inseparability in service innovation 38
inside-out open innovation 183
Institute of Management Science & Strategy of Zhejiang University 80
institutional design of innovation: active innovation 429–430; governance of innovation 416–424, *417, 419, 422*; innovation management 417–418, *425*, 425–428, *426*; introduction to 415–416
institutional situation of responsible innovation 316–318
intangibility in service innovation 38
Integrated Innovation Maturity Model (I2MM) 502–505
Intel 225

Index

intellectual leap in serendipity 345–346
intellectual property (IP): alliances, networks, and innovation 467–468; article profiles 459–466, *460*, *461*, *462*, **463–465**; intangible assets and innovation 466–467; introduction to 6, 457–458; management and innovation 470–472; patenting 468–470; study methodology 458–459, **458–459**; summary of 473–474; university technology transfer 472–473
intellectual property rights (IPRs) 171, 380, 457
interactive leadership 116
interconnectedness of smart products 278
interdisciplinarity 92
interface management of innovation 365–367
internal incentive systems 215–216
internal innovation 189–191
internalization of explicit knowledge 64
International Institute for Management Development (IMD) 394
internationalization 66, 140, 152, 353, 386, 416, 466–467
International Organization for Standardization (ISO) 81
international standardization 81
Internet+ age 91–94, **92**
Internet of Things (IoT) 297
interorganizational relations: corporate innovation and 387–389; ecosystems and 384–387; introduction to 377; modularity and labor divisions 377–379; strategic alliances 383–384; university as engine for 379–382
intra-industry convergence 301
intra-inter-firm networks 153
intrinsic motivation 57, 58
invention and innovation 30
iSIM (Integrated Service Innovation Method) **499**, 499–500
ISO 50500 series of innovation management 487–490, **488–489**
ISO/TC 279 innovation management 495
iteration 93

Japanese semiconductor industry 205
Japan Innovation Network (JIN) 82
Jin Chen 102
Johnson & Johnson 31
Jugaad innovation 50
Jung, Carl 394

K-nearest neighbors algorithm 255–257, *256*, *257*
knowledge-base theory 63–64, 186
knowledge boundary-crossing processes 204
knowledge inertia 398
knowledge-intensive business services (KIBS) 379, 550
knowledge management 134

knowledge-related micro processes 56–57, *57*
knowledge sharing 118, 135, 198–199
knowledge transfer offices (KTOs) 381
knowledge viewpoint of open innovation 191–192
Koestler, Arthur 394
Korean Telecom 394
Kuhn, Thomas 49, 174, 394

labor division of innovation 377–379
laminated object manufacturing (LOM) 240
laser engineered net shaping (LENS) 240
leader-member exchange (LMX) 125
leadership: ambidextrous leadership 124–125; authentic leadership 126–127; characteristic leadership 116–117; commitment of 85; developmental leadership 128–129; directive leadership 114–115; entrepreneurial leadership 128; family leadership 122–123; female leadership 129; humorous leadership 125–126; interactive leadership 116; introduction to 113, **114**; participative leadership 115–116; paternalistic leadership 123–124; of R&D&I Management 491; shared/distributed leadership 122; strategic/CEO leadership 121; strategic management of innovation 113–129; structuring leadership 127; transactional leadership 118, 120–121; transformational leadership 117–120
lead-user method 211–212
Lean Product Innovation Management 508–509
Lean Startup 509–510
Lean startup methodology 79
learning base theory 186
learning systems 65–66
Leifer, Richard 47
Liang Mei 102
Licensing Executives Society (LES) 408
licensing of professionals 408
Li Keqiang 94
Living Lab Methodology 512
logistic regression 257
Logitech 273
low-fidelity materials 239
low-fidelity prototyping 246, 248, 249, 267
LTS (Large Technical System) 35
lucky iron fish 272, 274, 275

machine learning algorithms 255–258
management audit 516–517
management development *397*, 397–398
"Management of Innovation" (Burns, Stalker) 74–75
management system standards (MSS) 66, 81
Managing Innovation (Tidd, Bessant, Pavitt) 79
Manifesto for Agile Software Development 279
Mann, Horace 344

manual external defibrillators (MEDs) 224
Marshall, Barry 349
Ma Yun 91
McClelland, David 563
McKim, Robert 22
McKinsey Global Institute 4
memory and knowledge 60–61
mergers and acquisitions (M&A) 109–112, 398
merit-based ethical responsibility 310, 312
methodologies for innovation management: design thinking 510–512; InnoCamp model 512–513; Lean Product Innovation Management 508–509; Lean Startup 509–510; Living Lab Methodology 512; MEVGIT methodology 507–508; MIM3 methodology 505–507; Very Lean Startup Method 510
Methodology for Evaluating the Value Generation of Information Technology (MEVGIT) 507–508
Methodology of Innovation Management for Obtaining the Level 3 of I2MM (MIM3) 505–507
Micro-Electro-Mechanical Systems (MEMS) acceleration sensor 225, 226
Microsoft 14
microwave market 231
miniaturization strategy in disruptive innovation 222–223, 226, 228
Ministry of Economy, Trade and Industry (METI) 82
mini-washer market 231
MIT Commission on Industrial Productivity 525
MIT Sloan Center 181
Miyamoto, Shigeru 18
models for innovation management: Innovation Capability Maturity Model 502; Integrated Innovation Maturity Model 502–505; Integrated Service Innovation Method **499**, 499–500; introduction to 498–499; Open Business Model 504–505; Open Innovation Maturity Model 500–502; Statistical Model for Measuring the Business Model Innovativeness 504
modern portfolio theory 581–583
MOD station ecosystem 385
modularity of innovation 377–379
modularization 232, 234
momentum serendipity 349
motivation and knowledge 57–59, **58**, 62
multinational corporations (MNCs) 140, 270, 272, 469–470, 552–553
"My Pril-My Style" idea competition 212
mysteries of creation 393–394

nanotechnology: in China 330–332, **331**; in Europe 328–330; responsible innovation and 325–332; summary of 332–337, **333–335**; in United States 325–328, *326*
Nanotechnology Research and Development Act (2003) 309
Nash equilibrium rate of investment 137
national competitiveness 4–6, **5**
National Economic Council 3
national innovation systems (NIS) 386, 387–389
National Nanotechnology Initiative 325–326
National Natural Science Foundation of China 330
National Research Council 325, 326
National Scientific Fund (NSF) 325
national standardization 81
Nature (Rodríguez, Mingyan, Fisher) 328
need identification phase 272–273
need information 207–208
negative binomial regressions 140
Netherlands Organisation for Scientific Research (NWO) 435
netnography 208, 212
network-based crowdsourcing 182
networked systems 75–76
network traffic 93
neuroimaging studies 19–20
neurons/neuroscience 17
new institutional economics 318
new product development (NPD) 237, 239, 281–282, 367–369
Newton, Isaac 344
NightScout project 169–170
Nintendo 224–225, 226
North Carolina State University 80
Norwegian Research Council 436
not invented here (NIH) 180, 214–215
not sold here (NSH) 180
NP Series of R&D&I Management 498
NSD research stream 281–282

observation-related patterns of serendipity 347
Office of Science and Technology Policy 3
Open Business Model 504–505
open call/indirect search 209, *209*
open direct search 208–209, *209*
open innovation: business management practices 195–197; business R&D internationalization 416; classification of 183; collaborative innovation 181–182; conceptual comparison of models 180–182; defined 403; ecosystems and 280; governing innovation under 418–424, *419*, *422*; impact on innovation performance 187–189; infrastructure 421; intellectual property rights and 471; internal *vs.* external innovation 189–191; management implications of 194–195; network-based crowdsourcing 182; organizational implementation of 192–194; policy analysis 198–200; reaching business

maturity 197–198; technological innovation 183–187
Open Innovation Maturity Model 500–502
open innovation practices: categorization of 208–209, *209*; competencies 212–216; crowdsourcing 210–211; culture for 215–216; idea contests 209–210, **210**; lead-user method 211–212; methods of 207–212; netnography 212; not-Invented-here syndrome 214–215; organizational information roles 214; organizational prerequisites for 213–214; partnerships 204–206; social enterprises 206–207; summary of 216
openness to accident 354
open-source software 172, 176
operating processes of R&D&I Management 492–493
operation and maintenance (O&M) technologies 428
operation-specific implications 107
operation-wide implications 107
organisational stability 398–399
Organisation for Economic Co-operation and Development (OECD) 27, 31, 108, 153, 171, 389, 406, 519
organizational asymmetries 132–133
organizational commitment 116–117
organizational information roles 214
organizational innovation management: acceleration of 369–370; chief innovation officers 371–372; creativity and fuzzy front end 363–365; high-performance innovation teams 372–373; interface management 365–367; new product development 367–369; strategic management 113, 129; summary of 373–374
organizational knowledge processes 58
organizational learning 64–65, 111
organizational memory 60–61
organizational needs in technology innovations *566*, 566–568, *567*
organization of innovation management *425*, 425–428, *426*
organization systems in innovation management *84*, 84–85
Oslo Manual: Proposed Guidelines for Collecting and Interpreting Technological Innovation Data (1992) 27, 519, 524, 532
outbound increase 421
outbound open innovation 183

paper prototyping 246, 248, 249, 266
paradigm shift in innovation 49, **49**
participative leadership 115–116
partner network 42
partnerships in open innovation 204–206
Patagonia company 23

patents/patent system: antitrust and 136–137; behaviors and innovation 139; intellectual property 468–470; introduction to 135–136; spillover effect 140; strategic management of innovation 135–141; summary 141; technology transfer 138–139
paternalistic leadership 123–124
people-centric innovation 410
people-centric technology transfer 404–411
people management and cognitive disinhibition 23–24
performance evaluation of R&D&I Management 493
perishability in service innovation 38
personal factors in serendipity 354–355
pharmaceutical industry 138
Philips Medical Systems (PMS) 224
planning concept 350
planning of R&D&I Management 491
plasticity in brain 18
platform awareness 93
policy analysis of open innovation 198–200
positioning school view of management 75
pride-of-authorship effect 210
prior knowledge in serendipity 346, 354–355
proactiveness in entrepreneurship 146
process innovation 36–37, 78–79
process management 97, 132, 134, 420, 469
producer innovation paradigms *171*, 171–174, 176–177
product development 273–274, 524
Product Development and Management Association (PDMA) 82, 367
product innovation 33–36, 365
product-server dimension 98
project leaders 402–404
proprietary rights 136
prototypes 238–239
psychological empowerment 119–120
public funding of universities 381
public value in responsible innovation 320

Quadruple Helix Innovation 10
quality culture 14
quick prototyping 246, 248, 267

radical innovation 44, 44–47, *45*, **46**
rapid prototyping 246, 248, 267
reflexivity in responsible innovation 315–316
refrigerated containers sector 230–231
regional competitiveness 4–6, **5**
Rehau company 273
Renaissance thinking 3
Rensselaer Polytechnic Institute 80
requests for proposals (RFPs) 211
required resources in accelerators 370

research and development (R&D): business application aim 422; business R&D internationalization 416; collaborative work 407–408; competencies and 213; convergence in innovation 301–302; in entrepreneurship 146; expenditures 6; facilities in China 269; globalization of 298; in incubators 423; innovation and 12–13, 31–32, 418–424; intensive high-tech industries 187; interface management 365, 366–367; internal *vs.* external innovation 190–191, 196; mergers and acquisitions 110–111; nanotechnology 326; Nash equilibrium rate of investment 137; open innovation 180–181, 193, 194–197; patent system 139, 140; servitization of manufacturing 40; SKIN model 550; strategic management of innovation 108; substantial (radical) innovation 422–423; universities, impact on 380–382; walk-around manager 402; *see also* disruptive innovation R&D strategies

research and development and innovation (R&D&I) management system 81

research and innovation offices (RIOs) 381

researchers-entrepreneurs 399–400

resource-based theory (RBT) 75, 148, 150, 383, 469

resource viewpoint of open innovation 191

responsible development (RD) 101

responsible innovation: anticipating requirement of 314–315; assessment standards of 318–321, *319*, *320*; attribution analysis of 310–312, **311**; connotation of 309–310; construction elements of 312–316, **313**; inclusion element 312–314, **313**; innovation management 99–103, **100**, **101**, *102*, *103*; institutional situation of 316–318; introduction to 307–308; nanotechnology and 325–332; origin of 308–309; reflexivity in 315–316; research methods/levels 324–325; responsiveness of 316; theoretical framework of 321–324, **322–323**, *324*; transnational practice of 324–332

responsible research and innovation (RRI): agent-based modelling 551–552; dimensions of *438*, 438–440, *440*; frameworks of 101; human brain stimulation 442–451; introduction to 435–436; as meta-responsibility 436–442; networks of 440–442; summary of 451

responsiveness of responsible innovation 316

revenue streams 42

reverse product cycle 281

rights-based harmless principle 310

risk-taking in entrepreneurship 146

Röntgen, Wilhelm Conrad 344, 349, 350

sanctum serendipity 348
SAPPHO Project 527
Schumpeter, Joseph 26, 146

Science Lessons (Binder) 404
Science Policy Research Unit (SPRU) 35
search concept 350–351
Securities Data Corporation (SDC) Platinum 109, 110
selective laser sintering (SLS) 240, 241
self-awareness of leaders 126–127
self-developed core technology 6
serendipity and innovation: aspects and elements of 345–350; boundaries of *350*, 350–351, **352**; intellectual leap 345–346; introduction to 343–344; management of 353–357, *358*; origin and definition of 344–345; patterns of 347–350, **348**; personal factors 354–355; prior and follow-up knowledge 346; research in management literature 352–353; social and contextual factors 356–357; strategic advantage 346; summary of 357; surprise/accidental encounter 345

service development phase 273–274
service industry digital age innovation 281–282
service innovation 37–41, **39**, 119, 282–283
service management innovation 41
service model innovation 41
service process innovation 41
service product innovation 41
service technology innovation 41
servitization of manufacturing 40
shared leadership 122
Shaw, George Bernard 18
Sherman Antitrust Act (1890) 136
simplicity 92
simplification strategy in disruptive innovation 223–224, 227, 228
simulations in agent-based modelling 539–540, 545–547
SKIN model 548–553
small and medium enterprises (SMEs): agent-based modelling 550–551; entrepreneurship 141–144, 152; human factors in 395, 405; perceived barriers 484; radical innovation 46; simplification 227
Smart Growth strategy 99
smart prototyping: AI system development 250–259; brief overview 238–243; data collection 243–250; data exploration 250–252, **251**; data visualization 252–255, **253**, *254*; efforts related to 241–243, *242*; experimental research 243–246, *244*, *245*; experimental setup 246–249, *247*, **249**; findings 249–250; framework *242*, 242–243; introduction to 237–238; limitations/further research 262; machine learning algorithms 255–258; materials, tools, and technologies 239–241, *240*; performance of models *258*, 258–259, *259*; prototypes, defined 238–239; research approach 243; summary of 259–262, *260*, **261**, **262**

social enterprises (SE) 206–207
social factors in serendipity 356–357
socialization 64, 93, 301
social network services (SNSs) 300
social network theory 61
social responsibility 309
societal needs in technology innovations *566*, 566–568, *567*
solution information 207–208
Sony Corporation 14, 206
space in accelerators 370
Spanish Association for Standardisation and Certification (AENOR) 81
spillover effect 140
spin-offs 112–113, 408–410, *409*
spontaneous radioactivity discovery 350
stage-gate model 78, 279
stakeholder-orientation 107
standard operating procedures (SOPs) 450
standards for innovation management: BS 7000 Design Management Systems 495–498; CEN/TS 16555 standard 494–495; introduction to 479; ISO 50500 series 487–490, **488–489**; ISO/TC 279 innovation management 495; lack of 482–485, **486–487**; NP Series of R&D&I Management 498; problems with 480–485, **486–487**; UNE 166002 R&D&I Management 490–494; value generation of 480–481
start-up organisations 370, 395, 408–410, *409*
Statistical Model for Measuring the Business Model Innovativeness 504
Statute of Monopolies 135
stereolithography apparatus (SLA) 240, *241*
STI mode of technological innovation 185–186
strategic advantage in serendipity 346
strategic alignment 420
strategic alliances within innovation systems 383–384
strategic/CEO leadership 121
strategic insights in technology innovations 576–578, **577**, *578*
strategic management of innovation: core competencies and 129–135; corporate strategy 109–113; entrepreneurship 141–153; introduction to 77, 107–108; leadership and 113–129; mergers and acquisitions 109–112; patents/patent system 135–141; spin-offs 112–113; summary of 153
strategic maps in technology innovations **578**, 578–589, *579–581*, *582–583*, *584–588*
Strategy for American Innovation 3
Structure of Scientific Revolutions, The (Kuhn) 49
structure perspective on innovation management 77
structuring leadership 127
substantial (radical) innovation 422–423
sudden cardiac arrest (SCA) 224

Super Mario Bros. game 18
support in accelerators 370
support of R&D&I Management 491–492
surprise encounter in serendipity 345
Sustainable Development Goals (SDGs) 49
sustainable innovation 52, 94, 96, 276, 525
Suzlon 229
systemic innovation 379
systems approach to innovation management: academic works on 79–80; adaptive and networked systems 75–76; common themes 82; consultants and industrial research reports 81–82; elements of 85–86; exposition of 74–75; feedback processes 86; implications for 86–87; introduction to 73; national and international standardization 81; organization systems *84*, 84–85; performance evaluations 86; principled outline of 82–86, **83**; process perspective 78–79; reasons for 73–74; selected frameworks from literature 79–82; strategy perspective 78; structure perspective 77

tacit knowledge 64
tank gauging machines 223–224
target customer segments 42
Tata Motors 228
Tata Research Development and Design Centre 229
team culture 14
technical capacity accumulation 528, **529–532**
technical knowledge workers 396–400, *397*
technique for order preference by similarity to an ideal solution (TOPSIS) 241
technological convergence 298–299
technological innovation 183–187
technological innovation audit (TIA): applications of 532–534, **533–534**; background 516–518; core process 523–525; introduction to 516; management audit and 516–517; methodological support for 517–518; metrics for 518; modeling of 518–523, *519*, *520*, *521*, *522*; organizational environment 527; performance audit 532; process audit of 523–532; product development 524; resource supply 527–528; supporting system 525–532; technical capacity accumulation 528, **529–532**; technology acquisition 523–524; technology strategy 525–527, *526*
technological revolution 3
technology acquisition 523–524
technology assessment (TA) 436
technology clustering 568–567
technology diffusion 388
"technology-economy-society" pattern 3
technology innovation: candidate scenarios 574–576, *575*, **575–576**; decision factors 571–574, *572*, *573*; diffusion of 388; external

Index

forces 572–573, *573*; forecasting relationships 569–571, **570**; human needs model 563–565, *564*, *565*; implementation policy implications 583, *584–588*; introduction to 560; leadership and innovation 29; life-cycle of 7; management of 134; methodological emphasis 560–563, *562*; modern portfolio theory 581–583; organizational and societal needs *566*, 566–568, *567*; overview of *28*, 28–29; patent system and 138–139; strategic insights 576–578, **577**, *578*; strategic maps **578**, 578—589, *579–581*, *582–583*, *584–588*; systematic framework 561–563; systems approach 560; technology clustering 568–567
technology strategy 525–527, *526*
technology transfer offices (TTOs) 381–382, 406, 408, 411
Theory of Economic Development, The (Schumpeter) 26
three-dimensional printing (3DP) 240
time horizon in accelerators 370
Tinkerers: The Amateurs, DIYers, and Inventors Who Make America Great, The (Foege) 3
top-down lamination mechanism 318
Total Innovation Management (TIM) 80, 82
total quality management (TQM) 41
transactional leadership 118, 120–121
transactive memory systems 129
transformational leadership 117–120
transistor radio 222–223
transnational practice of responsible innovation 324–332
Triple-A System 279
triple helix perspective of innovation systems 388
two-staged least squares (TSLS) 140

ultrasound machine (USM) 231–232
UNE 166002 R&D&I Management 490–494
United States nanotechnology 325–328, *326*
university, as engine for innovation 379–382
university-firm collaborative research 405–407, *406*

university-industry collaboration (UIC) 380–382
university technology transfer 472–473
U.S. Horizontal Merger Guidelines 110
U.S. Patent Act 135
user dimension 97–98
user-driven innovation 551–552
user-first thinking 91–92, **92**
user-supplier relationship 301
utility in managerial practice 553–554
UTStarcom Personal Handy Phone 47

vacuum tube 222
value of innovation 3–15
value proposition 42
VAM (Valuation Adjustment Mechanism) agreement 91
venture capital (VC)-funded innovations 45
venture capitalists (VCs) 409
Very Lean Startup Method 510
Viagra discovery 349
visible design parameters 378
voice of the customer 207

walk-around manager 402
Walpole, Horace 344–345
Wang Jianlin 91
war games 225
Watts, Christopher 545–547
Wii game console 224–225, 226
Winter Olympics (2018) 394
work behavior-related patterns of serendipity 347
workflow systems 366
work organization in accelerators 370
World Economic Forum (WEF) 28, 297
World Intellectual Property Organization (WIPO) 395
Wu Xiaobo 50

Xerox 205
Xiangshan Science Conference 332
x-ray discovery 349

Zhang Ruimin 14